Don Carlos Buell
. . . .

CIVIL WAR AMERICA
Gary W. Gallagher, editor

Don Carlos Buell

· ·

MOST PROMISING OF ALL

Stephen D. Engle

THE UNIVERSITY OF NORTH CAROLINA PRESS : Chapel Hill & London

© 1999 The University of North Carolina Press

All rights reserved

Designed by Jacquline Johnson

Set in New Baskerville by Running Feet Books

Manufactured in the United States of America

The paper in this book meets the guidelines for
permanence and durability of the Committee on
Production Guidelines for Book Longevity of the
Council on Library Resources.

Library of Congress Cataloging-in-Publication Data

Engle, Stephen Douglas. Don Carlos Buell : most promising
of all / by Stephen D. Engle. p. cm.—(Civil War America)

  Includes bibliographical references and index.

  ISBN 0-8078-2512-3 (alk. paper)

1. Buell, Don Carlos, 1818–1898. 2. Generals—United States
—Biography. 3. United States. Army—Biography. 4. United
States. Army of the Ohio—Biography. 5. United States—
History—Civil War, 1861–1865—Campaigns. 6. Tennes-
see—History—Civil War, 1861–1865—Campaigns. 7. Ken-
tucky—History—Civil War, 1861–1865—Campaigns.
I. Title. II. Series.

E467.1.B78E54 1999   99-18485

973.7′471—dc21   CIP

Portions of this work appeared previously, in somewhat
different form, as "Don Carlos Buell: Military Philosophy
and Command Problems in the West," *Civil War History*
41, no. 2 (June 1995): 89–115 (reprinted with permission
of the Kent State University Press); "Generalship on Trial:
Don Carlos Buell's Campaign to Chattanooga," in *Civil
War Generals in Defeat*, ed. Steven E. Woodworth (Lawrence: University Press of Kansas), 95–117, © 1999
(reprinted with permission of the publisher); and
"Success, Failure, and the Guillotine: Don Carlos Buell
and the Campaign for the Bluegrass State," *Register of the
Kentucky Historical Society* 96, no. 4 (Autumn 1999)
(reprinted with permission of the society).

03 02 01 00 99   5 4 3 2 1

For Stephanie, Taylor, and Claire

Contents

· ·

Illustrations & Maps

· ·

Preface

· ·

Upon Don Carlos Buell's death one newspaper editor prophesied that the "future historian will do justice to General Buell, to his qualities as a commander on the field." A century later that journalist would be disappointed that Buell had evaded a biography since his death. Still, historians have done justice to Buell's qualities as a Union commander in the western theater of the Civil War. Regrettably for Buell, however, the consensus of that assessment would have one believe that Buell's lack of aggression and initiative had ruined him, that he feared combat more than he feared defeat, and that he was not the general to march and fight while living off the country. According to his historical epitaph, he never marched as the enemy marched, lived as the enemy lived, or fought as the enemy fought. Consequently, in the celebration of the Union victory, there remains no celebration of Buell's role in it.

In some respects the story of Buell as commander of the Army of the Ohio in the West conjures up images of George B. McClellan, the famed commander of the Army of the Potomac and onetime general in chief of the Union armies. Contemporaries and scholars wrote essentially the same kinds of epitaphs upon Buell's death as they had written on McClellan's passing. Some loved Buell; some hated him. One newspaper correspondent considered Buell as much of a misunderstood genius as McClellan, concluding that one day the country would "rise up in the majesty of the sustained honor . . . and call these men blessed." This praise, of course, never materialized. In fact, condemnation instead of commendation of Buell has grown with the passage of time. Thus, it is easy to imagine Buell as the "McClellan of the West." In contemplating Buell's life as a soldier and his place in the Civil War, however, I thought of the context and circumstances that brought Buell to the Union high command in the war and what led to his dismissal. Thus, if McClellan and Buell had essentially remained the same as commanders, I sought to answer why Buell refused to change and what was different about the war during his tenure that might suggest why he was shelved from command in November 1862. This of course allowed me to consider the shifting nature and conduct of war and the Union war aims at a critical period in the conflict. Therefore, the context of Buell's tenure became as intriguing as Buell himself, which made him more attractive as a topic. Though Buell was not a Ulysses S. Grant or a William T. Sherman who grew in insight as the war went on, the Union learned from his failures as a commander, just as it would learn from Grant's and Sherman's many successes.

Of course, in any life an understanding of the person is best found in original, primary sources. Unlike McClellan, Grant, or Sherman, however, Buell was uncooperative with his biographer. He left behind only a fragmented set of personal papers, most of which, though useful, are still difficult to read. He did, however, contribute to the *Battles and Leaders* series published two decades after the war. Still, I often wished Buell had written his memoirs or even his own story, as did McClellan, since it would have allowed a more complete understanding of his motives for what he did and how he thought. Regrettably, the absence of this kind of personal legacy forced me to make conclusions about Buell the man from the sources relating to Buell the commander, because he left so little around which to construct anything more. Perhaps this fact alone has left him without a biographer for a century. The only significant work on Buell is James Chumney Jr.'s 1964 dissertation, "Don Carlos Buell: Gentleman General," completed at Rice University, which briefly chronicles his Civil War career. Chumney's work places Buell in a considerably more favorable light than what follows in these pages. Still, I learned a great deal from Chumney's insights. Gerald Prokopowicz's Harvard dissertation, "All for the Regiment: Unit Cohesion and Tactical Stalemate in the Army of the Ohio, 1861–1862," provides a thorough and perceptive examination of the army Buell commanded. Although historians of the war have devoted obligatory space to Buell in discussing the battles of Shiloh and Perryville, for the most part his failures proved him unworthy of any significant study. Consequently, Buell's complete story has never seen the light of day.

Part of this obscurity also stems from the fact that the personal papers preserved by the Buell family fail to provide answers to the questions the biographer most often asks: What was at the core of his character? Did he calibrate the use of violence? Did he think he could control war through the policies he and McClellan adopted? What exactly were his racial, social, and political views? Did he actually care about the ultimate meaning of the war? Apparently, Buell related little of his social life because there was little to tell. Thus, trying to make Buell appear colorful was difficult, as was penetrating his innermost thoughts. He had neither the brilliance of Henry W. Halleck nor the dash of McClellan nor the instincts of Grant or Sherman.

Though as a junior officer in the regular army he fraternized with his officer friends, he remained for the most part a self-absorbed, distant, and private man. As a commander of the Army of the Ohio, Buell never strolled through camps and chatted with enlisted men. The army he created never came to know him. In attempting to turn the army into something that resembled himself, he created a machine that was disciplined but lacked an emotional attachment to its commander. He was unable to create a mystique about the Army of the Ohio, and he displayed no endearing qualities his men could turn to when they doubted his decisions. Though he was simple in his habits, he was too thorough the professional to appear inviting to his men. He had little capacity for motivating soldiers. Too frequently he gave orders, not explanations, and he could never distinguish sufficiently between the plodding regular soldier and the high-spirited volunteer, often failing to acknowledge the volunteer soldier as someone entitled to any greater consideration. He was too inflexible in his thinking, and though personally brave, he lacked the instincts to take risks with his army. Ultimately, Buell's conservative temperament, habitual caution, and lethargy; his unwillingness to subordinate military desires to political considerations; and his efforts to wage the war as a contest to restore the antebellum Union rather than as a contest that would bring considerable social change to the slaveholding South brought about his demise as a field commander. Buell was removed from command because he had failed to win on the battlefield at a time when politicians were judging success only in terms of simple victory.

Still, with all that I came to know about Buell, in the end I wondered whether or not he would recognize himself in this biography. I concluded that if he did, he might not like what he read about himself. Nonetheless, however his actions may be judged for good or ill, Don Carlos Buell stood among the senior northern commanders early in the war who gave shape to the course of the war in the West. His role and significance in the war at that time were as important as, if not more important than, McClellan's or Halleck's. Contemporaries charged him with being sympathetic with the secessionists, but in truth no one was more loyal and patriotic. As a conservative Democrat who owned slaves before the war and who clearly had ties to the South, Buell remained a staunch supporter of the Union. The Union Buell fought to preserve would have included slavery, not so much because he thought it morally justified but, rather, because he came to believe that southerners should be left alone to solve the slavery dilemma. Abolitionism threatened public order, Buell feared, and in the process would threaten the constitutional guarantees of citizens loyal to the Federal government.

Buell's importance in the war was clearly connected to the Union's passage through a difficult time in reconciling public and political thought with military operations, particularly in the West. Perhaps no other Union commander's career provides as good an opportunity to examine civil-military relations, command relationships, and the changing nature of war in the West as does Buell's. His limited-war-for-limited-goals attitude and lenient reconstruction policies were in harmony with the Lincoln administration's initial desire to fight a war of resistance and not liberation of slaves. Throughout his tenure in command, Buell remained consistent in his beliefs about waging war simply to repress the rebellious segments in the South and not to subjugate the people of the entire Confederacy. Of course, his handling of the war issues in the West provided the Lincoln administration with examples of how not to fight for success. He was a practitioner of limited war because he firmly believed that the war could be won without devastating the countryside or disrupting the lives of civilians who chose not to participate actively. It would be more difficult for the Union to restore itself, Buell believed, if the southern states were ravaged by invading Federal armies that trampled the rights and liberties of civilians.

Since this is the first biography of Buell to appear, I am sure some readers may feel I have not adequately explored his life; others may feel I am too critical. My appraisal will undoubtedly generate controversy among scholars who see his conduct in the western campaigns in a more favorable light. Whatever the case, I trust the questions raised with regard to Buell and his conduct will provide points of departure for understanding the evolution of the war in the West.

Acknowledgments

Research and writing seem such individual activities, though it is only because I recognize my own limitations in both that I imposed on others to help me complete this book. I wish to acknowledge the many institutions and friends who helped me over the past seven years. Karen Voshall labored tirelessly to assist me in sorting out and copying research materials while completing her own graduate work in sociology. Claire Fuller Martin helped me obtain pertinent manuscripts in the Illinois State Historical Library. The entire staff of the Florida Atlantic University interlibrary loan department deserves special recognition for accepting and filling what was surely a mountain of requests. Frankly, Usha and Ken deserve medals. The students in my graduate seminars also deserve recognition for indulging me when I veered from the topic and toward Don Carlos Buell. In the summer of 1992 I was fortunate to receive a University Foundation Grant that provided funding for numerous research trips. That same year I received the James Haas Fellowship that allowed me to spend considerable time at the U.S. Army Military History Institute, where Dr. Richard Sommers assisted me greatly in locating relevant manuscripts. He also invited me to his personal library, where he, Ed Haggerty, and I discussed the war for what seemed like hours. I want to thank Dr. Sommers and the Harrisburg Civil War Roundtable for supporting my interest in Buell.

In my search for any living relative of Buell who might have some family papers, I was fortunate to discover that, indeed, at least one existed, Sheila Tschumy. Not only was Sheila excited about my work, but she also provided me with manuscripts that helped me to piece together some of Buell's personal life. Librarians, curators, park historians, and museum directors around the nation, of course, made my work easier. Steve Towne at the Indiana State Archives generously came through with some invaluable materials on Indiana governor Oliver P. Morton. Mike Meier allowed me to impose on him, yet again, and directed me to the relevant files in the National Archives. Alan Aimone of West Point provided me with Buell's cadet material. James Ogden III came through at the last minute when I discovered that Buell materials existed at the Chickamauga and Chattanooga National Military Park. Jim Holmberg at the Filson Club also provided invaluable assistance. John Adler of Harpweek granted me permission to use copies from his private collection of *Harper's Weekly*. In addition to these persons who distinguished themselves in helping me, the staffs at the following repositories also deserve thanks: Chicago Historical Society, Claremont Graduate School, Huntington Library, Illinois State Historical Library, Indiana Historical Society, Ohio Historical Society, Rice University, Tennessee State Archives, University of Chicago, University of Kentucky, University of Michigan, and Western Kentucky University.

From the earliest stages of my research, I was fortunate to discover that there was some interest in Don Carlos Buell. Numerous historical associations and Civil War societies invited me to present papers that allowed me to put some of my initial ideas in writing. John Hubbell published some of my early thoughts on Buell and his philosophy of war in *Civil War History*, and our discussions have helped me in conceptualizing Buell in this regard. That article benefited from the judicious comments of Brooks Simpson, Bill Piston, and Herman Hattaway. Steve Woodworth graciously invited me to do a chapter on Buell in his work *Civil War Generals in Defeat*, which profited from Mark Grimsley's insights. Tom Appleton, editor of the *Register of the Kentucky Historical Society*, also published some of my ideas on Buell and the Kentucky campaign. During my Fulbright year in Germany, Hans Jürgen Grabbe, my host professor, invited me to present a paper on Buell to the American Studies Conference in Würzburg. Other persons who shared their insights and advice on Buell include departmental colleagues John O'Sullivan and Mark Rose. John Childrey facilitated the mountain of copies that needed to be made to send out to readers and the press. More than that, he listened unconditionally to whatever I had to say about Buell, when asked.

Still, there are those scholars/friends who willingly took the time to read initial drafts of chapters or the entire manuscript and whose comments helped me to develop a conceptual framework and from whom I learned a great deal. Three persons in particular lent me wise counsel, and the book benefited from their collective efforts. I have had the inestimable good fortune of utilizing the keen insight of John F. Marszalek. John deserves a special thanks for committing himself to a task similar to Grant's before Petersburg in the summer of 1864. It did not take him all summer, but he nonetheless read the initial draft of the entire manuscript. I shamelessly took advantage of his patience and intuition simply because his previous works are models of scholarship. His careful reading of every page, pointing out things that should be removed or added, definitely enhanced the final product. Stephen V. Ash also read the civil war chapters and made invaluable suggestions. I was also fortunate to discover that Larry Daniel was interested in my work on Buell. After Larry and I shared our thoughts on Buell and the Army of the Ohio, Larry graciously offered to read the manuscript. I want to thank him for his careful and judicious comments, which made me re-think some of my conclusions. Stacey Allen read and commented on the Shiloh chapter and finally convinced me that Buell did not save Grant at Shiloh. David Coles, who befriended me in graduate school many years ago, continues to serve as an initial critic. His incomparable knowledge of the war is matched only by his selflessness as a scholar. As always, he put aside his own work to read someone else's. Fortunately for me and the reader, this book is vastly improved thanks to the efforts of such out-standing scholars.

I will always be indebted to Professors Jim Jones and Joe Richardson, who in their own professional lives prove to be model teachers and scholars. In addition, I should say a long-overdue thanks to my under-graduate professors Ralph Sherrard, Jerry B. Thomas, and John E. Stealey, who unknowingly inspired a young student to become a historian by simply being exciting and engaging teachers.

Gary W. Gallagher suggested the University of North Carolina Press to me as a possible publisher and provided valuable advice. I wish also to thank the anonymous readers who evaluated the manuscript for the University of North Carolina Press, and copyeditor Stephanie Wenzel, whose careful eye saved me from embarrassing mistakes. This simple ac-knowledgment can in no way adequately thank those persons men-tioned above. Still, with all their assistance, I take sole responsibility for any errors or shortcomings.

My wife, Stephanie, deserves special thanks for giving her time freely to read my work and advise me. She is truly a scholar in her own right and a gentle but honest critic. I must confess that after all these years I continue to be enhanced simply by being in her presence. My two chil-dren, Taylor and Claire, are to be commended for unknowingly provid-ing me with the distractions that sometimes are too frequently brushed aside. Of course, this book could have been finished in less time, but I would have missed out on more important things, such as throwing a baseball with my son or simply walking alongside my daughter riding her bike. These are things that delayed the final product, and I am a bet-ter person for choosing to be distracted.

Stephen D. Engle
Boca Raton, Florida
December 1998

Don Carlos Buell

CHAPTER ONE

Life on the River

Among the people who sailed from Huntingdonshire, England, to Dorchester, Massachusetts, in the autumn of
1630, the most prominent figure was William Bevilles Sr., a religious
enthusiast who refused to subscribe to the tenets of either the church of
England or the pope of Rome. Upon landing in the New World, he
changed the family name from Bevilles to Buell, and he later moved
from Dorchester to Windsor, Connecticut. The Buells of New England
founded towns and owned large tracts of land; they were lawyers, judges,
ministers, and doctors—men of distinguished political reputations and
prominence. They served in the War of Independence and the War of
1812 with distinction. Their celebrated blue-blooded pedigree included
kings of England—Henry III, Edward I, II, and III—and writers and
philosophers such as Thomas Paine.[1]

The Buell children of the early New England generations were rigidly disciplined in the Puritan dogma. Well educated, they attended college in Europe or in the Northeast at Harvard or Yale. The character of the Buell family reflected a sincere devotion to religion, education, tradition, gentility, and the qualities that revealed strong convictions in making actions conform to beliefs. That same character shaped the Buell progeny of the eighteenth and nineteenth centuries as well.[2]

Born in upstate New York in 1764, Salmon Buell, the grandfather of Don Carlos, was the consummate Puritan disciplinarian. As an Ithaca lawyer, senator, and judge of the Court of Appeals of New York, Salmon represented the finest tradition of the Buell ancestry. At age sixteen he served in the Revolutionary War. He was later educated at Yale and became politically connected and prominent in the most distinguished social circles in Ithaca, New York. His first marriage in July 1785 to Joanna Sturtevant of Connecticut was equally as rewarding and fertile as his career. The union produced ten children. Among the seven sons was Don Carlos Buell's father, Salmon A. Buell Jr., born in Ithaca in August 1794. The family lived in Ithaca until they migrated to Marietta, Ohio, in 1816 and later to Cincinnati.[3]

When the War of 1812 broke out, Salmon Jr., at age sixteen, mustered into the volunteer service under the auspices of his uncle Timothy Buell, who resided in Marietta. Shortly after the war Salmon Jr. moved to Lowell, Ohio, just a few miles north of Marietta on the banks of the Muskingum River, and engaged in agriculture. Lowell, or Buell's Lowell as it was later called, was a Buell family foundation. Perez Barnum Buell came west with his brother Salmon Buell Jr. in 1816 searching for opportunities in the newly opened Ohio country. He laid out the plan for the village and started a trading center for agricultural products. The two brothers became influential in the economic development of the community by expanding agricultural activity and production by loading surplus wheat, corn, cider, and other products on keelboats and floating them to New Orleans. After 1822 they drove cattle, horses, sheep, hogs, and sometimes turkeys overland to Baltimore. This activity attracted steamboat travel, and Lowell quickly became a prosperous community.[4]

In Marietta, Salmon Buell Jr. met his future wife, Elizabeth, the daughter of his Uncle Timothy. Evidently Timothy Buell and Salmon Buell Sr. were half-brothers, so Eliza, as she was called, and Salmon Jr. were distant cousins. They were married in Marietta on April 13, 1817. Meanwhile, Salmon's younger brother Perez married Eliza Rector, a Virginia belle, in 1818. She brought with her to Lowell a black woman named Fannie Fitzhugh—Aunt Fannie to later children. Expecting to raise many children, the two newly married brothers built a brick house on the Muskingum River bank, where their families lived together. Shortly after, Salmon and Eliza produced their first son, Don Carlos, born March 23, 1818. The baby was named for his uncle Don Carlos, the first of Salmon Buell Sr.'s seven sons. Carlos had been a promising young lawyer in Ithaca, but he died in the War of 1812 on the Canadian frontier. On February 26, 1822, Sallie Maria was born, and then came Auriela Ann, born February 27, 1822.[5]

Nestled at the confluence of the Muskingum and Ohio Rivers, Marietta was the county seat of Washington County. It was first settled in Ohio under the authority of the New England Ohio Company, and its settlers were of New England origin. In 1820 the county's population was barely 10,000, with Marietta as the largest city, numbering almost 2,000 residents. According to one local resident, there were few places in the country that could compare to Marietta in "point of morality and intelligence." Merchants filled the streets and markets with the business of the shipping industry, but the river city essentially supplied the wants of a rich agricultural region of diversified productions in corn, wheat, oats, potatoes, dairy products, fruit, and wool.[6]

As a small boy growing up on the banks of the Muskingum River, Don Carlos Buell was disciplined by the daily rigors of farm life. As soon as he was old enough to gather eggs or feed the livestock, he was put to quick and rigorous work by his father and uncle, who managed to make a modest living as farmers of corn, wheat, and other market crops. As the oldest boy of the combined Buell families, young Carlos toiled by his father's side in the fields while his mother took care of his two younger sisters. The daily routine of maintaining the family enterprise instilled in the youth the value of land and the responsibility and discipline that came with the kind of hard work that farm life required. Living close to the land meant living close to God to the Catholic family, who replenished their souls through regular churchgoing. Don Carlos was close to his father, and on occasion Salmon Jr. would kindle his son's interest with stories of his war exploits.[7]

In his youth Carlos became good friends with his younger cousin Thomas, with whom he lived, and William M. Scottsman, a neighbor. Occasionally, after the early morning farm chores were done, Salmon would allow his son an afternoon of free time, and together the boys would race down to the banks of the Muskingum and spend a pleasant afternoon fishing, swimming, or just relaxing. The horses on his father's farm also caught Carlos's attention, and although still quite young, he

The Muskingum River below Lowell, Ohio, ca. 1890, Buell's birthplace and home before he moved to Lawrenceburg, Indiana, in 1823 to live with his uncle (Courtesy of the Ohio Historical Society, Columbus)

eagerly wanted to ride. He would have this love for thoroughbreds all his life.[8]

The year 1823 marked a turning point in the life of the Buell family. In the late summer a cholera epidemic broke out in Lowell, and in August the extended Buell family lost three members to the epidemic, including Carlos's father and two cousins, Thomas and Sally Almeria. It was a devastating loss to the family and to what was then a tiny community. The death of his father left the young boy utterly downcast and emotionally desolate, and he grieved with a melancholy that was not easily shaken. The demise of his cousin Thomas, his closest playmate, was equally distressing, since he lost the best friend who might have shared his sorrow. Carlos never forgot that day, when, indeed, decisions were made that affected the rest of his life.[9]

The period following Salmon Buell's death proved difficult for the family. Don Carlos's mother, Eliza, tried to make the best of the farm, and her father and her in-laws saw to it that the farm continued to produce and that the children were well provided for. Still, as the only male in the family, Carlos had no role model, and his father's death left a profound void in his life for several years. Perhaps seeking to provide some stability in the family, Eliza got remarried three years later, to George Dunlevy, the clerk of Washington County. By this time Carlos was eight years old, and in light of the recent marriage, his mother and his grandfather, who then lived in Lawrenceburg, Indiana, decided that the young boy should be reared by his uncle George Pearson Buell, who also lived in Lawrenceburg. Of Buell's father's five brothers only two were living. The ties between Carlos and his mother weakened as he became the "foster son" of his uncle and because her marriage eventually produced four children—Harriet Eliza, George Wake, David, and Julia—to whom she had more immediate responsibilities. Although Buell's sisters, Sallie and Auriela, were still quite young when he departed for Indiana, he always kept in touch and remembered the kinship that began in the small village on the banks of the Muskingum River.[10]

Born in Ithaca, New York, on August 18, 1801, George Pearson Buell was Judge Salmon Buell Sr.'s youngest son. He had moved to Indiana with his father in 1820. In connection with his brother-in-law Luther Geer, who had been a wealthy merchant in Utica, New York, George brought a large stock of goods to the village of Lawrenceburg and initiated a pork business. Upon his arrival George Buell began purchasing all the hogs in the surrounding country, had them slaughtered and packed into barrels, and transported them by makeshift boats to New Orleans and then to New York.[11]

In the early 1820s George Buell proved so successful in his pork trading business that Lawrenceburg became a home market for this agricultural product, and farmers in the Miami Valley began to engage extensively in it. The small town established a monopoly of trade in pork packing and shipping to distant markets, exceeding and preceding this branch of business at Cincinnati. Among his most prominent associates was Amos Lane, a distinguished attorney and business entrepreneur who sat on the board of directors of the Lawrenceburg Farmers and Merchants Bank. This business association brought together George Buell and Ann Lane, the daughter of the honorable Amos Lane. In 1824 the couple married.[12]

A promising businessman and devoted husband, George Pearson Buell appeared the logical choice to rear his young nephew and mold him into a fine young man of high moral character. When Don Carlos arrived in Lawrenceburg in the autumn of 1826, he surely had an uncomfortable feeling. Still, his new environment shared a common bond with the village he left behind: the farm life, the river, and horses.

Situated on the east bank of the Ohio River in Dearborn County, Lawrenceburg occupied a broad expanse of fertile bottomland just across the river from Tousytown, Kentucky. The population numbered fewer than a thousand people, but it grew in size and diversity with the market success of the pork and later beef trade. In the 1820s the town boasted nine mercantile stores, a distillery, a drugstore, three taverns, two brick churches, three schools, a brick courthouse, a stone jail, and two printing offices, each of which issued a weekly newspaper. From the success of the pork industry, many merchants formed substantial businesses in shipping, dry goods, and commercial trading to accommodate the changing market economy.[13]

The change from a small house in a rural community with only a few crowded rooms where the noise of his younger sisters and cousins reminded Don Carlos constantly that he was not alone, to a largely empty house with only his aunt's companionship made him long for the days when his father awoke him at the crack of dawn to work. His early life on his uncle's Lawrenceburg farm was not the same, since its pork industry reflected more of a business venture than a gentleman's farm.

As a child Carlos was self-absorbed and introverted, and he developed a shy personality. He was forced to carve from his reserved demeanor a way to survive outside the farm and get along with other children—new children. He was no longer secure in his environment; he was a loner and a newcomer in a town where other children looked at him with suspicion. Usually undemonstrative and quiet, he nonetheless displayed an emotional intensity when he had to prove or defend himself. Shortly after he arrived in Lawrenceburg, the town bully, Joseph Danagh, challenged him to a fight. One cool autumn morning at the town pump the friends of both contestants formed a ring, and fists began to fly. Within seconds the lads were rolling around on the ground, and when it was over, the farmboy had demonstrated his mettle by beating the bully. He had proven himself in a fight, and from that experience came self-confidence and peer respect. He learned early that firm resolve, determination, and an unyielding defense could make up for lack of physical size. He also had inordinately rigid perceptions of right and wrong, or justice and injustice—no doubt a reflection of his father's firm hand. Once he made a decision, he clung to it tenaciously.[14]

If the days were not long enough for him in Lowell to complete all that needed to be done on the farm, Carlos now found time to ponder his new surroundings. Some of his new friends regarded him as a great playmate and school fellow, while others described him as "generally resolved and a taciturn lad" but a "most genial and companionable fellow." He excelled in the boyish sports of the time, "was a fearless hunter and noted as the best ice skater in the region."[15] On Sundays the Buells attended the Catholic church, and Carlos attended Sunday school, where he made new friends and strengthened his religious and moral convictions. Just as he was getting accustomed to his new environment, however, change again disrupted his life. As a prominent businessman, Uncle George could now afford the large family he and his wife desired, and within a decade they produced seven children.[16]

Shortly after moving in with his uncle, Carlos entered formal schooling. Education naturally captured the young boy's interest if not enthusiasm. He was probably first educated at the school that was kept for a time in an old frame building on High Street. Samuel H. Dowden, characterized as a "Virginian of intelligence," and Mrs. Stevenson were probably among his first teachers. During his school years he demonstrated a decided aptitude for mathematics and a predilection for drawing, and he improved his proficiency in equestrianism. Morals and manners were an important part of his daily regimen, as the instructor placed particular emphasis on the development of moral character. These methods were naturally founded on long-standing New England educational practices and philosophy. He was soon schooled in the tenets of republicanism: moral and civic virtue, equality, citizenship, and patriotism. These lessons, combined with his religious belief in an omniscient and almighty God who ruled the events of the universe with interminable wisdom, gave him the goals to be reached through religion. He would, however, have his own ideas about how to reach them.[17]

After the completion of the old Presbyterian church on Church Street in 1830, the basement served as a schoolhouse. Buell was probably among the first pupils educated in the new facility. As a student he "made fair progress" and was regarded as "a promising boy of excellent moral habits, and remarkable for his sturdiness of purpose."[18] Still, he was a serious student and a well-cultivated and proper young gentleman, exceedingly mannerly, polite, and respectful of authority. He spent most of his leisure time engaging in outdoor pursuits and horseback riding, which became a habit. In 1833 the new Lawrenceburg High School was opened. Graded schools were not formally organized and established in Lawrenceburg until 1856. Buell attended the high school until he was sixteen, when he entered the dry goods store of John P. Dunn and Company as a clerk. Dunn was also a representative to the state legislature from Dearborn County, and Buell's employment in Dunn's store over the next three years gained him the respect of even the most prominent Lawrenceburg citizens. At the dry goods store he made the acquaintance of a young lady, "Miss Mary Ann," who lived in a small town near Lawrenceburg. Soon the two fell in love.[19]

It was during these years that either Buell began to think about the

military or his uncle considered it for him. Though quiet, as a determined young man, perhaps driven by a desire for discipline and order
in his life or by a pathetic search for the family he never had, he decided
to make a career in the military, since that appeared to be the one area in
which he could develop his intellectual talents. His uncle may have
wanted his nephew to have the advantages of a college education and
the discipline of military life. Buell's high moral character and sense of
right and wrong had been shaped by his intense religious beliefs and by
a Puritan work ethic instilled in him at a very young age. Surely those
qualities would serve him well in the military. No doubt the prestige of
attending the U.S. Military Academy and the lure of higher education at
the government's expense also influenced his decision to join the military as an officer.[20]

Securing an appointment to the U.S. Military Academy at West Point
was not as difficult as it might have been had he remained on the farm
in Lowell. Because of his uncle's prominence in business and in political
circles in southeast Indiana, acquiring the necessary endorsements of
the highest political officials for his nephew's admittance into the academy was relatively easy. In late December 1836 Indiana Congressional
Representative Amos Lane penned a formal letter of recommendation
to Acting Secretary of War Benjamin F. Butler for an appointment to
the academy on Buell's behalf. Lane's letter referred to this Dearborn
County youth as "an orphaned boy about 18 years [who is] very immi-
nently qualified to enter the institution, with all the requisites in disposition, in habits . . . and [discipline] for a soldier." "I have known him
from a small boy," wrote Lane; "he is the grand son of the late Judge
Buell of Cayuga Co. N.Y."[21]

In early January 1837 Representative Lane penned another letter to
Butler enclosing some additional testimonial on Buell's behalf for an
appointment to the academy. The enclosed letter had the signatures of
several prominent residents of Lawrenceburg and Dearborn County.
Their flattering letter expressed great confidence in the young store
clerk and reflected the high regard these men had for Buell. "Don Carlos Buell," they wrote, was "a young man of correct business habits of
good morrals and from constitution, form and disposition eminently
calculated for a soldier." They believed he would be "an ornament to the
institution and the army."[22]

In late March Buell learned that he had been accepted at West Point.
On April 3 he acknowledged receipt of his conditional appointment
and began to ponder the rigorous curriculum and entrance examinations. Because his tenure at the old Lawrenceburg school provided him

with only a modest common schooling, he worried about the June entrance examinations. Although very diligent, Buell was not a particularly exceptional student, and his limited education was a worry. He honed his skills for the tests and read as much as he could to make up for his deficiencies.[23]

In 1837 the academy's entrance examinations were not designed to exclude. Candidates had to be in good physical condition and demonstrate rudimentary proficiency by reading two and one-half lines from a history book, by writing a dictated sentence on the blackboard, and by defining a fraction. Furthermore, each potential cadet received free tutoring prior to taking the examinations, and anyone who failed the first time in June could try again in August, provided his congressman had not named another candidate in the interim. The result was that even poor boys without the benefit of a formal education had an opportunity to get in. Almost every cadet who had the equivalent of a high school education passed easily, but as a result of the ineffectiveness of the screening devices, more than a quarter of those admitted failed to graduate.[24]

The academy required that all candidates arrive within the first three weeks in June, and it was during that time that Buell, among more than 100 other nervous, excited, and curious would-be cadets, landed at the West Point wharf. When Buell departed the boat and placed his baggage on the horse-drawn carriage for the journey up the hill to the school, the midwestern farmboy entered a world of military precision, regimen, and rigidity. It would be nearly three decades before he became a civilian again.[25]

Superintendent Sylvanus Thayer was no longer in command of the academy when Buell entered, but during his fourteen-year tenure he had created the Thayer System. His achievements earned him the title Father of the Military Academy. During Buell's first year Maj. Rene De Russy was the academy's superintendent, and for his remaining three years Buell came under the tutelage of superintendent Maj. Richard Delafield.[26]

After making his required appearance in the adjutant's office to present his credentials, Buell was ordered to the quartermaster, where he was issued the bare essentials to survive barracks life. In the interval between his arrival and the entrance examinations, Buell divided his time between the classroom, where for four hours daily, cadet instructors tutored him in arithmetic and grammar, and the parade ground, where student drillmasters taught him the fundamental military skills. Even before he had been fitted for a uniform, Buell was living the life of a cadet. The drilling and tutoring ceased temporarily around June 20 while the new cadets took their physical and mental examinations.[27]

Probably to his relief, Buell passed the academic examinations easily, and he similarly passed the physical requirements. Since a cadet under four feet, nine inches would not be admitted, Buell was pleased when they measured him at five feet, three and one-half inches and about 150 pounds. Although small in stature even by 1837 standards, his boyish frame belied a great physical strength that was at once displayed by his firm handshake. After being found fully qualified, he was sent to the quartermaster, where he drew his cadet grays. Although cadets were assigned to quarters according to company, they could chose their roommates, and in contrast to modern custom, cadets of different classes could room together. It is uncertain, however, who Buell's roommate was, since he never mentioned it, and neither did others who attended the academy during his time.[28]

During this period of West Point history, the academic faculty attempted to turn out not only Christian gentlemen but also Christian soldiers, so it emphasized the virtues of duty, loyalty, honor, and courage. The academy required of every individual rigid conformity to its standards, and the superintendent severely reprimanded or dismissed those unwilling to comply. Beyond the academy's demanding rigid discipline the curriculum was not intellectually stimulating. Still, of the more than 100 cadets admitted to the academy in 1837, only 52 ever graduated.[29]

De Russy's last year as superintendent made Buell's first year at the academy as relaxed as he would ever find it. The superintendent tried to make life pleasant for the cadets, instituting, for example, a ball at the end of summer encampment. As a plebe, Buell probably went alone. He was, after all, in love with Miss Mary Ann, to whom he would become engaged while at West Point. Although he spent his summer vacations in Lawrenceburg and corresponded with her regularly, his days at West Point must have been marked by the disappointment of not seeing her more often.[30]

After the two-month summer encampment, Buell was assigned to his barracks. His time was scheduled to the minute. He arose at 5:30 A.M., ate breakfast, studied and attended classes until 1:00 P.M., broke for lunch, studied again until 4:00 P.M., and read and wrote letters until dinner at 6:00 P.M. Cadets studied until lights were ordered out at 9:30 P.M. On weekends and during free time cadets could be found at Benny Haven's local tavern in nearby Buttermilk (Highland) Falls, where the food, drink, and atmosphere made life a little more bearable. Although academy authorities frowned on such practices, Benny's was one of the few places where cadets could unwind.[31]

When Buell began his academic career in the early summer of 1837, he was one among more than 100 freshman plebes who would undergo hazing and "devilment" at the hands of upperclassmen. Those who made it through the summer entered the academic sphere hoping to endure the rigors of the curriculum and the noted Thayer System of discipline. Buell's fellow students in his first year included some of the most famous future Civil War figures. Fourth Class mates included Pennsylvanians Josiah Gorgas, John F. Reynolds, and James Totten, Nathaniel Lyon of Connecticut, and Joseph B. Plummer of Massachusetts. Among the fifty-eight remaining members of the Third Class were Ohioan William T. Sherman, or Cump as his friends called him, and Corp. George H. Thomas of Virginia. The thirty-three-member Second Class included 1st Sgt. Henry W. Halleck of New York. First Class cadets included Ohioan Irvin McDowell, Georgian William J. Hardee, and Louisianan Pierre Gustave Toutant Beauregard, who was at that time an assistant teacher of French and ranked second in his class.[32]

The summer encampment taught Buell the practical aspects of professional training and the functions of a private. He learned how to pitch a tent, parade, shoot on the rifle range, march, and ride over long sweeps of countryside, something he very much enjoyed. He endured the initiation process and the practical jokes and the irritation of personal service to older cadets.

After summer encampment Buell was transferred to B Company Corps of Cadets, and the academy's curriculum tested his intellectual abilities. The most onerous part of cadet life, Buell soon learned, was the severe discipline, and he had considerable trouble adjusting to the environment and curriculum. The scope of mathematics alone was extremely broad, and the attempt to cover a lot of ground in a short time exacted a heavy toll on the cadets, producing more academic casualties than any other discipline. Buell, however, was among the fortunate cadets who fared well in this subject.[33]

Overall, however, cadet Buell impressed none of his academic instructors in his first term, failing to establish himself as a bright young soldier in the eyes of his academicians. Though Buell was conscientious, he unfortunately developed a pattern of delinquency that brought him close to dismissal more than once. He made an impression on his senior military compatriots by being one of the few plebes to be arrested during the fall of 1837.[34]

He continued his studies of mathematics and French into the next term, and his frequent delinquencies also continued. Buell made it into the Register of Cadet Delinquencies no less than thirty times his second term, and his activities must have earned him quite a reputation among his superiors and classmates. His delinquencies included missing French class; not carrying his gun correctly; neglect of duty, a frequent occurrence; being late for dinner; late marching on guard; absence from drill; answering improperly at a parade and at roll call; not dressing properly; and talking in ranks. Authorities relied on an intricate and comprehensive system of punishments and demerits to enforce discipline. Demerits, although closely associated with chastisement, were actually assessments against the cadet's grade in conduct, whereas punishments entailed loss of privileges, confinement, extra duty, and expulsion. At the end of the day at parade, the adjutant announced the delinquencies that had been recorded for the day. Consequently, Buell's name quickly became synonymous with that record.[35]

When Buell entered the academy Third Class, cadet William T. Sherman remembered that he was a "slender, high-strung" lad, but Sherman certainly could not have predicted the degree to which that energy would be channeled into positive or, in this case, delinquent activity. Given Buell's shy demeanor and his desire to graduate from the academy, it is certainly surprising that he manifested this kind of behavior. His disposition did not change once Buell left home for West Point, but his activities his first year reflected the degree to which the young Indiana farmboy was willing to adapt to the academy's demanding curriculum and rigid discipline. True, he may have had a lot of energy, but being disciplined into compliance became something he, like other cadets, learned well because he resisted it so much. Although the Register of Cadet Delinquencies suggests that he was in trouble frequently with the same cadets, no record exists that might indicate Buell's relationship to those cadets. He made few friends while at the academy, and even those he might have befriended were never mentioned in his personal correspondence either during his cadet days or after. One of the few times he may have tried to cultivate a friendship was during his many extra hours of retribution with those who had been punished for the same offense.[36]

Buell completed his first year at the academy with a less than promising record. His grades in math and French were mediocre and did not help his standing in the Fourth Class. He ranked 47 out of 82 cadets who completed the plebe year, but he received 183 demerits his first year, placing him 178 out of 218 cadets. The academy allowed a maximum of 200 demerits before dismissal. Had Buell not earned such a high number of demerits his first year, he might have ended his plebe year at a higher academic rank. While Buell certainly wanted to become a second lieutenant, he was neither overly ambitious in his study habits nor preoccupied with the desire to impress his instructors by strengthening his intellectual capacity. This, however, would change once he left the academy. Perhaps the only deed Buell performed during his first year that merited some honorable recognition was what he did in removing the library books and other philosophical and chemical apparatus from the building known as the Academy when a fire broke out on February 19, 1838. Interestingly enough, Buell had just been released from confinement to his room when the blaze erupted and the Corps of Cadets was ordered to retrieve the materials.[37]

Buell's mediocre academic standing coupled with his poor disciplinary record did not diminish the academy's effect on his character. Like all cadets, he shared the same military experience. West Point purposely made life hard for the cadets in order to turn out finished soldiers. The full schedule, the constant supervision that removed temptation, and moral exhortations at chapel every Sunday all helped keep Buell out of serious trouble and safe from expulsion his first year. As a plebe, Buell was not allowed to join the recently formed Dialectic Society, and his reserved manner would certainly have precluded him from participating in the debating clubs. Most likely he spent his spare time brushing up on his French and drawing, since he became quite good at both. He evidently had a flare for the artistic and cultivated an aesthetic character.[38]

At the end of his plebe year, on the first day before summer encampment, he began what became his worst year at the academy. He received demerits for not being properly dressed on the grounds. For this offense he was confined to his tent and given extra duty. Within three weeks he received his severest punishment—eight demerits—for using profane language, something that was totally out of character for Buell. This incident could have resulted in expulsion from the academy, but instead he was confined to prison. Twice in August he received further severe punishment for being late for chapel. Even before beginning the fall term, cadet Buell had accumulated enough demerits to warrant a visit to the superintendent's office, which resulted in a severe reprimand and warning from Major De Russy.[39]

After the summer encampments, Buell began his second academic year as a member of the Third Class, now only sixty-eight strong. Among the more prominent Civil War figures who had graduated that June were Beauregard, McDowell, and Hardee. Incoming plebes included William S. Rosecrans of Ohio, John Pope of Illinois, Abner Doubleday of New York, and Earl Van Dorn of Mississippi. Although not a close friend, John Pope, who saw Buell almost every day, remembered that

Buell made quite an impression on other cadets. Buell was a "short, square man, with an immense physique and personal strength," wrote Pope, adding that he was "very erect, had a dark, impressive face and black eyes, and from something in his bearing and general appearance always gave the impression that he was much taller and larger than he really was."[40] Buell trusted no one and possessed a "frigid deportment," Pope added, and was "from the beginning a man of note at West Point, not because of his intellectual capacity or his social qualities, but rather because of something in his appearance and bearing which indicated great force of character and prompt resolution. He was in no respect social in his habits, but appeared always to be self-absorbed. He was extremely reserved in his demeanor and very silent and reticent if not at times forbidding in his manners." Pope regarded Buell as the consummate student even after West Point, "not . . . in a college sense," but rather as "a steady and close reader of history and books on military subjects." He concluded that in the pre–Civil War period, Buell "was probably as well posted on military subjects as almost any officer in the army."[41] Although during the Civil War Pope attributed this extremely reserved manner, bordering at times on haughtiness, more to painful diffidence than to natural coldness of temperament, as a cadet Pope appears to have been impressed with his ranking classmate.[42]

When Buell began his second year, Maj. Richard Delafield became the superintendent. Delafield had graduated first in his 1818 class, and shortly after he had received a commission in the Corps of Engineers. Under his instruction the academy's strict disciplinary measures were restored and all possible amusements and recreations removed. "Dicky the Punster," was the nickname he earned by making sarcastic puns. He was constantly bustling around the post, instituting changes, looking for troublemakers, and investigating petty occurrences. In the case of Buell, the superintendent would not have to look very far. The two quickly became acquainted.[43]

Buell would have to show marked improvement in discipline in his second year if he wanted to be removed from Delafield's list of delinquent cadets. In his second year Buell again took courses in mathematics and French. Although he made only modest gains in French, his grades in mathematics improved considerably. His second year curriculum, however, introduced him to another difficult area of the educational sphere—English grammar—which he evidently had difficulty mastering. Drawing, though, continued to spark his interest and perhaps helped defuse his anxiety over his inability to master his other subjects. The curriculum was utilitarian, not aesthetic, and included lettering, topographical drawing, signs, and symbols, which would provide the foundation skills for engineering courses. Buell excelled in drawing, and it no doubt excited him to discover that he had mastered at least one of his courses. His January examinations were a little easier, and the grades sent home to his uncle George Buell reflected his maturing academic abilities. In math he ranked 21 out of 82; in French, 49; English grammar, 44; and drawing, 14.[44]

Although it appears that he had made some modest strides in his educational endeavors, by March Buell had amassed 169 demerits. After the demerit roll had been compiled and forwarded to the chief engineer, Superintendent Delafield observed the names of the cadets who appeared to be on their way to expulsion. No stranger to the list of delinquencies, Buell's name was among those at the top of the list, and Delafield chastised him personally. He let Buell and other delinquent cadets know that "as they [prized] their warrants, let this timely admonition suffice to recall to their recollections the consequences of a continual violation of the regulations."[45]

At the end of Buell's second year his June examinations placed him 45 out of 68 remaining cadets. The Register of Conduct listed him as having received 183 demerits, and he was ranked 219 out of 229 cadets. It appeared that each term his delinquency record severely and consistently diminished his academic record.[46]

When Buell entered his third year, only fifty-eight cadets remained in his class. Among the most noted seniors who graduated were Sherman and Thomas, while incoming freshman plebes included Ulysses S. Grant of southern Ohio, or Sam as he was called. As a member of the Second Class Buell took courses in chemistry, philosophy, and drawing for the entire year. From his record it appeared that chemistry was Buell's worst subject. In philosophy he fared better, yet he continued to excel in drawing. In his spring term, probably on the recommendation of his superiors, he added conduct to his curriculum and received a passing grade.[47]

Both his January and June examinations reflected his modest intellectual development, but his 110 demerits for the year, the most of any other Second Class cadet, earned him a rank of 199 out of 232. Consequently, his academic rank suffered. He was 33 out of a class of 55 cadets. Once again he made an appearance at the office of the superintendent and received a warning about his future at the academy.[48]

In his senior year Buell had to be careful not to acquire too many demerits, since as an upperclassman his activities were even more closely monitored. This was the year for instructors and authorities to see if they had indeed turned Buell into a Christian gentleman and a soldier.

The number of demerits increased to the highest level for any offense during his final year, and to remain at West Point Buell would have to reach a compromise between what was required by military discipline and what he was willing to do. Though the academy had instilled in the cadet a strong character, he evidently put his own sense of right and wrong against the academy's strict regimen. Toward that end, he met his final year head on.[49]

The day Buell reached his First Class year was surely one of his happiest at the academy. Of the original 117 cadets who had entered in the summer of 1837, only 53 remained and 52 would graduate. Although a First Classman, he was not presumptuous enough to disassociate himself from the incoming plebes, though they did not have the appearance of a distinguished group. Indeed, among the class of 1844 there were not any cadets who would later distinguish themselves in the Civil War, except Winfield Scott Hancock of Pennsylvania. Hancock made an unforgettable impression on Buell, who remembered him as a "fair-haired, handsome boy, well-bred, good-tempered, and manly," who "looked even younger" than his sixteen years. Evidently Hancock made such a favorable impression on Buell and the other First Classmen that he was "one of the few Plebes who [was] at once taken into good fellowship by the older class, and was a special favorite with my [Buell's] most intimate friends."[50]

The capstone of Buell's academic program at West Point was Dennis Hart Mahan's class in military and civil engineering and the science of war, which First Classman took daily. In the fall Buell focused on civil engineering, and in the spring he concentrated on military engineering. The degree to which Buell's military thinking was influenced by Mahan's teachings at the academy is difficult to ascertain, largely because only a week was devoted to the art and science of war. Mahan drew on the French experience and the philosophy of Swiss military theorist Antoine Henri Jomini, who had derived a set of operational principles from his analyses of Frederick the Great and Napoleon. Like Jomini, Mahan firmly advocated the use of reason in military matters, so much so that students nicknamed him "Old [Common] Sense." He preached that the occupation of territory or strategic points was more important than the destruction of armies. Buell no doubt listened attentively when Mahan lectured on the need for a professional army. Beyond that, however, Mahan's influence was limited. Although it appears unlikely that one course would so influence a student that it would continue to govern his thinking years later, a case can be made that Buell, inspired by Mahan, became a careful and studious reader of military philosophy after graduation from the academy. As he matured into a disciplined soldier, his thinking on military philosophy matured as well. As he developed fixed ways of conducting his life in the military, so too would his reasoning become fixed in political and military matters. His rigid upbringing and conservative religious and social views simply reinforced this thinking and deterred him from deviating from whatever he thought right.[51]

In addition to his engineering courses, Buell enrolled in ethics, artillery, equestrian, infantry tactics, and more drawing. He also took artillery and sword exercises, both of which appealed to him since they were among the few areas in which he received a decent grade. Unfortunately, neither his conduct nor his ability to follow simple military codes had improved. He received 193 demerits in his senior year, the most of any cadet in 1840–41. That record alone distinguished Don Carlos Buell from his fellow classmates at the academy.[52]

When graduation arrived in June 1841, Buell finished 32 out of his class of 52. His mediocre grades and celebrated record of violating the academy's military codes probably earned him a reputation as a nonconformist. His record placed him apart from those who were chosen to join the elite Corps of Engineers. He evidently did not possess the natural intellectual abilities of those students who distinguished themselves by graduating at the top of the class. In fact, because the government offered high-ranking cadets the choice of which branch of the military they wished to enter, those of the lower ranks were routinely assigned to the infantry to fill the void left by the best and the brightest of the academy who chose more specialized branches. Buell was not surprised that his rank assigned him to the infantry.[53]

Although in later years many cadets developed a nostalgia for the academy, Buell never mentioned his tenure at West Point, perhaps because that time was not the most favorable of his life. Only a few persons remembered Buell in their postwar reminiscences, perhaps because he kept to himself socially. His mediocre record indicated that he barely tolerated the strict regimen, and his unruliness attracted the unfavorable attention of the superintendent. His accumulation of demerits reflected his inability either to conform to strict military discipline or to accommodate himself to the circumstances there. In short, he was a better leader than a follower and flirted with insubordination as a result. Learning to be disciplined did not come easily for Buell, but he never forgot the value of discipline itself. If he disagreed with his superiors, he made his objections known. His grades suggested that he certainly did not find his work effortless. With the exception of drawing and military tactics and strategy, the tedious memorization did not stimulate his mind; in fact, it stifled his imagination and reduced his intellect to book knowledge. He had, however, impressed Mahan, who saw potential in Buell. In the summer of 1861, when George B. McClellan was in command of the Army of the Potomac, Mahan wrote him that among those officers whom McClellan might look to for assistance was Buell, since Buell had impressed him as one who would make a future general. Despite his academic record, Buell proved during the war that he had absorbed the simple fundamentals that Mahan taught him about Jomini.[54]

As unimpressive as his grades were, and as ungovernable as his demerits made him seem, the academy still made an impression on Buell. Like most graduates of his time, he believed he was one of a special group, superior to ordinary mortals. The experience of surviving the academy for four years indicated he wanted to be among those professional officers who would shape the regular army. Still, the academy failed to strip away his modest and unassuming reserve and his genteel attitude. As he matured into a man and a soldier, his capacity for conforming to the mental demands of military discipline grew. Buell would learn to become a more disciplined soldier, since graduation from the academy established his life's work in the army. Indeed, his military education was just beginning.[55]

CHAPTER TWO

Seminoles and Severity

Whatever youthful innocence cadet Buell possessed during his tenure at the U.S. Military Academy, his graduation from West Point at age twenty-three marked its end. The army would have him for the next few years whether he liked it or not. He was surely eager to be away from the academy, since it stifled his imagination and shaped his behavior—something his excessive demerits indicated. He may have been comfortable among his fellow cadets, but he developed few close friendships. Part of his problem was that Buell had no talent or capacity for cultivating useful relationships. His serious manner often repelled people.[1]

While the highly ranked members of the West Point class of 1841 entered the army in the Corps of Engineers, dragoons, ordnance, or the artillery, Buell began his military duty in the Third U.S. Infantry along with three other members of his class, Richard H. Bacot, Israel Bush Richardson, and William T. H. Brooks. On July 1 Buell was appointed second lieutenant, Company F, and after a postgraduation furlough, he was ordered in early October to report to the commanding officer at Fort Columbus, on Governors Island, New York, which had essentially become the holding place for officers and soldiers heading south to join their respective regiments in Florida. Once mustered into the infantry, the young lieutenant boarded a vessel in New York harbor and in the late summer headed for Florida and the Florida War.[2]

By the time Buell arrived in Florida in the fall of 1841, the Second Seminole War had been in progress over five years, though the 5,000 American soldiers had succeeded in subduing most of the small bands of natives. Still, America's growing dissatisfaction with the war, the indiscriminate brutality of the Indians, malaria and yellow fever, and the suffocating heat combined to drain the American ranks. The unusually high number of officer resignations reflected the low pay and unpopularity of the assignment, and Buell was one of many green lieutenants sent to fill the void.[3]

Fort Stansbury was Buell's Florida destination. Located on the Wakulla River twelve miles south of Tallahassee, the fort was established during the Seminole War when most of the area's plantations were stockaded against Indian attack. Upon his arrival, Buell reported to Maj. Henry Wilson, commander of the Third Infantry. Buell was the only new regular officer commissioned to his unit, and a significant amount of responsibility for its leadership naturally descended upon him. He quickly recognized that responsibility and leadership began with acting the role as well as believing in it. At the time of Buell's arrival the regiment totaled 691 soldiers who patrolled the western part of Florida, an area extending between the Suwannee River and the western boundary of the state.[4]

The Third Infantry had arrived in Florida in October 1840 and by the end of that November had concentrated at Fort Brooke (Tampa Bay). For the next two and a half years the regiment endured its share of hardships and rigorous duties. From Fort Brooke the companies of the Third were dispersed to numerous detached posts and camps throughout middle and west Florida and along the Georgia border. Constantly engaged year-round, they scouted the surrounding country and swamps in search of small bands of marauding Indians.[5]

Lieutenant Buell participated in these operations, although his military expeditions were limited to minor patrols to seek out remaining Indians. These patrols usually lasted several days and rarely took him out of north Florida. Other soldiers of the Third stationed at Fort Stansbury went on twenty-five-day boat expeditions to the Aucilla, Wacissa, Econfina, and Fenholloway Rivers and to the mouth of the Suwannee. Although some 600 men engaged in these activities, 220 usually reported sick from dysentery. Of the approximately 60 men in Buell's company, under the command of Capt. Henry Bainbridge, frequently about one-third were sick. Bainbridge was often on detached service at another post, while 1st Lt. John H. Eaton, Buell's immediate superior, spent most of his Florida tour (1841–43) on detached service at the U.S. Military Academy. Consequently, Buell assumed more than his share of command. He was assigned to Fort Aucilla, a few miles east of Tallahassee between the Aucilla and Wacissa Rivers. In the fall and winter of 1842–43 he led several scouting forays into north Florida. He participated in no major engagement with the Indians, however, and thus shared little of the glory of other companies that had already borne the brunt of fighting the "savages."[6]

Although his initial tenure in Florida was uneventful, Buell made a lasting impression on at least one of his subordinate soldiers. Sgt. John H. Kendall recalled his impression of Buell in November 1841 as a serious professional officer. "As long as I live," he wrote Buell many years later, "I think I shall never forget the time on 'company drill' at Camp Carter or 'Fort Ocilla,' Florida. . . . You marched up to the right of the company and brushed off with your gloved hand a gadfly (I think it was called) that was stinging my bare chin until the *tears* ran down my cheek —you let me bear the torment for a while, and I believe that you almost bit your lip to keep from smiling."[7] Kendall also recalled another instance when Buell let him off easy for allowing two prisoners to escape. Under the circumstances, Kendall remembered, Buell informed him that "we were *all* glad to be rid of them."[8] Though Buell displayed a soft side toward regulars, he would not, however, share the same attitude with volunteers in the Civil War.

It was an easy lifestyle for a green lieutenant fresh out of West Point and pleasantly different from the rigidity and suffocation of the military academy. Buell no doubt relished his freedom, but he took his official responsibilities seriously. Because only a few of his classmates were assigned to the Third Infantry, and none to his company, he probably enjoyed little camaraderie. Although he wrote little of his days in the land of swamps and alligators, Buell seems barely to have tolerated his tour of duty in Florida. He abhorred the widespread corruption of the civilian interpreters and guides who secretly sold ammunition covertly to the enemy. Moreover, he was frustrated that his insignificant assignment was wasting his military schooling. Although he had trained for war, he now failed to encounter it, or at least the kind of war he had learned about at West Point. Perhaps the winter weather proved for Buell the only saving grace of his first military assignment, since it was a far cry from the dreary winters he had spent along the Hudson at the academy.[9]

By January 1842 the war had essentially ended. Although Buell considered the conflict a gigantic waste of time, he nonetheless gained invaluable field experience. He encountered a significant lack of discipline among the soldiers of his unit, which he no doubt blamed on its previous commanders. He had come to view discipline as defining the soldier and, therefore, a unit, an ironic conclusion since his record at the academy revealed that he had found it difficult to conform to the kind of rules he now expected his own men to accept. On the Florida frontier, Buell became convinced that combat was ill defined, since the guerrilla tactics were the ruling condition. In such a state of battle, discipline was that much more necessary.[10]

Nothing at West Point had prepared him for Florida. Battles were not always fought between two rival professional armies as envisioned by Antoine Henri Jomini, Marshal Saxe, and Dennis Hart Mahan, but between peoples. The Seminoles fought with their entire society, and they attacked not merely enemy soldiers and civilians; they even killed their own to avoid enslavement. At the same time the Indians survived because necessity made them use the strength, supply, and defense of the wilderness. Consequently, U.S. army commanders had to rely on knowledgeable scouts and guides and adopt techniques that struck at the nerve centers of the native society and its villages, crops, and herds. Buell drew lessons from his initial tenure in the combat zone, not the least of which was the value of discipline in conducting campaigns.[11]

After the pacification in the summer of 1842, the bulk of the army pulled out of Florida, though Gen. William Jenkins Worth remained behind to capture any remaining Seminole chiefs. The Third Infantry, now under the command of Lt. Ethan Allen Hitchcock, took part in these operations. Hitchcock was a former aide to the secretary of war and a rigid disciplinarian. Under orders from Worth, Hitchcock besieged the surrounding country by land and water with boats, dragoons, and infantry. In these operations Buell received his last significant assignment in Florida. In early January 1843, on the Ocklockonee River, west of Fort Stansbury, the soldiers of the Third successfully rounded up Seminole chief Pascoffer and his band of fifty-one Indians. The soldiers were skillful and energetic in fighting the Indians and, according to one source, "were seconded by the zealous exertions of the officers of [the] regiment," including Buell.[12] Hitchcock boasted in his diary that he was certain "Worth [had] not seen movements better executed these many years—not even in his own regiment."[13] Whether true or not, the Seminole War was over, and the Third Infantry was transferred to Jefferson Barracks, Missouri. Buell prepared to move to St. Louis.

Though Buell failed to earn a brevet for his service in Florida, he did gain invaluable experience by commanding a company. His leisure allowed him time to develop competence in all his tasks. He also became acquainted with other officers, including William Lear, Henry Bainbridge, Douglass S. Irwin, Philip N. Barbour, William S. Henry, and Lewis Craig. Nevertheless, he was relieved when on April 5 his brief tour of duty in the piney woods of north Florida ended and he and his company boarded the steamer *Ben Franklin* at Port Leon for their journey to the Midwest. The Third Infantry arrived at St. Louis on April 22, 1843. The unit established regimental headquarters at Jefferson Barracks ten miles below the city in the largest military post in the country at that time, home for sixteen companies of infantry.[14]

For the most part, the change from the Florida frontier to garrison duty along the Mississippi proved a welcome relief, although garrison duty resembled the rigid atmosphere of the military academy. Up every morning before sunrise for breakfast, reveille, and dress parade, Buell would sometimes also pull a night of guard duty supervision. The truth of the matter was, however, that after 9:00 A.M. he had little to do. Officers mostly had to depend on themselves for recreation, and their conversations were often of tactics, their tours in the Seminole War, or the days at West Point. At least Buell was not alone, since a few of his West Point acquaintances were at Jefferson Barracks as well.[15]

In the summer of 1843 the Third and Fourth Infantries were formed into a school for brigade drill under Col. Stephen Watts Kearny, commander of the Third Military Department and a thorough disciplinarian. The soldiers were so intensively drilled and disciplined during the summer and fall of 1843 and the winter of 1843–44 that the brigade gained a reputation as one of the best in the army. Buell, no doubt, was beginning to see a pattern of how officers handled soldiers.[16]

On June 3, 1843, Buell's career took a turn for the worse, as he unceremoniously lashed out at a soldier. Despite his own unruly attitude and cast-iron will, Buell was intolerant of those who had not cultivated the characteristic he believed crucial in the making of a soldier: firm discipline. Evidently, on the morning of June 3, Pvt. James P. Humphrey, a noted troublemaker with an ungovernable disposition, was late to reveille. As punishment, Buell directed the first sergeant to order Humphrey to police behind the company quarters. According to Buell, "It was a course I had been in the habit of pursuing under similar circumstances."[17] Later that same morning the sergeant reported to Buell that the private was not carrying out his orders. Buell ordered the sergeant to have Humphrey report to work when he returned to quarters. When the private came back, he continued disobeying the sergeant's orders. When Buell was informed, he ordered Humphrey to his headquarters, worried that the private's insubordination would have an injurious effect on the excellent discipline of his command.[18]

When Humphrey arrived at Buell's headquarters, Buell glared at him. Although short, Buell must have made an impressive appearance. His stocky frame and husky voice reflected a man whose words were sharp and his actions uncompromising. He asked Humphrey why he had been late. The sullen private responded that he "had something else to do." Buell's temper flared. He stepped to within a pace of the soldier and said in a rough manner, "What do you mean, sir?" The soldier leaned back and in an insolent tone remarked, "Don't you touch me, sir," or words to that effect. Buell grabbed the soldier's collar, and Humphrey seized Buell by the throat and began to choke him. In a moment of rage Buell drew his sword and repeatedly slashed it down on Humphrey's head. As he had as a boy, Buell refused to remain passive when physically challenged. The injured private clutched his head while leaning over to pick up the piece of ear and clump of hair that had been sliced off. "You will repent this, sir!" he shouted as he cowered near the floor. Buell responded, "Silence, you son of a bitch!"[19]

In his testimony Humphrey claimed that Buell had not only thrown him against the wall but had also attempted to run his sword through him. Although several soldiers who witnessed the scuffle declared that Buell had not attempted to run Humphrey through with his sword, their testimony did indicate that Buell had been furious and rough with the private, both physically and verbally. Buell's overbearing nature surfaced as he questioned witnesses. Although the company physician determined that Humphrey's wounds were minor, rumors spread throughout Jefferson Barracks that Buell had not only thrown Humphrey to the ground and cut off his ear but also had tried to kill him. Buell's reputation for sternness now assumed a more violent tone. He set a harsh precedent for command in his company, showing just how far he was willing to go to force his soldiers to conform to his standards.[20]

The Buell case raised the eyebrows of military and civilian officials all the way from the lowly private to the president of the United States. While the government tried to keep the case secret, the *Army and Navy*

Chronicle, a prominent service journal, published a report on it. Buell was arrested and ordered to stand trial for charges of "unofficial-like conduct," with Colonel Kearny ordering a court. On June 12 Maj. William W. Lear of the Third Infantry convened the court-martial. Besides Lear, twelve members served, mostly junior officers of the Third and Fourth Infantries. One of the members was Richard H. Bacot, Buell's former classmate who had served in the Seminole War with him.

The trial lasted a few days, and Buell took full advantage of his opportunities to appear before the court, conducting himself like a lawyer. In a succinct and carefully reasoned closing defense statement, Buell deeply regretted that his conduct as an officer had been called into question. In an emotional reprisal of the events he stated, "I had hoped when I entered the service, that the pride I felt in the profession I had chosen in purpose [*sic*] to all others, and a wish to prove myself not altogether unworthy of the commission with which the President had been pleased to honor me, would enable me to shake my official conduct on, at least not to deserve the censure of my superiors."[21] He expressed confidence in the court's ability to reach the honorable conclusion. His chief concern was that "the service . . . has arrived at such a deplorable state of discipline that an inferior can not only commit the most flagrant act of insubordination, but, after having committed it, with unblushing effrontery, he cries out against the grievances which have been, as he conceives, inflicted upon him by the conduct of his superior . . . whose sworn duty it is to use his 'utmost endeavors' to preserve order and regularity whenever his duty may call him to act."[22] He further added that even though the court might find him innocent of the charges, the entire incident was a "blot on [his] character as an officer, which neither time nor any future course of [his would] be able to obliterate."[23] After deliberation, the court attached no criminality to his actions and found him not guilty. On June 19 it honorably acquitted him. Buell was released from arrest, and the court was dissolved.[24]

The severity of Buell's actions, however, caused the War Department and Maj. Gen. Edmund P. Gaines, Kearny's replacement as commander of the Third Military District, to take notice. On July 1, 1843, Asst. Adj. Gen. Samuel Cooper ordered Major Lear to reassemble the court to reconsider its decision. Gaines likewise directed the court and brought the matter to the attention of higher authorities, including Gen. in Chief of the Army Winfield Scott, Secretary of War John M. Porter, and President John Tyler, all of whom disapproved of the court's findings. The previous year Scott had issued orders denouncing officers' illegal punishments of enlisted men and ordering the court-martial of those who used methods beyond his orders. Buell's actions and the decision of the court, therefore, conflicted with these new military procedures. Gaines ordered the court to state on what authority of law or orders they justified Buell's actions in striking a soldier so severely. Furthermore, Gaines wondered whether the members of the court were not biased in Buell's favor, since many had either served with him or had come to know him in some capacity while at Jefferson Barracks.[25]

The court grudgingly reconvened on July 5 and, after brief deliberation and reexamination of their earlier proceedings, found Buell innocent again. In its statement, however, the court went beyond its assignment. Ethan Allen Hitchcock, who was disturbed about the request to reassemble, prepared a declaration regarding the functions and role of a military tribunal. He argued that "the Rules and Articles of War nowhere give authority to any officer to demand from a court-martial reasons for its decisions, still less to dictate what its decisions 'must be' in any case."[26] The members of the court, all junior officers, were uncomfortable about reconsidering Buell's case and were worried that military superiors were trying to use the influence of their rank to secure decisions they wanted.[27]

Criticism of the decision in Buell's case, Hitchcock wrote for the court, appeared almost entirely to be predicated on the assumption that Buell's blows on Private Humphrey were a designed punishment. Furthermore, critics implied that Buell had deliberately taken Humphrey from the guardhouse to punish him by striking him with his sword, and the court was required to show the law that authorized him to do so. The members of the court, Hitchcock wrote, regarded these premises as invalid. Because its initial findings were rooted in the fact that Buell was justified in his actions whether he was authorized to strike the private or not, the court had awarded judgment in favor of the lieutenant. Compelled by a like sense of duty to themselves and respect to the high function they were discharging, the members stood by their initial decision.[28]

General Gaines disapproved of the court's decision and its justification. He declared that Buell was a commissioned officer with the advantages of a military education, "sufficient to justify the hope that by a vigilant and faithful discharge of his duty *according to the Rules and Articles of War*, he may rise to the highest command of the army." Moreover, Gaines said that in the spirit of military law he would allow the tribunal the opportunity to correct its errors.[29]

Gaines was obviously upset about the court's interpretation of military law and tried to use his authority to force it to concede to his wishes. He reminded the members of his duty and the sacred responsibility of his oath in carrying out military law and that both he and the court were not independent of those restraints. Finally, he ordered Buell to return to duty but added that while he respected Buell as a young officer, Buell should not have punished the private by going beyond the law, no matter how disorderly the soldier. He urged Buell to follow strictly the military codes of discipline to "confine the disobedient; if necessary, iron them; but never strike them with a sword, or any other weapon, without clear case of mutiny."[30]

The matter was hardly over. General Scott now became concerned about the results of the proceedings. He declared that the findings of the court "show great perversity, which it is feared may be common on the same subject (flogging) among the younger officers of the Third and Fourth regiments of infantry." "To correct the perversity, and to vindicate discipline," he added, "now requires serious measures."[31] He pointed out that the previous year in a similar case an officer of a higher and distinguished rank was sentenced to three months' suspension. "Buell, without any claim to indulgence," Scott said, "is *honorably* acquitted by the court."[32] Scott was so disgusted that he laid the matter before the secretary of war with his recommendation for reconvening the court.[33]

Secretary of War John M. Porter responded by ordering yet another reconsideration to be held on August 15. He was deeply concerned about the precedent that might be set in cases of this nature, since it might do great injury to the service. On receipt of the order, the court reassembled, but instead of proceeding to trial, Hitchcock and the members charged the government with an attempt to intimidate the court. In a letter to the president, Hitchcock alluded to General Scott as "some subordinate authority," whereupon Scott responded by accusing Hitchcock of attempting to "stimulate disobedience" and expressed indignation at what he considered a "miscarriage of justice."[34]

As the bureaucratic battle continued over the legal issues of the case, Buell resumed his duties, though the affair affected him privately and publicly. Hitchcock, however, would not let the incident end and wrote to President Tyler almost a year later, challenging the secretary of war's reasoning in the Buell case. Tyler, however, apparently had more pressing issues than a fatiguing legal issue involving the army and paid little attention to the affair.[35]

In any event, the case against Buell illustrated that he had impressed his comrades with his highly principled integrity and military bearing. Those who acquitted him and then stood by him despite immense pressure had evidently come to respect the young lieutenant as a man and soldier of principle. Even General Scott recognized this fact when he commented that Buell "bears a high character in his regiment for intelligence and moral and military deportment."[36] Perhaps this was true, but Buell nevertheless was now a marked man. He had a reputation as a strict, almost brutal disciplinarian. This reputation preceded him wherever he went.

In the meantime, Private Humphrey was confined at hard labor for the balance of his enlistment, with a ball and chain attached to his leg. The court ordered that he forfeit all pay and allowances except what he owed the sutler and fifty cents per month for his washing. At the end of his enlistment, it was ordered that "his head be shaved and he be drummed out of the service."[37]

The case continued to elicit worry among civilian officials, and Porter feared that public outcry against Buell's actions might taint the character of the military. Moreover, Gaines and Gen. Roger Jones, through General Cooper, worried that because Buell was a West Point graduate, his behavior might reflect poorly on the disciplinary measures being instituted at the academy to force soldiers to comply with orders. Toward that end, Buell's case became a political matter in the fall of 1843, generating correspondence between military and political officials. In December General Scott's opinion on the Buell case finally encouraged the president to get involved by making a statement to put the matter to rest. Tyler declared emphatically, "I can see no good to the service in again requiring the Court to pass upon the case. . . . Let all further proceedings, therefore, against Lieutenant Buell, for the offence with which he is charged, cease."[38]

Buell had always enjoyed a limited social life, but he decided to be even less social during the legal affair. He had emerged from obscurity as a soldier who possessed a good record but also one whose uncompromising attitude reflected a firm resolve and inflexibility in matters of discipline. Though he had not cultivated serious relationships with fellow officers, he had managed to impress some of his comrades, who evidently maintained considerable admiration for him, since the facts of the case clearly indicated that his actions deserved at least some minimal sentence. Whatever the case, for such a short duration in the army, Buell had suffered more than his share of controversy, most of his own doing.[39]

By the fall of 1843, with the court-martial case essentially behind him, Buell resumed the duties of his rank. He drilled his company, logged daily reports, and slowly drifted back out of the center of attention. He was soon recognized, however, among the other officers of the Third and Fourth Infantry Regiments, as a thorough disciplinarian.[40]

In early May 1844 the Third Regiment was transferred to Camp Wilkins, an old Indian reservation in Louisiana adjacent to Fort Jesup, about midway between the Red and the Sabine Rivers. The regiment had been ordered to become part of the American forces congregating to occupy Texas after it voted to be absorbed by the United States. The newly organized Army of Observation came under the command of Gen. Zachary Taylor, who after nearly four decades of relative obscurity unexpectedly found himself quite popular in the approaching war with Mexico.[41]

As the summer of 1844 wore away and the cool days and colder nights of fall and winter descended on the Louisiana delta, the soldiers of the Army of Observation spent their time drilling and anticipating the results of the coming election and the annexation of Texas. That fall the presidential election, which pitted Tennessean James K. Polk against Kentuckian Henry Clay, decided the question of annexation. It is unclear whether or not Buell favored annexation, since he never mentioned it. He was a decided Democrat, however, and though he may not have favored annexation, he probably cast his vote for Polk, who won. The following March, when the Senate approved annexation, the Polk administration assured Texas officials that a 3,000-man army would march to protect their newfound claim.[42]

By July 1845 Texas had formally agreed to annexation, and President Polk ordered the 3,000-man Army of Observation to Corpus Christi. Hitchcock's Third Infantry arrived in early August and helped to establish Camp Corpus Christi, or Fort Marcy, on the southern shore of the Nueces River, the first federal fort on Texas soil. Buell's Company F had now come under the command of Capt. Henry Bainbridge. The presence of U.S. troops on the edge of the disputed territory farthest from the Mexican settlements was not sufficient to provoke hostilities. To be sure, there was much talk of war with Mexico as Lt. Ulysses S. Grant remembered the foreboding sentiment, "We were sent to provoke a fight, but it was essential that Mexico should commence it."[43]

The prospect of war naturally excited Buell, since it could provide him with the chance to redeem himself from the debacle in St. Louis. With the promise of action also came the opportunity for advancement. There was much talk in his camp about a conspiracy to create new slave states, and he was undoubtedly troubled by the U.S. invasion of a foreign country. As much as he may have disapproved of the U.S. Army's actions in Florida, he could be convinced that it was a just policy. Buell possessed high regard for decisions made on principle, and the mood of an approaching war, which had thus far been undefined, inherently concerned him. Anxiety descended on the Third Infantry as the summer heat bore down on the soldiers preparing to enter the domain of the Mexicans.[44]

The experience of the Seminole War and the confrontation with Private Humphrey provided indications of the die Buell had cast for himself as an officer. He began to show some of the features that would later become a distinguishing part of his personality. He displayed tremendous energy and seriousness when it came to even the smallest task, and he had no trouble assuming more than his share of responsibility. Though a quiet man with a shy demeanor and great self-control, he proved that he was capable of using violence, particularly when provoked. For Buell, discipline was not merely for training or controlling the troops but also for the molding of a soldier's gentlemanly conduct. Perhaps the most important of Buell's maturing features was the pride he developed for the army's professionalism. Since his departure from West Point, Buell had come to value and represent the professionalism involved in soldier making that he apparently failed to learn as a cadet. This came from setting and enforcing the rules of the soldier, which meant setting in himself the finest example of an officer and hence a gentleman. The Mexican War would reveal yet another distinguishing feature of this promising officer.

CHAPTER THREE

The War in Mexico

A s the sweltering summer heat of 1845 descended on Corpus Christi, so did the U.S. Army. The gathering of soldiers comprised the largest assembly of U.S. regulars since the Revolutionary War. Corpus Christi became the center of excited interest throughout the United States and Mexico. The Third Infantry was the first regiment to occupy Texas soil. Other than Hitchcock, the cast of senior officers was an undistinguished group of commanders: Maj. William W. Lear and Capts. Edmund B. Alexander, Henry Bainbridge, Philip N. Barbour, Daniel T. Chandler, Lewis S. Craig, William S. Henry, Robert Hazlitt, and Lewis N. Morris. Together these officers had molded the soldiers into a professional regiment, universally known as the "Buff Sticks" because of its clean soldierly appearance at all times. Buell continued to serve under Captain Bainbridge.[1]

On August 6 Taylor changed the name of his force to the Army of Occupation, reflecting the government's desires and the military's responsibilities in the area. It was a laborious task to concentrate the fragmented regiments into something resembling an army. Even the landing of the troops at Corpus Christi was nothing short of a miracle. Taylor arrived on August 15 and described the scene to his daughter as "quite an imposing one."[2]

Accustomed to crude frontier conditions, it was natural for "Old Rough and Ready" to assume the troops were relatively healthy and comfortable at Corpus Christi. By the end of September, however, the summer heat had taken its toll. The weather fluctuated abruptly between sweltering heat during the day and windy, piercing cold at night. The lack of wood made campfires infrequent, and the brackish water was barely drinkable. At one point almost 20 percent of the men were sick, and about half suffered constantly from mild diarrhea. Those who were well enough found outlets at the gambling halls and the grog shops that skirted the camp, which an officer in the Eighth Infantry characterized as "the most murderous, thieving, gambling, cut-throat, God-forsaken hole[s] in the 'Lone Star State.'" Increasingly the men paid more attention to mischief than duty, and "some, if not many, of the officers gave up acting like gentlemen."[3]

Buell, however, never gave up acting like a gentleman; indeed, he possessed tremendous moral restraint, and he realized that military life was essentially his career. Thus, discipline and readiness became his means of defense against unpredictability. In Hitchcock he saw a more senior example of himself. Hitchcock had played a key role in Buell's defense at Jefferson Barracks and took it upon himself not just to reveal the impropriety of the commanding general's orders in requesting a retrial but to come to the aid of a young officer who had demanded respect and discipline of his subordinates. Buell saw in Hitchcock not only someone who could change his direction but also someone who confirmed what he already believed. Moreover, Buell had learned a thing or two about military discipline from Hitchcock during his days at Jefferson Barracks, and now at Corpus Christi he again came under the careful eye of the rigid practitioner. As commander of the Third Infantry, Hitchcock was second to none in bringing order to chaos, and his junior officers greatly respected him as a commander and benefited invaluably from observing his leadership.[4]

Whether or not Buell believed that the government was just in planting a force in Texas, he was certainly aware of Mexico's opposition to the U.S. government's operations in the area. He must also have heard of and shared expressions of reservations about General Taylor's leadership abilities. Some officers worried about his lack of interest in training the troops, while others were amazed at his failure to investigate potential future operations. Although Buell made his own decisions in such matters, it seems reasonable that he, too, harbored silent reservations about America's move to Texas and about Taylor's abilities.[5]

Many officers and men enjoyed the rampant frolicking in the midst of grave military matters, but the serious Buell thought that riding a wild mustang was about as much excitement as he wanted. He explored the Texas frontier with former academy friends and the officers of the Third and Fourth Regiments, including those from his Florida and Missouri days. He became friends with Phil Barbour, Lewis Craig, and Lewis Morris, and together they spent many evenings strolling through camp discussing military theory and war. When Hart's Theatrical Company arrived from Savannah that fall, the evening show, *The Lady and the Devil*, was the main attraction among the soldiers. Horse racing also drew considerable attention, and some men even acquired mustangs from nearby herds or from Mexican horse sellers. Buell exercised his riding abilities when he had the time and engaged in the horse races. Still, he was careful to maintain a professional bearing and distance from the enlisted men.[6]

By mid-October Taylor's command had grown to almost 4,000 soldiers organized into three brigades commanded by General Worth, Lt. Col. James S. McIntosh, and Col. William Whistler. Though there were several West Point-trained, junior ranking officers, many senior officers lacked formal military instruction, and those that had training were dispersed among the several regiments.[7]

That autumn saw heavy rains followed by a cold spell in late November. According to Taylor's own account, the sun did not shine on the shores of Corpus Christi Bay for the first two weeks in December. Conditions in the ranks worsened as the soldiers huddling under the sullen Texas skies to escape the driving wind and rain became irritable and found the temptations of grog shops that much more appealing.[8]

Although Taylor had been on orders since he arrived at Corpus Christi to be prepared to advance on short notice, a month's delay in moving revealed the commanding general's unfeigned lack of effort in keeping his troops ready. Nonetheless, when he did move forward, he did so with a cautious vigor. In early March the army started the 150-mile journey to the old Spanish city of Matamoros. Hitchcock had become ill before the march commenced, and Capt. Lewis N. Morris assumed command of the Third Infantry. Because Captain Bainbridge was on detached service, Buell was placed in temporary command of Company F. Though they passed through magnificent western terrain, the soldiers experienced difficulty in dealing with long marches and torturing thirst.[9]

By late March Taylor's army reached the north bank of the Rio Grande opposite Matamoros and hoisted the Stars and Stripes to the sounds of "Yankee Doodle" and the "Star-Spangled Banner." Buell, like many soldiers, had believed that before the army reached the river they would have a fight, so he and the others stared anxiously across the river at the Mexican colors flying in the wind and the 200 or so persons watching their every move. Many of the U.S. soldiers saw Mexico for the first time. Though sick himself, Hitchcock was nonetheless confident in his regiment, boasting in his diary that he could do "anything with the 3d Infantry, for every officer and every man knows his place and his duty."[10] Lt. Robert Hazlitt agreed, saying that "a better little army than this never took the field."[11]

The Americans were nervous about the unfamiliar surroundings, and rightfully so. They were 200 miles from nowhere, and rumors from anxious outposts that Mexican soldiers had crossed the Rio Grande to the northern side kept them in a state of alarm. The arrival of 3,000 Mexican soldiers at Matamoros, threatening war unless there was an American withdrawal to the Nueces River within twenty-four hours, further darkened the clouds of war hovering over the city. On April 23 the Mexican government declared war on the United States, and immediately Gen. Anatastio Torrejon with 1,600 cavalry crossed the Rio Grande a few miles upstream of Taylor's camp. When the Mexicans ambushed an American patrol, Taylor reported to Washington that "hostilities may now be considered commenced."[12]

By early May the armies had maneuvered into combat positions, and the silence of the prairie was broken on May 1 by the eruption of Mexican artillery opening two days of battle at Palo Alto and Resaca de la Palma, which the Americans won decisively. These victories, however, hardly ended the conflict; in fact, the U.S. government had not even declared war yet. On May 12 Congress consented to Polk's declaration of war without the knowledge that Taylor had already won a decided victory against the Mexicans.[13]

In these first battles the Third Infantry lived up to its reputation as one of the most well trained regiments. In his official report Taylor commended it for its gallantry in holding the right wing. Buell's actions in these battles proved him a brave, but not reckless soldier. He received two flesh wounds on the first day of battle, and for his gallantry in leading a charge on the second day he received the bar of first lieutenant.

These battles marked Buell's first combat experience, and they taught him valuable lessons. First and foremost, courage came with a heavy price. He had been engaged in skirmishes with the Indians and had seen men die before, but not in large numbers. While the Seminole War had frustrated his learned abilities, the battles of Palo Alto and Resaca de la Palma allowed Buell the opportunity to combine his military training and previous combat experience. Although the underbrush and ravines essentially determined how the battle would be fought, Buell still had a practical lesson in tactics and strategy while in actual combat on the Texas prairie. Strict discipline and precise movements usually predicted success.[14]

After Palo Alto and Resaca de la Palma, Taylor decided to move to Monterrey, but delays kept the army at Matamoros for weeks. While in camp the Third Infantry was reorganized, and Buell's company increased to about seventy men, counting the sick and absentees. Buell was among the small group of officers, and by now he could count Barbour, Morris, Craig, and Hazlitt among his close friends. After the rigors of the last month, the men enjoyed the leisure of camp life. They shared letters from home, newspapers, and good cigars frequently. Still, the trouble with camp life, wrote Lieutenant Hazlitt, was not the "tiresome marches" but that "it was too easy and sometimes monotonous."[15] Still, Buell found drilling a way to keep his men focused.

Although the lack of supplies and troops delayed the Americans' 100-mile advance to Monterrey for over a month, the influx of short-term volunteers presented Taylor with more immediate problems. The volunteers had come for "glory and good time" but arrived without weapons and with a natural resistance to any kind of military discipline. The correspondent to *Niles National Register* characterized these recruits as the most "graceless and lawless spirits" in the army.[16]

These volunteers presented an especially troublesome problem for an officer like Buell, whose attitude toward strict discipline dominated his military thinking. The lack of discipline among the new soldiers no doubt discouraged him. Like most West Pointers, Buell entertained an inherent distrust of the reliability of volunteers, however much he acknowledged their courage. The only security he had was the knowledge that he was training them as best he could. He had to instill in them an instinct to follow orders, immediately and unquestioningly, to ensure their effectiveness and safety in combat. Thus, to some he seemed a martinet, but he sensed that his outfit would see action frequently, and his harsh regimen was nothing more than essential preparation. His reputation from the affair at Jefferson Barracks preceded him, and it

was only a matter of time before the volunteers learned of the lieutenant's response to indifference to military protocol and conformed to his
standards.[17]

The army moved out for Monterrey in late June and arrived at Camargo in early August. The combination of Camargo's inhospitable location and the suffocating heat and humidity made camp conditions in-
sufferable. The volunteers channeled their energies into coping with
the brutal prairie elements, and it calmed their restless energy. In preparation for the Monterrey campaign Taylor divided his 3,200 regulars
into two divisions under David L. Twiggs and Worth, with 3,000 volunteers to follow. The Third Infantry was in the First Division under Twiggs
and was brigaded with the Fourth Infantry and under the command of
Col. John Garland. Buell, however, was by this time acting assistant adjutant general of the First Division.[18]

The promotion to Twiggs's staff reflected the favorable impression
Buell had made on his superior as a company commander and combat
soldier. Like Buell, Twiggs had an unappealing manner but could get
the most out of his men. In Buell, Twiggs no doubt saw a young proficient lieutenant who had the same ability. Whether or not Buell welcomed the change from being company commander to being on the
general's staff, he surely recognized that the opportunity to assume
more responsibility reflected the confidence Twiggs had in him.[19]

About mid-September Taylor's Army of Occupation came upon Monterrey, the city of 10,000 inhabitants perched on the north bank of the
Santa Clara River. To the 7,200 Americans the city appeared a solid
fortress. More alarming to Taylor, however, was the report that the Mexican army had swelled to about 7,300 soldiers. Taylor considered Monterrey a key objective in his campaign in northern Mexico, so he prepared to give battle.[20]

On September 20 Taylor ordered Worth's division to undertake a daring flanking movement against the western defenses while Taylor himself commanded the remainder of the army in its demonstration against
the citadel and the eastern approaches along the river. In torrents of
rain the American army moved into position, spending a miserable
night in the cold. The following day dawned clear and hot, and soon
Worth's sweeping march, characterized by a series of sharp, bloody, and
confused engagements, opened the way to the Saltillo Road.[21]

Taylor, meanwhile, could not boast of such success, taking on heavy
losses as the infantry tried in vain to move forward against the "Black
Fort." Realizing the only hope for success was to commence shelling the
fort, Taylor's batteries unleashed a tremendous barrage on the mon-

strous structure. The soldiers of the Third Infantry tried unsuccessfully to find cover in the cornfields and were forced to endure tremendous fire. Lt. William S. Henry declared that in their "utter ignorance of . . . locality, we had to stand and take it."[22] Barbour was instantly killed, and the Third's commander, William Lear, was severely wounded. The Mexicans, apparently surprised by the willingness of the Americans to take heavy casualties, began to waver as Taylor called up reinforcements. The Americans fought hard a few more hours; but the Mexican artillery proved overwhelming, and by 5:00 P.M. Taylor had ordered the army back.[23]

Taylor's force rested on September 22, and consequently Worth assumed the burden of continuing the American assault and forced the Mexicans out of the city during the night. Worth's men had shown a masterful exhibition of courage and expected to finish the battle the next day. Although both armies were exhausted from the previous days' combat, both wings of the American army engaged in vicious close combat with the Mexicans the following day, ultimately forcing the Mexicans to surrender the city. The Mexican force left Monterrey on September 26, beaten but not defeated.[24]

In what Gen. Winfield Scott later called "Three Glorious Days," the Army of Occupation suffered but few casualties, about 530 men. The Third Infantry, however, lost 52 men out of an effective force of 262, and 6 of its 14 officers were killed, including Lear, Barbour, and Morris as well as Lts. Douglass Irwin and Hazlitt.[25]

Buell went through the battle physically unscathed, although he was shaken by the considerable loss of the regiment's leadership, since about 50 percent of its commanders had been killed. He witnessed personal acts of bravery as the soldiers and other officers tried unsuccessfully to save the lives of their comrades. Moreover, the loss of comrades with whom he had endured the past months and in some cases years naturally grieved him. Lear and Irwin, for example, had served as members of a court-martial that four years earlier had acquitted him. Barbour and he often strolled the camp conversing about the latest news. With the loss of junior commanders and the preservation of his own life, Buell emerged as an officer who reacted skillfully to combat "in exposed positions." During the Monterrey campaign Lt. Cadmus M. Wilcox discussed the impressions Buell had made on his men. "Buell," he wrote, "was frequently seen on horseback, but whether mounted or on foot, the eye always followed him as he passed, attracted by his fine soldierly air and a natural easy dignity of manner."[26]

Apparently that manner again caught the eye of Twiggs, who had witnessed Buell's administrative and now combat gallantry. Twiggs praised Buell highly for his "valuable and meritorious services" at Monterrey, and the lieutenant would be breveted a captain in the months to come. Although he would have preferred to keep Buell on his staff, Twiggs realized that considering the high numbers of casualties among officers, it would be better if Buell returned to the Third Regiment. The loss of the regimental adjutant Lieutenant Irwin made Twiggs's decision all the more logical, since Buell's staff experience would serve him well in his new role as regimental adjutant. The command of the Third reshuffled after Monterrey, and its leadership now fell to Captain Bainbridge, a friend of Buell's from his days at Jefferson Barracks. Bainbridge had also served on Buell's court-martial and was well aware of the lieutenant's mettle.[27]

Though Taylor was eager to move ahead, in mid-November Gen. in Chief Winfield Scott had ordered him to remain in Monterrey while Scott organized a force for a campaign against Mexico City. Scott's rearrangement ultimately divided the army and sent Taylor to the northern region of Mexico, where in February he successfully defeated Gen. Antonio López de Santa Anna at the battle of Buena Vista. Scott himself decided to capture Vera Cruz by land and by sea. He was determined to take the coastal city and organized his forces into three divisions comprised of Twiggs's and Worth's regulars and Brig. Gen. Robert Patterson's volunteers. The entire landed force numbered over 8,500 men.[28]

The investment of Vera Cruz took twenty long days, and the Third Infantry played an important part in the city's capitulation. While Worth and Patterson initiated the encirclement, Twiggs's troops completed it, hacking their way north toward the village of Vergara and seizing the northwest passage out of Vera Cruz. By the end of the fourth day, Twiggs's soldiers reached the village. For the next two weeks the siege was essentially a duel between Mexican and American artillery, but on March 21 Scott ordered the heavy guns of the American fleet to commence bombarding the city. Mexican and even European authorities requested Scott to cease firing so that the foreigners and noncombatants could escape. The general refused, and on March 29 the Mexicans formally surrendered.[29]

Within ten days Scott started his advance westward. This time Twiggs's division was the vanguard commencing the movement, and by the time his troops started forward in early April, General Santa Anna had returned from Buena Vista and had consolidated his forces in defense of the nation's capital. Concerned with the news that the Americans were advancing, Santa Anna himself caught up with the Mexican soldiers, some 12,000 strong, and guided them to a pass in the mountains near the small town of Cerro Gordo.[30]

By mid-April Twiggs had reached Cerro Gordo, and on April 18 the Mexicans attacked with a fierce assault. While the infantrymen fought bayonet to bayonet, the Mexican artillery heated up, and a long and deafening artillery duel commenced across the hilltops of La Atalaya and Cerro Gordo. The Americans stormed the hill of Cerro Gordo and took it. Meanwhile, the rest of Scott's forces reached the village of Cerro Gordo, surprising and overwhelming the Mexicans. By ten o'clock both the hill and the village had fallen to the Americans; thousands of Mexicans broke and ran like "stampeded cattle," perhaps hoping that rain might save them from utter disaster.[31]

Although the battle of Cerro Gordo lasted only about three hours, the Americans achieved a victory far more overwhelming than even Scott had expected. He boasted to Taylor that Mexico no longer had an army. About 200 Mexicans were killed, and almost 3,000 were taken prisoner. The Americans suffered about 450 casualties. The Third Infantry had 9 men killed and 26 wounded. In his official report Twiggs expressed his pride in the conduct of his men, at least half of whom were raw recruits. Besides the general good conduct of the regiment, he made specific references to Buell, who fought bravely under severe fire. Though he mentioned no specifics of Buell's actions, Capt. Edmund B. Alexander, the brigade commander, wrote, "I cannot speak in too high terms of the gallant bearing throughout the day," of Buell and Captain Craig.[32] Even Scott commended Twiggs's staff officers for their services.[33]

After Cerro Gordo, Scott inched his way to Puebla, 60 miles west of Jalapa and over 130 miles from Vera Cruz. As reinforcements arrived and his army swelled to almost 14,000 men, Scott made plans for their final campaign against Mexico City and a Mexican army estimated at 36,000.[34]

By early August Scott's 11,000-man army was organized for the advance to Mexico City, a week away. Generals Worth and Twiggs commanded the First and Second Divisions, followed by the divisions of Gideon J. Pillow and John Quitman. To the Americans the Mexican capital appeared impregnable. Santa Anna had crowded 36,000 troops inside the city and prepared his defenses. The city lay amid a series of marshes and lakes, with three causeways as the only routes of entry. The Americans would have to seize the causeways before advancing to the city's gates. Santa Anna fixed his sights on defending those entries.[35]

The army approached from the south until they reached an impassable lava bed called the Pedregal. Santa Anna's base, Churubusco, lay on the northern edge of the huge field; Scott's base, San Agustin, lay on the southern edge. In the two days of fighting, August 19–20, Worth forced his way around the eastern side of the Pedregal toward San Antonio and Churubusco, while the divisions of Twiggs and Pillow cut their way around the southwest side near Contreras. The stormy night of August 19 caused Santa Anna to withdraw northward from his advanced position to San Angel, and the Americans moved closer to battle.[36]

At dawn on the morning of August 20 the Americans under Twiggs and Pillow surprised the Mexicans with a brief but murderous assault. The soldiers showed no mercy as they chased the fleeing Mexicans out of the village of San Angel and down the turnpike to Coyoacan. The battle of Contreras ended almost before the day began. One officer pulled out his watch and declared, "It has taken just seventeen minutes" to effect this rout.[37] When Scott arrived at San Angel, he ordered his army to press on to Coyoacan and Churubusco to support Worth. By late afternoon on Friday, according to Hitchcock, a "tremendous fight came off." Worth secured the Churubusco bridge, and Twiggs's forces under Capt. Edmund B. Alexander of the Third Infantry seized by bayonet the strongly fortified Convent of San Mateo (San Pablo), from which they could draw cover. Two other brigades crossed to the north side of the Churubusco River and secured the village of Portales and a main causeway to Mexico City. The battle of Contreras and Churubusco had achieved at least one of Scott's objective—the seizure of a main causeway—but at a heavy cost to his army.[38]

Santa Anna had suffered a devastating defeat; he lost an estimated 4,000 killed, wounded, and missing men, and 3,000 were captured. The Americans also sustained the highest numbers of casualties since coming to Mexico. Over a thousand were either killed, wounded, or missing. Twiggs's division had been in the thick of the fighting, and Scott commended the regiment's gallant efforts in his official report. Buell had been in the fierce and close fighting in front of the works surrounding the convent. Apparently when others hesitated to overlook the enemy positions, Buell had scaled the redoubt, and a musket ball hit him, passing through the upper part of his chest near the right shoulder. Upon witnessing this courageous act, Captain Alexander allegedly said, "There has fallen the bravest man in the army."[39] Daniel F. Frost, a lieutenant in the Regiment of Mounted Rifles, was with Buell's outfit at the battle of Churubusco and recalled that the "Mexicans got the best of us that day. The Mexicans were in a large field of corn which was higher than our heads and we did not know what kind of fortifications they were behind and there was no chance to find out. Finally, Buell climbed on top of an adobe house and reconnoitered. We kept yelling to him to come down, and when he dropped we felt sure that he was killed. We afterward found that he was shot through the body. It was not expected that he would live, but in six weeks he was on duty again."[40] Buell's actions that day so impressed Lieutenant Frost that even years later he declared, "I have never known but one man whom I thought was absolutely ignorant of what it was to be afraid. That person was . . . Buell, who I am certain, was the bravest man it was ever my fortune to know. . . . He was a magnificent specimen of manhood and was strong as a person could find in a day's journey."[41]

For his actions that day Buell became universally known among the junior officers in his regiment as "the bravest of the brave." Indeed he was. Even Buell's superiors were impressed with his actions. Both Twiggs and Capt. Persifor E. Smith credited Buell for displaying a "coolness and activity under the circumstances."[42]

Buell was not among those comrades who in September ran up the American flag in Mexico City signaling the end of the military conflict. His wound was painful and slow to heal, and it was in "great measure due to his great physical strength" that he survived at all. He had been among the first to step on Mexican soil and had endured the rigors of the prairie. He had seen considerable combat and no doubt wanted to witness the capitulation of the Mexican capital by a victorious American army, a testimony to the services of thousands of soldiers like himself. The Mexican War did not formally end until February 10, 1848, when U.S. and Mexican officials signed the Treaty of Guadalupe Hidalgo, restoring peace between the two countries.[43]

Although he spent the winter with his regiment in Mexico City, in early March Buell left for the United States, passing through Lawrenceburg and Aurora, Indiana, where he spent a brief period. Finally, he made his way to Marietta, Ohio, to his family's farm and to his mother. As a soldier wounded in a war so distant, he may have wanted to relieve her anxiety about his well-being. Whatever the case, the seclusion and serene atmosphere of his mother's Ohio farm along the banks of the Muskingum River were certainly a welcome reprieve from the last two years.[44]

Buell evidently kept up a correspondence with his relatives and friends, but his relationship with fiancée Mary Ann had become strained. His life in the military during these early years gave him little opportunity to continue a long-distance romance, and she finally ended the engagement but not the friendship. By the time he returned to Ohio and Indiana, his performance in the war had made him famous among the townspeople, and word of his gallantry and wound had preceded him. Buell would remember several immediate details about the war, not the least of which was the loss of his horse, a companion of almost six years. Even Congressman Amos Lane knew of Buell's loss and offered to replace the animal.[45]

Certainly the Mexican War was a series of defining moments in Buell's maturation as an officer and a leader. It was an education for Buell, and he learned invaluable practical lessons by trial and error. He certainly did not go unnoticed. For his gallantry at Churubusco he received a major's brevet. He emerged from the war a skillful combat soldier who had earned the respect of his fellow soldiers and understood more clearly the troublesome tactical and logistical burdens of moving an army through a hostile countryside. He got his first indoctrination in conciliation and its implications for the army. He prided himself on being a strict disciplinarian and became universally known in the army as a professional officer. Even when he was compared to Hitchcock, Twiggs, and Worth—masters of discipline—his efforts on and off the battlefield seemed to measure up. The professional pride and manner of his superiors made a great impression on him. And to those in the regular army whom he impressed, Buell was a fine example of character and devotion to duty.

CHAPTER FOUR

A Career Man during Peacetime

In many ways life in the peacetime army was more rewarding for Don Carlos Buell than the Mexican War had been because at this time he rose in rank and influence. In late January 1848, upon learning of a vacancy, Buell wrote to Adj. Gen. Roger Jones requesting an appointment to the Adjutant General's Office. He received overwhelming support from his immediate commander, Capt. Edmund B. Alexander, who enthusiastically wrote that Buell's "gallantry and capability combined render him so highly qualified for the [position]."[1] Capt. Persifor Smith also supported Buell's application, asserting that while Buell served under him in Mexico, "no officer in this army [had] displayed more gallantry, nor [was] any one more capable of the duties of the office which he desires to hold."[2]

In mid-February, however, Buell's physical condition worsened. The bullet he received at Churubusco had crushed the principal bone in his shoulder, and the wound was not healing properly. If he wanted to live and keep his arm, he would have to change climate. Buell, therefore, returned to the northern states for several months. During the spring and summer he recuperated on his uncle's farm in Lawrenceburg, Indiana, and made a trip to Marietta to see his mother and sisters. In May, however, he wrote to the adjutant general that his shoulder was progressing and that he expected to be well enough to return to the army within a month. Evidently his flair for administrative and organizational detail had impressed his superiors so much that upon his return in July he was assigned to the Adjutant General's Office in Washington as acting assistant adjutant.[3]

This assignment was uneventful compared with campaigning in Mexico, but it was no less important to Buell. He developed into a proficient officer who could make the wheels of organization operate with an exacting precision. Because of that skill, he would spend the next ten years at posts throughout the country. The days of filtering through voluminous paper and moving from post to post brought him in touch with high-ranking military and political officials. To relieve the daily tedium of bureaucratic red tape, he continued to ride what he described as "the finest horse in Indianapolis" and occasionally traveled to New York, Marietta, and Lawrenceburg. Though he and Miss Mary Ann were no longer engaged, they still corresponded with each other. It was clear, however, that Buell would never return to Lawrenceburg, and Miss Mary Ann would not leave to become the wife of a career soldier.[4]

In early January 1849 Buell was assigned to the Sixth Military Department at Jefferson Barracks as assistant adjutant general. He welcomed his new assignment, which placed him under the authority of his old division commander, David E. Twiggs. Jefferson Barracks was the army's gateway to the West, since almost all military units assigned to western duty stopped at St. Louis before moving to their frontier posts. As departmental commander, Twiggs was responsible for establishing new forts in his department and maintaining smooth operations at the existing ones by supplying them with competent administrators. Buell's abilities would quickly be put to use.[5]

Captain, soon to be Major, Buell spent the next two years attending to the mundane chores of the adjutant's office. He labored over the details of courts-martial, procured supplies, combated the cholera epidemic, and dealt in relations with the Indians. Perhaps the only significant highlights of this period were his reacquaintances with former cadets from his days at the U.S. Military Academy. In September 1850 William T. Sherman was assigned to the Third Artillery at Jefferson Barracks, and Capt. Winfield Scott Hancock was regimental quartermaster. These men eventually had their offices in the same building. In the fall of 1849 Buell introduced Hancock to Almira Russell, the daughter of a prominent St. Louis merchant, and the following January the couple married. Buell, Orlando Wilcox, and Anderson D. Nelson were Hancock's groomsmen.[6]

In mid-April 1851 Buell was assigned to the Department of New Mexico and departed St. Louis for the long journey west. Passing through Fort Leavenworth, he met Capt. John Pope, who had recently been appointed chief topographical engineer of the Ninth Military District and had also been ordered to Fort Union. Pope and Buell had been at West Point together, and Pope had been just as impressed by Buell's manner at the military academy ten years earlier as he was at Fort Leavenworth. As they traveled across the Sante Fe Trail, Pope apparently came to know Buell quite well. "I . . . had of necessities and opportunities of seeing and knowing him," he later wrote, "which a life time in cities would not have furnished, and I came to have the greatest respect and regard for him."[7] "He was a man of tremendous passion, which he evidently kept under control," Pope observed, "but his passions were of a generous and manly character, and had no quality of vice for meanness." "He was," concluded Pope, "a man of the tenderest domestic life and affections, a pure, upright and most honorable man, capable of great things."[8]

Perhaps the most significant aspect of Buell's transfer to the Southwest was the separation he endured from Margaret Hunter Mason, with whom he had fallen in love. Though his engagement to Miss Mary Ann had ended because of his military career, being a professional soldier also had its advantages in fostering new associations. Given the professional circles of Jefferson Barracks, it was not surprising that he had made the acquaintance of Margaret Hunter "Maggie" Mason, who was prominent in St. Louis society. Her husband was the distinguished Brig. Gen. Richard Barnes Mason, twenty-one years her senior and a career military man, who had succeeded Stephen Watts Kearny in 1847 as military governor of California and for a short time was commander of Jefferson Barracks.

Mason had died at Jefferson Barracks in late July 1850 during a cholera epidemic. His widow took a liking to young officer Buell because he embodied several characteristics of her first husband, particularly his harsh bearing and professional manner. Both men were career soldiers,

Don Carlos Buell as a young lieutenant in the regular army (Courtesy of the
Filson Club Historical Society, Louisville, Ky.)

Margaret Buell, formerly married to Richard Barnes Mason, who died in 1850 at Jefferson Barracks, St. Louis, Missouri (Courtesy of the Filson Club Historical Society, Louisville, Ky.)

disciplinarians, and principled to the point of violence. While Mason may have been more highly spirited than Buell, both men were no less determined to bend another man's will by whatever means necessary.[9]

At first glance the thirty-three-year-old Buell cut a somewhat dashing figure, though his stiff demeanor made him appear distant. His small but compact frame betrayed a man of considerable vigor. His carriage was erect, his step was measured, and his sharp voice bordered on arrogance. His air was quiet and easy and was calculated to avoid attention. His dark blue eyes possessed a firm expression, steady and unmoved in the midst of excitement. His light brown hair had thinned considerably since his cadet days, and his beard was full but neatly trimmed. He stood about five feet, eight inches and possessed an "almost herculean strength in his arms." More impressive than his physical features, however, was his favorable reputation as a daring, gallant soldier and leader among his men.[10]

Apparently Don Carlos and Maggie began their courtship sometime in either the late fall or early winter of 1850–51, several months after the death of her husband and shortly before Buell set out for New Mexico. The couple were the same age, but Maggie had two daughters, fifteen-year-old Emma Twiggs Mason and thirteen-year-old Elizabeth Mary Ann Sally Mason, or Nannie, named for her father's three sisters. Emma's middle name honored her uncle David Twiggs, who had married Maggie's sister. Thus Buell, after he married Margaret Mason, became the brother-in-law of his former commander. Both girls always kept their father's name, but they grew quite attached to Buell, who loved them dearly.[11]

The courtship between Buell and Mason was so compelling that Buell returned to Jefferson Barracks in the fall of 1851 to marry Maggie on November 19. She had inherited $20,000 and eight slaves from her husband, and this property, combined with Buell's $2,500 worth of real estate, allowed the couple to live comfortably. After the wedding they traveled back to Fort Union.[12]

The marriage proved to be a happy one, and it certainly domesticated Buell. He became stepfather to two daughters of a man he had always respected, and he saw to it that the girls were raised properly. He also became the owner of eight slaves—four mulatto men and four black women—suggesting that he had little difficulty accepting the peculiar institution. The Buell family slave, Aunt Fannie Fitzhugh, had helped raise him as a child, so slavery was not new to him. The fact that Maggie was an Augusta, Georgia, native and an experienced slave owner helped to reinforce his attitude toward the institution. Though there is no recorded evidence of how he treated his slaves, Buell seems to have readily assumed the role of a master.[13]

In the autumn of 1852, Buell was assigned to the Eighth Military Department comprising the southeastern portion of Texas, with headquarters at Corpus Christi. Daniel M. Frost, a friend from the Mexican War, was glad to hear that Buell was coming to Texas. He wrote to his wife in St. Louis that Buell was a man of "good judgement and will be of much use."[14] Because Buell was a career soldier, his family traveled extensively and had to endure the hardships of living on frontier military posts. Fortunately, Margaret had become used to the military life during her first marriage.[15]

On the trip to Corpus Christi, Buell and a young lieutenant in the Corps of Engineers, George B. McClellan, came to know each other. McClellan had been acting as Gen. Persifor Smith's aide on his tour of frontier posts and in October 1852 had been assigned to survey the rivers and harbors on the Texas coast. His survey headquarters were to be at Corpus Christi. He and Buell met in the little town of Indianola,

Texas, in Matagorda Bay, where McClellan was in charge of a small schooner. McClellan "blindly volunteered to take Major and Mrs. Buell" to Corpus Christi. "They are very pleasant people indeed," McClellan wrote his sister, "but I shall have to regulate my moments to suit her comfort, instead of making a straight track, without regard to wind, weather or day of time." "When I offered to take the major (one of the best men in the army)," he wrote, "I did not know that the madam was with him." When McClellan realized the couple's entourage included eight slaves and twelve trunks, he wondered "why will people get married."[16]

Along the way McClellan's vessel repeatedly grounded, no doubt because of the extra weight of Buell's entourage, and he constantly jumped overboard into about three feet of water to heave the small schooner out of the mud. After first watching, Buell decided to jump in himself. The two officers did duty almost the entire way as "mud marine[s]," working their way through the troubled waters and poling through the shoals and quicksand toward Corpus Christi.[17]

Both men were West Point graduates, but while McClellan had been president of the Dialectic Society, the intellectual elite of West Point's upperclassmen, Buell had spent a considerable portion of his time confined to his quarters for numerous demerits. McClellan's father was a distinguished surgeon, while Buell, though possessing a prominent New England pedigree, was raised on a farm and was an orphan. McClellan graduated from the military academy five years after Buell and was attached to the elitist Corps of Engineers. Buell spent his initial military years as a foot soldier in the swamps of Florida, fighting Indians. The Mexican War, however, provided the common experience for them, and as combat soldiers they earned three brevets each for gallant and meritorious conduct. They had seen perhaps the heaviest combat of the Mexican War at Churubusco and for their efforts had emerged from the obscure lower ranks to be known as men of distinction.[18]

The key attraction between Buell and McClellan was the professional pride and bearing they both exhibited on and off the battlefield. They shared a military education that through the trial-and-error experience of the Mexican War they had refined into an uncompromising military philosophy. At the core of this philosophy was a rigid belief that war was something that was recorded in books and that was fought in conformity to a fixed pattern, which emphasized preparation and discipline. Too many times Buell, like McClellan, insisted that certain rules in war must always be followed. When McClellan met Buell, McClellan regarded him as one of the best men in the army because he possessed many traits McClellan admired, including military discipline and accountability. The friendship they began that fall of 1852 was the beginning of a long and fruitful relationship that carried into the Civil War.[19]

During Buell's tenure in Texas, he made trips back to St. Louis and New York, where his stepdaughters were going to school. On one occasion his usually pleasant journey ended abruptly in disaster. Early in the morning of February 16, 1854, he boarded the steamboat *Kate Kearney* in St. Louis, and as the boat was backing away from the wharf, its boilers exploded. Many prominent citizens of St. Louis and soldiers on furlough were onboard, and according to one witness, people "were thrown high in the air and [descended] upon the hull a confused mass of shivered timbers, and dead and wounded people."[20] Buell was burned, and although he was buried in the wreck of the shattered boat, as a newspaper later reported, "he quickly emerged."[21] "Stunned, burned and bleeding, as he was," wrote the witness, Buell nonetheless "seized a fire bucket and addressed himself to the extinguishment of the flames that had begun to break out from the wreck, as calmly as if he had not been a victim of the catastrophe."[22] This witness reported years later that on that day, "by his own exertions in the midst of the appalling scene, and by his coolness in organizing the efforts of others, [Buell] succeeded in saving the wreck from fire, and many of his fellow sufferers from a horrible death."[23]

Thomas Tasker Gantt, Buell's friend and attorney from Missouri, wrote to Emma Mason in New York of the incident. Gantt informed her that her stepfather had been seriously injured and that because he had inhaled a great deal of hot steam, he would not get to New York. Upon hearing of the accident, Buell's good friend Winfield Scott Hancock went to the hotel where Buell was recuperating and found him "so seriously injured as to be scarcely recognizable."[24] When Hancock learned that Buell and another gentleman "through gallantry and personal exertions" were responsible for saving many onboard the ship from death, he went to the editor of the St. Louis *Missouri Republican,* who had already written a brief article on the explosion, and demanded that he further accord to Buell an article more appropriate to an officer's heroic actions. The editor followed up his initial brief comments with fulsome words of praise for Buell's actions:

> As a matter of justice to a gallant gentleman, now on a bed of suffering, it should be known that after the explosion occurred on board of the *Kate Kearney,* nothing saved the boat from being entirely destroyed by fire . . . but the personal exertions of Major Buell . . . assisted by another gentleman whose name is unknown. . . . It is certain

that several persons who were wounded, if not others, who are now alive, would have perished but for such prompt and efficient action. In times of danger, presence of mind in a soldier is expected; but it is thought that under the circumstances Major Buell's conduct deserves especial notice.[25]

Hancock's determination to see that Buell received due recognition for his bravery reflected his considerable esteem for Buell, and according to his wife Hancock shared the "highest respect and admiration for . . . Buell."[26] After a few days in the hospital, Buell was released and continued his journey to New York. Those who witnessed this incident were undoubtedly impressed by Buell's coolness in danger and methodical adaptability to emergencies. His display of self-sacrifice revealed his courageousness in putting the safety of others before himself.

The *Kate Kearney* incident, however, was not the only indication of Buell's willingness to put himself in jeopardy to save others. In the summer of 1854, yellow fever ravaged Corpus Christi, and George F. Turner, the only surgeon at the post, died. Buell sent his wife away, and in June he himself fell desperately ill. He sent a telegram to Margaret saying, "Do not be anxious. I shall soon be up again. Do not think of coming," but she returned to Corpus Christi anyway.[27] Fortunately, Buell recovered, and then he and Margaret devoted themselves to nursing the sick. Many soldiers remembered that altruism, and because of it and his other responsibilities to the department, "he won the respect of all officers of the army in the Department."[28]

In the autumn of 1855 the headquarters of the Department of Texas were moved to San Antonio, and Buell traveled there in late October. Concerned over the Comanche threat to the frontier settlements in Texas, the War Department ordered the 700 men of the Second U.S. Cavalry Regiment from Jefferson Barracks to Texas in late October. When Col. Albert Sidney Johnston arrived, he commenced intense warfare and within a short time crushed the Indians. Although he did not accompany the scouting and combat missions against the Indians, Buell nonetheless ensured that the new headquarters maintained the highest standards. In his inspection report on the Department of Texas, Col. J. K. F. Mansfield wrote that Buell had put the San Antonio headquarters "in excellent order." Under the direction of Buell, he noted, "there appears to be great regularity and system in all its particulars and the books and records neatly kept."[29]

Buell remained Johnston's assistant adjutant general until mid-December 1856, when, for an unknown reason, he was transferred to the East. Perhaps he and Margaret wanted to be near their daughters. Buell and his wife enjoyed the trip from St. Louis through Indianapolis to New York and then to Washington and Baltimore before reaching Troy in February 1857. Buell was quite impressed with his new surroundings, describing Troy as an "altogether clever town." He traveled through upstate New York extensively, taking advantage of the "pleasant resorts within our borders," and eventually made it to Canada to broaden the cultural realm of his daughters.[30]

During the summer of 1857 Buell drew on the services of his friend William T. Sherman, officer turned banker, about some business transactions in California. Sherman had been stationed there in the Mexican War and had been an aide to Gen. Richard Barnes Mason. Since Sherman and Buell had known each other since their cadet days at West Point, their mutual trust formed the basis of a close bond between military men. That trust extended into business transactions as well, and Buell relied on Sherman to make his financial investments in California and to see that his wife's investments from her previous marriage were handled well. In July Buell inquired about some real estate outside Sacramento, and Sherman counseled him over the proprieties, ultimately saving Buell from financial loss. Buell appreciated his friend's graciousness in handling his business transactions in California, and when Sherman later desired to return to the army, Buell acted on his behalf.[31]

In September Buell was transferred back to the Department of the West, and he arrived in St. Louis in early December. In the meantime Margaret, certainly no innocent regarding the protocol of a military wife, penned a formal letter on Buell's account to Joseph Lane, a prominent politician from Buell's hometown in Indiana. Wanting to speed up the military chain of command, she wrote,

> I feel that I can rely on [the] kind promise you made me some three years since to procure [Carlos's] advancement in the army. . . . Maj. Buell is devoted to his profession and is ambitious of preferment. I would urge you assistance my dear general and have resolved to ask you if you can aid me to accomplish my desire for the promotion of Major Buell. . . . I must ask your pardon for trespassing on your time and patience but this matter of promotion lies close on my heart— General and if you could only gratify me in this great desire for his promotion, I will be under great obligations to you.[32]

Margaret's letter certainly demonstrated that she was a seasoned military wife who knew how to use the political arena to advance her husband's career. Why she decided to act at that particular moment is difficult to determine, but her letter had no effect. It is difficult to fathom Buell, a man of considerable reserve and an officer who shunned attention, writing such a letter or encouraging his wife to do so regarding his promotion, whether or not he thought he deserved one. It was not in his nature to request for himself such honors. Having been married to a general of distinction, perhaps Margaret had greater ambitions for her husband than he had for himself. Whatever the case, it would be some years before he received a promotion.[33]

After a brief tour in the Department of Utah under Albert Sidney Johnston, who was attempting to suppress the Mormons, Buell was transferred back to St. Louis. From his desk at St. Louis he witnessed the increase in hostilities among the rank-and-file soldiers during the winter of 1858–59, a result of the clash between free-state and proslavery groups over Kansas's admission into the Union as a slave state. As in Utah, his duties were not exciting, but the hostilities over slavery were now more present to him than before, particularly since he owned slaves. What leisure he had was spent with his wife and reading and studying military history. As a student of military history, over the years he had acquired a small collection of books on European warfare.[34]

In February 1859 Buell was ordered to the War Department. Adj. Gen. Samuel Cooper had confidentially informed Buell that Secretary of War John Buchanan Floyd needed an experienced army officer for a "Special Assignment." Floyd required someone who was thoroughly acquainted with the details of the service and on whose judgment in military matters Floyd might confidently rely. Cooper enthusiastically recommended Buell with the "full conviction in my mind that your acceptance will gratify him." He encouraged Buell seriously to consider the opportunity. It would require a significant amount of labor, but he would find the position agreeable. Moreover, Cooper added, "it will promote the interests of the service," and "I think you ought not to refuse."[35]

Cooper was certainly aware of Buell's industry and the fine job he had done at his various posts since being appointed to the Adjutant General's Office. His reputation as an organizer and administrator was well known. Cooper was perhaps looking for an opportunity to reward Buell for his industry over the past years, and the secretary of war's request was timely. "I will say nothing about the advantages which [this position] may open to you in after years. I trust you will give me a favorable response."[36]

On February 2 Buell penned a letter back to Cooper expressing his gratitude for being considered. He thought, however, it would be wise for Cooper to make the final decision about recommending someone to the secretary of war before Buell simply offered his assistance to Floyd. Cooper appreciated Buell's discretion and recommended Buell's services to Floyd. Floyd agreed that Buell would be suited for the position, and Buell was ordered to Washington, arriving in mid-March.[37]

Comparing his new assignment to those of the preceding few years, Buell no doubt relished his new surroundings despite the unsettling situation confronting President James Buchanan's administration. Though Buell had previously been unconcerned about the workings of the nation's political machinery, he was no stranger to governmental bureaucracy. Having served as assistant adjutant general for the past ten years, he was not immune to the politicization of the military. As a career soldier, however, he possessed an ardent dislike for politics, since it often muddled the operations of military commanders seeking to carry out the duties of command.[38]

Like most military men, Buell harbored partisan views regarding the crisis of the 1850s, especially since the past ten years had made him sensitive to the political use of the military. Considering Buell's upbringing in a small midwestern town that was staunchly Democratic and thoroughly entrenched in the reform movements of temperance and religion, his political conservatism and allegiance to the Democratic Party were not difficult to understand. He probably voted for James Buchanan, the compromise Democratic candidate in 1856, since, like army friends such as Sherman, he believed the candidacy of Republican John C. Frémont posed serious questions about the future integrity of the office. The new party's free-soil ideology was little more than an antislave stance, which made conservative Democrats, even from the North, uncomfortable. The fact that Buell's wife possessed animosity toward Frémont from the California days when he and her previous husband had been archenemies might also have played a role in Buell's decision not to support the Republican candidate.[39]

As a slave owner himself, Buell was surely sensitive to the issue. His sentiment regarding slavery was not a mystery, since he had at least tolerated being a master for the last eight years. His wife's southern background and attitude surely played a role in his stance on slavery, sectionalism, and politics. Her long marriage to Richard Mason of Virginia was also significant; she had been extremely fond of the Mason family and in particular Senator James M. Mason, whom she considered a brother. Senator Mason was part of the Senate block that in 1854 had strong-armed President Franklin Pierce into signing the Kansas-Nebraska bill that repealed the ban on bondage in that territory. In the War Department Buell was in a position that certainly made him more conscious of the severe abolitionist opposition to slavery. He sensed how powerful sectionalism was, and he never wavered in his conviction that the preservation of the Union was the paramount objective.[40]

Although it is not clear exactly what his special assignment entailed, Buell considered his selection as a mark of confidence in his abilities as an officer. After a few days he realized that his appointment had something to do with the secretary of war's desire, or perhaps Cooper's desire, to maintain better the War Department's records, considering the inevitable crisis looming in the near future. John Floyd, former governor of Virginia, was careless in handling the public affairs of the War Department, and as a result of his neglect, the office and his subordinates were in a constant state of confusion. It was becoming more apparent to administrators and military superiors that Floyd was the wrong man in a critically important War Department and that an experienced administrator such as Buell might facilitate the operations.[41]

Though he could not be sure how long his assignment would last, Buell must have found his position in Washington a welcome reprieve after his travels of the past several years. His new authority provided him with the opportunity to advance himself and help his friends. In the summer of 1859, when Sherman began seriously contemplating a return to the army, he wrote to Buell about his chances. Sherman asked Buell to recommend him for any available vacancy in the Paymaster's Department. "Was I ten years younger & had I not four children," he wrote, "I would be too proud to ask any favor of anybody."[42]

Although Buell realized Sherman's worth as a soldier, he was not able to recommend him for a job in the Paymaster's Department because all such posts were filled politically. Instead, Buell told Sherman that he might be able to help him by putting in a word to the secretary of war, but "it would be practicing an unusual imposition." Although Buell clearly recognized that in "these times everything turns on political or other influence," he encouraged Sherman to seek the position on his own.[43] Buell confessed that "though it may worsen your opinion of [me] . . . [it will] cure my conscience to admit that I am a poor politician."[44]

He did, however, inform Sherman that the new Louisiana Military Seminary was looking for a superintendent, and that if he was interested, Buell would be delighted to recommend him for that post, since the position was "as honorable as any man could desire."[45] George Mason Graham, the chairman of the board of the newly created seminary, was a half-brother to Richard Barnes Mason and had fought with Buell in the Mexican War. He had sent Buell an advertisement of the superintendent position. Buell responded with a letter declaring that "of all men of his acquaintance Major Wm. T. Sherman, lately resigned from the army . . . was the most perfectly qualified for the position."[46] According to Graham, when Buell told him that Sherman was the man for the job, he knew he "need not look any farther."[47] Buell's attachment to Graham, coupled with the affection Graham's half-brother had had for Sherman during their military service in California, certainly made the difference in Sherman's chances for the superintendency.[48]

When Sherman finally applied for the post, Buell wrote an impassioned ten-page letter on his behalf. In it Buell expressed the admiration and "warm personal regard" Sherman had received from General Mason for his efforts while in California. Sherman, Buell said, although possessing an "active [emotional] temperament," was "practical, laborious, conservative and decent." Moreover, he wrote that Sherman's disposition and character "in the military or private life, or in business, or in any respect as a man of honor, is without reproach. . . . I do not doubt for a minute that the institution would be fortunate in such a selection."[49]

In August 1859 Sherman became superintendent at the Louisiana Military Seminary, his appointment due in part to the efforts of his friend in the War Department. The following month Buell penned Sherman a long letter of advice regarding his new position. It was clear he regarded the training of military cadets as most important. Buell wrote to Sherman that his ideas "haven't cost me much," but that "if they are worth any thing you are heartily welcome to them."[50]

In mid-October when John Brown and his band raided the U.S. Armory and Arsenal at Harpers Ferry, Virginia, all of Washington was thrown into a frenzy. From that time until Abraham Lincoln's election as the sixteenth president in November 1860, Americans revealed their attitude toward slavery during the summer political campaigns and at the autumn polls. In these turbulent months Buell and Sherman corresponded about the operations of the military seminary and the contentious activities of the Thirty-sixth Congress in the winter of 1859–60. Sherman's brother, John, an Ohio moderate, had been nominated Speaker of the House, but his endorsement of *The Impending Crisis*, written by Hinton Rowan Helper in 1857, forced the House into a two-month-long speakership contest that eventually ended in the election of William Pennington of New Jersey. This struggle dramatized the political divisions in Congress over slavery. During the crisis Sherman wrote to his brother that when he became Speaker he would need friends, and he could therefore count on his army friends such as Buell for honesty and sincerity.[51]

Sherman and Buell shared a like mind over the brewing crisis. "I suppose you are sick and tired of politics," Sherman wrote to his friend; he hoped that "a time may come in our day when men of action will govern and not men talkers."[52] Knowing that Buell himself was suspicious of the more radical Republicans, Sherman declared, "I suppose John Sherman is so black a Republican that you would not be seen in his company." Still, Sherman wanted his brother to meet Buell, if for no other reason than to "know some real substantial military gentlemen not for title but for real information that all Ohio people need in army matters of which from their locality they must be ignorant."[53] Buell and Sherman also shared similar views regarding the Union. Their patriotism was tied to its continuation, and while Sherman believed that the Democratic spirit, which substituted mere "popular opinions for law," was the real trouble, Buell was concerned that the destruction of a nation by disorder and secession would result in complete ruin.[54]

In the summer of 1860, Buell, with the aid of Secretary of War Floyd, helped facilitate Sherman's acquisition of weapons and ammunition for the 200 cadets at the military seminary. Buell was obviously excited about Sherman's venture and his decision to remain as the seminary's superintendent. He read with delight of Sherman's progress with the new cadets. From the War Department Buell did whatever he could to accommodate Sherman's requests. It did not take much prodding to get Floyd excited about sustaining Sherman's efforts because, as a southerner, Floyd certainly viewed it as a political necessity to supply the South militarily as the clouds of war approached.[55]

Working in the War Department under Floyd made a profound impression on Buell, particularly because he was surrounded by men of diverging political opinions. Besides Floyd, Buchanan's Cabinet was comprised of politicians ranging from elderly and haughty Secretary of State Lewis Cass of Michigan and strongly pro-Unionist Postmaster General Joseph Holt of Kentucky and Attorney General Jeremiah Black of Pennsylvania, to fiery Secretary of the Treasury Howell Cobb of Georgia and forceful Secretary of the Interior Jacob Thompson of Mississippi. The most loyal advocates of the South were Cobb, Thompson, and Floyd. Buell, however, proved to be loyal and trustworthy and received the confidence of the secretary.[56]

As a conservative Democrat Buell had a choice for whom to cast his vote in the coming election. The summer political campaigns reflected the sharp divisions that had plagued the party for almost a decade. The ideological divisions over slavery and states' rights splintered the party into three distinct factions. The only northern candidate was Illinois senator Stephen A. Douglas, who had supported the concept of popular sovereignty in the Kansas-Nebraska affair and in his 1858 debates with Abraham Lincoln. As a consequence he had alienated himself from southerners and appealed mainly to the northern wing of the Democratic Party, and Buell almost certainly voted for him.[57]

Lincoln won a decided victory that November, and in the weeks between his election and the opening of Congress in December, Secretary Floyd continued to ponder the delicate question of how to protect U.S. forts in Charleston. Because Winfield Scott was in New York, Floyd was forced to determine the best course of action himself. Rather than reinforcements he sent a new commander, Maj. Robert Anderson, to Fort Moultrie in hopes of appeasing the populace. Although he was a slave owner, Anderson was a Union man opposed to secession. When he arrived at the fort in mid-November, he found himself in charge of two small companies in a tattered and dilapidated garrison.[58]

Anderson was expected to defend Forts Castle Pinckney and Sumter as well as Moultrie. In his comprehensive report of November 23 to Washington, however, he informed Floyd that "the Clouds are threatening . . . , and the storm may break upon us at any moment."[59] He urged the secretary of war to act in the strictest secrecy. "I will thank the Department to give me special instructions," he wrote, "as my position here is rather a politico-military than a military one."[60]

Charleston was in a state of incessant hysteria, and this placed Floyd and Anderson in a precarious position, since it was difficult to determine what might happen. Floyd knew the value of Fort Sumter, and on December 7, 1860, he summoned Buell to his Washington residence to discuss Anderson's predicament in Charleston. After a brief discussion he ordered the austere and methodical Buell to Charleston to inspect Anderson's situation and convey instructions. Floyd had Buell commit the instructions to memory for personal delivery to Anderson. During the interview it became apparent that whether from "prudential reasons or because of the difficulty of providing for every contingency," Floyd wanted Anderson committed to a defensive policy only. Furthermore, Floyd wanted nothing in writing, neither his instructions to Buell nor Buell's findings. Whatever unexpected problems might arise, Floyd believed he could count on Buell to judge for himself the best course of action. Moreover, it was obvious that Buell, too, was a slave owner who maintained southern sympathies, and this fact made his selection all the more judicious.[61]

Buell arrived in Charleston on December 9 and probably felt like a man in the wrong place at the wrong time. From the way Charlestonians talked it was clear to Buell that they intended to seize Fort Sumter "with or without state sanction." Buell immediately recognized the danger to Anderson's forces and the strategic implications of losing Sumter. Sailing across the harbor to Moultrie, he found unenthusiastic soldiers who felt that a timid administration was abandoning them to angry citizens. Capt. Abner Doubleday recalled that when Buell arrived, he did not sympathize much with the troops in the garrison and instead expressed his disapproval of the defensive positions, since they might irritate the people. For that comment Buell surely received some resentment. After all, according to Doubleday, "I thought the remark a strange one, under the circumstances, as 'the people' were preparing to attack us."[62]

Apparently unaware of this resentment, Buell, escorted by Anderson, made an inspection of the three forts and observed the situation carefully. He had planned to leave Charleston after he finished his inspection, but Anderson persuaded him to spend the night at his headquarters at Moultrie. That night Anderson apprised Buell of his hazardous position. Buell presented Anderson with Floyd's instructions, which essentially amounted to a liberal explanation and rationalization of general policy, rather than explicit orders.[63]

After discussing with Anderson Floyd's instructions and the possibility of abandoning Moultrie and moving to Sumter before the secessionists did, Buell became even more conscientious. On the morning of December 11, just before he left Moultrie, he said to Anderson, "You ought to have written evidence of these [Floyd's] instructions." He then determined to do what the secretary of war had resisted: he composed a written memorandum of Floyd's verbal message. The most important part of the memorandum instructed Anderson to avoid unnecessary acts that would provoke aggression, but at the same time it authorized him to take steps against what he believed was "tangible evidence of a design to proceed to a hostile act."[64]

Buell was convinced that Fort Moultrie was already in danger and agreed with Anderson that if he did occupy Fort Sumter, that installation would soon fall. This decision unquestionably influenced his interpretation of the secretary's instructions and his decision to write Anderson the memorandum. In Buell's estimation it was necessary for

Don Carlos Buell as a lieutenant colonel in the Adjutant General's Office
(Courtesy of the U.S. Army Military History Institute, Carlisle, Pa.)

military rather than political purposes to hold on to Fort Sumter. The political consequences were inevitable, he thought, and thus moving into Sumter under whatever pretense would at least allow the army to save the fort. As Buell handed a copy of his memorandum to Anderson, he added a meaningful remark: "This is all I am authorized to say to you, but my personal advice is that you do not allow the opportunity to escape you."[65] He also made some further suggestions, "all looking to the contemplated transfer of command."[66]

Buell's written instructions and final remarks portrayed Floyd in a more favorable light than Anderson had previously held him. The secretary of war was not deserting Anderson but was offering him deliverance, or so it seemed from Buell's memorandum. Unwittingly Buell made himself a pivotal character in the Charleston drama, since his unauthorized written instructions appeared contradictory to the president's promise, would baffle Floyd, and placed the burden of decision on Anderson. After leaving Moultrie on Sunday morning, Buell stayed another night in Charleston and witnessed more of the Charlestonian temper. "There was everywhere," he thought, "evidence of a settled purpose" to secede and to have the forts of the South.[67]

When Buell returned to Washington a day later, he reported to Floyd on his observations and his discussion with Anderson. On his way out of the secretary's office, he left a copy of his written instructions to Anderson with the chief clerk of the War Department. Whether Floyd read the copied memorandum is uncertain.[68]

Whatever uneasiness Anderson had felt about the Buchanan administration prior to Buell's arrival, Buell had given him complete authority to move from Fort Moultrie to Fort Sumter—not simply when attacked but whenever he had "tangible evidence" of such a design. Because Charleston was overflowing with tangible evidence, Anderson had in effect been told he could move to Sumter whenever he thought best. On the same day that Buell left for Charleston, Buchanan had pledged to maintain the status quo in Charleston harbor.[69] On December 21, the day after South Carolinians seceded from the Union, President Buchanan finally read Buell's instructions to Anderson. Floyd did not get around to looking at it until that date, when he endorsed it, saying, "This is in conformity to my instructions to Major Buell," and handed it to the president.[70]

Buchanan was uncomfortable with the language of Buell's memorandum, and he instructed the secretary of war to send another communiqué to the major. Significantly, Floyd chose not to send Buell again and instead dispatched Capt. John Withers, a Tennessean, also in the

Adjutant General's Office. Buchanan ordered Floyd to soften the orders. When Anderson received the secretary's latest words of guidance, he became furious. Buell's message had allowed Anderson to decide for himself when and how to act. Now the administration was drawing back.[71]

South Carolina's secession from the Union on December 20, 1860, certainly provided tangible evidence for Anderson. The palmetto flag now flew over Charleston, and demands increased that the forts be turned over to the state's jurisdiction. He decided to move to Sumter on Christmas evening, counting on the day's festivities to divert Charlestonians. Bad weather, however, caused him to postpone the move until the following day. That same evening he reported to Adjutant General Cooper that it was a necessary step "to prevent the effusion of blood."[72] Necessary though it surely was, Anderson's move stunned Floyd, who immediately sent a communiqué to Anderson demanding that he "explain the meaning of [his] report."[73] When Buchanan learned that Anderson had moved, he, too, was furious, claiming that the move was "not only without but against my orders."[74]

Buell realized Anderson's precarious state and considered making a move for military reasons more important than the political consequences. In the postwar years, several persons inquired as to the motivation behind Buell's interpretation of Floyd's instructions to Anderson. Buell, however, denied any deliberate attempt on his or Floyd's part to provoke hostility.[75]

On the afternoon of December 27, Buchanan met with his Cabinet, which had undergone some reshuffling due to the activities at Charleston and was moving rapidly toward a strong Unionist position. On his way to the Cabinet meeting Floyd met Buell in the hallway and announced to him, "This is a very unfortunate move of Major Anderson. It has made war inevitable." "I do not think so, sir," replied a stunned Buell, defending his fellow officer, "On the contrary, I think that it will tend to avert war, if it can be averted." Floyd responded, "It has compromised the President."[76] The meeting was stormy, and Floyd charged that Anderson and probably Buell had disobeyed orders and that Fort Sumter should be withdrawn. Buchanan refused. Moreover, whatever honorable pledges the president had made to the South Carolinians were no longer in effect once South Carolina seceded. He also reached a conclusion regarding Sumter and South Carolina's departure from the Union: he would resist secession.[77]

The "great secession winter" was perhaps one of the longest and gloomiest in American history. Floyd's scandals, Buell's written memorandum to Anderson, South Carolina's secession from the Union, and finally Anderson's move to Sumter all combined to make the following months for the outgoing and the incoming president a time of turbulence and suspense. Although he remained in the War Department long enough to see Lincoln inaugurated, Buell drifted back into relative obscurity. As the events of that winter unfolded, he was made lieutenant colonel and became the third-ranking officer in the Adjutant General's Office. He had witnessed considerable strife during his military career over the issue of slavery and had lately heard the bitterness expressed in the legislative halls, in the press, and in the War Department. In fact, he himself had been the target of such passions. He knew too well the results of such civil strife. As he read the daily dispatches coming in from the South, he must have pondered the vexing problems facing his country and the possible role he would have in solving them. Sherman contemplated the coming crisis to his brother, and in questioning which way some of his friends in the army may turn, he confidently told him that Buell was friendly to the Union and "would give you notice of any opening."[78]

CHAPTER FIVE

A Soldier Is a Gentleman,
and Honor Is His Name

When Buell graduated from West Point in the summer of 1841, he received some valuable advice from Aunt Fannie Fitzhugh, not a person likely to advise a cadet fresh out of a military school. She had helped rear him from birth until he had left for Lawrenceburg to live with his uncle. She was delighted to see the young lieutenant when he returned to Ohio on a postgraduation furlough, displaying the transformation from a rough-and-tumble farmboy into a well-mannered, polished cadet. As he had bade goodbye to Aunt Fannie on his way to Florida, she embraced him and said, "God Almighty Bless ye. . . . A soldier is a gentleman and honor is his name."[1]

Buell was taken with this "brief and homely, but comprehensive and exacting" definition of a soldier and used it to guide his conduct. Because he left civilian life as a youth, the army defined his life. Indeed, it became his family. He never seriously considered returning to civilian life but did not disapprove of those professional soldiers who did. One of Buell's acquaintances described him during the late 1850s as a man whose "word was even better than his bond . . . and that one of his grandest characteristics [as a soldier] was never to say a word derogatory to anyone."[2]

He had come a long way from the small town of Lowell to the War Department. He had been at the center of the whirlwind of events in Charleston harbor in December 1860, although Floyd blamed him for Anderson's move to Fort Sumter. What became clear from Buell's mismanagement of the Charleston crisis was that he was too much the soldier for the delicate civil-military blend necessary in Washington to suppress sectional tendencies. Though he hoped to escape from the crisis in Charleston with nothing more damaging to his professional reputation than President James Buchanan's displeasure, the new secretary of war, Joseph Holt, decided it best to utilize Buell's talents in another department as far from Washington as possible. He ordered Buell to report to the Department of the Pacific by late mid-May to serve as assistant adjutant general.[3]

Ordinarily Buell would have welcomed a new assignment, especially one that got him away from what he considered the disdainful political intrigue of Washington. As events moved toward war, though, he wanted to be near the action. Six hundred miles south, delegates from seceded states met in early February at Montgomery, Alabama; drafted a temporary constitution; transformed the convention into a provisional congress for the new government; and elected a provisional president and vice-president. Few deliberative bodies have done so much so quickly and so smoothly, with less time out for oratory. When Jefferson Davis was elected provisional president on February 6, 1861, Buell began contemplating when and where he would command. He hoped to be offered a high place in the army. He had a lofty opinion of himself in military matters, and he remained loyal when several of his comrades abandoned the service. Moreover, he knew that few others matched the range of his experience.[4]

The tensions in Charleston harbor erupted on April 12, a month after Lincoln's inauguration. The southern firing on the fort must have jarred Buell, considering his instructions to Anderson just four months prior. Despite Buell's military prominence, his friend George B. McClellan clearly overshadowed him and all other officers. Upon the firing on Fort Sumter, McClellan became the most sought-after former officer in the North. On that same spring day Buell's Uncle George from Lawrenceburg wrote to him and inquired as to what role his nephew might assume. Although Buell could only hope it would be a prominent role, he meanwhile remained a major assigned to a relatively remote department where only the inconsequential appeared to be happening.[5]

Although Buell was at the center of military decision making in the War Department, the abolitionist atmosphere in Washington hardly agreed with him. While living in Washington Buell and his wife had apparently felt obliged to dispose of almost all of their slaves, since the census records indicate they retained only one of the eight slaves they had owned for a decade. While they may have been influenced by the pressures of abolitionism that had increased in Washington during the past decade, it is unclear as to why or how the Buells disposed of their slaves. Perhaps their belief that Washington would be a permanent home convinced them that keeping more than just a domestic servant would prove as much a burden as a blessing, especially in Washington. By this time Buell's stepdaughters, Emma and Nannie, had outgrown their adolescence and, consequently, their dependence on servants. Moreover, Buell's status as one of the highest-ranking officers in the Adjutant General's Office may have been a factor in his decision, despite his attitude toward slavery.

The tremendous exposure to abolitionist ideas that had increasingly descended on the political arena in Washington prior to the firing on Fort Sumter may also have influenced Buell's decision, but it certainly did not affect his racial views. Indeed, it may have hardened them. The attitude of the officers corps toward slavery was reinforced by the army's proclivity to avoid sectional conflict. But because little correspondence exists regarding Buell's racial views, it is difficult to know exactly what he thought at the time and whether or not he was able to distinguish between slavery and southern secession. His marriage to a southerner and his prolonged service in the slave states also helped to foster his acceptance of the institution.[6]

Whatever the case, it would be hard to imagine that Buell's racial beliefs were atypical of those of his army friends such as Sherman and McClellan. If he believed that blacks were inferior to whites, he would not have been unusual. His experience with slavery as a youth naturally influenced him, and his increasing exposure to the institution as he moved from department to department, coupled with his deep association with the military, surely developed in him the racial views of the inferiority of blacks prevalent in the army. In his association with slave owning, he apparently adopted the view that blacks should be slaves and that their inferiority precluded them from equality with whites. Because his principles dictated his politics, Buell's strict adherence to the rules and regulations of the military, especially military law, coupled with his precise manner of thinking, helped to instill in him a conservative view of the rights of civilians and a strict view of the Constitution when it came to slavery.

Abolition was probably abhorrent to him since it threatened the public order, and as a slave owner it threatened his otherwise safe and regimented life. He had little tolerance for the radical agitations of abolitionists and northern defiance of the Fugitive Slave Act. As a strict constitutionalist, Buell thought slavery was protected by the guarantees of all citizens' rights to property and individual freedoms, and he vowed to defend those rights even if it conflicted with the political policy of the Lincoln administration. He simply considered disunion a greater evil than slavery. His southern views accompanied him to California and into the Civil War.[7]

The Buells arrived in San Francisco on May 20, 1861. The salubrious California climate was a refreshing change from the frigid Washington winter; the environment offered a complete change from the nation's capital. The intense internal strife that had characterized Washington was not altogether absent on the West Coast, but still the Buells settled into a docile life. The Department of the Pacific had been unusually quiet under the command of Albert Sidney Johnston, even in the midst of national crisis. As the clouds of secession hovered over Texas, rumors began to surface in San Francisco about Johnston's Texas loyalties and southern sympathies and his alleged connection to a conspiracy to form an independent Pacific republic that would assist the Confederacy. Whether the rumors were true or not, Johnston resigned on April 9, the same day Texas joined the Confederacy. What Johnston did not know, however, was that President Lincoln, unable to clear up the rumors about Johnston's involvement in the conspiracy and unwilling to lose California if they proved true, had already sent Gen. Edwin V. Sumner to relieve Johnston as departmental commander.[8]

Buell assumed his new duties under Sumner, a commander he had served under in the Department of Utah three years earlier. Johnston left a well-organized and disciplined department when he departed, so Sumner's and Buell's transition was somewhat eased. Within a few weeks, however, the task of keeping peace in the ranks became increasingly difficult. Aside from the mundane daily chores of recording desertions from the army, maintaining supply lines, carrying out routine courts-martial, and monitoring Indian affairs, about the only welcome news Buell received was the order of his promotion to lieutenant colonel dated May 11.[9]

As the northern and southern armies began mobilizing back east, Buell carried out the laws of the Constitution. As men such as Albert Sidney Johnston and Buell's brother-in-law David Twiggs began to leave the ranks to side with the Confederacy, Buell's task of keeping order was made more difficult, but his loyalty to the Union remained. He promptly ordered commanding officers of military posts to report to his office for the execution of War Department General Orders No. 13 requiring officers of the army "to take and subscribe a new oath of allegiance to the United States."[10]

As the mobilizing of volunteers into the northern army became more overwhelming with each passing summer day, it became apparent that officers with organizational ability were needed. The Confederate victory at First Bull Run on July 21 made Gen. Irvin McDowell the North's first sacrifice to the Lincoln administration's dissatisfaction with defeat. Fresh from his victories in western Virginia, Gen. George B. McClellan assumed prominence in the eyes of the administration and in public opinion. Severing western Virginia from the Confederacy was a major feat because it buoyed up the region's attempt to create a separate Union state. McClellan became an overnight military hero, lauded by politicians and the press alike.[11]

When McClellan took over the Department of the Potomac and the defense of Washington, he realized the overwhelming burden of organizing a large army, especially in an atmosphere of a looming Confederate attack on the capital. The ill-trained and undisciplined soldiers and the poor and unenterprising officers convinced him that he had to appoint professionally trained West Point officers, or what he called instructed officers.[12] He had to include in his thoughts his old Texas acquaintance Buell. Indeed, West Point professor Dennis Hart Mahan had written to McClellan in early August and discussed the former cadets he had considered as future leaders. "I had marked a small group of you for future generals," he wrote, "and the luck has been . . . that I find some of you turn up as I had hoped."[13] To his regret Simon Bolivar Buckner, P. G. T. Beauregard, and William D. Smith had become generals, more than likely because they joined the Confederacy. Mahan also expressed his regret that Buell, whom he had down as a future general, had not reached that rank. He warned his former student not to let "those miserable nests of petty intrigues, the Washington Bureaus, keep good men out of the way."[14]

This estimation of Buell merely reinforced what McClellan already knew. Buell was desperately needed for his organizational and administrative talents. Toward that end, McClellan got Buell a command in his department. On August 9 Buell made the journey back to Washington. Longtime Missouri friend Thomas Gantt had written to Buell from St. Louis before his departure that it was just a matter of time before Buell's appointment to a higher command. He was glad to learn that his friend had been summoned to Washington, especially after the Union defeat at Bull Run. "I hail it as an auspicious omen for the country," Gantt wrote, "that the services and the capacity of such men as you, are recognized and called for by the Government." "So long as armies [are] committed to the [mis]management of journalistic or political generals," he observed, "nothing but disaster was to be looked for. . . . Great things are expected of *McClellan*, Buell, Sherman, etc."[15]

Though he was a combat amateur, Buell was eager to participate in the Civil War. He had proven himself a capable junior officer in the Second Seminole War, had distinguished himself on the battlefield in Mexico, and had so impressed his superiors that he gained staff command in the War Department. His subsequent thirteen years in the Adjutant General's Office reflected his flair for administrative detail and rigid adherence to military protocol. More than anything else, however, Buell's lifetime commitment to the professional army was complete. The military was the only life he knew, and not supporting the Union in the rebellion was unthinkable. The army's regimen had shaped the innocent farmboy into a soldier whose principles dictated policy. For over twenty-four years Buell's military career was a constant evolution of mobilization, accommodation, and definition. He had neither asked for nor obtained so much as three months' leave of absence since he left West Point.[16]

Buell arrived in Washington in late August, received his promotion to brigadier general, and became one of the most sought-after officers in the Federal army. Brig. Gen. Robert Anderson, at that time commander of the Military Department of Kentucky, had been recruiting loyal citizens out of Kentucky to his headquarters across the river in Cincinnati. As a native of the Bluegrass State, Anderson's task was to lead loyal Kentuckians against the secessionists, but he lacked a staff and resources to do so. As New York journalist Henry Villard put it, "The political situation in the state was stirring and threatening," and Anderson had spent the summer assembling enough soldiers to form the core of the Army of the Ohio. His operations in Kentucky were vital to the Union, since Kentucky had not yet decided in favor of secession and President Lincoln

Commanders of the Army of the Potomac, September 1861 (*left to right*): William F. Smith, William B. Franklin, Samuel P. Heintzelman, Andrew Porter, Irvin McDowell, George B. McClellan, George A. McCall, Don Carlos Buell, Louis (Ludwig) Blenker, Silas Casey, and Fitz John Porter (Courtesy of the U.S. Army Military History Institute, Carlisle, Pa.)

wanted to maintain the status quo. It was Anderson's move to Fort Sumter that had helped precipitate the Civil War, and his actions in Kentucky might end it. Learning that Buell had been ordered east, Anderson wrote to Secretary of the Treasury Salmon P. Chase that he must have him. Instead, Anderson eventually got an old Fort Moultrie friend, William T. Sherman, who in mid-August had also been promoted brigadier general of volunteers.[17]

About the same time that Anderson asked for Buell, McClellan made the same request. "I am sure you will appreciate my motives in being so anxious to retain the services of such officers as Genls Buell, [George] Stoneman etc," McClellan wrote to Lincoln, "whose appointment I asked for with special reference to service in this army—on the efficiency of which depends the fate of the nation."[18] Two days later McClellan wrote to Secretary of War Simon Cameron demanding that Buell and John F. Reynolds be appointed to his Department of the Potomac. McClellan had more clout with his superiors than did Anderson, and the alleged imminent danger to Washington made Buell more immediately useful there than in Cincinnati. He reported to the Army of the Potomac on September 11, three days after McClellan's request.[19]

Buell took the field in the second week of September as a divisional commander in the developing Army of the Potomac. McClellan had decided that as northern volunteers came into the army, the division would be the largest command unit. He also established instructional schools for the volunteer regimental and company officers. Part of

Buell's initial responsibilities as a division commander, therefore, were to instruct his subordinate officers in field drills, tactics, and military protocol.[20]

In mid-September Buell arrived at Camp Brightwood near the home of transplanted Missouri politician Francis P. Blair Sr., about eight miles outside Washington. There he received the officers of his division, who stood, saluted, and continued to stand until Buell left the tent. While this element of military etiquette was rudimentary for Buell, it made him appear a bit of a martinet. Rumors circulated through camp about the new commander, and it became clear that Buell's arrival confirmed what soldiers had heard. The stocky commander had a deep chest, trunklike forearms, and a measured step. His nose was aristocratic, and his piercing blue eyes, sunken and close, were separated by deep vertical lines reflecting the burden of his duties and the seriousness that he brought to every issue. He was cautious and deliberate by nature and maintained an icy reserve and a professional distance from subordinates and soldiers alike. The almost herculean strength in his arms allowed him to "lift a weight at arm's length that would seem too much for one of twice his weight and muscle." His appearance at age forty-three reflected much of what the division lacked: a tone of discipline, organization, professionalism, and experience. He possessed an intellectual rigidity, conservative political views, a methodical industry, and a strict adherence to discipline and was a "good christian man." A contemporary described him as "stoutly built, erect and firm on his feet, straight, looked you squarely in the eye, had an air of self-possession, yet kindly expression, reserved manner, a good listener, quiet, yet firm in his decisions, a rigid disciplinarian."[21]

Shortly after lunch Buell said a few brief words and then reviewed and inspected the men for three hours in the hot sun, the longest review and drill session they had yet experienced. Capt. Joseph Keith Newel of the Tenth Massachusetts Volunteer Infantry recalled that the combination of the intense drill and heat caused "some of the men [to fall] out of the ranks," no doubt cursing the new commander they would ultimately come to respect.[22]

Buell's division was comprised of Batteries D and H, First Pennsylvania Artillery, and the brigades of Brig. Gen. Darius Nash Couch, Lawrence Pike Graham, and John James Peck. He had no cavalry attached to his division, which bothered him greatly. As autumn advanced and the weather remained favorable, the drilling continued. As one Massachusetts volunteer recalled, "These were rather days of work than of excitement."[23] What made Buell's task of exercising his men more difficult were the numerous cases of typhoid fever and measles and the complications associated with what one soldier called King Alcohol.[24] Occasionally some drunken Maryland cavalrymen, firing their revolvers and carbines, would arouse the camp and disrupt the soldiers' otherwise dull routine.[25]

On September 29 some minor movement began in the vicinity of Tennallytown, Maryland, so Buell ordered four companies of the Tenth Massachusetts to Fort Slocum. He arrived shortly after the men and ordered them to garrison the fort. Buell left his horse in charge of a Company A man while he went inside. Thinking the opportunity a good one to obtain a quick drink, the man leaped on Buell's horse and started for Grave's store a mile away. Realizing what had happened, the general's staff followed in hot pursuit. Buell always rode the finest and fastest thoroughbreds, and his Red Oak far outdistanced the pursuers, allowing the man his drink. The staff caught up to the soldier on his return trip and escorted him back to camp as a prisoner. Buell had the soldier perform a week's restitution "mounted on the head of a barrel, carrying on his back a knapsack full of sand," apparently an argument for total abstinence.[26]

Time passed in an uneventful manner in early October. The troops, however, were anxious to move, and so were members of Lincoln's Cabinet and congressional leaders. The grand reviews that McClellan staged incited in some senators and the public a desire to see the Army of the Potomac take action. The men in Buell's division were discouraged by the constant issuance of orders that were countermanded only after preparations to march had been made. After only a brief time, camp life had grown fatiguing. "I am getting weary of marching orders," wrote an exasperated Pvt. Elisha Hunt Rhodes of the Second Rhode Island, "and wish that we could move, for we have been in Camp Brightwood for two months, and I know every tree within two miles of camp."[27]

About the only excitement Buell's division experienced that fall at Camp Brightwood, beyond the constant alerts that the Confederates were about to storm Washington, was the arrival of Governors John A. Andrew of Massachusetts and William Sprague of Rhode Island; and the president himself reviewed the Army of the Potomac in mid-October. Buell accompanied Lincoln, Sprague, and Andrews on their tour through his camp, and after the end of exercises, he complimented his brigade and regimental commanders for their good work.[28]

One officer especially had caught Buell's attention, not only because of his military talents but also because he had piqued the interest of Buell's oldest daughter, Emma Twiggs Mason, who often accompanied her father through the camp. Col. Francis "Frank" I. Wheaton, a surgeon of the Second Rhode Island, had served on the U.S.-Mexican border survey in 1855 and three years later accompanied the First U.S. Cavalry in the Utah expedition. Recently he had led the Second Rhode Island at First Bull Run. His abilities as a surgeon and an officer had impressed his superiors, including Buell, who apparently overlooked the fact that his pedigree failed to include a West Point education. The soldiers also had confidence in Colonel Wheaton and regarded him as a fine commander. At age twenty-eight he was three years Emma's senior. The couple met during the summer when Buell became a divisional commander, and they courted during the fall. Emma was accustomed to socializing in military circles, and it was a natural assumption that she would take the hand of a soldier—certainly an officer—in marriage. In early November she and Wheaton became engaged.[29]

All was quiet along the Potomac River for weeks until Sunday, October 21, when at Balls Bluff, near the town of Leesburg, Virginia, just forty miles upriver from the nation's capital, Col. Edward Baker attempted to dislodge a brigade of Mississippians and Virginians from the town. The Confederate rout of Baker's force resulted in the colonel's death and the loss of more than half of his 1,700 men, killed, wounded, or captured.[30] The incident was a shameful display of inept leadership, and McClellan used the debacle to undermine commanding general Winfield Scott. In the midst of complaints that the Union army was suffering from inertia due to Scott, McClellan explained to a triumvirate of Radical senators—Benjamin Wade of Ohio, Lyman Trumbull of Illinois, and Zachariah Chandler of Michigan—that Scott was the impediment to a more spirited war.[31]

McClellan's lobbying to gain control of all the Union armies worked, despite his having done little to merit high esteem and confidence. When Scott renewed his application for retirement, Lincoln accepted it. When Lincoln called on his new military chief, McClellan responded that he felt as if "several tons were taken from my shoulders." Lincoln expressed his concern about McClellan's increased responsibilities as general in chief and as the commander of the Army of the Potomac, but McClellan confidently replied, "I can do it all."[32] Buell wrote to McClellan, congratulating him and expressing great confidence in his ability to meet his new responsibilities. He also expressed his great satisfaction that McClellan had gained his new position through his "concurrent belief in fitness," as opposed to the shallowness by which others had apparently gained rank.[33] As a conservative Democrat, however, McClellan would need the only thing Lincoln could really offer a military commander who appeared to have everything: the president's political shield against the Radicals and against public opinion.[34]

Although McClellan boasted publicly that he could do it all, he confessed to his wife that he felt the "need for some support."[35] Information from the field confirmed what he already knew: the western commands needed considerable attention. Little had been done to resolve the lack of coordination in the West, and McClellan decided to organize two departments out of the vast territory west of the Appalachian Mountains. He extended the responsibility of the newly created Department of the West to his leading rival, Henry Halleck, a favorite of Winfield Scott's and his choice for the position of general in chief. With headquarters in St. Louis, the department included Missouri and that portion of Kentucky west of the Cumberland River. Halleck was to restore order from the chaos left by John C. Frémont.[36]

McClellan's decision to appoint Buell to the newly created Department of the Ohio, which included Tennessee and the rest of Kentucky, was a selection of a more delicate nature. When McClellan had requested information from all the departments, Sherman in the Department of the Cumberland had sent alarming news, not so much about the Confederates but about his own state of mind. From the day he arrived in Louisville, headquarters of the Department of the Cumberland in early September, Sherman was convinced the Union had little hope of success. He continually lamented the condition of the troops, the weakness of his position, and the uncertainty of the enemy's size or designs. According to Col. Benjamin F. Scribner of the Thirty-eighth Indiana, during a September council of war Sherman said that the enemy was about to overrun Louisville and that the men had better make up their minds to "die right here." He was ready to "fight them down to our stubs."[37]

By mid-October about the only thing Sherman was sure of was his need for 200,000 troops to go on the offensive in Kentucky, shocking Secretary of War Simon Cameron, who was passing through Louisville on his way from St. Louis to Washington. Sherman made no secret that he was "forced into command of this department against my will." His overly pessimistic view of affairs in Kentucky, coupled with his desire to return to his old brigade in Washington, made his removal easier for McClellan. Moreover, the rumors that swept through the newspapers claiming that Sherman was insane made McClellan's decision appear almost a necessity. Thus, McClellan made the decision to send Sherman to Henry W. Halleck in St. Louis and replace him with Buell.[38]

McClellan expected great things from Buell, since he saw in Buell some of the same qualities he himself possessed. But while Buell shared McClellan's temperament, he scarcely had a hint of his charm or popularity. Whereas McClellan involved himself directly in politics early in the war, Buell tried to remain apolitical. He apparently never believed that politics or popularity were useful to a soldier. In the position that Buell assumed that fall, however, he would be forced to make bold decisions about how to deal with politics and with civilian authorities during the war.[39]

The word that Buell was leaving the Army of the Potomac spread throughout his division like wildfire. His soldiers had grown accustomed to the austere commander and his rigid ways, his persistence in disciplining them, and his strict adherence to the highest professional standards. Whether they liked him or not, they could not deny his success in molding hundreds of civilians into one of the finest divisions in the Army of the Potomac. The Massachusetts boys in his division considered themselves fortunate to have soldiered under the precise eye of General Buell, who had made them into a fine regiment of fighting blues. Buell had labored on this division, according to the correspondent to the *New York Times*, "with indefatigable zeal from early dawn till late at night."[40] The day before he left command he held his first review, which was "declared a splendid success for only thirty days of training." Moreover, wrote this enthused observer, "The assiduous devotion of Gen. Buell to his work may be judged by the fact, though his encampment is not over four miles from his home, he has not slept one night under his roof since he assumed the command."[41] Those who had grown fond of Buell expressed regret about his leaving. Elisha Hunt Rhodes, who had recently been appointed a clerk in division headquarters, replied that while he considered Buell a martinet, the general was "undoubtedly a good soldier . . . and I rather like his style."[42]

The relative obscurity and uneventfulness of Buell's position in the Union army during the autumn of 1861 ended with his reassignment. Sherman was happy to give up his responsibilities in Kentucky, and Buell was equally glad to take them. Buell and Sherman were good friends, and Buell was certainly distressed by the discrediting effect of the rumors characterizing Sherman as insane. Whatever Sherman was that fall, he was not insane, although the press continued to hound him even after he left Louisville.[43]

If Buell sought reassurance about his new responsibilities, he did not have far to look. "I trust I need not repeat to you," confided McClellan, "that I regard the importance of the territory committed to your care as second only to that occupied by the army under my immediate command."[44] With this friendly gesture of confidence were McClellan's authoritative overtones of policy and procedure, which served to highlight the political aspects of Buell's assignment in Kentucky. "The military problem would be a simple one," McClellan advised Buell, "could it be entirely separated from political influence." "It is possible," he counseled, "that the conduct of our political affairs in Kentucky is more important than that of our military operations." He added that Buell should "constantly bear in mind the precise issue for which we are fighting," which was the preservation of the Union and the restoration of the government in the seceded states. This, McClellan declared, could only be done by "religiously respecting the Constitutional rights of all." Buell was not to interfere with but, rather, to protect the domestic institutions of Kentuckians. Nothing but the "dictates of military necessity" should cause Buell to depart from McClellan's instructions.[45]

As for strategy, McClellan urged Buell to remain on the defensive and secure the railroad from Louisville to Nashville while he moved the mass of his army rapidly through Cumberland Gap or Walker's Gap to Knoxville. This, McClellan argued, would allow Buell to cut the railway between eastern Virginia and the Mississippi and enable the loyal citizens of East Tennessee to rise in support of the Union.[46]

On November 12 McClellan sent Buell another letter reiterating his earlier instructions but placing more emphasis on a campaign into East Tennessee. "The main point to which I desire to call your attention," McClellan wrote, "is the necessity of entering Eastern Tennessee as soon as it can be done with reasonable chances of success." Still, he repeated to Buell that the army was fighting only to preserve the Union, and it must religiously respect the constitutional rights of all.[47]

McClellan spoke in absolutes and with clear direction, and fortunately Buell, too, thought in absolutes. He was a painfully conscientious man and cemented McClellan's policy firmly in his mind—perhaps too firmly. McClellan and Buell had conversed long and fully on the subject of military operations, and each man greatly respected the other's intellectual abilities and judgment. "My confidence in your judgement is so great," wrote McClellan, "that I will not dwell further upon the necessity of keeping me fully informed as to the state of affairs, both military and political."[48]

Although he had faith in Buell's judgment, McClellan was keenly aware of Buell's political liabilities. He hoped that by making it absolutely clear to Buell that the politics of his command were as important to Union success as his military operations in the Bluegrass State, he might overcome this liability. McClellan emphasized what Buell already knew about politics and the military—the two were inextricable during war—and whether or not Buell liked the degree to which politics affected military operations, he would be forced to accommodate political considerations. McClellan's desire to help Buell was ironic, since McClellan's own record regarding political-military relationships was not great. McClellan also made it clear that it was the policy of the Lincoln administration to extend constitutional guarantees to Kentuckians not identified with the rebellion—a message that endured with Buell long after the administration abandoned it. But perhaps the most important message McClellan sent to Buell was that in regard to the local institutions, only the dictates of military necessity should cause him to depart from the spirit of McClellan's instructions. In this, Buell was apparently allowed to determine for himself what was military necessity.[49]

Although the fall of 1861 was a rather calm time in Buell's life, it was the beginning of a new era for him as a commander. His division in the Army of the Potomac was the largest unit he had ever commanded. To assume management of an entire department and army in a state where loyalties were bitterly divided was surely overwhelming. His predecessors, both of whom he regarded as fine and capable military men, had buckled under the pressure. Robert Anderson, fatigued from his Fort Sumter activities and the strain of operations in Louisville, resigned his position to Sherman on October 8. A month later Sherman suffered an emotional collapse, partly resulting from the mountain of responsibilities as a departmental commander. The omen of misfortune that hung over Louisville was surely uninviting.[50]

Although Buell may not have learned anything new that fall as a division commander beyond what he already knew about leadership and command, he thought the war was a peculiar one, and his views about the way it should be conducted became more pronounced after he assumed his new command. Fundamental to his beliefs about the war was his recognition that the Union was not fighting a foreign enemy but a people with whom the North hoped to live in peace and harmony. Therefore to accomplish what were essentially reconstruction efforts, the duty of the military was to suppress every recognizable armed force and to respect the constitutional rights of those civilians who had not taken up arms. In this way the Union army could achieve two results simultaneously: suppress armed resistance and protect unarmed civilians.

The Lincoln administration fought the war on the theory that secession was unconstitutional and, therefore, the southern states still lived under the Constitution. Congress concurred. The passage of resolutions in July 1861 sponsored by Kentuckian John J. Crittenden and Tennessean Andrew Johnson affirmed that the United States fought with no intention of "overthrowing or interfering with the rights of established institutions of the [seceded] States" but only to "defend and maintain the supremacy of the Constitution and to preserve the Union with all the dignity, equality, and rights of the several States unimpaired."[51] As long as Buell and the administration were in harmony about the kind of war they were waging, Buell would have little trouble reconciling his military policies with the national or political policies of the administration.[52]

Though Buell would take with him to Kentucky a well-cultivated military philosophy that was twenty years old, his success in the peacetime army came from following orders and regulations. He would have to outgrow his adjutant background and move his thinking beyond the mere fundamental and tactical to strategical, geographical, and political concerns. What sort of strategy should he adopt? Should he cultivate a political neutrality? What if he disagreed with his friend McClellan? These questions gave him much to think about on his mid-November train ride from Washington to Louisville.

CHAPTER SIX

Napoleon Buell

T he seeds of Union discord were sown early and deep in the West in the autumn of 1861. The two protagonists were Buell and Halleck. Though his prewar experience paled in comparison with Halleck's, Buell was considered one of the best officers in the regular army, particularly as an organizer, administrator, and disciplinarian. Fellow officers labeled him brilliant, but he lacked Halleck's intellectual gifts. In the shadow of the scholarly Halleck, Buell had considerable advantages: he had more practical ability in military field organization, shared the same "soft war" views as General in Chief McClellan, and more importantly, was closer to McClellan than Halleck ever was. The fact that he owned slaves perhaps made him more popular among Kentuckians. In other words, Buell possessed a McClellan-like attitude when it came to shaping armies and conducting war, particularly in the politically sensitive environment of the border states. Lincoln apparently also regarded Buell highly for the Kentucky appointment, since he had no objections.[1]

Unfortunately, both Buell and Halleck lacked that flamboyance of leadership that McClellan exhibited; yet both men shared a high degree of professionalism and intensity of purpose, and neither man possessed a small ego. Buell, Halleck, and McClellan all demanded strict discipline. All were administratively inclined, and all shared a common temperament, military philosophy, and conservative view of the war. None of them doubted that the war would be a limited one fought along traditional lines. All believed the best way to win the war was through a series of long campaigns in which maneuvering rather than fighting would determine success.[2]

The fact that Halleck had been McClellan's rival for his position as general in chief placed Buell in a difficult situation. Buell had received appointment to the more significant department, militarily and politically, and Halleck was jealous. He thought himself more qualified than Buell for the Department of the Ohio, if not the post of general in chief. Halleck and Buell probably only knew each other from their West Point days, but Buell was no doubt familiar with Halleck's military reputation and his works on military theory. But while Halleck had abandoned the military for a more lucrative life in business, Buell had remained through the California gold and land craze of the 1850s and had earned his rank and appointment through his military activity rather than by any flare for writing about military theory.

Buell was not as ambitious as Halleck, in part because he did not have to be. By mid-November, Kentucky, not Missouri, was the crucial border state for the Union. Like Halleck, Buell merely wanted to govern his own department independently, without subordinating his operations to any other departmental commander. But considering the vast terrain of the West, Halleck and Buell had to act in concert. The fact that there existed a degree of rivalry in their early relationship made such agreement difficult. Still, the maintenance of their successful military association would have as much to do with their conservative personalities as with their professional attitudes.[3]

Buell's professional attitude was the result of a lifetime in the military. By 1861 he had been a soldier longer than he had been a civilian. His outlook stemmed from his gentlemanly character and conduct and his application of pride and strict discipline to everything he undertook. Over the years he had developed a cast-iron self-discipline in the routine duty he performed in the Adjutant General's Office. Unfortunately, these admirable qualities also made him too systematic and impaired his originality. His conception of an officer's responsibility was to live and command in accordance with high standards of the gentlemanly codes of the military. A contemporary of Buell's wrote that he was the "beau ideal of a West Pointer. . . . Small in stature, he was so soldierly of bearing that he seemed of full height."[4] Buell "impressed all with an air of business and confidence," another contemporary said.[5] Because the military regimen kept his thinking precise and focused on the systematic care of small details, it made him more suited to the unimaginative tasks of organization and administration than to those assignments requiring postulation, risk, or chance. In short, Buell's years as an adjutant general had required little originality but had developed systemization, a fixed way of doing things.[6]

Buell's attitude came to shape much of his nonmilitary thinking as well. He believed in a strict interpretation of the Constitution and viewed the military as an instrument not of public policy but, rather, of constitutional guarantees. In fact he thought, as did McClellan, that because the war was actually politics of reconstruction, then commanders should make policy for the politics of war. Buell lived a life of regulations and protocol that instilled in him habits and traditions not easily changed. He was modest, unassuming, and quiet, and he never swore and seldom drank. He never outgrew his taciturn youthful demeanor, which repelled casual observers. As a commander he had to learn to inspire and motivate men, but his austere manner and cold reserve made him appear unfriendly and unapproachable. This conservative attitude, reserved deportment, and lack of political savvy became more acute when the war became more political. Buell himself even recognized his limitations as a commander and wrote to his wife shortly after assuming his new post that he did not want to disappoint those who had placed him in this position. "I have only a few instincts," he confessed, and "you will comfort and soothe me in case of failure, but they [the country] will not."[7] Still, he was confident he was the man for the job.

The states of the upper South—including Kentucky, Missouri, Maryland, and Virginia—did not share the certitude that was at the heart of Buell's being. Though Unionists held a slim majority in these states, a slight change in political or military circumstances might allow the determined secessionist minorities to prevail. Although Kentuckians had relied on the Mississippi River to channel their commerce south and east in the antebellum period, railroads increasingly redirected their trade North by way of the Ohio River. With those goods went a substantial political allegiance. As the natural boundary between North and

Though small in stature at five feet, eight inches and weighing roughly 155 pounds, Don Carlos Buell was endowed with incredible strength, which he demonstrated by picking up his wife, who weighed some 140 pounds, and holding her out in front of him before placing her on the mantel of a fireplace. (Courtesy of the U.S. Army Military History Institute, Carlisle, Pa.)

South, the Ohio River could be used as a defensive barrier by the Union against the Confederacy, but only if Kentucky stayed in the Union. The fact that two of the Ohio's navigable tributaries, the Cumberland and the Tennessee Rivers, flowed west through Kentucky and Tennessee increased the importance of the waterway. Wisconsin governor Alexander Williams Randall advised President Lincoln that control of the Ohio River was "a matter of absolute necessity, not only for the Northern border States but for all the Northwestern States."[8] Kentuckian William B. Shanks, who was a correspondent to James Gordon Bennett's *New York Herald*, agreed that "serious disasters" would result from the Union's loss of the Ohio.[9]

Shortly after the firing on Fort Sumter, Kentucky's Governor Beriah Magoffin announced formal neutrality and warned both Union and Confederate governments not to enter the state without invitation. Still, Lincoln understood the importance of the Bluegrass State. "Kentucky gone," he declared, "we can not hold Missouri, nor, as I think, Maryland. These all against us, and the job on our hands is too large for us. We would as well consent to separation at once, including the surrender of this capitol."[10] It was understandable, then, why Lincoln was reported to have said that while he hoped to have God on his side, he must have Kentucky, since it came with the Ohio River. The editor of the *New York Times* echoed this sentiment, saying, "Kentucky has suddenly become a field of exceeding interest in the war."[11]

Located at the crossroads of several strategic lines, Kentucky's neutrality was sure to be short lived. In the summer of 1861 both Union and Confederate governments established military camps just outside the state's border. Magoffin allowed Confederate recruiting agents to enter the state while simultaneously rebuffing both Lincoln's and Davis's calls for volunteers. He also allowed Brig. Gen. Simon Bolivar Buckner to mobilize the 4,000 men of the Kentucky State Guard. Sailor-turned-soldier William Nelson was instrumental in organizing a "Home Guard" to counter the state militia. By July Nelson's troop had so increased in size and strength that he established Camp Dick Robinson not far from Frankfort, the state capital. The rapid buildup of Union forces in Kentucky caused Cameron to expand the Department of the Cumberland, headquartered at Cincinnati, to include all of Kentucky and Tennessee.[12]

The political victory in the summer elections placed the state under Union control, essentially marking the end of political neutrality. Kentucky's loyalty allowed Lincoln the opportunity to use the Ohio River as a Union defensive barrier against the Confederacy and a point of de-

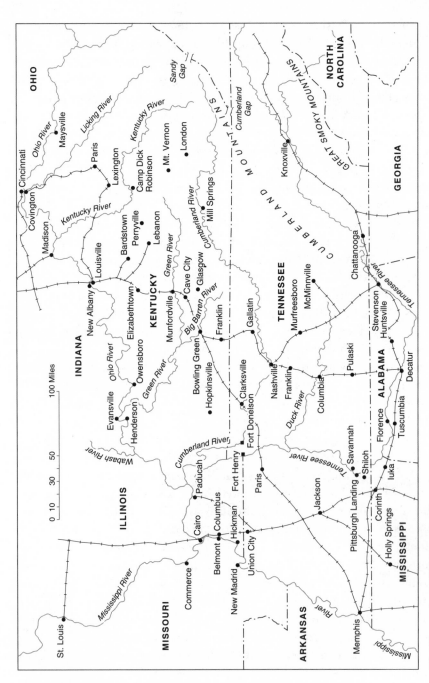

The Kentucky and Tennessee theater

parture for an advance into the region of loyal Tennesseans—namely, East Tennessee. In early September, with the entry of Brig. Gen. Leonidas Polk's Confederates into Columbus, Kentucky, on the Mississippi River, General Anderson and Indiana governor Oliver P. Morton urged Federal authorities to remove political restrictions on raising troops or moving them into the state. Lincoln acquiesced, and Anderson, in an action reminiscent of his move from Moultrie to Sumter the previous winter, transferred his headquarters from Cincinnati to Louisville. After that, Morton declared to Secretary Cameron that the "war in Kentucky has commenced." On September 18, loyal Kentuckians officially declared their support for the Union, which prompted those not loyal to the Union to join the Confederacy.[13] As the gray skies and crisp air signaling the approaching autumn descended on the Bluegrass State, military operations heated up. War had come to Kentucky, and so had Don Carlos Buell.

Buell arrived in Louisville on November 15, 1861, and found the newly designated Department of the Ohio just as McClellan had described it: chaotic. According to Shanks, "Instead of being an organizer, Sherman was a disorganizer."[14] But the chaos was not solely due to Sherman. Buell faced the problems typically inherent in organizing new departments and new armies early in the war. Yet it was just the kind of assignment that would allow him to apply everything he knew about the military. Buell's new role placed him in a critical situation. Shortly after he arrived, a delegation of 200 Kentuckians led by ex-governor Magoffin and Senator John Breckinridge passed an ordinance of secession, formed a provisional government, and became the thirteenth Confederate state.[15]

The orders creating the new Department of the Ohio caused some confusion in the West for Buell and his rival across the Mississippi. Neither Halleck nor Buell was at all familiar with the countryside, and neither man knew exactly where his departmental authority ended, since Halleck's command reached to the banks of the Cumberland River but applied only to Kentucky. Buell's orders made him responsible for the states of Ohio, Michigan, and Indiana; that portion of Kentucky east of the Cumberland; and the entire state of Tennessee, which had yet to be divided. The fact that the Tennessee and Cumberland Rivers changed departments as they crossed into Kentucky was apparently insignificant in the fall of 1861. Whether the departmental commanders would cooperate sufficiently to prevent the confusion from causing operations to halt was a question for the future.

In November Buell's challenge in holding on to the Bluegrass State was obvious. He was responsible for defending a 300-mile line from Cumberland Gap through inhospitable terrain to Bowling Green, where the Louisville and Nashville Railroad junctioned with the Memphis and Ohio, to Columbus, Kentucky, on the Mississippi. An anxious public demanded of Buell in Kentucky the same things it demanded of McClellan in Virginia: quick and effective movement.[16]

Louisville was in a state of confusion when Buell arrived, although it was not on the verge of capture as Sherman had insisted. Just the day before, the *Louisville Daily Journal*, in announcing Buell's arrival, had expressed a reservation about his academic standing at West Point but concluded that a "low grade in college may show want of scholarship and want of capacity . . . [but] it is what a man accomplished in the actual battle of life that gives him character."[17] The correspondent to the *Cincinnati Commercial*, apparently responding to the Louisville paper, declared that Buell had previously distinguished himself in war by his "marked ability and courage."[18]

By the time of Buell's arrival, Sherman had concentrated what forces he had in and around the city to prevent an imminent Confederate attack. He was convinced that Johnston was making "herculean efforts" to strike a great blow in Kentucky. He even halted Brig. Gen. George H. Thomas's advance toward the Cumberland Gap, fearing falsely that Confederate General Felix Zollicoffer was moving toward Louisville with overwhelming forces. Though Thomas was eager to advance into East Tennessee, Sherman ordered him to remain at Crab Orchard until he received instructions from the new departmental commander. Then he ordered Thomas to retreat "farther back" toward Louisville.[19]

Certainly there was an element of awkwardness when Buell arrived, since he was a close friend of Sherman's. Despite the circumstances, both men were glad to see each other; Buell broke the tension with a compliment about the progress Sherman had made in training the recruits. "Sherman," he declared, "you should be a major general."[20] Any tension between the two men dissipated before the task facing Buell. He was unconvinced that the future looked as "dark" as Sherman had described it. The situation in his new army, however, did little to relieve his apprehension about the city's security. Shortly after Buell arrived, he telegraphed McClellan that Sherman's fears about an attack were unfounded. Ironically, however, Sherman's fear, rather than Buell's optimism, encouraged Cameron to begin building up forces in the department.[21]

Buell's arrival inspired great enthusiasm. "Anderson was a gentleman of no mind," wrote the *Chicago Tribune* correspondent. "Sherman is possessed of neither mind nor manner. We are thankful now that we have a man who combines both." The *Cincinnati Commercial* congratulated the press on escaping from the "peevishness, prejudice and persecution" of Sherman, the "perfect monomaniac on the subject of journalism."[22] Sherman himself had previously thought he might feel more comfortable "if some more sanguine mind" were in Louisville, since as he confessed to Thomas, "I am forced to order according to my convictions"—convictions many were beginning to question.[23] Buell indeed had the conviction that Sherman lacked. Nonetheless, he would first have to restore order to relieve the apprehension of Louisvillians and do it with inherited subordinates, none of whom he knew.

Shortly after Buell arrived, he and Sherman rode out to Camp Nolin south of Louisville to review the troops under the command of Ohioan Brig. Gen. Alexander McDowell McCook. McCook had been a student and tactical instructor at West Point and had led the First Ohio in the Battle of First Bull Run. He now commanded the First Division in the newly designated Army of the Ohio. The two men returned to the Galt House, and Sherman turned over his command. Sherman knew better than anyone that there was truth in the rumors that "the care, perplexities, and anxieties of the situation had unbalanced my judgement and my mind."[24]

The following day Buell wrote McClellan a lengthy private letter describing the situation in his department. In their frequent correspondence the two commanders addressed each other as "My Dear Friend," Buell unknowingly injuring Sherman's feelings by opening these letters in his presence. Sherman was not friendly with McClellan and had never received any correspondence from the general in chief, except for a few curt telegrams. When Buell suspended Thomas's retreat from the East, Sherman saw the regiments he had previously ordered arriving with Buell, and he grew increasingly depressed.[25]

Buell tried to be fair to Sherman. He told McClellan that the condition he found himself in was so "inextricabl[y] confus[ing]" that it made even writing about it difficult. The problems were clearly larger than just the "disorganization" of Sherman. He informed McClellan that getting his department into shape would require considerable work. He also expressed concern about confronting Albert Sidney Johnston's forces, especially since the Federals in his department were scattered and exposed. Moreover, he stated he was aware that his task was to penetrate Tennessee, but in reality he believed that the true course was to threaten Johnston at Bowling Green and then strike for Nashville. "The loyalists in East Tennessee," he argued, "would be as effectively released [with a move toward Nashville] as though you [McClellan] were in their midst." He closed his letter by requesting from McClellan two gunboats, adding that while he needed some reinforcements, "that's not quite equal to demanding 200,000 men," which Buell knew Sherman had requested.[26]

Buell's initial letter to McClellan highlighted several important points. First, he made it clear that while he was cognizant of the political importance of relieving loyal Tennesseans in East Tennessee, he believed that moving his army into Cumberland Gap would be injurious to it. The political desires of taking East Tennessee would have to wait. He was reluctant to take on Johnston, considering the Union army's condition, even though Johnston's army was also in a wretched state. Given the fact that Buell had left McClellan only two days before, it was odd that he had changed his mind about East Tennessee so quickly.

Buell's reluctance to move immediately to East Tennessee and instead aim for Nashville revealed his Jominian philosophy. For Buell, reflecting the nineteenth-century theorist, war was a limited and leisurely exercise to be conducted by professionals who emphasized preparation over movement. "Success," he argued, "must be rendered reasonably certain if possible—the more the better." He contended that "if the result is reasonably uncertain, battle is only to be sought when very serious disadvantage must result from a failure to fight or when the advantages of a possible victory far outweigh the consequences of probable defeat." "These rules," he stated, "suppose that war has a higher object than that of mere bloodshed, and military history points for study and commendation to campaigns which have been conducted over a large field of operations with important results and without a single general engagement." Jomini could not have said it better. Buell accepted these principles and never deviated from them throughout the war.[27]

Buell requested that Sherman delay his departure for a few days to make the transition easier, and under the circumstances he "commenced to concentrate a little." He expected to be ready for operations relatively quickly. He had to be ready because McClellan expected action and was sending four more regiments for Buell to use in advancing to Cumberland Gap.[28]

Buell had other ideas. The organization of his army was paramount in his mind. With tremendous energy he plunged indefatigably into shaping the Army of the Ohio and into establishing his kind of discipline. According to one contemporary, Buell began at once "creating an efficient army out of the raw material at hand."[29] East Tennessee would have to wait.

When Buell took over the department, he inherited an ailing army. He had only two organized divisions of approximately 23,000 soldiers under McCook and Thomas. McCook's division was spread out south along the road to Bowling Green, and Thomas's spread out east toward Cumberland Gap. Of the two, Thomas was the more qualified to command. He had graduated twelfth in the 1840 West Point class and had probably known Buell at the academy. Like Buell, he had been brevetted in the Mexican War. Unlike Buell, he advocated immediate movement into East Tennessee and concentrated all his energies for a march in that direction. Unfortunately, his command was poorly equipped, lacking transportation, adequate staff officers, and funds. Still, his recruiting efforts in eastern Kentucky proved successful, and East Tennesseans, particularly Senators Andrew Johnson and Horace Maynard, urged him to move into their region. As a regular army man, fresh from the well-trained Army of the Potomac in northern Virginia, Thomas was naturally concerned at the lack of discipline he found in his division and the raw recruits. Nonetheless, he was willing to advance into East Tennessee.

Thomas had already moved his headquarters and supply depot to Crab Orchard in order to improve his position for the expected advance into East Tennessee. Within a week after arriving at Louisville, however, Buell ordered Thomas back to Lebanon on the railroad to move his supply base from Cincinnati to Louisville, which cut the distance of moving supplies by half. Meanwhile, as Thomas continued to make preparations to move, loyal East Tennesseans became more impatient of the delay and urged Andrew Johnson to press Thomas for immediate action.[30]

While Thomas prepared for a move into East Tennessee, 4,000 soldiers under General Nelson, nicknamed "Bull" for his overwhelming size, strength, and ungovernable attitude, mustered in eastern Kentucky near Maysville. Because of his hot temper, Nelson had made enemies of influential politicians around Louisville, so Sherman had sent him out of the city. He quickly became a similar problem for Buell. Buell, however, would come to tolerate Nelson's temper and disruptiveness, since the Bull exhibited the qualities that Buell most admired in an officer. He was a thorough disciplinarian, and he was loyal.[31]

In addition to Thomas's and Nelson's divisions, there were some forty other Kentucky regiments or fractions of regiments lamentably scattered throughout the state and also trying to recruit additional men. According to Buell, many of these soldiers, "in fact nearly all, of them were not yet mustered in" and were without "arms, equipments or proper organization."[32] Only some of the men in the cavalry regiments were armed with muskets, a few had pistols, and there was not a carbine among them. The cavalry was so bad that Gen. Albin Schoepf later questioned whether he would ever obtain a regiment of "*reliable* cavalry."[33] In the infantry the soldiers carried arms of two or three different calibers, and many of these were of foreign make and unfit for service. Supplies and equipment were largely deficient and defective, and there was not transportation enough to sustain 20,000 men on a march for more than two days. There were not enough trained officers to deal with these men, and those newly appointed junior officers were functioning as generals in anticipation of promised promotions.[34]

It became painfully clear to Buell that he would need to overhaul thoroughly the command structure of the Army of the Ohio to centralize authority. He found the department just as editor William Shanks had described it: "a mob without head or foot, or appropriate parts."[35] Compared with Halleck's and McClellan's in the adjoining departments east and west of Kentucky, Buell's situation was critical, given the heavy responsibility he had. His army was only 30,000 strong for a 300-mile front that stretched through rugged terrain. Sherman had made the same argument. With 60,000 soldiers, Halleck's department had twice as many men, and his front stretched only about 100 miles. McClellan's 100,000-man army was the largest of all Union armies, yet he had the smallest of the three departments. For Buell, this was a difficult situation, one that under the best of circumstances could prove troublesome.[36]

Like McClellan, Buell was a perfectionist. With the one leverage that his predecessor had been denied—control of the new troops being raised for his command—he quickly transformed the army into the very image of its commander, a body with definition and direction. Buell directed all the lines of communication and supply from the armies in the field from Cincinnati to Louisville. He insisted that camps be carefully selected and well drained. Though there was no shortage of applicants for positions within his army, Buell's expectations of receiving competent or perhaps experienced staff officers and a regiment of regular cavalry further darkened his outlook for the immediate future.[37]

Buell made it a rule not to organize the brigades by states but, rather, to represent as many states as possible in each brigade. He was careful to ensure that each brigade contained regiments from at least two states, which would maximize his authority of the unit and minimize the authority of the governor. Apparently the political situation in his department convinced him that this arrangement would reduce the opportunity for state governors to interfere in military affairs—"an arrangement," Buell declared, "which was attended with the happiest results in the discipline and tone of the army." He abandoned the modern command structure of a "corps" and, instead, peered back to the eighteenth century and to French military writers to organize his army into sixteen brigades that shortly were assembled into five divisions. The brigades numbered from one to sixteen consecutively, and even though they were organized into divisions, it was clear that Buell wanted to be able to command them as separate units under his personal control.[38]

The soldiers themselves had mixed feelings about Buell's arrangement. Benjamin F. Scribner of the Thirty-eighth Indiana believed that the new commander's system of organization tended to "destroy the national spirit" in favor of state pride. Wesley Elmore of the Tenth Indiana wrote to his parents of his dissatisfaction with his regiment being brigaded with "Green Kentuckians."[39]

Creating an army in a state with divided loyalties was not an easy task. Buell tried to select commanders, when he could, whom Kentuckians would find more acceptable, particularly in regard to their views on slavery. Naturally, his decisions did not go uncontested. Some commanders and politicians believed that Buell himself had received command for political reasons. Maj. Gen. David Hunter, for example, was "very deeply mortified, humiliated, insulted and disgraced" by Buell's appointment. He complained to Cameron and Lincoln that he had not received the command of the Department of the Ohio because of his views on slavery and his support for emancipation. He claimed that Buell became commander because he and McClellan supported slavery. In his usual soothing and gracious manner Lincoln responded, "'Act well your part, there all the honor lies.' He who does *something* at the head of one Regiment, will eclipse him who does *nothing* at the head of a hundred."[40] Lincoln was not criticizing Buell; he was merely trying to convince Hunter that his services were important.

Buell created an army that looked like it belonged to Kentucky. Still, he was careful to select commanders with military experience and organizational ability. Of his first fourteen brigade commanders, only Thomas J. Wood (Fifth Brigade) and Richard W. Johnson (Sixth Brigade) were active in the regular army. Cols. Joshua W. Sill (Ninth Brigade), Jacob Ammen (Tenth Brigade), and Milo Hascall (Fifteenth Brigade) were all West Point graduates but civilians by the time of the war. Those brigade commanders who had some military experience included Brig. Gens. Samuel Carter (Twelfth Brigade), Albin Schoepf (First Brigade), Lovell Rousseau (Fourth Brigade), and James Scott Negley (Seventh Brigade) and Cols. Mahlon D. Manson (Second Brigade) and John Basil Turchin (Eighth Brigade). The remaining three brigade commanders—Col. Robert L. McCook (Third Brigade), Col. Charles Cruft (Thirteenth Brigade), and Brig. Gen. Jeremiah Boyle (Eleventh Brigade)—had no military experience.[41]

By the end of his first two weeks in Louisville, Buell had made some progress in establishing himself as the central authority for the army. He required a thorough record of every regiment's officers—general, field, and staff—and of each regiment's equipment and ammunition down to the last mule and bayonet. He demanded that regimental commanders report weekly on the amount of ammunition and that quartermaster and commissary chiefs report not only on what they possessed but also where they obtained their supplies and the anticipated difficulty of increasing supplies if necessary. Buell wanted to make sure that his quartermasters were not procuring supplies through illegal means. He ended the election of officers, prohibited infantry officers from riding when on the march, and banned buggies and family carriages from camp.[42]

Buell firmly, almost severely, impressed discipline on the volunteers. As Shanks put it, Buell was "too much of a regular."[43] He expected the newly mustered volunteers to attain perfection in "appointment, organization, drill, and all that routine duty to which he had been accustomed in the old army."[44] His "highest aim was to make good soldiers of his command, and everything that detracted from this, as straggling, pillaging, disobedience of orders, he regarded as unworthy of a soldier, and meriting prompt and stern punishment at his hands."[45] He considered that the "stricter the obedience to orders the better for the soldier."[46] One veteran wrote that Buell's strict discipline resulted in Buell's gaining "much personal unpopularity" among the soldiers because they did not understand him.[47]

Buell's regular army background made him insensitive to the volunteers, who by that time had organized themselves and elected their own officers. He had trouble motivating men and was more concerned with the physical and theoretical appearance of an army than with a soldier's goodwill. James F. Mohr of the Fifth U.S. Artillery considered Buell's insensitivity toward the soldiers terrible. "It is awful the way we are treated at presant," he wrote, "it is a shame for regulars nay more—we are treated worst than Hogs here. . . . It is a sin for Officers to mistuse there soldiers as we are used."[48] Pvt. Roderick Hooper of the Seventeenth Ohio Volunteers disagreed. He argued that though they "have had some pretty hard times," he thought the "dumb sesech . . .

have not got the energy about them [to fight] that the Ohio and Indiana boys has."[49]

Buell considered discipline central to a soldier's survival in combat. The more disciplined an army, the better the chances for its survival. Naturally, soldiers viewed such harsh disciplinary measures as more life threatening than life saving. Realizing that most of the regimental officers had never given a military command, Buell attempted to set up "camps of instruction," as McClellan had done in the Army of the Potomac. He also provided manuals for the new officers. The Army of the Ohio, however, continued to lack a centralized training system, which was a serious consequence when it came to coordinating the actions of the other units.[50]

Buell made the troops painfully aware that discipline was of paramount importance by forcing them to adhere to strict regulations. He inspected companies regularly, and the inspections were meticulously thorough down to the last cartridge box and tin cup. All officers on duty with troops had to appear in uniform, and those leading troops in the field encamped with their men. Women were prohibited from camp and from accompanying troops in the field. Citizens applying for permission to visit the camps greatly annoyed Buell, and while it pained him not to grant their wishes, the rules had to be enforced.[51]

Shortly after Buell's arrival in the city, a woman correspondent to the *Indianapolis Daily Journal,* outraged by Buell's orders expelling women and relatives from camp, wrote a scathing letter to the general. "We doubt not but that it gave General Buell exquisite pleasure to issue this order," she lamented, "for once in our life we are thankful that we are a woman, exempt . . . from being governed by military despots."[52] Buell's hard drilling and training no doubt made many of his soldiers wish they were women. Still, constant drilling prepared the men for obedience, teaching the soldiers what George Herr of the Fifty-ninth Illinois referred to as the "habit of implicitly obeying orders," which to citizen soldiers, he added, came "slowly and with a sense of irritation."[53]

Marching required no less obedience. Soldiers marched in neatly formed ranks for over an hour, and no one could fall out without permission. Buell forbade any visiting, even if a soldier's home was nearby. The father of Illinois colonel Ulysses S. Grant thought such discipline was excessive, but Grant wrote to his sister that while it may have been a "little inexcusable in Gen. Buell not to allow troops to stop for a few hours when near their homes . . . [father] should recollect that Gen. Buell was not on the spot to see the circumstances fully and does not know what necessity may have existed to have got the troops through by a certain time."[54] Whatever appeared inexcusable to civilians or the rank and file had little influence on Buell's attitude anyway.

Buell also made the army more mobile by reducing the amount of baggage for camp equipment for each officer and soldier. Furthermore, he ordered infantry officers to dispose of their personal horses and march on foot with their men. Even generals would have to march unescorted. Buell's insistence on following closely the fundamental military codes was his way of preparing to meet every contingency in war.[55]

Perhaps the cornerstone of Buell's command philosophy was the fact that he alone made decisions affecting the army. All official correspondence proceeded through regular military channels and passed across his desk. He alone authorized the transfer of soldiers and arms, accepted resignations, and granted leaves. Moreover, he prohibited officers from making proclamations or other similar addresses to the public. To strengthen his authority over the soldiers, Buell cited the Constitution, particularly Article Two, Section Two, which gave the president authority over volunteers when called into actual service. He also cited the congressional acts passed on August 5, 1861, that subjected volunteers to the rules and regulations governing the regular army. Thus, the rules for the chain of command were clear, and governors and other politicians were excluded.[56]

Buell did not just explain the laws, but he relentlessly enforced them. When Indiana governor Oliver P. Morton complained about the poor condition of an Indiana regiment to Buell, Buell rebuked the unit's commander for appealing to the governor without authorization from headquarters. Unfortunately, however, Buell refused to see most regimental commanders over some military matters. Thus, colonels and soldiers took their complaints either to the press or to their governor. The editor of the *New Albany Daily Ledger* highlighted soldier complaints against Buell, writing that no one had business with Buell "except Division commanders through whom all matters for consideration are to come." Buell "follows the chain of command," declared the editor.[57] Maj. Joseph Warren Keifer of the Third Ohio wrote to his wife that he, like many soldiers, had yet to see Buell. "He keeps to himself very closely," he observed, "and in no case consults with his officers not even his division commanders."[58] Apparently sensing frustration over not getting to see Buell, Capt. William C. Moreau wrote to Morton asking for the governor's assistance regarding his transfer.

As Buell was made aware of such requests, he immediately saw a need to stifle such communications by insisting his troops follow the chain of command. He became so disturbed at these problems that he wrote to

Morton himself requesting that the governor impress upon soldiers the need to go through the proper channels. A chagrined Morton agreed to comply with the commander's request.[59]

Buell also saw to it that military forms were filled out completely and thoroughly. When they were not, he returned them, chastising the responsible person. When Gen. James S. Negley, Seventh Brigade, submitted an improperly completed certificate of disability, Buell sent it back with a scolding remark. Officers who failed to maintain strict discipline over the rank-and-file soldiers also caught Buell's wrath. In the event that soldiers committed illegal acts against civilians, Buell demanded an explanation from the commanding officer.[60]

Another major issue was the daily barrage of newspaper reporters clamoring for something to write about the new commander and his intended operations, especially what he had in mind for East Tennessee. As a division commander in the Army of the Potomac, Buell had been shielded from the press. As the commander of an entire department, however, he was in the spotlight. The austere Ohioan met this issue in the same way that Sherman did, and consequently he, too, had poor press relations. Buell disliked journalists because he considered them a hindrance to the military effort and merely the voice of politicians unqualified to judge his plans. Consequently, he stifled reporters and thus hoped to stifle political opinion. According to journalist Henry Villard, Buell "held the same views regarding war correspondents as General Sherman, and would not allow them to approach him on any ground."[61] Approaching Buell was as useless for reporters as it was for colonels. Instead of encouraging among war correspondents self-censorship of the military news, Buell sought to censor the correspondents himself by simply refusing to meet them. At one point, it was alleged, he authorized the arrest of his own relative George P. Buell, army correspondent to the *Cincinnati Times*, for publishing and writing reports not authorized through proper military channels.[62]

If Buell had not lived the same kind of life he demanded from his soldiers, they would probably have rebelled at his severe discipline. But Buell practiced what he preached, and the men came to respect that quality in him. If he refused to see the common soldiers and the lower-ranked officers in his headquarters, he at least shared the simple food and life of the camp. He worked longer and harder than anyone else, which was partly why few soldiers saw him. While he genuinely cared for his soldiers, men saw little compassion in his eyes and heard no comfort in his tone on the few occasions they encountered him. This, however, did not wholly determine their opinion of him. He had a dignified presence, and during inspections he made a favorable impression on the men. Major Keifer, who eventually got a chance to see the commander from a distance during a review and inspection, liked the "appearance of Buell *very much*."[63] Keifer was perceptive enough to realize that "the troops here need discipline. They are here in most cases raw regiments under *Political Officers*."[64] He concluded to his wife that "everything is being done that is possible to thoroughly discipline the army," though he feared that "our operations will be delayed on account of the condition of the troops." "Genl. Buell is much embarrassed," he added, "but seems determined to make the most of the [men] possible."[65]

In his November 22 letter to McClellan, penned the day after Sherman departed for St. Louis, Buell wrote of the progress he had made in shaping his command, indicating that there was much to do. Regarding the problems he encountered with newly elected Ohio governor David Tod, Buell wrote, "The Governor evidently looks upon all Ohio Troops as his army. He requires, I am told, morning reports from them, and their quartermasters to forward their returns to him." Furthermore, Buell wrote that every colonel and brigadier general "has his personal establishment or army." Buell wanted to make McClellan aware of these "little items," as he called them, to illustrate to the general in chief "what sort of organization and subordination has existed in these remote parts."[66]

Buell rectified these little items of command, but he failed to see the huge implications of wrenching civilian volunteers from the very head responsible for supplying them to the Union cause. Governors were an important element in the war effort since Lincoln counted on them to supply the Union armies. What Buell considered to be "extraordinary" in the daily exchange between governors and commanders was actually quite common and typical in the army as a whole. Even Jomini would have appreciated that.

Though the War Department had made it clear that governors were responsible for appointing all regimental officers, they shared this authority with the president and the soldiers themselves. Some governors took advantage of this patronage to buoy their strength in the state legislature by rewarding friends and weakening political enemies. Some midwestern governors such as Illinois Republican Richard Yates and Oliver Morton had appointed officers with the idea of trying to forge an alliance of Democrats and Republicans by commissioning colonels from both parties.[67]

Despite the abuses by some governors in appointing officers, Lincoln did not want to jeopardize his relationship with midwestern Republicans and frequently sided with governors in their disputes with commanders. Thus, by the time the Buell arrived in Louisville, the relationship between the president and state governors was a delicate one, strengthened when governors got their way and weakened when they did not. More importantly for Buell, though, Lincoln came to rely on them, for better or worse, and consequently they exercised more influence with him than did Buell.[68]

Despite these facts, Buell set out to sever the ties that bonded soldiers to their politicians. He failed to realize what Jomini recognized as a crucial element of war: politics. The way Buell saw it, the governors had fulfilled their patriotic and legal responsibility in providing the army with volunteers, and when those civilians mustered into the army, that responsibility ended. For Buell, becoming a soldier meant recognizing military authority first and foremost and severing all connections with civilian life. He gave neither volunteers nor governors consideration simply because they supported the Union cause. He never understood that these loyalists represented the backbone of the war effort. Limiting the state governors' attachment to their soldiers proved as much a curse as a blessing in his attempt to centralize authority in the Army of the Ohio, since increasing his control over the army meant limiting political control. In December, for example, before he left for Washington, Governor Morton wrote to Buell inquiring about the commander's intentions for the troops forming in his state. Buell did not reply.[69]

Buell's desire to solidify his command and subordinate political to military control revealed a crucial aspect of his philosophy of command, that of either failing or perhaps refusing to see the truly political nature of the Civil War. There was no question that he needed to centralize the authority of the Army of the Ohio, especially since the large numbers of volunteers and political appointments made him suspicious of how these recruits would perform in combat. Buell's organizational scheme, therefore, was fundamental to the overall success of his command, and limiting the control of governors was essential to establishing a functioning army. Still, he became almost dictatorial in his daily governance of the army.

Though McClellan himself had a flawed notion of civil-military relations, he sought to help Buell overcome this disability, or at least make Buell aware that he had one. While McClellan was general in chief, their friendship allowed Buell to get away with his foibles. The reaction to Buell's behavior would change in later months, when McClellan was replaced. Then Buell's superiors came to regard his apolitical and conservative attitude as having a direct impact on his ability to command in a war that was rapidly changing its course. Buell's apolitical attitude illustrated a striking dissimilarity between him and McClellan. Whereas McClellan directly involved himself in politics to try to dominate those making military policy, Buell did not. McClellan knew Buell had a disdain for politics, so he added some friendly advice as often as he could to keep Buell aware that the war directly involved state and federal officials whether he liked it or not. McClellan used considerable tact in stressing political matters while allowing his friend to exercise his own judgment in military strategy.[70]

Buell assured McClellan that he was carefully studying the country and that the unreasonable expectations of the newspapers would not at all disturb him. In Buell's judgment, "a commander merits condemnation who, from ambition or ignorance or a weak submission to the dictation of popular clamor and without necessity or profit, has squandered the lives of his soldiers."[71] But newspapers and state governors were not the only parties clamoring for movement in Buell's department. The demands came from much higher up, from McClellan himself. On November 23, Buell, in passing on to McClellan an unconfirmed report that Zollicoffer had crossed the Cumberland River at Gainesboro, Tennessee, probably on the way to Bowling Green, wrote, "I have a letter from the Adjutant-General. Have you seen cause to curtail my discretion?"[72] Indeed, McClellan had become concerned about Buell's inaction and thought some prodding was in order.

CHAPTER SEVEN

East Tennessee

McClellan was not the only one concerned about Buell's hesitation to move east. The editor of the *Cincinnati Commercial*, though impressed by Buell's military pedigree and abilities to command an army, commented that the chief anxiety regarding the new commander was whether or not he "has the *go* in him."[1] The editor was not alone in his apprehension. Nothing irritated the president more than the fact that Confederates occupied the loyal region of East Tennessee, and he wanted Buell to bring the region under Union control immediately.

Though Lincoln's political reasons for wanting East Tennessee were obvious, he also saw the military advantages, particularly since Tennessee would bear the burden of the upper South defense of the Confederate heartland. In his Plan of Campaign written at the beginning of

October, the president declared that he wished troops to seize a point on the Virginia and Tennessee Railroad near Cumberland Gap, then guarded by Zollicoffer's 4,000 Confederates. An advance through Cumberland Gap and capture of Knoxville, located on the East Tennessee and Georgia Railroad, would cut a vital Confederate railway in the West and would put the Union army between the secessionists and what Lincoln aptly phrased their "hog and hominy."[2]

The importance of Union occupation of East Tennessee manifested itself in many ways during the summer and fall of 1861, and the situation required delicate measures. Since Fort Sumter, Tennessee, like other border states, had become a stepchild of the Union and of the Confederacy, being neglected by the Union at one end and by the Confederates at the other. The Civil War forced the states of the upper South into a period of redefinition regarding their political ties. Much of this reflected the economic relationship between the border states and the northern states. The political and economic internal divisions proved crucial in the border states, and the interplay between loyalty and location was most visible in Tennessee, as the Civil War threatened to sever the bonds of traditionality.[3]

The first state elections under Confederate rule the previous August reflected the polarization of Union sentiment in East Tennessee. Unionists elected Thomas A. R. Nelson, Horace Maynard, and George Bridges to the U.S. Congress in direct violation of Tennessee governor Isham G. Harris's order to elect Confederate congressmen. The results prompted Harris to adopt a "decided and energetic policy with the people of that section." General Zollicoffer, a prewar journalist and politician who commanded the Department of East Tennessee, enforced such a policy. He initially vowed to protect the constitutional rights of citizens in the region in his attempts to suppress treason and to prevent Unionists from establishing political and military organizations. In the fall, however, he abandoned that policy.[4]

Zollicoffer's policy changed by November because the situation in East Tennessee had changed. The Reverend William Blount Carter, an influential Tennessee Unionist, had earlier met with Lincoln, Cameron, and McClellan and presented a plan for removing Confederates from East Tennessee. The scheme was to prepare the way for a northern invasion by destroying nine key bridges on the railroads connecting East Tennessee with Georgia, Virginia, and Middle Tennessee. McClellan and Lincoln favored the plan, and Carter thought he had convinced them to invade East Tennessee as soon as possible. By early November when no official move had occurred, Carter's separate Unionist bands destroyed five of the designated bridges. Thus, by the time Buell arrived in mid-November, the sabotage on the bridges, which was intended to loosen the Confederates' grip on East Tennessee, had merely hardened Confederate policy under Zollicoffer. He commenced a policy of severe repression. Rumors that Confederate soldiers summarily shot or hanged captured Unionists enraged the Union War Department and Congress.[5]

The East Tennessee loyalists suffered greatly from the November uprising, despite the fact that some considered it a "noble, elating spectacle." Many Unionists cowered for days in cellars, caves, or woods as the "reign of terror" prevailed. Confederate officers also executed five men for bridge burning. Confederate secretary of war Judah P. Benjamin thought it "would be well to leave their bodies hanging in the vicinity of the burned bridges."[6] The editor of the *Cincinnati Commercial* disagreed. He published a letter, "Read-Hot with Wrath," from an East Tennessean who fumed that he was tired of waiting to be protected by the Union army. "God grant that the day be not far distant," the letter read, "for we are all tired and weary, and sick of the everlasting cry that we are not ready, wait a little longer. Yes, watch and pray, and wait, to what purpose? For the secession soldiers to devastate our fields, slaughter our live-stock . . . burn our houses, insult our wives and daughters, and ruin them forever, and all time."[7]

The constant pressure to get Buell into East Tennessee quickly, then, was easily explained. Unionists had incurred the wrath of the Confederates for sabotaging the railroad bridges and they feared for their lives. They viewed Buell as their savior, and the longer he delayed, the more he drew fire from those unconvinced he could not redeem East Tennessee. Brig. Gen. Samuel Powhatan Carter, whom Lincoln sent to Kentucky to assist in organizing and training the recruits from East Tennessee, was among the unconvinced. He was the cousin of the Reverend William Carter and demanded that Buell move east. He had previously written his commander General Thomas about the plight of loyal East Tennesseans, urging an immediate movement to East Tennessee. "Many of them have been lying out in the woods to escape their enemies," he wrote, "but as the season advances they will be driven to their houses, and be forced into the rebel ranks or carried to prison."[8]

Although both Sherman and Thomas had made some progress toward relief of East Tennessee, Buell halted operations in that direction until he could complete the organization of his army. Irritated by the lack of response on the military's part, and equally frustrated by Buell's apparent lack of sympathy, Carter decided to write Tennessee congressman Horace Maynard in hopes of getting some satisfaction. "We are all inclined to think that help will be deferred until it is too late to save our people," he wrote. "This ought not to be so." He added, "I have no information as to the plans of General Buell. Can you not get those in power to give us a few more men and permission to make at least an effort to save our people?"[9]

Lincoln had every intention of saving East Tennesseans, and he expected from Buell what McClellan had achieved in western Virginia: to hold on to the regions that had voted against secession. Given the hostile circumstances, both Lincoln and McClellan expected Buell to strike at East Tennessee before winter. While in Washington, Buell had seen it that way, too, since he had helped to frame his own instructions for the Department of the Ohio, which he carried with him to Louisville. He was to bring more of Kentucky under Union control, defeat Johnston's army, and march to East Tennessee to relieve that region's loyalists. Not only did all of this have to be done simultaneously but also, as McClellan phrased it, while "religiously" respecting the "constitutional rights of all."[10]

In Washington Buell had given every indication that he was serious about advancing through Cumberland Gap. But in Louisville the logistical difficulties alone overwhelmed him. This problem, combined with his undisciplined army, and with winter fast approaching, caused him to decide against moving into East Tennessee until things looked less foreboding. McClellan also gave Buell an opportunity to exercise his own judgment. He ended a lengthy letter of instructions with a gesture of confidence in his friend. "If the military suggestions I have made in this letter prove to have been founded on erroneous data," Buell was, "of course, perfectly free to change the plans of operations."[11]

Although McClellan's letter might have left Buell with the impression that he could exercise freedom of judgment in developing strategy for an East Tennessee advance, it was clear, at least in McClellan's mind, that Buell could not change the destination of his movement or delay it indefinitely. As Buell surveyed the situation in Kentucky, however, he believed he had to make significant changes. The four mountain ranges—the Pine, Little and Big Black, and Cumberland—that rose in eastern Kentucky were difficult to get through. The absence of a railroad leading from his supply base at Louisville to East Tennessee would force him to rely on horses and mules to haul supplies to feed and equip his army. For Buell this fact alone was enough to seek another point of departure to East Tennessee. When combined with poor dirt roads that wound around the mountain ranges through tortuous creek and river valleys in a barren countryside vulnerable to raiders throughout its length, the

Don Carlos Buell as commander of the Army of the Ohio (Courtesy of the Ohio Historical Society, Columbus)

hardship of getting to Knoxville was too much of a sacrifice to the army to sustain loyal East Tennesseans. Even if he did traverse the countryside, there were few towns in which to store supplies, and he was not prepared to requisition. He believed that even under the best circumstances his amorphous army was in no shape to move. Besides, the real difficulty lay in not only getting to and seizing East Tennessee but also in holding it once there.[12]

Why Buell had not balked at an East Tennessee campaign from the beginning was curious. Perhaps he did not want those who placed him in command of the department to question their selection, or perhaps he had his sights set on another point of departure and wanted to lay out the logistical difficulties to McClellan from Louisville to justify modifying his plan. Once he arrived in Louisville, Buell came under the influence of Kentuckian James Guthrie, pro-Union president of the Louisville and Nashville Railroad. A large portion of the rail line's 286 miles passed through Kentucky and across the boundary southward for 45 miles to Nashville. Guthrie acted as an adviser to Buell and impressed upon the commander the importance of an invasion south over his line. If Buell moved south, his troops could recover the railroad and use it for transport as they drove the Confederates out of Kentucky. Guthrie also wanted Sherman back in command under Buell. Though the president considered sending Sherman back to Kentucky, he left the decision to McClellan, who evidently let the issue die. Given what little he had to work with in terms of competent officers, Buell surely would have welcomed Sherman's return, his controversies notwithstanding.[13]

The more Buell considered the possibility of striking directly at East Tennessee, the more troubled he became. Thus, what appeared on a map to Buell and his superiors as a simple hurdle became the deterrent to the whole plan. Buell's emphasis on strategy throughout his tenure allowed the difficulties of creating the means to achieve objectives to overshadow the accomplishment at the end. To Buell, the difficulty of getting an army through Cumberland Gap would not be worth the strategical success of capturing Knoxville. So, he reconsidered his plans for East Tennessee because obstacles appeared more difficult at close range.[14]

There was no more critical obstacle for Buell than Andrew Johnson. The Tennessee senator had worked tirelessly in the congressional session the previous summer to promote an advance into East Tennessee. He had repeatedly encouraged both Sherman and Thomas to undertake such a venture, but neither commander got the chance to carry it out. Thus, by the time Buell arrived, Johnson's patience had worn thin with military commanders apparently unsympathetic to a move toward East Tennessee. Johnson was touring Kentucky and Ohio between congressional sessions, and within a week after Buell's arrival in Louisville, the two men discussed the East Tennessee expedition. Buell apparently thought he had succeeded in convincing Johnson that logistical difficulties precluded him from undertaking an advance at that time. He wrote to McClellan that he had talked "freely" with Johnson and that he thought Johnson was satisfied regarding postponing the expedition.

Johnson may have been pacified, but he was unconvinced that logistical difficulties outweighed the lives that would be lost if East Tennessee remained in Confederate hands. It was an embittered determination that the exiled Tennessee senator carried back to Washington for the second session of the Thirty-seventh Congress. Johnson had every reason to be angry, since his property, including his slaves, had been confiscated; two of his sons, Robert and Charles, and his son-in-law, Daniel Stover, had been arrested; and his wife remained with their youngest son, Frank, in the region. Johnson had one thing on his mind that December: the liberation of East Tennessee.[15]

Buell was as determined as Johnson. "I shall be prepared to do anything you think best," he told McClellan, "after you hear what I propose." Buell was not going to be disturbed by "unreasonable newspaper clamor" or allow McClellan's confidence in him to be shaken. He had by no means totally abandoned the idea of the East Tennessee advance; in fact, he found "some attraction in it." But unless McClellan or the president absolutely required the movement, he had not "determined on it absolutely." He promised that if they did, he was willing to carry out the advance "with all my might."[16] In short, Buell still was not ready to move.

He also had strategical reasons for not wanting to make the campaign. He considered mobilizing for a thrust at Bowling Green and Nashville and then striking at East Tennessee. He favored Nashville as the point of departure for his campaign east for two reasons. First, he considered it more strategically valuable to the Union than Knoxville, because it was a manufacturing center and transportation junction and was positioned on the Cumberland River, which he also intended to use. Second, and more importantly, Nashville was linked to Louisville and Knoxville by rail and was closer to his army than Cumberland Gap. The agriculturally rich countryside from Louisville to Nashville contrasted sharply with the barren roads to Cumberland Gap. Moreover, with Nashville in Union hands, the Confederates defending East Tennessee would be outflanked; when they abandoned the region, he could march in unopposed. It might take longer to get to East Tennessee this way, but he felt more certain of achieving his ends.[17]

Buell kept confidential his proposed plans for East Tennessee or for any other advance. Shortly after arriving in Louisville, he had employed the services of intelligence agent John Lellyett, a staunch Nashville Unionist forced to leave his state in July 1861. Lellyett's job was to keep Buell informed about what was going on in Kentucky and Tennessee. Buell was so secretive, however, that he kept even this informant in the dark about his plans, eventually frustrating him with his cryptic nature.[18]

Buell also kept his subordinates in suspense regarding his plans. General Thomas, whom Buell trusted, was disappointed at Buell's determination to keep his intentions to himself. Thomas complained that Buell had "not communicated any of his plans to me, but requires that I shall keep my troops together and be prepared to move promptly in any direction."[19] Buell urged McClellan to exchange correspondence informally rather than through the official channels, since he had an "enormous respect for secrecy in military operations." As a thirteen-year veteran of the Adjutant General's Office, Buell knew only too well that in the AGO, "there is no secret."[20] He urged caution in discussing such delicate issues also because he did not trust politicians, who would have easier access to his views regarding East Tennessee, particularly Andrew Johnson.

Though Sherman still insisted that Buell's responsibilities would require 200,000 men, Buell wired McClellan that he was "quite content to try with a good many less." The Confederates, he argued, posed no immediate threat, but he was aware that Zollicoffer and Episcopal-bishop-turned-general Leonidas Polk at Columbus on the Mississippi could easily reinforce Johnston. Besides, a Confederate concentration would prove more an advantage than a problem to the Federals. "As for his attacking," asserted Buell, "I do not intend to be unprepared for him, yet I should almost as soon expect to see the Army of the Potomac marching up the road."[21]

If Buell had convinced himself that the situation in his department required a movement on Bowling Green and Nashville, as opposed to Knoxville, and that he had mollified Andrew Johnson, he certainly failed to persuade McClellan or Lincoln. His stubbornness in maintaining that the true route of advance was through Middle Tennessee to Nashville gave the president the impression that he was unsympathetic to East Tennesseans and their needs. Despite Buell's solid logistical and strategical rationale, a chagrined McClellan continued to urge Buell east. The general in chief liked the sureness of his friend's plan, and if put in Buell's situation, he might have considered the same route. But in Washington the political forces descended heavily on him, and he was convinced that political urgency, more than military practicality, should inspire Buell to move. Invading East Tennessee quickly and directly, Buell's army could not only cut a major railway supplying the Confederates in Virginia, but from Knoxville it could assist in McClellan's campaign against Richmond.[22]

The hard facts of the problem were that Buell, much like Sherman and Thomas, knew that the road to East Tennessee was long, hard, and barren. Buell also saw the value of occupying Middle Tennessee and defeating Johnston's Confederates before heading east. What Buell failed to perceive was that Johnston, commanding the Western Department, could hardly concentrate enough strength to strike at Louisville, as Sherman had earlier insisted. By late November the Confederate commander had fewer than 40,000 poorly equipped and mostly untrained troops. Johnston's mission, like Buell's, was the protection of a vast and diverse geographical region from Columbus, Kentucky, on the Mississippi River to Cumberland Gap in the east. Though he concluded that Nashville was the most alluring target for Buell and perhaps the main route for Union penetration, he had to defend three other routes of Union invasion along the Mississippi, the Tennessee and Cumberland Rivers, and Cumberland Gap.[23]

With 12,000 troops, Polk was responsible for defending against the Union approach along the Mississippi, Tennessee, and Cumberland Rivers in the western end of the department. Though his preference for defense was Columbus on the Mississippi, he neglected Fort Henry on the Tennessee and Fort Donelson on the Cumberland. The geographical center of the entire Confederate line and the gateway into the Confederate heartland lay at Dover, Tennessee, where these two rivers flowed to within ten miles of each other. At the opposite end of the department in East Tennessee, Zollicoffer's "beggarly force" of roughly 4,000 men guarded against a Union advance toward Cumberland Gap. Gen. Simon Bolivar Buckner's 4,500 soldiers occupied Bowling Green.[24]

At a time when idleness got more attention than action, Buell's emphasis on preparation appeared to cast him in the shadow of McClellan, who was just as idle. It also served to reinforce what was strikingly similar and frustratingly troubling about them both: movement was secondary to preparation. Still, McClellan continued to emphasize "that political and strategical considerations render a prompt movement in force on Eastern Tennessee imperative."[25] Despite the logistical problems, he insisted to Buell that a movement on Knoxville was absolutely necessary. The editor of the *Cincinnati Commercial* was more direct, charging that if the Union did not rescue the East Tennessee loyalists, "it ought to be damned by every loyal man in the country."[26]

To impress upon Buell just how important the movement was, McClellan wired him that reinforcements were forthcoming. In addition, McClellan increased his literary pressure on Buell to the point of questioning Buell's judgment and complaining at not having heard from him. "What is the reason for concentration of troops at Louisville? I urge movement at once on Eastern Tennessee, unless it is impossible. No letter from you for several days. Reply." "I still trust to your judgement," he ended a November 27 letter, "though urging my own views."[27]

Herein lay part of the problem in getting Buell to move. McClellan's barrage of messages always contained some comment that gave Buell independence of judgment. Why McClellan tolerated Buell's inactivity, considering the fact that he was counting on Buell to buoy his own proposed movement, was curious. His patience revealed the friendship between the two men, as well as the tremendous respect McClellan had for Buell as a commander. Buell was his senior by eight years and had considerably more practical experience in the field. Buell was also held in high regard throughout the regular army, and McClellan used considerable tact in not wanting to slight a commander of Buell's caliber by simply ordering him to East Tennessee and thus overruling his judgment.

After a delay of four days, Buell confessed to his friend on November 27 that he had not written frequently because there was little definite he could say. He told McClellan to regard the concentration at Louisville not as a defensive position but merely as a base from which he would launch his operations and thus have the advantage of "bringing everything under my eye." Buell preferred Lebanon over Lexington as a point of departure, since Lebanon was linked to Louisville by rail and was closer to Nashville.[28]

Buell had changed his strategic vision of operations in Kentucky and Tennessee since his previous discussions with McClellan. Now he wanted to establish a force in front of Bowling Green to hold Buckner. He also envisioned two columns moving into East Tennessee by Somerset and by London while he moved on to Nashville. Additionally, Buell advocated moving two flotilla columns up the Tennessee and Cumberland Rivers to strike at the weak batteries at Forts Henry and Donelson, while a strong demonstration was made on Columbus by the Mississippi River. There were more details to all these operations, but Buell cavalierly informed McClellan, "You can imagine them all."[29]

George B. McClellan, commander of the Army and Department of the Potomac and general in chief of the Union army from November 5, 1861, to March 11, 1862. McClellan was a close friend of Buell's who shared the same belief in limited war for limited goals. (Courtesy of the U.S. Army Military History Institute, Carlisle, Pa.)

For Buell's strategy to work, however, he needed help from Halleck. Buell believed that a well-coordinated strategy between himself and Halleck would enable the Union to hold on to Kentucky while penetrating deeper into the southern heartland. East Tennessee, he thought, could only be reached and, more importantly, occupied by moving through Nashville and establishing communications with the Ohio River by way of the Tennessee Valley.[30]

Buell also perceived that Halleck's movement in the western part of the state, simultaneous with his own movement in Middle and East Tennessee, would force the Confederates to divide their forces. He wanted to avoid a demonstration in the direction of East Tennessee until he could be assured that Halleck would move as well. He "studiously avoided" any movements and, in the meantime, informed McClellan, "'We are lying around somewhat loose' and I shall not care much if some of our fragments have to look sharply after themselves." "We have occasional stampedes," he added, "but I do not allow myself to be much troubled about them." Buell appeared to be troubled more by his own desire to remain inactive than by the actions around him.[31]

In Missouri Halleck had his own problems. Appointed the same day that Buell was, he was charged with restoring order to the chaos left by John Frémont. To compound his problems, Halleck had to deal with an utterly demoralized Sherman, who appeared "stampeded," as Halleck put it.[32] In hopes that a few weeks' rest would restore Sherman, Halleck gave him an indefinite leave of absence. Besides, Halleck was not in the least encouraged about moving into western Tennessee. "It seems to me madness," he wrote. Just as Buell was reluctant to move into East Tennessee, so was Halleck loath to move into West Tennessee.[33]

By the end of November it was clear to Buell that his operations in the West were subordinate to McClellan's operations east of the mountains. Furthermore, he attempted to shift responsibility for an East Tennessee advance back to McClellan by arguing that any move into that region be coordinated between himself and Halleck, and only the general in chief could effect such an arrangement. On November 30 Buell wrote McClellan confidentially, stressing such coordinated action. Buell made it sound as though his advance east was contingent upon Halleck's move into West Tennessee. This would divert Confederate attention away from East Tennessee, he thought, by directing the Union's focus of operations to the West, where the potential for Union success was greater and more militarily significant for the Confederacy.[34]

Meanwhile, Buell had succeeded in providing the organizational framework that gave shape to the once ill-defined mass of soldiers. His administrative talents, sharp eye for detail, and firm resolve in seeing to the completion of every task displayed his strength as a commander. As the troops continued to come into the city, they went into camp about five miles outside Louisville under the direction of Gen. Ormsby Mac-Knight Mitchel, whom Buell referred to as "attentive and subordinate." Mitchel was an 1829 West Point graduate and had taught mathematics there after graduating. Now, at age fifty-two, Mitchel's lanky frame belied a tremendous endurance. Perhaps the qualities that best endeared him to Buell were those that made him a "great economizer of time and rigidly punctual." "General Mitchel knew everything about an army from the linchpin of a wagon to the most important implement of warfare," wrote a contemporary.[35] Perhaps what Buell liked least about Mitchel was the fact that he had a bodyguard with whom Buell was obliged to interact, as did several commanders. Still, Buell trusted and respected him.[36]

Mitchel was the kind of commander Buell could rely on to impress the firm hand of the military on raw recruits. But apparently he played that firm hand too far with surly Bull Nelson in late November when he sent orders to some of Nelson's troops. Though Nelson had been in Mitchel's camp less than a day, he caused a commotion over this alleged insult and complained "with all the intensity of expression for which that officer was distinguished." Though this affair was inconsequential at the time, Nelson would prove to be an even greater curse to Buell in the future.[37]

After the troops mustered in at Louisville and were sent through Mitchel's training camps, Buell took little time in positioning them within the department. The organization of the army satisfied Buell, though he remained suspicious of volunteers and complained of insufficient staff and officers. He wrote to McClellan, "I should pay myself a very high compliment if I hoped to come up to the expectations which you first formed." "I am afraid," he confessed, "I shall have to ask a little patience."[38] If McClellan had any patience with any subordinate, it was surely with Buell.

Two days after Buell sent McClellan a long letter detailing his plans, November 29, McClellan responded with great assurances of Buell's intended operations for Tennessee. "I fully approve of your course and agree in your views," he wired Buell. In a follow-up letter McClellan added some words of confidence: "I now feel sure that I have a 'lieutenant' in whom I can fully rely. Your views are right. You have seized the true strategic base, and from Lebanon can move where you will." But, as always, McClellan's expressions of confidence in Buell's judgment contained a message of political consequence. "Keep up the hearts of the Tennesseans," he wrote. "Make them feel that, far from any intention of deserting them, all will be done to sustain them." McClellan also added a few practical words on how Buell's operations would sustain his in the East, proposing that he attempt two movements, "one on Eastern Tennessee, say with 15,000 men, and a strong attack on Nashville, as you propose, with, say 50,000 men." "Unless circumstances render it necessary," McClellan added oddly, "do not strike until I [too am] ready. Should I be delayed, I will not ask you to wait for me."[39]

As important as McClellan made Buell's operations seem, they were always subordinate to his own. McClellan closed his letter by assuring Buell that he would take the necessary steps in carrying out Buell's wishes for the two flotilla columns on the rivers. If he had not pacified his superior regarding East Tennessee, Buell had at least convinced McClellan that a move along the Tennessee and Cumberland Rivers was worth undertaking.[40]

Lincoln, however, had other ideas. He continued pressuring McClellan to get Buell to move into East Tennessee by using the letters from General Carter pleading for relief. Senators Maynard and Johnson placed Carter's correspondence in Lincoln's hands, and the president forwarded the missives to McClellan with an attached note that read, "Please read and consider." It was clear that Lincoln wanted Buell to get the message and used his general in chief as a prod. McClellan sent these letters to Buell in an attempt to further rouse him.[41]

McClellan encouraged Buell to overlook any "slurs" he had incurred for his inactivity regarding East Tennessee and urged him to send with the "least possible delay, troops enough to protect these men." "For the sake of these Eastern Tennesseans who have taken part with us," he advised Buell, "I would gladly sacrifice mere military advantages."[42] Still, Buell could not be budged.

Perhaps in reminding Buell that the political was more important than the military expediency concerning East Tennessee, McClellan was Machiavellian. While he was in Washington, the administration's political sensitivity toward East Tennessee certainly was foremost in his mind. Thus, perhaps not wanting to devalue the political importance from Washington's perspective or to reduce Buell's independence of judgment regarding East Tennessee, McClellan continued to allow Buell essentially a free hand in making decisions in the West, which also made him the target for criticism. Whatever the case, McClellan wanted Buell to do something. He closed by reassuring him of his "utmost confidence and firmest friendship" and by placing a reward on a movement to East Tennessee, saying, "If you gain and retain possession of Eastern Tennessee you will have won brighter laurels than I hope to gain."[43]

CHAPTER EIGHT

The Politics of Command

Gaining brighter laurels did not interest Buell. If it did, he would have noted that Lincoln wanted East Tennessee under Union control and would reward the successful commander for its possession. While it was true that few things could spark Buell, the constant barrage of communiqués prodding him east, coupled with the letters from Carter to Maynard, certainly aroused his anger. It was bad enough that he repeatedly had to justify his unwillingness to advance, but the fact that a subordinate officer had written to a politician was simply intolerable.

Buell was greatly concerned about politicians knowing too much about his plans because he distrusted them. Toward that end, he continued to urge McClellan to correspond confidentially, further tightened the reins on what his division commanders knew about his plans, and of course limited the independence of his subordinates to keep the enemy "profoundly ignorant" of his movements. He authorized his subordinates to engage in active operations to the extent necessary to appease those who demanded that he do something. He kept so many people in the dark about his operations that a correspondent to the *New York Times* complained he could not even get basic information. "They have been organizing . . . so quietly," he wrote, "that we are only able to gather, from scattered hints in newspaper correspondence, who are the division and brigade commanders."[1]

In early December 1861, despite the hurricane of issues swirling around him, Buell completed organizing his army. He pulled the brigades together, dividing his army into five divisions. Thomas commanded the First Division, McCook commanded the Second, the Third Division was commanded by Ormsby Mitchel, Bull Nelson commanded the Fourth Division, and Thomas L. Crittenden commanded the Fifth Division. True to his word, McClellan added to Buell's army two fully armed regiments of cavalry and additional infantry from the Northwest, all to convince Buell of his department's priority in the West. Even while McClellan was presuming that Buell would move on Nashville, he added that Buell should send "something into East Tenna as promptly as possible." He ended, "I tell the East Tenna men here to rest quiet—that you will take care of them & will never desert them."[2]

McClellan's comment concerned Buell because he had repeatedly told McClellan that it was impractical to advance into East Tennessee, but McClellan promised just that. Not surprisingly, Buell avoided any detailed discussion of East Tennessee with his superior. On December 8 he penned McClellan a long letter thanking him for his earlier encouragement about the true strategic base of his operations and for the expressions of confidence in his judgment. "Such encouragement," he wrote, "would make a good lieutenant of almost any man, and robs him of all credit, no matter what he may accomplish." Referring to the East Tennessee expedition, Buell added that a "good programme does not always result to our satisfaction, but I shall work very hard not to disappoint your confidence altogether."[3]

Buell had disappointed McClellan and he knew it, and to justify his inaction, he described the daily problems in organizing the army. He complained that the quartermaster's department did not live up to his expectations and that he was greatly in need of staff officers and brigadiers, whom he "loath[ed] to nominate" until he knew the men better. Almost a month had passed, and he still continued to suffer the annoyance "from the officiousness of Governors." These governors, he wrote, "send their staff officers to look after the interest of their troops, exchange their arms without my knowledge, and keep up a communication in other matters which they have no business with." While he was annoyed by these actions, he boasted that he would quickly be able to "correct" these political-military problems "entirely."[4]

Morton had long been an advocate of an invasion of East Tennessee and used the *Indianapolis Journal* as his personal and political voice to stir up support for such an advance. On Morton's influence, and the influence of governors in general, Buell would write, "all the influence these [governors] exercised on the government and on the soldiers in the field was more of a menace to the country than an undisciplined army."[5]

When Buell finally referred to another problem—the enemy—it was evident that the Confederate army was of little consequence compared with the difficulties of organization and governors. Regarding the burning of the Bacon Creek bridge on the road between Bowling Green and Louisville by some of John Hunt Morgan's cavalry, he calmly responded, "We are beginning to be a little animated," meaning these were merely inconsequential, though amusing acts.[6] To keep the road to Bowling Green secure, he dispatched General McCook's division to Bacon Creek to repair the bridge and sent Brig. Gen. Reverdy W. Johnson's Sixth Brigade ahead to Munfordville north of the Green River to prevent the destruction of that bridge. Buell wrote that further damage "would have embarrassed my prospective movements, and so I have had to put aside the inertion which I was anxious to pursue for the present." He did not want to give the impression to the enemy that he was concerned about their activities, especially since he wanted to conceal his plans until he was ready to move in mass. These movements, he wrote, "will stir up our neighbors a little, but it cannot be helped."[7]

As Buell remained content to stay put, Zollicoffer moved across the Cumberland River from Mill Springs to the north bank at Beech Grove, which placed him in the path that Thomas had chosen for getting to East Tennessee. Apparently Zollicoffer was as encouraged as East Tennesseans were discouraged when Thomas carried out Buell's November 19 orders to move from Crab Orchard back to Lebanon. At that time Buell had declared that Zollicoffer was making demonstrations to stop the Union blockade of the coal trade on the Cumberland and would do "no great harm."[8] Thomas and Schoepf, however, were not so cavalier, particularly since Schoepf continued to lack reliable cavalry in a region that begged for it, and Thomas knew the roads to Somerset were in wretched condition.[9]

Buell's attitude in these instances reflected his desire to continue to emphasize preparation over movement. He thus demonstrated one of his strengths and ironically one of his weaknesses as a commander. "I do not mean to be diverted more than is absolutely necessary from what I regard as of the first importance—the organization of my forces, now little better than a mob," he wrote to McClellan. "I could fritter the whole of it away in a month by pursuing these roving bugbears."[10]

Refusal to counter the enemy made it appear as though he saw preparation as an end, not a means. Unlike Sherman, Buell regarded the enemy as an inconvenience in his organizational efforts rather than as a major threat. For Buell, rules were a way of keeping order. The fact that he was conservative merely added to his severity in enforcing the rules, his guiding military principle. These rules would usually prevail in the end, because in his mind they minimized the unpredictability of war. Therefore, he emphasized a scientific approach to warfare including a blueprint of plans, diagrams, and rules. If there was any chance or risk within this framework, it was only supplemental to what appeared to be already predictable. Buell strove for a calculated war, in which every move was contemplated and absolute care was given to logistics, administration, and detail to maneuver for favorable situations for his army, rather than for fighting from strategic positions. "If precaution and the observance of rule diminish the number of battles, and sometimes miss the accidental success which folly or recklessness might have gained," he contended in Jominian logic, "it is nevertheless true in the end they usually triumph."[11]

By early December the Army of the Ohio had swelled to about 70,000 soldiers, of whom roughly 50,000 were able for duty. Anticipating movement toward Zollicoffer, the bulk of Thomas's First Division remained at Lebanon, while his remaining forces were scattered at Somerset under Schoepf, at London under Carter, and at Columbia under Boyle. McCook's Second Division continued to face Bowling Green at Bacon Creek, with a brigade at Munfordville to protect the bridges. Nearby to the north was Mitchel's Third Division at Elizabethtown on the railroad. Crittenden's Fifth Division was near the confluence of the Ohio and Green Rivers near Owensboro, and Nelson's Fourth Division remained scattered in eastern Kentucky.[12]

As the Army of the Ohio continued to take shape, Buell attempted to fend off the persistent political pressure for the relief of East Tennessee. Both Horace Maynard and Andrew Johnson had written to Buell on December 7, informing the general that they had met with President Lincoln and General McClellan, and that both fully concurred with them in respect to the East Tennessee expedition. "Our people are oppressed and pursued as beasts of the forest," they declared, and they were looking to Buell "with anxious solicitude to move in that direction."[13] Buell responded honorably to Maynard the following day, acknowledging receipt of this letter and assuring the senators that he indeed recognized his imperative duty in bringing relief to the loyal Tennesseans. Significantly, he said nothing of his plans.[14]

Not satisfied with Buell's response or the response from his superiors, Maynard decided to press Buell's subordinates. Knowing that Thomas looked favorably upon a movement east and had repeatedly pressured Buell for permission to move in that direction, Maynard wrote to him that "there is shameful wrong somewhere; I have not yet satisfied myself where." He added, "You are farther from East Tennessee than when I left you nearly six weeks ago."[15] Maynard was distressed, and he took it personally that he could not bring relief to East Tennesseans, so much so that he was "ashamed to look them in the face."[16] His heart bled for Tennesseans suffering from "Nelson and the measles and . . . nakedness and hunger and poverty and home-sickness." Maynard encouraged Thomas to act without Buell's authorization: "I cannot approve your determination simply to 'obey orders.' "[17]

Despite the evident pressure from his military superiors and politicians, Buell considered the situation in East Tennessee more annoying to him than life threatening for the residents. Because he did not want to move into East Tennessee for logistical reasons, he apparently convinced himself that the loyal East Tennesseans suffering the depredations committed by the Confederates could hold out. "Constancy will sustain them," he affirmed, "until the hour of deliverance." "I have no fear of their being crushed," he assured McClellan on December 10. The "allegiance of such people to hated rulers, even if it could be enforced for the moment, will only make them the more determined and ready to resist when the hour of rescue comes."[18] The dark realities of the situation in East Tennessee were not going to hinder Buell's organizational plans or his plans to campaign south, as long as somebody else had to overcome obstacles. To be sure, when the hour of deliverance arrived for East Tennesseans, Buell would not be the man to deliver them.[19]

Buell was able to avoid a direct confrontation with McClellan over the East Tennessee expedition because McClellan respected Buell so much. "I have the most confiding letters from Genl. McClellan," Buell wrote his wife, "though he wants me to be a primary object of what I think ought to be secondary. However, He will not disapprove I think."[20] As McClellan danced around giving Buell an order to move to East Tennessee,

Buell continued to debate McClellan in soothing terms. On December 10 he once more defended his justification for not moving into East Tennessee and in the same breath assured McClellan that he would pursue his friend's views "with as much zeal and hopefulness, and perhaps more energy, than if I entirely concurred in them." He added, "You do not know me well yet if you think I cannot do this."[21]

If anyone knew Buell, it was McClellan, and he knew that Buell was intractable when he thought he was right. Buell thought he was right about not sending Federal forces into East Tennessee. He even advised McClellan as to what Halleck should do below Cairo. Halleck should make a demonstration on Columbus and the Mississippi on such a scale that it could be converted into a real attack if necessary. While Buell confessed that he knew nothing about the quality of the troops, the officers, or the terrain, he was confident that the expedition would require nothing more than "ordinary nerve and good judgement and ability to command men."[22] "The object," he lectured McClellan in Jominian fashion, "is not to fight great battles and storm impregnable fortifications, but by demonstrations and maneuvering to prevent the enemy from concentrating his scattered forces." "In doing this," he added, "it must be expected there will be some fighting; it may be pretty good fighting."[23] Almost any ordinary commander could carry out the operation if he simply followed the rules, Buell believed. If only McClellan could get Buell to practice in East Tennessee what Buell preached for Halleck in West Tennessee.

If anyone needed a lecture on the "object" of war, it was not McClellan. The "Young Napoleon" understood the situation in the West and agreed with Buell's recommendation. He simply had more pressing political matters at hand. The second session of the Thirty-seventh Congress had opened, and McClellan's own chronic idleness came under severe attack. The general in chief's impassivity had attracted considerable attention. "All quiet on the Potomac" was no longer a soothing characterization regarding the enemy but, rather, an alarm for those politicians tired of military inertia. In his friend's misfortune there was some good fortune for Buell. The president had spent the autumn with McClellan patiently reasoning with the general, flattering his ego, and shielding him from critics. In December, however, during the second session of Congress, Lincoln found it more difficult to defend his general in chief. The formation of the Joint Committee on the Conduct of the War heated up the war in the rear by setting its sights against military inertia.[24]

Buell's idleness, therefore, also came under attack, though not to the same degree as McClellan's, since operations in the East continued to get more attention than those in the West. But Lincoln was concerned with Buell's inactivity. In his message to Congress in December he was so desperate to get Buell into East Tennessee that he advocated the construction of a railroad at government expense from eastern Kentucky to either Cumberland Gap or the Tennessee state line near Knoxville. Like the Radical Republicans in Congress, Lincoln began to cast the two commanders in the same light. The fact that they were both Democrats certainly did little to enhance their positions with Republicans, particularly since by December the Democratic Party had entrenched its conservatism, tradition, and defense of the Constitution with regard to the war, when Republicans were seeking new directions to encourage economic, social, and governmental change to win the war. Consequently, at a time when Democrats generally opposed the president's path to victory, Buell, like McClellan, came to represent in the army what Democrats represented in politics. As the new year approached, congressional discussions turned to expanding the war and minimizing the professional soldier's control over the government's army.[25]

On December 10, 1861, the same day the Federal Congress appointed the Joint Committee on the Conduct of the War, the Confederate Congress admitted Kentucky to the Confederacy's jurisdiction as the thirteenth state. Confederate Kentuckians elected George W. Johnson the state's first provisional governor. The predominance of Kentucky's Unionist government hinged on Buell's ability to move south and push the enemy back into Tennessee. McClellan knew this, and he decided to follow Buell's suggestion and order Halleck's troops to move in concert with Buell's. Buell had essentially made up his mind about the advance on Nashville and was simply stalling for the spring offensive. Halleck, however, unconvinced he could supplement Buell's operations in Kentucky, remained quiet, except to say that he did not have enough troops to assist Buell.[26]

December was a curious month for Buell. He continued to keep Mc-Clellan well informed of the army's preparation and of its troubles and demanded better support from the quartermaster's department. When the War Department proposed to reduce his authority by transferring responsibility for the Big Sandy River valley in eastern Kentucky to Brig. Gen. William S. Rosecrans's Department of West Virginia, Buell thought it unnecessary. Eastern Kentucky had little strategic value for either side, but it possessed a significant population and was important for Buell's potential advance into East Tennessee. He had already organized a brigade under Col. James A. Garfield, a "promising officer" of the Forty-second Ohio, to guard the area. Apparently these dispositions convinced Cameron not to transfer the valley. When Garfield met Buell at the Galt House in Louisville to discuss eastern Kentucky, Buell impressed him. "He is a direct, martial-spirited man," Garfield wrote, "and has an air of decision and business which I like."[27] Confessing that he knew little of the country in that area, Buell wisely entrusted the management of the expedition to the young officer's discretion.

With the exception of the attack on the bridge at Bacon Creek and Zollicoffer's movement north of the Cumberland, Buell wrote to McClellan, "we are doing pretty well." By mid-December Buell had concluded that Zollicoffer either was retiring across the Cumberland or was prepared to do so at the approach of any superior force. "Any more formidable demonstrations against him," he wrote, "would only harass my troops and derange my plans."[28] The resistance to any formidable demonstrations and Buell's "policy of quiet" caused a disillusioned colonel to write that his commanding officer "did not care if some isolated posts were occasionally raided by the enemy."[29] William Grose of the Thirty-sixth Indiana of Jacob Ammen's Tenth Brigade wrote that the soldiers in his regiment were fearful "that the war would end and they would not get into a fight."[30] In fact, Buell himself had earlier written that some of the "fragments" would have to fend for themselves. He kept his brigades and regiments, which he frequently inspected and maintained in constant readiness, in "objectless dispersion" until he was ready to move, "the day and hour of which he proposed to keep to himself."[31]

The sound of cannon near Munfordville, however, broke the silence in Buell's department in mid-December. On December 17 Buell received word that a regiment of Johnson's Sixth Brigade had been involved in a skirmish at Rowlett's Station south of Munfordville. The Thirty-second Indiana, comprised largely of German immigrants, defeated the Arkansans and Texans under Brig. Gen. Thomas C. Hindman. Buell was elated that his men had engaged the enemy and, from all reports, had defeated the "roving bugbears." The affair near Munfordville, which resulted in the death of eight Federals and thirty-three Confederates, caused the poised commander to glibly remark, "The little affair in front of Munfordville was really one of the handsomest things of the season. Our neighbors in part begin to show signs of being interested."[32]

The affair at Rowlett's Station was proof that when Buell was ready to show fight, his men would do well. What the *New York Times* characterized as the "most brilliant National victory yet achieved" had broken the quiet that had loomed along the Ohio all season. Lincoln, the residents of Kentucky and Tennessee, and the press also expressed concern over the lack of activity in the West. The *Chicago Tribune* declared that Buell "has the best men the West can furnish, and can have more if there is need for them; only the West will require that they be used against the enemy, and not, as under his insane predecessor, for self-destruction."[33]

Kentuckians were apparently so worried about the welfare of their state that the state legislature was considering a bill for raising 20,000 twelve-month volunteers for Kentucky's defense. Kentucky Congressman Charles Wickliffe wrote the Ohio general to solicit his views on the subject. The departmental commander strongly opposed the measure, arguing that it would not produce efficient troops. He further remarked that "troops whose obligations are tacitly confined to sectional object are not apt to conform efficiently to a control whose object is national."[34] Buell was also quick to point out that while the war remained within Kentucky's borders, "it should have entirely the character of civil war."[35] Buell's argument reflected his desire to keep the war safe and the authority of his department centralized.

The national goal was just what Lincoln was contemplating when McClellan came down with typhoid fever on December 23. McClellan was the first witness scheduled to appear before the Joint Committee on the Conduct of the War when he took ill. Some Radicals were hoping for McClellan's natural death because it would relieve them from having to use the political guillotine against him. For nearly two weeks while the general in chief remained bedridden and ineffective, the high command functioned only on matters of daily routine. Buell similarly continued to labor over every detail in molding his army to his standards. After using every minute of daylight to travel, inspect, and review the army, he labored at his desk long into the next morning writing dozens of telegrams.[36]

On the same day that McClellan was diagnosed with typhoid, Buell penned a long and detailed letter to Adj. Gen. Lorenzo Thomas. His efficient force was about 70,000 men, he wrote, and despite some problems with incoming regiments, "the condition of things, I feel assured is changing." He still faced "one of the greatest evils" of his command —the "ill-judged interference" of governors. He confidently asserted that his enforcement of the "proper means of administration" would soon correct the problems of command and communication.[37]

Buell continued to advocate defense of his department's eastern region and invasion of Middle Tennessee, just the opposite of what McClellan and Lincoln had been insisting on for the past three months. He considered it wiser to trust that there would be no invasion from the east. Besides, though he knew that there were communities in which Confederates dominated, Buell believed that most Kentuckians were loyal to the Union, since some 20,000 troops were being organized for his army and it could be expanded. Thus, moving into Middle Tennessee would be much easier and less risky than heading east.[38]

Whether demonstrating unhappiness with Buell or not, McClellan extended the command of Ulysses Grant to include that part of Kentucky west of the Cumberland River, along with southern Illinois and a few counties in Missouri south of Cape Girardeau. Grant was an 1843 West Point graduate, as undistinguished as Buell had been at his graduation two years before. Though his conduct in the Mexican War won him considerable distinction, Grant's peacetime service and civilian life went unrecognized. Still, when the war broke out, he became colonel of the Twenty-first Illinois Volunteers; within a few months he became brigadier general, and by November he had been baptized by fire at Belmont. On the day after Christmas, Grant wrote to Buell apprising him of his new boundaries and offering his cooperation. Whether Grant realized it or not, he was now between a rock and a hard place or, rather, between Halleck and Buell.[39]

As 1861 ended, Buell wrote the general in chief that he had been very busy but was satisfied that "very few men accomplish as much as is possible, and I cannot assume to be an exception."[40] George H. Thomas, however, seemed willing to undertake the expedition east that Buell complained he was unable to do. At Christmas Buell went to Lebanon to discuss any advantages of a move on Zollicoffer and into East Tennessee. The capture or defeat of the Confederates would surely threaten Johnston's Nashville base, as well as the Richmond supply line. Both consequences appealed to Buell, particularly since he hoped Halleck would soon move into West Tennessee. Thus, with Johnston's flanks threatened from both ends, he would have to reduce the Nashville defenses, which would allow Buell to capture easily the Tennessee capital.[41]

There were disadvantages to striking at Zollicoffer as well. Poor roads and tormenting weather made for inhospitable conditions and would slow any march no matter how determined the commander. In fact, Zollicoffer, realizing the vulnerability of his army positioned on the north side of a swollen river, had wanted to recross the Cumberland and had been waiting for the resources to do so, but impassable roads, harsh weather, and lack of supplies precluded this. Buell thought of the unpredictability in such an advance, and though his forces had been successful at Rowlett's Station, Thomas needed more troops to overcome Zollicoffer and move into East Tennessee.[42]

After returning from Lebanon, Buell was encouraged by Thomas's enthusiasm for movement, particularly since he confessed to McClellan that it "startles me to think how much time has elapsed since my arrival and to find myself still in Louisville."[43] This was an amazing assessment for a commander who, despite the logistical conditions, had only himself to blame for not going anywhere. Still, it represented a departure from his previous views. McClellan's letter of December 29 also helped Buell make his decision to advance toward East Tennessee. Though too feeble to manage the war or see the president, McClellan mustered enough strength to write Buell of the ongoing discussions in Congress. "Johnson, Maynard, &c., are again becoming frantic," he warned Buell, "and have President Lincoln's sympathies excited. Political considerations would make it advisable to get the arms and troops into Eastern Tennessee at a very early day." But as usual, McClellan eclipsed his demand by adding, "You are, however, the best judge."[44]

For someone who was not easily influenced by political pressure, Buell at least proved he could use politics to his advantage. The combination of Thomas's encouragement and McClellan's impassioned letter convinced Buell of what Lincoln and McClellan had been unable to: the time had come to start an advance toward East Tennessee by removing Zollicoffer. Buell respected Thomas more than any other subordinate and greatly trusted his ability and judgment, and after considering both aspects of the move, convinced himself that he had more to gain than to lose. If Thomas succeeded in defeating Zollicoffer and crossing the river, Buell might send him forward to East Tennessee. This would relieve Buell from the mounting political pressure against him in Congress and perhaps silence his critics. If Thomas failed, it would confirm the correctness of his reluctance to move into East Tennessee. In other words, whether Buell intended Thomas's strike at Zollicoffer to be the beginning of a larger campaign to East Tennessee or not, he certainly did not mind if it looked that way to politicians. He would have to reassess the situation depending on the outcome against Zollicoffer. Whatever his thinking, he had finally consented to move toward East Tennessee, and the news surely startled McClellan as well as the president. When he wrote to McClellan, however, Buell put a qualifier on the expedition. "It is impossible to fix a time," he wrote, since "so much depends on the circumstances which may arise in the meantime."[45] That day, however, Buell allowed Thomas to fix a time to strike. Thomas was so convincing that Buell wisely allowed him independence of judgment due to the impossibility of foreseeing how conditions might change his plans. The decision was left up to Thomas, but the circumstances could change at any minute.[46]

Having sent Thomas on his way, Buell had done as much thinking about East Tennessee as he was going to do. He now concerned himself with activities in Middle Tennessee and Kentucky, particularly the Confederate concentration at Bowling Green, which he believed had the potential to snowball from 25,000 to 50,000 or 60,000 men. This, Buell argued, would "increase our work vastly," unless cooperation between himself and Halleck was speedy.[47] He continued to emphasize to McClellan that "all the force that can possibly be collected should be brought to bear" on West Tennessee. The center of the Confederate line —where the Memphis and Ohio Railroad crossed the Cumberland and Tennessee Rivers—"is now the most vulnerable point." It was so vital, Buell contended, that it was the "most strategical point in the whole field of operations."[48] If the Union could penetrate it and secure the rivers where the railroad crossed them, Federal armies could defeat the rebels because of "access through the two rivers to the very center of their power."[49] Demanding that he must have more troops to carry out his part in the operation, Buell sent a telegram to McClellan at 3:00 A.M. on December 29. It contained a stark order: "Don't acknowledge this, however, but act on it."[50]

As winter descended on East and West, Johnston's Confederates continued to contemplate Buell's possibilities for a move south. Though Zollicoffer remained on the Cumberland River essentially blocking the way to East Tennessee, Thomas was preparing to march to remove him. Meanwhile, Johnston as well as Polk continued to keep a careful eye on Halleck, headquartered up the river at St. Louis. At the time Halleck complained he was unable to march, but he certainly realized the strategic significance of Columbus. Because there was more talk than action regarding advancing on the center of the Confederate line where the Cumberland and Tennessee Rivers passed from Kentucky into Tennessee, Johnston remained less concerned about the defensive works at Fort Henry and Fort Donelson. Both were only partially complete by the end of December and wholly undergarrisoned, because Polk made the works at Columbus his priority. If Union forces in the West could effectively harness their strengths and target the Confederates' weakness, they could prove successful.[51]

Lincoln had given considerable thought to the strategy of the war, and his perception of it reached far beyond Virginia and beyond politics. Unencumbered by concern for a particular army or theater of operations, the president understandably approached military strategy on the level of productive collaboration. "The war was moving," wrote Bruce Catton, "and Mr. Lincoln felt that the men whom he had appointed to direct it ought to be moving with it."[52]

CHAPTER NINE

Delay Is Ruining Us

By the New Year of 1862 the Civil War had shifted significantly. The members of the Thirty-seventh Congress who had convened the previous July in a special session had consented to give the president the reins in running the war until they met again in six months. By the time of their second session in December, however, Congress was satisfied with neither the administration's handling of the war nor the generals' handling of the armies. It turned the session into a debate on the war effort, its direction, and its generals—a debate that revived party politics. The Republican majority sought to make the abolition of slavery a wartime measure and desired more action and new direction. Because neither the president nor his generals had taken the lead in achieving victory, Republicans decided to take it from them.[1]

The Joint Committee on the Conduct of the War, headed by Ohio Republican Benjamin Wade, owed its creation to the old assumption that civilians should leave military matters to military men. The committee members were frustrated with those commanders who were not moving forward. Though McClellan was the most prominent of these leaders, Buell might just as well have been, since he represented in the West what McClellan did in the East. The committee not only subjected sluggish Union commanders to more direct accountability to political authorities; in wanting to abolish slavery, it attempted to expand the government's initial war aims. Thus, the Union's war policy that initially had little to do with ending slavery had by December moved closer to adopting a policy on the practice. "Slowly but surely," the war was moving into a new phase, wrote the editor of the religious-based *New York Independent,* and "the Administration is drifting into the right attitude toward slavery."[2]

The war took a turn politically because it was standing still militarily. As Democratic generals who remained inactive, McClellan and Buell produced what Democrats sought to maintain politically—the status quo, particularly regarding slavery. Thus, Buell's reluctance to move into East Tennessee came to be seen in the context of larger issues of inactivity. Editors and politicians alike linked the inertia of the generals, particularly McClellan and Buell, to their training at West Point. Some critics, such as Ohio senator John Sherman, concluded that a West Point education had not "infused into the Army the right spirit to carry on this war."[3] Illinois senator Lyman Trumbull was more blunt, arguing that it was the academy's education alone that caused the war to "[languish] as it has."[4] New York journalist Horace Greeley boasted that anyone with common sense was competent "to decide questions of hastening or deferring operations against the rebels."[5]

To politicians who sought to oversee the conduct of the war, McClellan and Buell appeared more interested in managing war than fighting it. Naturally, this attitude had some foundation. A West Point education emphasized that war was a professional's business, since it demanded the knowledge of fixed rules and complex stratagems best understood by trained men. Theory dictated that the only hope of military strength for the nation resided in the ability of the army's officers to make professional soldiers out of the material at hand. This would take time and effort, since it involved intensive training, thorough knowledge of an extensive body of literature, and organization and discipline. Consequently, professional soldiers required volunteers to perform maneuvers they were incapable of performing and became cautious of the troops in whom they lacked confidence. West Point cadets absorbed this concept of war from the writings of Baron de Jomini, who had served with Napoleon a half-century earlier. Though he emphasized offensive warfare, he stressed maneuver. It was the maneuver that required a high degree of discipline and precision. As cadets, Buell and McClellan as well as Halleck had been exposed to these principles. As commanders they advocated them.[6]

New technological developments in weaponry and the character of the American armies in the post-Napoleonic era forced some theoreticians to reconsider Jominian principles. New weapons in the hands of poorly trained militiamen and civilian volunteers on the offensive would quickly teach frightful lessons about Jomini's philosophy. In his class on engineering, West Point instructor Dennis Hart Mahan introduced the ideas of entrenchment in the field, from which soldiers could launch attacks and to which they could retreat. The emphasis on fortifications and preparation by Mahan and maneuver and discipline by Jomini formed the core of military philosophy for McClellan, Buell, and Halleck. The problem, however, particularly for all three commanders, was that the application of these principles to the war became easy to identify and label: slow in movement and short on results.[7]

For many politicians the annoyingly slow prosecution of the war and the absence of fighting spirit had increasingly become an explanation for why the war stood still. Politicians, and perhaps much of the public, came to believe that commanders such as McClellan and Buell not only lacked fighting spirit, but that they also lacked appreciation for the anti-slavery and political implications of the war they were waging. It was not enough that Union generals failed to move, thought House Republican leader Thaddeus Stevens. The administration's strategy would never fully conquer the Confederates until the war became more than just a rebellion. The Union should aim to bring about revolution to "inspire the grand idea of liberty, equality and the rights of man." If many Americans were fighting for a compact, Stevens argued, the Union was "fighting to rivet the still stronger chains of slavery."[8]

Thus, Congress began to resent commanders unwilling to recognize a shift in war policy and attempt to harmonize their military goals with the political goals of the government, even more so when they were Democrats. At a time when Lincoln wanted to keep war limited to specific goals, he wanted more movement from his generals because he wanted to end the rebellion without starting a revolution. He had in December admonished Congress that the war must not degenerate into a "violent and remorseless revolutionary struggle."[9] The fruits of victory would be easier to digest if the war was kept a conflict of armies and not societies.

If Lincoln's generals did not prove capable of winning his war, however, Congress would soon shift the war's aim from suppression of rebels to include liberation of slaves.[10]

Buell was not fighting the war for the Republican Party and certainly not for the abolition of slavery. He was a conservative Democrat who owned slaves. The orders outlining the policy for his department had been clear and straightforward, and they had come from the president himself. The preservation of the Union, as well as the maintenance of constitutional principles, was at stake, and he could not bring himself to think that the abolition of slavery was a precondition to ending the war. As determined as he was to discipline his army, so was he determined to keep the government's directives in proper perspective with the goals for his army. Even while Congress debated policy over the political direction of the war, Buell remained firmly wedded to the initial objects of the conflict. His idea was Jominian in theory: display his troops proportionally "to the obstacles and resistance likely to be encountered, calm the popular passions in every possible way, exhaust the enemy by time and patience, display, courtesy, gentleness, and severity united, and particularly deal justly."[11] Escalation was a last resort. In six short months the pace of war had quickened before Buell even started, and two months after taking command, the commander was already one step behind.

The military standstill in the winter of 1861 inspired the desire for change, but it also highlighted one of the fundamental command problems that would plague the Union army in the months to come: cooperating with civil authorities. Attorney General Edward Bates also wondered at "the slowness of our military movements" in the West but concluded that it resulted from "an evident lack of system and concentrated intelligence."[12]

Just as the administration hoped for the best for the new year, Buell hoped that his superiors would let him do his own thinking about East Tennessee. His department had been a stepchild to the East, but Buell's actions had not. He continued to receive weekly, if not daily, reminders of what was expected of him during that turbulent winter despite logistical problems and the weather. He celebrated the new year as just another day, busily poring over maps and correspondence from his subordinates. The new year began, however, just as the old year ended: with the pressure for action. This time, however, the pressure came not from East Tennessee but from West Tennessee.

As McClellan remained immobilized by his illness, the disheartened president sought to get Buell and Halleck moving. The *New York Times* had forecast in December that, given their credentials, these two commanders would "have driven the last spoiler out of Kentucky and Missouri by January 1."[13] At the time, Lincoln had no reason to doubt that prophecy. Even Radical Republican Senator Charles Sumner, who was not particularly fond of Buell's insensitivity toward political desires, characterized him as an "able general" and implied to a friend that Buell was about to bring victory to the Union in the West in a "decisive battle in Kentucky."[14]

Wishful thinking though it was, both Lincoln and Sumner really wanted only cooperation. Hoping for good news in the new year, the president wired both Halleck and Buell asking them if they were in concert. He queried Halleck that if Buell moved on Bowling Green, "what hinders it from being re-enforced from Columbus?" Lincoln answered his own question for Halleck, saying, "a simultaneous movement by you on Columbus might prevent" the enemy from reinforcing in Buell's front.[15] In other words, the coordination between the two commanders would help accomplish the overall objective in the West.

On the first day of the new year, the president reemphasized his call for collaboration between the western commanders, but McClellan had separate goals for both. To Buell, Lincoln wired, "I think you better get in concert with General Halleck at once."[16] To Halleck he wired the same about Buell. The president's message no doubt reflected his frustration, but pressure from Congress played a role, too. From the Joint Committee on the Conduct of the War he felt the pressure to make abolition a war measure at a time when the Union armies stood still. This was Lincoln's war, however, and he was determined to keep the task of conducting it in his hands. Productive collaboration between Halleck and Buell was as important to Lincoln as getting them to move.[17]

Lincoln was certainly aware of the rivalry between the two western commanders for overall command in the West, and their disdainful separation from each other. Buell wrote to a beleaguered, though anxious Lincoln that there was "no arrangement between General Halleck and myself," though he had been assured by McClellan a few days before that Halleck "would make suitable disposition for concerted action."[18] Before midnight on the same day Buell dashed a note to Halleck to arrange cooperation with him.[19]

An exasperated Halleck wrote to Lincoln that he was not yet ready to cooperate with Buell. Perhaps he would be ready in a few weeks. He told Lincoln that he had fully informed McClellan of his situation. He summed it up plainly for the president. "Too much haste," he declared, "will ruin everything."[20] To cover his bases Halleck informed Buell that he had "no instructions respecting cooperation." Furthermore, all of his

Henry W. Halleck, known in the regular army before the war as "Old Brains"
for his impressive intellect. He succeeded John C. Frémont in November 1861
as commander of the Department of the Missouri and in March 1862 was
appointed to command the Department of the Mississippi, which made Buell
his subordinate. In July 1862 Halleck was made Lincoln's chief of staff.
(Courtesy of the U.S. Army Military History Institute, Carlisle, Pa.)

available troops were in the field, except those at Cairo and Paducah. To withdraw troops from Missouri was "almost impossible," he concluded.[21]

A vexed president simply could not understand this unproductive collaboration. Coming on the heels of McClellan's illness and the final days of a turbulent congressional session that was eager to blame the president for the failure of others, the tiresome lack of cooperation between the western commanders sank Lincoln to the pits. Attorney General Bates was among the most frustrated Cabinet members. "If Halleck can only cooperate," he lamented in his diary, "we may [stand] to win advantages decisive of the war. But I fear the arrangements are not as perfect as they ought to be."[22] Though Bates blamed Halleck, Lincoln considered Buell equally responsible for the impasse. Each man's inflexible determination to run his department without interference from political bosses or rival commanders led Lincoln to conclude that there were two separate wars being waged in the West, one in Missouri and one in Kentucky. This he simply could not tolerate.

Following Lincoln's lead, McClellan's first communiqué of the year to Halleck emphasized cooperation. "It is of the greatest importance," he stressed, "that the rebel troops in Western Kentucky be prevented from moving to the support of the force in front of Buell."[23] Though McClellan insisted on the importance of not allowing this reinforcement to occur, he certainly must have considered the fact that anything that deterred Buell in moving into East Tennessee would affect his own ability to move south into Virginia. Thus the object apparently was to keep things in perspective; what happened in the West was subordinate to operations in the East.[24]

Buell tried to consider the overall scheme, but seeing beyond his department was difficult for him. To Halleck he wired, "I do not understand the difficulties in Missouri," though he confidently assured him that "the great power of the rebellion in the West is arrayed on a front, the flanks of which are Columbus and Bowling Green and the center about where the railroad between those points crosses the Tennessee and Cumberland Rivers."[25] Though he continued to think that the only practical route for a powerful offensive into East Tennessee ran over the railway to Bowling Green, Nashville, and Knoxville, Buell also argued that the real choice for breaking the Confederates' entire line in the West was where his and Halleck's departments joined each other and where Kentucky and Tennessee met.[26]

In case Halleck had not determined that this was the key to breaking the Confederate stronghold on the West, Buell provided a page-length description of the situation as he saw it and, more importantly, how he saw it for Halleck. "The attack upon the center should be by two gun-boat expeditions, with, I should say 20,000 men on the two rivers," he wrote. Moreover, it would be important to "break the railroad com-munications, and if possible, that should be done by columns moving rapidly to the bridges over the Cumberland and Tennessee." "I say this much," he concluded, "rather to lay the subject before you than to pro-pose any definite plan for your side. Whatever is done should be done speedily, within a few days."[27]

If Buell was trying to be tactful, the tone of his message failed to show it, since he was instructing one who considered himself a master strate-gist. Besides, the strategy was apparently so obvious that commanders later could hardly contemplate that the idea had ever been ignored. Buell was informing "Old Brains" what he, and certainly others, may have already known. Buell, however, had no way of knowing that Hal-leck had conceived of the combined river and land assault, particularly since Halleck had not officially discussed it with him.

In his message to the president, Halleck confessed that he knew noth-ing of Buell's intended operations, never having received any infor-mation in regard to the general plan of campaign. He expounded on the problems he was encountering in Missouri, lamenting that the "au-thorities at Washington do not appreciate the difficulties with which we have to contend here." Comparing himself to "a carpenter who is re-quired to build a bridge with a dull axe, a broken saw, and rotten tim-ber," he reiterated what he told McClellan the month before: "it would be madness" to attempt to assist Buell.[28]

Halleck evidently knew more than he was willing to acknowledge, and what he knew, he condemned. He argued that a simultaneous move on Bowling Green by Buell and on Columbus by his forces was same strate-gic error that produced the Bull Run defeat. "To operate on exterior lines against an enemy occupying a central position will fail," he con-cluded, "as it always has failed, in ninety-nine cases out of a hundred."[29] Besides, Halleck had as much difficulty organizing his army to defend the vast region west of the Mississippi as Buell complained he was having east of the river. Moreover, he was reluctant to move because Ulysses S. Grant was the top-ranking officer in the Kentucky area and Halleck thought him reckless, particularly since at Belmont he had been lucky to escape.[30]

The same day he laid out his theory to the president, Halleck wrote to Buell in the same vein that the whole plan was theoretically doomed, since it was simply a "plain case of exterior lines." Buell, however, did not intend for Halleck to move on Bowling Green from Paducah or Cairo.

He merely wanted him to make a demonstration on Columbus and use the Cumberland and Tennessee Rivers to penetrate the Confederate center. If possible, depending on the condition of the forts, Halleck should make his way to Nashville. He wanted to strike at the Confederate center along the rivers and the flanks, Columbus and Nashville. Not only was this reasonable strategy, he thought, it was practical, and it came essentially from the president himself. For once Buell and Lincoln were in agreement about simultaneous movements on Bowling Green and Columbus.[31]

Buell liked Lincoln's idea because it placed him in a better situation to move on Bowling Green and Nashville. He liked it even more because it diverted attention from East Tennessee. Just when it appeared as though Lincoln was focused on the uncooperativeness between Halleck and Buell, a two-line telegram from the president put things into perspective for Buell. "Have arms gone forward for East Tennessee," he wrote. "Please tell me the progress and condition of the movement in that direction. Answer."[32]

It was the "Answer" that pinned Buell. Lincoln wanted answers not explanations, and Buell had none. Though he spoke of the "contingencies" that subordinated Lincoln's desires, the fact was that he had sent Thomas on his way toward the Cumberland River at the end of December to meet Zollicoffer. Still, the advance was extremely slow, and Buell complained that his preparations had been "delayed far beyond" even his expectations. A frustrated Buell, however, let it slip that it was his "sympathy for the people of East Tennessee and the anxiety with which you and the General-in-Chief have desired it than by my opinion of its wisdom as an unconditional measure." "As earnestly as I wish to accomplish it," he continued, "my judgement has from the first been decidedly against it."[33]

Despite sending Thomas to meet Zollicoffer, therefore, Buell had not changed his mind about East Tennessee. He had told McClellan all along that he intended to send two columns to East Tennessee. It was the problems of logistics and the choice of advance that had first deterred him. Now he had new explanations for why he could not envision any military or strategic worth to the invasion: the position of the Confederates had changed.[34]

To give Buell some idea of the depths of his anxiety and the personal pain of his burden as commander in chief, Lincoln penned a letter back to the recalcitrant commander. He was gracious in saying that he was "not competent to criticise [Buell's] views," and that he wrote merely "in justification of myself." "I cannot see why the movement on East Ten-

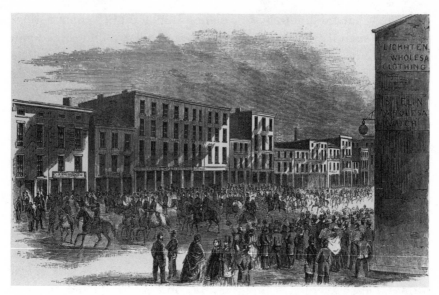

Buell's bodyguard (*Harper's Weekly*; photograph courtesy of Harpweek)

nessee would not be a diversion in your favor rather than a disadvantage," he argued, "assuming that a movement toward Nashville is the main object."[35] Of equal importance, Lincoln reemphasized the political considerations, since he knew Maynard and Johnson would desire to know the reason for the delay. "My distress," he concluded, "is that our friends in East Tennessee are being hanged and driven to despair, and even now I fear are thinking of taking rebel arms for the sake of personal protection."[36]

Buell's letter to the president and Lincoln's response aroused a still-feeble McClellan to pen a confidential letter to Buell expressing his disappointment. At the time there were few things closer to McClellan's interest than the East Tennessee advance, and he reemphasized to Buell that the "political consequences of the delay of this movement will be much more serious than you seem to anticipate." McClellan was extremely sorry to learn that Buell had "*from the beginning attached little or no importance* to a move in East Tennessee." "I had not so understood your views, and it develops a radical difference between your views and my own, which I deeply regret."[37]

Whether or not McClellan really understood what Buell meant when he confessed that "from the beginning" he had attached "little or no importance to a movement into East Tennessee," he knew that Buell's actions spoke louder than his words. In an attempt to put things into perspective for McClellan as well as the president, Buell spoke frankly again. He had decided to subordinate the East Tennessee advance to more pressing concerns now confronting him. McClellan decided to do some confessing as well. Whether he was sincerely concerned for East Tennesseans or simply wanted to please the president, he finally came around to the truth of the matter. To "My Dear General," he wrote, "My own advance cannot, according to my present views, be made until your troops are solidly established in the eastern portion of Tennessee."[38]

Certainly McClellan and Buell had discussed this strategy two months earlier in Washington, which was why Buell's stark confession was all the more disturbing. McClellan thought he and Buell had seen eye-to-eye concerning East Tennessee. McClellan did not like the message, and he no doubt harbored a resentment for the messenger. And while one of the strengths of their friendship was their respect for each other's professional judgment—so long as the ends remained the same— McClellan's patience with Buell began to wane. The general in chief continued to envision Buell's advance into East Tennessee as a benefit to his own plans in Virginia; thus, operations in the West loomed large for McClellan's operations in the East.[39]

Regardless of his motives for not advancing into East Tennessee, Buell's candidness with Lincoln and McClellan cost him dearly, and a week passed before he wrote either again. The fact that Johnson and Maynard had seen the letter and had descended on Lincoln certainly came as no surprise to Buell. Sentiment was strong for action, and the public was starved for some kind of victory. What Buell failed to take seriously, however, was that these politicians were not only dissatisfied with his apparent lack of sympathy for East Tennessee, but also, like other politicians, they were fed up with commanders managing rather than fighting the war.[40]

Buell considered himself pressed from two sides. The president wanted him to join with Halleck at one end of Tennessee, and on the other end he was being forced to walk backward into inhospitable terrain. He tried to maintain his initial focus of getting to Bowling Green and Nashville without jeopardizing his relations with McClellan. In keeping all this in perspective, it became easier for Buell to forget that the Army of the Ohio he had created was the army of the people. He continued to hold tight the line between civilian and military authority, even when it might have meant, for him, doing the wrong thing militarily for the right political reasons to fulfill the president's desires.[41]

Two telegrams of January 7 from the president and his defamed secretary of war Simon Cameron, whom Lincoln was on the verge of replacing, reflected the complexity of Buell's dilemma. Just as Cameron wrote, "We are exceedingly anxious to have some result in Kentucky; especially towards East Tennessee," so wrote Lincoln, "Please name as early a day as you safely can on or before which you can be ready to move southward in concert with Major-General Halleck." "Delay is ruining us," Lincoln lamented, "and it is indispensable for me to have something definite."[42] Buell could surely have given the president something definite, but he refused. He was not going to commit more troops than Thomas's toward East Tennessee, and he was not going to cooperate with Halleck until he was ready.

At a time when the president needed answers, he was getting explanations why Buell could not provide them. On January 9 he forwarded Buell's previous telegram of noncompliance to McClellan with an endorsement on the back: "I send the within copy of dispatch from Gen. Buell, with the remark that neither he nor Halleck meets my request to name the DAY when they can be ready to move."[43] The following day he expressed his woes on the back of Halleck's equally disheartening January 6 telegram: "It is exceedingly discouraging. As everywhere else, nothing can be done."[44] The same day, as if to liberate himself from this burden of frustration, he tempted Quartermaster Gen. Montgomery Meigs to share the hardship by asking a question to which he wanted not an answer but, rather, consolation. "General," he grumbled, "what shall I do? The people are impatient. Chase has no money; . . . the General of the Army has typhoid fever. The bottom is out of the tub. What shall I do?"[45]

Even if the president had an answer to his own questions, the war situation required action. McClellan, Buell, and Halleck all saw obstacles in the woods, while Lincoln was trying to get them to see the forest itself. His dreary summation was as discouraging as the desolate winter weather. Through the fog of confusion, Old Brains was beginning to demonstrate clever ways of making Buell look even more uncooperative and sluggish while presenting himself as an example of cooperative Union leadership. He told Buell one thing and the president another.

When Halleck wrote Lincoln on January 7, he said that he had written Buell the previous day, asking him to "designate a day for a demonstration" near Columbus, something he knew would please the president. In fact he had not yet written that letter. That telegram did not go out to Buell until four days later. When he did wire Buell on January 10 asking him to designate a time, he said that his troops at Cairo and Paducah were ready to advance on Mayfield, Murray, and Dover, but he added that Buell should take his time because he wanted to increase the size of the force. In the meantime, using the excuse that he had not heard from Buell, Halleck ordered Grant in command of the Cairo and Paducah force to fix his own time for an advance into Tennessee. Perhaps it was just an oversight on Halleck's part, but in light of their rivalry, a misrepresentation of the facts looked to be a clever scheme to undermine Buell, whether or not anyone recognized it at the time.[46]

McClellan had his own problems with Halleck over the withdrawal of troops from Missouri, and the two exchanged bitter words. The unpleasantness between them did little to help Buell. Buell was hoping to get Halleck to cooperate and knew trying to get Halleck to do anything outside his department was difficult. Significantly, Buell was pulling some tricks of his own. Realizing that Thomas was preparing to meet Zollicoffer, he ordered him to send some newly mustered Illinois regiments into garrison at Cairo and Paducah. "Raw troops," he claimed, "do not add much to our strength for active operations. Why not send them into garrison at Cairo and Paducah, and let the older troops take the field."[47] A conscientious Thomas was not altogether sure he could do this, particularly since Cairo and Paducah were in Halleck's department. Thus, Thomas wrote to Halleck asking if this met Halleck's views. Certainly it did not, since it looked as though Buell was sending troops he had no use for to Halleck.[48]

From January 10 through 13, on the advice of Quartermaster General Meigs, the president held what amounted to a council of war to try to put a bottom back in the tub. Lincoln invited Treasury Secretary Chase; Secretary of State William Seward; Postmaster General Montgomery Blair, a West Pointer turned lawyer; Assistant Secretary of War Thomas A. Scott; and Gens. Irvin McDowell, William B. Franklin, and Montgomery Meigs. This council had direct implications for Buell, though he knew nothing of it at the time and most of the agenda focused on the Army of the Potomac. McClellan appeared on January 13. When Chase asked him where and when he intended to advance with the Army of the Potomac, McClellan replied that it was necessary to act first in Kentucky and that he was pressing Buell on that. As for his own plans, he was unwilling to reveal them to anyone, declaring, "No general fit to command an army will ever submit his plans to the judgement of such an assembly." When asked if he had set a time for the advance, McClellan confirmed that he had. With that information, Lincoln said, "On the assurance of the General that he will press the advance in Kentucky, I will be satisfied, and will adjourn the Council."[49]

McClellan's bullish refusal to reveal his plans epitomized his arrogance and disdain for political interference. He had steadily become his own worst enemy, and it certainly did little to enhance Buell's position in the eyes of McClellan's opponents that he was tied to him. McClellan had also laid the entire movement of the war on Buell's shoulders and required of his friend something he himself was unwilling to do: acquiesce to political dictates and move.[50]

One of Lincoln's strengths as commander in chief was that he knew how to handle command relationships. Since Lincoln had not convinced Buell with political appeals, he tried to explain his thinking on a level Buell could more fully appreciate—a military level. On the same day the council of war ended, Lincoln wrote Buell and described in simple mathematics and principles his view of the military situation:

> We have the greater numbers and the enemy has the greater facility of concentrating forces upon points of collision; that we must fail unless we can find some way of making our advantage an overmatch for his; and that this can only be done by menacing him with superior forces at different points at the same time, so that we can safely attack one or both if he makes no change; and if he weakens one to strengthen the other, forbear to attack the strengthened one, but seize and hold the weakened one, gaining so much. . . .
>
> Applying the principle to your case, my idea is that Halleck shall menace Columbus and "down-river" generally, while you menace Bowling Green and East Tennessee. If the enemy shall concentrate at Bowling Green do not retire from his front, yet do not fight him there either, but seize Columbus and East Tennessee, one or both, left exposed by the concentration at Bowling Green.[51]

Though he explained this idea to Buell, he also confessed that "unless I should put them in the form of orders," he would "blame [Buell] to follow them contrary to [his] own clear judgement."[52]

On the last day that Lincoln's war council met, Buell wired his "Dear Friend" a modest apology concerning his earlier letter to the president when he had written that he attached little importance to the movement into East Tennessee. He told McClellan that moving to Bowling Green, instead of East Tennessee itself, would more effectively force the Confederates to abandon the region. Though Buell fully expected success in his campaign to Nashville, the task could be more successfully accomplished if he had "say in all 120,000 men," reminiscent of Sherman's earlier request.[53]

Upon returning to his office from the council of war, McClellan found Buell's telegram and dashed a letter of desperation back concerning political pressure. "You have no idea of the pressure brought to bear here upon the Government for a forward movement," he told Buell. "It is so strong that it seems absolutely necessary to make the advance on Eastern Tennessee at once."[54] Though he made it appear to Buell that politicians were clamoring for the East Tennessee advance immediately, he failed to acknowledge that the real pressure came for movement in the East, not the West. It was McClellan the politicians were after, not Buell. McClellan merely shifted the burden of responsibility from his department to Buell's, and with it he passed along the political guillotine.

McClellan reiterated what had been clear to Buell since November: the possession of the railroad in East Tennessee would prevent the main army from reinforcing in McClellan's front, and it was politically desirable. Halleck's refusal to make a demonstration on Columbus had also become a reason why Buell should direct his attention away from the West and toward the East. To illustrate how important Buell's advance had become, McClellan was even willing to abandon his initial orders protecting the rights of citizens. McClellan advised Buell to hire private wagons and teams to facilitate and expedite his operations, or if the people "will not freely give them, why, then, seize them. . . . It is no time now to stand on trifles."[55]

The pressures or trifles of war were unraveling McClellan and descending more heavily on Buell, and Buell knew it. As he continued to wrestle with McClellan, Halleck, and Lincoln over the proper strategic deployment of his army, the fact still remained that his army stood still. With the exception of Col. James A. Garfield's defeat of Humphrey Marshall's Confederates on January 10 at the forks of Abbott and Middle Creek near Prestonburg in eastern Kentucky, Buell's soldiers continued to battle the miserable winter weather, perfecting regimental drill and maneuvers, waiting for something to happen.[56]

Nothing proved more discouraging to the army than inactivity. The real enemy was disease. The sickness in camp, wrote Capt. Alexis Cope, resulted from "being compelled to remain for so long a time inactive in our muddy and disagreeable camps."[57] Col. John Beatty of the Third Ohio echoed these sentiments: "I fear the winter will send many more to the grave than the bullets of the enemy for a year to come."[58] General McCook brought this to Buell's attention in a January 10 message, saying, "Working the men will prove a great sanitary measure."[59] The machine that Buell had created in the Army of the Ohio was ready to move, but its commander was not. Despite the hardships, Buell continued to collect fresh troops and supplies and by mid-January had completed the organization of twenty-three brigades into five divisions.[60]

It was mid-January before the Union command in the West began to move. When it did, it moved slowly, almost crawling, and its movement was a response not only to the Confederates but also to the intense pressure from Washington. General Zollicoffer, who had reentered Kentucky in early December, was still positioned at Beech Grove on the north side of the Cumberland River and also at Mill Springs on the south side of the river. Generals Johnston and George B. Crittenden, brother of Thomas L. Crittenden of Buell's army and who had been recently appointed to supersede Zollicoffer as departmental commander, foresaw the hazard of dividing his force between Mill Springs and Beech Grove, particularly since the river continued to rise. Zollicoffer had for several weeks wanted to move south back across the river but lacked the boats and supplies.[61]

For weeks in December, however, Buell had promised McClellan that the roving bugbears were not going to deter him from organizing his army and that any "formidable demonstration" against Zollicoffer, stranded along the Cumberland, or anyone else for that matter, would only harass his troops and derange his plans. Buell had been aware of the enemy's position for over a month, and yet he failed to realize that Zollicoffer was quite vulnerable on the north side of a river he had little hope of recrossing until supplies arrived. Buell's failure to order Thomas to attack in December was probably one of the reasons why the Confederates had remained in that position for as long as they had, despite weather conditions. They had no fear of an offensive from Buell. Had Buell pursued the Confederates as vigorously in early December, when he knew of Zollicoffer's position, as he was willing to do in mid-January, he might have captured the rebels. At a time when the enemy was as unprepared as his own force, Buell continued to emphasize preparation over movement largely because the weather continued to be as inhospitable as the Cumberland Mountains.[62]

Thomas had departed Lebanon on January 1 with Colonel Mason's Second Brigade and Colonel McCook's Third Brigade and for over two weeks had marched barely four miles a day. The severity of the march must have convinced Thomas that Buell's idea to move on Nashville and then on to East Tennessee would prove more successful even if it took longer. The roads were the worst Thomas had ever seen, and the 600 wagons were often axle deep in the mud. The march seemed endless. Still, some soldiers were enthused about proceeding. As William Bircher, a drummer in the Second Minnesota put it, "We were really going towards the enemy."[63]

On January 13 Thomas wired Buell from his camp near Webb's Crossroads that Buell should consider a move down the Cumberland River toward the Tennessee capital to cut enemy communications and bring his soldiers much-needed supplies. Buell, however, was content with Thomas's snail-like pace. On the same day Buell wrote McClellan that the "presence of Zollicoffer at Mill Springs," though an "obstacle," was not "altogether unfortunate, as it affords a reason for sending a considerable force to that point."[64] From what information he had, Buell fully expected success from Thomas, advising him that if he saw an opportunity, he should "lose not a day." At the same time he wrote to McClellan that to destroy Zollicoffer entirely was perhaps "too much to calculate upon." Four days later he wired Thomas that Zollicoffer's force "must be captured or dispersed."[65]

Buell was fortunate to have a subordinate willing to risk the battle that he complained he was unable to undertake. Though the roads were horrible and the pelting rains and sleet were fierce, Thomas's nearly 5,000 Federals pursued the march for over two weeks to Logan's Crossroad, eight miles west of Somerset and nine miles north of Zollicoffer's camp at Beech Grove. He arrived January 17 with two regiments each of the Second and Third Brigades. General Carter's Twelfth Brigade followed a few hours behind. Thomas had ordered Schoepf's 4,000 men at Somerset to follow close behind once he descended on the enemy entrenched along the river. A heavy downpour on the night of the January 18 flooded the banks of nearby Fishing Creek, preventing Schoepf from keeping up. Thus, Thomas's force was divided by the swollen creek, as Zollicoffer had been by the Cumberland. Sensing the vulnerability of the Union force, Crittenden gave up trying to recross the Cumberland and instead decided to surprise Thomas by making an overnight march on the eighteenth to unite his Confederates north of the river before Thomas could be reinforced. The rains slowed the march, though, and the Confederates did not arrive until dawn on the nineteenth, tired, rain-soaked, and discouraged. By all accounts the night of the eighteenth was incredibly dreary. Col. Judson Bishop of the Second Minnesota Volunteers recalled that it was the "darkest night and the coldest and most pitiless and persistent rain we ever knew," and he took some comfort in knowing that the enemy was "at least as wet and cold and wretched as he was himself."[66]

The battle of Mill Springs opened in darkness and rain. The firing of Confederate muskets about half past six signaled the surprise attack on Thomas, though the Union commander was hardly surprised. The battle began as an exchange of distant musketry fire between Union pickets and the approaching Confederates, but soon the battle lines drew closer.

As the rain turned to drizzle, dawn broke through the dense woods, mist and smoke revealing the close proximity of the fatigued combatants. Visibility was so poor that Zollicoffer, who was "pathetically nearsighted," lost his sense of direction and unknowingly came upon Union colonel Speed Fry of the Fourth Kentucky. Zollicoffer's aides fired on Fry, who shot back and killed the Confederate commander. The death of their leader cracked the spirit of the already beleaguered Confederates.[67]

Both sides hammered at each other for over an hour until Carter's brigade arrived from the east. The rain ceased, and McCook ordered the Ninth Ohio Volunteers, comprised mainly of Germans, to charge with bayonets. An already retreating Confederate line caved in to a full retreat. Thomas re-formed his lines about eight o'clock and took up the chase. A few scattered shots continued as the Federals pursued the exhausted Confederates for ten miles back to their fortified camp on the Cumberland River. Once there, the Confederates caught the ferry across the river to safety. General Schoepf arrived on the battlefield a few hours later and chased the remaining rebels, who scattered throughout the countryside, deserting in large numbers. According to Thomas Small of the Tenth Indiana, the firing ceased about midday. "We gave them a good whipping and sent them back to the river," he wrote jubilantly.[68]

The completeness of the victory provided proof that Buell was finally moving. It gave him the much-needed confidence to pursue the Confederates across the Cumberland River. "The instructions of Gen. Buell," wrote the editor of the *Louisville Daily Journal*, "show that he is fully master of the situation."[69] Indeed, such characterizations proved as much a curse as a blessing to Buell, since they seemed to indicate he would now begin the major advance to East Tennessee.

The impassability of the roads leading into East Tennessee, however, still hindered the enthusiasm he and Thomas now shared "to follow the enemy," as Buell ordered Thomas to do. The retreating rebels devouring all available forage gave Thomas the idea that his forces might move down the river and cooperate with the main army moving against Bowling Green. He tempered this idea with the suggestion that Carter's brigade might advance east to encourage the citizens and to take them arms and ammunition that Lincoln desired they have. Though Buell thought well of the latter campaign, he remained content not to undertake it.[70]

Though the battle of Mill Springs was not a great battle in terms of numbers engaged, its significance cannot be dismissed nor its forecast overshadowed. Not only did it weaken Johnston's defensive line; it revealed that Johnston's Confederates could be whipped. The victory went a long way toward restoring the morale and confidence among the soldiers. They realized that they were capable of handling combat maneuvers even under inhospitable circumstances. Indiana Hoosier Harrison Derrick boasted to a friend about a week after the battle, "I don't believe I ever spent happier hours than when the battle was raging."[71] An Ohio captain who had earlier complained of inactivity wrote to his wife after the battle, "We are beginning to feel that there is yet some life in our army."[72]

The Mill Springs victory also breathed new life into a deflated administration. The new secretary of war, Edwin M. Stanton, acknowledged on behalf of the president what he called a brilliant victory on January 20. Stanton also took the opportunity to declare his views on the purpose of the war. It was one of "attack, pursue and destroy."[73] Buell's congratulations to Thomas came four days after what he called an important victory. The completeness of the conquest impressed him, and he saw it, no doubt, as an opportunity to appease both McClellan and Lincoln. To McClellan he merely used Thomas's own words to describe the outcome by sending the Virginian's initial dispatch declaring the rout of the enemy. Within the next few weeks the Senate confirmed Thomas's nomination as brigadier general.[74]

Even in his congratulatory message, however, Buell's attitude toward rewards reflected his desire to maintain professional standards and not let the frenzy of victory sway his soldiers. "The question of rewards," observed Buell, needed to be "treated with very great caution," since it was one that "produces jealousies and dissatisfaction in a regular army, and, composed as ours is, may lead to a most injurious condition of things." Thus, Buell suggested that rewards for services in battle "be conferred exclusively by brevets, leaving the full promotion (to the grade of brigadier) to flow exclusively from fitness for the office as shown by service."[75]

Obviously, Buell did not want to reward men who had by risk distinguished themselves in battle and yet who had failed to demonstrate soldierly qualities away from the battlefield. Even in victory, Buell maintained a desire to reward only those who had been consistent in their soldierly bearing. Being a good soldier not only meant performing well on the battlefield. It was determined by the moral courage one displayed in the ranks as well.

Perhaps the most important outcome of the Mill Springs battle was that Buell had consented to send Carter's brigade to Cumberland Gap. Interestingly enough, earlier the same week Buell had written McClellan that "the plan of any colonel (referring to Carter) . . . for ending the war by entering East Tennessee with his 5,000 men light . . . while the rest of the armies look on, . . . is in the aggregate simply ridiculous."[76] Apparently the prospect appeared less ridiculous in light of the victory at Mill Springs.

On January 26 Buell ordered Carter to "seize and hold Cumberland Gap" by moving back through London and eastward as "rapidly as possible." He gave the commander explicit instructions for the campaign regarding the discipline of his troops. "As a matter of policy," he wrote, "if for no other reason, and in order not to excite the rebel authorities to increased persecution of the loyal people by way of retaliation, you are to refrain from any unnecessarily harsh course toward the former." Carter was to restrain his troops "from committing outrages upon persons or property, and to make no arrests, unless of those who [were] engaged in war against your command or who [were] otherwise working actively against its comfort or safety."[77]

Modest though it was, Carter's advance marked the beginning of the much desired and anticipated attempt to get at East Tennessee. As Confederate senator Landon C. Haynes of Tennessee put it to President Jefferson Davis, "There is now no impediment whatever but bad roads and natural obstacles to prevent the enemy from entering East Tennessee and destroying the railroads and putting East Tennessee in a flame of revolution."[78] After months of prodding, Buell had finally moved with the war toward East Tennessee, but Thomas received the laurels and the president's confidence.

CHAPTER TEN

War without Warring

By the new year Simon Cameron's administrative shortcomings and unsavory associations as well as the overwhelming demands of war forced Lincoln to replace him in February with Edwin M. Stanton, a Pittsburgh attorney who had reluctantly consented to President James Buchanan's appointment as attorney general just before Christmas 1860. Stanton certainly knew Buell, since Buell had been the special envoy in December 1860, and Stanton had come to Anderson's and Buell's defense regarding the move from Fort Moultrie to Fort Sumter.[1]

As secretary of war, Stanton inherited a post that had generally been a liability to Lincoln, since the office itself was ill defined and, once the war began, the ambiguity had led to corruption under Cameron. Stanton's incorruptibility, driving energy, and bluntness equipped him admirably for the demands he assumed and helped him teach generals who had acted independently of the civilian secretary that they were subject to civil authorities and had better harmonize military operations with political goals. Though Union generals would eventually gain the offensive spirit the public eagerly awaited, Stanton saw his position as one that could prod them into action. For Stanton, the only way to win the war was to engage in it. Stanton found the Joint Committee on the Conduct of the War useful in energizing generals.[2]

McClellan was well aware of the political criticism of his inaction, and he blamed the inactivity on the weather. The inability to campaign in Virginia, however, opened for McClellan the possibility of shifting the main offensive from Virginia to Kentucky. On January 26 he wrote to Stanton confidentially that he was thinking of transferring a major part of the Army of the Potomac, as many as 70,000 troops, to Buell's department. Though he confessed he was not "fully committed" to the idea, he called on Stanton to "put the machinery in motion to ascertain exactly how many troops we can move per diem hence to Kentucky."[3]

McClellan never elaborated on the details of this idea, but he must have hoped he could get more cooperation from Halleck and Buell if he personally went to the West. He apparently thought that more troops would overcome the logistical problems caused by Kentucky's bad weather. McClellan's reasoning is difficult to fathom, however. Buell complained as much as McClellan about impassable roads, flooded rivers, and rain deterring his operations. Perhaps McClellan thought that he could advance to East Tennessee and redeem himself in the eyes of Congress and the administration by cutting the Confederacy's main east-west railway, or that he would finally order Buell to do it for him. In light of the victory at Mill Springs, McClellan might have persuaded himself that the Confederates in the West were less of a fighting force than those in the East. In any case, he would soon abandon this idea, but he recognized that the West possessed the strategic key to overall Union success. More importantly, he never lost faith in Buell.[4]

Because of the completeness of Thomas's Mill Springs victory, Buell wrote the adjutant general that it was "proper" for Washington officials to assume that his success would be followed rapidly by other successful operations. But the weather in late January had stalled his plans to forge ahead, and he abandoned any hopes of a quick advance. He had sent McClellan an embarrassing number of telegrams justifying his immobility and now thought the adjutant general of the army might be pleased to see an end to the tiring excuses. Buell explained that when he had ordered Thomas to head toward Zollicoffer a month ago, the roads had been in good shape. The weather had transformed them into streams of mud, precluding any advance beyond Somerset. Still, his efforts, he believed, were not "altogether without fruits." Buell felt assured "that the difficulty of moving large bodies of troops in the winter . . . will be rightly appreciated."[5]

Buell's logistical problems were rightfully appreciated, but by the wrong people. Lincoln, McClellan, and East Tennessee politicians appreciated Buell's difficulties, but they had come to expect negative news from him. Buell was aware that members of the Joint Committee on the Conduct of the War and now Stanton cared less for logistics and more for forging victory through a closer relationship between military and political leaders. In his defense Buell wrote the new secretary of war a nine-page letter, including maps, explaining in careful detail his attitude toward East Tennessee. He stated "candidly the difficulties in the way of the object you have so much at heart" and claimed that while he did not want to disappoint the president, logistical problems simply made any attempt to advance into East Tennessee impossible.[6] In addition, he complained to Stanton about the lack of cooperation from Halleck. Stanton immediately felt the deflation of hope that the president and Congress had endured since November. As always, wrote an Ohio soldier, for Buell there was "a lion in the way."[7]

Though the transfer of troops commanded attention for a few weeks, it quickly dissolved, partly because of a startling order issued by Lincoln on January 27. "President's General War Order No. One" called for a "general movement of the land and Naval forces of the United States against the insurgent forces."[8] It directed the armies in Virginia, in western Virginia, in Kentucky, and in Illinois, along with the gunboat flotilla on the Mississippi River, to be ready to move by February 22. Lincoln issued this order hoping to cause McClellan to reveal his plans. In substance, McClellan planned to flank the Confederates out of northern Virginia and to carry the war at once to the region of the Confederate capital. This thrust would be coordinated with advances by Buell and Halleck in the West. It was a solid plan and not altogether unlike Lincoln's earlier idea.[9]

As baffling as Lincoln's order was and as earnest as McClellan now appeared to be, the fact was that war was about to erupt in unexpected quarters, which made the transfer of troops unnecessary. Whatever Halleck and Buell may have thought about the true strategic line in the West, it was clear that neither commander was inspired enough to put thought into action until someone did it for them. The two men had explained to McClellan how penetration along the Cumberland and Tennessee Rivers should develop, yet neither commander was willing to sacrifice the operations in other parts of his department or to compromise his own ideas about the strategy. Thus, while it appeared to be a weakness for the Confederacy in the West that the Tennessee and Cumberland Rivers reached inland from the north toward its center, it also became a weakness for the Union command, since the true strategic line was the same place where authority was divided.[10]

Though the 700-mile Cumberland was not as strategically significant as the Tennessee for the Union, its southernmost navigable point reached Nashville, a city that was significant. Buell knew this, and if McClellan transferred troops to his department, they could be used to advance on Nashville via water while he advanced over land to Bowling Green. The Tennessee River, however, penetrated deeper into the Confederacy and traversed a line out of the Great Smoky Mountains of North Carolina and Tennessee, running southwest and west from Knoxville to Chattanooga and Decatur, Alabama, and toward Corinth, Mississippi, then north to Pittsburg Landing and Fort Henry before draining into the Ohio River at Paducah. It also intersected the most important communication and transportation link between the Confederates east and west of the Appalachian Mountains, the Memphis and Charleston Railroad.[11]

Throughout the fall and winter the Lincoln administration, for strategic as well as political reasons, had urged movement from Buell on the eastern portion of the line to get at Knoxville. The western portion of the line, however, offered the more feasible opportunity, since both water and rail could be used to threaten the Confederates from two simultaneous advances. For whatever discussions that went on during late 1861 regarding a move along the rivers, the fact was nobody consented to undertake such an operation, at least no one who had the authority to do so. Buell could not move up the river because it was not in his department. Halleck simply refused, since he argued he was not prepared.[12]

Buell's ideas, like Halleck's, had been maturing for some time. For weeks he had envisioned a three-pronged Union advance coordinated by Halleck and him. He would strike at Bowling Green while Halleck simultaneously struck at Columbus and steamed up the Cumberland and Tennessee Rivers to where the railroad intersected them. If the river campaign proved successful, then perhaps Halleck might also send his force farther upstream to Nashville. Whatever the case, Nashville remained the objective, and thus the main line would be overland by rail. Buell wanted to convince Halleck of this. The struggle was over whose advance would take priority and who would assist whom. Buell wanted to keep Bowling Green and Nashville as his sole prize while Halleck aided him by threatening the other points of the Confederate line. Oddly enough, it appeared as though Buell was more eager to move than Halleck.[13]

The responsibility, however, for a move up the Tennessee and Cumberland Rivers would have to come from Halleck, since it was his department, at least until the advance reached Tennessee. He had complained throughout January that he would not be ready to cooperate with Buell until some time in February. He had sent Grant and Flag Officer Andrew Foote, commander of the river gunboats, to investigate the western end of Johnston's line. The two men had seen the weaknesses of the Confederates at Forts Henry and Donelson and had been clamoring for action against them. Halleck was reluctant not only because he had convinced himself that his troops were in no condition to move, but more importantly, he had little faith in the commander who would undertake the mission prescribed by Buell.[14]

Grant was perhaps the most unlikely commander for Halleck to rely on to lead the coordinated land and river assault. But he had no choice. Halleck, perhaps jealous over Thomas's victory in Buell's department, finally consented two days after the Mills Springs victory to allow Grant to visit and make a case for movement up the rivers. Like Buell, Halleck had little time for the advice of subordinates, and even less for those in whom he lacked confidence and respect, particularly men who in appearance, according to one historian, "looked more like the town joke than a great soldier."[15] Still, Grant had trained his men well and was ready to move when others were not, but he failed to persuade Halleck.[16]

Fear, more than the urging of McClellan, Buell, or Grant, was the great motivator that finally inspired Halleck into action. McClellan's January 29 telegram, short thought it was, managed to strike a chord of anxiety in Old Brains that was not easily shaken. The telegram alerted Halleck that rumor had it that Confederate general Pierre Gustave Toutant Beauregard was expected to go to Kentucky with fifteen regiments. This alarmed Halleck into putting into action, though prematurely, what he and others had been thinking about for several weeks.[17]

Halleck no longer considered Buell's suggested dual advance up the Cumberland and the Tennessee "madness." What had been madness all along was not that Buell's idea was bad strategy but that the Union forces in the West were so scattered that to cooperate with Buell meant that Halleck's force in Missouri would be weakened. This "pepper-box strategy," as Halleck called it, would be fatal to the Union. He had earlier observed to McClellan that politicians were no doubt responsible for the distribution of forces to satisfy political expediency and that the "want of success on our part [was] attributable to the politicians rather than to the generals."[18] With Stanton as the new secretary of war, Halleck felt confident that some suggestions could be made in regard to operations in the West. He decided to make them.

Halleck's reconsideration of Buell's idea to move up the Cumberland and Tennessee, "making Nashville the first objective point," also led him to conclude that the operation on the rivers was "the great center line of the Western theater of war."[19] The problem was that the great line flowed from his department into Buell's and with it the path to victory. He was concerned that Buell would claim a victory by capturing Bowling Green and Nashville, a triumph that Halleck had helped to create by sending expeditions up the Tennessee and Cumberland Rivers. Halleck had come to see Buell's plan favorably, but he did not want Buell to take the upper hand in directing the campaign.[20]

Buell never intended for a double force of either his army or his and Halleck's army to arrive simultaneously at Nashville or Bowling Green. He wanted those prizes for himself. He merely wanted Halleck to strike at Columbus while also sending a force up the twin rivers toward Dover to keep the Confederates from reinforcing Bowling Green and Nashville. Buell considered the capture of Nashville the great prize in the overall objectives in the West, and thus he believed the main line of operations should remain his. From Nashville he could more easily get at Knoxville, McClellan's and Lincoln's pet objective. Halleck disagreed.[21]

Whatever reconsiderations Halleck made, the stark outline was now before him. Buell might gain overall command of the West not only because of his friendship with McClellan but also because Thomas's Mill Springs victory added leverage to his appointment, especially considering the fact that the advance had opened the way to East Tennessee and with it the way to Lincoln's heart. Thus, Halleck knew he must do something to counter the success of his rival as well as establish his forces in Tennessee before Beauregard arrived.

On January 30 Halleck put an end to the strategic inertia. Though he had previously informed McClellan that an advance up the rivers should not be undertaken with less than 60,000 men, he now ordered Grant's 15,000 soldiers and Foote's naval forces to start immediately for Fort Henry. Halleck was determined to be the master of the situation and gave Grant a limited objective and virtually no freedom of movement.

He suggested to McClellan that Tennessee be added to his department. This would not only enlarge the area of his command and allow him to oversee the entire operation as it progressed farther into Tennessee; it would also subordinate Buell's operations. Halleck wanted to start and finish the engagement and claim sole victory, as opposed to starting the operation and then allowing it to end outside his domain. McClellan ignored this request and, instead, sent Buell a map of Tennessee to make sure he knew the terrain.[22]

The same day, Buell, referring to John Lellyett, notified McClellan and Halleck that "an intelligent and well-informed person" in Paducah claimed that due to the flooding of the river, Fort Henry could be taken by gunboats within two hours "with perfect safety."[23] Buell, not knowing Halleck's plans, was telling Halleck what he already knew. He wrote Halleck, "Please let me know your plans and force and the time, &c."[24] Halleck sent a curt telegram back that he had already ordered movement against Fort Henry and the railroad between Columbus and Dover. He would later telegraph the day of investment or attack. Halleck wanted to make his operation appear more important than Buell's getting to Bowling Green, and at the same time he wanted to be able to draw on Buell for help.[25]

Though for two months Buell had urged Halleck to move into Tennessee and had in fact said that Fort Henry could be taken in a matter of two hours, when the maneuver actually commenced, he was shocked over its haste. He was particularly upset at not having been consulted first. "Do you consider active co-operation essential to your success," he queried Halleck, "because in that case it would be necessary for each to know what the other has to do." He closed with a threatening bit of advice for Halleck that his operation "ought not to fail."[26]

Naturally, Halleck's uncooperativeness incensed Buell, since he was not ready to move, certainly not with haste. Though he had convinced himself that a movement into East Tennessee would be futile, he had nonetheless arranged his army to make it look like he might head in that direction. Part of this arrangement had to do with his desire to make it appear that political reasons forced him to move to East Tennessee, and, in part, he wanted to keep his movements concealed from the enemy until he was wholly ready to strike at Bowling Green. Thus, to shift his army quickly to aid Halleck would be impossible, or at least Buell thought so. On the same day that Buell received Halleck's telegram about sending Grant to Fort Henry, Buell stopped General Schoepf from crossing the Cumberland River and heading toward East Tennessee, something he knew he would have to explain to Washington.[27]

Cooperation between Buell and Halleck was essential for success in the West, but the two men were irascible and too much alike, which oddly enough, made it difficult for them to work in unison. As departmental commanders of vast and diverse regions, both were saddled with positioning parts of their armies to satisfy political pressure, both locally and nationally, without the ability to concentrate the whole. For two perfectionists who conceived of war in terms that minimized risk and maximized security, it was mentally and emotionally exhausting to rely on subordinates, many in whom they lacked confidence, to carry through such measures. Thus, caution and thorough preparation had become the means to increase the safeness of war. For Halleck the rivers had become the safest means of advancing, but he lacked confidence in Grant. For Buell, the rail was the only way to advance, though he could not convince the administration to let up on East Tennessee. Halleck discounted the importance of Nashville, as always, and saw Buell playing a role in his river advance. Buell emphasized the importance of the river advance but simply could not see beyond Nashville or the importance of Halleck's advance over his own. Both commanders campaigned by map, and neither was interested in going after the enemy. Instead, in Jominian fashion, they wanted to occupy certain points. Thus, cooperation would only be forthcoming whenever Buell or Halleck was willing to relinquish the importance of their objects.[28]

Exactly one month after the president had demanded that Halleck and Buell cooperate in the West, the two departmental commanders were still sparring over how to comply. On February 1 Halleck penned Buell a short note with a large message: "co-operation at present not essential."[29] He added that if Buell would send him his plans, he would try to assist him. This shallow display unnerved Buell, who the same day wrote McClellan a lengthy and carefully worded letter regarding his frustration with Halleck and his chronic problems with the advance to East Tennessee.

For someone who wanted to distance himself from the expedition to East Tennessee, it was odd that Buell initiated the discussion. It had been two weeks since Buell and McClellan had discussed the advance, and the exchange had ended on a desperate note, with McClellan emphasizing Buell's ignorance of the political pressures in Washington. Buell had sensed McClellan's genuine disappointment and had actually made a modest attempt to move troops toward East Tennessee. In a perfunctory gesture, he sent General Carter's brigade to advance to Cumberland Gap, and he feared it would be compelled to fall back. As for the people suffering the depredations, Buell wrote that the East Tennesseans were loyal and would remain so, "though submitting to the power that has subjugated them." "They will rise whenever they can see themselves properly supported and we can put arms in their hands," he affirmed, "but not before in any efficient manner." "It would be cruel," he thought, "to induce them to do so on any other conditions." "For the reasons I have stated," he ended, "I have been forced reluctantly to the conviction that an advance into East Tennessee is impracticable at this time on any scale which will be sufficient."[30]

Certainly this was not news to McClellan or anyone else hoping to see Buell's army appear in East Tennessee. He had been "reluctant" since mid-November. Buell merely wanted to justify his position on the subject yet again. The general in chief had exhausted his patience, having apparently failed to convince Buell that political considerations were becoming increasingly vital to the Union high command. Buell avoided a confrontation with his superiors over political and military considerations not only because McClellan and Lincoln continued to respect his judgment, but also because they had no one else to send there.

Buell resumed lobbying for his Nashville strategy. The plan had not changed, nor had his expectations for movement from Halleck. He outlined for McClellan his proposal to move immediately against Bowling Green in combination with an attack up the Tennessee and Cumberland and an effective demonstration against Columbus. The first objective was to carry Fort Henry, Dover, and Clarksville and to destroy the railroad bridges across the waterway. With these goals accomplished and Nashville threatened, the resistance at Bowling Green would give way; otherwise the struggle at that point would be protracted and difficult. Buell said, "We shall be dependent on the railroad, which must be repaired as we advance" and would take ten days.[31]

Buell also aired to McClellan his frustration about Halleck's uncooperativeness, charging that when he had first proposed teamwork, Old Brains had answered, "I can do nothing." Now, complained Buell, Halleck had ordered an advance without consultation and had curtly responded that cooperation was not essential. For a man who seldom revealed his emotions, he could hardly conceal his anger at Halleck. "I protest against such prompt proceedings," exclaimed Buell, "as though I had nothing to do but command 'Commence firing' when he starts off." It was obvious that Buell wanted to be the one to give orders about Halleck's movements, especially since he had conceived of the plan and had written to McClellan about it at length for the past two months. He just needed more time to repair the railroad. Obviously Buell and Halleck had different interpretations of "the sooner the better." That would certainly explain why Buell complained of being pushed into action when he wanted to move immediately on Bowling Green anyway.[32]

Though it appeared that Halleck's swiftness had, for the moment, saved Buell from the trouble of moving into East Tennessee, the possibility of being pushed into premature action troubled him as it always did. Whatever the case, when Buell finally sent his letter, Stanton acknowledged it by passing on words from McClellan saying that the general in chief approved of Buell's proposal. If vigorously prosecuted, it would not fail. Stanton added that McClellan desired cooperation, concluding "that your two heads"—Halleck's and Buell's—"together will succeed."[33] Whatever military genius the two men possessed together, however, their lack of cooperation eclipsed it.

In addition to Grant taking Fort Henry, Halleck envisioned him capturing Fort Donelson and cutting the railroad from Columbus to Bowling Green. He explained that as easy as the operation appeared, muddy roads, poor mortar boats, and gunboats not worth "half the money spent on them" would handicap his venture. Buell, however, saw great advantage in using the gunboats, especially since, from what he knew from Lellyett, the river was quite high and they could run past the batteries at night without great risk. Grant knew this as well, since he had previously sent Brig. Gen. Charles F. Smith, in command of Paducah, on a reconnaissance mission up the Tennessee. Smith returned with the belief that Fort Henry could be taken with two gunboats.[34]

Despite Halleck's angering him, Buell decided that he would have to advance into East Tennessee to keep the Confederates debating in which direction they should send reinforcements. On February 2 he sent Thomas a telegram filled with questions, all indicating he wanted movement into East Tennessee at once. To Thomas, Buell's bafflingly uncharacteristic urgency was puzzling, particularly since only two days before he had stopped Schoepf's movement until further orders; more puzzling was that Buell knew the answers to his questions from Thomas and had the previous day just explained to McClellan in a three-page letter why the East Tennessee campaign would fail. Evidently, Buell wanted to seize the opportunity to move into East Tennessee while Grant advanced toward Fort Henry. Whatever the case, Buell was beginning to show signs of urgency.[35]

Over the next few days no less than two dozen dispatches passed between Halleck, McClellan, and Buell revealing a troubled high command. Friendship, egotism, conservatism, rivalry, and jealousy all characterized the relationship between these three commanders. Halleck began the swirl of communiqués by informing McClellan that Grant was on his way and had landed troops three miles below Fort Henry. Old Brains's nerves began to crumble. The more he thought about Beauregard's 15,000 Confederates and Grant's recklessness and his small force, the more anxious he became. He wrote to Buell on February 5 asking for a diversion at Bowling Green.[36] A rebuffed Buell wrote back, "My position does not admit of diversion. My moves must be real ones and I shall move at once unless restrained by orders concerning other plans." Buell added that progress toward Bowling Green would be slow; it would probably be twelve days before he got in front of Bowling Green, since he was forced to repair forty miles of the railroad as he advanced.[37]

Getting little satisfaction from Buell, Halleck wrote McClellan asking for some Ohio regiments. He worried about the report that 10,000 men had left Bowling Green to reinforce Fort Henry, and he feared that with such additional strength the Confederates might overcome Grant. McClellan then prodded Buell to help Halleck either by demonstrating on Bowling Green or by sending him troops. Buell, however, continued to reiterate that a demonstration was impractical. He consented instead to send Halleck a brigade but wrote to Halleck, almost as if he were demanding proof, that he would send it only if Halleck "absolutely" required it. He ended his curt acquiescence with words he had uttered six days before: "You must not fail."[38]

From the barrage of telegrams it became painfully clear that Buell was not going to make a demonstration on Bowling Green and he was not going to aid Halleck by sending any more than a brigade. He needed to explain why. On February 5 Buell wrote to Halleck that he regretted they could not have consulted earlier on the campaign that Halleck had commenced, which was an important part of Buell's overall plan for the West and which he had previously laid out for Halleck. In an attempt to make Halleck feel he had prematurely commenced his part of the plan, Buell elaborated on his reasons why at present he could be of only limited help. He bemoaned the fact that McClellan and Washington had not let up on their demands for an East Tennessee campaign, and while he was not confident in its success, he had nonetheless positioned his troops to make it look like he would eventually advance. Now that Halleck had commenced the river campaign with haste, Buell confessed that his troops had "been thrown somewhat out of position." He concluded to Halleck that "the work which you have undertaken is therefore of the very highest importance, without reference to the injurious effects of a failure." "There is not in the whole field of operations," he ended, "a point at which every man you can raise can be employed with more effect or with prospect of as important results."[39]

Buell never fully appreciated the political significance of East Tennessee as being the most important field of operations in the West—at least from Lincoln's point of view. As much as Buell wanted to distance himself from the matter, it simply would not go away. Hoping to gain some understanding from McClellan, Buell wrote the same day: "I am unwilling to seem to swerve from the execution of your plan without advising you of the meaning of it and knowing that you will acquiesce in the necessity for it."[40]

If McClellan was prone to anything, it was being sympathetic to Buell. The following day he wired Buell: "I fully appreciate the obstacles. Same thing here."[41] McClellan continued to be torn between his friendship and respect for Buell and fulfilling Lincoln's political desires to liberate East Tennessee. Now, in light of Halleck's commencing the Fort Henry campaign, the East Tennessee advance, which Buell had earlier written was impractical, would have to wait. Still, as much as Halleck needed a quick diversion to aid the operations against Fort Henry, he would not deviate from what he already considered the most practical advance to Bowling Green—rail. Buell hoped Halleck had "weighed his work well," lecturing McClellan that Halleck should have thought of all the contingencies in striking at Fort Henry in haste and should be prepared to handle the consequences if it failed. It was almost as if Buell wanted Halleck's river mission to flop, if only to teach him a lesson.[42]

Buell was not the only one who would have been happy to learn of Halleck's defeat. Given the friendship between McClellan and Buell, and McClellan's ambition to continue to manage the Union armies, it would not be difficult to imagine that McClellan wanted Buell, not Halleck, to bring about the great victory in the West. Buell had no ambition for a higher or larger command—he certainly did not want McClellan's position—and thus McClellan felt no threat from him. In fact, Buell might even help McClellan maintain his position as general in chief, since political leaders might be convinced that despite military inertia in his own department, McClellan was at least successful in getting Buell to move in what was considered by Lincoln a most important department of the war. McClellan had promised such movement at Lincoln's council of war three weeks earlier.

At a time when it was clear that Halleck could use reinforcements, McClellan, though disappointed in Buell's delay to get to East Tennessee, agreed with Buell's summation of the situation in the West. He urged Buell to draw in whatever troops he needed from Ohio and Indiana, Governors Tod and Morton having been instructed to be of aid. Had Halleck read the dispatches between Buell and McClellan, he would have been furious to find that Buell was urged to ask for more troops at a time when Halleck was being requested to give them up. Confessing to McClellan that he had not been totally ready to move and was forced to draw from Missouri every available man to aid Grant's operation, Halleck thought that Grant's movement was best in light of the expected arrival of Beauregard. His words of desperation apparently struck a chord in McClellan. He questioned Buell about changing the main line of operations from Bowling Green to Forts Henry and Donelson, where progress was sure to be made. This would have huge implications for both commanders, shifting as it did the main offensive from Buell's control to Halleck's. Unfortunately, McClellan refused to take a decisive role in deciding what should be done and who should do it, so nothing happened.[43]

Hoping to relieve some of Halleck's anxiety, McClellan wrote to him late in the day assuring him of Buell's assistance. In addition, McClellan had placed nine more regiments at Buell's disposal to send to the Tennessee River, as Halleck had suggested, or to use himself if he could advance on Bowling Green. The general in chief closed by asking Halleck if a sudden dash on Columbus was practical should Buell send more troops. For a man who appeared in such desperate straits, Halleck confidently replied that if he had 10,000 more men he could "take Fort Henry, cut the enemy's line, and paralyze Columbus." "Give me 25,000," he added, "and I will threaten Nashville and cut off railroad communication, so as to force the enemy to abandon Bowling Green without a battle."[44] Clearly, Halleck had his sights on the entire West. McClellan did nothing, however, waiting to hear from Stanton and his assistant, Thomas A. Scott, about the grand transfer of troops from the East to the West.

In late January Stanton had sent Assistant Secretary of War Thomas A. Scott to the Midwest to examine the possibility of McClellan's transfer of troops. By early February he had made his rounds, visiting the midwestern governors and discussing the transfer. As a former vice-president of the Pennsylvania Railroad Scott had studied carefully all the logistical considerations. He wrote to Stanton that the transfer of 60,000 troops from Washington to the Ohio River could be accomplished within five to six days, though he still needed Buell's views on the matter.[45]

On the afternoon of February 6 Scott arrived at Buell's Louisville headquarters, and the two men discussed McClellan's intentions. Scott found Buell impressive. Middle age had been good to the austere Ohioan. Though his features appeared more worn, revealing the intensity of his purpose, his confidence was as commanding as was his tone. Scott's characterization of the general as "a very superior officer—calm, prudent and with great power to control," confirmed what he already knew of Buell. Buell cut quite an impressive figure as an officer, and though he had not been without his critics in the press, many journalists in the Midwest would have agreed with the correspondent to the *Nashville Republican Banner* who characterized Buell as "a first-rate officer, a dangerous foe, and among the best purchases made by the Yankee government."[46]

Lincoln may have been as impressed with Buell as Scott was, but Buell's refusal to advance into East Tennessee tempered his favorable attitude. After all, impressions were one thing; disappointment was quite another. Had Buell been the only disappointment to the administration, it might not have loomed so large, but Lincoln was plagued by military frustration that appeared to be systemic in the winter of 1861–62.

Scott knew firsthand of the president's disappointment and the criticism brewing in Congress over Buell's noncompliance. A glance through the numerous dispatches on the commander's desk from his subordinates quickly convinced Scott that bad weather and impassable roads had indeed immobilized Buell's army. Moreover, Scott spent considerable time with Buell and Capt. James B. Anderson, the superintendent of the Louisville and Nashville Railroad, who with James Guthrie, president of the railroad, easily convinced the former railroad vice-president that Buell's advance into East Tennessee was simply a physical impossibility because of the wholly inadequate transportation facilities.

Guthrie had continued to urge Buell to invade the Confederacy along his railroad and tried to convince Stanton, through Scott, that Lincoln's earlier idea of constructing a railway into East Tennessee was as impractical as was Buell's advance. Both activities would require too much time and exhaust too many resources, and in the case of Lincoln's plan, there simply were not enough supplies. Scott was so sympathetic to Buell's logistical problems that in his initial report to Stanton from Louisville he enclosed a memo from Buell's chief of staff, detailing the transportation problems. It was not that Lincoln or Stanton needed firsthand confirmation of any of these facts, but Buell simply wanted to make sure Scott could testify on his behalf. Buell also complained to Scott that better coordination between himself and Halleck was essential, since once Grant left Kentucky, he was operating in Buell's department. Halleck made no attempt to put Grant in contact with Buell, and thus Buell would have to go through Halleck to find out what Grant was doing while in his department.[47]

Buell was anxious to increase the size and efficiency of his army by concentrating new recruits in regular camps for disciplined training near the front. He told Scott that a column of "30,000 to 50,000 good soldiers from the Army of the Potomac" would enable the Federals to take and hold a good position between the Tennessee and Cumberland Rivers at a point that would cut the railroad line connecting Johnston's central position at Bowling Green with the Mississippi River stronghold at Columbus, Kentucky. Once this was accomplished, Buell could destroy the Confederates at Bowling Green while Halleck disposed of the rebel force at Columbus. Meanwhile, the Potomac column could advance up the rivers, Nashville could be occupied, and "with Nashville for a base of operations the so-called Southern Confederacy could be effectually divided, and with reasonable facilities our armies could be able to accomplish great work south and east of that center."[48]

Buell clearly thought the key to winning the war not only resided in the West but also in his department. So did Scott, who not only informed Stanton that the transfer of troops from the East should take place, but also that these soldiers should be given to Buell. He added that Halleck must cooperate absolutely and entirely with Buell's plan. Stanton gruffly replied that he had sent Scott on an inspection and information tour, not on a tour to make policy suggesting command. At that point Scott began to sense that Stanton favored Halleck over Buell, no doubt because of Buell's association with McClellan and his inactivity.[49]

Fortunately, Foote and Grant would do for Halleck what Thomas had done for Buell: move and fight. As the Union forces ascended upriver to Fort Henry on February 5 and 6, Halleck, McClellan, and Buell continued to orchestrate strategy from a map and over wire. Buell kept his promise and telegraphed Halleck that he would send a brigade as well as two regiments from Indiana and six from Ohio, though these troops were raw and without any organization. After a day of fatiguing correspondence and strategic posturing, Buell wrote to McClellan at midnight that Halleck's whole move, "right in its strategical bearing," was commenced "without appreciation—preparative or concert—[and] has now become of vast magnitude."[50]

Though Buell conceded that he was thinking of changing the main line from Bowling Green to support Halleck's operations on Fort Henry, he would have to do it in the face of 50,000 if not 60,000 men, and the move was hazardous. One frustrated critic of Buell wrote after the war that the Ohioan was requiring conditions for his safety and that of his army as numerous and as great "as the Russian Government would take in these times of anarchy and misrule for a movement of the czar from one of his capitals to another."[51]

CHAPTER ELEVEN

The Laurels in Tennessee

Fortunately the army and navy were better at collaborating than Buell and Halleck. Foote, like Grant, believed in combined operations and had joined with Grant in bombarding Halleck with telegrams urging the undertaking of the Fort Henry expedition. For weeks the two officers had urged movement before the water in the Tennessee receded, thus preventing a quick attack with gunboats. Johnston had been preoccupied with the need to defend Columbus, where he believed the Union attacks would come, and had never personally inspected the twin river forts. He had predicted in late January that the Federals would soon attack Fort Henry and Fort Donelson and then would move on Nashville. He knew Buell would move on Bowling Green and thus heavily fortified the city anticipating the advance. Johnston expected Buell to flank the Confederates out by coming up the

Cumberland River but did not have the manpower to defend against such a maneuver. Thus Grant and Foote had known for several weeks Johnston's worst fear: the Federals would penetrate the Confederate line on the rivers.[1]

The combined Union assault easily forced the surrender of Fort Henry on February 6, but not until after the 2,500-man garrison fled twelve miles cross-country to Fort Donelson. On the morning of February 7, Buell awoke to alarming, and no doubt annoying, news from Halleck: "Fort Henry is ours."[2] To McClellan, Halleck wrote the same but added, "The flag of the Union is re-established on the soil of Tennessee." In an attempt to display his military prowess, thanks to Foote, as well as flaunt his victory in the face of McClellan, he boldly ended, "It will never be removed."[3] For a month the gray skies and bitter cold of a dreary midwestern winter had mirrored the lack of warmth and cooperation between the departmental commanders in the West. As Federal gunboats headed up the Tennessee River, Halleck saw the crisis of the war floating with them and shifting from Buell's department to his.[4]

Neither Grant nor Halleck wasted time in lauding their victory. The same day that he boasted to Buell of the success on the Tennessee River, Halleck also informed Buell that it was "all-important that we hold our position and advance toward Nashville."[5] Just a few weeks before, Halleck had considered the advance of two armies on the same point as madness. If Halleck could hold Fort Henry and move up the Tennessee and Cumberland Rivers, Buell would have little difficulty in taking Bowling Green, since, Halleck argued, the Confederates would be forced to abandon the Bluegrass city and fall back. Moreover, Halleck thought, and logically so, that the Confederates would try to regain their lost advantage at Fort Henry. If they did not, they would be making a mistake.[6]

In light of these considerations, Halleck asked McClellan to order Buell to attack or at least threaten Bowling Green. At the very least, Buell's demonstration would force the Confederates to abandon that city. Halleck's telegram contained a message that would endure for several weeks. "If you agree with me," he wrote McClellan, "send me everything you can spare from General Buell's command or elsewhere."[7]

McClellan's congratulations that evening, besides saying that Halleck's operations had caused the "utmost satisfaction" in Washington, included a suggestion that Buell take the line of Tennessee and operate on Nashville while Halleck turned toward Columbus. To Buell he penned the same thing. McClellan was not thinking of reducing forces in Kentucky to strengthen Halleck's campaign. There was still East Tennessee to think about.[8]

The same day the Union flag was raised at Fort Henry, Buell congratulated Halleck on his success, though he was still miffed at not being consulted in a victory within his own department. In light of Halleck's success, his tone toward Buell now modified a bit, and he claimed he regretted not informing Buell of Grant's departure earlier. He had "not abandoned caution for idle cause," nor had he intended to disregard Buell's operations or his feelings. It was McClellan's telegram about Beauregard's arrival that spurred him into action. "Although not ready," he wrote, "I deemed it important to move instantly." Now he wanted Buell to help him in completing what he had started. "The enemy has the railroads, and we must use the rivers," he wrote.[9]

Buell was not biting, however. After returning to his headquarters that evening, he wrote with exasperation to McClellan: "I cannot, on reflection, think a change of my line would be advisable." He hoped Grant would not require further reinforcements, but he was willing to go if necessary. The following morning he wrote McClellan that he was concentrating and preparing but would not "decide definitely yet," though it was not exactly clear what Buell was supposed to decide.[10]

Two days after the fall of Fort Henry, February 8, the same day Grant informed Halleck that he would take Fort Donelson, Halleck wrote McClellan hoping for answers that might give him the authority he desired. If McClellan wanted Buell to come to the Cumberland River to take command of the expedition on that river to Nashville, it would present some problems. Halleck had intended to use William T. Sherman in that capacity, and since Sherman outranked Buell, he proposed an idea that would produce unity of command.

"Create a geographical line," he recommended, "to be called Western Division . . . [and] composed of three departments." These included the Department of the Missouri, composed of the present Department of Kansas and the states of Minnesota, Iowa, Missouri, and Arkansas, which he would give to Gen. David Hunter, and the Department of the Mississippi, including the remainder of the present Department of the Missouri and West Tennessee, which he would give to Ethan Allen Hitchcock, a retired old regular army officer living in St. Louis, provided Hitchcock's health had improved enough to be appointed as Halleck had requested, or Sherman, whose health, he added, had "greatly improved." The Western Division would also include the Department of the Ohio, to be the same as at present with the addition of East Tennessee, which Buell would command. "This would avoid any clashing of interests or difference of plans and policy," he concluded. Of course all of these commands would be under one general head, and Halleck held out that position for himself, though modestly confessing that he had no desire for any larger command than his current one.[11]

McClellan would have none of it, but this did not stop Halleck from continuing his barrage of telegrams to McClellan asking for assistance from Buell to move on the Cumberland or Tennessee. "Give us the means," he argued, "and we are certain to give the enemy a telling blow." He also wrote Stanton that since Buell was "stuck fast in the mud" and would be for several weeks, why not send him to command a column on the Cumberland? Halleck pleaded for McClellan to send men, emphasizing that his expedition would succeed, "*if they will give me the forces which are now useless elsewhere.*"[12] For a commander who had just been greatly relieved to hear of the success at Fort Henry, it seemed strange that now he was willing to stake his reputation on his ability to win the war if Buell consented to come to the Cumberland.

The War Department, however, continued to think that Buell's plan was the most likely to succeed and that as a commander of a major offensive operation, Buell seemed less likely than Halleck to panic in the face of a crisis. Besides, Halleck's plan, assistant war secretary Scott thought, was merely a scheme to discredit Buell.[13]

Buell had been preparing either to come on the line of the Cumberland or Tennessee and reinforce Grant, who was moving toward Fort Donelson, or to move on Bowling Green. He started Mitchel's division along the railroad for the long-awaited march south toward Bowling Green on February 10. By February 13 his division had progressed unopposed beyond Dripping Springs to Bell's Tavern, where Mitchel was informed that Bowling Green had been evacuated. To the rest of the Army of the Ohio, Buell sent orders to be ready. He directed Thomas's First Division back to Lebanon as promptly as possible: "I may want you immediately."[14] He also shifted Wood's Sixth Division from Lebanon to Bacon Creek. In addition, he ordered Crittenden's Fifth Division to Smithland and Nelson's Fourth Division to come under Halleck's command at Smithland. Capt. Alexis Cope of McCook's Second Division, stationed at Bacon Creek repairing the bridge over the Green River, recalled that Buell's orders gave the impression "that we were marching to meet some emergency and that it was necessary to get to our destination as soon as possible."[15]

Buell was still waiting to see what developed on the Tennessee, particularly since Fort Donelson had yet to fall as Halleck had expected. Though his gut feeling was against it, Buell said he was willing to move on the line of the Cumberland River or the Tennessee River; but it would take time, and he needed something concrete from Halleck about when and where their forces would unite. Moreover, McClellan, not Buell, would have to effect such a move, and McClellan was not altogether sure that Halleck's forecast for the fall of Fort Donelson was accurate. Grant's forces had taken more time than Halleck had expected in getting to Fort Donelson. Thus, McClellan wanted Buell to watch the developing situation carefully. Buell was unsure, too, and he queried Halleck to make sure Old Brains knew what he was doing.[16]

Halleck apparently knew what he was doing. On February 13 he wired Buell that the joint land and naval attack would be made on Fort Donelson either that evening or the following day. His urgency, then, to have Buell assist was easily explained. He urged Buell to come and take immediate command of the Cumberland column. He also asked McClellan if he could spare some troops from the Department of the Potomac.[17]

As reinforcements from David Hunter's army began to show up to aid Grant, swelling his total forces to around 25,000, Buell thought the real urgency was not to aid Halleck so much as it was to watch the enemy to see if they were going to make a stand at Fort Donelson or Bowling Green or would abandon both places to concentrate at Clarksville or Nashville. Whatever the case, Nashville was still the primary target for Buell, and McClellan wanted to keep it that way.[18]

It soon became clear to Halleck that he would get no satisfaction from either McClellan or Buell regarding the reinforcement of the Cumberland line. With the news that Bowling Green was completely evacuated, Buell informed Halleck that although he had made arrangements to operate up the Cumberland to Nashville, the evacuation "makes it proper to resume my original line on Nashville."[19] Buell had the same day ordered General Nelson's division at Elizabethtown to embark for the Cumberland in case Grant needed him, but he would not hesitate to recall him if Grant was not in danger. He also wrote to McClellan detailing his intentions and describing the disposition of his troops for striking at Nashville, but he complained that "armies with the appliances which are necessary to make them successful cannot move over dirt roads in the winter with quite as much facility as a man takes the cars at Washington and goes to Baltimore."[20] The general in chief supported him fully: "The movement on Nashville is exactly right."[21]

After briefly pondering what was exactly right and wrong about the Buell-McClellan proposed movement on Nashville, Halleck concluded that it was just plain "bad strategy." Though early in the day on February 15 he boasted that the "siege and bombardment of Fort Donelson" were "progressing satisfactorily," by late afternoon it became a military necessity that he have more troops, since the rivers were apparently the only way to get to Nashville. By eight o'clock that night he had received Buell's plan to head toward Nashville, and as McClellan was the master strategist, Halleck decided to air his opinion to him.

Halleck argued that a combined Buell-Halleck operation on the rivers could easily take Clarksville, where the Confederates were concentrating. From there they could move on Florence, Alabama, cutting the railroad at Decatur. This would force the Confederates to abandon Nashville. "Give me the forces required," he bragged, "and I will insure complete success."[22] The same day he wrote Buell an almost identical telegram that began, "To move from Bowling Green to Nashville is not good strategy," and ended, "Come and help me, and all will be right."[23]

If Buell was offended by Halleck's lecture on what was and was not good strategy, he never let on to Halleck that it ruffled him. He merely vented his frustrations to McClellan. Halleck's confidence was impressive, though Assistant Secretary Scott had reservations about his motives. What he had earlier suggested to Stanton, he now confidentially wrote: "There is evidently a little desire on the part of General H. to out General B."[24]

Apparently Halleck cared little about offending the general in chief of the armies, since he was informing McClellan, who fully agreed with Buell's strategy, that it was wrong. Moreover, his boasting that he could ensure complete success if things were done his way smacked of pure egotism, since it looked as though he was saying that McClellan and Buell were obstacles toward bringing about complete success in the West. McClellan responded late that same evening that Buell's advance on Nashville via the railroad was not bad strategy. In fact, he thought capturing Nashville was vitally important. To make sure Halleck knew who was running the war, he concluded that the "Decatur movement and one on Memphis are the next steps in my programme." He closed by recommending that Halleck make himself available at the telegraph office, as Buell had been expected to do, to "come to a full understanding" about the direction of the war in the West.[25]

On February 16, though the real war was being waged at Fort Donelson, the Union command continued waging war over strategy. Halleck stepped up his criticism of the advance on Nashville. He confidently concluded to McClellan that "we shall regret it." "Think of it before you approve," he contested. "Fort Donelson and Clarksville are the keypoints. Since the evacuation of Bowling Green, the importance of Nashville has ceased." "Fort Donelson is the turning point of the war," he argued, "and we must take it at whatever sacrifice."[26] Buell and McClellan, however, continued to think that Halleck's operation was mainly a diversion to the capture of Nashville, and so did the Confederates.[27]

Neither Buell nor McClellan was willing to let a sure capture of Bowling Green and Nashville disappear simply because Halleck thought it was bad strategy. In fact, McClellan wrote to Stanton, who needed some encouragement, the same day: "We have a brilliant chance to bag Nashville."[28] Perhaps sensing that his official Executive Mansion letterhead was needed to emphasize to Halleck the importance of Nashville to Union interests, the president urged "full co-operation" between Buell and him. But apparently what was lacking with regard to the move on Nashville was Halleck's spirit, or at least Lincoln thought so. He begged Halleck to "put your soul in the effort."[29]

Halleck had certainly not put his heart into acting in concert with Buell. He had kept Buell in the dark regarding Grant's exact whereabouts and troop strength, and though Buell had already consented to send Halleck Nelson's 10,000-man division, he needed more precise information regarding Grant's actions at Fort Donelson before he committed more resources. He knew from Lincoln and McClellan that Fort Donelson was about to fall, but he needed to hear fully from Halleck. It appeared as though Halleck's lack of communication with Buell was his way not only of limiting Buell's interference with Grant's objectives but also of taking his frustration out over Buell's movement to Nashville. Whatever the case, Halleck still refused to put Grant in communication with Buell, even though Grant continued to operate in the latter's department.[30]

Albert Sidney Johnston knew exactly where General Grant was on February 16. He was at Fort Donelson wreaking havoc on the Cumberland River stronghold. Though it had taken him longer to organize the march from Fort Henry to Fort Donelson, Grant had finally gotten his army there by February 12. Over the next four days he managed to repeat what had occurred at Fort Henry. His capture of Fort Donelson was considered, thus far, the greatest victory of the war. The telegraph wires that had been hot with communications between departmental commanders orchestrating war for the past two weeks suddenly were transmitting the victorious news from an obscure general: "We have taken Fort Donelson" and with it "from 12,000 to 15,000 prisoners, including Generals Buckner and Bushrod [R.] Johnson."[31]

The news sent Confederates in Kentucky and Tennessee into a panic. George W. Johnson, Kentucky's Confederate governor, wrote his wife that "the time of our severest afflictions has now come—our state is about to be abandoned by our armies."[32] Indeed it was. Johnston had ordered Gen. William J. Hardee's 17,000 troops from Bowling Green to Nashville, which had paved the way for Buell's army to move into the city. As the remnants of Hardee's Confederates, reduced by sickness during the icy retreat from Bowling Green, plodded into the Tennessee capital, they frightened the people with news of Buell's savage troops closing fast upon their rear. Panic descended on the city as the war abruptly came upon its residents.[33]

Halleck was elated at the news of Fort Donelson, and though still urging McClellan to order Buell to move on Clarksville via the Cumberland River instead of Nashville via rail, he parlayed his recent successes into more command for himself. "Make Buell, Grant, and [John] Pope major-generals of volunteers," he wrote on the afternoon of the seventeenth and, as if to make himself the sole architect of the victories, added, "and give me command in the West. I ask this in return for Forts Henry and Donelson."[34] This statement was an odd one for a commander who earlier in the day, before learning of Grant's success, had written to McClellan that what was happening at Fort Donelson was "the crisis of the war in the West," and that he was "certainly in peril."[35]

McClellan would have none of it. If anyone were to command the western armies, McClellan would have Buell, not Halleck. Buell was already heading for the great prize in the West. By February 14 Mitchel's division had filed through Munfordville, where McCook's division was repairing the Green River bridge, and had moved into Bowling Green. Mitchel had hoped to get to the city before the Confederates burned the Big Barren River railroad bridge, but he was too late. Upon his arrival he found the city evacuated, and signs of a hasty retreat were everywhere; fortifications were empty and ablaze, and the bridge was destroyed. Through his field glasses Mitchel could see the Confederates in the distance as they marched south to join Johnston at Nashville. As one Ohio captain wrote his wife, Bowling Green, or the "Gibraltar of the Southern Confederacy," as he called it, was "a city Confederates had," all along, "claimed that all the Lincoln forces combined could not take."[36] Yet, the city fell without a shot.

Because of his continued disagreement with Halleck, Buell decided to recall Nelson's division, which he had already ordered to Halleck. If reinforcements were to go anywhere, they should come to support Buell, since the Confederates would no doubt throw soldiers from all quarters east and south to defend Nashville. Ignoring the requests of Halleck, Buell suggested that he and Old Brains meet at Smithland and visit Grant to study the situation and work things out personally.[37]

Halleck only continued to press the Ohioan, informing him that he had asked the president to make Buell a major general to remove all questions of rank. "The battle of the West is to be fought in that vicinity," wrote Halleck. He pleaded, "Don't hesitate. Come to Clarksville as rapidly as possible. Say that you will come, and I will have everything there for you." "Help me and I will help you," begged Halleck. "We came within an ace of being defeated," he told the hesitant Buell. Had it not been for the help of Hunter's reinforcements during the Fort Donelson crisis, Grant would surely have been defeated. His words of desperation continued: "It is evident to me that you and McClellan did not at last accounts appreciate the strait I have been in." "Don't stop anyone ordered here," he demanded, "Help me, I beg of you. . . . You will not regret it. There will be no battle at Nashville."[38]

Though Grant had just captured two Confederate forts and about 15,000 men and overwhelming supplies, for Halleck it was a feat that was as worrisome as it was impressive. His panic about the Confederates concentrating at Clarksville, however, appeared to be unwarranted. To convince him that there would be action at Nashville, not Clarksville, Buell sent Halleck General Mitchel's report from Bowling Green that the Confederates were falling back from Clarksville and were concentrating a heavy force at Nashville. In the meantime, Secretary Scott, who had been to St. Louis, where Halleck filled his ears with the problems of Buell's plan, had returned to Buell's headquarters to explain Halleck's views. On the day he arrived in Louisville, February 19, Scott reviewed the messages from Bowling Green, as well as those from the commander's informant, John Lellyett, and concluded that Buell, not Halleck, needed reinforcements. He wired McClellan to get them moving.[39]

Not surprisingly, Halleck remained unconvinced that Buell needed more troops. On the same day that Scott arrived in Louisville, Halleck sent no less than a half-dozen telegrams urging Buell to order his troops back to him. Buell, however, had stopped Nelson's division at Smithland and ordered him to return. This information exasperated Halleck, who wired Stanton, asking him to intervene on his behalf. Though Stanton disliked Halleck, he liked Buell and McClellan even less and, consequently, was willing to support Halleck in conflicts with Buell. Thus, Stanton countermanded Buell's order halting Nelson. Buell was miffed, as was McClellan, since Halleck went around them both to get what he wanted. Still, Halleck's fear apparently moved Buell. He decided that simply to relieve the panic-stricken commander he would cooperate a little. He asked Halleck to specify his needs. Halleck responded that he thought it best that Buell move on Clarksville from Bowling Green and then continue up the Cumberland to Nashville. Buell, of course, disagreed.[40]

Halleck continued to ask McClellan for command of the West, a move that he said would enable him to "split secession in twain in one month." On the evening of February 20, he wrote, "I must have command of the armies in the West. Hesitation and delay are losing us the golden opportunity. Lay this before the President and Secretary of War. May I assume the command?"[41] Complaining that Buell "acted like a dog in the manger," he even went so far as to ask Scott, who was still in Louisville, to assume the responsibility of ordering Buell to accommodate Halleck's desires.[42] But he waited in vain. As diplomatically as he could, McClellan responded that Buell at Bowling Green knew more of the situation than Halleck at St. Louis. Moreover, his mind had been made up; Nashville was the key. He would wait to hear from Buell before laying Halleck's request for overall command before Lincoln, who was emotionally distraught because of his son's illness, or before Stanton, who was recovering from a mild stroke.[43]

Clarksville fell on February 20. Halleck's panic now seemed unnecessary, and his incessant demands were all the more annoying to McClellan. Buell entered Bowling Green the same day, and McClellan added an inducement for him to capture the Tennessee capital: "Have your commission as Major General on the field of battle in taking Nashville."[44]

Halleck's complaints about Buell's noncompliance with his requests reflected his animosity for both McClellan and Buell. Had Buell cooperated more swiftly and fully when asked, griped Halleck, Columbus and Nashville would now be flying the Union flag. The Confederates obviously had made a mistake and "lost the golden opportunity" when they had not fallen back from Bowling Green to Clarksville, where they could have driven Grant out of Fort Donelson as Halleck had contemplated. Cooperation from Buell would force the enemy to surrender Columbus and Nashville. To effect quick cooperation from Buell, and win Stanton's favor again, Halleck wrote the secretary of war that he must control Buell's army. "Give me authority," he demanded, "and I will be responsible."[45]

The western theater of the war never left Stanton's mind and for good reason—Halleck never let up. Halleck's confidence and ambition impressed Stanton, and the evacuation of Bowling Green appeared to vindicate his strategy. Conversely, Buell's lack of vigor disturbed the secretary of war. He confessed to Scott, "As soon as General Buell fights a battle or makes any decisive movement with the large force under his command, I will be glad to recommend him for major general."[46] More irritating was Buell's lack of direct communication. Stanton complained to Scott that Buell "communicates nothing to the department, nor even acknowledges communications made to him, by me, the department knows nothing of his operations except what appears from the newspaper."[47]

Stanton's accusations were not exactly true, but his irritation was nonetheless real. Buell, following the military chain of command, corresponded frequently with McClellan, his immediate superior, who passed along the information to Stanton. Besides, during much of February Scott had been in Louisville discussing at length strategy in the West and had sent almost daily letters to Stanton of these discussions. But Buell continued to trust only McClellan, which increasingly put him at odds with the secretary of war. By remaining more loyal to McClellan and less flexible in his thinking, Buell rubbed an already impatient Stanton the wrong way. The friendship between McClellan and Buell, which had earlier appeared to work in Buell's favor regarding East Tennessee and his insistence on advancing to Nashville, was now beginning to work against him, since Stanton was convinced the two commanders shared a like attitude about strategy and remained inflexible in considering the wishes of either the administration or other commanders. Stanton was also beginning to show contempt for Buell's dilatory behavior. He had hoped McClellan would change his mind about sending Buell to Nashville and instead send him to aid Halleck, but McClellan continued to defend Buell's strategy.

As much as Stanton and perhaps Lincoln may have wanted to give Buell overall command, neither was willing to consent to his wishes, nor did they think it advisable to change the departmental organization. Whatever strategic problems existed, they believed full and zealous cooperation between the commanders could overcome them.[48] Besides, Buell had accomplished nothing to compare with Halleck's Donelson victory.

By February 22 the Army of the Ohio was marching on Nashville to do what Buell and McClellan wanted—force the city to surrender. But these had been monotonous weeks, even before the fall of Bowling Green. Col. Benjamin F. Scribner of the Thirty-eighth Indiana remembered that for the soldiers "the winter was a severe one."[49] Sickness, in the form of typhoid and measles, had pervaded the Army of the Ohio. Hit with rainy, "biting cold" weather and repetitious drilling, the soldiers remained, as Gen. Ormsby Mitchel put it, "mud-bound," waiting for something to happen. George H. Thomas confessed to Buell as he approached Bardstown, "It rained as I never saw it rain before."[50] The military inertia caused a frustrated Mitchel to complain in early February, "It rains, then it snows a little, then it freezes a little, then thaws a good deal, and finally everything on the surface of the ground seems liquid earth, and our cavalry horses have the scratches to such a degree that half of them are this day unfit for service. All this from being compelled to remain in the same spot."[51]

Remaining in the same spot caused Ohio surgeon Henry H. Seys to complain to his wife in late January that camp life was so dull that his fellow officers passed the time arguing over how many weeks they had spent in camp. The arguments stemmed from the fact that it was "almost impossible to tell one day from another."[52] Charles Briant of the Sixth Indiana recalled that he passed the "long, dreary winter evenings" with "nothing to read, nothing to do."[53] During these monotonous days of inactivity about the most excitement many of the soldiers had was pitching the new Sibley tent, which greatly reduced overcrowding and disease, or getting new Springfield and Enfield rifled muskets.[54]

During these indistinguishable days of hardship, the army grew in quality and continued to perfect the regimental and brigade drills prescribed by Buell. One newspaper correspondent declared that Buell "leads as great an army in the West as McClellan does in the East."[55] The problem was, however, that neither army had been led anywhere. What seemed like an endless advance to Nashville not only tested the ability of the men to sustain a long continuous march but also their confidence in their commander. Writing from Elizabethtown in February, Illinois captain R. Delavan Mussey commented to a friend, "We have, all of us, large confidence in Buell." And while he thought the soldiers would see no fighting, he recalled the blind British writer John Milton's famous line: "They also serve who [only] stand and wait."[56]

The men of McCook's division were among those who stood, watched, and waited. These were trying times for officers and soldiers, and many grew discouraged. Colonel Scribner recalled that many soldiers in McCook's division were "utterly disheartened" and that "complaints, mutterings and even threats prevailed." Times were particularly discouraging for these men because they had spent weeks at Munfordville repairing the railroad bridge over the Green River and, "weary of the monotony of camp life, . . . had longed for marching orders," only to watch Mitchel's Third Division pass over the bridge first on its way toward Bowling Green and Nashville on February 13.[57]

Even a trained army had difficulty moving from place to place in winter weather, particularly if it had not experienced a long march. The journey to Nashville was the army's first major advance of any distance, and numerous problems plagued the army inexperienced with enduring such treks. In the seemingly endless and bottomless muddy roads, wagons continually got stuck. To complicate matters, Samuel Thomas Davis of the Seventy-seventh Pennsylvania pointed out in his diary that "carcasses of mules and horses had been thrown into the various ponds along the route in order to render the water unfit to drink."[58] Thus, the experience taught commanders and soldiers alike that the only way to perfect the march was to march, and the more the better. These problems, however, seemed particularly odd for an army that had been training during this stationary time.[59]

Buell himself was with Mitchel's lead division about thirty-seven miles from Nashville when reports arrived that the Confederates were evacuating the city and making a stand at Murfreesboro. McCook's division followed Mitchel's for a total of 25,000 men making their way to Nashville. Wood's Sixth Division was ordered forward, as were Jeremiah Boyle's and Sanders Bruce's brigades. Thomas's division was heading to Louisville to travel down the Ohio River and then up the Cumberland. Nelson's Fourth Division had made it to Paducah and had begrudgingly come under the command of William T. Sherman. Nelson was furious because he had his sights set on taking Nashville before Buell reached the city. As he sat in Paducah for two days awaiting orders, his impatience grew. General Crittenden's division had been detained at Calhoun just below Owensborough by Buell's orders to hold the Lower Green River. For the capture of Nashville, Buell had drawn on the resources of his entire department, an army of about 50,000 fighting men. In addition, he called on Halleck to move up the Cumberland with his gunboats, and he sent some transports to Louisville to pick up Thomas's division, which was due to arrive any day.[60]

Now it was Halleck's turn to be uncooperative. If Nashville was going to fall anyway, Buell would not need his help, particularly since Buell, realizing that Fort Donelson was about to fall, had refused to aid Halleck. To James B. Fry, Buell's chief of staff, Halleck said that he could not understand "how you want boats sent to Louisville to transport troops up the Cumberland. We have no transports to spare. On the contrary, I have asked Assistant Secretary Scott to send down all he can spare."[61] Frustrated, Halleck wrote to Stanton that "if it is thought that the present arrangement is best for public service, I have nothing to say."[62] But he did.

Getting no cooperation from Halleck, Buell had Fry use McClellan's

James B. Fry, Buell's chief of staff during his tenure in command of the Army of the Ohio. Fry was a West Pointer and veteran of the Mexican War. In 1863 Fry was appointed provost marshal general for the Union. After the war he became one of Buell's supporters. (Courtesy of the U.S. Army Military History Institute, Carlisle, Pa.)

authority. The general in chief was being pulled from all directions, particularly since Lincoln had not let up on East Tennessee. While McClellan confirmed to Buell that he would have Halleck "give you all the aid in his power in our operations on Nashville," he closed his support saying, "We must not lose sight of Eastern Tennessee."[63] McClellan did not want Buell to abandon totally the East Tennessee offensive, particularly since action in that vicinity would aid McClellan in the campaign on which he was preparing to embark. He boasted that "if the force in the West can take Nashville or even hold its own for the present I hope to have Richmond and Norfolk in from three to four weeks."[64] Thus, he asked Buell on the afternoon of February 25, "Cannot Garfield reach the Virginia and Tennessee Railway near Abingdon [in southwest Virginia]?"[65] Garfield's situation at Piketon along the Big Sandy River, however, was desperate. The river was cresting at nearly sixty feet, the highest flood waters in over thirty-five years, trapping Garfield's brigade. Under the circumstances Buell remained content with leaving Garfield alone, particularly since eastern Kentucky had been cleared of Confederates and loyalty appeared on the rise.[66]

McClellan also pressed Halleck to support Buell's imminent capture of Nashville. Halleck begrudgingly sent General Smith at Clarksville with five regiments to join Buell, and once the Federals occupied the city and Buell felt secure, Buell returned them.[67]

Sunday, February 23, precisely one week after the fall of Donelson, Mitchel's advance guard under Col. John Kennett reached Edgefield, on the side of the Cumberland River opposite Nashville. It was a beautiful springlike day in Nashville, belying the miserable week of almost continuous rain, apprehension, and panic that had ensued when Fort Donelson fell. Those disheartened residents who had not fled the city gathered along the river to watch the anticipated arrival of the Union troops. In the absence of a bridge, which the Confederates had destroyed, and with no orders from Buell, the detachment from Kennett's cavalry did not cross the river. Fearing the troops might be preparing to open fire on the city with long-range guns, the anxious residents urged Mayor Richard B. Cheatham to get in a rowboat, cross the river, and deliver the city to the Federals to save it. Surprised to find only a squad of cavalry and no guns, Cheatham persuaded the Ohio captain in charge not to attack the city. Buell arrived on the night of February 24 with the remainder of Mitchel's division, but he did not intend to cross the river until he could do so with a sufficient force "to run no great hazard." Even in his triumph, he remained distressingly cautious.[68]

Tuesday was a "bright, glorious day," according to a soldier in the Sixth

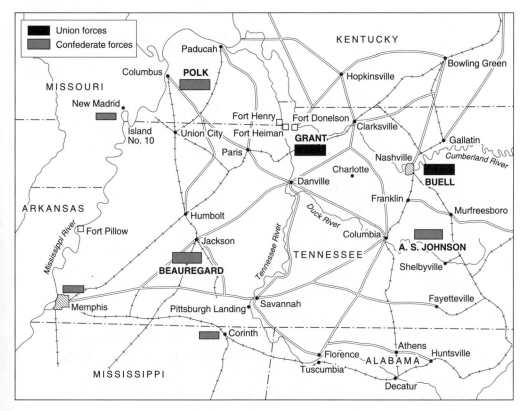

The situation in the West in February 1862

Ohio aboard the *Diana*, headquarters for Nelson's division. Just before
9:00 A.M. the steamer approached the wharf at Nashville, and "hundreds
of eager eyes from the decks . . . were straining to catch the first glimpse
of the distant city."[69] A crowd had assembled to see the troops land, and
northern and southern eyes gazed upon each other. It was a proud day
for Nelson, who at the head of his soldiers marched ashore to the "in-
spiriting strains of Dixie from the drums and fifes of its field music."[70]

Nelson's troops were the first actually to set foot in Nashville, and
soon after, Old Glory was hoisted above the Tennessee capital. Shortly
before 11 A.M. the mayor and a committee of citizens called on Col.
Jacob Ammen, commander of the Tenth Brigade of Nelson's division,
for a pass to enable them to speak with Buell and ask for terms of surrender. They were granted permission. There were no violent demonstrations, and though Buell wrote that the mass of Nashvillians "appear
to look upon us as invaders," he had seen "several strong indications of
loyalty in individuals." Buell's terms were generous, and according to

Secretary Scott, who accompanied him, the interview was "entirely satisfactory to all parties." To Stanton he wrote of the outstanding news, "Nashville was taken possession of to-day."[71] Soon after the conference, Buell and his staff crossed the river and established headquarters initially in the St. Cloud Hotel. Nashville was occupied.[72]

Buell was given the city before he even set foot in it, and consequently he was the butt of criticism. The *New York Daily Tribune* charged that Buell should have moved simultaneously with Grant, and that because he had not, he had allowed the Confederates, first at Bowling Green and then at Nashville, to evacuate the city uncontested. Though it could be argued that the *Tribune* was unduly harsh on Buell, particularly in light of all that had been achieved, this could not be dismissed as merely criticism of unreasonable expectations. The editor's tone reflected the frustration that the capture of Nashville had not resulted in the capture of the army defending it. True to Jominian doctrine, however, Buell considered the occupation of places more important than defeating armies.[73]

In a display of bold independence, Grant, who had yet to communicate with Buell but who was anxious to meet him, came to Nashville early on February 27, without Halleck's permission, to meet Buell and convince him that he was in no danger. Both Grant and Foote had wanted to move from Clarksville further upstream, but Halleck had kept them at Clarksville. Instead of finding Buell during the day, Grant found New York journalist Henry Villard, anxious to do a story on old "Unconditional Surrender." Grant stayed in the city only a few hours, but long enough to see the city and pay his respects to the widow of ex-president James K. Polk.[74]

When Grant returned to the wharf, he met Buell. Grant was unconvinced that the Confederates posed a serious threat and in a brief but crisp conversation told Buell that, based on his information, the enemy was demoralized and retreating. Buell argued back that perhaps Johnston meant to return, particularly since there was fighting just ten miles southeast of Nashville. Grant responded sharply, "Quite probably; Nashville contained valuable stores, of arms, ammunition, and provisions, and the enemy is probably trying to carry away all they can." "The fighting," added Grant, "is doubtless with the rear guard who are trying to protect the trains they are getting away with." Buell disagreed and continued to think Nashville was in danger, saying that he "knew" this to be the case. "Well," remarked Grant, "I do not know; but as I came by Clarksville General Smith's troops were embarking to join you."[75] In a brief few minutes at the wharf, Buell and Grant had managed to offend each other at a time when both needed friends.

Buell wrote to Halleck of his good fortune in possessing the "Gibraltar of the South," but added that the Confederates were just thirty miles distant, in greatly superior numbers. His estimate of the Confederates just a few hours' march away revealed that Buell, like Halleck, remained overly cautious. Buell had pressed his army to get to Nashville, but he arrived with only 18,000 soldiers. Until the remainder of his army showed up over the next ten days, Johnston's 30,000 Confederates made him anxious. The capture of Nashville was one task; holding on to it was quite another. He sent a communiqué to General Smith the same day warning that if the enemy should assume the offensive, his force was inadequate. Smith thought Buell's apprehension bordered on the ridiculous, but as ordered, he proceeded to Nashville against Halleck's wishes. Buell sent Smith back to Clarksville as soon as the rest of the Army of the Ohio trickled into Nashville.[76]

Even if Halleck was unconvinced about Buell being in danger, he nonetheless acquiesced to Buell's wishes, and the two gunboats on the Cumberland at Clarksville proceeded with what remained of Thomas's division upriver to Nashville. Halleck also agreed to send General Crittenden's division back to Buell as well. The remaining divisions of the Army of the Ohio arrived by water or were ferried across the river by Nelson's steamers over the course of the next week and a half.[77]

The size of Buell's force mirrored the importance of Nashville. The city was one of the largest and most important in the Confederacy and, as one recently arrived Union soldier put it, was simply "a very fine city."[78] About 17,000 inhabitants resided in the Tennessee capital, and according to Henry Villard, who accompanied Nelson's division there, Nashville "impressed me more as that of a Northern than of a Southern city."[79] The Tennessee capital was the nexus of important rail and water connections. River traffic flowed north to Cincinnati and Cairo and south to the heart of the Confederacy. Railroads extended north to Louisville, south to Decatur, and east to Chattanooga, Knoxville, Atlanta, and beyond.[80]

Nashville's location was only partly the reason it was a great prize. In the midst of a wartime boom, the city enjoyed tremendous economic benefits. Its factories produced military ordnance, munitions, and supplies ranging from saddles and sabres to belts and uniform cloth. All Kentucky now seemed safe in Union hands, the Mississippi was open as far as Island No. 10 on the Kentucky-Tennessee border, and strong Union forces stood in central Tennessee.[81]

Nashville (*Harper's Weekly*; photograph courtesy of Harpweek)

In truth, Buell had been given the city; he had not taken it. In fact, Foote believed his naval forces had been purposely retained at Clarksville in order to let Buell's army descend on the city first. After sending the rest of Buell's forces up the river, however, Halleck retained the remaining gunboats, since he believed Buell's army was sufficient to hold Nashville once there, or if not, Grant, Foote, and Smith would be in a position to come to Buell's rescue. Grant had found the success at Fort Donelson a personal triumph, but Buell found the capture of Nashville a hollow victory. He had wanted the city since he arrived in the West, and now he had it. The operations of Foote and Grant had made possible the capture of Bowling Green and Nashville, and Buell knew it. Halleck, however, claimed to be the master strategist of both, and this certainly rubbed Buell raw, even if he never revealed it. Johnston's army had fallen back to the Tennessee River and, according to reports, was concentrating about thirty miles away at Murfreesboro, though it was expected to relocate at Chattanooga. With spring fast approaching and Union morale restored, Johnston knew the Union would try to capitalize on its recent victories and continue to press deeper into the heartland. As Grant predicted to his wife, Julia, a week after the Donelson victory, "Sesech is now about on its last legs in Tennessee. I want to push on as rapidly as possible to save hard fighting."[82]

February 1862 proved a banner month for the Union. The effect of the twin-river campaign and the capture of Nashville was inspiring, since it made politicians and the critical public forget about the debacle at First Bull Run. The use of the river for military purposes proved that the key to winning the war in the West resided in the experience of warring as much as theory and reason. This meant that Buell would have to overcome his extreme cautiousness and uneasiness about going on the offensive and actually engage in war to learn from it. He would have to use his army not simply to maneuver, but to fight.

In a long winter cast with shadows of military inertia and frustration, the three outstanding victories helped Lincoln put the bottom back in the tub. Washington had not expected success from the West, particularly such stunning success. Buell had been stubborn, and Halleck even more so. Few people, in Washington or in the West, could understand how Grant, an obscure officer commanding a small undisciplined army, had achieved such success over Johnston's Confederates, while McClellan's well-equipped and well-trained Army of the Potomac remained idle. Though Halleck had earlier predicted dismal odds for any operation on exterior lines against an enemy occupying a central position, Grant apparently banked on the one time out of a hundred that the operation might succeed. Thus, while to both Union and Confederate officials the capture of Nashville might have appeared more significant than the fall of the river forts, the laurels in Tennessee that McClellan expected Buell to claim by capturing Knoxville were claimed by Grant, who despite his poor relationship with Halleck, had proven successful. Like Thomas after Mill Springs, Grant was promoted, but to major general. Halleck, meanwhile breathed a sigh of relief and would shortly be named overall commander in the West. Buell had what he wanted. It was McClellan who obviously wanted more for Buell than Buell wanted for himself.[83]

CHAPTER TWELVE

Nashville Occupied

The capture of Nashville proved to be for Buell and Lincoln a curse as well as a blessing, since it accentuated the perils of civil-military problems. The conflicting views of civil and military authorities over what was the true political intent of the war and how the political policy of the government could be carried out by the government's armies became more acute as a result of the Union's victory. In the first year of the war Lincoln never doubted that the aim of the conflict was to preserve the Union, and that his initial reconstruction efforts would merely be an attempt to reintegrate the southern states back into their proper relation with the Union. Thus, what he sought to gain with reconstruction guided the process of how the war should be waged. Lincoln wanted so desperately to restore civil government in the seceded states rapidly, rather than force southerners into submission, that he was willing to carry out his reconstruction efforts at the first chance of an occupied region or city.[1]

Lincoln's attitude reflected the beliefs of Federal policymakers at the outbreak of the war. Motivated by the assumption that secession was an elitist-led conspiracy, the Union adopted a conservative conciliatory policy. That a large portion of southerners were loyal Unionists tyrannized and silenced by the rebel oppressors held wide currency in the North. The North viewed Federal armies as agents of freedom for these loyalists subjugated to tyranny. Any attempt by the Union army to punish southerners or interfere with their social institutions would serve to jeopardize the lives of southern Unionists and alienate others. These intentions and assumptions had created the basis for the Union's policy of conciliation. By late February, however, the war was almost a year old, and attitudes had changed.[2]

Though Lincoln would have greatly preferred to have extended the privileges and guarantees of the Union government to the staunchly loyal mountaineers of East Tennessee, he was, by what one historian has called "an accident of war," presented with the opportunity to allow the citizens of Nashville and Middle Tennessee to begin participating in civil processes. The president was apparently convinced that even in a region where slavery and Confederate sentiment were deeply entrenched, the latent unionism of Middle Tennesseans would surface if only allowed the opportunity. Thus, the occupation of Nashville presented larger political considerations for the entire unoccupied and unreconstructed South.[3]

The president's first attempt to implement political reconstruction efforts in Tennessee placed a severe burden on an already strained alliance between civil and military authorities. Even a favorable and productive relationship between politicians and commanders would not have made easy the sheer demands of having to deal with the civilian population, slavery, the local economy, and Confederate property. These issues were the most prominent of the war effort in Tennessee and aggravated and further retarded civil-military relations in the West. They forced politicians and commanders to redefine the political intent of the war, which had, until now, remained subordinate to military concerns.[4]

This turning point caught Buell off guard, and he continued to follow the government's policies conceived when the war was in its infancy. But while the larger implications of Nashville's occupation would be played out over several months at higher levels, Buell faced the immediate task of attempting the state's first reconstruction efforts. The favorable position Buell had initially maintained in Washington as a result of his close relationship with McClellan, Chase, and Stanton waned when McClellan fell out of favor and Buell's slowness came to be viewed in the larger context of commanders unwilling to bend to political considerations. His constant refusal to move into East Tennessee and his lack of aggression and appreciation for the true political intent of the war increasingly hurt him. Now he would be faced with balancing the political and military aspects of war in a region that was simply not favorable for or receptive to Lincoln's reconstruction ideas. Ironically, had Buell seized the East Tennessee region where loyalty ran high, his task at reconstruction might have been made easier.

When the Federal army arrived in Nashville in late February 1862, residents shared mixed emotions about what to expect. Though a considerable number of the citizens fled the city, a majority remained; but under the circumstances they were surely uncomfortable. In West Tennessee Grant had declared martial law, and it was assumed that the same policies would prevail in Middle Tennessee. This alone was alarming. Nashville was almost lifeless when Buell's army arrived, and as James B. Shaw of the Tenth Indiana put it, the city appeared as though "all who could go, had 'skedaddled.' "[5] A correspondent to the St. Louis *Missouri Republican* wrote that Nashville had become "mutilated terribly by war —silent streets, market places empty, stores closed. Ruin appears at every step. . . . Union feeling—there is none, and people do not pretend to show any."[6] Pvt. George Botkin of the Forty-fourth Ohio, however, saw another side of the arrival in Nashville: "We were welcomed by the residents with thanks and tears of joy and gladness."[7] Capt. Thomas J. Wright of the Eighth Kentucky recalled that the slaves who had gathered along the river to witness the day of jubilee "made many demonstrations of joy, clapping their hands, swinging their hands and patting and dancing."[8] Lyman S. Widney, in Nelson's division, recalled that the slaves "hung on the fences along the road in Sunday attire and gazed for the first time upon the Yankees with open-eyed wonder."[9]

Buell was perceptive enough to realize that whatever their sympathies, Nashvillians desperately needed less war and more order. He had convinced Mayor Cheatham that he had no intention to "rob, burn or murder" the people, and to give proof, he pledged safety and protection to the populace "both in their persons and in their property," as well as aid in the enforcement of local police regulations.[10] On February 26, the day after taking the city, Buell issued what became the most controversial orders of his command, General Orders 13a, or his "Roasting-ear Orders," as some called them.[11] Besides congratulating the troops for restoring the "national banner to the capital of Tennessee," Buell took the liberty to remind his troops of the conduct they had observed and were still to pursue. "We are in arms," he declared, "not for the purpose of invading the rights of our fellow-countrymen anywhere, but to maintain the integrity of the Union and protect the Constitution under which its people have been prosperous and happy."[12]

As painfully conscientious as he was, Buell laid out in considerable detail his principles for the occupation of Nashville. No longer would aid to the enemy be viewed with indifference, but only authorized persons could take action against it. Peaceable citizens were not to be molested "in their persons or property," and "any wrongs to either" would be "promptly corrected and the offenders brought to punishment." Moreover, if public service should require the use of private property, "fair compensation" would be allowed. "No such appropriation of private property" was to be made "except by the authority of the highest commander present." Soldiers were "forbidden to enter the residences or grounds of citizens . . . without authority," and no arrests were to be made "without the authority of the commanding general." He reminded his soldiers that the "most frequent depredations" were those committed by "worthless characters, who straggle from the ranks on the plea of being unable to march; and where the inability really exists, it will be found in most instances that the soldier had overloaded himself with useless and unauthorized articles." Buell concluded his general outline by emphasizing that the government provided "with liberality all the wants of the soldier," and those who sought more than what the government provided during this occupation would be placed in positions where they could not "bring shame on their comrades." Of course, officers were not spared from these rules, and anyone who sought to enhance his personal comfort would be "held to a rigid accountability."[13]

Buell sincerely hoped to convince errant southerners that his army was not representative of an allegedly wicked northern society that many in the South feared. Instead, he wanted to prove that his soldiers represented the best of a democracy, which meant they would uphold constitutional guarantees of private citizens in war. General Orders 13a was Buell's attempt to accomplish two important, though quite conflicting, tasks. First, he wanted to ensure that his army would act responsibly in Nashville in conducting an occupation of a southern city. Second, he wanted to maintain an atmosphere that was favorable to regaining the daily functions of life both in business and among the private residents. Neither political nor military authorities, whether in Washington or Nashville, had any experience with military occupations of this nature, and the immediate expectations of the mayor and the larger political expectations of the president handicapped Buell's attempt to restore citizens to the Union. Buell was so concerned over discipline in his army that he could only consider the routine duty and law. He failed to recognize the difference between professional and volunteer soldiers. In an attempt to uphold the rights of private citizens, he detailed Col. Benjamin F. Scribner of the Thirty-eighth Indiana to preside over a board to determine whether the vast quantities of stores in Nashville were private or public property.[14]

Influenced by the words of Governor Isham Harris, before he fled the city, that the Federals were ruthless invaders, cut-throats, and vandals, Buell's conciliation came as reassurance to the townspeople. If Buell had anticipated some backing for the Union, it was not physically evident; few residents welcomed the Yankees, and no flags hung in support. A correspondent for a New York paper wrote, "The people were benumbed, stupefied at the change, as though they hardly yet appreciated the fact that it was Stars and Stripes, instead of the Stars and Bars, that hung from our flag-staff."[15] Whatever Union sentiment there was, the Confederates had overpowered and suppressed it. Whitelaw Reid, correspondent to the *Cincinnati Gazette* writing from Nashville, perceptively warned his readers that before the Union could again claim popular support in Nashville, citizens "must be assured that the power of the nation is re-established throughout the State beyond peradventure." In his own metaphorical way he added some prophetic words regarding the attitude of southerners loyal to the Union, stressing that only when a return of the Confederate army was no longer feasible would the change be permanent: "One swallow doesn't make a summer."[16] The *Memphis Daily Avalanche* was more sarcastic about Buell's policy, saying, "What virtue there is in the favorite appliance of 'soft sawder.' "[17]

Though Buell was optimistic about a change in attitude and encouraged by some loyal demonstrations, he was nonetheless concerned about the president's reconstruction efforts. On February 28 he penned a note to McClellan professing that he had "reason to hope that a great change will take place speedily in the attitude of the Tennesseans, in both the manner of the military and political policy to be observed."[18] Here was the cornerstone of Buell's command. His army was an extension of good Union government, and no sacrifice was too large for his army if it presented a favorable image to the citizens that a well-disciplined army was tangible evidence of the Union's desire to support the civilians' constitutional rights. But Buell was greatly worried about what Washington would do with the fruits of war in Tennessee. He did not want his to become an army of occupation. "As a matter of great importance and delicacy," he warned McClellan, "I would advise you to use all the means you have to induce the President to pursue a lenient course, and as far as possible to reconstruct the machinery of the General Government out of material here. . . . Deference to the recommendations of the most reliable Union people here would be advisable."[19] Still, there is no evidence that McClellan ever discussed Buell's views with Lincoln.

If Lincoln had really wanted to restore civil rights and government to Middle Tennesseans, he would have allowed elections to produce a provisional governor, but he apparently was not convinced a loyal man could be produced, or at least not one acceptable to Congress. Moreover, he had to satisfy the demands of Congress, particularly the Committee on the Conduct of the War, seeking any opportunity to expand the Union's war aims. Thus, he looked to appoint someone from the South who had held office before the war and who remained loyal. He also had East Tennessee loyalists to think about. He had to choose someone from that region or lose their support. Consequently, Lincoln not only had to make a controversial decision to appoint a military governor; he had to decide just who might be a logical and judicious representative. Fortunately the presence of Andrew Johnson in Washington made Lincoln's decision easier.

While much of the nation's attention focused on Nashville, the reappearance of newspapers in the city after a week of suspended publication masked the assumption that normal life had returned to the captured Tennessee capital, since occupational control had yet to be fully tested or defined. One thing was certain, however: Buell was in full control of Nashville, and he thought he was in control of reconstruction as well. Assistant Secretary of War Scott wrote Stanton, "Buell's course has been very prudent and conciliatory which I think the present temper of these people absolutely requires."[20] True to his pledge, and despite the unruliness of most Nashvillians, he allowed county elections to be held on March 1 and ordered the provost marshal's guard to police the city to ensure peaceful procedures. He also pledged to purchase large portions of supplies from that region, provided he could obtain them on terms as reasonable as from other sources. By that time he could breathe a sigh of relief about Albert Sidney Johnston's army, who, Buell reported to Halleck, was preparing to head toward the Tennessee River and either Decatur or Chattanooga. An air of composure descended on Buell, and he began to feel more secure about holding on to Nashville. Gentleman that he was, he called on the widow of former president James K. Polk, was received politely, and visited for an hour.[21]

Buell earned the immediate, though grudging respect of the Tennessee rebels, who had earlier witnessed the undisciplined mobs of Confederate troops fleeing the capital. Pvt. DeWitt Clinton Loudon of the Seventieth Ohio wrote shortly after arriving that the residents were expecting the Yanks to "kill all the men and carry off the women and niggers."[22] Buell, however, not only arrived with a completely disciplined army, but his occupation policy allowed citizens to resume daily life. Margaret L. Lindsley of Nashville wrote to her grandmother in Louisville that Buell had accomplished wonders, saying the general "came in at night, the troops were in perfect discipline, and completely amazed the poor duped people here by their orderly behavior."[23] She added that they had been duped because the "people really believed that the soldiers would not stop till they had *murdered the women and eaten the children*; but when it was seen that they took nothing *without pay*, the people were rejoiced to *sell*, for money of any kind has long been a marvelous sight here." She boasted that the "Federals have interfered with no one whatever, and have behaved much better than the rebel army."[24]

Ellen C. McClung, another resident, wrote to her mother that "Gen. Buell keeps his troops out of the city, & tries to keep them [under] restraints; he has promised to protect private property & so far has done so."[25] Another pleased observer was so impressed that he wrote the War Department in Washington that Buell's men were "truly gentlemen— gentlemen of a high order in all their bearing."[26] He added, "The retreating [Confederate] army did much damage on leaving, burnt our bridges, some steamboats, & c. We citizens did all in our power to prevent this destruction. . . . I never felt more secure in my life, both in property and person [under Union occupation]."[27]

A few days later Buell moved his headquarters from the St. Cloud Hotel to the abandoned mansion of George W. Cunningham, a local merchant who had taken refuge farther south when Nashville fell. The remainder of Buell's troops trickled through the city and were finding large quantities of public provisions. A private resident wrote that as the soldiers came through the city, one noticeable difference between the two armies, besides their appearance, was that the Confederate troops would shout to the crowd, " 'G—d D—n you, stand back here, or I will blow your heads off.' " According to the correspondent, the Union soldiers would say politely, " 'Ladies and gentlemen, please stand back.' "[28] Even some of the citizens who had fled during the panic returned to the city after a week of Buell's policy. For the first time in several weeks Buell was able to relax without the immediate pressure of marching and felt a sense of accomplishment. On the evening of March 2 he calmly wrote McClellan that the city was "quiet and orderly."[29]

McClellan probably would have wished for as much in Washington. The general in chief was under unyielding pressure from members of the Joint Committee on the Conduct of the War to take action to demonstrate that the Army of the Potomac was capable of doing what the government expected of it. Despite the pressure, however, McClellan continued to correspond with the western commanders about their future movement, and he encouraged cooperation between them. He emphasized the magnitude of holding on to Nashville and targeted Chattanooga as a "very important point to gain," as though accomplishing these tasks would be simple. Of course a Federal occupation of Chattanooga would have greatly pleased Washington. But it was 140 inhospitable miles from Nashville, and Buell, using the railway, would have had to secure the line all the way from Louisville. McClellan scratched the old wound of East Tennessee, urging Buell to "push Carter forward as rapidly as possible."[30]

McClellan was as relentless about getting something to happen in East Tennessee as the president was about movement on the Potomac. Buell fired off a dispatch of excuses the following day, saying that as much as he wanted to assist his neighbor, he could not "get exactly at what Halleck [was] doing."[31] He thought an interview with Halleck and McClellan might be productive. Scott, who was with Buell in Nashville at the time, wired Stanton the same message. "If General McClellan could be spared for a week," he wrote, "I think it would be of great service to have him visit Louisville, and by appointment call Generals Buell & Halleck to that point for collaboration."[32] Halleck replied that events were "pressing on so rapidly" that he could not be away from the telegraph office.[33]

Buell expected Carter to unite with Garfield after the latter chased the Confederates entirely out of Kentucky. The most important matter at hand, and certainly the most alarming from Buell's standpoint, however, was the fact that the president had decided on the appointment of a military governor for Tennessee. Buell feared any appointment, especially since he was convinced that most citizens of the state, if not coerced into submission, would cooperate with the Union army commanders in restoring local government and maintaining law and order. He implored McClellan to intervene with Lincoln: "Use all your persuasion against the appointment of a military governor for Tennessee. It will do incalculable harm. Beg the President to wait."[34]

For someone who appeared to have political disabilities, Buell was perceptive enough to realize that the appointment of a military governor would mean military government in his department. In the first place, he was concerned over what appeared to him to be a hasty decision and a fragile attempt by the administration to restore loyal Tennesseans to the Union politically without considering the effect this decision might have on the residents of the entire region. In Buell's mind, an incomplete military occupation would not sustain political restoration and, consequently, would jeopardize otherwise innocent civilians. Common sense told him that should the Union army be forced out of the region, civilians who had professed loyalty while the military was there would incur the wrath of the enemy when the army left. Thus, there was great anxiety about developing Union sentiment incautiously. Maggie Lindsley trembled when she thought of the possibility of a reverse—"that the Confederates should ever get back here." "Then," she feared, "*our* doom is spoken—either flight—beggary or, remaining, death."[35] The death of several loyal Tennesseans punctuated what was already known.

Buell also had serious reservations about the obvious conflict of power he would have with a military governor in carrying out his military strategy. Would Tennesseans resent the imposition placed on them by a military governor and retaliate against the army? Surely those who chafed at the thought of being forced into submission might consider taking an active part against the invaders. "Wars of invasion," wrote Jominian disciple Buell, "always difficult, become tenfold so when the people of the invaded territory take an active part against the army." "These considerations are of such importance to success," he added, "that there is no exception to the rule of securing the neutrality if not the friendship of the population [in rebellion]."[36] Therefore he adopted a lenient reconstruction attitude in Nashville, which reflected his desire to uphold the constitutional rights of southerners, including the protection of their slaves, which in turn would protect his army in the field and perhaps undermine the enemy's leadership by encouraging civilians to support the Union. He moved with great caution, hoping to convince the Nashville rebels that he would not trample on their sensibilities. Buell had an interview with the editor of one of the city's newspapers and encouraged him to support the Union. Secretary Scott was present during the interview and concluded that the paper would "change its course gradually and in a few days give reasons for supporting the Union cause based upon the generous and liberal treatment on the part of the Government—a treatment so widely different from that they had been taught to expect."[37]

Buell gave citizens every opportunity to express their loyalties and their disloyalties, even to the point of personal insult. On one occasion, however, he was not so tolerant. According to a newspaper correspondent, Buell was riding his horse through the streets of Nashville one day and came upon an aristocratic lady, "Mrs. W.," who lived in what was described as a "fine large house." When she saw Buell approaching, she stood in an open door, waved a rebel flag toward him, and shouted, "Hurrah for Jeff Davis and the Southern Confederacy!" Buell reined in his horse, turned to the lady, "touched his hat with all the courtesy and suavity for which he is remarkable," and surveying the fine house from top to bottom with the eye of a connoisseur, quietly remarked, "An excellent house for a hospital." In less than two hours every room was full of sick soldiers, and Mrs. W. was requested to take care of them. The correspondent sarcastically applauded her upon her "blessed privilege of ministering to the needs of suffering patriots."[38]

Buell was able to distinguish between tolerable and intolerable disloyalty. No one expected him to hold everyone accountable for their past loyalties, but an invitation to former Democratic presidential candidate John Bell to return to Nashville was not one of his more popular gestures. Drawing a line between loyalties was much more easily done for those who had supported the Union since the war's inception and who had suffered at the hands of the Confederates. Nashville loyalists who wanted to see traitors punished naturally resented Buell's lenient policy, and he ran a tremendous risk of alienating them the longer his army stayed in Nashville. Still, Buell prepared to deal with civil disobedience and guerrilla activity. Persons who reacted to the Union presence by burning Union supplies or more violently by killing Union pickets found that Buell was willing to execute them as outlaws. On one occasion when John Hunt Morgan's band of cavalrymen slipped into the city disguised as Union troops and burned the steamboat *Minnetonka*, Buell responded by threatening to execute some of the captured horsemen, though in the end no one was hanged.[39]

Buell's lenient attitude toward reconstruction was a direct result of his initial attitude that the Civil War would be a war with limited goals. His military philosophy that emphasized, above all else, discipline and preparation over movement reinforced this limited approach. Besides, he was better at managing than waging war and was at his best when it came to bureaucratic red tape. A lenient reconstruction policy could help keep war safe by appeasing rather than antagonizing the enemy. With Nashville in his possession, Buell had the opportunity to make a broad statement about the kind of war the Union should be waging and the potential dangers sure to occur in the kind of war Congress was eager to wage. In his conciliation policy perhaps Buell played politics of his own—the politics of pragmatism and idealism—practical in its application and idealistic in its expectations. But because Buell lacked an improvisational ability and limited himself too strictly to the military side of his duties, he would be caught between doing what he thought was right and changing war aims. Consequently, just when he thought he had caught up to the war, it shifted again.[40]

Bull Nelson shared the vision of incalculable harm that Buell predicted. He agreed that reconstruction ought to be fostered in Middle Tennessee by the support of men who could elect their own leaders. When it was known publicly that Senator Andrew Johnson would be appointed military governor, Nelson, despite having been in Nashville only a few days, strenuously objected. He had corresponded with Secretary Chase about affairs in Kentucky and Tennessee since the previous summer and fall and hoped he could convince Chase to change Lincoln's mind. He had apprised Chase of the situation in Nashville during the last week of February and emphasized how astonished the residents were to see neither soldiers nor officers in the city. Buell had forbidden troops to enter the city. Nelson reported that only one drunken soldier had stumbled into the streets, and he was promptly arrested and severely punished. He was optimistic about expressions of loyalty from Nashvillians, saying that although the Union army had been in possession of the city a few days, "the tide has already turned" and Nashvillians "seem to be awakening from some unpleasant dream." He urged Chase to advise Lincoln to allow Tennesseans to elect their own political leaders. "*Do not send* Andy Johnson here in any official capacity," he cautioned. "He represents a party! Let him come as Senator if he wants to. He is too much embittered to entrust with a mission as delicate as the direction of a people under the present circumstances. It will be better if the people here choose a Governor."[41]

Perhaps Scott, who had traveled with Buell from Louisville to Nashville, best characterized the situation regarding the appointment of Johnson. He agreed about the need for a provisional government and urged that a "wise and prudent man" be appointed as military governor. He recommended former Tennessee governor and now general William Campbell. Buell no doubt agreed with the recommendation, since he appeared willing to appease the wealthy elite "who have been heretofore aiding the rebellion—in many cases from sheer necessity."[42] Rumors had begun to circulate even before the capture of Nashville that Buell had appeased prominent secessionist leaders by allowing them to return to their homes.[43]

William Nelson, nicknamed "Bull" for his overwhelming size and strength, commanded the Fourth Division of the Army of the Ohio, and in July commanded the Army of Kentucky engaged in organizing the defenses of Louisville. Nelson supported Buell's attitude toward discipline, limited war, and conciliation, which earned him the wrath of governors as well as congressmen. He was shot and killed by Brig. Gen. Jefferson C. Davis in September 1862 in the Galt House Hotel in Louisville on the eve of the battle of Perryville. (Courtesy of the U.S. Army Military History Institute, Carlisle, Pa.)

Three days later when Scott learned that Lincoln was considering Johnson, he protested, arguing that many of Johnson's supporters were now secessionists and that the senator had been opposed to the Confederates for so long that he would have trouble reconciling rebels to their former allegiance. Scott could feel the pulse of the city and observed to Stanton that many residents feared Johnson would be vindictive toward them. The editor of the *Memphis Daily Avalanche* predicted great disappointment for Johnson, who was "radically rotten on the negro question." "We think the North," the paper added in another editorial, "wholly miscalculates on this point."[44] Animosity was so bitter toward Johnson in Nashville, Scott informed Stanton, that his life might be in jeopardy. The situation was such that as an "out & out Union man, and one politically opposed to everything concerning the Southern Confederacy," Johnson was not suitable to Nashvillians. Besides, Buell was "managing matters with great prudence," and the people feared that Johnson would rule them "with despotic power."[45]

Both Scott and Nelson concluded that Johnson's coming to Nashville would seriously injure relations between civil and military authorities. The military governor not only cultivated a more determined distaste for the military and military red tape during these cold months but was impatient and resentful toward Buell for not advancing into East Tennessee. And even a city as large as Nashville would never seem smaller than when these two conservatives collided over reconstruction policy. "I anticipate," wrote a perceptive Maj. Joseph Keifer, "that there will be no harmony between Johnson and Buell." "Buell," he added, "is one of those men who is good at watching and waiting."[46] Johnson was not; he was brusque and fast acting.

In late February and early March congressmen focused on the Federal occupation of Nashville, and most approved Lincoln's decision. The editor of the *New York Times* best summarized the situation: "Gov. Johnson undoubtedly has a most difficult task before him . . . and it will require discretion as well as nerve and courage to lead the State safely through this period of transition."[47] The accident of war was not capturing Forts Henry and Donelson so much as it was embarking on reconstruction in perhaps the most unreceptive region of the state.

Johnson was surely embittered about the situation in Tennessee, and he had reason to be. He believed Buell could have seized East Tennessee just as easily as he had Nashville, and his unwillingness to do so left the most loyal region in the state in Confederate hands. Johnson was a Democrat, a former two-term governor of Tennessee, a current member of the Committee on the Conduct of the War, and, more importantly, the only southern senator to have remained loyal while his state seceded. On March 4 Johnson became the nation's first military governor with the Senate unanimously attaching the military rank of brigadier general to his political appointment. Notice of the appointment came by way of Stanton, who in a brief but sweeping statement of his duties notified Johnson that he had the authority "to exercise and perform *within the limits of that state,* . . . the powers, duties and functions pertaining to the office of Military Governor (including the *power* to *establish all necessary offices and tribunals,* and *suspend* the *writ* of Habeas Corpus) during the pleasure of the President, or until the loyal inhabitants of that state shall organize a civil government in conformity with the Constitution of the United States."[48] The president had given Johnson authority to exercise and perform the powers, duties, and functions pertaining to the office of military governor, but the fact remained that there was no precise definition of that office. Still, Lincoln had sent Johnson to get loyal state government functioning again and politically restore Tennessee to the Union as quickly as possible.[49] Two days after Johnson's appointment, Buell confided to McClellan that a provisional government "would be injudicious at this time. It may not be necessary at all."[50] He objected to the very concept.

Whatever clout Buell thought McClellan had in Washington, he was apparently unaware that it had waned considerably since the end of the year. He was simply not tuned in to high-level political matters in Washington. McClellan was in no position to make recommendations to the president about Tennessee, particularly not on behalf of a commander who, though he was in possession of Nashville, had not seized the most loyal region of the state where such a selection as military governor would have been less controversial. McClellan was quick to point out to Buell that Johnson's appointment and the provisional government was the president's idea, arguing that "I think your dispatch advising against it arrived too late."[51] Had Buell cultivated a political relationship with others in Washington, or perhaps endeared himself to someone like fellow Ohioan Chase or even Stanton, he might have had more influence. Buell, however, remained constant in his uninviting demeanor and continued to keep a distance from politicians. More importantly, he strove endlessly to keep politicians distant from his army, and Johnson had already interfered with his command.

Buell's strong conviction that the occupation of the Tennessee capital would tap a huge reservoir of Unionist sentiment in Tennessee was not altogether unrealistic. He believed that "thousands of hearts in every part of the State will swell with joy to see that honored flag reinstated in a position from which it was removed in the excitement and folly of an evil hour; that the voice of the people will soon proclaim its welcome, and that their manhood and patriotism will protect and perpetuate it."[52]

General Mitchel, who had initially been impressed with Buell, was among those who formed an unfavorable opinion of his reconstruction policies. As the officer next in rank in Buell's department, Mitchel had made a favorable impression on the Army of the Ohio and its commander because, as Col. John Beatty of the Third Ohio described him, "Mitchel is military."[53] He never swore, never drank, and was indefatigable. These were qualities that immediately endeared him to Buell. Buell had been so impressed with Mitchel, in fact, that he invited him to headquarters on several occasions to discuss military strategy. The two men spent many late nights debating the strategy and policy for the war in the West. Buell treated his subordinate "with marked attention," but while he valued Mitchel's advice, he quite often declined to take it, particularly when it came to the issue of slavery and war aims.

By early March, however, Buell's lack of zeal for the political aim of the war had frustrated Mitchel, and he lamented that Buell's "want of iron firmness and irresistible energy in the execution of the projected expeditions" was responsible for a more aggressive war. His unsuccessful attempts the previous year to acquire an independent command from Buell and head toward East Tennessee simply added to his frustration. The rejection of his recent plea to move on Nashville quickly and farther south before the railroad bridges could be destroyed compounded his resentment. Moreover, Buell's apparent affinity with Nelson, whom Mitchel hated, annoyed him. To make matters worse, Nelson and Buell were in full agreement regarding a conciliatory policy in Nashville, while Mitchel believed General Orders 13a was simply intolerable.[54]

Mitchel, however, did not limit his frustration to only Buell. He was among those regular army officers who resented McClellan and believed that his conservative success had slighted them in matters of promotion and, in fact, had limited the war politically. They embraced the Radical position, or gave that impression, to gain support from the Joint Committee on the Conduct of the War for their own military fortunes. They rendered military gossip, biting criticisms, and eventually, vehement denunciations of Buell to Cabinet members who would naturally share it with the members of the Joint Committee. Mitchel wrote confidentially to fellow Ohioan Secretary Chase about affairs in Tennessee. He knew that it was no secret that all of Washington was chagrined to the point of embarrassment over Buell's refusal to move into East Tennessee. Mitchel also knew that the committee was trying to eliminate

Ormsby MacKnight Mitchel, who taught mathematics at West Point and astronomy at Cincinnati College before the war, commanded the Third Division of the Army of the Ohio. In March and April 1862 Mitchel's division advanced into northern Alabama while the rest of the Army of the Ohio headed toward Pittsburg Landing and fought the battle of Shiloh. Once one of Buell's advocates, Mitchel soon lost patience with Buell's slow pace of campaigning and his policy of conciliation. He ultimately became one of Buell's harshest critics. (Courtesy of the U.S. Army Military History Institute, Carlisle, Pa.)

conservative commanders from the army, and he opened an old wound by condemning Buell's blunder of suspending this expedition. "That mistake," wrote Chase, "as well as many others, must be made good by future achievements."[55]

Buell's consistent unwillingness to carry out the wishes of the administration seemed all the more disturbing and suspicious in light of his current policy protecting the rights of southerners. Mitchel had been with Buell, the Nashville mayor, and the delegation calling itself the Committee of Citizens when Buell assured them "in the most positive terms of full protection for themselves and their property; for which protection, no return was demanded from them." Mitchel was convinced that this "extreme leniency" would "work evil and not good." It would not inspire Unionism but, instead, stifle it. In Middle Tennessee there were thousands who, "only require[d] a little pushing to come out Union men." But Nashvillians, he argued, "fear the return of their military masters, and they wish to have a good excuse to make for their change of sentiments, in case it be necessary."[56] "If I had the management," he boasted to Chase, "I would disarm all the citizens of the state, . . . [and] invite them to manifest their loyalty by coming forward and taking the Oath of Allegiance." "The poison of rebellion," he explained, "has penetrated deeply into the systems of our Southern people. . . . It needs some powerful antidote, and it can be more readily applied through the pocket than in any other way."[57]

Mitchel certainly had reason to question Buell's policy. When a civilian shot an officer in his division as a result of what Mitchel apparently deemed too much civilian liberality, however, he lashed out at Buell. Administering the oath of allegiance, or at least arresting those whose loyalty was doubtful, Mitchel claimed, would be more useful in distinguishing loyalty from disloyalty. Of course Mitchel's ideas impressed Chase far more than they did Buell, who was determined to "reach a class of persons who are not hostile to us although not warmly our friends."[58] Besides, according to Buell, Mitchel's officer might not have been shot had he been more cautious or acted more responsibly. Obviously, placing the blame for such instances on the soldiers of his command infuriated Mitchel and fed a budding opposition to Buell. Mitchel was so disgusted by Buell's policy that he asked Chase to inquire about a transfer for him.[59]

The small but growing opposition to Buell manifested itself mainly in Mitchel's division. Rumors circulated the camps that Mitchel disagreed with Buell's policy and timidity. Major Keifer of the Third Ohio hoped that Buell's policy would be changed for the better once Johnson arrived. "Nashville is second only to Charleston in her rebel proclivity," he wrote his wife. "I predict the policy of Genl. Buell will be promptly changed for the better. . . . We must punish the secesh of this place and state in a more *severe* and *summary* manner."[60]

As the initial weeks of occupation passed, Buell continued to regroup his army as it came into Nashville and made preparations to move south, though he was not exactly sure where. He offered to aid Halleck at Columbus, but by the end of the first week in March, Columbus had fallen, John Pope was investing New Madrid, and Halleck had learned that Beauregard was fortifying Corinth with 20,000 men. As Halleck predicted, the war in the West was moving in the direction of Memphis, not toward Chattanooga or even back to Nashville, where Buell had anticipated it might shift in light of that city's fall. He invited Buell to "come to Savannah or Florence" and bypass Decatur as McClellan had advised and Buell thought appropriate. If the Confederates had destroyed the railroad and bridges in their rear, how could they return to menace Buell at Nashville? Thus the tug-of-war continued between Halleck and Buell over the true strategic design for the West, and as often as he could, Old Brains complained that others simply could not see what he saw. To Secretary Scott he griped that "I cannot make Buell understand the importance of strategic points till it is too late."[61] To his wife he was less charitable, connecting Buell with McClellan and Stanton as culprits in denying him due credit for the successes of Henry, Donelson, Nashville, Columbus, and New Madrid. "The newspapers give the credit of these things to Stanton, McClellan & Buell," he fumed, "but fortunately I have recorded evidence that they even failed to approve them after I had planned them."[62]

Though Scott had earlier visited Halleck and confided to him Buell's intentions for the West, Halleck failed to realize that Scott and Buell shared more than an acquaintance. They shared a similar strategic view that contrasted with Halleck's. Halleck's monotonous complaints to Scott did not cause him to drop his support of Buell. If he considered Buell a self-absorbed and somewhat insensitive commander, Scott nonetheless respected and admired him. He was apparently one of the few persons able to win Buell's trust and perhaps the only favorable political connection he had to Washington. "I am much gratified to hear of the promotion of General Buell," wrote Scott. "He is a prudent, wise officer, and his whole heart is in the cause & will bring success in his Department." "He is not so fast and dashing perhaps as some others," he added, "but his army is disciplined." Scott concluded to Stanton, "His moves are made with caution and well supported; and I believe that positions once taken by him will never be yielded if you will give him the aid from time to time in a military way that his Department may require."[63]

In the meantime, Halleck was busy being annoyed by Grant, who was allegedly drinking again and who had recently gone to Nashville without authority. Buell contemplated helping Halleck in western Tennessee but continued to urge a meeting in Louisville. Scott reinforced this sentiment, telegraphing to Halleck that Buell "wishes to aid any important movement."[64] But as much as Buell pledged his support, he made excuses as to why Halleck should not expect too much. Buell bemoaned that his concentration was incomplete due to the difficulty of crossing two formidable rivers. Though not prone to accepting rumor as truth, Buell acknowledged that the talk in Johnston's camp was that he and Beauregard were expected to unite at Fayetteville twenty-five miles south of Murfreesboro and then attack Nashville.[65] Buell, therefore, delayed aiding Halleck until he could be assured of his coming to the Tennessee River. Meanwhile, a frustrated Halleck waited and complained.

To be sure, Halleck never expected much from Buell. In a note the following day to Scott, as if to instruct the incompetent Buell, he laid out the obvious Confederate line in the West and bluntly told Scott to inform Buell that the center was Savannah and that Buell "should move immediately, and not come too late, as he did at Donelson."[66] These kinds of attacks on Buell's judgment reflected the animosity Halleck felt toward the Ohioan. It would be hard to imagine Buell not having a similar contempt for Halleck, although according to Scott, he hardly ever shared his feelings about Old Brains. Instead, he maintained incredible self-restraint.[67]

On the same day that Johnson boarded a train in Washington on his way to Nashville, Buell received favorable reports from General Carter at Cumberland Ford that "upwards of 1,000 East Tennesseans have arrived in this vicinity, the great mass of whom have entered the service."[68] At the same time he heard from a waterlogged Garfield, who had finally recovered from the effects of the flood in the valley of the Big Sandy, about the rise of Unionism in eastern Kentucky. Writing from Piketon, Garfield observed that "there has been a marked change in favor of the Union among the citizens [in] Buchanan, Wise, Scott and other counties." "At the foot of the Cumberland Mountains, within the last few weeks," he added, "several public meetings have been held to express their attachment to the Union."[69] Naturally, reports like these helped to confirm what Buell thought all along about loyalism in the South, provided his army acted in accordance with his desires for conciliation.

Though Buell remained steadfast about imposing a lenient occupation on the residents of Nashville, acting in accordance with the desires of General Orders 13a was easier said than done. The arrival of Buell's army not only tapped into the latent, but mild loyalism in the area but provided a haven for runaway slaves. Fugitive slaves in the camps of his army had been a problem from the beginning of his command, but they had gradually increased in number as his army moved south. Kentucky judge James R. Underwood, chairman of the state House Military Committee in Frankfort, wrote to Buell in early March about the problem of fugitive slaves. Buell assured Underwood that "the mass of this army is law-abiding, and that it is neither its disposition nor its policy to violate law or the rights of individuals in any particular."[70]

Whereas in Kentucky the majority of slave owners were loyal to the Union, many Middle Tennessean slave owners were not. This gave Buell more incentive to stand by his orders excluding slaves from the ranks. Still, he ran the risk of alienating loyalists and his soldiers when he supported the constitutional guarantees of Tennesseans sympathetic to the Confederacy. Federal policy precluded interference with slaves, and most Federal officers complied, many believing slaves were a nuisance anyway. Buell never had or desired to have a chance to deal effectively with the slavery issue. Though he thought loyal men should have their slaves, he turned away all slaves from his camps, even those belonging to secessionists, since their presence not only demoralized the army but also caused a drain on supplies. Besides, Buell thought that showing respect for the institution might convince Confederates that the antislavery intentions of the North were not widespread. Some of the soldiers still found use for them, particularly those in Mitchel's division. Buell's "let-alone policy" encouraged the residents to visit division and brigade commanders with reclamations. "So strong were the pro-slavery proclivities of all division commanders, that . . . [Buell] was hardly ever troubled with the case of a runaway." One New York correspondent was ashamed to say that some of these officers responded "with a zeal and alacrity both humiliating and disgusting." Without identifying the commander, he wrote that one general "even kept a regular register of such contraband for the benefit of those who would come in search of them."[71]

Circumstances of a more serious nature arose when large numbers of slaves appeared in the camp of General Mitchel's Third Division. John Beatty, an officer in the Third Ohio, observed that the army had the reputation of being abolitionist and that "the colored folk get into our regimental lines, and in some mysterious way are disposed of that their masters never hear of them again."[72] While he could not explain exactly what happened, he gruesomely and sarcastically commented that it was entirely possible that the "two sawbones, who officiate at the hospital, dissect or desiccate or boil them in the interest of science, or in the manufacture of the villainous compounds with which they dose us when ill."[73] When the owners tried to reclaim their slaves, they were prevented from doing so and in one case were maltreated and injured by some of Mitchel's men.

When these slave masters complained to Buell, he decided to make an example of the division, thinking it necessary that the discipline of his command "shall be vindicated." Consequently, Buell ordered Mitchel either to allow the masters to reclaim their slaves or to "release and expel the negroes from your camp." Furthermore, Buell declared, "no fugitive slave will be allowed to enter or remain in your lines."[74] Beatty was among those officers who obeyed the order promptly and commanded all the slaves to assemble at a certain hour on March 16 to be turned over to their masters. The "scamps," he feared, "took advantage of my notice and hid away, much to the regret of all who desire to preserve the Union as it was and greatly to the chagrin of the gentlemen who expected to take them handcuffed back to Kentucky."[75] It did not take long for the large number of slaves in and around Nashville to figure out that the Union army was not the army of freedom many apparently thought it was, at least not in March 1862 and certainly not in Buell's force. Thus, once commanders enforced the return of slaves to their masters, the number of runaways in Buell's camps decreased.

Though Buell's fugitive slave policy was not atypical among Federal commanders at this stage in the war, his directive became a topic for campfire discussion, and officers made speeches to privates, some defending and some condemning the policies of their superior. Rumors spread that Buell sympathized with the South and the institution of slavery. Col. James B. Steedman of the Fourteenth Ohio recalled that news circulated among the camps in Nashville that Buell had relatives in the city. On one occasion while Steedman was on picket duty, a citizen approached him and said that the residents liked Buell very much and that if "all our officers were like Gen. Buell we would not have any trouble with the people." This resident further reported that Buell had an aunt in Nashville with whom he had lived in early life, and that Buell had visited her often. Steedman said that the woman assured the resident that "everything was right; that special protection would be given to the peculiar institution, and that he had no apprehension on that scene." Of course these rumors were not true, but nonetheless, when combined with Buell's conciliatory policy, they cost him the respect of some of his soldiers. Moreover, these campfire discussions were shared with those at home and eventually found their way into the press.[76]

Mitchel, who had employed slaves as spies, was completely opposed to Buell's policy, as were many of his soldiers. Edwin Payne of the Thirty-fourth Illinois recalled that while his regiment was encamped at Camp Andy Johnson outside Nashville, "considerable indignation amongst the men was created" by Buell's order.[77] "All discussion of the slavery question was prohibited," he wrote, "and all of the rights of owners were carefully observed as to the 'peculiar institution.' "[78] Of course it was not that Buell simply enforced the return of slaves to their masters, but as in all things, he carried out the letter of the law to its fullest extent. To add insult to injury, he issued general orders for the return of slaves at a time when Congress was favoring legislation prohibiting such returns. Naturally, Buell's attitude did little to win him friends in Washington, particularly among members of the Committee on the Conduct of the War.[79]

The war in the West had commanded considerable attention in Washington. Claiming to be the architect for the success at Forts Henry and Donelson and now with the New Madrid campaign reaching a climax in his favor, Halleck let it be known that his was the only department where things favorable to the Union were happening. If given the resources and authority, he might totally overrun the Confederates in that region. With Buell's best friend at the helm of the government's armies, however, Halleck could get no satisfaction. Whether or not McClellan wanted to keep Halleck subordinate to himself, equal in responsibility to Buell, or simply far away from Washington, one thing was clear: his friendship with Buell had blinded him. McClellan was also cautious of Halleck because he was the only officer in the army who had aspirations of reaching general-in-chief status.

Disgust for McClellan's inept handling of the command situation in the West had finally convinced Lincoln to make some changes in that region. In near-desperation he had Stanton, on March 7, ask Halleck what areas he would desire in a new Western Department. Halleck replied that he wanted most of the area west of the Alleghenies. He then exploded to McClellan on the evening of March 10, pointing out the true strategic line in what was now his new department. He was utterly dumbfounded that "General Buell should hesitate to re-enforce me." Halleck had never supported three independent commands in the West and finally having won approval over McClellan, boasted, "You will regret your decision against me on this point. Your friendship for individuals has influenced your judgement. Be it so. I shall soon fight a great battle on the Tennessee unsupported, as it seems, but if successful it will settle the campaigns in the West."[80]

Halleck's good fortune would not be official for a few days, and in the meantime, Buell could revel in his own promotion to major general for capturing Nashville. He learned of his good fortune informally through Scott. Stanton wrote to Scott on March 8, no doubt begrudgingly, that the "President is much pleased with the cautious vigor of General Buell, and relies upon that to guard, above all things, against any mishap by premature and unsupported movements." He reminded him also that Lincoln "expects cordial concert of action between him [Buell] and general Halleck."[81] That the president was pleased with anything about Buell was a testament to the general's ability to subvert the wishes of the president and McClellan without intruding on his friendship with the latter.

Johnson was in Cincinnati the day the Senate confirmed Buell's nomination. The new military governor traveled by boat to Louisville and along the way composed a letter to Buell asking for suggestions about the time or manner of his arrival in Nashville. Buell responded that he should not expect "to be received with enthusiasm but rather the reverse." He suggested that Johnson "enter the city without display" and that he should travel by rail, the quickest route.[82] Johnson and his companions arrived in the Tennessee capital on March 11, and Buell escorted them into he city.[83]

Johnson had come to Nashville unconcerned about cultivating the trust or friendship of anyone, least of all Buell. In his letter of instructions to the new governor, Buell sought to disabuse him of any unrealistic expectations. "I have seen and conversed somewhat frequently with the most prominent Union men in and around Nashville," he wrote, adding that "they are true, but the masses are either inimical or overawed by the tyranny of opinion and power that has prevailed, or waiting to see how matters turn out. They will acquiesce when they see that there is to be stability."[84]

Buell had remained busy trying his best neither to incite more aggression from Confederates nor to alienate loyalists. Though the city was under occupation, Buell had not wanted to impose an ugly atmosphere of subjugation on its residents. The real and most identifiable enemy clad in gray had left the city. Whether or not Buell and Johnson shared the belief that a handful of villainous leaders had manipulated the white masses into secession, Johnson had other ideas about how to reconcile them back to their proper relation to the Union. With an "olive branch in one hand and the Constitution in the other," the former governor embarked on a new program and a speedy restoration of Tennessee, whose epitaph had a more stark message: Traitors must be punished and treason crushed. According to journalist Henry Villard, who was traveling with Nelson's division, Johnson had "too violent a temper and was too much addicted to the common Southern habit of free indulgence in strong drink." "These failings," he concluded "really unfitted him for his task."[85]

As Johnson launched into his war on traitors in mid-March, Buell and Halleck continued their battle against the enemy and against themselves. Although the two commanders agreed on few things, they both recognized that it was vital to the Union's strategy in the West to sever the Memphis and Charleston Railroad, one of the South's main east-west arteries. Buell thought marching due south from Nashville toward Huntsville, Alabama, was the surest and safest route. Halleck, however, wanted Buell's army to use the rivers and float down the Cumberland River from Nashville to the Ohio River, and then travel back up the Tennessee River to join Grant, whose army was already advancing south along the river. Buell wrote to Scott, en route to Halleck's headquarters, about these plans. Halleck's idea made sense, particularly in light of the speed and efficiency displayed by his army in the recent river victories, but Buell was not convinced that Halleck's strategy was more sound than his own. He resisted for several days.[86]

As recalcitrant as Buell was, the odds were against him. On March 11 Halleck won a decisive victory in the West in the form of Presidential War Order No. 3, which abolished the Department of the Ohio and put Buell's forces, along with Grant's, under Halleck's command. Without knowledge of the new arrangement, Buell continued to insist that Halleck should concentrate on Florence. "If you occupy that point," he pointed out, "I will re-enforce you by water or join you by land; otherwise I may detach too little to serve you, or else so much as to endanger Middle Tennessee."[87] Buell was not prepared to endanger Middle Tennessee, not only because Johnson would need a force to hold on to Nashville, but also because he needed to maintain his communication and transportation links with Louisville. "The possession and absolute security of the country north of the Tennessee, with Nashville as a center," he argued, "is of vital importance, both in a political and military point of view. Under no circumstance should it be jeopardized."[88]

Much to his dismay, Buell found out about the new arrangement in the West from Lincoln on March 12 and from Halleck the following day in the form of General Orders No. 1. The new letterhead read, "Hdqrs. Department of the Mississippi." To soften the blow, Halleck wrote to

Buell, his new subordinate, calmly assuring him that the "new arrange-ment of departments will not interfere with your command."[89] Despite Halleck's gesture of good intentions, it was clear that Buell would now have to accept his superior's strategy of combining forces. But there was more. The president's War Orders No. 3 also relieved McClellan of the command of the other departments, since Lincoln ordered him back to the field as the commander of the Army of the Potomac. To be sure, po-litical pressures against McClellan had developed since he assumed command in the summer of 1861 and helped to bring about his demo-tion. Not only did McClellan continue to oppose Lincoln's handling of the war, but also he failed to get the war moving in harmony with the government's expectations. Lincoln's new directives prompted Major Keifer of the Third Ohio to write, "I think Halleck is second to none of our Genls." He also had cause to reconsider McClellan's prominence, saying, "I *think* I have changed my mind somewhat in reference to Genl. McClellan."[90] Obviously, so had Lincoln.

With McClellan out of the way, Halleck could not only deal directly with Lincoln and Stanton, but also he could direct the war in the West. Buell lost his only advocate in Washington when McClellan headed for the field. Lincoln, no doubt fatigued by McClellan's unproductiveness and tortured by the entire military command system that led to more headaches and less activity, decided to direct the armies himself. His or-ders explicitly made the executive mansion, and the War Department, the center of policy and communications for the entire army. In the weeks to come, a retired Ethan Allen Hitchcock would be summoned to Washington and made Stanton's assistant. Though his professional army colleagues admired Hitchcock, and he had come to Buell's defense dur-ing his first court-martial trial at Jefferson Barracks some twenty years before, he had aged considerably, was in poor health, and had recently shown an interest in everything except the practice of war. Whatever the case, no longer was anyone watching out for Buell in Washington.[91]

With Johnson his military equal, Halleck his new chief, and his close friend McClellan superior only to the Army of the Potomac, a dumb-founded Buell had little to look forward to, since he was no one's fa-vorite in Washington. It must have given Halleck as much delight as it gave Buell grief to know that "Little Mac" was essentially demoted by the same order that gave Old Brains command in the West. Naturally, Buell questioned the events of the past few days, but what was foremost in his mind was why McClellan had been sent to the field.

Certainly in the opinion of the Radical Republicans, who were seek-ing to recast the conduct of the war by simply getting rid of McClellan and others like him and by promoting the emancipation of slaves and reinforcing the confiscation of property, Buell's influence in the conservative clique was second only to McClellan's. Though he continued to maintain a nonpolitical attitude, he had at the beginning of the war, according to one source, offended the Radicals by saying that he did not know what the war was about—at least that was how his comment was perceived by the press. What more careful observers noted was that Buell confessed at the time that he did not know which party was right and which was wrong in the great struggle confusing the country.

Whatever the case, as a friend of McClellan's it was naturally assumed he was closer to Peace Democrats whom Johnson and the Radicals considered traitors. Buell had faced the suspicion and enmity of the Radicals since the summer of 1861 when he was assigned a division in McClellan's army. The fact that his relative through marriage was David E. Twiggs, the controversial professional army officer turned Confederate, and that his wife had been married to Richard Barnes Mason of the Virginia Masons caused the Radicals to suspect his loyalty. His ownership of slaves and support of the Democrats in 1860 simply confirmed what they wanted to believe about the doughface commander. Now, in light of his recent policy of conciliation, the snowball of opposition toward unreceptive and unaggressive generals that had formed the previous year began its descent. If anyone had reason to be concerned about what had happened to McClellan, besides McClellan, it was Buell.[92]

With few endearing qualities, at least to politicians, and the political pressure mounting against his view of limited war and lenient reconstruction, Buell was now in a position in which his coarse manner would rub directly on those for whom he had the least amount of respect and yet who had the most political clout. Buell had not seriously been considered for overall command in the West, not only because the Radicals would not hear of it, but also because he simply failed to impress Stanton or Lincoln as being able to get the war moving in the direction they wanted. They saw more vigor in Halleck and too much McClellan in Buell, and what was initially deemed a blessing for the Union high command had now become a curse. Too much preparation for a war that was quickly passing them by and too little support for the government's political aims were becoming the criteria for unacceptability as a commander. The war took a severe turn for Buell, who would need to prove his mettle as a commander and even a supporter of the Union beyond a shadow of a doubt.

The spring rains came early in Middle Tennessee, and they reflected the melancholy that Buell must have felt. The capture of Nashville, hailed as one of the great accomplishments thus far in the war, and his promotion to major general were certainly eclipsed by the defeat he felt with McClellan no longer his superior and Andrew Johnson giving political and military orders in his domain. Buell was caught in the middle of a war of egos and politics, and neither sat well with him. Nashville was essentially the forbidden fruit of the Confederacy for the Union in February 1862. To acquire it would mean to subject the nation to a most difficult transitional and experimental phase in the war, that of forcing civil and military authorities to carry on a productive relationship while carrying out political reconstruction. If Halleck represented one message about the war, Johnson's appointment reinforced an even larger message: civilians held the reins of war. And while that had not bothered Buell all that much in the previous year, he no longer commanded a department in which he could make policy. He simply headed an army that carried out orders from Halleck.

Buell never accepted the political realities of Johnson's appointment. This attitude reflected his political outlook and was deeply rooted in his traditional military philosophy. Whether it was Buell's lenient policy toward unreconstructed southerners, his slowness to advance on East Tennessee, or his simple lack of appreciation for Johnson's political power, the Ohio-born West Pointer proceeded to annoy the military governor. One thing was for certain: he misjudged just how much clout McClellan had lost and Johnson had gained in Washington during the course of six months. This shift should have signaled to him a shift in the war's priorities. Had he been more aware of the governor's political clout, he may have been more in tune with the political nature of the war and certainly more discreet in his dealing with those unreconstructed southerners. Even Major Keifer recognized that the capture of Nashville was a turning point in the war. "I predict," he wrote to his wife, "the whole character of war will be changed."[93] He was right. It was important during this transitional phase that the Confederates be given no opportunity to benefit from any lack of initiative by the Federals in maintaining the offensive.

CHAPTER THIRTEEN

American Waterloo

It was simply a matter of time before Buell and Andrew Johnson clashed over the occupation of Nashville. The duel was more than just a power struggle, since it pitted two conservative men with contrasting attitudes on reconstruction. Johnson came to Nashville with little intention of cultivating the cooperation of southerners. He did not have to, since he was merely the carrier of a message initiated and supported by Lincoln, the War Department, and Congress. By presenting the military government as an instrument for restoring the state to the Union, Johnson sought to reward those who had remained loyal since the previous year and to demonstrate by example what would happen to those who refused to seek refuge under military government. Naturally, Buell's attitude of conciliation, or "let-alone policy," as the *New York Weekly Tribune* characterized it, irritated him. Buell had allowed residents to carry on in the manner to which they were accustomed, and this infuriated Johnson. Thus, before Johnson could embark on his restoration, he first had to undo what Buell not only had allowed but had encouraged.[1]

Johnson's list of reconstruction items was long and included government control of the press and the invocation of Tennessee's long-standing constitutional requirement that all officeholders take an oath to support the U.S. Constitution. While the military governor asserted his control over the press and municipal government, the city was swarming with soldiers who presented Johnson and Buell with a more serious problem: Who was in control of enforcing the government's policies?[2]

Johnson may have approved of Halleck assuming command of the entire West, but he was, nonetheless, greatly distressed over how the new arrangement would affect East Tennessee, which had been placed under John Frémont's new Mountain Department. Just a few days after his arrival, Johnson and Horace Maynard expressed their lamentations to Stanton: "For God's sake do not divide East Tennessee into two military departments. We have suffered enough already from a conflict of military authorities."[3] When Johnson sought clarification of the availability of military personnel to enforce the orders he might issue as governor, Buell allowed his inquiry to sit on his desk for days until he thought of a judicious response. In the meantime he sparred with Halleck over more pressing matters.

An inspired Halleck was on the move, and he needed to know what kind of support he might expect from Buell. On March 14 Buell reported that his force in the Department of the Ohio numbered 101,737, including eight regiments that were still with Grant. Due to the severity of the weather and wet conditions, about 30,500 men were sick and absent, leaving 71,233 present for duty. His army was clustered in eastern Tennessee at Cumberland Gap, where General Carter had been debating Buell's views regarding the best line of operations. Halleck had already agreed to send Grant to Savannah; he had to, since all his information confirmed that Johnston was concentrating his army in the vicinity of Corinth, Mississippi. On March 16, exercising his newfound authority, Halleck wired Buell to move his forces by land to the Tennessee as rapidly as possible, since Grant's army was concentrating at Savannah. Just in case Buell was at all hesitant about his ideas, and to make sure Buell fully understood what was expected of him, a vexed Halleck added the charge, "Don't fail to carry out my instructions. I know that I am right."[4]

Halleck never missed the opportunity to boast that he was right, even when he was not, and he always made it appear that he fully understood the enemy's movements, even when he did not. This time he was right, and he urged Buell to communicate with Grant and Smith as soon as possible, expressing a willingness to send Buell whatever materials and workmen he needed to facilitate these operations. Buell convinced Halleck that instead of using the rivers to get his army to Savannah, an overland march was shorter, would take less time, and would be more secure. Besides, his troops could use the discipline of the march. The closest and most secure route from Nashville to Savannah wound over a road that covered 120 miles, but less than half of those miles ran along a turnpike through Franklin to Columbia on the south bank of the Duck River.

Before he departed Nashville, Buell finally responded to Johnson's letter seeking clarification about the availability of soldiers to enforce his orders. Not wanting to totally disregard Johnson, Buell replied that troops under his command would be instructed to comply with Johnson's requisitions for Nashville's defense. He also mentioned that such requisitions, however, must be subordinate to whatever plans he had for the army's operations. To reassure Johnson of Nashville's defense, Buell visited him at his home and argued that the Tennessee capital would not be captured. Buell remembered that Johnson was shocked over the small size of the garrison and pondered to himself "of what consequence is my fate in this conflict."[5]

Whether or not it was necessary for Buell to emphasize the fact that Johnson's decisions would have to be subordinate to military considerations, it was nonetheless important for Buell to attempt to define civil and military relations during Nashville's occupation. William G. Brownlow, the Knoxville zealot, had been expelled from East Tennessee by Confederate authorities and had arrived in Nashville to support Johnson's military governorship. It did not take Buell long to realize that Johnson's tactics, and the small nucleus of his equally zealous supporters, would surely turn the countryside against his army, and he worried for its safety. Toward that end, Buell placed Brig. Gen. Ebenezer Dumont, a former Indiana politician with Mexican War experience, in command of the troops in Nashville. Dumont's position involved tremendous responsibility and a "mass of detail" that Buell could not even begin to convey in writing. Though probably not the wisest choice, due to Dumont's drinking problem, Buell charged him with preserving "the most rigid discipline" among the soldiers, "enforcing the protection of private property, and [seeing] that when the rights of citizens had been unnecessarily encroached upon, the depredators . . . instantly arrested and brought to punishment." In all of these responsibilities, however, there were no instructions for Dumont to fulfill the desires of the military governor. In the event that there were questions regarding the confiscation of property after the Confederates left the city, Buell reminded the Board on Property that under the laws of Congress only civil tribunals had the authority to provide answers.[6]

Buell also made arrangements to expedite rail service from Nashville southward to support the army's operations at Nashville and below. Buell selected Kentuckian John B. Anderson, whom Buell knew from Louisville, to be the "master of transportation" for the Nashville and Chattanooga and the Tennessee and Alabama Railroads. To ensure that he would be closer to his main headquarters, Buell ordered them moved from Louisville to Nashville.[7]

Nashville and Middle Tennessee were sufficiently protected by a garrison of 18,000 men under Brig. Gen. James Negley, and Johnson was adequately accommodated. Thus, Buell proceeded to put his army in motion for Savannah and in communication with Charles F. Smith, who in response to Halleck's orders had in the second week of March occupied that community on the east side of the Tennessee River. Buell sought to preserve the fruits of his previous victories by positioning his army at various points in Middle Tennessee. Within two weeks he also concentrated the scattered forces stationed in eastern Kentucky into a new division, the Seventh, commanded by Brig. Gen. George W. Morgan, and ordered it to seize Cumberland Gap and penetrate with "zeal and discretion," into East Tennessee. With Nashville in Union hands, Buell had no excuse not to pursue an East Tennessee advance. He ordered Mitchel's Third Division to Murfreesboro and Fayetteville to accomplish what he originally conceived for the whole army. Buell heard rumors of an enemy concentration of twenty-five to thirty regiments, and he reminded Mitchel that his force could be mobilized at any time for "an advance or defense, if necessary."[8]

Though sending Mitchel's division toward the Memphis and Charleston Railroad weakened the army, it was perhaps justified by the fact that it meant sending the army's second most winded, conceited, and vainglorious commander along with it. Only Nelson rivaled Mitchel when it came to arrogance, but Nelson remained supportive of Buell long after it proved injurious to his own reputation. What bothered Buell about Mitchel was that in his drive to get on with an offensive, Mitchel often turned critical of Buell, justifiably so, for not keeping pace. Furthermore, Buell was aware of the increasing difference of opinion he and Mitchel shared about past operations and the policy of conciliation. The decision to dismember his division, which by this time included a small but critical core of opinion regarding Buell's let-alone policy, indicated that Buell was aware of Mitchel's attitude. Perhaps he considered Mitchel's division the most disciplined, and thus more likely to survive in northern Alabama with the least amount of trouble. Whatever the case, his army was further reduced to 37,000 to aid Grant. In the meantime, Andrew Johnson continually harassed Buell, Halleck, and Stanton to have still more men assigned to Nashville, which placed Buell in a difficult situation, since any additional troops redirected to Nashville meant weakening another strategic point in Tennessee.[9]

Buell's army finally got under way on the night of March 15 by a rapid march of the cavalry to secure the bridges in advance, particularly the Rutherford Creek bridge and the Duck River bridge, which were then still guarded by the enemy. McCook's rank allowed him to lead all divisions of the army out of Nashville along the Central Alabama Railroad toward Columbia, under orders from Buell to "move forward steadily and as rapidly as you can without forcing your march or straggling."[10] McCook's departure was followed in successive days by the divisions of Nelson, Crittenden, and Wood. Thomas's First Division was the last to break camp and did not leave Nashville until April 1. As the army set out along the narrow road to Corinth, Buell remained in Nashville until March 25. Besides planning for the safety of Nashville, he had given thought also to East Tennessee. On the tenth he had received a letter from Lincoln, who in referring to the Confederate withdrawal from the lower Potomac had written, "The evidence is very strong that the enemy in front of us here is breaking up and moving off. . . . Some part of the force may be destined to meet you. Look out and be prepared."[11]

The president was right, or at least Buell thought he was, since he wired Halleck five days later that Brownlow had brought word that Gen. Kirby Smith was at Knoxville with eighteen regiments from Manassas and had seven others at Cumberland Gap. A week later Buell informed Stanton that Garfield, having driven Marshall from eastern Kentucky, was taking three of his regiments to Bardstown to join Carter's force already moving toward the gap.[12]

Halleck expected Buell to arrive at Savannah sometime before the last week of March, and so he wrote to Grant, whom Halleck had recently restored to command of the army and who had reached Savannah March 17. Halleck wired Grant that "the temper of the rebel troops is such that there is but little doubt but that Corinth will fall much more easily than Donelson did."[13] Grant's eagerness to resume the offensive, however, did not move the more cautious Halleck. "By all means," Halleck wired back to the frustrated subordinate, "keep forces together until you connect with General Buell, who is now at Columbia. . . . Don't let the enemy draw you into an engagement. Wait till you are properly fortified and receive orders."[14]

Halleck had reason to be cautious, since Buell had been plagued by a change in the weather. Heavy rains, high water, and the destruction of almost every bridge on the turnpike, including the Duck River bridge at Columbia, hindered his advance. To make matters worse, the river was at flood stage. Though Buell confidently remarked to Halleck, "I shall lose no time . . . in reaching General Smith," his optimistic expressions were precursors of disappointment, disaster, or vexation. The time necessary to construct a permanent frame bridge across the river would delay his getting to Smith and Grant an estimated four or five days. He planned to head out in "two or three days," carrying the telegraph line forward. He asked that an additional line be started from Savannah to meet him. Because the countryside could not feed his army, he wanted large supplies of forage to be transported to Savannah for his arrival.[15]

As Buell's army moved farther south from Nashville, Governor Johnson grew increasingly alarmed about what force would remain in the city and, more importantly, what would be done with it. Buell's earlier message apparently had not sat well with the governor, and realizing he would get more satisfaction from the War Department, a frustrated Johnson wrote to Stanton on the morning of March 21, asking "to what extent I can rely for the military forces necessary to execute such orders as in the discharge of my official duties I may deem expedient, prudent, and proper to make." He boasted that all was "working well" and that a "great reaction is going on." As soon as the Confederate soldiers were driven out of Tennessee, the state would "be overwhelmingly Union."[16] Stanton promptly wrote to Halleck the following day emphasizing the president's desire that Johnson "have adequate military support," and that he should make arrangements to place an officer in command who would "act efficiently and harmoniously with Governor Johnson."[17] This would be more easily said than done.

Two days before he left Nashville, Buell wrote Halleck a lengthy telegram, in part to justify the delicate position regarding the defense of Nashville and in part to justify the position of his troops. He reiterated what he had written over a week before—Nashville was vulnerable from three directions, by direct route from Knoxville, by the Chattanooga Railroad, and by the Decatur Railroad—and he had taken precautions to prevent the potential Confederate advances along these routes. This helped explain why he sent Mitchel south to Huntsville to cut the Memphis and Charleston and why the protection required more troops than Halleck could spare. Besides, Buell was convinced that a "considerable force" was collecting in East Tennessee. As for Middle and East Tennessee, Buell wrote, "We are working somewhat in the dark . . . for we do not know yet what is being done with the Virginia army." In case transports to cross his force over the Tennessee River were not available, he ordered a pontoon bridge carried by steamer to Savannah, since he had "seen something of the difficulty and delay in ferrying a large force with its trains."[18] Indeed he had, but apparently he believed, though falsely, that building a bridge across the Duck River at this point was faster.

Late on March 26 Buell reached the vicinity of Columbia, a town of 3,500 residents some forty-two miles south, where his army had been forced to camp. There he made the acquaintance of several residents, including Lizzie Rogers, who claimed he was "as nice a gentleman as I have ever met."[19] Even while he rested, however, he worried that his predictions to Halleck about Nashville might come true, so he directed Wood's Sixth Division to go no farther than Columbia when it did leave Nashville. This left only four divisions to move to Grant's support.

The situation at the 180-foot-long Duck River bridge turned out to be much worse than Buell expected. Rains and light snow had transformed the stream into a raging river nearly 40 feet deep and 200 yards wide. He hoped the bridge would be completed by the time he arrived. The process proved so embarrassingly slow, however, that Buell ordered the construction of a temporary pontoon bridge to be used until the frame bridge was completed. For someone who thrived on meeting every contingency, that Buell had not prepared for this crisis earlier was inexcusable.[20]

Buell's insistence on carefully rebuilding the Duck River bridge rather than immediately forging an improvised crossing delayed the army almost two weeks. At the time the delay must have seemed reasonable to Buell, since neither Grant nor Halleck indicated that there was any need to hurry. Indeed, the contrary was true. Halleck indicated to Buell that battle would be avoided until the Army of the Ohio arrived to support Grant: "I propose to join you as soon as you reach the Tennessee."[21] Perhaps the only encouraging news for Buell was that Halleck had finally received his letter from almost two weeks before and thought he and Buell agreed "in every respect as to plan of campaign, except perhaps the column on the diverging line to Stevenson [Alabama]," which Halleck thought divided Buell's force "too much."[22] Whatever the case, Buell informed Halleck, "I have studied pretty much every contingency, and have kept the object of concentration, wherever necessary, constantly in view."[23] The only cause for Buell's concern at Columbia, beyond the bridge repair, was the information that Grant had crossed to the west bank of the Tennessee River at Pittsburg Landing. He had assumed that Grant was still safely camped at Savannah, with the broad Tennessee River between his army and the nearest Confederates. Grant's situation, however, failed to inspire Buell to quicken his pace.[24]

Though Buell thrived on meeting every contingency, some things he simply could not control, such as weather and communications. Messages between Halleck, Grant, and himself had been so remarkably and seriously interrupted that Buell thought the whole matter worth investigation. What made it seem stranger was that Halleck had not received any of the dozen messages Buell had sent since March 14, though Buell received Halleck's messages within a day or two of writing. By March 29, however, the problem had apparently been corrected, as Halleck and Buell exchanged communiqués on the same day. Though Buell never let on precisely when he learned that Grant was on the west bank of the Tennessee River, he remarked to one of his staff officers while at Columbia on March 27 that it surprised him very much to learn that Grant had landed on the west bank of the river. Whatever, the case, Halleck confirmed that the enemy was concentrating at Corinth, and Buell should do the same at Savannah or Pittsburg to be ready to attack. "Don't fail in this," warned Halleck, "as it is all-important to have an overwhelming force there."[25] Buell responded, "We will waste no time."[26]

As it turned out, communications were working again on March 29, and both bridges were ready to use the same day. As luck would have it, the river had also dropped to a fordable level. Observing the slow work on the permanent frame and the pontoon bridge, Buell became frustrated, and when Nelson asked his permission to cross with or without a bridge and get on to Savannah, Buell granted it. Late that evening the impetuous Nelson explained to Col. Jacob Ammen, one of his brigade commanders, that he would cross in the morning. When Ammen asked about the bridge's completion, Nelson replied that the bridge was not completed but that the "river [was] falling, and damn you, get over, for we must have the advance and get the glory." The next morning Nelson ordered his troops to make bundles of pantaloons and drawers, attach them to their bayonets, secure their cartridge boxes around their necks, and ford the still-dangerous river. It was Nelson's nature to be the first to arrive on any scene, but he was not the only commander showing a sense of urgency in forging ahead. "By God," wrote Edwin Hannaford of the Sixth Ohio, "we must cross the river at once, or Grant will be whipped."[27]

While the Union command had problems of communication, Governor Johnson had little trouble in getting through to the secretary of war. He grossly exaggerated to Stanton: "This place, as I conceive, has almost been left defenseless by General Buell."[28] To Johnson, the weakness of the Federal forces in and around Nashville was a standing invitation for Confederate raiders. The situation gave Johnson the impression that Buell was not only incompetent but also a traitor. His fears were not altogether without reason, since a few weeks earlier the raiders of John Hunt Morgan's cavalry had come close to capturing Nelson while the commander was in Nashville. Still, Morgan could hardly do any damage to Nashville. As much as Stanton might have wanted to get involved, he referred Johnson's telegram to Halleck. Thus, Buell had to think about not only what he was moving toward but also what he was leaving behind. In neither case did he feel comfortable with who was giving the orders.[29]

Stanton was also attempting to determine operations in the East by obtaining information from Buell in the West. He wanted to know what could be expected in East Tennessee and how soon. Buell replied that every man was now required for the operations in Middle Tennessee and the concentration on the Tennessee River. Stanton did not interfere, and Buell continued his advance toward Savannah. To resolve the problems of guarding prisoners under his command, Buell had to take along a division he had originally planned to leave at Columbia, which ultimately meant diminishing the force near Nashville. Johnson was not happy.[30]

On Tuesday, April 1, the Army of the Ohio was still pulling out of Columbia, some eighty miles from Savannah. Before he left, Buell informed Halleck and Grant that he would concentrate with Grant's forces on Sunday and Monday, April 6 and 7. Neither Halleck nor Grant doubted Buell would fulfill this promise, since his army had resumed the advance beyond the river. It helped that Nelson's vanguard reached Savannah on Thursday, April 3, and established communications with the main division still some distance behind. Even then, Grant's message back to Nelson, according to later reports by Buell and his officers, was, "There is no need of haste; come on by easy marches." As for an attack, Grant wrote to Sherman, one of his commanders encamped at Pittsburg Landing near Shiloh Church, "I look for nothing of the kind."[31]

Though Buell had ordered a rate of march for the rest of the army that would bring his men to the Tennessee River in top condition by the beginning of the next week, Nelson pushed on and entered Savannah in the late morning of April 5, much to Buell's relief. Grant was upriver at Pittsburg Landing when Nelson arrived, but he returned shortly after. The discussion at the Cherry mansion was brief; Nelson asked permission to press on to Pittsburg Landing, but Grant told him to pitch his tents at Savannah. Later in the afternoon, Grant rode back to Nelson's camp and went to the tent of Col. Jacob Ammen of the Tenth Brigade. Grant declined to dismount, as he had been severely injured when his horse had fallen on him the previous evening when he was on his way to another meeting. In an answer to Ammen's remark that his troops were not fatigued and could continue the march to Pittsburg Landing, Grant replied, "You cannot march through the swamps; make the troops comfortable; I will send boats for you Monday or Tuesday, or some time early in the week." He added confidently, "There will be no fight at Pittsburg Landing; we will have to go to Corinth, where the rebels are fortified." "If they come to attack us," he ended, "we can whip them, as I have more than twice as many troops as I had at Fort Donelson."[32]

A few hours after this meeting, Buell himself rode into Savannah. He had left the bulk of his staff at Columbia and had ridden off two nights before with Colonel Fry, his chief of staff; Charles L. Fitzhugh, an aide-de-camp; and an orderly. From his camp three miles west of Waynesborough on the night of April 4, he wrote Grant that he would arrive in Savannah the following evening, where he hoped they could discuss preparations for the move on Corinth. Because the new command arrangement in mid-March had given Halleck overall control of the West, Buell naturally assumed that Grant, in charge of Halleck's main army, would be authorized to take the general command of the combined forces. Also, by date of commission to the rank of major general, Grant outranked Buell. He was right, though no one had communicated this to him before his arrival at Savannah. On Saturday Grant wrote to Buell that the enemy was "at and near Corinth." Grant was encouraged by Sherman's telegram that he did not "apprehend anything like an attack on our position."[33]

Grant was not at his headquarters when Buell rode into Savannah at sundown on April 5. Instead Buell found Nelson, and it was fortunate that he did. Though Halleck and Buell had planned all along that Buell's force would concentrate at Savannah, Buell received Halleck's approval that Waynesborough, thirty miles from Savannah, would be the point of concentration. Nelson's haste in getting to Savannah, therefore, encouraged Buell to keep the original plan and allowed all divisions to come to Savannah. Ammen called on Buell at his headquarters and no doubt informed him of the brief conversation he had had with Grant in Nelson's presence. Consequently, Buell felt no urgency to meet

Grant that evening and thus did not inform him he had arrived. Instead he decided to meet Grant the next day as he had planned. Riding over thirty-five miles of rough roads had no doubt exhausted him. Still, this was odd behavior for one who thrived on military protocol. After all, Grant was his senior. In his postwar article "Shiloh Reviewed," however, Buell argued that he had been "only a few hours within the limits of his authority, and I did not look upon him as my commander."[34]

If the Union had not seen the urgency of concentrating at Pittsburg Landing, the soldiers of General Johnston's southern army certainly had. Thanks in part to P. G. T. Beauregard, the Confederates seized the initiative Halleck had surprisingly given them, and the "great battle of the war" that Halleck had predicted to Stanton would be fought in southwest Tennessee was about to commence. Two miles or so beyond the Federal pickets, the Confederates had deployed their lines for battle and rested on their arms. Shiloh Church, the little meetinghouse used by local Methodists, was only a mile away.[35]

Because the road at Columbia forked south to Decatur, southwest to Florence, and west to Savannah, Johnston and Beauregard had to be sure of which route Buell would take before deciding to counter the advance. When the two commanders learned that Buell was heading for Savannah with 30,000 men to unite with Grant, they knew they had to act quickly. Here was the opportunity to attack Grant's army before the Federal forces came together, and Beauregard urged seizing the initiative. In fact it was rumored that Buell himself unintentionally contributed to this decision. In a story related by James Garfield to Salmon P. Chase later in the year, Garfield recalled that while Buell's army was in the vicinity of Columbia, the soldiers filled their canteens and watered their horses in a stream near the home of Jerome Pillow, brother of Confederate general Gideon J. Pillow. Pillow caused such a disturbance that a lieutenant arrested him and sent him to the colonel commanding the regiment. The colonel was an admirer of a Nashville woman who was the niece of Pillow, and he discharged Pillow. Pillow returned home, mounted his horse, and then rode to Buell's headquarters and complained that a slave had escaped and was somewhere in the army. Buell allowed him to search for the slave, permitting him to ride throughout the army and observe it. Satisfied he had an accurate estimate of the Union army, Pillow took off for Corinth and informed Beauregard of its size and the rate of Buell's advance. With this information, Beauregard and Johnston decided to attack.[36]

Whether Garfield's story was true or not, Johnston was hesitant at first, arguing that his army was not prepared to advance. However, a more promising opportunity could not be found. Grant rested on the west side of the swollen Tennessee River at Pittsburg Landing in a virtually unguarded position, and his reinforcements were still streaming into Savannah on the opposite side. The decision was made, and the Confederate army set out on the dirt roads from Corinth on the afternoon of April 3. The army consisted of four corps under Gens. Leonidas Polk, Braxton Bragg, William J. Hardee, and John C. Breckinridge. Johnston's battle orders were read to the regiments as they marched from Corinth. "The eyes and hopes of eight millions of people rest upon you. . . . You are expected to show yourselves worthy of your lineage."[37] The Confederates planned to strike the Federals before they were reinforced.

When word of Buell's arrival finally filtered back to Grant, the commander decided to take an early breakfast and ride out to meet him on Sunday morning, since he had scarcely a hint of a general attack. In the calmness of the predawn, however, even before Grant arose, the battle that was to become known as Shiloh began. As Grant sat down for breakfast around 7:00 A.M., he heard the artillery upriver. He hastened toward the *Tigress*. Before the boat cast off upstream, Grant composed a hasty note to Buell that he was on his way to Pittsburg Landing and that their meeting was canceled. He also sent a note to Nelson, encamped at Savannah, to move his division to the riverbank opposite Pittsburg Landing.[38]

About 9:00 A.M. Grant docked at Pittsburg Landing nine miles upstream from Savannah. He had expected a battle for some time and had focused his mind on commencing it, but not that day. Consequently, he had not positioned his army to receive what he intended to deliver. On his way upriver to the landing, he had passed Crump's Landing, where Gen. Lew Wallace, commander of his army's Third Division, had been stationed to threaten the Mobile and Ohio Railroad and deny Confederate access to the heights at Crump's Landing. From the steamer Grant shouted orders to Wallace to ready his division for a march upstream and await further orders. The Army of the Tennessee had arranged its camps with no notion of developing a defensive line, and the impenetrable darkness further impaired pickets and scouting patrols. The newly mustered and untried troops of Sherman's Fifth Division and Benjamin M. Prentiss's Sixth Division positioned south of the Purdy Road nearest Corinth bore the brunt of the attack.[39]

The thousands of screaming Confederates who charged out of the woods near Shiloh church that morning surprised the unsuspecting Federals, but the surprise was not wholly complete. Several hours before sunup on April 6, Col. Everett Peabody, commanding Prentiss's First

Brigade, sent out a patrol that ultimately engaged the advance units of the Confederate battle line. After about an hour of fighting, the patrol fell back, creating enough noise to alert the rest of the Sixth Division, which scurried into formation. The men of Sherman's division also leaped from their breakfasts and grabbed their muskets. Sherman jumped in the saddle and rode forward to see what was happening; within seconds a volley rang out, killing his orderly and causing him to exclaim, "My God, we're attacked!"[40]

By this time Prentiss's men were fighting stubbornly on the left, while Maj. Gen. John McClernand's more experienced men filled the gap between Sherman and Prentiss, and Brig. Gens. Stephen Hurlbut and W. H. L. Wallace sent reinforcements to the hard-pressed divisions. By the time Grant rode to the front, the fighting had reached an intensity unparalleled so far in the war, and men were swarming to the rear by the hundreds. Johnston and Beauregard had committed nearly 44,000 men early in the day, yet Grant remained calm and in control, bolstering his battle line that stretched from the Tennessee River on the left to Owl Creek on the right. He sent for Lew Wallace, but Wallace took the wrong road and had to countermarch, arriving too late to participate in the day's fight. Another message reached Nelson, presumably already sloshing through the swamplike terrain, urging him to "hurry up your command as fast as possible."[41]

Like Grant, Buell was finishing breakfast on a Sunday morning that was "as lovely and beautiful as any sung by the poets," when he heard the sound of artillery up the river. He had heard this sort of firing the previous two mornings and had no reason to believe that a major engagement had begun. Buell wanted to establish personal contact with Grant that morning and decided to call on the commander to discuss what would be the order for the battle that was to come at Corinth. Before he left camp, he sent orders to the divisions in the rear to leave their trains and push forward rapidly to concentrate for the crossing of the Tennessee. About 7:00 A.M., as Buell and Fry walked to the white brick mansion on the river that Grant used as his Savannah headquarters, the firing upriver became more intense. When they arrived, instead of finding Grant, who was just pulling away from the dock, they encountered Gen. Charles F. Smith, who though crippled from a leg wound, was in fine spirits. When Buell asked the whereabouts of Grant and the nature of the firing, Smith informed Buell that Grant had gone to Pittsburg Landing to survey the situation and that the noise was nothing more than a skirmish of pickets. At first Buell thought the same thing, since it sounded like the firing of the past two days. Grant's orders to

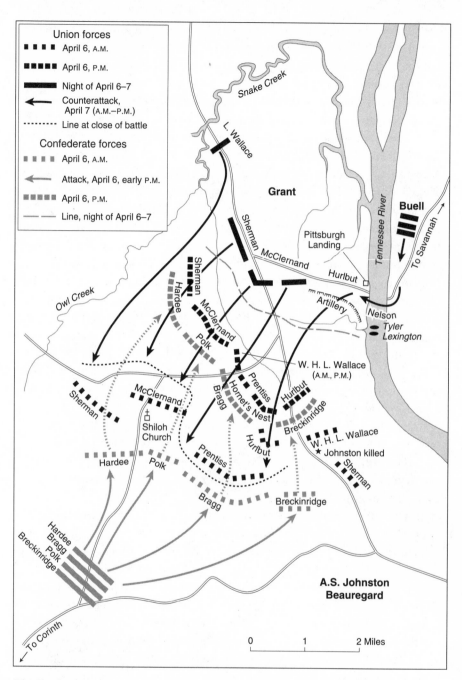

The Battle of Shiloh

Nelson to march opposite the landing for ferrying across the river, however, gave Buell reason to pause. Grant himself had recognized the swampy conditions along the river bottom; the roads were so waterlogged that artillery and wagons would have to be left behind and carried forward by steamers. Nelson sent his staff into Savannah in search of someone who could guide them upriver.[42]

The orders to bring forward the regiments caused great anticipation throughout the ranks of the Army of the Ohio. The opening of the battle of Shiloh was exciting for soldiers who had not "seen the elephant." Though most volunteers were impatient with dawdling professional generals conducting the war, Buell's slow descent to Nashville and Savannah rendered the anticipation for combat more acute. For over a month George R. Weeks, a surgeon in the Twenty-fourth Ohio, had waited patiently for Buell to move more aggressively. "I am tired of the system of warfare, known and characterized as 'masterly inactivity!'"[43] Colonel Ammen wrote that his officers and men were "more diligent" in preparing to march than ever before, as "preparation for parade and review is abandoned and all attention is given to what is required in battle."[44] Todd M. Oliphant, chaplain of the Seventy-eighth Ohio, wrote that the sound of battle went through his comrades "like an electric shock, all men were excited."[45] "Instantly," recalled Charles C. Briant of the Sixth Indiana, "each man grasps his gun more firmly . . . the speed is doubled; the mud is not in the way any more."[46] For many, however, fear eclipsed the excitement of getting to the battle. "Thinks I to myself," wrote Samuel B. Franklin, "now pretty soon we will know what war is."[47] "No one goes into a battle without fear," concluded Presley Judson Edwards.[48]

For the men of Nelson's Fourth Division, the anticipation would have to endure all day. Apparently there was more to finding a guide and making accommodations to meet Grant's initial orders than Buell or Nelson anticipated. Both men waited for several hours before starting out, despite having received orders throughout the morning of the intensifying battle. Some of the men in the Fifty-first Indiana were indignant about Buell's apparent negligence as he listened to distant guns. Whatever could have caused a delay of over four hours has been the subject of debate since the battle itself. Henry Villard, who was with Nelson, recalled that Nelson did not receive Grant's order until noon. James McDonough provides perhaps the most charitable justification of the delay, arguing that perhaps Buell believed that "nothing more than a hard skirmish between outposts of the armies was taking place."[49] Buell explained years later in his article on Shiloh that Nelson "waited only for the services of a guide to march by land."[50]

Both men recognized the impassability of the road leading to a point opposite the landing; thus they waited and looked anxiously for the smoke of river transportation and in the meantime searched for a competent guide. One soldier in Nelson's division recalled that the commander "chafed like a lion caged."[51] After four hours, with no transports in sight and a portion of the officers and men returning from surveying what lay before them, Buell and Nelson turned to greet a "large, fine-looking Tennessean." He professed to be a "strong Union man and a desperate hater of rebels" and claimed to possess knowledge of every pass through the swamp. He volunteered to lead the division through the seven-mile "labyrinth of roads" along the river bottom between Savannah and Pittsburg. Buell, therefore, ordered Nelson to march through the swamp.[52]

Buell decided to steam upriver. Along the way his boat met a vessel descending the river, and it chugged alongside while a sailor handed him a letter from Grant. Here, for the first time, Buell learned of Johnston's attack. Grant's words of urgency read, "The appearance of fresh troops in the field now would have a powerful effect, both by inspiring our men and disheartening to the enemy. If you will get upon the field . . . it will be more to our advantage, and possibly save the day to us."[53] As his boat continued farther upstream and approached the landing about 1:00 P.M., he witnessed what must have been a most shocking scene. "Seeing the elephant," as contemporaries called experiencing combat, probably appeared more like a stampede of elephants. At the mouth of Snake Creek, fugitives were swimming across in a frenzy. As some soldiers of Grant's army fled to the rear and cowered under the bluffs at the landing, Buell was utterly dumbfounded. "A confused mass of various regiments," as he recalled, numbering between 4,000 and 5,000 men swarmed the riverbank.[54]

Aboard the *Tigress*, Buell met Grant, whom he had not seen since their verbal exchange in Nashville, and who must have presented quite a sight just having come from the raging battle. He was still limping and relying on crutches from the fall of his horse. Raising his battle-worn sword scabbard, he remarked to Buell that he had just come from the front. Though Buell "did not particularly notice" the damaged sword, he never forgot that Grant "manifested by manner more than in words that he was relieved by my arrival as indicating the near approach of succor." He "appeared to realize that he was beset by a pressing danger," Buell remembered, and he lacked the "masterly confidence" credited him after the battle. Though it would be hard to imagine Buell's exact thoughts at the time, it is easy to conclude, as Larry Daniel has, that "perhaps Buell took some perverse pleasure in seeing Grant, the lauded hero of Fort Donelson, in his present nasty predicament."[55]

The two men consulted briefly, and Buell requested his superior to send steamers to Savannah to bring up Crittenden's division, which had arrived during the morning. As the two men left the boat together, Buell's attention was drawn to the soldiers cowering under cover of the bank, their faces marked by the ash of several hours of the fiercest fighting anyone in either army had ever seen. Soldiers were swimming across the Tennessee, floating downriver clinging to whatever would carry them away, and climbing aboard the boats returning to Savannah. Naturally this scene made quite an impression on him, so much so that Grant recalled in his postwar article on Shiloh that it "no doubt . . . impressed General Buell with the idea that a line of retreat would be a good thing just then." As Grant wrote in his memoirs after the war, "The rear of an army engaged in battle is not the best place from which to judge correctly what is going on in front."[56] Buell, according to Grant's aide John Rawlins, asked Grant what preparations he had made for retreat, to which Grant, not wanting to appear defeated, replied, "I have not yet despaired of whipping them, general."[57]

Up to this point Buell had seen neither the front nor the rear of battle, except during the Mexican War. The sheer chaos caused him to berate the cowards, "trying to shame them into joining their regiments." According to Grant, he "even threatened them with shells from the gunboats near by." In his own words, however, Buell concluded that "all efforts to form the troops and move them forward to the fight utterly failed."[58] Grant and his staff galloped to the front. Buell walked toward the bank, directing his troops down the road to the landing. He later came upon Col. James M. Tuttle, a brigade commander in Grant's Second Division, and asked about the battle plan. "By God, sir," a bemused Tuttle replied, "I don't know."[59]

As Buell tried to direct the fugitives of Grant's army back to the battle, Nelson finally started moving toward the river. It took him almost as long to reach a point opposite Pittsburg Landing as it had to find a guide and prepare to march. During this time Grant pondered not only the whereabouts of Nelson but also of Lew Wallace. He visited each of his division commanders and tried to reinforce the main line as the numbers of casualties and stragglers increased. Informed that Sherman and McClernand had been forced back still farther, he formed a line of reorganized stragglers and a few guns along the ridge west of Pittsburg Landing to make a final stand if the battle came closer to the river.[60]

Meanwhile, Albert Sidney Johnston went to the front of the Confederate right to rally the exhausted troops. He decided to lead a bayonet charge on the far flank of the Hornet's Nest, as the Confederates called the wooded thicket, and as the rebels stormed forward in the midafternoon, Johnston was struck in the leg by a bullet that severed an artery and caused him to bleed to death almost before he or anyone else realized he had been injured. The command passed to Beauregard. Throughout the afternoon the southern commanders launched at least seven separate full-scale assaults, but Prentiss held firm. Finally, at 3:30 P.M., Beauregard decided to blast the Hornet's Nest with sixty-two field guns that stretched for a half-mile. The horrendous hail of iron drew the white flag from Prentiss giving up 2,200 men, though it was hardly noticeable as the smoke descended on the battlefield. It was 5:30, and not even the setting sun could have saved them.[61]

With the sun going down, Beauregard concluded that not much more could be effectively accomplished, so he refused to authorize a final assault in the gathering twilight. Though he did know it yet, Lew Wallace's lost division was arriving, and Nelson's troops were crossing the river. Late that evening and into the early morning, while rain persisted, steamboats busily ferried Nelson's men across.[62]

The scene that met the soldiers of Buell's army as they arrived at Pittsburg Landing was frightful. The landing and the bluff above were covered with the terrorized segments of Grant's army. As each reinforcement-laden steamboat landed, Ambrose Bierce of the Ninth Indiana observed, "this abominable mob had to be kept off with bayonets."[63] Henry Villard, who had accompanied Nelson's men, found himself amid thousands of "panic-stricken" and "uncontrollable" soldiers, "all apparently entirely bereft of soldierly spirit, with no sense of obedience left, and animated by the sole impulse of personal safety." Fear had become the great motivator, and it was contagious.[64] According to New York journalist William Shanks, when Sherman's soldiers finally realized that Buell's men had arrived, they shouted, "Buell! Buell!—here come Buell's veterans."[65] "This sight," wrote an inspired Jesse Drew, "was all that saved Grant's army."[66]

The tremendous chaos caused the stragglers to tell the men of the Army of the Ohio wild rumors about what had happened on the first day of what was then the war's hardest-fought battle. A swarm of Confederates had surprised Grant at dawn and had brutalized the Federals, driving them back to the river's edge. The thundering herd of faint-hearted stragglers warned Buell's men that the same fate, or worse, awaited them at the front. After sloshing through the mud for several hours, Nelson was in no mood to tolerate such poltroons, and in his belligerent manner "asked permission to open fire on the knaves," whom he found "insensible to shame or sarcasm" or even to his own inimitable cursing.[67] Buell denied permission of course, and Nelson arrayed his mounted staff officers in a tight formation and ordered them to draw their swords. Nelson charged, "cutting through the mob of runaways who tumbled over each other in abject terror," one of Nelson's aides recalled.[68] In response to the warnings of " 'Oh, you'll catch it when you get over the hill there!' 'Oh, boys, I pity you!' 'You'll never come back again, comrades—mark that!' " they replied, " 'Fall in here; this is a good regiment; it's not going to run, neither!'"[69] When his men had finally made it to the top of the bank, Nelson met Buell. "You have had the advance throughout the march," said Buell, "and here, General, is your opportunity."[70] With that, Nelson called his men into line and proceeded forward.

Grant made quick use of eight companies of Col. William Grose's Thirty-sixth Indiana at the head of Ammen's brigade, deploying them along the Pittsburg Landing–Corinth Road to support a semicircle of guns that were trying their best to stop a last Confederate assault on the Union left. As the screaming Confederates came crashing through the underbrush, the overwhelming outburst drove the Federal gunners on the left of the circle from their pieces. At this critical juncture the soldiers of Grose's regiment let loose with a severe volley, causing the Confederates to falter. A combination of infantry, artillery, and gunboat fire, as well as bad terrain, ultimately forced the graycoats to fall back. With that, the fighting ended for the day.[71]

Across the lines, Beauregard did not have Grant's good fortune of fresh troops, though his men had much to feel confident about. Beauregard shared this confidence; in fact he inspired it. The next day's fight would simply complete the victory that Johnston had started. Without knowledge of Buell's arrival, the Confederates naturally concluded that the Union army would retreat during the night. In fact, a cavalry report from northern Alabama led Beauregard to believe that Buell was heading in that direction. Apparently Buell's decision to send Mitchel there had paid off, despite Halleck's reservations. Confederates returned in mass south of the Hamburg-Purdy Road to Sherman's and Prentiss's captured camps, putting over a mile between them and the Federal front. Now that the sunken road lay in the rear of the advance, the shortened line could be strengthened for a final assault that would shove Grant's army over the bluff and into the Tennessee.[72]

The only reprieve soldiers on both sides enjoyed was darkness, and lightning flashes and the ceaseless firing from Union gunboats in the

Tennessee disrupted even that. The boats lobbed shells throughout the night to keep the Confederates from sleeping. The rain came down steadily and at times with a vengeance, drowning out the wailing sounds of the wounded and dying men who literally covered the ground. Unlike Beauregard, Grant wrapped himself in a poncho and slept in the field with his men. He shared the confidence of his Confederate counterpart, but for different reasons. He was determined to counterattack the next morning. Though his army had been driven back, its position was stronger, since it still possessed the advantages of terrain, and because a large portion of Confederate troops would have to cross steep backwater ravines to assault the Union line. Moreover, his artillery remained powerful, including the eight-inch shells of two gunboats, *Tyler* and *Lexington*. Buell's arrival with almost 13,000 fresh troops that swelled to almost 18,000 by the day's end also provided Grant the advantage of numbers, as he could place the men of the Army of the Ohio alongside almost 25,000 pounded but willing survivors who had fought the first day. He had another sizable force along the river to draw on if he became desperate, but he chose not to rely on them in plans for the next day.[73]

Just after sunset, Buell and Fry walked the line to gain information and inspire the men, though motivation was scarcely one of Buell's strong suits. To the right of the Army of the Ohio they passed through the broken fragments of Hurlbut's, McClernand's, and Sherman's divisions. The scent of cigar smoke no doubt drew them to a tree, where they found Sherman resting. Buell had not seen Sherman since the red-headed general had left Louisville under a cloud of controversy. Though Sherman had been in the thick of the fighting all day, Buell remembered that "Sherman never appeared to better advantage." "There was the frank, brave soldier," he recalled, "rather subdued, realizing the critical situation in which causes of some sort . . . had placed him, but ready, without affection or bravado, to anything that duty required of him." Buell asked for information about the ground in front, and Sherman, handing Buell a small map, related what he knew about the enemy's position and strength. He also remarked that Grant intended to attack in the morning and that Buell was expected to position his army on the left of the Corinth Road. Sherman remembered that Buell was nervous, remarking that he "seemed to mistrust us" and "did not like the looks of things." Buell, however, recalled that Sherman's explanations on that occasion were briefer "than would ordinarily be expected from him." While he indicated he was glad to see Buell, Sherman also hinted that victory would have been certain even without Buell's army. Buell regarded this as a poor way to welcome him, since he provided Grant with a decided tactical advantage.[74]

As night descended on Pittsburg Landing and the soldiers of Grant's and Beauregard's armies sought safety, the commanders busied themselves by directing men into battle positions. Buell, meanwhile, returned to the landing and ordered brigades into battle positions all during the night. The remainder of Nelson's men made their way to their stations just to the right of Ammen's brigade, north of the peach orchard, where the troops of Hurlbut, Prentiss, and Wallace had fought and been pushed back. In their front they peered out at the peach orchard and the ravine where Johnston had fallen. Despite what they had heard, Nelson's soldiers were determined not to be defeated.[75]

On a night that was as "dark as a stack of black cats," and in a steady downpour, the men rested on their arms. Buell stayed awake all night and after walking Nelson's front line, he made his way back to the landing and found the advance of Crittenden's division arriving by steamboat. Thousands of demoralized soldiers blocked their way onto the landing, and Crittenden had difficulty getting his men off the boats. The "entirely demoralized soldiery" so "disgusted" him that he asked Buell's permission to use the bayonet to drive the stragglers away, explaining that "I did not wish my troops to come in contact with them."[76] Buell refused and finally led Crittenden's men himself through the mob and up to a position in the woods one half-mile from the landing, where they "stood to [their] arms" until 5:00 A.M. Buell then led them personally to the right of Nelson's division, where they peered toward the ominous Hornet's Nest.[77]

Meanwhile, McCook's division, which had dropped its train and hurried along the cluttered road in the dark, poured into Savannah and was to be ferried upriver by early morning. The same transport steamers also carried the artillery. Buell realized that his other two divisions, hurrying along by forced marches, probably would not arrive in time for action that day, although Thomas J. Wood's men would arrive in the late afternoon. When Buell came upon the brigade of William B. Hazen, the Ohioan's poised demeanor gave Hazen every indication that Buell expected his army to perform gallantly the next day. Moved, Hazen later wrote, "Nothing in war impressed me more."[78]

From his own observations, Buell expected little help from the Army of the Tennessee the next day. From what he saw along the riverbank and at the landing, he had little reason to expect anything else. From the first, he and Grant did not discuss any coordinated counterattack.

Buell commanded his own army with no plan of coordination with Grant. There was no tactical plan, "simply an understanding [between Buell and Grant] that they would assume the offensive . . . and the Army of the Ohio should take the left of the field."[79]

The divided command on April 7 was unusual, but not when viewed in the context of command relations in the West. Halleck dwarfed Grant, though it was Grant who gave Halleck the success needed to claim overall command in the West. Buell had been McClellan's favorite, despite Halleck's antagonism, and had maintained a senior and favorable position since coming to the West. Grant, however, had been too busy to be impressed by either Halleck or Buell. Although the first day's chaos at the landing may have discouraged Grant, who also thrived on discipline, he never doubted his ability to pull off a victory, particularly in Buell's presence.

That Monday morning the burst of field artillery from the Union lines signaled a change in the direction of the battle. As the sun tried to press through the early morning fog and the noise intensified, Union general Prentiss, who had surrendered the day before and was sharing Sherman's headquarters with Beauregard, sat up in bed and brazenly declared, "There is Buell! Didn't I tell you so?" It was Buell, just as Prentiss had gloated.[80]

Grant wasted no time that morning in doing what he was best at when it came to fighting: seizing the offensive and throwing everything he had at the enemy. Buell did the same. This time 45,000 men in eight divisions swarmed at Beauregard. When the battle opened, the fighting swirled once again about the Bloody Pond, the peach orchard, and the Hornet's Nest. Buell ordered Nelson's men simply to meet the enemy, because as he later stated, "My entire ignorance of the various roads and of the character of the country at the time rendered it impossible to anticipate the probable disposition of the enemy."[81]

If it was his misfortune "to know nothing about the topography in front," the Confederates had a similar misfortune, as they did not even attempt a night reorganization. At first Buell's men encountered only pickets and scattered detachments. Not until reaching the peach orchard and the densely wooded Hornet's Nest did they meet solid resistance. Nelson's men were the first to advance about 5:00 A.M., but Buell halted them to wait for Crittenden. While Nelson's and Crittenden's infantry exchanged volleys with the enemy across the thicket, McCook's men came quickly into line on Crittenden's right. Now the Army of the Ohio occupied a front of one mile, its left anchored on the Tennessee

River and its right ultimately extending to the middle of McClernand's camp of the previous day.[82]

Even had Buell been a disciple of fighting, the battlefield of Shiloh would not have been his choice. Most of the area was heavily forested with broad-leafed trees and, in places, a thick undergrowth. The landscape was cut by numerous ravines and skirted by several creeks. Under the best of circumstances the terrain limited the kinds of tactical orders he and his division commanders as well as brigade and regimental commanders could give. The rain-soaked conditions limited the use of artillery, and thousands of soldiers clustered and intermingled within a few thousand yards of one another. This combination of factors made tactical maneuvering virtually impossible. Consequently, the battle was a series of assaults and counterassaults in which success was determined by the sheer number of reinforcements and the ability of Nelson, McCook, and Crittenden to exhibit physical courage and inspire their men to charge against the Confederate line under tremendous fire. The terrain so impeded Grant's cavalry that commanders simply broke the regiments into small scouting parties.[83]

Nelson was as aggressive as he was obnoxious, and his division set the tone for the day's fighting. His men advanced and were pushed back throughout the day. When Buell noticed his left falling back, and Nelson without artillery, he immediately restored it with two rifled batteries of the Fourth and Fifth U.S. Artillery, which poured a terrific fire into the Confederate line, staggering it. After a short lull in the firing the Confederates attempted to advance; but Union artillery proved too much, and Hazen's brigade stormed the cannoneers and captured the batteries.

In the center Crittenden was having his share of trouble. Not only had his slow pace held up Nelson's advance, but even when his men had successfully charged a thicket, driving away the Confederates, he ordered the men back to their original position for fear that his flank was exposed. When the Confederates countered, Buell diverted one of Crittenden's well-placed guns to fire on them. All day Buell rode along the lines positioning his regiments and, according to one Iowan, "inspired confidence as he rode . . . and addressed words of cheer to his troops."[84] Such presence near the front line naturally endangered Buell, and he came close to being shot several times. Those accompanying him, such as aide-de-camp Almon Rockwell, found shells exploding all around them. Rockwell recalled that the "balls [were] whistling all about us."[85]

As they charged across the battlefield, Buell's men encountered something more gruesome than the faces of the dying: the faces of the dead from the previous day. The men of Jacob Ammen's Tenth Brigade, who during the march through the swamp the previous day had been concerned that the fight might be over before they arrived, witnessed horrible scenes. An Ohio soldier recalled, "The gory corpses lying all about us, in every imaginable attitude, and slain by an inconceivable variety of wounds, were shocking to behold, but they made no sign and claimed no recognition; their sufferings were over."[86] A private in the Fifteenth Ohio remembered that the dead and wounded on the ground "looked heavy to us new soldiers."[87] Seeing the amputated limbs outside a field hospital cured the volunteers of the Twenty-Ninth Indiana of their desire for combat.[88]

While Buell's left and center pressed forward, his right, McCook's division, fought in the vicinity of Duncan Field and McClernand's old camp on either side of the main road leading from Shiloh Church to the landing. By midday the Confederates directed their attack to this point, and it soon developed into the critical part of the battle. During this time "only three cowards . . . ran away," wrote artilleryman James F. Mohr.[89] Sgt. Edwin Payne of the Thirty-fourth Ohio recalled that the sounds of battle "began to give us a new experience. . . . We began to realize that we were earning our thirteen dollars a month."[90]

By noon the entire Confederate line had been forced back to a position along the Hamburg-Purdy Road, but not until soldiers had fought back and forth over the same ground several times in what seemed to be the bloodiest fighting of the day. Here "I saw for the first time," reported an impressed Sherman, "the well-ordered and compact columns of General Buell's Kentucky forces, whose soldierly movements at once gave confidence to our newer and less-disciplined forces." "Here," he added, "I saw [Col. August] Willich's regiment advance upon a point of water-oaks and thicket, behind which I knew the enemy was in great strength, and it enter it in beautiful style." "There arose the severest musketry fire I ever heard, which lasted for some twenty minutes, when this splendid regiment had to fall back."[91]

When Willich's German-American regiment had been repulsed, Sherman witnessed Rousseau's Fourth Brigade of McCook's division advance "beautifully" and enter "these dreaded woods." Rousseau's men "moved in splendid order steadily to the front, sweeping everything before it, and at 4 P.M. we stood upon the ground of our original front line and the enemy was in full retreat."[92] From these observations Sherman concluded that it was McCook's "splendid division from Kentucky" that "drove back the enemy along the Corinth road, which was the great central line of this battle."[93] Charges and countercharges epitomized the severe fighting that raged from 10:00 A.M. until 4:00 P.M. Grant's three divisions supported McCook.

The Confederate ranks were dwindling, and the rear of Beauregard's army began to look like Grant's the day before as a stream of battle-weary stragglers flowed backward. From his headquarters at Shiloh Church, Beauregard watched the ebb and flow of battle and realized his army could no longer maintain its position. At about 2:30 in the afternoon, with his ranks "perceptively thinned under the unceasing, withering fire of the enemy," Beauregard prepared to retire. Withdrawal was not easy. Collecting the broken organizations of the infantry and artillery and posting them in defensive positions so the army could pass through to the rear was not easy work. Getting to the wounded and carrying them off made leaving the battlefield dangerous. The rain picked up after dark. The road back to Corinth was littered with discarded wagons, artillery, and all the tools of war no longer needed to carry out a retreat. Most of the Confederates had had enough of the war. As one Tennessean penned in his diary, "I shall never forget how I felt that day . . . knowing that with the early tomorrow many of us most likely would pass away."[94]

The Union soldiers also had seen enough of the war. They were too exhausted to pursue the vanquished until the following day, and even that effort was halfhearted. Grant had not prepared for pursuit of the enemy; indeed it was all he could do to defeat him on the battlefield. Two raging days of battle had thoroughly exhausted Grant's men, and Buell's soldiers, fatigued after a grueling march, a sleepless night, and a hard day's battle, had no desire to chase an enemy protected by excellent cavalry. Grant ordered Sherman to ascertain if the Confederates were in full retreat or posed a threat of attack. Because the rains continued, the artillery normally used to support such a retreat was ineffective. Forrest, however, waited at Fallen Timbers six miles down the Ridge Road, where he ambushed Sherman's pursuers. He was wounded in the process and galloped off.[95]

The battle of Shiloh ended as it began: shockingly. Dead bodies demonstrated the result of the surprise and tactical blunders. One Ohio soldier concluded that the scenes after the battle "would have chilled the blood of the most cold hearted."[96] Although scenes from this battle may have convinced soldiers that the war was nearing its close, they persuaded Grant that only total conquest would end the conflict. That Buell did not see for himself Grant's conclusion reflected his inability or refusal to learn from the war. Shiloh baptized the soldiers and the country to the unlimited ways men could be killed. The first newspaper reports of the battle were made before the smoke of the strife had even rolled away. As one New York correspondent put it, "The great battle of Pittsburg will stand forth in bold relief upon the page of future history, as one of the most bloody and obstinate of the century, and by far the greatest our young Republic has ever known." "Everywhere was mad excitement," he scribbled, "everywhere was horror."[97] Some soldiers, such as Corp. Alexander Varian of the First Ohio, found the "awful grandeur of a raging battle" as invigorating as getting to the field of battle itself. Referring to his musket as "The Widow," Varian wrote to his wife, "She spoke to the Rebels 31 times during the day—I think to some purpose."[98] The exhilaration of the charge inspired Thomas Prickett of the Ninth Indiana to write, "I never felt so good in my life, I thought we were just going to play smash with them generally."[99] The New York correspondent himself wrote that when "arms, legs and heads were torn off, a grim smile of pleasure lighted up the smoke-begrimed faces of the transformed beings who witnessed the catastrophe."[100]

To those who fought at Shiloh, "full-scale" hardly described what happened. James A. Garfield, commander of the Twentieth Brigade, attempted to explain the unpleasant truth of what he had seen to his wife. "No blaze of glory," he wrote, "that flashes around the magnificent triumphs of war, can ever atone for the unwritten and unutterable horrors of the scene of carnage."[101] Like Garfield, most soldiers, North and South, were perfectly satisfied never to see another battlefield. Even for a seasoned veteran like Nelson, the battlefield was a "*shocking sight, a heartrendering sight*," as he related the combat to Treasury Secretary Chase. "War is an emanation of Hell," he wrote.[102] Describing how his brother was killed, young Torah Sampson wrote to his mother, "I have all ways want[ed] to see one battle field and now I have seen it and I never want to see another one."[103]

In the days following the battle, Thomas's division arrived at what Andrew F. Davis of the Fifteenth Indiana called "the Waterloo field of the American Continent."[104] The warm sun had caused such an "intolerable stench arising from the battle field," wrote Samuel Davis of the Seventy-seventh Pennsylvania, that his brigade moved far away.[105] Even officers who had become accustomed to seeing the dead after battle were completely unprepared for the grizzly sights of bodies churned into the ground by artillery and wagons, and burned-to-death soldiers pinned under fallen leaves. "We had *expected* to find dead and mangled bodies on the field," one soldier wrote, "and our minds were prepared for the spectacle but we were not prepared to come in sudden contact with that naked and ghastly mass of human flesh."[106] Passing through the woods assisting some relatives searching for a fallen soldier, Chaplain Todd Oliphant recorded, "Let a dark veil be drawn over the scene."[107]

After the battle that gave the Union its first taste of a large-scale contest in the West, the soldiers hailed Buell as the savior of Shiloh. In the days immediately following the battle, when he passed by a command, soldiers responded uncharacteristically favorably toward him, cheering him and raising their hats and weapons on his behalf. William H. Clune of the Sixth Iowa concluded that "General Buell [was] the hero of Pittsburgh, and from what they say of his management yesterday [he] could go to bed and forget more generalship in one night than Gen. Grant ever knew."[108] Gen. James Blair Steedman recalled that it was "very difficult to suppress cheers as General Buell passed the men." Buell's popularity was surprising, since his men generally considered him "too exclusive."[109] Because he remained with his men at the front during the battle, busily barking out orders and positioning his brigades, they gloried in his presence. Buell led by example, "expos[ing] himself freely," and some soldiers thought he had taken over the command of the entire army. His presence alone gave inspiration to men as he "superintended forming the line of battle." "Genl Buell," wrote Nelson to Chase, "great Genl Buell for great he is."[110]

Lovell Rousseau agreed. "We have entire confidence in him in all things," he wrote to Chase. On the battlefield, "he was present, and fixed upon the line of battle for my brigade . . . and he watched the field & his troops all day. His presence greatly cheered his men."[111] When Buell arrived, "the change seemed to be miraculous," wrote Sgt. Harold White of the Eleventh Iowa. "For the first time we could perceive the difference between a soldier, for such Buell assuredly is, and an imbecile."[112]

Buell never claimed any personal credit for Shiloh in the immediate aftermath. On the evening after the battle, he confided to his wife that he and his army believed they had saved Grant:

> I am writing you from the field . . . of battle, the greatest in the size of the armies engaged that has ever been fought on this continent. Nor is it without a great result, in this, that it saved the army of General Halleck, commanded by General Grant, which otherwise was doomed to destruction.
>
> It is the voice of his [Grant's] entire army, as far as I know, that they were lost. . . . I mean to state these facts very simply and briefly in my report, and let the world form its own conclusions as to what credit my troops are entitled to.[113]

At the time, what else could Buell conclude? The scene at the landing made it appear as though the soldiers of Grant's army had been completely overwhelmed or surprised by a larger Confederate force. The limited knowledge of the terrain and of the disposition of the Confederates further led Buell to this conclusion. Of course some officers and soldiers were more adamant than others about who won the battle and the cause for the overwhelming number of casualties. Crittenden's aide-de-camp Louis M. Buford was quick to state his opinion, which was prevalent throughout Buell's army. He admonished a correspondent not to believe the newspapers applauding Grant. "Grant was badly whipped," he wrote to his brother, "and if we hadn't have come to his relief when we did[,] his entire army would have been taken prisoners or [drowned] in the Tennessee River."[114] Rousseau was a more severe critic of the press. "I see already that the papers are filled with reports as fabulous as any of the vagaries of Don Quixote," he fumed. In order to vindicate the "'truth of history,'" Rousseau wrote a lengthy letter to Secretary Chase arguing that Grant's placement of the army on the west side of the river before Buell arrived was not simply a blunder but "the most stupendous crime of this age," and that "the blood of fifteen hundred brave men, cries aloud against the act." He concluded by saying, "This battle has blown to the winds, all our admiration for Gen. Grant."[115]

It did not take long for the world to draw its own conclusions about what happened at Shiloh. Not surprisingly, even Grant's own men criticized him for the unpreparedness. Timothy Blaisdell complained that Grant was an "imbecile" who "had caused the whole thing."[116] Such imbecility caused Charles Tompkins to lament, "Our Genl [Grant] ought to be compelled to serve as a private for the rest of his life."[117] Nelson lashed out to Chase in a long-winded letter that Shiloh was a "blunder on our part arising from the sheer stupidity of our Generals." Though he considered Sherman the hero of the Army of the Tennessee, calling him the "soul of the battle" and the "*achilles of Sunday*," he blamed him for neglecting his pickets. On Grant's role, Nelson wrote, "I say XXXXX–XXXXX Consider it said."[118] Garfield was a gentler critic, saying, "Grant seems to have been surprised at Shiloh by some criminal neglect, not yet explained."[119]

Though Buell was not negligent, he nonetheless received his share of criticism as well. The editor of *Frank Leslie's Illustrated*, for example, argued that "if Grant was careless, negligent and criminal, so too was Genl. Buell slow, inefficient and criminal." The editor claimed that Buell knew of Grant's position and "dawdled through Tennessee."[120]

For years after the battle the controversy focused on the criminal neglect of picketing and whether Buell saved the day or not. Whatever the day's results, Grant had the situation under control by the time Buell arrived. Still, the Ohioan's arrival not only made the attack of the second day an obvious assumption for both commanders; it also ensured victory. This debate obscures the importance of the performance of Buell's army under tremendous combat, the likes of which they had never witnessed. In spite of going into combat with only a portion of his army, almost no knowledge of the terrain, and no definite communicated battle plan from his superior, Buell had the Army of the Ohio perform excellently. Though Buell was personally on the field all that second day, it was the individual bravery and leadership of his division and brigade commanders that played a critical role in determining the outcome. The correspondent to the *Cincinnati Commercial* wrote, "Gen. Buell's troops were, in drill and appearance, the superiors of those under Grant." "There was the light of battle and promise of victory in the faces of every division of Buell's troops."[121] Sherman, McClernand, and Wallace specifically paid tribute to the men of McCook's brigade. All that Buell had demanded of his soldiers since the previous November was finally put to the test at Shiloh. The discipline and order had paid off handsomely in the battle as the men fought like veterans. If the soldiers had criticized him earlier as being a martinet, they had their lives to thank for his leadership. As Nelson aptly put it, "The labors of Genl Buell all the long winter [now] bore ripe fruit, discipline led. . . . The Army of the Ohio is an Army."[122]

Buell's words of praise after the battle confirmed what his men already knew. They had by forced marches pressed forward with "alacrity and zeal" and essentially saved "their comrades of a sister army imperiled by the attack of an overwhelming force." Their "gallantry" and "persevering courage" were virtues that an impressed Buell said "point to a great service nobly performed." But even in these words he reminded his men that "such results are not attained by individual prowess alone." Their subordination, careful training, efficiency, and readiness learned from obedience to orders from and the labors of division, brigade, and regimental commanders had "given them a brilliant page in history."[123]

Shiloh had a sobering impact on Buell's army. For the first time, he and his men shared an experience that humbled officers and privates alike. Yet he remained the distant leader. He failed to personalize his praise to make the soldiers feel as though he was one of them or that he even acknowledged that because they were volunteers, they were entitled to special commendation. Buell praised not the soldiers themselves, their commitment to the army, or their patriotism but, rather, their performance and appearance.[124]

Nelson, Rousseau, and Jacob Ammen were among the officers who carefully observed the firm hand Buell held over his army. Ammen was with Buell on the night of April 6, and the commander's tone, manner, and attention to detail impressed him. It appeared for a moment that whatever attractive and endearing qualities Buell had were best displayed on the eve of battle. At least that was how Ammen saw it. "Buell is indefatigable," he wrote, "careful of his men, cool in battle, labors hard to get the best positions, and sees and examines for himself."[125] Rousseau said Buell "has the best organized and best drilled army of volunteers that ever existed, made so largely by his own untiring exertions."[126]

Besides reporting to Halleck that Buell had arrived and fought the second day of the battle, Grant failed to comment further on Buell's contribution, since anything more than that would be an admission of his own surprise. What he did not say reflected the divided command of the battle. Even though Grant and Buell knew who was in charge of all the forces, the two men continued to think of their own armies as separate. Grant gave Sherman tremendous credit, and rightfully so. Sherman had impressed Grant by his willingness earlier to waive his seniority and come up to Donelson from Paducah. The two had developed an understanding before the battle, and Shiloh forged their friendship.[127]

That friendship extended into the postbattle debates and articles recounting what had happened at Shiloh. Not surprisingly both Sherman and Grant argued that they were not in the midst of defeat. Not only had they not been surprised; they had not been beaten, but simply forced back to the river. Sherman said his share as well. Shortly after the battle, he commented to his brother that the charges of surprise were "all simply false." Grant and he were "always ready for an attack."[128]

Later in the year Sherman repeated to a friend that the Army of the Tennessee was not surprised, defeated, or demoralized. He criticized Nelson for making such harsh characterizations of the conditions along the river on the evening of April 6, saying that because Nelson, who "would blow somewhat in his favor," created "harsh allusions" of the situation, he had misled the public about the battle.[129] For someone who stood by Grant's story of not being surprised or beaten, Sherman later had a different attitude about seeing Buell at sunset on the evening of the first day. "I admit that I was glad Buell was there, because I knew his troops were older than ours and better systematized and drilled, and his arrival made that certain, which was uncertain before."[130]

Buell said little about the battle until after the war, but Fry, his chief of staff, proved to be relentless in trying to put the Army of the Ohio's contribution into proper perspective. Not only did Fry try to restore Buell's reputation during the war, his postwar book *Operations of the Army under Buell* was an attempt to re-open and settle the debate. The editors of *Century Magazine* as well as scores of participants, including Braxton Bragg, who thought Buell's role had been invalidated by the success and prominence Grant and Sherman went on to claim, encouraged Buell to write his version of the conflict, in which he portrayed himself as the savior of Shiloh. Though he claimed that the "history of the battle [had] virtually been written in the official reports," he wrote the article, which according to friend Thomas Gantt, "closed the controversy about Shiloh." He returned to the battlefield many years later as a member of the Shiloh National Military Park Battlefield Commission, though the controversy was never resolved.[131]

By the time news of Shiloh reached the East, the Lincoln administration had heard scores of rumors and demanded an explanation regarding whether or not "any neglect or misconduct of General Grant or any other officer contributed to the sad casualties that befell our forces on Sunday."[132] Halleck, who had hurried to Shiloh, found it expedient not to discuss the battle but, rather, to soothe Washington by concluding that "the enemy suffered more than we did."[133]

The Confederates had suffered more than the Federals, though the sheer numbers of men killed and wounded overwhelmed both sides. With a combined force of about 65,000, Grant's and Buell's casualties numbered just over 13,000, including killed, wounded, and captured or missing. Despite the prebattle estimates that his army was 60,000, 80,000, or even 100,000 men strong, Johnston really had 44,000 engaged, and his army suffered nearly 11,000 casualties. An eager northern public, anxious for victory, had a combat-tested hero in the West. No longer would McClellan and grand maneuvers dominate the front page of the northern press, but fighting—brutal fighting—as all eyes had a new standard with which to gauge success. Because it happened on the way to Corinth, Shiloh was not the end of anything for the Union but, rather, the beginning of something larger militarily and politically. The army would move on, as would the war.[134]

CHAPTER FOURTEEN

The Northern Mississippi Blues

Whence Halleck arrived at Shiloh on April 11, 1862, the fact that the Confederates had left the battlefield only slightly diminished his irritation with Grant. Since Halleck had restored Grant to command, the surprise reflected poorly on the general in chief. It probably pleased him little that Buell had allegedly saved Grant's army. The rumors of Buell's timely arrival pulling victory from the jaws of defeat passed through the ranks for weeks and fed his indignation. Not surprisingly, wrote a New York correspondent, there was "much ill feeling perceptible between the respective commands of Generals Grant and Buell on the score of the great fight."[1] Halleck was so inflamed by the accusation that he falsely declared to Stanton, "Every division had notice of the enemy's approach hours before the battle commenced."[2]

Whatever Halleck believed personally, he realized that the battle of

Shiloh happened along the way to Corinth. The Confederates had re-treated twenty-five miles south to the Mississippi city, where they could gather reinforcements. Corinth was a sleepy little railroad junction, though one of the South's most vital crossroads. Thus Halleck, the orig-inal disciple of maneuvering for success, set his sights on not attacking and destroying the Confederate army but on capturing the junction. As Charles B. Tompkins put it, "Genl Halleck intend[ed] taking Corinth without firing a musket."[3] In the weeks following the battle, he assem-bled over 100,000 soldiers, summoning John Pope, recently hailed for his victory at New Madrid on the Mississippi River. Halleck organized his massive army into three grand wings.[4]

Though Halleck gave Buell little recognition for his role at Shiloh, he must have been impressed with his army's performance. He gave Buell the center wing in his grand strategy, though he ordered Thomas's di-vision to Grant's army, which formed the right wing of the massive force. Though Thomas had missed Shiloh, Buell regarded the Virginian as his best division commander, and he resented losing him. Nelson was aggressive, but his belligerent attitude won him more enemies than friends. With Thomas gone, Buell was left with the divisions of McCook, Nelson, Crittenden, and Wood.[5]

Buell was not the only one who resented a reduction of the Army of the Ohio. The loss of Thomas also frustrated Andrew Johnson, since it reduced the force from which he could draw troops for the defense of Nashville. After Buell departed Nashville, Johnson had busied himself not only with making Nashville a treasonless city but also with tampering with the forces under Buell's command. It was an odd situation for John-son and Buell, since Halleck was in command of the entire West yet never felt compelled to get involved in the delicate negotiations be-tween the two men regarding the government's reconstruction efforts. Halleck simply shifted the responsibility to the Ohio general by for-warding to him all correspondence on the matter. It could be argued that Halleck did not want to interfere in what was essentially Buell's charge, but he surely limited Buell's discretion in other areas of com-mand. Nonetheless, Buell continued to be torn between Johnson's de-mands for cooperation and Halleck's move on Corinth. Halleck proba-bly took some perverse pleasure in allowing Buell a free hand in these matters, since it would further expose his political liabilities to the ad-ministration. Halleck's refusal to get involved was a testament to the continued unproductive command relationships in the West.[6]

In the weeks following Shiloh, Johnson and Buell continued to spar over the defense of Nashville, the move into East Tennessee, and Buell's conciliatory policy; the mutual animosity escalated. Johnson never hesitated to draw on his military authority, frequently calling on Adj. Gen. Lorenzo Thomas and flooding Secretary Stanton with messages. Of course he made use of his political allies as well, since he knew political considerations continued to influence the defense of Nashville and the necessity of an East Tennessee movement. In late April he complained to Senator Horace Maynard that Buell had ordered the Third Minnesota away from Nashville and in doing so was "substantially surrendering the country to the rebels." "My understanding," he wrote on April 24, "was that I was sent here to accomplish a certain purpose. If the means are withheld it is better to desist from any further efforts." Of course the fault was Buell's alone. "You are well aware of General Buell's course in regard to Tennessee from the beginning to the present moment."[7]

What particularly infuriated Johnson was that he had specifically implored Buell not to withdraw this or any other regiment because removing these soldiers "will destroy confidence in the Union men and inspire on the part of Rebels insolence and arrogance."[8] Buell reasoned, however, that the troops coming into the city would replace any regiments removed, and that it would "not do to let the Enemy close around your city before we begin to drive him away."[9] Besides, Buell correctly considered the campaign for Corinth more vital than reinforcing Nashville.

Fortunately, Buell finally got some support from Halleck, but only because Old Brains considered Johnson's request potentially damaging to his drive to Corinth. "I have answered the Secretary," he told Buell, "that we require every available man on this line, and that to send troops back to Nashville to accommodate Governor Johnson would be releasing our grasp on the enemy's throat in order to pare his toe-nails." Still, Halleck left the disposition of troops east of the Tennessee River to Buell's judgment.[10]

Buell handled the disgruntled governor as best he could. In an attempt to appease him, he wrote, "I am anxious to gratify you but you will see the propriety of making all other considerations yield to that disposition of the troops which is necessary for the security of Nashville . . . & Middle Tennessee."[11] To Halleck, however, he replied that the disposition of his troops in Middle Tennessee was necessary to defend the region and to support Mitchel. Besides, the military operations were far more important "than the gratification of Governor Johnson, whose views upon the matter are absurd."[12] In light of the recent battle they might have been; but politics still played a critical role in campaigns in the West, and Johnson continued to have more clout in Washington than Buell.

On April 25, when Buell ordered the Sixty-ninth Ohio away from Nashville after Stanton had specifically ordered it to Johnson, the governor went straight to the president, proving he was as relentless as Buell was stubborn. "Petty jealousies and contests between generals wholly incompetent to discharge the duties assigned them have contributed more to the defeat and embarrassment of the Government than all other causes combined," he complained. To be sure, he had not forgotten the long winter of military idleness. "If I can be sustained," he added, "in carrying out the object of the administration in restoring Tennessee to her former status in the Union, and in not being dependent upon staff officers and brigadier-generals, it can be accomplished in less than three months." "I want a reply from the President," he demanded, asking Lincoln to call on Senator Maynard about "how matters have been managed . . . in connection with the military."[13] Lincoln merely passed on the governor's concerns to Halleck, who in turn passed them to Buell.[14]

Johnson was not the only commander bothering Buell and bending Secretary Stanton's ear. Ormsby Mitchel found it useful to bypass Buell, partly out of necessity, and apprise the secretary of war of the situation in northern Alabama. Mitchel's division had missed Shiloh because his army had been given the thankless task of penetrating into the Confederacy to Murfreesboro, farther south to Fayetteville, and down to Huntsville, Alabama, on the Memphis and Charleston Railroad. With the Union and Confederate armies gathering between Corinth and Savannah, it was unlikely that he would see much difficulty from the enemy—so unlikely that Mitchel became involved in the sale of contraband cotton and schemes such as the unsuccessful attempt to steal a Confederate locomotive near Chattanooga.[15]

By mid-April the bulk of Mitchel's division had arrived at Huntsville and was holding a line 125 miles deeper into the Confederacy than any Union commander had previously penetrated. On April 17 he communicated to Stanton that his operations extended from Stevenson on the eastern end of the road to Tuscumbia on the west. Mitchel was eager to move against Chattanooga or Knoxville and complained to a friend that he was tired of depending on others, referring to Buell, "who are moving [too] slow," for orders. "The entire war has been moved too slow," he griped.[16]

Stanton, Chase, Halleck, and Lincoln were all surprised that Buell had ordered Mitchel to burn the Bridgeport bridge over the Tennessee River when it looked like the opportunity to get to Chattanooga had finally arrived. Buell, however, had two reasons for ordering the destruction of the bridge. First, Mitchel convinced him that his division was vulnerable to a large Confederate force rumored to be hovering around Chattanooga, and second, Buell concluded that the Memphis and Charleston Railroad would hardly be a proper communication line for his army to move against Chattanooga. As Buell knew only too well, seizing Chattanooga was one thing, but occupying it was another matter altogether, no matter how bold Mitchel appeared. As Halleck's army settled lethargically into its move against Corinth in late April, Mitchel urged Buell to send a portion of his main army to occupy Tuscumbia on the south side of the Tennessee River. Halleck agreed, but it was clear he would not reduce Buell's main army to accommodate either Mitchel or Johnson. Instead, Halleck assumed Buell could simply rearrange the forces in that region without affecting the main army. Consequently, Mitchel had to abandon the line from Tuscumbia to Decatur and pulled his right flank back to Athens. Instead of Tuscumbia, Mitchel turned east toward Stevenson and determined to make that his main objective.[17]

As Mitchel turned east in late April, giving the impression he was still eager to head to Chattanooga, Halleck, having reorganized his army, was starting south. To keep Grant stripped of power, Halleck made him second in command, which naturally irritated Grant because Thomas assumed command of the Army of the Tennessee. The reorganization also annoyed Buell, since it left him with only three divisions, one of which was composed almost entirely of new regiments. What made him angrier was that Thomas, a former subordinate, had a larger command. With only 18,000 men Buell calmly expressed his displeasure to Halleck: "You must excuse me for saying that, as it seems to me, you have saved the feelings of others very much to my injury."[18] Since this happened at the same time that Johnson was clamoring for defense of Nashville and Mitchel was imploring Buell and Stanton for reinforcements in northern Alabama, Buell was distressed. Yet Halleck did nothing to relieve that anxiety.

Shiloh impressed Halleck enormously, so he was determined to keep his army tightly concentrated and thus gave virtually no independence of judgment to his subordinates. Halleck positioned pickets well in advance of the main body, repaired roads, maintained communications, and utilized entrenchments as the army moved forward toward Corinth. The army set out on May 4, and according to Halleck, it would be in front of Corinth by the following night. Yet steady rains, swollen creeks, narrow dirt roads, and low, sodden terrain severely impeded progress. It took the massive force almost a month to get to the position Halleck forecasted it would reach in one day. This was Buell's kind of campaign —slow, steady, and safe—so he approved.[19]

During the advance to Corinth the friction between Halleck and Buell that had recently waned heated up again. In the span of five months Buell had gone from departmental commander, where he had independence in making policy decisions, to a subordinate with the smallest command in an army commanded by someone who had yet to see combat. It did not help the relationship when, in mid-May, Buell offended Halleck on two occasions. First, he failed to entrench when ordered, and second, he delayed the army when he surveyed the ground he was to occupy. On May 17 Halleck sharply reprimanded him for a delay. "You were ordered to move at 8 o'clock this morning. . . . I do not understand the reason for the delay." Buell responded that it was imperative to examine the ground in his front and thought Halleck would "approve of a modification which we," implicating Pope, "thought necessary." Halleck lashed back that Buell was "entirely mistaken" if he thought he could assume such independence. After receiving dispatches from a disgruntled Sherman and Pope, as well as from Thomas, Halleck sent another dispatch to Buell, chiding, "Your not moving this morning, as agreed upon, has caused great embarrassment." An outraged Buell fired off a dispatch the following day. "I certainly have intended to carry out your instructions," he maintained, "but where they have not been specific I have supposed that you expected me to exercise my own judgement." Here was the martinet challenging the opinion of the master. Buell was not accustomed to being kept on such a tight leash. Halleck's remarks wounded his pride.[20]

Mitchel's situation in northern Alabama proved equally aggravating, but for political reasons that involved not only East Tennessee but also Buell's conciliatory policy. Mitchel's correspondence with Secretary Chase indicated that Buell would not allow him to move across northern Alabama and into East Tennessee. It appeared to Stanton and Chase that Mitchel was as energetic as Johnson in moving operations ahead, while Buell remained uncooperative. Mitchel's occupation of Huntsville pleased both Chase and Stanton. "Your spirited operations," wrote Stanton, "afford great satisfaction to the President." Thus, Washington had already been given a sense of optimism in getting to East Tennessee, but not by Buell.[21]

If Buell had thought detaching Mitchel's division from the main army was a good thing in February, by May it proved to be a liability. Mitchel's private correspondence with Chase and Stanton, as well his family, re-

Buell's army crossing Lick Creek toward Corinth (*Harper's Weekly*; photograph courtesy of Harpweek)

vealed that he had ambitions far beyond repairing railroads in Alabama, and his assessment of the circumstances often included delight with himself for keeping things in order at the expense of Buell. On one occasion, according to Col. John Beatty, commander of the Third Ohio, Mitchel "determined to make all understand that he was the greatest of living generals."[22] If only he could contact Buell, he might make his superior a believer, but for some unexplained reason, either Buell never responded or his dispatches were lost. Whatever the case, Mitchel's exasperation with Buell continued and increased. "He is the *slowest* person I ever had the misfortune to be associated with, and [he] tries my patience in the severest manner almost daily," Mitchel wrote to his family. "I wish I had the management of this war for just thirty days! Here now I shall be compelled to wait! wait!! wait!!!"[23]

Mitchel's division had been independent for almost three months by the time Halleck's army began crawling toward Corinth, and in that time he had exercised considerable freedom with regard to civilians, slavery, and the reopening of the cotton trade between loyal planters and northern merchants. Mitchel and his troops remained critical of Buell's slowness and policy of conciliation, and the deeper they marched into the Confederacy, the more the soldiers complained. They were not forged in battle with the other divisions, and consequently their experiences in the field with disloyal civilians fueled a frustration they had felt since leaving Nashville.

Mitchel's men initially encountered signs of loyalty along the march south, and when they arrived at Huntsville, Col. John Beatty wrote that while the women tended to be outspoken in their hostility to the Union, the men of the town had "settled down to a patient endurance of military rule." "They say but little and treat us with all politeness," he added.[24] The Union presence, however, soon invited trouble. Either individually or in small partisan bands, southerners wreaked considerable havoc on the soldiers by disrupting supply trains, sniping at soldiers as they passed on trains, or simply forcing them to pay exorbitantly high prices for anything they needed to survive. These activities forced Mitchel, already unsympathetic to Buell's conciliatory policy, to deviate completely from the prescribed code of General Orders 13a. In many cases this simply took the form of allowing his soldiers to administer suitable retribution on individuals who had perpetrated crimes against the army. This included arresting or hanging the culprits or burning the homes of those directly connected to such crimes. Colonel Beatty made it his policy to seek revenge every time his men were the targets of unsolicited and violent acts.[25]

As depredations continued against his soldiers, Mitchel's attitude hardened. Instead of protecting the rights and property of southerners, he sought Old Testament vengeance. On May 2, after learning that some townspeople had assisted a Confederate cavalry attack on a Union regiment, the troops under Col. John Basil Turchin, a Russian army veteran known for his disregard of secessionist property owners, entered the town of Athens. Turchin invited his soldiers to sack the town. The men pounced on the opportunity, breaking into stores, stealing valuables, firing shots into the homes of the locals, and making sexual advances on female slaves. When Mitchel learned of these outrages, he simply admonished Turchin, since arresting an entire brigade would prove difficult. Two months later Buell ordered Turchin court-martialed. In the meantime, the violence at Athens simply incited more attacks on Union soldiers marching through northern Alabama. More importantly, it became the most celebrated event of Buell's tenure in command.[26]

Even while Buell himself focused on the campaign to Corinth, his policy toward fugitive slaves had failed, inviting open criticism. Although

Buell's policy of returning fugitive slaves had been in tune with other commanders and harmonized nicely with his desire to pacify southerners into not taking up arms against his army, after March 27 it violated a congressional mandate that prohibited the return of fugitive slaves. Buell, however, continued to follow a policy of turning slaves away from his lines. He insisted that his officers keep fugitives out of his army. As Mitchel found, few southerners were receptive to his advance deeper into the South, and the only friends the soldiers had were slaves. He found them so useful that he pleaded to Stanton that it was an "absolute necessity" to protect slaves from their masters. Soldiers occasionally deceived their superiors about slaves in their ranks, often presenting them as free blacks from the North who had accompanied their regiments into the army. On one occasion during the occupation of Huntsville, several officers in Mitchel's division, prompted by their disgust at being forced to turn away slaves, went to the commander's headquarters, laid their swords on the table, and objected to the orders, declaring they would not obey them. Mitchel agreed with the officers but defused the situation by responding that the only alternative would be to have the slaves arrested. The situation was so divisive that Maj. Joseph Keifer of the Third Ohio wrote to his wife that slaves were often shot by their masters if they were caught soliciting relief from the soldiers. "The negroes think very hard when they are forbidden to come within our lines," and many were not persuaded by the bayonet to return to their homes. "They said they would sooner be killed in the army than by their masters and overseers," remarked Keifer.[27]

What made the situation more critical for Buell was that some of Mitchel's soldiers, like Mitchel himself, had lost faith in Buell's policy to win back southerners to the Union, and they also held more Radical views toward emancipation. "There is no disguising the fact," declared Keifer, "that slavery is the issue, that has brought on this war."[28] Mitchel wrote to Secretary Chase that although he could not agree with Chase before the war started that slavery would have to be ended, now that the war had come, he wrote, "I shall be rejoiced to see slavery driven from the national jurisdiction."[29]

Although at first opposition to Buell's policies was centered in a few, but vocal regiments such as the Third Ohio, Buell himself soon came under fire for maintaining his conciliatory attitude long after it was unpopular with his men and the administration. While many soldiers might have agreed with Ohio private John Fox that "a greater evil could not exist than to free the negro at this time," as spring turned into summer and troops were forced to adhere to a policy some were questioning, it was not long before soldiers felt that Buell's conciliation was no longer feasible and that their commander was out of touch with the political realities of the war and the administration's desires.[30]

James Garfield was among those who concluded Buell's policy was out of tune with the increasing shift in favor of freeing the slaves. Commanding the Twentieth Brigade, Garfield was in Thomas Wood's division of the Army of the Ohio during Halleck's drive to Corinth and made some perceptive observations illustrative of that shift. With each mile the army moved south, he became more exasperated with the proslavery proclivities of Wood and more sensitive to the issue of slavery and to the latent loyal support of southerners to the Union. "In one thing I fear we have been mistaken," he wrote his former college friend J. Harrison (Harry) Rhodes. "We have believed in a suppressed Union sentiment in the South. . . . The fact can no longer be denied that the white slave interest is inveterately hostile to the Union, and I am most thoroughly persuaded that the Union can never live in these states, except upon the 'broken body and shed blood' of slavery."[31] He was angry that there was a persistent and almost universal attitude among leading officers, as seen clearly in their words and by their acts, that the whole question of antislavery was "taboo." "A command in the army is a sort of tyranny," he fumed, "and in a narrow and ignoble mind engenders a despotic spirit, which makes him [the commander] sympathize with slavery and slaveholders."[32]

At the same time there was a feeling among many soldiers in his brigade who possessed antislavery sentiments that their own liberties had been abridged. Garfield noted that more and more soldiers had become sympathetic to the slaves as a result of their march deeper into the Confederacy, and they were "linking slavery and the rebellion together in an indissoluble bond." In Garfield's estimation, Buell's policy of conciliation had worked to harden the attitudes of the rank and file regarding slavery. Thus, the olive branch of protection and constitutional guarantees that Buell employed to entice southerners back to the Union appeared to be working against him, since it infected a few regiments with anticonciliation and antislavery ideas. Beatty concluded that "there must be a change in this regard before we shall be worthy of success."[33] Keifer added that "his [Buell's] intentions may have been good, or his instructions from McClellan compelled him to act as he did." Eventually, he concluded, "the War Department [would] sanction a more summary and sanguine policy, that has been tried in vain in what was once Buell's

Dept." Consequently, Buell would be "quietly laid on the shelf."[34] Buell's refusal to think that slavery more than disunion was the real reason for the war would cost him the respect of many of his soldiers.

Indeed, it would seem that the southern reconciliationists in whose loyalty McClellan, Buell, and even the administration professed to believe had apparently ceased to exist by the summer of 1862. Buell's army of conciliation was having difficulty in finding civilians receptive to the idea. Thus, it would appear that although Federal policymakers could project attitudes, they could not control war. But where McClellan and Lincoln were motivated into thinking that such a policy would force southerners to rediscover their loyalties, Buell's attitude of conciliation was motivated more by wanting to keep his army unharmed by guerrillas. Meanwhile, Mitchel did what he could to keep the offensive under way and on May 20 wrote to Buell that the expedition to capture Florence "has been very successful."[35]

Buell did what he could to accommodate Mitchel, urging upon Stanton the need for more troops in Tennessee to assist him. By late May, however, conditions in Mitchel's command had deteriorated so much that Mitchel asked Stanton to transfer him to the Army of the Potomac. Stanton denied his request. Though it seemed insignificant at the time, being forced to remain where he was, under Buell's command, added to Mitchel's rancor about how war was being waged in that region. Conciliation was the message, and Buell was the messenger. Mitchel resented both.[36]

Even if word reached Buell that Mitchel sought a transfer, he could not be bothered. By late May, an entrenched John Pope just outside Corinth was ready to bring battle immediately if Halleck desired it. Still, Halleck moved with extreme caution, wanting not to bring on battle but, rather, to force Beauregard out. Halleck was about to close the chapter on the Corinth campaign. Or so he thought. One soldier wrote to his wife, "One thing certain he will not be taken by suprize as general Grant was at the battle of Shiloh."[37] For weeks the army had inched its way toward the tiny hamlet to within two miles of Beauregard's entrenchments. Halleck meticulously prepared for every contingency. By May 27 Halleck finally consented to move forward and ordered Buell to make a reconnaissance "to ascertain the position and strength of the enemy's works." Buell had faced these works for three weeks but, on Halleck's orders, began a gradual advance on the right and left, warning his lieutenants to keep him fully advised of all movements. After a while the army halted and waited. It took two days for something to develop within the "continuous wall of steel around the town." On May 29 Halleck visited Pope's camp, where he found the enemy building a concentration against his left wing. Thus Halleck and Pope agreed that a move on their left would bring on the engagement. Late that night Halleck wrote to Buell that Pope would be attacking in the morning.[38]

The shelling in Corinth at sunrise on the morning of May 30 merely covered the noise of the last trains carrying whatever remained of Beauregard's army out of the town. The ruse was complete. The Confederates had abandoned Corinth and were heading south on the road to Mobile. The soldiers' shouts echoing back to Pope each time a train ran into Corinth were for empty cars, which actually took the troops out of town. Huge siege guns—"Quaker guns"—facing Union lines were merely peeled logs painted black. Not long after sunrise Pope had discovered the completeness of the ploy and two hours later had sent some cavalry and artillery in pursuit. That afternoon Halleck found an empty town. A short distance inside the Confederate breastworks Halleck noticed a blue uniform stuffed with straw hanging by the neck from a scrubby tree limb. Nearby a pine board was nailed fast, and on it were traced in barely legible letters, "'Halleck outwitted—what will old Abe say?'" After a brief glimpse, Halleck rode on.[39]

Halleck was just as surprised at Corinth as Grant had been at Shiloh. Though the press and the bulk of his soldiers ridiculed and hounded him for not bringing on an engagement, he had achieved a victory, and quite a significant one, too. James Easton of the Eightieth Ohio wrote to his family that if the Union in the West continued to "do as well as we [are] it would not be long till the war would be over."[40] Stanton called it a "brilliant and successful achievement," which "gives great joy over the whole land."[41] From a strategic standpoint it was a great victory. The Union army was concentrated at the key railroad center of the Confederate heartland, and Halleck could move troops in any direction.[42] To Sherman the campaign had a special significance, since Halleck had achieved without fighting "a victory as brilliant and important as any recorded in history."[43] The campaign merely confirmed what Buell believed all along: caution should never give way to idle cause, preparation and maneuver were the keys to winning great victories without bloodshed, and finally, defensive rather than offensive thinking was safer in the enemy's countryside.

Though Halleck had been completely deceived, he could have pursued Beauregard, but he chose instead to focus on repairing railroads, organizing his department, and improving the health of his army. The swampy roads, destroyed bridges, difficulty in getting supplies, and relentless heat of the approaching Mississippi summer made his decision appear all the more judicious. Because the Tennessee River was falling, Halleck turned his attention for the next week to opening the railroads for communication and supply, fanning out his three wings, which he quickly restored to independent commands, for pick and shovel duties. Buell, Pope, and Grant, who had requested a transfer but decided to stay on, assumed leadership of their old armies, with Thomas commanding a division in Grant's Army of the Tennessee. He remained at Corinth. Sherman was ordered to repair the railroads to Memphis, and John McClernand was detailed to rebuild the bridges on the line to Columbus, Kentucky, which Halleck saw as his main supply route. Pope was ordered to repair the railroads south of Corinth, and Buell was sent east to open the railroad to Tuscumbia and then to Decatur. Halleck predicted that the original Army of the Ohio would soon move farther in that direction and wanted Mitchel to cross a small force at Decatur to repair the road and communications to meet Buell.[44]

Although Mitchel had been hampered by Confederate guerrillas, Washington continued to be impressed by his energy in maintaining the stretch of roads, even more so because he still harbored a desire to get to Chattanooga. In fact, in early June a portion of Mitchel's command under James Negley fought a brief, but sharp engagement with the Confederates near Chattanooga and turned them back toward the city. Mitchel was so encouraged by this that he gave Negley the authority to take the city if he deemed it prudent and wired Buell that every effort should be made to hold Negley's position on the Tennessee River opposite Chattanooga. This news convinced Halleck that an offensive campaign following Mitchel's swift lead would bring Chattanooga under Union control and long-awaited restoration to East Tennesseans. Thus, Halleck was anxious for Buell to finish what Mitchel had started. After two months' experience of independent living in northern Alabama, however, Mitchel was worried that Buell would not march fast enough to sustain an attempt to take Chattanooga.[45]

As Halleck thought of the best line of operations for Buell's army during the coming summer, he was hesitant about moving with haste to reinforce Mitchel without securing a lifeline of supplies. Thus, Halleck concentrated on the other end of Mitchel's line. He considered using railroads, since rivers, lowered by the heat of spring and summer, no longer served as useful arteries of operations in the West as they had done in February. Because several rail lines connected at Corinth, this had certain advantages for the Union and disadvantages for the Confederates. Halleck realized that reliance on the railroad would require protection and reconstruction of the roads as Buell's army advanced, but with sufficient cavalry and engineering crews, these obstacles could be easily overcome. Besides, Buell's march straight across northern Alabama would keep Confederate Kirby Smith at Knoxville from uniting with the rebels in Mississippi. Lincoln was so delighted that he extended Halleck's Department of the Mississippi to include the whole states of Tennessee and Kentucky. This should have relieved Buell from dealing directly with Andrew Johnson regarding the defense of Nashville, but Halleck simply divided the region and the responsibility into two districts: the District of Ohio under Buell and the District of West Tennessee under Grant.[46]

Though Halleck's was an impressive plan, Andrew Johnson simply wanted it accomplished quickly and without jeopardizing Nashville. The governor's frequent reminders, of course, added to Halleck's ordering Buell to Chattanooga. "If poor East Tennessee could be relieved," he implored Halleck, "it would produce a thrill throughout the nation." The loyalists in that region, he argued, were "being treated worse than beasts of the forest, and are appealing to the Government for protection." "God grant that it may be in your power ere long to extend it to them," he pleaded.[47] Halleck replied that "East Tennessee will very soon be attended to[.] we drive off the main body of the enemy before we can attack his other Corps." Metaphorically speaking, Halleck argued that "the head must be attended to first & the toe nails afterwards."[48] If nothing else, Old Brains at least renewed Johnson's sense of optimism.[49]

Johnson was not the only governor who criticized Buell. Never at a loss to lament to Buell about the poor condition of his troops, Indiana governor Oliver P. Morton was disgusted by Buell's lack of attention to his soldiers at Cumberland Ford. Out of the 900 soldiers of the Forty-ninth Indiana, only 200 had reported for duty during May. Morton complained that his soldiers suffered daily from a lack of supplies, an unhealthy location, and overwhelming sickness. "Humanity and justice demand," he wrote, that the regiment must be ordered to Lexington, where the men could get supplies and be properly nursed. Buell was certainly sympathetic to the condition of the regiment but informed Morton that an investigation would determine what and when something should be done. He refused Morton's request.[50]

Of course Morton's demands signaled to Buell that having his army back did not come without a sacrifice. Kentucky Union congressmen had convinced Stanton and Lincoln that the Union's grip on the Bluegrass State had loosened over the past few months, and Stanton authorized Gen. Jeremiah T. Boyle to command a portion of troops to secure the state. During the Corinth campaign, Brig. Gen. George Morgan had assumed more independence, having been forced to raise troops in East Tennessee and communicate directly with the secretary of war. Though Halleck had been given full control over the two states, Lincoln was "anxious to have speedily some definite information" from Buell on these subjects.[51] Buell responded that although there was considerable cause for "prudent and prompt action," there was no need for "serious anxiety," since the occupation of Corinth, which stripped Kentucky and Tennessee of almost all Union troops, had effectively withdrawn all Confederate troops as well. Besides, what troops he had left in Tennessee when he marched to Corinth were positioned for defense of Nashville and Middle Tennessee.[52]

On June 10 and 11 Buell and Halleck conferred over the East Tennessee campaign, and just as McClellan had done the year before, Halleck laid out the destination. This time, however, it was Chattanooga, and he would get there via the Memphis and Charleston. Like Halleck, Buell believed railroads had certain advantages for offensive campaigns, but the Memphis and Charleston was not Buell's first choice. He thought it simply could not be sufficiently protected to move his army as quickly as Halleck desired. From the inception of the plan, Buell believed that Halleck's insistence on the Memphis and Charleston was the most serious impediment to his progress. Logistical problems alone would plague the army with every mile it advanced east. The fact that the railroad ran through a southern countryside that for eighty miles was south of the Tennessee River, was already inflamed by Mitchel's advance, and was susceptible to Confederate raiders compounded his anxiety. The spring heat had cursed Mitchel's advance, and an intensifying summer sun would only exaggerate the problems already encountered by his army stuck in northern Mississippi. What loomed important to Buell about Chattanooga was what Mitchel had earlier concluded to Chase: "To capture the City prove[s] an easy matter. The question was now to hold it and secure the safety of my little army."[53]

These logistical problems, combined with Buell's attitude of limited war, conciliation, and lack of aggression, worried Halleck but did not alarm him. After all, Buell possessed some qualities Halleck liked. He was painfully cautious, and if he needed reinforcements, he could draw on Thomas's 8,000 soldiers at Corinth or Morgan's 10,000-man division at Cumberland Gap. Halleck no doubt pondered the political importance to his own career if East Tennessee could be redeemed.[54]

Buell opposed Halleck's proposed line of advance so much that he tried to convince Halleck that a concentration at McMinnville might be a better point of departure. Not only would this position him closer to his supply base at Nashville, but also the Tennessee River could protect his right flank. Because Halleck directed Buell to draw supplies initially from Memphis, which had fallen to the Federals on June 6, via the Memphis and Charleston Railroad, Buell would have to repair the heavily wrecked railroad as he advanced, at least until he reached Mitchel. Relying on a railroad he had little faith in anyway and being forced to repair it as the army moved would lead to all sorts of problems, Buell worried. If Morgan could strike at Knoxville and Mitchel at Chattanooga, Buell could move the bulk of his army into Middle Tennessee along the Nashville-Decatur Railroad to Murfreesboro, then cross the Cumberland Plateau at McMinnville and head south to Chattanooga. This would march his army toward his supplies and presumably back into a region more sympathetic than northern Alabama to the Union army. At first Buell's powers of persuasion seemed to work on Halleck, as they had done on McClellan when it came to East Tennessee, but on June 11 Halleck changed his mind. "After fully considering the whole matter," he wrote, "I am satisfied that your line of operations should be on Chattanooga and Cleveland or Dalton instead of McMinnville."[55]

Because there were no written orders to Buell recounting specifically what had been discussed between the two men regarding the move from Corinth to Chattanooga, Halleck later denied issuing orders forcing Buell to repair the railroad. The fact was, of course, that he had explicitly directed that the Memphis and Charleston Railroad be prepared for supply and communication purposes. Whatever the case, once Halleck made up his mind, there was no changing it. No longer could Buell's powers of persuasion stall the advance. Unlike McClellan the previous winter, Halleck simply ordered Buell east.[56]

From February until early June 1862, Buell enjoyed as much prominence in the war as he would experience as a result of his association with the victories achieved by the Union armies in the West. He continued to maintain discipline over his army and had done nothing to diminish his reputation. If the previous disputes with Lincoln concerning East Tennessee and with Halleck over the river campaigns in February had distanced him from Washington and had encouraged no new friendships within the administration, he at least still retained a prominent command. Midwestern governors, however, continued to meddle in the affairs of his army, and Johnson flooded him with letters of desperation about his undefended capital city.[57]

If Buell had done nothing further to antagonize the governors supplying troops to his army, he had done nothing to accommodate them either. The most critical aspect of the campaign to Corinth was that it gave the soldiers time as they marched each mile to crystallize their attitudes not only about slavery but about conciliation as well. In the weeks and months ahead, the "Southern summer" heat would bear down on his army as it inched its way toward Chattanooga, and Buell would experience war of another kind. If it was true, according to the *Boston Traveller*, that Buell was more a "Cabinet rather than a Field General" and "belong[ed] to the class of military men who don't know what the war is about," then his march to Chattanooga would have to go far in convincing his superiors that he was worthy of their praise and that he did know what the war was about, or at least that he knew how to win it.[58]

CHAPTER FIFTEEN

The Chattanooga Campaign

L ocated on the Tennessee River and connected by rail to numerous southern cities, Chattanooga was undeniably important. With the "Mountain Citadel" in Union hands, the Federals would be better positioned to prevent a Confederate invasion of Middle Tennessee or Kentucky, hold on to the South's chief source of coal, and control three key railroads vital for Confederate traffic east and west. Though Halleck intended Buell to use the Memphis and Charleston Railroad, Buell also considered using the Nashville and Chattanooga. Lincoln understandably considered the city vital to the Union's effort, but the problems of the campaign matched its importance.[1]

Halleck could have enhanced Buell's campaign not only by presenting a realistic set of circumstances but by eliminating some of the obstacles in his way. Forcing Buell to draw on Memphis for supplies handicapped the campaign, not only because the army would be forced to repair the railroad as it advanced until it reached Mitchel in northern Alabama, but also because Halleck diverted the bulk of his engineer forces to the roads to Columbus and retained one of Buell's divisions at Iuka, keeping it from joining the main army for weeks. Additionally, he overlooked the difficulty of getting the railroad operating again, which required not only repairs but also running locomotives. After sending a considerable force to bolster Samuel Curtis in Arkansas, Halleck placed the rest of his army in summer quarters, with no other intended duty than that of covering the line between the two rivers. Nonetheless, he assured Buell, "I will do everything in my power to facilitate your movement."[2]

Even while Halleck was ordering Buell to use Memphis for his supplies, the Ohio commander was already thinking of alternatives—Louisville and Nashville. The Nashville Railroad that joined the Memphis and Charleston at Decatur, Alabama, was important because its junction was just north of the Tennessee River. Another branch of the Nashville Railroad also connected with the Memphis and Charleston north of the river at Stevenson. With the intention of using Decatur and Stevenson as supply depots as he moved east, Buell ordered Mitchel and Nashville Railroad Superintendent John B. Anderson to put the roads coming out of Nashville in order. But keeping two railroads open also doubled his work, doubled the delay, and doubled the number of guards necessary to protect the rails.[3]

The northern Mississippi and Alabama countryside from Corinth to Decatur just south of the Tennessee River was, as one Indiana soldier recalled, dry and barren with "dust so thick you could taste it." "With the mercury up to a hundred," the first of Buell's problems was that the scorching summer heat was draining the Tennessee River.[4] The river above Eastport, Mississippi, was getting so low that Buell doubted whether supplies could be landed at Florence farther upstream to meet his army when it arrived there. He suggested, therefore, that supplies be unloaded at Eastport, transported overland south about six miles to Iuka, and then put on the railroad and hauled into Tuscumbia. All this was necessary because the supplies coming down by water from Louisville had to halt at Eastport, and because the railroad to Memphis was inoperable as a supply line, largely due to a lack of locomotives. Halleck cautioned Buell that even those locomotives that were running were only half-repaired and were normally not used for transporting supplies but, rather, men and material to repair bridges.[5]

Another immediate problem for Buell was keeping his cavalry mounted.

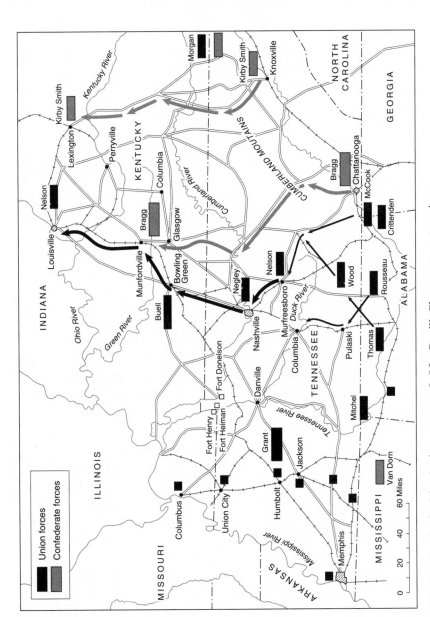

The situation in the West in the summer of 1862: Buell's Chattanooga campaign and advance into Kentucky to catch Braxton Bragg

His army had a history of insufficient cavalry, and its failure to keep the railroad and railroad workers protected from guerrillas revealed not only that the army lacked horses but just how inadequate it was when it was mounted. Though these problems may have been anticipated by Halleck and Buell, neither man foresaw how much of an impediment they would become as the weeks wore on. What made things even worse was that Mitchel reported from Huntsville that "large bodies of the enemy are passing almost daily en route for Chattanooga."[6] True or not, the Confederate cavalry was constantly on the move, which fed a fear on the part of northern troops that kept Buell immobilized.

To lessen the burden of the march, Buell physically lightened the load of his army and sought to ensure that his soldiers maintained the discipline and gentlemanly conduct for which they had been known in Middle Tennessee. On June 15 he issued General Orders 24, a compilation of former orders, including General Orders 13a, reminding the soldiers not to violate the constitutional rights of citizens as they moved across the Confederacy. What Buell called "my policy" had become nauseating for some soldiers. The men of the Forty-fourth Indiana, for example, referred to him as "Old Double Eye," since they thought he had eyes in the back of his head as he rode from the rear of the army to the front noting irregularities as he passed. Still, it did not keep soldiers of the Second Indiana, McCook's division, from stealing corn from a local resident at Florence.[7]

By mid-June Buell was camped near Florence on the north side of the Tennessee River across from Tuscumbia. The divisions of Crittenden and McCook were slowly making their way toward Tuscumbia, where they could cross the river to Florence. Wood's division alone did most of the railroad work. It was assumed that supplies would follow closely behind, forwarded from Eastport via Iuka by the divisions of Thomas and Nelson. As the army continued east toward Decatur, Buell anticipated that supplies would be sent from Nashville via Columbia and Athens, but there were serious problems. Capt. Judson D. Bingham, Buell's Nashville quartermaster, had difficulty coordinating the transporting of supplies, since the railroad could be used only as far south as Reynold's Station, twenty-three miles south of Columbia, where there was a break in the road that forced them to rely on wagon trains for forty-five miles to Athens.[8]

The chief problem Buell anticipated in being dependent on Memphis for supplies was that although his army could move, it could move only as fast as supplies could reach it. In the meantime, Mitchel tried to accumulate provisions at Huntsville but complained of being compelled to disperse his force to protect supplies coming south along the Nashville-Decatur Railroad. His division was spread from Athens to Stevenson and still was holding Jasper, Tennessee. For someone who had been itching to head east for weeks without hesitation, Mitchel's frustration was understandable. Even Buell was relating to Halleck that he thought it important to "expedite the movement of [his] troops so as to get them across the Tennessee at the earliest possible day." Buell related, however, not that he was anxious to get to Chattanooga but that both Nelson and Mitchel reported that the Confederates were hovering around his flank ready to take advantage of "any disorder in our arrangements," while another force was also moving in the direction of Chattanooga. To maintain the safety of his army, he argued that the road from Bear Creek, near the route from Tuscumbia to Decatur, which ran south from the Tennessee River, was "greatly overrated," and although he had a brigade repairing it, he had also made arrangements for his divisions to move north of the Tennessee and then east toward Decatur and Huntsville.[9]

Halleck would not budge. "It seems to me," he reasoned, "that by repairing the road to Decatur, then moving light, your supplies following you by rail, you can reach Chattanooga sooner than in any other way."[10] While he did not object to Buell moving his army north of the river, Halleck saw no risk in moving to Decatur over the railroad, since it was the shortest and safest route and would keep his forces on the same line. Meanwhile, Nelson learned of a sizable Confederate force moving up from the south, and George Morgan was telegraphing that he was about to attack Kirby Smith and possibly take Cumberland Gap. Buell had good reason to think his army might do well to cross the Tennessee.[11]

As if Halleck and Buell did not have enough logistical problems, Governor Johnson decided it was time, yet again, he lamented his woes to the commander of the West. He complained that Nashville had "been left to a very great extent in a defenseless condition," which kept alive a "rebellious spirit," and he hoped Halleck would not only replace the provost marshal and others sympathetic to southerners, but also pursue with more energy the move into East Tennessee.[12] Halleck passed on the governor's concerns to Buell, and in cases where Johnson required more troops, Halleck called on Stanton to appease him. The next day Halleck received a more alarming telegram from the president. "It would be of both interest and value to us here," he stated, "to know how the expedition toward East Tennessee is progressing."[13]

About all Halleck could say to Lincoln on June 21 was that Buell's column was at Tuscumbia. He wrote to Buell, however, that he was not satisfied with his progress.[14] Though it would appear that Halleck himself was partially to blame for the lack of progress because he expected too much too quickly, he would never admit it. Instead he simply argued that negligence had caused some of the delay. He repeated to Buell that the railroad from Tuscumbia to Decatur be put in order, and in a separate dispatch urged Buell to take care of the matters in Nashville to appease Johnson.[15]

Buell replied the same day that he was also dissatisfied with the slow progress, but his work had been greater than expected. Buell had never liked the idea of using the Memphis and Charleston, and he concluded plainly that he had "derived no benefit from the road worth naming." Of course Buell had concluded as much to Halleck two months before, with apparently no affect on Old Brains.[16] As for Johnson's problems, he wired back that he would investigate the situation, since charges of disloyalty were simply "frivolous and absurd."[17]

As spring passed into summer, Buell's army was shamefully stretched along a railroad that no one in his command viewed beneficial to getting anywhere, much less to Chattanooga. Nelson and Thomas were preoccupied with the threatening movements of the Confederates, which delayed their advance. Mitchel continued to have problems accumulating supplies at Athens, as did Captain Bingham. About the only good news Buell received during this time of frustration was that George Morgan had driven the Confederates from Cumberland Gap and, with sufficient cavalry, expected to sweep East Tennessee. But Buell had no cavalry to send him, which prompted Morgan to wire back, "I might as well be without eyes as without cavalry."[18]

Mitchel tried desperately to hold Stevenson, hoping Buell could get the army there and use the railroad coming out of Nashville. He feared that if he abandoned the town, the Confederates would destroy the bridges his division had repaired. Thinking he could get reinforcements from the East faster than from Buell, the determined Mitchel asked Stanton to send whatever the government could spare. But Stanton replied that although Lincoln regarded the Chattanooga campaign only second in importance to the advance on Richmond, McClellan's drive on the Confederate capital required every available man.[19]

In the meantime, Buell used considerable industry in setting up ferries to cross the Tennessee River at Florence and Decatur, but low water in the river continued to prevent the freight boats from navigating beyond Eastport. For several weeks, supplies were hauled from there by wagon train to Iuka, where they were placed on the railroad and pulled to Tuscumbia and then on to Decatur, where they were again ferried across the Tennessee and then reloaded on railroad cars, eventually to catch up to the army. Still, his industry was eclipsed by the wizardly Confederate cavalry that frustrated his march across northern Alabama. With his supply line cut and unsuccessful in procuring forage for his animals, Buell's operations slowed to a crawl. The great blessing Halleck had conceived in using the Memphis and Charleston had become a curse.[20]

It was clear from the beginning, however, that even if the railroads had been opened to travel, Buell's sudden demand for supplies would have severely burdened them. The lack of adequate quartermaster and commissary officers coupled with the size of his army, which required 300 tons of food and forage daily, further plagued Buell's operations. McClellan's Army of the Potomac had absorbed almost all available quartermaster and commissary officers in its push toward Richmond. Moreover, after getting the railroad repaired, Buell had difficulty bringing forward that tonnage of supplies.[21]

As the summer heat bore down on the Alabama countryside, Buell was trying to feed his 40,000-man army and hundreds of animals by relying on 300 miles of railroad that simply could not carry that volume of supplies. As James Garfield wrote to his wife, "It is very severe on our poor boys to march in such hot weather in this sultry climate."[22] Not only did the men suffer, but so did the animals. What further compounded Buell's problems was that his army was the only western force that contained slightly more horses—which were not as well suited to hauling supply trains—than mules.[23]

Buell's attempt to protect the railroad forced him to disperse his troops, and the tormenting heat and shortage of water greatly reduced his present-for-duty strength. Not only did the 14,000 officers and soldiers absent without permission compound his problems, but also the one-year volunteers who had enlisted in July 1861 were due to muster out of service. Desertions had also increased. In short, although Buell's army was pursuing the offensive, his attempts to stabilize his logistics transformed his army into a fragmented mass of railroad laborers, watchmen, and ill-trained paper bureaucrats. Nonetheless, Halleck wrote to Stanton that the campaign was progressing and that Buell's army was moving east through a "healthy region" and should penetrate into Georgia as far as Atlanta.[24]

By the end of June, Buell had arrived at Huntsville, a town that, according to Col. John Beatty of the Third Ohio, was as handsome as Decatur was ugly.[25] Buell expected to find rations for his soldiers, but the men found nothing. He had hoped that by opening the Nashville-Decatur Railroad he might be able to get supplies to his army faster, but enemy cavalry disrupted the Elk River bridge. Despite the obstacles, Captain Bingham and Thomas Swords, commissary officer at Louisville, used considerable industry in complying with Buell's request, but neither man was in a position to meet the demands of the army's requisitions. Thomas's division, still detained by Halleck, was spread from Iuka to Tuscumbia and burdened with hauling supplies, which caused Buell to think that perhaps Halleck was more enthused about opening railroads than getting to Chattanooga quickly.[26]

While Buell was in Huntsville, he and Mitchel finally sat down to discuss the campaign to Chattanooga. Over three consecutive days for several hours at a time, the two conferred over the best strategy in getting there. The first meeting lasted over four hours, and Mitchel recalled Buell as being his "usual uncommunicative self." The session ended without any decision. Buell simply folded up his map, and the officers adjourned. For three days Mitchel counseled an immediate advance and encouraged Buell to go to Bridgeport to survey the situation, but he refused to go. Buell valued Mitchel's opinion, though he declined to take his advice. At the end of the third meeting, Mitchel, having failed to convince Buell to advance quickly, stormed to his tent and requested a twenty-day leave of absence. Shortly after, Stanton ordered him to Washington to await a new assignment.

Mitchel's was a significant departure. It demonstrated not only to the soldiers but also to the administration that he was willing to protest Buell's lethargic campaign. For a commander who "*believe[d] in hunting the Rebels*, and disturbing their repose," Mitchel's characterization of Buell as "one of the most hesitating and slow men he ever met" hardly did justice to his frustration. Buell continued to find reasons why his campaign was impossible, and Mitchel was fed up. This gave Buell the opportunity to replace Mitchel with Rousseau, a Kentucky native known for his proslavery views.[27]

On June 30 Stanton sent Halleck an alarming message that, because of the situation near Richmond, it was absolutely necessary that 25,000 men be transferred from his force to the East. What made it even more alarming was that this transfer was to occur with no change in Buell's campaign to Chattanooga. Halleck hated these kinds of requests, largely because McClellan always seemed to get what he wanted at the expense of someone else. The same day Halleck wired back that it would be exceedingly difficult to detach so large a force without jeopardizing his ability to hold West Tennessee and that "under the circumstances the Chattanooga expedition better be abandoned."[28] Halleck knew that the very mention of East Tennessee would raise the president's eyebrows, and in light of Halleck's conclusion, Stanton responded that the Chattanooga expedition must not be abandoned or diminished. Instead he concluded, "The President regards that and the movement against East Tennessee as one of the most important movements of the War, and its occupation as important as the capture of Richmond."[29] The soldiers to be sent east, therefore, would have to come from West Tennessee.

In the same message came Halleck's first indication from Washington that the administration was not pleased with the Chattanooga expedition. Lincoln thought the campaign, although slow, was so important that he wrote Halleck himself, saying, "To take and hold the railroad at or east of Cleveland, in east Tennessee, I think fully as important as the taking and holding of Richmond."[30] Motivated by fear that Lincoln would certainly draw on Halleck's rather Buell's army for the 25,000 men, and by Lincoln's displeasure at Buell's slowness, Halleck's next communiqué was to Buell, relieving him from using the Memphis and Charleston to draw supplies. He now expected Buell to make something happen quickly in East Tennessee or it would make him look bad after denying the president troops. Ironically, the same day, without knowing Halleck's change of plans, Buell informed him that the railroad to Decatur was completed. As luck would have it, however, there were no locomotives to pull anything forward.[31]

Oddly enough, what had happened to McClellan when Stanton withheld Irvin McDowell's troops from joining him in the Peninsula Campaign appeared to be happening to Halleck. "The defeat of McClellan near Richmond," he wrote to Buell, had forced the withdrawal of a large portion of his army, which "destroys the entire campaign." There was a "regular stampede" in Washington, and Halleck demanded that "there must be no stampede here." "We must hold on to all we have got and get a little more," he argued.[32] In light of McClellan's defeat at the Seven Days' battles, Buell's campaign now had special significance, and the pendulum of political and public opinion swung back to the West. Thus, Halleck continued to promise great things from Buell's expedition to Chattanooga, even under the most inhospitable circumstances. Yet he did nothing to disturb the Confederates while Buell marched east.

By early July the vanguard of Buell's army had advanced to within thirty miles of Chattanooga. Though the next leg of the journey for the troops would be through a country that Halleck had characterized as "healthy," Mitchel's 9,000 men, as well as 6,000 of Negley's soldiers, had stripped the countryside as they had passed through. These northern counties were normally highly agriculturally productive and, according to a prominent local resident, had supported the federal government in 1860 "with five Union votes to one secession." This confirmed why over 2,000 citizens from this region enlisted in the Union army—some enlisted in Buell's army during the campaign. The agricultural resources of the region, coupled with the Union sentiment, made marching through the area appear more a blessing than a curse, especially since Buell could now concentrate on getting supplies from Nashville. If Buell could keep the lines open, he might make it to Chattanooga within a few weeks. But with no river transportation and the country around Chattanooga unproductive, Buell knew that the railroad would be the only way to ensure that he could hold Chattanooga once there. Even though Halleck had released him from the Memphis and Charleston, the fact was that he had already committed considerable resources to making the road functional as a lifeline to Chattanooga. To revert to his original plan of moving to Chattanooga via Middle Tennessee would only further burden his army.[33]

Had the region abounded with crops and had Buell not been so determined to avoid relying liberally on the local resources even for his animals, he might not have relied so heavily on the railroad for supplies to support his advance. Although counting on the southern civilians to provide food for his soldiers would perhaps have undermined the loyal sentiment that he had been led to believe prevailed in northern Alabama, requisitioning forage for animals would have caused less distress among the locals.[34]

Buell did attempt to use some of the region's resources, such as bacon and cattle, but remained firm in his policy of securing items necessary only for the transportation of the supplies brought down from Nashville. Building and repairing bridges required lumber, and he attempted to open the sawmills between Huntsville and Stevenson to provide material for pontoons and a floor for the Elk River bridge that he complained was too weak for a locomotive. Although opening the sawmills was not a problem, getting the men to work them was, since they feared guerrillas attacking them at night.[35]

Meanwhile, Halleck was looking for explanations to send to Washington as to why things were going so slowly. This of course required that he find a scapegoat. He found one in Mitchel, since it was Mitchel, Halleck learned, whom Buell had ordered almost four weeks before to cross a locomotive and cars over the Tennessee to Decatur. Mitchel's failure to do so, Halleck argued to Stanton, greatly stalled things, since Halleck had no engines of his own to send Buell. The fact that Mitchel had already departed for Washington amid rumors that he had been speculating in cotton perhaps made it easier for Halleck to target him for the problems. When Lincoln asked for 10,000 troops, Halleck continued to appeal to him that if the force in the West was diminished, the Chattanooga expedition "must be revoked or the hope of holding Southwest Tennessee abandoned."[36]

After ensuring that his army had safely crossed to the north side of the river, Buell continued to forward his troops toward Huntsville and even sent a brigade to support Mitchel's position at Stevenson and Bridgeport. Fry continued to complain to Bingham that the army was still without forage. Nonetheless, while his army occupied Huntsville, Buell insisted that his soldiers not interfere with the ordinary business and trade of the town, except where marked disloyalty forfeited individual rights and transactions. To Boyle he wrote, "I am not afraid of Kentucky rising nor of any fatal public consequences, but I deplore the mischief that will be done to individuals."[37]

To emphasize his orders and perhaps make a summary example of transgressors, Buell ordered Col. John Basil Turchin and several others court-martialed for the plunder of Athens two months earlier. The trial itself was as controversial as the brigade's actions. Turchin and the officers of the Nineteenth and Twenty-fourth Illinois responded by resigning. Buell suffered enormously from his insistence that their men be punished, but under the circumstances he thought it had to be done. The trial hardened soldier animosity toward Buell and began to infect larger segments of the army as the campaign to Chattanooga forced the entire company to share the grueling experience of maintaining Buell's attitude of "war proper." Even if there had not been any reason previously to think that Buell was more than sympathetic to southerners, the court-martial of Turchin at least planted seeds of doubt, insubordination, and demoralization in more than a few soldiers about whether their commander was waging the same kind of war the administration or his soldiers thought he should be waging. Buell continued to sow the seeds of his own demise.[38]

Colonel Beatty served on the Turchin court and, seeing Buell at the trial, characterized him as "cold, smooth-toned, silent." Under Buell's soft war, wrote Beatty, the "star of the Confederacy appear[s] to be rising, and I doubt not it will continue to ascend until the rose-water policy now pursed by the Northern army [is] superseded by one more determined and vigorous." Though Turchin had gone to one extreme in carrying out a more vigorous punishment of rebels, Buell had been pursuing a policy amiable and pleasant, which according to Beatty, had proved fatal to the Union army. "Turchin's policy is bad enough," he wrote, "it may indeed be the policy of the devil; but Buell's policy is that of the amiable idiot." Beatty then characterized Buell's policy:

> He is inaugurating the dancing-master policy: "By your leave, my dear sir, we will have a fight; that is, if you are sufficiently fortified; no hurry; take your own time." To the bushwacker: "Am sorry gentlemen fire at our trains from behind stumps, logs, and ditches. Had you not better cease this sort of warfare? Now do, my good fellows, stop, I beg of you." To the citizen rebel: "You are a chivalrous people; you have been aggravated by the abolitionists into subscribing cotton to the Southern Confederacy; you had, of course, a right to dispose of your own property to suit yourselves, but we prefer that you would, in future, make no more subscriptions of that kind, and in the meantime we propose to protect your property and guard your negroes."[39]

The trial of Colonel Turchin represented the diverging opinions regarding Buell's policy of conciliation, since it helped to polarize the army into what Gerald Prokopowicz characterized as "hard" and "soft" war factions.[40] Mitchel had come under severe attack from the administration for not dealing properly with the guilty parties responsible for plundering the city in early May. Over two months had passed before Buell ordered a court-martial on July 5, and perceptions had changed considerably with regard to Turchin's activities. James Garfield, now a brigadier general, was appointed president of the court investigating the sack of Athens, and at first he was incensed by the "shameful outrages." "There has not been found in American history," he argued, "so black a page as that which will bear the record of General Mitchel's campaign in northern Alabama." By the end of the trial, however, Garfield concluded that what Turchin was really guilty of was "not dealing quietly enough" in retaliating against civilians who had actively committed crimes against the Federals.[41]

The evidence persuaded Garfield that Turchin was the victim, and if Turchin was the victim, why was Buell placing him on trial? This trial attracted considerable attention from the soldiers as well as the citizens of northern Alabama. Much to the displeasure of Buell's soldiers, the citizens were impressed by the general's wanting to see justice served on those who had abridged civilian rights. Buell demanded that Turchin be eliminated from the service, since the real issue was the plunder and outrage of indulgent and lawless individuals, which would have a greater effect on the morale and discipline of his army than on the citizens. "Such conduct," argued Buell, "does not mean vigorous war; it means disgrace and disaster." Yet, under the circumstances, trying to maintain discipline and morale for whatever reason had proved difficult in light of a more aggressive populace that seized every opportunity to prove they were not so easily reconciled as Buell had hoped. Consequently, Buell's view was no longer popular because it was no longer useful as a means of keeping his army unharmed. Soldiers probably questioned Buell's idea of vigorous war. Beatty, for one, was happy when Rousseau replaced Mitchel, since he "discards the rose-water policy of general Buell under his nose, and is a great deal more thorough and severe in his treatment of rebels than General Mitchel."[42]

The episode involving the trial was a turning point in Buell's tenure as a commander. Since the issuance of General Orders 13a in February, Buell had always considered conciliation a means to keep his army protected rather than an encouragement of southerners to rejoin the Union. Volunteers, however, had trouble accepting the fact that Buell's policy, inspired for whatever reason, had not brought about the desired result. Much of this perception had to do with the distance he maintained from the soldiers. Since assuming command of the Army of the Ohio the previous November, Buell had not cultivated a productive and useful relationship with his men, who as volunteers expected more consideration from their leader. He had not acquired any personal skills from his experience with a large army. Showing affection toward his men was not in his manner. He had tried to make them into machines, but many volunteers were increasingly reluctant to surrender any more of their civil rights to protect those of the South.[43]

In spite of his efforts to nationalize the army and redirect the allegiances of the men from home state politicians to military commanders, Buell had been unable to give them an identifiable leader in whom they could place new trust, beyond the confines of their regiments. He remained a stranger to his men, as did most of his division commanders. Some of this had to do with his personal makeup, and some with his military philosophy and attitude toward volunteer soldiers. His attitude on slavery only damaged further his reputation as a leader, since by the summer more and more soldiers had assumed a clearer abolitionist position. Although the bulk of the army remained indifferent to the institution in relation to the aims of the war, some, like Keifer, Garfield, and Beatty, made the direct connection. This group of officers, along with Jacob Ammen, shared many meals discussing Buell's policy. Garfield, for example, wrote to his wife that slaves not only suffered from their daily hardships but from "bitter disappointment" at not being allowed to seek refuge under the Union army. It appalled him when his division commander would send him an order to search his camps for a slave. In an act of defiance to his superior, but in accordance with the congressional mandate, Garfield responded that if generals wanted to return slaves, "they must do it themselves."[44]

The fact that he cared little whether his men liked him or not, and that he possessed little charisma or motivational skills, only exaggerated the perception his men had of him. He attended more to the smaller details of protocol and management of the army and less to the conceptual aspects of solving political or civil problems. The Chattanooga campaign appeared to highlight Buell's worst features. The Army of the Ohio mirrored his qualities as a commander, and his failure to cultivate a blind loyalty or, in the words of Gerald Prokopowicz, "create a mystique" about the army, added to the sense of alienation his soldiers felt, which consequently produced a lack of loyalty that might have been useful when his actions were called into question. The condition of the army, the inhospitable countryside, the suffocating heat, and the dismal transportation situation should have caused Buell to depart from the policy McClellan had outlined several months before. But apparently Buell was more rigorous than sensible in carrying out the government's initial policy. Even when soldiers skipped camp only to search for food, Buell had them arrested and ordered the camps to be more heavily guarded. Divisional commanders, such as Nelson, made the guilty soldiers run around a tree stump for twenty-four hours without stopping.[45]

On July 8 a telegram from Halleck gave Buell the first indication that the president was not pleased with his advance. "The President telegraphs that your progress is not satisfactory," warned Halleck, "and that you should move more rapidly."[46] Halleck certainly shared the president's frustration, though he did not reveal his personal feelings because, according to one contemporary, "it would have hardly been becoming in one who had taken thirty days to move an army, unopposed, twenty-five miles . . . to chide his subordinate after setting him such an example."[47] Even if Halleck could be charged with causing a share of the problem, the fact remained that Buell's campaign was slow.

Buell's march toward Chattanooga was so horrendously tedious that Braxton Bragg was uncertain of its objective. This fact, of course, was one of Buell's key principles in conducting offensive campaigns: conceal the objective from the enemy as along as possible. Nonetheless, Lincoln's dissatisfaction thoroughly disheartened Buell, since he thought his logistical nightmare was the chief cause of the delay and that Halleck had explained this to Lincoln. "I regret," Buell responded three days later, "that it is necessary to explain the circumstances which must make progress seem slow." He knew what Halleck had intended for him but argued that, given the difficulties of the supply problem, reaching Chattanooga quickly would be useless if his army were not in condition to fight when it got there.[48]

After elaborating on the logistical problems of compensating for the break in the railroad, Buell argued to Halleck, "The advance on Chattanooga must be made with the means of acting in force . . . otherwise it will either fail or prove a profitless and transient prize." Furthermore, Buell did not want his operations to jeopardize his army "nor its honor nor trifle with the lives of loyal citizens." Still, the general added, "The disaffection of the President pains me exceedingly."[49]

At the same time that Halleck and Lincoln expressed their displeasure regarding the slowness of Buell's campaigns, Andrew Johnson, still fuming about the uncooperativeness of Buell's Nashville subordinates, added insult to injury by expressing his views of Buell to the president. After elaborating on how Buell's staff had retarded the development of Union sentiment in Middle Tennessee, Johnson reminded Lincoln, "I said to you repeatedly in the fall, General Buell is not the man to redeem East Tennessee."[50]

Lincoln provided Buell with an indirect gesture of support by refusing to give Johnson a free hand. "Do you not, my good friend," he questioned Johnson, "perceive that what you ask is simply to put you in command in the West[?] I do not suppose you desire this. You only wish to control in your localities, but this you must know may derange all other parts."[51] Halleck also provided a slight display of encouragement on July 12 when he advised Buell to be more patient with the amateurs in Washington who had "no conception of the length of our lines of defense and of operations," especially since "the disasters before Richmond [had] worked them up to a boiling heat."[52] He closed by assuring Buell that his movements would be "properly explained" to the president. Four days later Halleck was appointed general in chief of the armies and became one of those impatient authorities in Washington.[53]

By mid-July, the slow, leisurely movement of the army as well as Buell's solicitous treatment of the population in an attempt to pacify southerners had disheartened soldiers and officers alike. Some soldiers simply could not understand why Buell continued to protect southern civilians when it was evident that these same people had assisted the Confederates with food, water, and reliable information. Although Buell had tangible evidence that more and more civilians had actively engaged in undermining the Union campaign, his policy remained the same. Letters revealing weariness, impatience, and hostility were also pouring home from the camps.

Major Keifer, for example, continued to write scathing letters to his wife regarding the general's conciliation program and his policy of delay. Under Buell's command, he wrote to his wife on July 5, "the most contemptuous rebel in this country has more claims upon his time and is entitled more of his consideration than any officer in his army." "We will rejoice to get away from his command," he declared "I . . . fear that unless more magnanimity is shown among our generals, we might just as well hang up the fiddle for this war." Three days later Keifer wrote, "We still hope and pray that we get out of Buell's command.— (Buell is either a weak imbecile man, or a *secession* sympathizer)."[54] Garfield echoed this sentiment, saying that it was "better in this country, occupied by our troops, for a citizen to be a rebel than to be a Union man." Like Keifer, he declared that there "must be a readjustment of our public policy and management."[55] "This war will last 400 years," one disillusioned Hoosier complained.[56]

Although Keifer's and Garfield's sentiments did not reflect the view of the entire army, a significant portion of the troops had become similarly disheartened. "I am not alone in my views on Buell," Keifer wrote. "Large numbers have resigned in consequence of some of his orders. Others will."[57] In the ranks, Buell's conciliatory policy appeared to favor southern civilians at a time when the soldiers were suffering from his unwillingness to forage more liberally or confiscate property. Under Mitchel's reign at least, wrote Keifer, southerners "feared the *rope*."[58] What was unfortunate for Buell was that although his policy stemmed from his desire to protect his army, discipline his troops, and protect the rights of citizens, it looked to his soldiers as though he was trying to woo southerners back into the Union.

By July this policy looked to many soldiers as though their commander cared more for the citizens of the South than for his own troops. "The citizens say to us," wrote Keifer, "that Buell is as good a secessionist as they want to see in our ranks." "Gen. Buell treats these miserable traitors most graciously . . . [when they should be] most soundly thrashed," he lamented.[59] As one Indiana soldier put it, Buell's policy "prejudiced the men against him." Col. Marc Mundy of the Twenty-third Kentucky recalled that when Buell ordered Turchin court-martialed, several officers expressed "great bitterness toward the commander of the army."[60]

Just as McClellan's failed attempts to get at Richmond brought him severe criticism, political leaders and newspapermen now turned their sights on Buell. It did not help that Confederate cavalry leader John Hunt Morgan had crossed into Kentucky and had made it halfway across the Bluegrass State, causing the residents and governors of Ohio and Kentucky to panic. Most newsmen blamed Buell. The Army of the Ohio's slow advance had become the reason for numerous problems in the Union war effort in the West. The editor of the *Indianapolis Daily Journal* questioned the whereabouts of Buell's army. "He has . . . the best appointed and best drilled army in the West," wrote the editor, "and for all the country knows of him, he might as well be in the middle of Brazil."[61] The editor of the *Daily Nashville Union* declared Buell the "master of inactivity" because of his snail-like pace across northern Alabama.[62]

That these two newspapers were among the most critical of Buell was not surprising. Both were the mouthpieces of the Governors Morton and Johnson. Some papers had been slow to criticize Buell for his policies and slow advance, but once they did, they were relentless and unforgiving. Some of this animosity had to do with Buell's uninviting attitude toward reporters themselves. Consequently, they made slighting remarks about his habitual reserve and unappealing demeanor. Thus soldiers and citizens alike who read these characterizations came not only to hate his attitude and policies but to dislike the commander himself. Not all reporters were offended, however. Kentuckian William B. Shanks continued to applaud Buell in his dispatches to the *New York Herald*. The *Cincinnati Commercial* and *Gazette*, for example, continued to defend Buell into July, as did the *Chicago Tribune*. Some correspondents characterized Buell's army as "infinitely superior to that of any other." As a commander, the editor of the *Gazette* wrote, Buell had "not reached his zenith." His army, he added, loved him "as the army of the Potomac is said to love McClellan."[63]

As encouraging as some newspapers appeared, in some cases editors were using discretion in what they allowed into their paper. On one occasion, for example, William S. Furay, reporter to the *Cincinnati Gazette*, wrote a private letter to the editor that read,

> Buell . . . cares more for guarding a rebel cabbage patch, or reenslaving a liberated negro, than he does for gaining a triumph over the enemy. . . . General Buell is so intensely pro-slavery that I have no doubt he would sacrifice every officer in his District, for the sake of returning to bondage a single slave. . . . The army is really in a paroxysm of terror, each man fearing he may be the next one arrested and punished for having offended some scoundrelly traitor. It is a common remark in the army now, that there is not a traitor in Huntsville or vicinity who would not be received at Buell's headquarters with greater consideration and respect than any Union officer.[64]

The fact that the letter never found its way into the newspaper suggests that the editors thought it damaging in the hands of politicians and soldiers. For an army already suffering from desertion and hardship, this kind of scathing criticism, common in certain papers, would only serve, in the editors' judgment, to diminish the morale of the army.

What was important about the press's coverage of the Chattanooga campaign was that the longer the march lasted, the more critical the press became. As more and more newspapers criticized Buell for protecting southerners, their circulation throughout the camps of Buell's army spread rumors against the general. At the same time the papers printed editorials favoring the "vigorous war" attitude. This gave the impression that the vigorous war policy was right and Buell's soft war was wrong. Colonel Mundy recalled that when the *Chicago Tribune* printed the orders of Gen. John Pope, who had recently transferred to the Virginia theater of war, authorizing his officers to seize Confederate property without compensation, to shoot captured guerrillas who had fired on Union troops, to expel from occupied territory any civilians who refused to take the oath of allegiance, and to treat them as spies if they returned, Mundy had a great deal of trouble controlling his command because his soldiers wanted to do the same. Although Pope did not shoot any guerrillas or expel any civilians, his policy concerning southern property was sanctioned from the top. Johnson had advocated for weeks that Stanton should "cause the Commanding General of this Dept. [Department of the Ohio] to issue an order similar to that of Gen Pope in Virginia in regard to subsisting &c. on the enemy." "The rebels," he declared, "must be made to feel to the weight & ravages of the War they have brought upon the country, treason must be made odious & traitors impoverished."[65]

One of Halleck's first orders as general in chief reflected the shift in attitude. He ordered Grant in western Tennessee to "take up all active [rebel] sympathizers, and either hold them as prisoners or put them beyond our lines. Handle that class without gloves, and take their property for public use." "It is time," he added, "that they should begin to feel the presence of the war."[66] In July the Thirty-seventh Congress culminated its second session by passing a law that expanded the army's handling of Confederate property. Though the Confiscation Act was a vague law declaring that traitors be punished by the confiscation of their property, including slaves, it nonetheless served its purpose. As soldiers debated these policies at length in camp, no longer was it deemed honorable that Union commanders protect the property rights of civilians. Instead, in the pragmatic opinion of Beatty, it would "at least, enable us to weaken the enemy, as we have not done thus far, and strengthen ourselves, as we have hitherto been unable to do."[67]

Of course McClellan deplored this new turn in the war and on July 8 instructed Lincoln in a memorandum, which might just as well have had Buell's name on it, on the proper conduct of war, which did not include the subjugation of the southern populace. "Neither confiscation of property . . . [n]or forcible abolition of slavery should be contemplated for a moment," he instructed the president. To use the army in capacities other than strictly military operations would disintegrate the armies. In Buell's case, however, it would appear that such a policy could hardly disintegrate his army any more than the policy he was currently pursuing.[68]

Though Buell never saw McClellan's memorandum to Lincoln, his thoughts were no doubt similar to McClellan's. Eight months before, Buell's McClellan-like virtues were considered attributes, but in the middle of July they had become serious liabilities, simply because Lincoln and the administration had deviated from their initial conception of the nature of the war. McClellan and Buell were losing Lincoln's support, as the president was tortured over reconciling an existing military policy with the changing nature of the war. Their attitude was no longer simply a matter of noncompliance but, in the eyes of Radical Republicans in Congress, threatening to the war effort. No longer was pacifying southerners and supporting their constitutional rights considered effective in encouraging them to rediscover their loyalties or in protecting Union armies. Buell's army was not the first to experience this change in attitude on the part of southerners, but it endured the effects of the shift throughout the summer.

On July 12 Buell received the good news that the railroad was repaired and that the following day a train carrying a load of supplies would be whistling for the crossing at Stevenson. Finally, Buell would be able to put his army back on full rations and move to Chattanooga with renewed strength. Although Buell would have two routes out of Nashville to move supplies, he continued to safeguard the railroad by placing work gangs all along the line. To protect the workers, he stationed a small force at Murfreesboro. Thus, Buell's attention remained almost exclusively on the critical problem of guarding the Union supply line—the means of getting to and holding Chattanooga.[69]

Good news from Buell always seemed to have a false sense of optimism. On July 13 Nathan Bedford Forrest, who had been hovering around McMinnville for some time, swooped down on Murfreesboro, destroying the depots containing all government supplies that could not be transported and wrecking the Nashville and Chattanooga railroad bridges in the immediate vicinity. The news was bad indeed, not the least of which revealed that Forrest had taken more prisoners than he had men. "We are living from hand to mouth," Fry telegraphed to the Nashville adjutant on July 14. The following day he wrote to the Louisville quartermaster that the army would starve unless there was more activity in throwing supplies forward.[70] One Ohio soldier recalled that it was "amusing as well as pathetic to see the men flocking to the commissary tent to feast their eyes on the piles of cracker boxes." But, as he observed, at least "the issue of crackers made a very agreeable change in the condition of the men."[71] When an exhausted quartermaster at Louisville suggested that if Buell could somehow find or produce bread for his army in Alabama it would lessen his burden of transporting it, Buell lashed back that not only was there no flour in the country, but there was also no necessity for depending on the country even if there was flour. "If we don't get supplies," he scolded Thomas Swords, "it can only be our own fault."[72] The crews had barely completed their repairs near Murfreesboro when Buell wrote to Halleck, "We will go to work again."[73]

When Lincoln summoned Halleck to Washington, Buell hoped he might be more useful in presenting the importance of not only getting Washington to understand Buell's logistical problems but also in procuring cavalry and supplies. Halleck, however, was of little use, and leaving Grant in command hardly helped Buell solve his problems. Grant and Buell had not improved their relations since Shiloh, and in matters that required cooperation, neither commander was anxious to collaborate.[74]

After trying every expedient, Buell reluctantly withdrew large infantry units from the advancing main army to fend off cavalry raids and guard key bridges. He went so far as to ask Stanton to request Pennsylvania governor Andrew G. Curtin to raise additional cavalry regiments, since the Anderson Troop, a Pennsylvania unit, which was Buell's bodyguard, was a first-rate outfit. As he had done for nearly two months, Buell positioned his army to counteract the movements of the Confederates, accepting the fact that his army would have to go on the defensive. He fanned out in a seventy-mile arc from Battle Creek to McMinnville to await provisions and Bragg's movements. Beatty, a brigadier general by now, besides complaining of the weather and Buell's "insane effort to garrison the whole country," commenced praying for salvation from the campaign and its commander: "Lord be with us and deliver us from idleness and imbecility."[75]

Before he left for Washington, Halleck finally released Thomas, who by the end of the month was advancing to Dechard. But even by deploying large infantry units, it was still next to impossible to clear Tennessee of Confederate raiders. Because the rebels had placed large cavalry forces back into Middle Tennessee, Buell finally shared Johnson's view that Nashville was vulnerable. Not only was the city threatened by the Confederates, but Nelson wrote Buell that since he left, the "hostility to the United States Government and the troops [had] increased 1,000 per cent." "It seems settled into a fierce hatred to Governor Johnson," he concluded.[76]

On July 21 Forrest struck again. He wrecked the bridges over Mill Creek, and Buell's troops remained on half-rations and his animals on even less. This prompted Buell to lament to Negley, oddly enough, that he should not confine his cavalry to "mere defense." "Put a little life into it," he demanded, "and destroy the marauding bands that hover about you."[77] Again the Union repair gangs went to work, and within a week they had the railroad ready to operate.

It was July 29 when the first train loaded with 210,000 rations pulled into Stevenson from Nashville. Another train followed the next day, and the troops went back on full rations—but it was too late. The ominous cloud that had hung over Buell's army since it began the campaign burst on July 28 when Brig. Gen. William S. Rosecrans confirmed Buell's suspicions that Bragg would concentrate at Chattanooga. At this point Buell was so desperate to get the bridges repaired that he wrote to Rosecrans that the "citizens should be required to furnish negroes for the work." What Lincoln, Halleck, Johnson, and Keifer had feared had happened. On July 31 Buell wired Halleck that Bragg had arrived at Chattanooga with about 30,000 soldiers, and from other reports Buell ascertained that they would head either to Nashville or into Kentucky.[78]

With the news that Bragg had reached Chattanooga and that he might go on the offensive, Buell faced the obvious question: Where in Tennessee should he concentrate? On July 31 he provided his own answer to Halleck, concluding that Middle Tennessee was now the Confederates' likely target. Thus McMinnville, his original idea, would be the best place to concentrate his army, but even that now was more easily conceived than accomplished.[79]

Meanwhile, Lincoln held a Cabinet meeting on August 3, and as Chase recounted in his diary, there was a good deal of conversation on slavery and the merits of generals. In Stanton's absence, Chase was perhaps the most outspoken in his condemnation of what he considered the needless defeat of McClellan and the slowness of Buell. As the discussion turned toward slavery, Chase expressed considerable displeasure at the antiabolitionist attitude of Buell and McClellan and suggested that they be removed. Lincoln no doubt agreed. It was probably during this meeting that he expressed to Halleck that "a McClellan in the army was lamentable, but a combination of McClellan and Buell was deplorable." Much to his dismay, however, Halleck wanted to retain them both. At one point William Seward asked Chase what he would do and whom he preferred to Buell. Chase refused to say but remarked that if he were president or secretary of war, he would confer with the general in chief and "require him to name to me the best officers he knew; talk the matter over with him; get all the light I could; and then designate my man."[80]

That evening Halleck and Chase had a private meeting, and the secretary modified his tone on Buell, now saying he was "slow but safe."[81] Despite his dislike for Buell's policies, Chase backed off because of a letter from Nelson in late July. Nelson argued that, by and large, the army experienced a favorable reception as it marched throughout the South, which prompted Nelson to conclude that conciliation was working. "The policy of General Buell," he concluded to Chase, "it seems to me, is that which will put this rebellion down soonest."[82]

The following day Halleck informed Buell that there was pressure in Washington to create a new department of Kentucky, Ohio, Illinois, and Indiana. Buell was obviously not meeting the expectations of the administration. Under the circumstances Buell thought it was not a bad idea and, if approved, wanted Sherman appointed to command. Halleck refused to give up Sherman, his most accomplished former subordinate, and waste him on a campaign that by this time was going nowhere.

Two days later Halleck provided Buell with a more severe message about the campaign: "There is great dissatisfaction here at the slow movement of your army toward Chattanooga."[83] Buell responded calmly the same day: "It is difficult to satisfy impatience, and when it proceeds from anxiety, as I know it does in this case, I am not disposed to complain of it." "My advance," he argued, "has not been rapid, but it could not be more rapid under the circumstances." His only solace was that he had "not been idle nor indifferent."[84] Though Buell's placid demeanor always masked his anxiety, this campaign had distressed him. He had not been indifferent or idle in his efforts, but a vastly superior Confederate cavalry plagued his supply lines. The heart of the matter was that the campaign was forcing him into an ideological position that made him uncomfortable about the changing nature of war. Buell encouraged Halleck not to be disappointed about Bragg's arrival at Chattanooga, since he was again concentrating and preparing to meet the Confederate.[85]

Lincoln's concern about the Chattanooga expedition was more than anxiety; it was downright consternation. After all, it was because of Buell's campaign that Lincoln had allowed Halleck to persuade him that great things could be expected if the force in the West was not reduced. Johnson also continued to voice his distress about the safety of Nashville. Buell, however, remained calm and positioned his forces to meet the rebels wherever it advanced. Even with 15,000 men on guard and garrison duty, Buell could still attack Chattanooga with roughly 30,000 soldiers. The concentration of his army could be accomplished in less than twenty-four hours to meet the Confederates. If, on the other hand, Bragg crossed the river, Buell would attack him. "I do not doubt that we shall defeat him," he remarked.[86]

Finally Buell was excited into action, but it was too late. The Confederates were heading north. "There is reason to apprehend," Buell wrote Governors Tod, Morton, and Yates, "another formidable raid into Kentucky at an early day."[87] Bragg would soon cross the river somewhere between Chattanooga and Decatur and head to Nashville. At the same time Buell informed Grant that he might need the two divisions Halleck designated for his disposal, but Halleck made no corresponding shift of troops from Grant to Buell. Halleck feared that 16,000 troops under Gen. Sterling Price at Tupelo left by Bragg to support Gen. Earl Van Dorn's men at Vicksburg might invade West Tennessee if Grant shifted his position.[88]

With the fear of a full-scale invasion into Kentucky increasingly on Buell's mind, Halleck's August 12 message could not have come at a worse time. Thinking he was doing Buell a favor, the chief of staff confided, "General, I deem it my duty to write to you confidentially that the administration is greatly dissatisfied with the slowness of your operations. . . . So strong is this dissatisfaction that I have several times been asked to recommend some officer to take your place."[89] As much as Halleck realized there was no one else with whom to replace Buell, he confessed that "the matter has been urged on me very hard on the ground that you were accomplishing nothing." He added that "the Government will expect an active campaign . . . and that unless that is done the present dissatisfaction is so great your friends here will not be able to prevent a change being ordered."[90] It was as Boyle wrote to Morton: "I fear Gen. Buell is in a bad fix."[91]

Halleck was not exaggerating. Chase, Stanton, and Johnson had had little faith in Buell to begin with, and the summer campaign merely confirmed what they believed all along. Other midwestern governors such as Morton, Yates, and Tod were beginning to lose faith as well, despite Buell's attempts to pacify them that all was not lost. The governors saw no reason to continue Buell in command. In July Morton visited Washington and encouraged Yates and others to join him in appealing to Lincoln. Johnson had been relentlessly pressing the administration to replace Buell with Thomas and probably would have been successful had Thomas been more ambitious for command. Johnson was tired of conciliation, emphasizing to Thomas, "There must be more vigor & the enemy made to bear the expense and feel the pressure of war. Leniency is construed into timidity, compromising to concession, which inspired them with confidence & keeps alive the fell spirit of rebellion."[92] But Thomas remained loyal to Buell even when it became a political liability for him to do so. He wired Johnson that the circumstances in the West made it impossible for the "most able General in the World to conduct a campaign with success when his hands are tied," and he assured the governor that Buell's "dispositions will Eventually [free] all Tennessee & Go very far to crush the rebelon entirely."[93] As for any friends he had in Washington, Buell had none, and by this time being a friend of McClellan's was certainly anything but an asset.

As if Halleck's news was not enough, that same day John Hunt Morgan, raiding almost at will in Kentucky, struck the twin tunnels seven miles north of Gallatin on the Louisville and Nashville Railroad, essentially isolating Nashville and rendering the railroad between Louisville and Nashville useless for nearly four months. This completely crippled Buell's supply line and stopped his efforts to effect a concentration to strike at Bragg. Under the circumstances he could not cross the Tennessee River but instead had to wait for the movements of Bragg. As punishment for the disaster he court-martialed the colonel responsible for surrendering Gallatin. Buell's army continued to deteriorate. Sickness and the shortage of forage and food took their toll. Still, even when he needed to use slaves for labor, he reminded his officers that "in taking slaves . . . try, if possible, to leave enough with the owner to do the ordinary and indispensable work about an establishment."[94]

By mid-August the stationary Union army had thoroughly exhausted the countryside of forage and provisions. Still, Buell reminded his officers that "in taking horses it must be done in such a way that orderly persons shall not be deprived of what may be necessary for their ordinary work."[95] Bragg, by contrast, had restored the morale of his soldiers, saying the army had "improved in health and strength and has progressed rapidly in discipline, organization and instruction."[96]

There was every reason to believe that Buell would shrink from forcing Bragg to battle. His army had been reduced if not in numbers, which it had, but considerably in spirit and now was decidedly forced to the defensive. His solicitous attitude was showing little sign of effectiveness in keeping his army safe, since many civilians continued to assist the Confederates, while the more daring engaged in guerrilla activity. Even when Robert McCook, one of his finest officers, was killed, he did not retaliate except to issue orders to hang every civilian caught as a guerrilla. Instead he continued to shift his army to watch the mountain passes into Middle Tennessee where Bragg would most likely appear, and he forwarded his supply depot from Stevenson to Dechard.[97]

By August 16 Kirby Smith, motivated by the success of Morgan's exploits, advanced from Knoxville through the mountains with about 12,000 soldiers on his way to Lexington. Though he was not exactly sure where Smith intended to strike, Buell supposed Nashville and then Kentucky. He sent Nelson to Louisville to take command of the new troops coming into the city, which would comprise the new but small Army of Kentucky, and defend Kentucky. Though belligerent and haughty, Nelson still enjoyed the confidence of Buell as the most thorough disciplinarian in the department and a man who possessed tremendous energy and ability.[98]

By mid-August it would have been difficult to increase the extreme demoralization in the Army of the Ohio. From the beginning of the campaign, Buell's march was "like holiday soldiering," with the average day's trek beginning at dawn and ending long before noon. Major Keifer considered Buell's policy of "*Watch* and *Wait*" frustrating and debilitating almost to the point of treachery.[99] Soldiers passed the monotonous and fatiguing days by discussing Buell's policies, searching for water and food without leave, abusing slaves, and passing rumors, all of which found their way into newspapers and letters home. A correspondent to the *Cincinnati Commercial* wrote, "It is no wonder . . . that the enlistment in Ohio and Indiana goes slow, when our boys write such matters home . . . [who] would like to be made watch[men] of rebel melon and potatoe patches."[100]

Buell's punishments for violations of the rules and the soldiers' physical condition greatly frustrated the men. Even the mildest infraction caught the wrath of officers in tune with Buell's policies. If a soldier was caught entering an enclosure for a drink of water, he was "ignominiously punished," wrote a reporter for the *Cincinnati Commercial*[101] "No one at all observant," wrote a correspondent to the *Cincinnati Gazette*, "can travel from Nashville to this point without being convinced that there is the most palpable antagonism between the policy of the General commanding the army, and the feelings and opinions of his entire army."[102]

On August 18 Halleck prodded Buell again with a more severe criticism of his want of action. "So great is the dissatisfaction here at the apparent want of energy and activity in your district," he wrote, "that I was this morning notified to have you removed. I got the matter delayed till we could hear further of your movements."[103] Buell replied the same day that he did not want Halleck to interpose on his behalf. Quite the contrary, the prideful commander argued that "if the dissatisfaction cannot cease on grounds which I think might be supposed if not apparent I respectfully request that I may be relieved." "My position," he added "is far too important to be occupied by any officer on sufferance." Furthermore, "I have no desire to stand in the way of what may be deemed necessary for the public good."[104] As someone who seldom tolerated excuses, even Buell would have chided or in fact relieved a commander unable to accomplish a designated objective.

The following day, upon learning that Bragg would definitely cross the river, Buell moved his headquarters to Dechard, which placed his army at the center of his line extending from Jasper to McMinnville. He waited for Bragg to appear out of the mountains. Bragg considered combining with Kirby Smith's army, fighting Buell south of Nashville, and then invading Kentucky. Smith, however, chose to move north independently and left Bragg to keep Buell from capturing Chattanooga or pursuing Smith into Kentucky. From scouts Buell learned on August 23 that Bragg intended to advance along the mountain road running through Altamont, McMinnville, and Murfreesboro. He ordered Thomas and McCook to concentrate at Altamont to meet Bragg and delay him until the rest of the army could be deployed. Still, Buell failed to maneuver his forces quickly enough to catch Bragg.[105]

When Nelson arrived in Louisville on August 23, he found his mission hampered by a recent decision by the War Department to create a new Department of the Ohio. Lincoln and Stanton decided to strip Buell of that part of his district north of the Tennessee border and east of the Tennessee River because they felt his army, bogged down in Tennessee, would be hopeless in protecting Kentucky. The new Kentucky jurisdiction fell to Gen. Horatio G. Wright, who was in Cincinnati. To clear up any misunderstanding, Halleck wrote Buell that the orders did not affect Tennessee or his army but simply those troops now being consolidated in Kentucky. When Wright arrived in Louisville, he technically replaced Boyle as departmental commander, but under Halleck's orders

Boyle was left in charge of the troops. Nelson's arrival complicated everything, since Buell had sent him to command the troops in Louisville forming the new army. Buell's problem was that he still needed to draw on Louisville for supplies.[106]

In a letter to Wright, Halleck rephrased the criticisms lodged against Buell while enticing Wright to get something going:

> The Government . . . is greatly displeased with the slow movements of general Buell. Unless he does something very soon I think he will be removed. . . . There must be more energy and activity in Kentucky and Tennessee and the one who first does something brilliant will get the entire command. . . . The Government seems determined to apply the guillotine to all unsuccessful generals. It seems rather hard to do this where the general is not at fault, but perhaps with us now, as in the French Revolution, some harsh measures are required.[107]

Halleck did not blame Buell for his predicament, but he avoided saying who could be faulted for it.

By the end of August Bragg determined to follow Smith, keeping his army between Smith's and Buell's, and headed north, using the terrain to conceal his movements until he came out of the mountains. Buell learned that Bragg was advancing with no less than 50,000 troops and had crossed the Tennessee and come over Walden's Ridge. But because Bragg used his cavalry to screen his army's movements as they passed out of the mountains, he effectively froze Buell into waiting, not only for Bragg to show himself but also for reinforcements from Grant. With his rations at risk of depletion, Buell considered the prospects for further advance and wrote Nelson an alarming telegram: "The most momentous consequences depend on your opening communications with Louisville without delay." Buell's tone alarmed Nelson and pushed him into a panic about the defense of Kentucky.[108]

On August 30 Buell gave up concentrating at McMinnville and settled on falling back to Murfreesboro, which put him back on rails where his army more easily could draw supplies from Nashville and reinforcements from Grant. The Union campaign for Chattanooga was finished, and the Confederate campaign into Kentucky had begun. All of this caused a frustrated McCook to lament, "Don Carlos won't do; he won't do."[109] The Confederates had been given what Halleck had wanted to avoid in June: the opportunity to regain what they had lost the past winter and spring. When Nelson clashed with Kirby Smith's troops at Richmond on August 30, it encouraged Bragg to bypass Nashville and move north to Bowling Green.

From the campaign's inception Buell stressed that his goal was not only to get to Chattanooga but also to be in a favorable position upon arrival. This meant that securing the means of getting his army to Chattanooga was more important than Chattanooga itself. In this he illustrated one of the hallmarks of his command: emphasizing preparation over movement. Buell worried over an incomplete military occupation, since it would not sustain political restoration and would jeopardize otherwise innocent civilians when the Union army had to leave. Had Buell not been so determined to secure the means of sustaining a permanent presence, he might have considered more seriously the desires of his superiors and thus minimized the political fallout. At a time when the president was judging generals by the standard of victory, Buell would have to prove himself capable of bringing about success as the test of merit.[110]

Perhaps there were other considerations in his failure to attack Bragg. In January 1863, in his cross-examination of Gen. Lovell H. Rousseau during his court of inquiry, Buell made several references to the superior discipline of the rebel army, which gave it an advantage over his forces; a superior steadiness under fire that the Confederates exhibited to his army; and the fact that they were easier to handle in battle. This reinforced Buell's contention that the conditions of the summer had so unraveled the discipline of his army that his men had been rendered inferior to Bragg's.[111]

Buell had been finding reasons not to go to East Tennessee since he took command. At the core of his reluctance was the fact that his actions might compromise his beliefs about waging war itself. Buell extended his policy of conciliation with every mile the army marched through northern Mississippi and Alabama. Buell did not want to alienate the citizenry, and thus he refused to live off the countryside or the people. Interestingly enough, when the Union soldiers closed to within range of Confederate pickets around Chattanooga, the soldiers engaged in a shouting match back and forth across enemy lines. A few soldiers, who still remained loyal to Buell despite their disagreement with his policies, would shout that southerners "had better begin to repent for a terrible Union disease, called Buell, is rapidly spreading in your direction."[112] When the Union soldiers asked how the Confederates liked some of their generals, such as Mitchel and Pope, the rebels had nothing good to say. When they asked about Buell, the response was, "'First rate, first rate,'" which caused one Ohio soldier to conclude perceptively that "one thing is certain—the officer who handles them as if he meant something has their ill will, while those who pursue the 'velvet policy' have their good wishes."[113]

Buell continued to believe that his army was an extension of good government and offered the olive branch whenever and wherever he could. In this he remained true to his belief in a limited war for limited goals, even when it became evident that many of his soldiers opposed it. The problem was that he was in a vulnerable position in the campaign when war turned hard. Indeed, it was as Major Keifer wrote to his wife in late August: "We are at a turning point in the war."[114] Thus, at a time when Buell held firm to his attitude about waging limited war, the Union had expanded the conflict and was prepared to apply new criteria to generals who proved unsuccessful in turning with it.

CHAPTER SIXTEEN

The Hell March and Battle for the Bluegrass

Buell blundered badly by allowing an army half his size to lure him away from Chattanooga without either side firing a shot. As one Ohio soldier wrote, "Bragg deliberately threw sand in Buell's eyes and then ran away from him, before Buell could see what was up."[1] As another soldier put it, "We were now aware that General Buell had been outgeneralled by Bragg."[2] Inspired by his success, the Confederate commander turned his mind to larger prospects, involving nothing less than a complete reversal of the entire military situation in the West. He planned to move into Kentucky. Kirby Smith's dash north and victory over Nelson at Richmond, Kentucky, on August 30 confirmed that the tide could be turned in the West. Nearly 7,000 Confederates scored a brilliant victory over a Federal force roughly the same size and captured over 4,000. Nelson himself was wounded and captured but later escaped.[3]

Bragg had guessed that Buell would retreat to the safety of Nashville and thus expose the central route into Kentucky. Once in Nashville, Buell quickly realized that Kentucky, and not the Tennessee capital, was Bragg's objective and that Louisville appeared the likely destination. Andrew Johnson thought much the same. To Lincoln he wrote that the general "would never enter and redeem the Eastern portion of this State" because he remained on the defensive and, consequently, was ruining Unionism in Tennessee. Johnson was even more outraged that Buell had not issued orders for carrying out the Confiscation Act. All of this led the military governor to conclude that Buell was "very popular with the Rebels," and it was the impression in Nashville that he "favors the establishment of a Southern Confederacy." As much as Johnson wanted to believe this exaggerated charge, he knew Buell was loyal to the bone. This, however, did not keep him from thinking that if Buell had wanted to undermine Unionism in Tennessee, he could not have pursued a policy more helpful to the Rebels than conciliation.[4]

The animosity Johnson felt for Buell had become well known among the soldiers and residents of Nashville. On one occasion, a resident remembered, Buell and Johnson had a "'very pretty quarrel'" resulting from a remark Johnson made while giving a speech at the capitol. He was drunk at the time and, pointing to some rocks near the capitol building, told Buell that "'his bones should bleach on those rocks.'" Buell replied that he intended to stand against Bragg at Nashville if necessary, but that if Johnson "'patriotically desired his bones to bleach there, nothing could be easier to him [Johnson], or more agreeable to himself.'"[5] Johnson's detestation of Buell passed through the ranks in the late summer. The governor's incessant ravings that Buell was a traitor found considerable reception among soldiers desiring a command change. "General Buell is a rebel at heart," wrote one soldier, "and has done all in his power to aid the rebel cause. His very acts show him to be one."[6]

Buell, however, remained unmoved by the rumors and attitude of the ranks. He remained focused on getting to Louisville before Bragg. "The condition of affairs in Kentucky," he concluded to Halleck, "seems to render something more absolutely necessary. I believe Nashville can be held and Kentucky rescued." At that point Halleck did not much care about the condition of affairs in Kentucky or Buell's conclusions, for that matter. "March where you please," he responded, exasperated, "provided you will find the enemy and fight."[7]

In light of Halleck's comment, Buell decided simply to get to Louisville quickly and uninjured by the enemy. Consequently, he sacrificed the region his army had occupied for a year. He left Negley's Eighth Division and 6,000 troops under Thomas behind to aid Johnson. In trying to reach Louisville ahead of Bragg, he marched his men more miles per day than ever before, some days as many as thirty miles. Bowling Green was the army's first destination. The tormenting summer heat, as suffocating as the dust of the roads, replaced the enemy annoyances. Both forced the men off the roads in search of water, which was scarce and stagnant when found. Dried up ponds and shrunken streams resulting from a pronounced drought made the Kentucky countryside as unfriendly as northern Alabama had been. More tormenting than the heat, dust, and lack of water was the lack of food. The army's pathetically depleted wagon train labored to keep up with the main body, but horses and mules were dropping as fast as the soldiers. Often the soldiers marched at night to avoid the sun, only to be consumed by bugs. Stragglers had to be made to march at the point of a bayonet until they fell exhausted, cursing those who would kill their own men.

Of course, for soldiers who had just months before marched across northern Alabama under similar conditions, solace could be found in the fact that they were marching toward their supplies instead of away from them, even if it meant giving up all they had accomplished over the year. "Marching almost naked and barefoot often at dead of night," wrote one Illinoisan, "the solitudes of the forest would ring with sonorous imprecations on 'Old Buell,' by the exhausted soldiers whose resentment found vent in curses upon a leader in whom they had no confidence."[8]

As Buell's army trekked north toward Bowling Green, Lincoln's vexation about the location of Bragg increased. To put the president's mind at ease, Buell wired him on September 10 that Bragg, with his whole force, was west of the Cumberland Mountains and that Nashville was secure. Smith's timely arrival at Lexington cut off Morgan's chances to unite with Buell. A combined Confederate army could be positioned either to capture Louisville, as important to the Union as Nashville was to the Confederacy, or to turn south against a numerically inferior army and, according to Bragg, "thrash them all."[9]

Bragg's invasion alarmed midwesterners. Smith's victory, Buell's retreat to Nashville, and the Confederates' crossing of the Kentucky state line inspired wild rumors and exaggerations that the Confederates would be at the gates of either Cincinnati or Louisville any day. The residents across the river in Indiana and Ohio fortified themselves and mobilized "Minute-men" and "Squirrel Hunters" for defense. Departmental commander Wright suspended business in Cincinnati, declared martial law, and ordered troops from Louisville to Cincinnati, despite the objection of General Boyle. The governors of Michigan, Wisconsin, Illinois, Kentucky, and Indiana all worried about Wright's desire to reinforce Cincinnati at the expense of Louisville. Governor Morton was so concerned that he went to Louisville to ensure that his Hoosiers were being properly handled. In the camps he found, much to his pleasure, considerable public censorship of Buell.[10]

By mid-September Buell was fully aware of Bragg's threat to Bowling Green, where the rebels destroyed the Union supply depot and then pressed north to rendezvous with Smith. Until he could be sure of Bragg's exact intentions, Buell left Thomas and 6,000 men at Nashville, which greatly relieved an overly anxious Johnson. On September 14 his dusty, parched, and partially demoralized divisions reached Bowling Green, just as Bragg's inspired soldiers, though "foot-sore and tired," passed through Glasgow some thirty miles to the east. Buell's timely arrival at Bowling Green did little to dispel the biting criticism and colossal dissatisfaction he had generated. For someone who just four days before had concluded to Lincoln that he would dominate Bragg's movements, Buell wrote Halleck that although he had ordered his army north, "movements of the enemy" had delayed it. This letter revealed part of the mental framework within which Buell conceived his advance into Kentucky. He could not decide whether he was coming or going. "I am not insensible to the difficulty and embarrassment of the position," he confessed, "but it must be so for [Bragg] also, and I hope it may result in his discomfiture and not ours."[11]

The discomfort, however, belonged to Lincoln and Halleck, the soldiers of the Army of the Ohio, and Buell's division commanders, most of whom were still harboring resentment about his earlier decision to fall back to Murfreesboro on the railroad rather than Sparta. The retreat had so outraged some officers of Thomas's division that they drafted a petition to Lincoln to have Buell removed. Though heedless of the petition, Thomas was aware of the unfavorable attitude toward Buell among some of his officers and men, and he tried to keep it from infecting the entire division. The demoralizing effects of the Chattanooga campaign and the yellow, acrid dust kicked up from the hot limestone pikes only made the disillusionment even more disheartening.[12]

Hard training and lean diets had conditioned Buell's soldiers to endure inconceivable hardships and, to their credit, they secured Bowling Green. Bragg's troops, however, despite the same hardships of heat, scarcity of water, and clouds of dust, pushed on another eighteen miles to Munfordville on the Louisville and Nashville Railroad, arriving on

September 15. When Buell learned that Bragg had reached Munford-ville, he delayed assisting the 4,000 troops stationed there under the command of Col. John T. Wilder. He was unconvinced that Bragg's entire force was there, since Wilder had not communicated with Buell but with General Wright in Cincinnati. In the meantime, Bragg arranged to have Wilder visit his headquarters to convince him that the Confederates would easily overrun the small Federal garrison, and on the night of September 16 Wilder agreed to surrender. The following day Buell learned of the capitulation, and though he had been anxious to pin down Bragg at Glasgow, the fall of Munfordville changed his mind. He would have to give battle at some other point, some other day.[13]

Munfordville's capitulation worsened Buell's hope of reaching Louis-ville. Not only had Bragg positioned his army squarely in Buell's path, but he hoped also to demoralize the Union army further by sending the 4,000 paroled prisoners to Buell at Bowling Green. He knew Buell's army was already disheartened from reading northern papers that had been unduly harsh on the general and his deteriorating relationship with his soldiers. Bragg had boasted to Richmond as Buell had only a few days before: "My position must be exceedingly embarrassing to Buell and his army." "My junction with Kirby Smith is complete," he added. "Buell [is] still at Bowling Green."[14]

Bragg's conclusions gave Richmond a false sense of opportunity. Bragg and Smith had not massed; in fact, the two were still a hundred miles apart. Moreover, Buell had not remained at Bowling Green; he was at Cave City, only ten miles south of Bragg. Significantly, too, Buell was marching toward his supplies and reinforcements, while the Confederates were moving farther away from theirs. If capturing Louisville had been Bragg's objective, as Buell thought, now even that seemed unlikely. Nelson had worked earnestly to fortify the city and organize the 30,000 newly mustered troops for its defense. Louisville was still dead in Buell's sights, while Bragg's undefined objectives in moving into Kentucky became even more unclear when he captured Munfordville and halted.[15]

Despite his obvious predicament, Bragg was determined to stay in Kentucky and fight Buell, but on the defensive. The ten-mile distance between the two armies concerned Bragg, simply because he assumed correctly that the Union army, numbering 35,000, was larger than his own force of roughly 28,000. Thus, he took up a defensive position just below Munfordville on the south side of the Green River. This gave Buell, whose first reaction was to send for Thomas at Nashville, the opportunity to seize the offensive. Now that he confronted Bragg's entire army, which from reliable sources was estimated at between 30,000 and 40,000, he would have to move cautiously, pondering whether he should attack before Thomas arrived. Always playing it safe, Buell waited, largely because he could overcome the entrenched position of the Confederates only with more troops. Buell was just as surprised as Bragg at the sudden inertia. On September 20, after Buell's failure to appear, Bragg turned to his exhausted supplies and soldiers. He withdrew from Munfordville and headed toward Bardstown, a tiny hamlet some forty miles southeast of Louisville. Buell regained the main road to Louisville and, realizing Bragg would soon unite with Smith, ordered a series of forced marches for Louisville the following day.[16]

Buell's refusal to fight Bragg at Munfordville stemmed from his belief that the Confederate's numerically superior army was in an entrenched position and, in part, from his conviction that getting to Louisville was more strategically important than fighting. Though he was personally not timid, he lacked aggressiveness. He considered discipline and caution more effective in winning battles, and Louisville offered both. Besides, the lack of discipline he perceived along the march caused him to fear his troops were not in condition to fight. Of course, discipline did not prevent taking the offensive, yet Buell never outgrew the fear that his men were not prepared to fight. In light of his campaign to Chattanooga, his desire to bypass Bragg and head straight for Louisville was not surprising. What he did not know, however, was that his lack of aggression at Munfordville had done irreparable damage. New York journalist Henry Villard recalled that "this scandalous incident produced a thrill of disgust and discouragement in our army."[17] For months rumors had been passing through the ranks that Buell was a traitor and a coward, and the Munfordville episode convinced soldiers that new hearsay that Buell and Bragg were brothers-in-law and had visited each other while near Munfordville were indeed true. Soldiers could see no other logical reason for not fighting.[18]

Halleck agreed that Buell was right in moving into Kentucky, but he griped, "I fear that here as elsewhere you move too slowly, and will permit the junction of Bragg and Smith before you open your line to Louisville." "The immobility of your army is most surprising," he lectured, "Bragg in the last two months has marched four times the distance you have."[19] Still, he worried about the increasing depredations his army had committed, leading him to conclude that the soldiers were in no condition to fight a general engagement. He was so concerned that the defeated Army of Kentucky and the new recruits at Louisville were no match for Bragg's army that he advised Nelson not to resist an attack from Bragg but to abandon the city and move down the river to the Salt River.[20]

Buell attempted to defend the pace of his march, but chronic impatience was hard to satisfy. He had not missed Halleck's chiding tone. "It might seem useless for me to answer the frequent charges of tardiness that are made against the movements of the Army of the Ohio," he argued, "though I think I could answer them with some effect." Bragg had not marched a greater distance since he departed from Chattanooga 200 miles away, and Buell's army had marched over 300 miles since leaving Corinth. Buell argued that disrupted communications and transportation had cramped his advance. In other words, matters beyond his control had plagued him since leaving Corinth. "I am not disposed generally to be very zealous in my own defense," he concluded, "but I ought perhaps to say this much."[21]

On September 25 the clouds of dust hovering over the long blue line of the Army of the Ohio lifted as the 35,000 soldiers trudged into Louisville. In some ways it was a sad homecoming, since the army had returned to the place it had left nine months earlier. "Thank God for the Ohio River and hard tack," exclaimed a member of the Second Minnesota.[22] The 1,700 wagons, most of which were empty, stretching almost seventeen miles behind the army, reflected the suffering of the troops. Thousands of soldiers had fallen during the march and straggled into the city days later. Since leaving Louisville the previous winter the army had campaigned over what must have seemed like thousands of miles, or as some thought, "to hell" and back. Their arrival dazed the spectators as the public could now comprehend how troops on the march and actively campaigning appeared. "Of all slouchy, slovenly-looking, mud begrimed ill clad human beings," wrote a newly mustered Indianian, "these veteran troops of Buell's old command were unmatched."[23]

Despite their suffering the soldiers had many laurels to boast of, including the capture of Bowling Green, Nashville, Corinth, and numerous smaller towns, all without firing a shot. At Shiloh they had been brutally baptized, though only for a day. For many soldiers, though, Bragg's advance into Kentucky forced them to reclaim the Bluegrass State, and it eclipsed their sense of accomplishment. The soldiers were also no closer to Buell as a commander than when they first laid eyes on him the previous autumn. They knew him only through the barrage of orders and stifling policies he cast on them in trying to make them soldiers. Few knew of his ability to incite engaging conversations on military theory or of his almost Herculean strength, which on occasion he demonstrated by lifting his wife, who weighed 140 pounds, at arm's length and standing her on a mantel shelf nearly as high as himself. Journalists were perhaps more perceptive in understanding the baffling relationship between the general and his men. While riding north through Elizabethtown on September 24, Cincinnati correspondent Joseph "Mack" McCullagh carefully observed the austere and disengaged commander.

> His dress was that of a brigadier instead of a major general. He wore a shabby hat, dusty coat, and had neither belt, sash or sword about him. . . . Though accompanied by his staff, he was not engaged in conversation with any of them, but rode silently and slowly along, noticing nothing that transpired around him. . . . Buell is, certainly, the most reserved, distant and unsociable of all the generals in the army. He never has a word of cheer for his men or his officers, and in turn his subordinates care little for him save to obey his orders, as machinery works in response to the bidding of the mechanic. There is in McClellan and Frémont an unaccountable something, that keeps this machinery constantly oiled and easy-running; but Buell's unsympathetic nature makes it "squeak" like the drag wheels of a wagon.[24]

The atmosphere in Louisville was not much different in appearance and attitude to Buell from when he had arrived the previous November. Seventy thousand Louisvillians panicked at the very thought of a Confederate invasion and expected Buell to relieve their fears. Buell's arrival in Louisville turned the tide for the Union war effort in the West, but it was also Buell who had allowed Bragg to seize the upper hand in the first place. The fact that his men could march at the pace they did confirmed that it was not the army's inability to fulfill demands placed upon it but, rather, the commander's inability or refusal to use effectively the machine he had created. Few people in the Midwest or in Washington could believe such an army living on so little could march so quickly and achieve so much in so little time.[25]

Unlike the relieved Louisvillians, the soldiers found only partial relief upon arriving in the city. The hostility over the Chattanooga campaign had not softened, and the thought of not fighting Bragg at Munfordville was only the most recent reminder that Buell was a cowardly southern sympathizer in collusion with Bragg, his brother-in-law. Threats of wholesale officer resignations passed through the ranks after Munfordville. Soldiers were convinced that "Granny Buell" purposely avoided Bragg because, as James Shaw wrote, he was "as good a Southern man as Jeff Davis."[26]

This attitude held wide currency in the army. Some soldiers wanted Lincoln to appoint secret agents to infiltrate the Army of the Ohio just to convince the administration that Buell was a traitor. "General Buell was by instinct, if not by birth," concluded an Indianian, "possessed of the *Chivalry* of the true Southerner."[27] The press was equally critical. Correspondent Mack had devoted columns of his reports to the *Cincinnati Commercial* to defaming Buell, frequently questioning his editors "how long an army of lions was to be commanded by a jackass." Junius Browne of the *New York Daily Tribune* continued to attribute the Union's failure to Buell's ineptitude. Reporters for *Frank Leslie's Illustrated* and the *Boston Journal* impugned Buell's loyalties, going so far as to reprint hearsay articles from other papers accusing Buell of not knowing what the war was about and of lounging around the Washington taverns before the war cursing the Black Republicans and "eulogizing slavery."[28] Even the New York *Independent* lashed out: "Treason or imbecility has kept intolerable Genl. Buell crawling to Nashville and then North."[29] Only the *Louisville Daily Journal, Chicago Times,* and *New York Herald* came to his defense, but little could be done to stop the avalanche of hostility toward him.[30] "He is a traitor" whose own men might shoot him, declared James Love. "It is spoken openly in the streets, by his own staff and by all the secesh fools that they are."[31]

Criticisms of Buell escalated into widespread hatred by the time he arrived in Louisville. "The whole country was aflame with anger" at Buell's failure to meet Bragg at Munfordville, one soldier wrote.[32] Lt. John W. Tuttle of the Third Kentucky penned in his diary that along the march to Louisville, "free use was made of the epithets 'traitor, tyrant, fool, and coward' with reference to Gen. Buell."[33] "That old poke-easy general of ours [Buell] has allowed the thieving rebels to overrun the best portion of the State and they are now in full possession of our homes," wrote a disgruntled Kentucky soldier.[34] If nothing more, wrote a soldier in the Tenth Indiana, "It was the desire of the army to get into an engagement . . . to relieve the monotony of constant marching."[35] "All we care now is to . . . thrash and drive the lousy devils out, kill or capture the whole army of thieves."[36] For thoroughly disheartened Indianian Thomas Small, the solution was simple: "Shoot him [Buell]—let us go."[37] Illinoisan R. Delavan Mussey concluded that in retreating north, "Buell has lost, by his vacillation and incompetence, nearly or quite all we have gained in Kentucky and Tennessee and Alabama during the last twelve months," and that every leading officer in his army agrees "*that he is either a Traitor or an Imbecile.*"[38]

The influx of thousands of ragged, soiled, and gaunt soldiers added as much to Louisville's problems as it did to relieve its fears, since the army would have to be replenished and reorganized if it were to defeat Bragg. For men desperate for food, loved ones, or simply to get out from under Buell, pillage and desertion in some cases became the order of the day, particularly since many soldiers had not been paid for almost six months. Buell only added to the problem by threatening to withhold their pay until after the campaign against Bragg was over. One soldier was so disgusted with Buell that he was strongly tempted to run away and join a Missouri regiment. There were even public insults. On one occasion at an elaborate birthday celebration in honor of Gens. William B. Hazen, James S. Jackson, and Nelson at the Galt House, in Buell's absence Senator John J. Crittenden proposed a toast to General McCook, whom he referred to as "the coming leader of the Army of the Ohio." This naturally offended those supporters of Buell seated together.[39]

For weeks Nelson had been preparing the city and its residents for what might be the worst of all fates of war, and when Buell arrived, Louisville instantly became the citadel of the West. His first order of business was to centralize authority in himself. He asked Halleck to make the appropriate structural changes; Halleck agreed. The Ohioan worked tirelessly reconfiguring the army. Realizing the need to restructure his conglomerated troops into distinct commands, Buell divided the men into three corps. He rewarded the ever loyal McCook and Thomas L. Crittenden, who had been promoted during the hasty reorganization at Louisville, with the leadership of the First and Second Corps, respectively. McCook had perhaps been the most impressed with Buell's energy over the last ten months. He never knew when the commander slept. Any defamations against Buell made in McCook's presence were immediately stopped, and on one occasion he arrested a newspaper reporter who had allegedly called Buell an "Ass." But while both remained loyal to Buell, the Chattanooga campaign exasperated McCook, and Buell's failure to fight Bragg at Munfordville completely disgusted him. The First Corps included the division of Lovell Rousseau and the newly added and mostly green Tenth Division under James S. Jackson. Crittenden's Second Corps comprised the divisions of Brig. Gens. William S. Smith, Horatio P. Van Cleve, and Thomas J. Wood.[40]

The Third Corps was undoubtedly the most colorful, since it comprised a peculiar combination of soldiers and commanders, many of whom chafed at the thought of fighting under Buell. Because Buell always shared an affinity for Nelson's ability to exact the most from his soldiers, and because Nelson was a senior officer with impressive combat experience, Buell named him commander of the Third Corps. Brig. Gen.

Albin Schoepf disliked Nelson and frankly hated Buell. He had once even threatened to shoot Buell for arresting some of Schoepf's men scrounging for food without orders. The previous December Buell had kept him on puppet strings in advancing to East Tennessee, and Schoepf resented that, too. The corps also comprised the largest contingent of Grant's former troops, including Brig. Gen. Philip H. Sheridan's Eleventh Division and Brig. Gen. Jefferson C. Davis's Ninth Division.[41]

Integrating 36,000 new levies, hurried to Louisville from northern communities, with the utterly fatigued veteran regiments proved confusing. The old troops remained demoralized. The stark contrast between what was and what had been the Army of the Ohio took on new meaning for those soldiers who, after peering at their comrades, surely considered returning home. "*Then*," wrote Asbury L. Kerwood of the Fifty-seventh Indiana, "we came with more than eight hundred men, but *now*... [there are] scarce three hundred able to bear arms."[42] As was his trademark, Buell displayed the administrative and organizational qualities for preparing soldiers that many had expected of him the year before. All this industry caused an impressed General Boyle to later write that "I have never seen, known, heard, or read of anything evincing more in the same length of time."[43]

In reorganizing the army, Buell confronted the same problems he had encountered the previous year. When Nelson had earlier arrived to command the newly mustered troops in Louisville, so had Governor Morton. For weeks Morton traveled back and forth between Indianapolis and Louisville, strolling through the camps conferring with soldiers from the Hoosier state. He made no bones about despising what he called the traitorous, proslavery Democrat commander, whose devoted friendship with McClellan made him even less appealing. Morton openly denounced him and used the *Indianapolis Daily Journal* to disparage the commander and influence soldiers. What Morton found more immediately displeasing than Buell's leadership was that many Indiana soldiers chafed at serving under Nelson, Buell's most abusive and ungovernable subordinate. Morton was not about to let Nelson abuse Hoosiers as he had so many others. The soldiers in the Indiana regiments that had been transferred to the Army of the Ohio did not welcome the opportunity to serve under Buell or Nelson. "The conduct of General Buell was a subject of bitter comment among the men who made the march from Nashville to Louisville," observed George Herr of the Fifty-ninth Illinois. "The men of Davis's division were particularly severe on the general."[44]

Part of this hostility stemmed from resentment over Buell's severe punishment on the march for even minor infractions of the rules. What made matters worse was that the battle of Richmond resulted in a bitter disagreement between Nelson and Brig. Gen. Jeff C. Davis. The sour-mouthed Nelson insulted Davis for negligence during the battle as well as for his lack of zeal in preparing Louisville for the enemy. He ordered him to Wright's department at Cincinnati. A rebuked Davis returned to Indianapolis, where for days he conspired to return the insult.[45]

Davis returned to Louisville with Morton, and on the morning of September 29 the two appeared in the lobby of the Galt House. They met Nelson on his way to see Buell. Davis demanded an apology. The profane and husky Kentuckian ordered him out of his sight, saying, "Go away, you damned puppy." Davis responded by snapping a crumpled hotel calling card in Nelson's face, which infuriated the general, who slapped Davis with the back of his hand. Nelson then turned and ascended the stairs on his way to Buell's room on the second floor. An enraged Davis obtained a pistol from a bystander, followed Nelson up the stairs, made a few remarks, and then shot him in the chest.[46]

News of Nelson's death blazed through the army and the city. Ohioan Charles Coburn wrote his father that "it [was] one of the best things that has ever happened in this department."[47] Kentuckians, however, had developed quite an admiration for "Old Bull" and considered taking revenge. Still, the killing did not surprise some of Nelson's own subordinate's, who knew he was a tyrant. Morton, however, and some of the more outspoken Indiana soldiers defended Davis, going so far as to propose him as commander of the Third Corps. Buell, distraught by the death of Nelson and concerned about other potential violence, ordered Davis arrested before he had another murder on his hands. In the end, Buell blamed Morton, whose influence he considered detrimental to good order and discipline. "The seeds of mischief," he later wrote, "always present in his extra-official conduct toward the Indiana troops, were now being sown with a vigorous but crafty hand, in the counsels at Washington and among the executives of other states."[48]

In the days following the murder, Buell could not spare troops for a court-martial and did not have time to draft formal charges against Davis, so he arranged for Washington to take care of the matter. Morton, however, managed to ensure that the affair got lost in bureaucratic red tape, and Davis returned to duty a few weeks later without having faced trial. Buell remarked to Fry that the "dignity of a State was abused by the attitude of its governor in the affair, and the authority of the general government was even more degraded by its condonment of the act—a condonment made virtually, if not actually, at his direction."[49]

Buell's immediate problem was filling the vacancies created by Nelson's death and Davis's arrest.

That same morning Col. Joseph C. McKibbin, one of Halleck's aides, hunted down Thomas and Buell and handed them orders removing Buell from command and replacing him with Thomas. Lincoln was tired of excuses, evasions, and lethargy, and his patience had snapped even before Buell had arrived in Louisville. The fact that Buell had been within ten miles of Bragg at Munfordville and had not fought him outraged Halleck and Stanton. Just a few weeks earlier they had ordered Buell to find the enemy and fight. The increasingly hostile atmosphere within the army, reflected in the scathing letters from soldiers and the public denunciations by officers, reinforced Lincoln's desire to remove Buell. Halleck, however, resisted. His desire to keep Buell in command manifested his lack of confidence in any other commander in the West for such an important position. Nonetheless, anticipating that Buell would not arrive in Louisville in time to prepare and fight Bragg, Lincoln had concluded to remove him on September 24.[50]

When Buell arrived in Louisville the next day, either Lincoln was impressed or Halleck was more persuasive than even he imagined, since they tried to stop McKibbin, en route through Cincinnati, from delivering the order. Assuming McKibbin would not make the delivery, Halleck had in the meantime given Buell the authority necessary to organize his army in Louisville, despite the previous departmental arrangements. Buell knew the War Department had been dissatisfied with his handling of the army for the last three months, and what stunned him about being removed was that it had not come sooner. In light of what he considered a rapid march through Kentucky and Halleck's granting of sole command, Buell thought he had at least mollified Union authorities and perhaps partially redeemed himself. Indeed he had, but on the morning of September 29, McKibbin, who never received the cancellation directive, delivered the orders. Based on less than a day's observations, he concluded, "I think it is fortunate that I obeyed instructions. Much dissatisfaction with General Buell."[51]

The unfriendly military atmosphere matched the inhospitable mood outside the army. The Northwest had become alarmed and dismayed when Smith and Bragg entered Kentucky and marched almost unopposed to within miles of the Ohio River. Then, too, Buell had sacrificed all the Union had gained over the course of a year with his abandonment of northern Alabama and most of Middle Tennessee. The Radicals were furious. Desperate to further his reconstruction efforts, Johnson

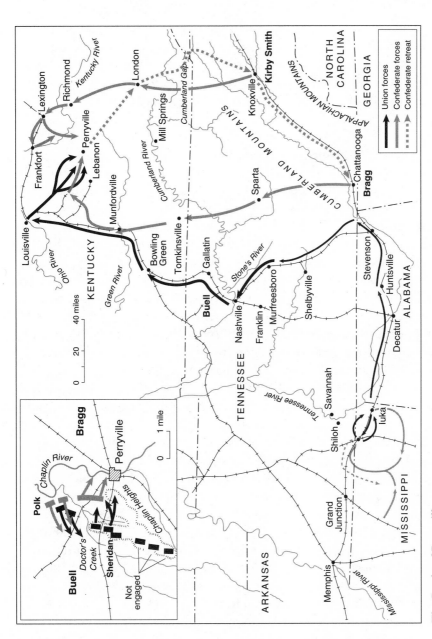

The Battle of Perryville

Union forces
Confederate forces
Confederate retreat

NORTH CAROLINA

GEORGIA

APPALACHIAN MOUNTAINS

Kirby Smith

Knoxville

Chattanooga

Bragg

CUMBERLAND MOUNTAINS

Kentucky River

Lexington
Richmond
London
Cumberland Gap
Mill Springs

Frankfort
Perryville
Lebanon
Munfordville

Cumberland River

Sparta

Louisville
Bowling Green
Tomkinsville
Gallatin
Stone's River
Murfreesboro
Shelbyville
Stevenson
Huntsville
ALABAMA

Ohio River
Green River
KENTUCKY

40 miles
20
0

TENNESSEE
Nashville
Franklin
Decatur

Buell

Tennessee River
Savannah
Shiloh
Iuka

MISSISSIPPI

Grand
Junction

ARKANSAS

Memphis

Mississippi River

Bragg

Polk
Chaplin River
Perryville

1 mile
0

Buell
Doctor's Creek
Sheridan
Chaplin Heights

Not
engaged

burned with a desire to eliminate Buell. Even more outraged than John-son was Morton. The Indiana governor went to Washington in early Oc-tober with the sole purpose of getting Buell out of the army. At one point James Garfield, recently sent to Washington, recalled a conversa-tion he had with Stanton, Chase, and Morton once the Indiana gover-nor arrived. They talked, Garfield said, like men "whose hearts [were] sinking in despairing shame at a condition which might so easily be remedied if only they were allowed to use bold and vigorous measures." According to Chase, Morton said that Buell was "utterly unfit for com-mand[,] . . . is slow, opposed to the [emancipation] proclamation, & has bad influence in every way."[52]

Morton also enlisted Governors Tod and Yates to get Buell removed. The three men demanded to know why he had not attacked Bragg, in the process misrepresenting his motives and in some cases his loyalties. Michigan senator Zachariah Chandler, one of Buell's original critics be-cause of the general's friendship with McClellan and his antiabolition attitude, made a trip west to gather tangible evidence of the Ohioan's unpopularity in his own state. "Buell's course," he concluded to a friend, "has simply exasperated, not demoralized the army of the West." A com-mand change would significantly increase morale.[53]

Kentuckians and those residents living across the river believed that Buell had arrived just in time to save Louisville. The state's senators, John J. Crittenden (despite making some snide remarks at Buell's ex-pense earlier) and Garrett Davis, and congressmen Robert Mallory and George W. Dunlap wired Lincoln requesting that Buell be kept in com-mand because only he had the "confidence of the people and the army."[54] When Thomas received his orders, he went to Buell's room and refused the command. But Buell encouraged him to accept, "since nothing remained to be done but to put the army in motion." Thomas, in a characteristically modest gesture, remained firm and continued to refuse. Though there was widespread dissatisfaction with Buell, many of the veteran soldiers and officers, including a majority of division and brigade commanders, supported him.

Thomas was perceptive enough to know that timing and circum-stances were critical in replacing commanders, particularly those al-ready preparing to advance. Neither were acceptable to Thomas, realiz-ing as he did that such a change would cause delay in attacking Bragg. As confident as he may have been about his own abilities, Thomas may have doubted his capacity to endure the same kind of political and pub-lic criticism that Buell had experienced for the last three months. He may also have concluded that Buell had done such irreparable damage

George H. Thomas, a Virginian who remained loyal to the Union, spent his initial tenure in the war in the East before being transferred to the West. He commanded the First Division of the Army of the Ohio and in January fought and won the battle of Mill Springs. He arrived too late to fight at Shiloh but accompanied Buell's army on the Chattanooga campaign during the summer of 1862 and the campaign into Kentucky in August and September. (Courtesy of the U.S. Army Military History Institute, Carlisle, Pa.)

to the army that it was in no condition to fight, and thus he refused to command what he thought would soon be a defeated army.

Thomas's refusal seems more curious in light of a conversation that allegedly took place at Munfordville. As some soldiers wrote, Thomas wanted to attack Bragg; but Buell refused, and he and Thomas quarreled. At one point during the heated discussion, Thomas called Buell a traitor and said that some of his own men were angry enough to shoot him. Buell then reportedly drew his sword on Thomas and made some remarks that ended the conversation. If true, this incident would seem to have made Thomas more than willing to get rid of Buell, but there is no way of knowing if the incident actually occurred.[55]

Washington was certainly embarrassed when Thomas refused a command the War Department thought he would naturally desire. In light of Buell's arrival at Louisville, Thomas's refusal, and the demanded patronage of the Kentucky representatives, Lincoln was forced to suspend Buell's removal. Among the more outspoken critics was Garfield, who complained, "Buell, removed one morning, for a year of unparalleled s[t]upidity and disaster, and reinstated the same evening at the request of a half dozen Kentuckians who misrepresent the army and the people of the whole West."[56] For anyone else, resumption of command, particularly by default, might have been an embarrassment, but Buell gave up and then retook command without so much as a whimper of protest. Because he had no emotional attachment to his soldiers, it was easier for him to keep his sense of public duty in perspective. His sense of detachment from the soldiers was not accidental; he worked at maintaining a distance between himself and the rank and file, and they reciprocated.[57]

Buell seemed to pay little attention to his firing and rehiring. He remained focused on what he considered the larger task of reconfiguring and rejuvenating the soldiers into an organized and disciplined army. Yet the War Department's public expression of no confidence further diminished his credibility with his men. It inflamed tension and increased the mutterings of mutiny and resignations passing through camps. What made matters worse for Buell now was that these volunteers found their resentment supported at home and in the War Department. Campfires had become venues for debating Buell's policies and loyalties. Unlike McClellan's Army of the Potomac, the Army of the Ohio was not his army. Buell cared little whether soldiers admired him; if they had, he would have probably thought he was doing something wrong. In the meantime, Halleck watched from a distance, waiting to hear that Buell had found and fought Bragg.[58]

Buell quickly made what he thought was a wise decision when he appointed Charles C. Gilbert to replace Nelson. That he passed over Thomas might seem incomprehensible, but not in light of the alleged conversation at Munfordville. Buell knew Gilbert from the regular army and as inspector general of the Army of the Ohio in the summer. Though only a captain, Gilbert had seen combat at Wilson's Creek and Shiloh and had, by what one soldier called "hocus pocus," been named a major general by General Wright, who was badly in need of professional help. Although Lincoln approved the promotion, Wright technically had no authority to make it, and Congress never did approve it. Gilbert, however, acted as a major general, though Buell was surely aware of Gilbert's lower rank. The army saw the appointment as favoritism, and it did little to endear Buell or Gilbert to a corps that included the troops of Schoepf, who hated Buell; Sheridan, a newcomer to the Army of the Ohio, who had asked for Nelson's corps; and those formerly under Mitchel who had long hated Buell. Nelson's death and Gilbert's appointment cast a shadow over the Army of the Ohio as it set out after Bragg.[59]

The Army of the Ohio marched out of Louisville on October 1 in what one soldier recalled as a perfectly enchanting scene. "Fairer skies or more delightful surroundings [an] army never had upon a march," wrote Albion Tourgée of the 105th Ohio.[60] "Could it have been painted on canvas it would have been beautiful," wrote George W. Morris of the Eighty-first Indiana.[61] The long blue lines of soldiers calmly winding through brown fields and rounded hills spotted with oak groves and golden hickories contrasted with the gleam of polished steel bayonets that caught the eye of the distant spectator. Years later Capt. Marshall Thatcher recalled that the march was "a grand pageantry of war."[62]

Not only did the soldiers give the appearance of confidence, but the sheer size of the army, roughly 77,000 men, was inspiring. Buell's strategy was also nearly perfect. But Buell remained unhappy, concentrating on the weaknesses of his forces. The inexperience of at least one-third of the soldiers, rallied by the frantic calls of governors and hastily trained, weighed heavily on his mind. Buell knew that in combat, particularly in light of what he had witnessed at Shiloh, panic could be contagious, and poorly trained soldiers were more susceptible to running.

Recognizing that Smith and Bragg were still sixty miles apart, Buell ordered two of McCook's divisions, about 22,000 troops under Joshua Sill and Ebenezer Dumont, to feign an attack on Frankfort. He wanted to deceive Smith and to protect Louisville. The main army, at a strength of 55,000, advanced to Bardstown, where Buell thought Bragg was with his main army. Buell believed he could defeat Bragg and then move against Smith. Even if Bragg elected to flee the vicinity instead of fight, he would still be driven northward, away from his retreat routes and into a position where he would be forced to fight. Though limited in its objectives, this was aggressive strategy for a commander like Buell who had been repairing and plodding along railroads. He had to be aggressive because Halleck wired him the day after he left Louisville, urging prompt action.[63]

After four days of hard marching through "blinding clouds of dust that darkened the sun," Buell's three main columns pushed Confederate pickets back through Bardstown and south toward a small country town called Perryville. Though Bragg was not deployed at Bardstown as expected, Buell had still managed to position himself between Smith and Bragg. Fortunately, Sill's deception worked better than expected, and Smith completely mistook his column for the main Union army and stayed at Frankfort preparing for battle. On October 4, the same day Buell arrived at Bardstown, the Federals drove the enemy pickets into Frankfort. When Buell learned of this success, he ordered McCook to have Sill and Dumont hurry to join the main army. Meanwhile, Gilbert's corps advanced along the Springfield Road to Perryville, skirmishing with Col. Joseph Wheeler's Confederate cavalry as it went. By the end of the day, scrimmaging turned into preparations for a full-scale battle within six miles of Perryville, where Gilbert's unit saw the Confederates to their front. The divisions of Sheridan and Mitchel deployed across the Springfield Road, with Schoepf in reserve.[64]

Buell rode with Gilbert's Third Corps as it pursued Bragg's army toward Perryville. These early days of October continued to be tormentingly hot and irritating, and some complaints from the rank and file stemmed from the lack of water "not fit for a horse or cow" and from the suffocating heat. There was water at Perryville, but the soldiers would have to fight for it. Along the way, however, Buell's unbending sense of discipline almost did him in. Riding along the dusty and crowded Springfield-Perryville road on October 7, he observed some stragglers foraging in a garden near a farmhouse. He ordered the soldiers to return to their regiments immediately, but one crass soldier refused to obey and continued washing his face with his canteen water. An angered Buell trotted over to the man and shouted at him. The frightened soldier sprang to his feet and reached for the bridle of Buell's horse, Red Oak. This sudden movement spooked the horse, which reared up and fell over backward on top of Buell, who was severely cut and bruised. It was a wonder he survived the spill. For days he could not sit or ride and was transported in an ambulance wagon wherever he went. In a spartan gesture, Buell refused to allow a doctor to wash his wound while water for his men was scare, but the men never knew of this self-sacrifice.[65]

Although lamed by the fall, Buell continued to direct the campaign. That evening, as the sun began to set, Gilbert's corps arrived near Perryville, and Buell deployed for battle three miles west of the village, facing what appeared to be Bragg's entire army. From a hospital wagon, just before dark he carefully directed the positioning of the center corps and then retired to his headquarters, a tent two and a half miles behind the line at the bottom of the hill near the Dorsey home. He had never initiated battle before, though he knew he had to because he had caught Bragg alone. To his front was Brig. Gen. William J. Hardee's wing of Bragg's army comprised of two divisions commanded by Brig. Gen. James Patton Anderson and Maj. Gen. Simon Bolivar Buckner and a portion of Maj. Gen. Leonidas Polk's wing comprising Maj. Gen. Benjamin F. Cheatham's division. The rest of the Confederate army was hastening northward to meet Smith.[66]

Buell anticipated that each of his corps would arrive at Perryville at about the same time—before 10:00 A.M. To make sure everything went according to plan, he issued specific orders that evening to bring up his other two corps during the night in time for the battle the next morning. But McCook's corps, moving through Mackville to the north, found the Taylorsville-Bloomfield pike, a rough country road that wound its way to Perryville, slow going and camped about eight miles from Perryville. Crittenden's corps, accompanied by Thomas, had detoured for water and by the evening was six miles back and to the south of Gilbert's corps along the Lebanon Road.[67]

Buell appeared to be perfectly situated, having maneuvered Bragg into a position to be destroyed by a larger force. A mood of confidence saturated army headquarters that night as Buell stayed awake poring over maps and anticipating daybreak. Shortly before midnight, the men of the Fifth and Seventh Arkansas watched from their concealed positions on the high ground near the Turpin house as Sheridan's men inched forward in the twilight along the Springfield Road, lured by Doctor's Creek. Now nearly dry and dusty, sprinkled only with pools of water, this creek contained the soldier's precious sustenance. Sheridan had ordered a reconnaissance and obtained encouraging news that his men could get to the creek. Buell and Gilbert approved such a move and gave Sheridan the task of seizing Peters Hill, which protected the creek. For several hours Sheridan successfully fought the Confederates for the high ground. By 6:00 A.M. he had pushed them back, and his men were able to fill their canteens. Sheridan established his headquarters at the Turpin house.[68]

Before the first streaks of dawn on October 8, Buell's soldiers were uneasy about the imminent battle. They debated who would launch the first assault in what was surely to be the battle for Kentucky. Concern led to fear that disaster would prevail if Buell lacked the boldness to finish what he had positioned his army to begin. Though it is not clear when they exactly met, some thirty officers from Crittenden's and Gilbert's corps assembled in secret at the home of a Rolling Fork resident and drafted a letter to Lincoln to remove Buell. Schoepf was apparently the ringleader, still suspicious of the high esteem Buell maintained in Kentucky. "If they admire him so much," he concluded, "he must sympathize with them some at any rate. . . . I would not like to trust him a great deal, and I have not the utmost confidence in him anyhow."[69] Though they never sent the letter, these officers had gathered to urge the sacking of the man who was to lead them in the upcoming major battle. Buell might have been confident; but his men were not, and their lack of faith in their commander did not bode well for Federal hopes at Perryville.[70]

Throughout the predawn hours, Buell waited anxiously for word that Thomas and McCook were moving their veterans into position. Neither McCook nor Thomas, however, had reported in person as ordered. As the sun cracked over the hills of the Kentucky bluegrass, it was clear something was wrong. Knowing his flanks were not in position, Buell waited for Bragg to bring on the battle. If not, he planned to postpone it until the following day.[71]

During the early morning, Buell waited as McCook's and Thomas's divisions, which had finally been informed of Buell's orders, raced to Perryville. He also looked for signs of an attack on his exposed corps before their arrival. In the distance, sporadic cannonading sounded, but nothing indicated a Confederate attack. What Buell did not know, however, was that Gilbert's corps was deployed along Doctor's Creek and, outnumbering all the Confederates in front, had run into striking resistance during the night from the enemy as a result of Sheridan's attempt to gain the pools of water in his front and the bluff ahead. Reacting to Buell's orders not to bring on a general engagement, Gilbert cantered to the front during the morning and, seeing the advanced positions of Sheridan's division, emphatically ordered the soldiers back to avoid bringing on a battle. Before Bragg's arrival, meanwhile, Hardee, poorly informed as to the exact location and strength of the Federals, had positioned Anderson's division in the center facing Gilbert and Buckner's division on his right near the confluence of Doctor's Creek and the

Chaplin River. Col. John H. Wharton's cavalry brigade protected Buckner's flank from across the Chaplin River. Cheatham's division and Col. Joseph Wheeler's cavalry made up the left and extreme flank.[72]

From sunrise until around 10:00 A.M. the Confederates and the Federals skirmished for the high ground and the water meandering through the small valleys. Sheridan succeeded in driving the Confederates across Bull Run and over the hill nearest the Chaplin River. About 10:30 a general lull in the fighting occurred. McCook's First Corps then appeared on the Mackville Pike. McCook had not yet reported to Buell and approached the battlefield with no sense of urgency. He failed to notice Sheridan's signal flags attempting to warn him of the presence of a Confederate army. When his cavalry scouts ran into skirmishers, McCook halted his column in the road. He ordered Rousseau to deploy his division in a defensive position adjacent to Gilbert's corps and then rode back to Buell's headquarters. Despite clear instructions, however, Rousseau delayed in the road and the heat before realizing not only that his position was vulnerable but also that the men were suffering from the heat. He allowed them to wander down to Doctor's Creek, blissfully ignorant of what was there.[73]

Buell's headquarters were over two miles from the front, and having heard nothing to indicate Bragg was preparing to attack an unsupported corps, he concluded that Bragg would not move until the following day. Just before noon Buell decided to postpone his own attack. At 12:30, just as Buell and Gilbert were sitting down to lunch, McCook sauntered into camp an hour after being spotted on the road. He reported that his two divisions were in the process of deploying and that there was no sign of the enemy except some cavalry moving toward his left.

Buell was relieved to see him and hear the good news. He was completely unaware that anything was going on in his front. He instructed McCook to join Gilbert's corps on the left as planned and to make a reconnaissance ahead to the Chaplin River to get water for his men. The battle would be fought the next day. At 1:00 P.M. Buell received the even better news that Crittenden was on the Lebanon Road and was preparing to move northward beyond the creek to take his position alongside Gilbert's right flank. Thomas had not arrived in person yet, but Buell expected him soon.

Though Sill and Dumont had not yet arrived, Buell's combined strength of 55,000 men, stretched along a six-mile front, seemed prepared for the next day's battle against Hardee's two divisions. Relaxing in his tent, Buell could not think of a better situation for battle. Though his leg bothered him, he would seize the moment tomorrow. In the meantime, he lay on his back reading, his staff overseeing soldiers carrying fence rails to his headquarters as punishment for picking apples without orders.[74]

While McCook was conferring with Buell, the moment had seized the Army of the Ohio, and the battle of Perryville had exploded, unbeknownst to Buell. Around 2:00 P.M. McCook's Federals were making their way down to the water when out of the listless woods came the screaming soldiers of Cheatham's and Buckner's divisions in a roaring charge intended to surround the Federal flank. For over a mile the Confederates pushed the Federals back, capturing fifteen guns in the process. From a distance Bragg peered out over the field anticipating that the entire Federal left flank was about to be routed.[75]

When McCook arrived back at the field and realized what was happening, he immediately called for help from Gilbert and reconfigured his line. After two hours the Confederate attack on the right flank of the First Corps had succeeded in killing or wounding hundreds of Rousseau's men. The Confederates had driven them back, but they were not scattered or defeated. Still, Rousseau and McCook bypassed brigade leaders and gave orders directly to the chaotically intermixed regiments.[76]

After William Terrill's brigade had been driven back, Col. John C. Starkweather's Twenty-eighth Brigade and the batteries of Capts. Asahel K. Bush and David Stone stalled the rout of the First Corps' left wing. With the Confederates in full pursuit of Terrill's men, the Wisconsin soldiers stood up and delivered a staggering blow, driving the Confederates until the troops and the batteries fell back to the original line, found supplies, and renewed the fight.[77]

Though Buell had listened to the sounds of distant artillery throughout the day, not until 2:00 P.M. did he reportedly listened for a moment in front of his tent to the dull rattle of musketry and remark impatiently that "the skirmishers were wasting entirely too much ammunition." Two hours later the intensity of the shelling drew Buell out of his tent again, causing him to remark to Gilbert, "That is something more than shelling the woods; it sounds like a fight."[78] This time Buell sent Gilbert to the front to see what was going on. Just as Gilbert galloped off, Horace Fisher of McCook's staff dashed into Buell's camp and informed him that not only was a battle raging against McCook's corps but heavy skirmishing and artillery duels had been under way since midmorning. Buell gasped in astonishment. Incapacitated by his injury, he could not gallop over to examine matters for himself.[79]

Peculiar atmospheric conditions and the rugged terrain had virtually deadened the sounds of battle raging on the left. This combination of factors was later referred to as the "acoustic shadow." Only slowly did Gilbert's corps to the right of the fighting realize what was happening and move to assist McCook. Gilbert's corps had repulsed Anderson's earlier attack but did not know when or if another assault would follow or at what strength. From his advanced position on the left, Sheridan looked across the valley and saw the Confederates sweeping westward, driving McCook's men back. He turned his batteries in that direction, heaving shells into the flank of the gray columns as they crossed his line of fire. This barrage threw them into considerable confusion and encouraged Gilbert to detach troops to go to McCook's assistance. When they had left, the Federals counterattacked with a brigade on his right flank and, fighting almost hand to hand, drove Anderson back to Perryville late in the day. Having advanced so far, the brigade commander put his batteries in position west of the town and, firing shells across the rooftops, engaged some rebel guns on the opposite side until darkness.[80]

Once informed of the fighting on his left, Buell tried desperately to bring his whole army into action and to exercise tighter control of the six-mile front. He ordered the reserve division of the center corps to McCook's aid and sent a staff officer galloping off with instructions for Thomas to move the right corps around quickly and attack the enemy's left. Though Thomas had not personally reported his position to headquarters, he heard an occasional rumbling of artillery but suspected it might be some Federals shelling the woods. When the fire had become prolonged, he had sent his chief of artillery to Buell to request further orders. Buell, however, believed it was only wasteful artillery fire. He merely sent the officer back to Thomas with instructions to make a reconnaissance to prepare for the next day's fight. About 3:00 P.M., heavy cannonading had prompted Thomas to communicate with Gilbert, who replied that he had encountered only slight resistance and was now encamping for the night. He had thought that Rousseau's division on his left had driven the enemy back across the lost ground. By then it was growing dark and too late for him to trap the reckless Confederates several miles to the left. As night fell, the Army of the Ohio had recovered its balance. Reinforcements from Gilbert had saved McCook, and one brigade had even turned the enemy's left and driven the Confederates out of Perryville. While the Confederates mauled McCook with equal numbers within a musket's range, Gilbert's 20,000 soldiers faced 2,500 rebels.[81]

When Buell conferred with Gilbert and Sheridan under a full moon that night over dinner, he revealed that only after 4:00 P.M. did he even known that a fight was going on. Sheridan was stunned and dismayed and concluded that Buell was "unconscious of the magnitude of the battle that had just been fought."[82] When Rousseau arrived later in the evening and informed Buell what had happened to McCook's corps, he, too, was dismayed at Buell's cool attitude. According to Rousseau, who called it the hardest battle he had ever seen, Buell "did not appreciate the fight we had." From a survivor of Shiloh's second day, Rousseau's words should have impressed Buell.[83] But Buell had simply not heard the battle; the acoustic shadow had kept the noise from him. Major Wright, of Buell's staff, "had heard no sound of battle" as he galloped off for the front shortly after four o'clock. As he came "within a few hundred yards, the battle of Perryville burst into view . . . wholly unexpected, and it fixed me with astonishment."[84] So Buell was correct in saying he had not known about the battle. Once he had known about it, however, he was not prepared to fight and thus missed the opportunity to prevent McCook from absorbing a frightful beating by sending reinforcements.[85]

Whatever Buell knew or did not know about the battle of Perryville, he could gather from surveying the battlefield the following day that the fighting had certainly rivaled the worst at Shiloh.[86] "The Rebel gray and Federal blue, lay commingled, often side by side," wrote James Shaw of the Tenth Indiana.[87] One Illinois soldier was so overcome with grief he could not bring himself to write his parents of the details except to say, "I saw some sights there I shall never forget."[88]

Some northern newspapers desperate to credit Buell for at least not losing the battle interpreted Bragg's departure from the field later that night as a Union victory. Though neither side acknowledged defeat, neither knew who had won, either. The editor for *Harper's Weekly* commented that it was remarkable that while the North criticized Buell, southern papers were equally critical of Bragg. Bloody and savage though the partial engagement was, the two commanders, who were thoroughly misinformed about the other's movements and strength, had brought it on. Although Buell had 57,000 men in the area, only a third of those troops fought. This fact alone caused soldiers openly to accuse Buell of disloyalty. Indiana artillerist Henry M. Kendall wrote, "I left Perryville with the idea that the sooner Buell was relieved of command of the Army of the Ohio, the better for all concerned."[89] "If any one had been fond of profanity," wrote an Illinois soldier, "and wished to hear vigorous denunciations . . . they should have heard the army of the Ohio, on the merits of the arch traitor Don Carlos Buell."[90] Some soldiers were so inflamed by Buell's mishandling of the army that they considered retaliating against him. David Smith of the Sixteenth U.S. Infantry wrote to his father that the "Army all think that old Buell is a Rebble and they say they will shoot him the first chance they get."[91] Officially the total Federal loss was placed at 3,696, while the Confederates sustained 3,396 casualties out of an effective fighting force of roughly 27,000 men.

Controversy immediately broke out in Buell's army. Thomas had not reported in person, and this neglect probably stemmed as much from his increased disassociation from Buell as from the need to look out for his soldiers. Even though he had refused command of the army, Thomas's flagrant independence in not reporting to Buell demonstrated his true feelings that he, too, had lost respect for the commander. Thomas knew a meticulous Buell liked to accommodate every contingency in war, and his incapacitating injury made him especially dependent on his subordinate commanders. Thomas may have also felt the army was too demoralized to fight, particularly since Buell's reinstatement had increased hostility toward him. McCook's misuse of his signal corps, which resulted in his failure to communicate with Buell upon becoming engaged, was particularly inexcusable. "What further precautions could be required," Buell argued several months after the battle, "except the presence of commanders whose duty to communicate with me was as well understood as though it had been prescribed in their commissions?"[92] Nelson's aggressive style, in light of Gilbert's lethargic leadership, might have inspired the raw recruits to fight.[93]

Despite being beaten back during the day, McCook's corps rebounded and had regained lost ground. Crittenden's corps was circling northeast around Perryville, rolling up the Confederate line to the north. Finally convinced that he had most of Buell's army to his front, Bragg, leaving dead and wounded behind, wisely abandoned Perryville after midnight to join Kirby Smith at Harrodsburg, a small town about ten miles northeast. Smith arrived the morning of October 10, and the combined army awaited Buell's movements. Buell concluded that the Confederates had consolidated their forces in Kentucky for a decisive battle, and he proceeded cautiously and refused to pursue Bragg. Buell's estimate of the enemy was 50,000, and though he himself had 60,000 and more when Sill and Dumont arrived, the fact that Bragg, with less than a third of his men, had wrecked an entire wing of the Federal army when it had been nearly as large as it was now persuaded him not to press the Confederates. So Buell did nothing except wonder, perhaps with amazement that Bragg's men could achieve so much, perhaps that his own men could not.[94]

Two days later Buell's Army of the Ohio was at full strength, and Bragg thought that lingering too long too close would jeopardize his army as well as the bountiful supply of goods and foodstuffs he had collected. He retreated across the Dick's (or Dix) River to Bryantsville on the tenth. Buell followed the same path, waiting for Bragg to act. The next day Bragg formed a line of battle near Camp Dick Robinson in case Buell attempted to cross the river, but Buell once more found the position too strong to risk attacking. For a full day Bragg stayed there, then on the following day, October 13, Buell circled around toward the south, threatening Bragg's Cumberland Gap supply line and retreat, so Bragg headed for the Cumberland Gap. On the evening of October 13 Buell learned that Bragg was probably falling back to Somerset and moved through Danville toward Crab Orchard to prevent a sudden rush on Nashville. Crittenden's corps was given the mission of keeping steady pressure on the Confederates all the way to London, forcing them to abandon hundreds of sick and wounded men. Once Bragg left the Bluegrass region near Crab Orchard and entered the rugged mountains of eastern Kentucky, it was too late for Buell to intercept him. For two weeks Buell chased the enemy another sixty-five miles without bringing him to bay, making it a total of some 320 miles of pursuit. Buell had allowed Bragg to escape without destroying his army. His failure to catch Bragg lost him the opportunity of his career. Soldiers of the Army of the Ohio had had enough of the "great big lump fish." "If Gen. Buell is not removed by the President—immediately," wrote R. Delavan Mussey, "the army will go to the Devil."[95]

Buell penned a brief report of the battle to the War Department that revealed his astonishment that he had been severely engaged. Stanton, Halleck, and Lincoln were equally amazed, not so much about the particulars of the battle, but at how he was unable to catch Bragg. Lincoln personally wrote Boyle to find out what Buell was doing. Boyle responded that Buell was pressing Bragg, but that was all he knew. Buell did not write Lincoln himself until a week after the battle. For someone as conscientious as Buell the tardiness spoke volumes. Lincoln would not like the news, so Buell included his excuse. "It is but proper that I should say that the present time is perhaps as convenient as any for making any changes that may be thought proper in the command of this army," he concluded. "It has not accomplished all that I had hoped or all that faction might demand; yet composed as it is, one half of perfectly new troops, it has defeated a powerful and thoroughly disciplined army in one battle and has driven it away baffled and disrupted."[96]

Buell was clearly expecting to be removed, but in case Halleck granted him another reprieve, he indicated the only strategy he was willing to pursue. He insisted that a movement into East Tennessee must be made by way of Nashville, and on military grounds he was right. His obsession with Nashville as the only means of getting to East Tennessee, however, was old and irritating to the administration. He again reminded Washington of the impossible supply problems to be faced in the mountains. "You are aware," he began as if Washington could forget, "that between Crab Orchard and Cumberland Gap the country is almost a desert." Bragg had retreated into the heart of the desert, depleting the resources as he had marched. "The limited supply of forage," he argued, "is consumed by the enemy as he passes. In the day and a half we have been in this sterile region our animals have suffered exceedingly." The already difficult roads would get progressively worse as winter approached, and the "route abounds in defiles in which a small force can retard the progress of a large one for a considerable time, and in that time the enemy could gain material advantages" by moving into Middle Tennessee. Besides, the governor of Kentucky demanded he take care of the depredations committed by his men in the Bluegrass State, to which Buell replied, "I shall spare no pains to correct these abuses."[97] As usual, Buell remained an adjutant general who enforced the rules of war when he should have been a commanding general wanting to fight.

Lincoln's administration would have been ecstatic had Buell utilized as much effort in getting to East Tennessee as he did maintaining discipline in his army. Even in Buell's own words the enemy regarded an invasion of East Tennessee as "the most dangerous blow at the rebellion."[98] Treasury Secretary Chase sarcastically wrote to Brig. Gen. Napoleon Bonaparte Buford that the "earth [was] a body of considerable magnitude—but moves faster than Gen. Buell."[99] Perhaps to entice him, Halleck wired Buell on October 18 that his victory at Perryville—a generous characterization on Halleck's part—had given "great satisfaction to the Government." The great object now was to drive the enemy from East Tennessee. "If we cannot do it now," he pleaded, "we need never hope for it." To fall back on Nashville had negative strategic and political ramifications.[100]

In a follow-up letter the next day, Halleck simply reiterated that the capture of East Tennessee "should be the main object of your campaign." If, as Buell reasoned, it was the heart of the enemy's resources, then Halleck challenged him to "make it the heart of yours." If Bragg could live in that region, so could Buell. Lincoln wanted Buell to "march as the enemy marches, live as he lives, and fight as he fights."[101]

Buell refused to budge, as he had for the last year. "We can give good reasons why we cannot do all that the enemy has attempted to do, such as operating without a base, &c., without ascribing the difference to the inferiority of our generals, though that may be true." He tried to dispel Washington's illusions that major supply problems could be solved merely by traveling light and living off the land. Frankly, there was considerably more to it. "The spirit of the rebellion enforces a subordination and patient submission to privation and want which public sentiment renders absolutely impossible among our troops," he argued, and it was because of these causes that the discipline of the rebel army was superior to his own.[102]

After almost a year Buell had not convinced himself that his soldiers, despite all his energies in shaping them into soldiers, were equal to the Confederates. Some men thought he lacked confidence in himself, since the attack mentality never fit Buell. He always had more excuses not to fight than designs to fight.[103]

On October 23 Halleck unequivocally rejected Buell's plan and finally laid out the real reason for demanding a drive into East Tennessee, which had nothing to do with Buell's strategy or his slowness: "To now withdraw your army to Nashville would have a most disastrous effect upon the country, already wearied with so many delays."[104] Congressional elections were near, and midwestern Republicans demanded defeat of the enemy lest the party lose prestige. Not only was Buell's hesitancy to wage a sensational campaign in East Tennessee embarrassing to the administration, protested several war governors, but the inability to destroy Bragg's army in Kentucky was even worse. "The butchery of our troops at Perryville was terrible," cried Morton. "Nothing but success, speedy and decided, will save our cause from utter destruction. In the Northwest distrust and despair are seizing upon the hearts of the people."[105] "With one voice, so far as it has reached me," Governor Tod of Ohio informed Stanton, "the army from Ohio demands the removal of General Buell." Stanton answered, "I had been urging his removal for two months, had it done once, when it was revoked by the President."[106] Horace White, chairman of the Illinois Republican Party state central committee, fumed to Lincoln, "If we are beaten [politically] in this state two weeks hence, it will be because McClellan and Buell *won't fight*."[107]

Lincoln could not afford to ignore these governors, particularly because militarily there were few reasons to vote Republican. Despite being characterized as victories, neither Antietam nor Perryville produced enduring success and inspired little support for the administration. Louisville merchant E. T. Bainbridge wrote Judge Advocate General Joseph Holt that "if some change does not soon take place, a storm

Edwin M. Stanton, who succeeded Simon Cameron as secretary of war in January
1862. When McClellan and Buell failed to perform adequately, Stanton was one of
the leading forces advocating their removal. After Buell was relieved of command
in November 1862, Stanton allowed him a court of inquiry to clear his name from
charges that he conciliated southern civilians to the point of treason. The court
ultimately found Buell guilty of no misconduct or treasonous activities. (Courtesy
of the U.S. Army Military History Institute, Carlisle, Pa.)

Andrew Johnson, Tennessee senator appointed military governor of Tennessee
in March 1862. As a southern Unionist Johnson remained loyal to the Union
and tried desperately to get Buell to move into East Tennessee to liberate the
oppressed Unionists suffering under the Confederate occupation. When Buell
refused, Johnson was so determined to eliminate Buell from command that he
contended Buell was a traitor. (Courtesy of the Tennessee State Archives,
Nashville)

Oliver P. Morton, governor of Indiana and among the most outspoken critics of
Buell's conciliatory policies and his ability to command (Courtesy of the Indiana
State Library, Indianapolis)

will arrise that will [consume] the whole state and produce a shock that
would be felt all over the Union."[108] The president's recently issued Emancipation Proclamation had alienated conservatives, including some soldiers in Buell's army. To retain a significant portion of the conservative
vote, Lincoln was willing to leave McClellan in command at least until
after the election. If western politicians were going to turn against him
because he maintained Buell, however, he would have to give in. Be-

sides, the North wanted victory whether or not its generals agreed with emancipation. And Buell was profoundly opposed to freeing slaves, since he viewed it a military inconvenience.[109]

Having already been removed once for failing to capture Bragg, Buell did little for his own cause with his excuses in late October. He expected, perhaps with too much confidence, that the merits of his strategy would soon become obvious to Lincoln. Armed with the support of Morton and other governors, Halleck ordered Buell on October 22 to occupy East Tennessee with all possible dispatch. "Neither the Government nor the country," he warned, "can endure these repeated delays."[110]

Buell knew that following his own strategic convictions would goad Halleck and Lincoln into removing him, but he could not convince himself that any other way was possible. Buell's latest conclusion that he felt the enemy's army was superior to his own was the last straw in the decision to remove him. After reading Buell's latest dispatch, the president convened briefly with Stanton and Halleck and decided to dismiss him. On October 30 Buell received orders removing him from command again. He read about his removal in the newspaper and wired Halleck that if his termination were true, he would like to know it, since "the troops were already in motion."[111] As lethargic as he had been about the previous month's sacking, so was Buell again unmoved. Before turning over his command to William S. Rosecrans, fresh from the battle of Iuka, his final act as a military commander was his farewell to the army. He laced his words with as much emotion as he could muster, saying that it was difficult to leave the army he had shaped and that he alone was responsible for not meeting the desires of the administration.[112] Buell's words, however, touched few soldiers. As one careful observer wrote, "He came to and left his soldiers a stranger to the feelings of all as well as the eyes of most."[113]

Before proceeding to Indianapolis to await further orders, Buell wrote to Thomas, a commander wondering why he had been passed over for leadership of the Army of Ohio, asking, "Can I do anything for you privately? . . . I can hardly flatter myself that I can do anything officially, though I would be glad to try."[114] Thomas had no use for Buell's patronage.

Even with all the condemnation, Buell still had supporters outside the army. James Guthrie, president of the Louisville and Nashville Railroad, read of Buell's dismissal in the newspaper and came to his defense: "The clamors of the press and of unfeeling men for more bloody fields, without regard to results obtained and reasonable future one, in my judgement should not prevail."[115] Unionist Theodore S. Bell, Louisville physician, wrote to Holt: "I doubt whether Gen'l Buell has his superior as a military administrator in this country. With Buell at the head of affairs here . . . we should have had nothing to fear."[116] The *New Albany Daily Ledger* was perhaps the newspaper most supportive of Buell and equally critical of the administration in removing him. The editor was outraged:

> The President, listening to a few political demagogues has removed Gen. Buell. . . . There can be no question, however, but that Gen. Buell has been greatly wronged by this act of the Administration. An able officer has been sacrificed to the clamors of a clique of intermeddling Governors and strategic editors, because he would not yield his own judgement to the demands of a pack of ignoramuses, who, because they happen to be "clothed in a little brief authority," take it upon themselves to dictate not only for what purposes the war shall be conducted, but the precise manner in which the Generals shall move their armies.[117]

What had prevailed was not so much the press or the desire for more bloody battles, but the government's desire to run its armies when its commanders had not. Even Rosecrans held Buell in high regard, despite disagreeing with his strategy. Upon accepting command of what became the Army of the Cumberland, Rosecrans wrote to Buell expressing his personal feelings about the whole affair:

> I know the bearer of unwelcome news has a "losing office," but feel assured you are too high a gentleman and too true a soldier to permit this to produce any feelings of personal unkindness between us. I, like yourself, am neither an intriguer nor newspaper soldier. I go where I am ordered; but propriety will permit me to say that I have often felt indignant at the petty attacks on you by a portion of the press during the past summer, and that you had my high respect for ability as a soldier, for your firm adherence to truth and justice in the government and discipline of your command.[118]

In anticipation of Buell's sacking, Morton was in Indianapolis preparing to depart for Washington again, this time accompanied by Illinois governor Yates. Northern governors were planning a convention in Washington in late October for the purpose of getting rid of McClellan and Buell and urging a more vigorous prosecution of the war. Until these demands were met, these governors would not furnish any more troops to the Union cause. Naturally, Buell's removal and the expected removal of McClellan excited them. "The removal of General Buell could not have been delayed an hour with safety to the army or the cause. . . . The action you have taken renders our visit unnecessary," Yates and Morton wrote to Lincoln.[119] Gen. John M. Palmer, influential among the Illinois Republicans, had counseled Lyman Trumbull for weeks that Lincoln's retention of Buell had proven disastrous and that any general was "a great relief after that *nightmare . . .* Genl. Buell."[120] Chase was more emphatic in his condemnation of Buell. "For months and months," he howled, "the Country has witnessed with pain & indignation the waste of opportunities and the sluggishness of movement which has characterized the action of Buell," caused, he "verily believed," by "Buell's proslaveryism."[121]

In what turned out to be a season of cleansing for the Union high command, Buell was simply another leader eliminated as Union authorities continued to reconcile the civil-military conflicts inherent in conducting a political war. He refused to accept the effective war the Union needed to wage. In his instructions to the new army commander, Halleck commented, "The time has now come when we must apply the sterner rules of war, whenever such application becomes necessary, to enable us to support our armies and to move them rapidly upon the enemy. . . . Neither the country nor the Government will much longer put up with the inactivity of some of our armies and generals."[122] Lincoln had guillotined Buell.

CHAPTER SEVENTEEN

Too Thorough a Soldier to Command One of Our Armies

Buell's immediate dismissal was met with mixed emotions, causing some of his supporters to characterize absurdly his military worth for the Union. Next to McClellan, Buell "justly ranks as the great military genius of the country," wrote an Indiana journalist in October 1862. According to Gen. Lovell Rousseau, Buell was "the greatest general on the American continent."[1] Apparently they had not read the *Indianapolis Daily Journal* or any number of other northern newspapers scathingly critical of Buell and McClellan, who was dismissed just eight days after Buell. The editor of the New York *Independent* devoted considerable space to condemning the two generals:

It is difficult to say which excelled in practical torpidity, Buell or McClellan. Whichever figure one contemplates it seems impossible that another should excel him in laborious uselessness. Both were insatiable in their demands, and both wasted immense resources without any important advantage. If there is anything yet to be exhibited of military insufficiency, some new man must be imagined, created expressly for it; for every conceivable part of insatiable demand and miserly retention of forces and means has been exhausted by the great Oriental *Vis Inertiae* and the Occidental *Vis Inertiae*.[2]

The comparison of Buell and McClellan was certainly not new. Throughout Buell's tenure, newspaper reporters and Radical Republicans had made frequent comparisons of these professionally trained, conservative Democrats who fought a limited war for limited objectives and who repeatedly thwarted Lincoln's attempts to make the war more aggressive and expansive. "I am well satisfied with the removal of Genl. McClellan," Major Keifer wrote to his wife. "I have for a great while placed McClellan and Buell in the same category."[3] Brig. Gen. Carl Schurz, prominent leader among German Americans, wrote to Lincoln in late November that it was unfortunate that the administration had sustained McClellan and Buell so long, particularly after "they had been failing;—failing not only in a political but also in a military sense."

> Will perhaps anybody assert, that such men as Mcclellan and Buell and Halleck have the least sympathy with you or your views and principles?—or that their efficiency as military leaders has offered a compensation for their deficiency of sympathy, since the first has in 18 months succeeded in effecting literally nothing except the consumption of resources with the largest and best appointed army this country ever saw;—since the second by his criminal tardiness and laxity endangered even the safety of Cincinnati.[4]

McClellan and Buell had shared comparable ideas on strategy even though they had disagreed about East Tennessee. Both were insensitive to the need to interpret military realities to politicians. Their arrogant secretiveness and opposition to threatening slavery, combined with their endless interest in preparing, fueled congressional hostility. Both were careful and methodical in developing military strategy, and both considered maneuvering more important than fighting. Like McClellan, Buell had become convinced that the Confederates were far superior in discipline to the Union army, and this fed the natural cautiousness of both men, resulting in avoidance of battles. Both had exhausted the patience of the administration in the winter of 1861–62 with their inactivity. The president had failed to make them understand the importance of aggressive warfare and victory. Neither commander was a practitioner of warfare on the enemy's resources but clung to limited war waged against only those clearly aligned with the rebellion. These commanders were intellectually unsuited to fight the first of the modern wars.[5]

Although the administration relieved Buell for not achieving battlefield success, the relentless criticism of him after the battle of Perryville led him to conclude that his removal was the result of vengeful politicians. Finally, Buell figured out the power of politics, but this revelation came only because he was on the losing end. For weeks newspapers had published articles impugning his character and his loyalty and undermining his reputation as a professional soldier. For Buell, however, being relieved for not winning was criticism he could accept, but being accused of sluggishness, ultraconservatism, defending slavery, and disloyalty was wholly ridiculous. If that had been the case, he thought, the Lincoln administration would have relieved him much earlier. Consequently, he requested a court of inquiry to exonerate himself from the public execution that he suffered in the press and to reclaim a favorable reputation. In the courtroom he believed he could educate and enlighten politicians on "war proper." In doing so, he made perhaps the last case for a brand of warfare that best suited his intellectual makeup but was already out of date. He asked Stanton if the proceedings could be made public, but Stanton denied his request. On December 1, less than three weeks later, Buell walked into the courtroom. In the meantime he returned to Indianapolis and Lawrenceburg, where he received an exuberant reception.[6]

In late November Buell traveled to Cincinnati, a city whose reporters had been among the harshest on him during his tour of command. Sensing that the residents might be unreceptive to him, Buell kept a low profile while preparing for the trial. After a few days, word spread through the city that Buell had arrived, and each evening crowds gathered before his terrace at the Burnett House to serenade him. On one occasion the Menter's Cornet Band performed several popular songs, including "Hail to the Chief." Loud and continuous calls for the general demanding "Speech! Speech!" finally drew him onto the terrace, accompanied by the city's mayor. Never one for words and taken completely by surprise, he simply thanked the group and afterward shook hands with the guests. The outpouring of support for Buell so impressed one local journalist that he concluded, "The future will do him justice."[7]

Were Buell to have justice, he would have to achieve it in the courtroom. Since Stanton and Halleck had granted Buell the investigation, they chose the officers who would conduct the proceedings. Stanton made it clear that these members were not only to justify Buell's elimination from command for his failure to pursue Bragg after Perryville, but they were also to condemn him for waging an unacceptable brand of war. Stanton intended to focus the inquiry on controversial issues throughout Buell's tenure, including his conciliation policy and his loyalty. Stanton ordered,

> You will please organize a Military Commission to inquire into and report upon the operations of the forces under command of Major-General Buell in the States of Tennessee and Kentucky, and particularly in reference to General Buell suffering the State of Kentucky to be invaded by the rebel forces under General Bragg, and in his failure to relieve Munfordville and suffering it to be captured; also in reference to the battle of Perryville and General Buell's conduct during that battle, and afterward suffering the rebel forces to escape from Kentucky without loss or capture; and also to inquire and report upon such other matters touching the military operations aforesaid as in the judgment of the Commission shall be beneficial to the service.[8]

Interestingly enough, the sole purpose of the investigation was to determine whether or not the actions of the Army of the Ohio produced enough evidence to indicate that charges be brought against Buell himself. Still, the commission, as broadly defined as it was, would find it difficult to obtain the conviction of Buell.[9]

To add a hint of treason to the investigation, Stanton directed Maj. Donn Piatt, judge advocate of the so-called Military Commission, to contact Governors Morton and Johnson. These governors had informed the administration that they possessed enough evidence to prove that Buell was downright treasonous in his conciliation of southerners. Johnson and Morton, as well as other politicians, had been relentless in their attempts to get Buell removed, and they also held considerable sway in the formation of the commission. "Those fierce War Governors, O. P. Morton and Andrew Johnson," Piatt later wrote, "had stuffed the ears of Secretary Stanton with stories of Buell's incompetence and disloyalty. He was a traitor they charged, and claimed to have conclusive proof of his treachery."[10]

Slandering Buell was one thing, but proving it was quite another. For all their bellicosity during Buell's tenure in command, neither Morton nor Johnson produced anything to help Piatt devise charges against Buell's loyalty. Thus, by default, Stanton endeavored to satisfy these politicians, hoping to convict Buell for his apparent wrongful operation of the Army of the Ohio. As Piatt informed his fellow board members on the first day of the proceedings, no matter how absurd some of the charges were or how the investigation proceeded, the outcome must be the same—they had been "organized to convict."[11]

Buell expected that those who sat on the commission would be prejudiced against him, Piatt's choice as judge advocate confirming his fears. As a former attorney and county judge of Hamilton County, Ohio, Piatt was articulate and clever, with a keen legal mind. Lew Wallace characterized him as a "sharp, quizzical man of the world—knows everybody and everything—is witty and Frenchy and not without talent. He is especially calculated to shine in society with his ready word and quick repartee."[12] The fact that he was friends with both Stanton and Secretary Chase made it clear that his selection was no accident. Friends warned Buell anonymously that Piatt, a journalist and intimate of Stanton, was "part of a commission packed for the purpose of slandering a great general." "You are deeply sympathized with," read one anonymous letter, "like the noble . . . Maclellan you too must suffer a crown of thorns."[13]

Compared to some of the other members on the commission, including Albin Schoepf, Lew Wallace, and Daniel Tyler, Piatt was tolerable to Buell. Schoepf and Tyler made no secret about their animosity toward Buell. Schoepf had once physically threatened Buell and had organized the petition to eliminate him from command before the battle of Perryville. When it became known that Schoepf was to serve on the commission, James Fry warned Buell that the Hungarian was a "deceitful person . . . so much so that he hardly seems a fit member of the commission."[14] Another of Buell's friends, Thomas S. Everett, sent Buell a newspaper that quoted Schoepf as charging Buell with disloyalty. Everett offered to be a witness, so he "*might* disclose facts which [would] open the eyes of the Department a little, and place the sin of disloyalty on another pair of shoulders."[15] He was never called to testify.

At sixty-five years of age, Daniel Tyler was an even more curious appointee. Although he was an 1819 graduate of West Point, he had been in civilian life for many years as a railroad man. Wallace was unimpressed with his pompous, sour demeanor and considered him, like Schoepf, an advocate of an "energized" war "quickly concluded" and "having no mercy for slow men or blunderers." The remaining two members of the commission, Edward Otho Cresap Ord and Napoleon Jackson Tecumseh Dana, whose military careers most closely followed Buell's own experience, proved more impartial toward the whole affair, which benefited Buell. Both had fought in the Mexican War, and both were quite conservative. Dana had known Buell at West Point and in many respects closely resembled him in temperament. Wallace described him as "refined and quiet—has a cool head, silent tongue, good judgement . . . just and honorable."[16]

The president of the commission was Indiana Hoosier Lew Wallace, whose close relationship to Morton made him incapable of being objective. As a professional officer and a student of war, Wallace was pleased to be a commission member, considering it a privilege that was "only a little less acceptable than field duty." He viewed the court proceedings as an education in the conduct of war.[17] Though at first unimpressed by Buell, he quickly came to appreciate his role in upholding not just his actions but the ideas of the "Old Army." Buell appeared like "a professor" who would lecture the court daily on his army's operations, justifying every order and policy. As president, Wallace was perfectly situated to "have things rendered explicitly" to his satisfaction.[18]

The Buell Commission, as it became known, proved to be the military school Wallace had envisioned. By referring to Buell as a representative of the old army, Wallace cast him in an unpopular role, his defense reflecting the ultraconservative philosophy of limited war for limited goals. In its questioning of witnesses, the six-member prosecution team made it clear that limited war was no longer in harmony with the government's political aims. They advocated a philosophy of aggressive warfare that promised results and victories by focusing not on the means of waging war but on the objectives in winning it.[19]

Though Stanton designated the investigation a military commission, it was clear he wanted to allow the prosecution as much latitude as possible to convict Buell and condemn his brand of warfare and, in doing so, to discredit McClellan also. Winfield Scott had introduced the military commission in the Mexican War as an unofficially recognized court to investigate offenses committed by American troops beyond the limits of law against the Mexican population. Though Scott intended it as a supplementary arm of military law, Stanton resurrected the concept but forgot the original intent. Unlike a court-martial or a court of inquiry, which had well-defined roles under the *Military Laws of the United States* and the *Revised Regulations for the Army of the United States*, the Buell Commission had no defined role, and its specific purpose was nebulous.[20]

This lack of definition became apparent on the first day of the trial, and it set the tone for a five-month clash of wills. Just as the lead witness began testifying, Buell entered the courtroom. Piatt immediately stopped the questioning and asked Buell to leave the courtroom while the commission went into secret session. Buell refused. Wallace, however, maintained that Buell himself was not on trial but, rather, "a series of operations conducted by him." Consequently, Wallace allowed Buell to enter but refused him the rights and privileges normally allowed a defendant. When Piatt attempted to swear him to secrecy concerning the proceedings, Buell objected to the absurd demand. Piatt again demanded he leave, but Buell objected. After a lengthy discussion the court finally granted him the privilege of attending the session and introducing witnesses, although he could not cross-examine them. Having more experience in these kinds of proceedings than any other court member, Buell heatedly lectured the six officers on his rights before a tribunal. The court debated the entire day and adjourned without reaching a conclusion, except to ask Stanton whether or not Buell could remain in court.[21]

Stanton decided to allow Buell to present his own defense, probably because he felt that Piatt would make short work of him. Though Stanton had hoped to keep the affair simple, Buell's addition as a defendant who was not charged with or accused of anything made for a lengthy and troublesome process. In characterizing the commission's purpose, Wallace remarked that it was "simply an investigation of general operations which certain officers of the Army are charged to make." Still, it would prove difficult to get the conviction Stanton desired.[22]

Stanton's startling decision to allow Buell to present a defense allowed the commission to analyze Union command in the West. Buell represented the limited war philosophy, which emphasized preparation, maneuvering, logistics, territorial occupation, safety of his army, and securing the means instead of the ends of his objectives. In condemning Buell the prosecution was concerned less with preparation and logistics and more with an aggressive, expansive brand of warfare that emphasized strategic objectives and the destruction of the enemy's military force as well as civilian morale. Thus, what was really on trial was Buell's ideological position of how war ought to be waged, a position that by now was considered passé.[23]

Buell's Chattanooga campaign was the most absorbing topic of the inquiry. The Army of the Ohio had marched over 250 miles through an inhospitable Confederate countryside that made it nearly impossible to move quickly. Long lines of communication, major rivers to cross, troops pathetically scattered to guard these lines, insufficient cavalry, and Confederate guerrillas and cavalry roaming at will all combined to stall Buell's operation. During the discussion of the campaign, Buell consistently asked questions that provided answers asserting that there was more success for his army in overcoming the logistical impediments than in fighting. The responses emphasized the positive side of Buell's brand of war. Buell produced enough courtroom testimony to prove beyond doubt that he overcame problems slowly but surely, even though Bragg reached Chattanooga first. Judge George W. Lane of Huntsville, Alabama, and Gen. William Sooy Smith, for example, argued that Buell's army successfully survived in an area that was bare of supplies. Lane testified that because planters in northern Alabama looked to cotton as the source of their revenue, grain was rarely grown, and in 1861 what little grain that was grown was scarce. When Albert Sidney Johnston's army retreated from Bowling Green and Fort Donelson in February and March and passed through northern Alabama, it levied contributions upon the country. Additionally, Ormsby Mitchel's army had drawn on whatever forage remained during his march toward Huntsville in the spring and summer. Not only was there a lack of forage, but also, according to Smith, the transportation lines available to Buell had been greatly damaged, and even when a railroad was opened for any distance, finding a locomotive able to haul supplies was difficult.[24]

Transportation and communication troubles combined with scarcity of supplies constituted only part of Buell's claim that his army had been successful in reacting to and surviving under dire circumstances. Gen. Thomas Crittenden, a defense witness, provided further testimony that praised the army's reaction to its problems. When his division arrived at Stevenson in mid-July, the same time Nathan Bedford Forrest had swooped down on Murfreesboro and cut the railroad line from Nashville, his soldiers had lived off half-rations for a month despite making "every possible exertion to obtain forage." Buell himself illustrated perhaps the best example of making accommodations to the conditions. Lt. Col. Francis Darr, a commissary officer, explained Buell's difficulties with river captains and the seemingly impossible problem of supplying troops by way of the Tennessee River in their march to Chattanooga, "because Union pilots then in the employ of the general were unwilling to undertake running boats to Tuscumbia."[25]

As much as Buell tried to emphasize the logistical problems of his campaign, the prosecution remained determined to contest his actions. Stressing an aggressive philosophy of war, the prosecution often trivialized Buell's logistical difficulties. Wallace, for example, could not understand why subsistence and transportation alone prevented Buell from reaching Chattanooga. He supposed that a temporary solution to the subsistence problem would have allowed Buell's army to get to Chattanooga. In other words, getting to Chattanooga might, in fact, have solved at least a part of his problem and could have allowed the army enough food to continue expeditions to destroy the Virginia and Tennessee Railroad.[26]

Piatt expanded this argument by targeting Chattanooga's vulnerability as reason enough to prompt Buell into forging ahead despite logistical problems. "It has been proved on the part of the Government and not denied by the defense," contended Piatt in his summation, "that the rebels were not in force at that time in either place, and had General Buell pushed on he would have taken the more important strategic points almost without resistance." "The lack of supplies," he concluded, "cannot justify a delay of a month or six weeks for repairs when that time would have enabled the army to seize and occupy a country rich as was East Tennessee, and inhabited by a friendly, loyal population."[27] Piatt used J. B. McElwee, a resident of Thea County in East Tennessee, to support his contention. McElwee recalled that at the time the Confederates considered abandoning the city, "My understanding from rebel soldiers and others was that they were going to surrender Chattanooga."[28]

Bragg's invasion of Tennessee and Kentucky also reflected contrasting and uncompromising views. In attempting to position his army effectively to counter Bragg, Buell thought that the best offense was a good defense. Thus, the invasion forced Buell to better position his army for an encounter, which essentially took the form of a retreat. He emphasized the necessity of the Army of the Ohio's steady retrograde movement west away from the enemy and toward Nashville in order to protect its lines of communication and supply. The fact that he had just spent two months strung out in the Confederate countryside no doubt played a part in his desire to fall back toward safety. The Confederate cavalry had wrecked Union supply and communication lines, including numerous railroad bridges, and Buell tried in vain to prevent such destruction. To support his contention that his army had to retreat toward Nashville to save its lines, he put former chief of staff James B. Fry on the stand to testify about the severe problems the Confederate cavalry caused his army during the summer. Fry argued that the communications of the Army of the Ohio had been "molested by the rebel cavalry" as Buell's army advanced. "The cavalry force of the Army of the Ohio," he argued, "was insufficient to guard against the dangers to which the Army was exposed by the operations of the rebel cavalry."[29]

Perhaps the best summation of Buell's intellectual position during the trial was his "sphere of offensive movements" doctrine. After the prosecution had questioned Gen. Jeremiah T. Boyle as to whether Buell was on the offensive or the defensive from the time Bragg crossed the Tennessee until the battle of Perryville, Buell redirected the examination. When questioning Boyle he began,

> Do you understand, general, that in all military operations the sphere of offensive movements is limited by certain circumstances, such as the amount of supplies and the distance to which you can carry supplies with the means available, and perhaps by other considerations also? Does it not follow, then, that an army may be on the defensive for everything beyond the sphere which is limited by these circumstances, and that within that sphere it may assume the offensive if an enemy should come within its reach?[30]

Piatt, however, was as focused on undermining Buell's philosophy as Buell was on emphasizing it. The opportunity and necessity of fighting Bragg eclipsed the logistical problems. Shortages of cavalry, supplies, and water were minor interferences in comparison with what could be gained if Buell brought Bragg to bay. Tyler used defense witness Gen. James B. Steedman's testimony to suggest that if Bragg could take on the offensive without water, Buell could defend without water.[31]

Having reasoned that Buell had been only inconvenienced in his attempts to get to Chattanooga, and that Bragg had been similarly hampered, the prosecution considered Buell's loyalty an important motivation for his lack of vigor. Buell, they argued, had made it a policy to inflate the strength of the enemy force to claim he was always outnumbered. When asked what the supposed reason was for Buell not fighting Bragg, Steedman attested that various explanations were discussed by the men, ranging from timidity and prudence to disloyalty. Further examination, however, produced a line of questioning about whether or not Buell enjoyed the confidence of his army during the campaign. Steedman argued that Buell enjoyed considerable confidence of the army until he fell back to Nashville, but that support steadily waned from that point on. The lack of confidence, he testified, led several soldiers, mainly officers and including Schoepf, to impugn Buell's loyalty. Upon hearing this for the first time, Buell was shocked but refused to dignify the charge of disloyalty with a response. Instead, his cross-examination simply remained focused on the problems of overcoming the means to carry out his objectives.[32]

Buell's sphere-of-offensive argument opened him to severe criticism from the prosecution. Piatt attempted to undermine Buell's doctrine in his questioning of defense witness Gen. Gordon Granger. Regarding Bragg's Kentucky campaign, Piatt asked whether the circumstances of a campaign were so varied and numerous that supposing what might have been regarding the campaign provided little light on the objective. What Piatt meant was that all commanders faced the same kinds of problems and that good ones overcame them. Almost as if Buell had instructed him, Gordon provided a Jominian answer that "the rules and maxims of war, combined with the experience such as a commander might have, may be fixed and infallible, and that all the great disasters that have happened to armies have originated in nineteen cases out of twenty . . . by deviating from them."[33] In other words, had Buell deviated from his cautious, methodical attitude about conducting his operations in accordance with the science of war, he would surely have failed. The fact was, however, Buell failed anyway. During the discussion of Sparta, Tennessee, as a place for Buell to meet Bragg, the prosecution considered only fighting Bragg and not the vulnerability of the Union army and limited supplies as justification for going to Sparta. Even George H. Thomas testified, when cross-examined by Buell, that although he should have "concentrated the army sufficiently to have fought at Sparta," he "did not know at the time anything about the state of supplies."[34] Thomas's answer proved Buell's point that logistics controlled objectives.

Discussion of Bragg's escape from Kentucky and Buell's pursuit produced the same philosophical distinctions between Buell's defense and the prosecution. Buell introduced witnesses who confirmed that the Army of the Ohio was virtually paralyzed in the pursuit of Bragg due to darkness, the need to reorganize and recuperate from the effects of battle, the junction of Bragg and Smith, and the need to be reinforced by Joshua Sill, as many of the troops in the army were green. Crittenden's testimony implied that the barren countryside and hardscrabble roads impeded progress even under the best circumstances. Prosecution witness Gen. Alexander McCook, however, argued that there was "no reason whatever" why the rebels were not "vigorously pursued."[35] But the vigor articulated by McCook and endorsed by the prosecution failed to consider certain realities. Gen. Lovell H. Rousseau, for the defense, highlighted an important aspect of pursuing incautiously, as "approaching Bragg was like hunting a 'lion in the jungle.'" Like Buell, Rousseau considered Bragg's army defeated but certainly not destroyed. "He had the best army for its numbers," he concluded, "that I ever saw."[36]

Rousseau's favorable characterization of Bragg's army opened another aspect of the campaign: Buell's conciliatory policy toward southerners. It was a topic that perhaps best underscored the difference of opinion that emerged during 1862 regarding the changing nature of war. Buell clearly favored a policy, as laid out in his General Orders 13a, that allowed for the protection of civil guarantees, including slavery, to southern citizens as a way not only to safeguard their rights but also to protect his army marching through the Confederate countryside. He did desire to see a reunified country living under one constitution, but he desired more the safety of his army. In closing arguments before the court he concluded that he had devoted his life to restoring the Union. He knew he was expected to defeat the Confederates and to respect the rights of the people insofar as it was possible. This had been his rule since taking command. Men in arms he treated as enemies; persons not in arms he treated as citizens of the United States.[37]

Buell's argument in support of his conciliatory policy drew upon the constitutional rights of the civilian in "civilized" warfare. Though it was common "among civilized nations to hold the inhabitants of the country responsible" for depredations and violent acts against the invading army, "I think noncombatants [should be] respected in their rights of property among civilized people." Buell took the view that partisan rangers and not the majority of the citizens were responsible for disrupting the army's lines. He made clear distinctions between persons who were enemies and those who were not. Buell incredibly even refused to accept the prosecution's definition of Nathan Bedford Forrest and John Hunt Morgan as guerrillas, since there was a difference in terminology between cavalry and what was properly known as "guerrillas."

Buell also targeted the ruthless Confederate policy toward loyal East Tennesseans to illustrate why his lenient attitude toward southerners was more appropriate in subduing aggressive activity. East Tennesseans had supported the Union largely because Confederates had mistreated them. Several defense witnesses, including Col. Marc Mundy, for instance, described the southerner as one who became not only a loyal Unionist under Buell's liberal policy, but a loyal Christian. When Mundy stopped depredations committed by his soldiers as well as by citizens, he received considerable support for his actions and found that the people "generally behaved as a loyal and Christian people."[38]

The prosecution naturally advocated a less discriminatory and charitable policy by arguing that because southerners sympathized and gave aid and comfort to the Confederate army, the citizens "have no rights which the [Union] Government is bound to respect."[39] Piatt emphasized that southerners were generally hostile and destroyed bridges and railroads and killed Union soldiers. The animosity of the local inhabitants had a direct connection to the subsistence problem. The prosecution generally concluded that Buell's soft policy tended to make the rebel citizen, if anything, more set against the Union than a harsher policy would have, since it betrayed weakness. To support this argument the prosecution called on East Tennessean William G. Brownlow, who testified that the citizens attributed "our forbearance toward them to cowardice and think that we are afraid of them."[40]

Buell's conciliatory conduct labeled him a southern sympathizer, since he continued to carry out this policy even when the government found it no longer useful. Buell's lenience toward southerners reflected a gullibility directly related to his belief that if the rights of southerners were protected, then his army would be protected.

> Wars of invasion, always difficult, become tenfold so when the people of the invaded territory take an active part against the invading army. A system of plunder and outrage in such cases will produce the same effect of hatred and revenge that such treatment does under other circumstances among men, and the embarrassments resulting from them to the invading army become of the most serious nature.
>
> These considerations are of such importance to success that there is no exception to the rule of securing the neutrality if not the friendship of the population as much as possible by just and mild treatment, and then, having given no good cause for hostility, to treat with kindness those who behave well and with severity those whose misbehave.[41]

The prosecution, however, had difficulty accepting Buell's distinctions. They would surely have agreed, however, with the sentiments of Nashville resident Lucy Virginia French, who concluded that "Buell [was] the only Yankee officer who will be even tolerated in Nashville."[42]

The trial ended in early May 1863 after more than five months of courtroom combat, which included daily sessions of grueling testimony of over seventy witnesses in three cities. For all the fatiguing depositions and the arguments over minute points of procedure, the prosecution concluded that despite being slow, unaggressive, inflexible, sympathetic to southerners and slavery, and not in harmony with the government's aims for waging or winning war, Buell could not be charged with any crime or misconduct that warranted court-martial.

On May 5, 1863, before reaching a decision, the Buell Commission allowed Buell to present a 70-page closing argument. It was a carefully and meticulously reasoned summation of his philosophy of war and his attitude regarding conciliation and slavery, and it covered every aspect of his army's operations from the day of his assumption of command of the Army of the Ohio. The complete court record of 721 pages comprises almost one entire volume of the *Official Records*. As soon as the court adjourned, the transcript was sent to Washington, where it sat unopened in a pine box for several years. Interestingly enough, only three weeks into the trial, Wallace complained to his wife that the trial was progressing terribly slowly. "Sometimes," he wrote, "it seems to me like the slow wearing away of [a] mountain, which I am doomed to see disappear grain by grain."[43]

Wallace's metaphor of watching a mountain wear away grain by grain was well conceived. Each day there appeared to be something that stalled the process. During February and March, for example, when the prosecution rested its case, Buell was allowed to introduce witnesses on his own behalf. This shifted the intent of the investigation, since Buell's first request was to call Governors Morton and Johnson. Piatt made little serious effort to have them summoned and instead arranged for depositions to be taken and read into the court transcript. Morton, however, refused to do even that.

On several occasions Buell was precluded from introducing evidence that exposed the prejudices of Morton and Johnson. At one point, in attempting to prove Morton hated him and had used the *Indianapolis Daily Journal* to discredit him, Buell cited an editorial in that paper that suggested Buell ought to be shot. The court took extreme exception to this evidence, striking it from the record and prohibiting Buell from making further accusations against Morton. Buell then attempted to expose the prejudiced attitude of Schoepf by introducing testimony that documented Schoepf's personal threat toward him. Piatt objected to the testimony, arguing that Buell should have voiced his concerns at the start of the investigation. Wallace, Tyler, and Schoepf agreed. Buell, however, knew nothing of the accusations at the time and was never given the chance to challenge members of the court. Piatt countered masterfully that because Buell was not on trial, he could not examine a member's supposed partiality. The heated dispute abruptly ended when Schoepf withdrew from the court. No doubt to maintain leverage in favor of the prosecution, Halleck ordered Ord dropped as well.[44]

Though Buell himself was not on trial, "the most extraordinary [feature] of the whole proceeding," wrote Wallace, "[was] the use he made of his privileges of appearance . . . and the lawyer-like capacity he unexpectedly developed. . . . His examination of witnesses, cross and original were masterful, his arguments brief and admirably worded and he allowed nothing to divert or excite him." Buell essentially became a professor "with daily lecture[s] giving the movements of his army and the reasons of them."[45] Afterward Piatt, impressed by Buell's strength of character, had a change of heart and admitted publicly that the Buell

Commission "sat as a matter of mere form" and was "such a farce that even Stanton was ashamed to promulgate its acts."[46]

Throughout the investigation Buell remained isolated from the commission and socialized with no one. At the beginning of a session, Piatt later recalled, Buell walked "into court in full uniform with sword on side to show that he was not under arrest and accompanied by two aides so well drilled and disciplined that they seemed a chorus ready at any moment to break into song."[47] Wallace remarked that "he would walk in and seat himself without a bow of recognition or a good morning; upon adjournment, he would gather his papers together, tuck his sword under his arm and exit, his chin a little elevated, his eyes studiously to the front."[48] Day after day he remained emotionally and mentally focused on the business of exonerating his reputation. Buell's defense reflected the meticulousness and seriousness with which he conducted the training of his army. Nothing distracted him from examining, alone, volumes of documents in preparing his case. "The labor he performed unassisted was prodigious," remarked an impressed Wallace.[49]

Buell's articulate and well-reasoned defense impressed even Piatt. Wallace had thought that, confronted with almost any other general in a similar circumstance, Piatt "would have distinguished himself," since he "had ability and showed it." But against Buell's cold demeanor, Piatt's strength "was of the silkfloss variety." "In the atmosphere of that cold nature," recalled Wallace, "humor could not live and wit was a plant too weak to flower."[50] Though Buell was not humored in the least by the investigation, journalist William Shanks did witness a brief glimpse of levity. After the war, he related that one December morning during a recess Buell "grew unusually lively in a playful controversy with a young daughter of General Rousseau, and perpetuated several rather comical jokes." "[Mrs.] Rousseau, utterly astonished at this unexpected liveliness on the general's part," recalled Shanks, "expressed her surprise by exclaiming, 'Why, General Buell, I never knew you to laugh aloud before.' 'Ah! My Child,' replied the general suddenly growing serious, 'you never knew me when I feel free to laugh as now.' "[51] Piatt later wrote that Buell conducted his side of the inquiry with "marked ability." His mere presence and line of questioning often "embarrassed and at time confused" the witnesses, many of whom had earlier criticized his ability. Even some of the members of the court were swayed by his character, but even Wallace observed that "it was his [serious] manner, of the kind to beget belief that all human interest was dead within him, the sympathies included."[52]

The press saw little room for humor either and continued to hound

Buell throughout the trial in an attempt to prejudice the public against him. The *Cincinnati Times* assailed Buell constantly, attacking not only his military but also his political character. The editor attacked Buell almost daily with abusive and vicious articles designed to assassinate his character and discredit him for the remainder of the war. His conservative views on the war and slavery and his connection to McClellan were all subjects that received tremendous attention. The *Louisville Daily Journal*, which supported Buell, contested these attacks, arguing that had Buell been an abolitionist and a Republican, he would not have suffered such abuse. These kinds of attacks injured his family and made the trial all the more painful and humiliating.[53] The *New York Daily Tribune* was also unhappy that Buell had not been convicted. The editors castigated the Lincoln administration for "postponing his removal so long."[54] All that the commission had proven was that Buell had "failed to do all that he might [have] done."[55]

After months of fatiguing testimony, the final opinion of the Buell Commission was that Buell had failed to do all he might have done, though it was not made public until after the war. In the absence of formal charges, the commission concluded that Buell (1) had failed to live off the country and possessed too many supply trains during his march to Chattanooga, (2) had let the opportunity to defeat Bragg at Perryville slip away due either to his absence from the field or to his ignorance of the condition of the battle, and (3) had failed to vigorously pursue Bragg after Perryville. He was not however, held responsible for the fall of Munfordville, nor were there were any charges against his loyalty. Finally, despite all the controversy that it had inspired, the commission concluded that Buell deserved neither blame nor applause for his conciliatory policy, since at the time it was the directive of the government. Shortly after the conclusion of the trial, Piatt was asked about the commission's verdict. Having been impressed by Buell and annoyed by the whole process, Piatt remarked, "Why the main fact developed is that Buell is too thorough a soldier to command one of our armies."[56]

In some ways Buell had won his only true victory of the war. It was a personal victory that restored his faith that despite considerable opposition and criticism, he had not compromised his principles in waging war. If victory was the test of merit, then Buell had not been successful in accomplishing the Union's objectives. Whereas Shiloh had taught Grant that war meant fighting, Buell continued to cling to the idea that maneuvering would prove more successful in the long run. As critical as the press continued to be of Buell, many of his friends were just as supportive. John Lellyett, for example, wrote Buell several encouraging letters during the trial, saying that those persons who had been carried away by all of the rumors regarding his loyalty and slowness as a commander were now coming to see that if "'Gen. Buell is too slow,' other generals are still slower and not half so sure." According to Lellyett, what had fed suspicion regarding Buell's loyalty by what he called the fanatics was that Buell's silence was interpreted as "giving consent in a qualified sense, to the imputation." "While you justly feel it a condescension to notice a charge so cruelly libellous and [obscure]," he wrote, "zealots imagine that your silence signifies that you are willing to be considered a rebel sympathizer." He encouraged Buell to make public his views in regard to a "vigorous and uncompromising prosecution of the war," which he concluded would "turn the tide" in his favor.[57]

In April Lellyett, like Buell, had become gravely concerned that the war had encroached more and more upon the rights of the people without regard to their constitutional guarantees and liberties. In the same letter he informed Buell that the Ohioan had suffered such public clamor because he exposed the "notorious nest of swindlers and speculators which had taken possession of Gen. Mitchel and north Alabama." "Then at once," he argued, "you were assailed with the utmost violence by the correspondents and the radical press—for rebel sympathy—guarding rebel property—tardiness and inefficiency—everything but the real matter of offense." Lellyett was so inflamed by the whole affair that he decided to write an article about the truth behind "a man of ability." Nothing in print ever appeared, though.[58]

Even William T. Sherman wrote to his brother John in Washington of the problems politicians had caused in the prosecution of the war, though he clearly was not supporting Buell. "You have driven off McClellan, and is Burnside any better? Buell is displaced. Is Rosecrans any faster?"[59] William Shanks wrote Buell, asking him for documents that would help in his later account, *Personal Recollections of Distinguished Generals.*[60] A few soldiers were so incensed that the administration had relieved Buell and not reinstated him that they offered their resignations and, in anticipation of Buell's return to command, hoped to serve under him again. Such sentiments were due in part, however, to the fact that Rosecrans had proved no more successful than Buell, and that Lincoln's Emancipation Proclamation had inspired considerable rifts among soldiers. "I wish to be with you [Buell] in any capacity," wrote Reverdy Johnson, "commanding a Brigade of white men . . . [instead of] a corps d'armie of 'niggers.' "[61] Political leaders from Kentucky drafted a resolution of thanks and presented it to Buell for driving Bragg from the state.[62]

On May 20 Buell sent Stanton a copy of his personal statement made on the closing day of the trial, remarking to the secretary of war that he knew of the plot to get rid of him. In response to Stanton's mishandling of the investigation, Buell wrote that he sought no position in the military "in which it might be thought I cannot promote the public welfare."[63] Stanton no doubt buried the pine box with the many other boxes from similar investigations and probably thought nothing more of it. Buell, however, actually benefited from the ordeal. His statement was so well conceived and well written that several northern journals and newspapers, encouraged by its tone, printed various sections of it. While some critics continued to discriminate against his brand of war, Buell had managed to influence some soldiers and officers with his attitude. Lellyett was so impressed that he encouraged Buell to utilize the principle journals of the North to publish his statement as a mandate on the war. "The mild dignified, forebearing tone . . . is calculated," wrote Lellyett, "to produce a most favorable affect upon the public mind; and the history of the campaign therein given will enable any man of sense to perceive that you have been right and those who have [criticized] you wrong."[64] Thomas J. Bush, a former staff member, wrote Buell that newspapers carrying his statement had circulated widely through the camps, and "the general opinion was favorable." He confessed, however, that some of this had to do with the disgruntlement the soldiers felt for Rosecrans, who, they complained, only "drank, ate opium and held mass."[65]

During the summer Buell traveled to see family and friends of the old army. Everywhere he visited, he was received with an enormously favorable reception among Democrats. When he stopped in Syracuse, New York, in mid-September 1863 to see the widow of his friend Gen. Edwin V. Sumner, he was serenaded and welcomed with a huge reception. As he walked along the streets from the residence where his family was staying to widow Sumner's house, hundreds of people gathered, including the mayor, and strolled alongside until Buell was forced to stop and greet the crowd. As the band played "Hail to the Chief," Buell received almost every citizen at the gathering before finally reaching widow Sumner's residence.[66]

Officially Buell was "awaiting orders" after the military investigation and hoped to be reinstated to a command worthy of his rank and seniority. The Union's war aims had expanded, though, and emancipation and confiscation had become essential preconditions to reconstruction. The fact that he agreed with neither of these policies, had failed to make friends in Washington, and refused to lobby for a new command or assume a subordinate role combined to give the administration ample reason to keep him on the shelf. Consequently, he spent the remainder of the war as a spectator debating whether or not he should write a history of his operations.[67]

Despite his flaws as a commander, Buell still had considerable military worth, and several commanders saw great benefits from his talents. During the summer, Sherman counseled Buell's friends not to write a history of the early war and instead urged Buell to return to the service in any capacity. As crazy as Sherman was supposed to have been in November 1861, he had survived severe criticism and had gone on to become a tremendously successful commander. He obviously understood what it took to win the war. Sherman's motivation for encouraging his friends not to write a history of the early conflicts had much to do with his friendship with Buell. Sherman was perceptive enough to realize that any such publication would only discredit Buell. In the fall of 1863, in his correspondence with J. Marcus Wright, assistant adjutant general in Louisville and Buell's former staff member, Sherman warned Wright that any such publication written during the war would "do General Buell greater wrong than his worst enemy could desire." Because Wright had been a member of Buell's staff, any history he wrote would be "construed as his [Buell's] act" and would prove "injurious to his well-earned reputation." "The time for history is after the end is attained," Sherman declared. "Like in a race," he concluded, "the end is all that is remembered by the great world. Those who are out at the end will never be able to magnify their importance . . . no matter how brilliant and important."[68]

Sherman had given Buell, through Wright, some invaluable advice and even made his comments part of the public record by putting his private letter into a military telegram. But it apparently offended Wright, who supported the idea of writing a history of Buell's exploits to exonerate him. Buell, however, understood perfectly the intent behind Sherman's warning and no doubt encouraged Wright not to publish anything on the Army of the Ohio until after the war. Sherman remained cordial to Buell, referring to him as "one of the coolest, most methodic, and patient men living," not to mention "one of the best, if not the best, practical soldier of our army."[69] That friendship waned after the war.

Throughout the remainder of the fall and the winter of 1863–64, Buell remained without a command partly because Stanton and Johnson continued to make sure he never returned to the field, at least not in the West. When it was rumored that Buell would be sent to Knoxville to take charge, in April 1864 Johnson penned a letter to Lincoln, saying,

"I trust in God that Gen Buell will not be sent to Tennessee. We have been cursed with him here once and do not desire its repetition."[70] He also wrote to Stanton trying to block Buell's return to the state, and Stanton assured him that there "was no design to put General Buell again in command in Tennessee."[71] In mid-April, when Grant asked Halleck and Stanton to restore Buell to command, Halleck replied, "I would like very much to see Buell restored to a command and have several times proposed him to the War Department, but there has been such a pressure against him from the West that I do not think the Secretary will give him any at present."[72] The following month Sherman informed Halleck that he needed a "bold, discreet major-general (not a Kentuckian) to command in Kentucky," and he wanted Buell.[73]

Stanton apparently had a change of heart in the spring of 1864 and invited Buell to Washington for an interview. The request from Sherman and Grant to see Buell reinstated no doubt played a part in Stanton's decision to extend an invitation to Buell. During the interview Stanton asked Buell to choose from several important commands. In an election year, returning Buell to any command might prove difficult, but at least Stanton made the gesture. Buell answered that before he would even consider returning to a command he demanded that Stanton formally and publicly exonerate him by disposing of the proceedings of the military commission. Buell's ultimatum annoyed Stanton, who refused to make the proceedings public, no doubt out of embarrassment that nothing had been accomplished. In mid-May, however, Stanton voluntarily offered Buell commands under Sherman or Gen. Edward R. Canby, commander of the Department of the Gulf. Buell declined both because they were not important enough. As Thomas L. Crittenden wrote to his nephew in December 1863, Buell was "greater within himself than . . . great achievements can make appear. His nature lifts him above all little things, & his pre-eminent justice is marvelous in these times."[74] Grant was disappointed in Buell's refusal to return to the field later, arguing, "The worst excuse a soldier can make for declining service is that he once outranked the commander he is ordered to report to."[75]

On May 28 Buell was mustered out as major general of volunteers and that same day resigned his commission in the regular army, though few in the public knew it at the time. For the first time in nearly three decades, he was a civilian again. Although his officer friends condemned him for not serving in some capacity, Buell considered his decision justifiable, since the positions offered him were hardly appealing. Buell remained without a command not only because he refused to take a subordinate position, but also because he refused to participate in a revolutionary struggle that waged war on the South's resources, including slavery. He explained his reasons for resigning to a former aide-de-camp, Almon Rockwell, in July:

I believed that the policy and means with which the war was being prosecuted were discreditable to the nation, and a stain upon civilization; and that they would not only fail to restore the Union, if indeed they had not already rendered its restoration impossible, but that their tendency was to subvert the institutions under which the country had realized unexampled prosperity and happiness; and to such work I could not lend my hand.

While there may have been more or less of personal ambition mixed up in the movement of Secession, as there must generally be in the management of political affairs, yet I do not doubt that it was mainly determined by an honest conviction in the minds of those who engaged in it, that the control of the Government had passed permanently into the hands of a sectional party which would soon trample on the political rights of the South. This apprehension was shared in by a very large portion of the people who did not favor secession, and who were so anxious for the preservation of the Union that even coercive measures, if tempered by justice and mercy, would not have estranged them. Under these circumstances the use of military force to put down armed resistance was not incompatible with a restoration of the Union with its former glories and affections, provided the means were employed in such a manner as to convince the people that their constitutional rights would be respected. Such a policy, therefore, in the use of force, if force must be resorted to, had the manifest advantage of weakening the power of the Rebellion, and strengthening the Government independently of the moral force which dignity and justice always lend to authority.

A policy which recognized those principles was wisely declared by Congress in the beginning of the war. . . . Unfortunately it was too often cheated of its own due effect by the intrusion of sectional rancor, and the injudicious or unfaithful acts of agents of the Government; and when, at the expiration of year, a system of spoliation and disfranchisement was inaugurated, the cause was robbed of its sanctity, and success rendered more difficult of attainment.[76]

Unfortunately for Buell, his reasons for not seeking command were made public in the summer of 1864, which further discredited him in the eyes of his superiors and Radical Republicans. In August 1864 the *New York Times* ran a copy of the entire private letter Buell had written to

Rockwell, no doubt further undermining Buell's credibility as a professional officer. Former West Point professor Dennis Hart Mahan attempted to rescue Buell, arguing that military and political etiquette ought to be observed in matters of placing senior officers in subordinate positions. Mahan only drew criticism upon himself. In response to Mahan's argument, an anonymous letter was sent to the *Times* severely berating Mahan and Buell. "The resignation of an officer," read the letter, "on the grounds that the Administration follows principles not approved of by the resigning officer, seems simply to amount to an outrage. The soldier belongs exclusively to his nation, and especially so in times of war."[77]

In the autumn of 1864 the presidential contest eclipsed the discussion surrounding Buell's resignation and sent him into obscurity. The Republicans had renominated Lincoln, but a number of their party leaders were calling for his replacement in light of the gloomy war news: long casualty lists coupled with stalemates around Richmond and Atlanta. The Democratic Party met at the end of August, declared in its platform that the war was a failure, and nominated McClellan. Buell supported McClellan in the presidential election, only to see him suffer defeat again. After the election McClellan wrote Buell and thanked him for his support and informed him of his resignation from the army:

> Well! The struggle is over [and] we have been thoroughly defeated! I accept the result and have resigned my commission — I fancy it will be very promptly accepted & that I shall soon be an independent citizen again. I trust that I have seen the last of public life & that I may hereafter live in peace & quietness. My only regret is for my country & my friends some of whom have suffered so much in consequence of their devotion to me — a debt I can now only repay by heartfelt gratitude, & unfortunately not by redressing their wrongs. But it is the will of God, & I submit without repinning.[78]

Years after the war, Buell revealed in his East Tennessee article his attitude about the nature of the conflict and why the Union army took so long to defeat the Confederacy. "Much," he claimed, "was due to the character of the contest." In arguing that the war was a revolutionary struggle, which often "inspired bold and desperate action" on the part of those who consider themselves revolutionaries, the southern soldiers recognized that because the odds were against them in terms of resources and manpower, they must find some means of prevailing. For Buell, that means was the southern soldier's passionate enthusiasm. The fact that the Union was forced to invade a hostile population placed the

Federal armies at a distinct disadvantage. "The simpler mode of life to which the bulk of Confederate troops were accustomed," he argued, "made them more contented with meager supplies." The lack of resources of every sort precluded the luxurious furnishings to which northern soldiers were accustomed. Other considerations also contributed to the duration of the war. The more rural conditions of the South and the institution of slavery, he argued, provided southern leaders with a sense of confidence that did not mean humility but produced subordination. Finally, he contended that southern women, even in agony of their heart, "girded the sword upon their loved ones and bade them to go." All of these influences "would give a confidence to leadership that would tend to bold adventure, and leave its mark upon the contest."[79]

Buell left his mark on the Civil War in the West by casting the Army of the Ohio in a mold that mirrored himself. Contemporaries assailed him for his inability or refusal to mature with the war and develop a flexibility of attitude that might have allowed him to cultivate a neutrality in handling the political side of war. His flawed conception of civil-military relations perpetually aggravated Lincoln, governors, and Radical Republicans. His failure to appreciate the volunteer as someone who deserved special consideration as a soldier, particularly with regard to discipline, was odd in light of his conciliation policy that extended special consideration to southerners. This failure had to do, in part, with his professional pride in making soldiers of civilians and, in part, with his lasting faith in the assumption, however oversimplified it was, that the mass of white southerners were loyal and would remain so if not burdened unnecessarily with war. Thus, he attempted to keep war proper and sustain moral justice by exempting southerners from retribution. Buell thought in absolute terms in a war that required a certain degree of fluidity. His insistence on conciliation after the administration abandoned it was not the only reason he was removed. He made mistakes in judgment and failed to grow as a commander, but Lincoln removed him because he did not produce results.

In the final analysis, it must be said of Buell that his flaws as a commander had as much to do with his military philosophy and his conservative temperament as with his incomplete idea of the nature of the Civil War. He understood that war was shaped by political policy; he simply remained steadfast in his conservative beliefs that limited war could achieve the desired political results. He refused to subordinate military operations to political necessities and to calibrate the conduct of his military operations to the incompatible policies of the administration.

For someone who viewed himself and the Union armies as agents of northern society, by his refusal to accommodate the changes in war policy he indicated his own personal dissatisfaction with the Union's shift in military directives. His unproductive relations with politicians were not merely clashes of wills but, rather, clashes of philosophical beliefs about the conduct of the war, which included his refusal to accept that any policy other than conciliation would not prove more destructive in the long run.

Buell could never see emancipation and confiscation as preconditions of reconstruction. He waged war not to refashion southern society by freeing slaves but, rather, to suppress the rebellion without simultaneously waging a revolution. He never abandoned his desire to preserve the Union by conciliating southerners and confining the war to the battlefield. Conciliation, conservatism, and limited war all became sacrifices to the Union's changing attitude that war was about revolution. Buell merely refused to depart from his initial conception of the Civil War and embrace the conflict that Sherman and Grant went on to fight and win. As a leader Buell had demonstrated great potential, and yet he tragically carried the seeds of his own demise. In short, Buell was Jominian to the core. Commanders were to train and maneuver armies and win victories that way, he believed. He avoided committing his army to battle because he might lose it. His mind was full of fear, and he tried to calm it through preparation. Still, as important as rules were to preventing problems, Buell never overcame problems. More importantly, he believed professional soldiers, not politicians, should run the war. Therefore, no matter what someone like Lincoln might say, Buell ignored it. To him, rules and regulations were more important than anything else, be it success, friendship, or victory. He never grew in insight as the war progressed. His mind was closed, so no one's perceptions or advice, no matter how valid, could get through. Buell was an adjutant general in his heart and soul and remained one even when he became a commanding general. Perhaps John Pope, reminiscing after the war, put it best when he said that of all the distinguished commanders who in the spring of 1862 were in Halleck's grand army descending on Corinth, Buell was perhaps "the most promising of all."[80]

Epilogue

After the war Buell turned to business. He and his wife searched for an oil field in Kentucky and ended up in Airdrie, in the Green River country. He took out an extended forty-year mineral and oil lease on 17,000 acres of the Alexander lands along the Green River in Muhlenberg County, where he spent the remainder of his life. Over the years he managed the oil business as the president of the Airdrie Petroleum Company. In the years immediately following the war, Buell drilled extensively for oil. When he discovered coal, he changed his plans and in the 1870s turned most of his attention to coal development. What farmland remained undeveloped he rented out to local farmers and sharecroppers.[1]

The genteel nature of rural Kentucky agreed with Buell, and he settled into a calm and contented life. He became close friends with some of the prominent locals, including Judge Charles Eaves, who handled all the legal affairs of Buell's enterprise. Though the transition from military to civilian life was easier than leaving Lawrenceburg to enter West Point, he no doubt missed the military, since the life of a soldier had been all he had known for nearly three decades. Always quiet, unassuming, and self-absorbed, Buell became as much a recluse in civilian life as he had been during the war, staying close to his estate. Though he devoted most of his time to his business enterprises, he still read, worked in his little carpentry shop, and rode. He became a great admirer of native trees and plants. His passion for fine saddle horses continued, and he was often seen riding his favorite steed, Shiloh, a gift from Civil War days. He and his wife frequently rode together, studying their vast property. Finally, he could enjoy in Kentucky a life beyond the army.[2]

The absence of military duty gave Buell the opportunity to fill his days with running the business and securing his place in the history of the Civil War. Though he had left the army in 1864, the controversy over his role in the 1862 campaigns in the West continued for years. His reputation had always been mixed, and his role in the war remained curious. No one could deny he had played a major role for the Union in the early part of the conflict, shaping the Army of the Ohio, capturing Nashville, and participating in the Shiloh and Corinth achievements.

Still, he failed to benefit favorably from these accomplishments once his liabilities as a commander proved more damaging to the Union's prosecution of the war. Thus, he did not bask in the glory of victory in the aftermath.

The battle of Shiloh attracted particular attention for Buell largely because it was one of the Union's greatest victories and because he could never accept partial credit for making it so. He never conceded to what he considered gross exaggerations of what transpired during those two spring days along the Tennessee River. Consequently, even in peace Buell fought a personal war against his detractors merely to secure his reputation and his place, and the reputation of his army, in the history of the war. He emerged from his characteristic silence and calm stoicism to provide counterarguments to those who charged that his army only added to the Union victory but was not the reason for it.

Even before the war ended, Buell became involved in what amounted to a public dispute with his old-friend-turned-critic William T. Sherman over the battle. In January 1865 the *United States Service Magazine* published a letter by Sherman, who was responding to a previous article that cast Buell as the savior of Grant at Shiloh. Because "life [was] liable to cease at any moment" and because he had witnessed certain truths about the battle, which were apparently "beginning to pass out of memory and form what is called history," Sherman wanted to correct the article.[3] Sherman did not like the fact that Grant was not assigned a favorable place in what was the "modern description" of the battle, and he decided to revise its existing history by mentioning these "truths" and thereby ensuring the historical accuracy of the events of those years.[4]

Sherman had taken particular exception to the passage in which the editor remarked, "but for the immediate and timely arrival of General Buell's forces, and the conduct of that officer, the disaster of the first day might not have been retrieved." In an attempt to vindicate Grant, Sherman explained that there had been no disaster the first day. He recalled that Grant had visited him at 10:00 A.M. during the first day's fight and remarked to Sherman that his division was "doing right" in vigorously opposing the enemy's progress. According to Sherman, Grant visited him again at 5:00 P.M. just before sunset, and after discussing the condition of affairs and concluding that the enemy had expended the "*furore* of his attack," they estimated their losses, approximated their troop strength, and decided to resume the offensive the next morning. Sherman argued that all of this transpired before Buell arrived, leaving it to be inferred that Grant had not made known to Sherman that he had seen Buell, that his troops were now arriving at the river, and that support was certainly to be expected from Buell's army. Furthermore, Sherman's troops in the front line had stopped the enemy by 4:00 P.M. and were preparing to assume the offensive the next day.[5]

Sherman also claimed that "there was no mistake" in debarking the army on the west bank of the Tennessee, and that it was not then a question of "military skill and strategy, but of courage and pluck." But even if there was an error, he said, it was not Grant's, but Charles F. Smith's, for Smith had selected the ground and positioned the troops before Grant succeeded to the command. Thus, not only had Grant done nothing wrong, he had overcome the first day's attack and was preparing to counter the next day whether Buell's army arrived or not.[6]

Buell decided that there were enough falsities in Sherman's "truths" to warrant a response, and he immediately penned a lengthy letter to the editor of the *United States Service Magazine*. The magazine, however, ceased publication that February, and Buell's letter was published in the *New York World*. Because the letter made its way into the newspaper, what might have been a discreet disagreement was aired publicly. Buell did not like the role Sherman assigned him in his response to the article, and he attempted to correct Sherman's vindication of Grant by claiming that the arrival of the Army of the Ohio was the only reason for Union victory. Buell asserted that Sherman's declarations to right the record of the history of the battle of Shiloh were remarkable misrepresentations of the facts, since they relieved Grant and Sherman from much of the responsibility that was supposed to rest on them. Sherman's truths virtually denied that the Army of the Tennessee was reduced to very strained circumstances on April 6 and made Sherman the dominant figure in the day's fighting. Buell contended that the "tide of popular favor has given too much weight to General Sherman's expressions to make it a gratuitous labor to expose his fallacies." Still, Buell aired his interpretation of the events of those two days not to incriminate Grant but, rather, to render what he considered a more accurate version of the events.[7]

Buell argued that during the Shiloh campaign, Grant's was not an independent force sent to occupy a certain point threatened by the enemy but, instead, was one of two armies that were to unite for a grand invasion against Corinth. Sherman's declaration, Buell argued, that the question was not one of "military skill and strategy, but of courage and pluck," may answer the purpose of a "clap-trap, but does not befit a man who aspired to the direction of armies." A greater mistake, Buell contended, was the neglect of all proper measures against the danger of the enemy, and he placed the blame squarely on Sherman. As far as what Grant and Sherman discussed and when they discussed it, Buell did not know, which in Buell's mind allowed Sherman considerable latitude and advantage in recasting the events. He did, however, acknowledge that when he visited Sherman shortly after dark, Sherman said nothing of any orders that he had received or what he proposed to do. In answer to Sherman's inquiry regarding Buell's plans, Buell said he told Sherman that he was going to attack the enemy at daylight, and that Sherman expressed gratification at this fact. At the time, Buell argued, he presumed that in the absence of any formal orders, and under the circumstances, he and Sherman thought there was nothing else to do but attack.[8]

It was not odd for Buell to respond to anything that had been said about his role in the war, particularly since he thought his trial had exonerated him from questionable acts. When it came to Shiloh, however, Buell was extremely sensitive about who received credit for the Union victory. Understandably, it was the one and only high mark in his military career, and he sought to preserve his place in the history of the war as Grant's savior at that battle. The fame heaped on Grant as the Union victor who emerged from the cloud of Shiloh eventually to force the surrender of Robert E. Lee no doubt made Buell's sensitivity about this one battle all the more acute.

Because Buell had not lasted the war and had in fact refused to participate after his dismissal, the public came to believe that it was entirely possible that Grant had done nothing wrong at Shiloh and that Buell had simply been in the right place at the right time to share the victory. Buell may also have felt that because of Grant's military successes after Shiloh, persons were likely to recast Grant more favorably during that battle as well. Whatever the case, it was not so much that Buell was jealous of Grant but, rather, that he had no tolerance for the injustice that Sherman created by his letter. "I have taken up General Sherman's letter with no pleasure," he wrote in a dignified manner, "but it was due to the army which I commanded that I should write what I have written." Marcus Wright, who the year before had encouraged Buell to write the history of the Army of the Ohio, was pleased that Buell had finally decided to vindicate himself instead of letting the records speak for themselves. "I need hardly say," he wrote, "that I was rejoiced to see you emerge from your customary silence, and remark the . . . spirited statements regarding Shiloh."[9] This letter signaled the beginning of a postwar feud between Sherman and Buell and, later, Grant over who was responsible for the victory at Shiloh.

Not only did Buell defend his role at Shiloh, but he also contributed ideas and official documents to others contemplating histories of the much-maligned army under his command. George H. Thomas was among the more prominent ex-soldiers who asked Buell to assist him in writing a history of the Army of the Ohio. Though the army's record was never written, Buell contributed his views, particularly since he thought it would do justice to the men who served. He also harbored ideas about writing his own history of the army. He inquired about the papers of William Nelson and others for inclusion in either Thomas's or his own projected history.[10]

Buell also found it necessary to correct rumors claiming that he never understood what the war was about and criticizing his leadership abilities, particularly when these assertions were made in public. In the summer after the war, during an appearance in Springfield, Massachusetts, Grant was quoted in the newspaper as accusing Buell of not knowing what the war was about and saying that although Buell was well versed in the theory of war, he knew nothing about handling men in an emergency. After reading the article, Buell sent Grant a copy of it and asked him to explain his comments. When Grant finally responded in December, he told Buell that when asked about Buell's ability to command in the presence of an enemy or battle, Grant responded charitably that he had "always thought, and frequently expressed the opinion that in that precise case you would do as well as almost any General that could be selected." Grant argued that he had said no such thing about Buell's heart not being in the war and regarded Buell "as earnest at the beginning of the war and whilst in command as any other officer engaged in it in the maintenance of the Government." He added, however, that Buell's published letter in July 1864, in which Buell refused to fight a war to end slavery, revealed that Buell wanted "the Union saved in a particular way, and that way [was] different from the one which was being pursued."[11]

The confrontation with Grant, coming on the heels of Sherman's letter, simply added to the animosity Buell felt for Grant and Sherman after the war. Though Sherman certainly reciprocated the feeling, Grant may have felt the same animosity for Buell, but he never publicly criticized him. In fact, Grant went to great lengths to correct any injustices done to Buell. In later years, when Grant was touring the world, he occasionally spoke about Buell. While in Hong Kong, he remarked that although Buell did not like him, Grant had "always borne my testimony to his perfect loyalty and his ability." Buell was a man, he said, "who would have carried out loyally every order he received, and I think he had genius enough for the highest commands; but, somehow, he fell under a cloud."[12]

Even in civilian life Buell had fallen under a cloud for his wartime exploits. Unlike Grant and Sherman, who shared a common background of past failure and newly achieved success in the war, Buell's career had taken the opposite path. When the war broke out, he had been among the most sought-after commanders in the Union and proved early to be one of the most promising of all officers. Still, he had only participated in, not contributed to, the Union's military conquest of the Confederacy. In fact, many critics came to believe he stood in the way of the conquest itself. At least that was the general opinion when he was relieved. He never shared the anecdotes between commanders or civilians about his war exploits and remained as self-absorbed in civilian life as he had in the army. There were no postwar trips to Europe, no glamorous appointments, and no part in reconstruction. His was a life devoid of national fame and notoriety.

Buell continued to suffer publicly from a damaged self-image wrought by his slowness and displeasure at fighting a war against the South and slavery. To assuage his personal honor and integrity and that of his army, he felt compelled to revive whatever little claim to fame he and his army possessed whenever he felt it obscured or challenged by others recounting the war. Moreover, Buell believed he had been wronged and persecuted by attacks like Sherman's, and that if he failed to reply to the accusations or critics, it would surely reflect an implicit acknowledgment of his own failings as a commander. Though he had had his day in court to rectify his status in the war, his own sense of justice denied him the opportunity to stand with those who laid claim to the victory. Thus, to further exonerate himself he engaged in refuting what he considered false accusations about his attitude regarding the war, his role, or the role of his army. Unfortunately for Buell, the cumulative effect of his corrections, no matter how significant he thought they would be to history, made him appear petty and self-serving and as uncompromising in peace as he had been in war. When it came to his role and that of his army, no compromise was acceptable in forming the history of the war.

Despite the lingering controversy over his abilities in the war, Buell settled into a pleasant and initially productive postwar life. Kentuckians were especially fond of Buell and seized opportunities to manifest this affection. In the fall of 1865 a committee of citizens of Lexington gave Buell a public reception to honor his "unsullied personal character and eminent public services." Such receptions demonstrated the state's fondness for him, and he felt an affectionate attachment to his adopted state.[13]

In 1867 Buell's conservative Kentucky friends urged him to seek the Democratic nomination for governor of the Bluegrass State. Richard R.

Bolling, a former attorney who in the election became clerk of the Court of Appeals, wrote to Buell insisting that if he ran for governor and William H. Wadsworth ran for lieutenant governor, the "*Conservative Union* men" of Kentucky would be successful in coming to power. Simply using his name as the Democratic candidate would place Buell before the public, which would induce all Conservative Union men to vote and thus carry the state. The Conservative Union Democrats endorsed President Andrew Johnson's policies in their spring convention and bitterly condemned congressional Reconstruction. Not surprisingly, Buell's popularity in his adopted state exceeded his interest in politics, and he refused the nomination.[14]

In the 1876 and 1880 elections Buell's friends again tried to secure him a political post, urging him accept the nomination as the Democratic presidential candidate, or at least the nomination for governor of Kentucky. "The South accords you the esteem and courage of her manly and candid sons," wrote one enthusiastic supporter, "because we know that you fought honestly for the Union and not for our ruin and conquest." Again, he refused.[15]

During these years education, not politics, interested Buell. He enjoyed the company of learned men and often attended lectures on various topics at Kentucky Agricultural College. In the early 1870s Buell sought a teaching position at the college. Although he was not given a faculty appointment, the college's Board of Commissioners made him a member, since he had shown considerable interest by supporting the agricultural endeavors of the college. He later compiled and introduced a schedule and report on discipline and administration for the college, which was adopted.[16]

In the early 1870s Buell sought a full pension, but this required that his name be cleared from the 1862–63 investigation. He petitioned Congress to take such action and wrote New York Republican Representative Roscoe Conkling asking for his assistance in getting a resolution passed to clear his name. When Congress requested the transcripts from the military commission that investigated Buell's operations, however, the War Department could not locate the pine box into which Stanton had stuffed hundreds of pages of testimony years earlier. The disappearance of the documents caused quite a stir, and the Military Affairs Committee summoned Buell and Andrew Johnson to Washington to testify regarding the whereabouts of the papers. Neither Buell nor Johnson had any idea as to their location. Johnson confessed that as much as he had quarreled with Buell, he had nothing to do with the commission's report and, in fact, had never seen it during his presidency. Finally, in 1874, Congress found the commission's documents, which exonerated Buell, and he received his pension.[17]

Throughout the 1870s and 1880s Buell continued his work in the coal industry. Unfortunately, however, when the Green and Barren Rivers Navigation Company leased the Green River from the State of Kentucky, the increased freight rate demanded by the new corporation nearly put Buell out of business, as he was unable to meet the prices of his competitors to whom a lower rate was given. Buell spent almost fifteen years fighting the corporation through the legislature to reduce the rates or terminate the lease. His long, hard, and time-consuming work resulted in the federal government purchasing the unexpired lease of the navigation company in 1888. The river was then reopened to the public.[18]

During these years the health of Buell's wife had deteriorated. When she died in August 1881, he was devastated. He grieved for months and made no public appearances. Though he seldom manifested compassion, the passing of his wife brought out the old commander's emotional side, and he composed a poem titled "Thou and I," a tribute to his undying love for her. His grief was compounded by the fact that although his fight with the Green and Barren Rivers company ultimately brought legislative success, his coal enterprise had in the meantime degenerated until he was destitute.[19]

By this time Buell was far too advanced in years to begin again his work of developing new mines. He became so reclusive after his wife's death that when an iron peddler agreed to purchase all the old pig iron and scrap iron around the furnace, the peddler, without Buell's knowledge, simply loaded his barge with not only the scrap iron but also the old machinery. All that remained from the once-prosperous business were two boilers. Consequently, Buell was left with virtually nothing to sell. During these years Buell spent much of his time reading, walking, riding, looking after his trees, and working in his carpentry and machine shop. He had a mechanical turn and constructed, among other things, a model of a large steam dish-washing machine, such as were used in hotels, which allowed one person to do the work of four. He applied for but never received a patent.[20]

Eventually, however, Buell compensated for the financial and emotional void in his life as several Civil War veterans had, by speaking at reunions of army veterans, lecturing at colleges, and writing about the war. Though he had never considered himself a speaker or a writer, he frequently contributed his ideas to those who sought to write histories of the war. In his correspondence to his comrades, Buell was meticulous about details and penmanship. The editor of the *Louisville Daily Journal* gave Buell an open invitation to write anything on the war. When Samuel W. Crawford sought Buell's views about Robert Anderson's move to Fort Sumter in 1861 for his *Genesis of the Civil War: The Story of Sumter, 1860–1861*, Buell defended Anderson. He confided to Crawford, however, that when he gave instructions to Anderson regarding any move, he was acting more out of the confidential nature of his relationship with Secretary of War John B. Floyd than any official authority. Buell also considered writing a history of the Army of the Ohio, and at one point even seriously considered writing a biography of George B. McClellan. Yet even he recognized that such a work "would require so much careful study" that he was not sure he would live to see its publication. The editors of *Century Magazine* encouraged him to write his autobiography or at least his memoirs, but Buell had no desire to tell his own story.[21]

Why he did not write his memoirs as other commanders had done remains a mystery, particularly since he was not satisfied with the role Sherman and Grant assigned him in their published works. Besides, he could have used the money. A volume on McClellan alone would have attracted considerable attention as well as speculation. It might also have given him the opportunity to write a favorable part for himself in the early part of the war and explain what led to their termination as commanders. Perhaps he saw little value in such a publication, since although he felt abused by Sherman and Grant, he maintained that if he were to be judged a success or failure as a commander, that conclusion should be derived from the official records of the war, a series that was already under way for publication. He had no need to be noticed beyond what the official records had indicated but only wanted his army's actions acknowledged appropriately. Whatever the case, he never composed either a history of his army or his memoirs.

The appearance of Sherman's *Memoirs* in 1875, however, sparked another round of debate over Shiloh and stirred Buell's acrimony. Buell was outraged, though hardly surprised, that he and his army had not been more favorably considered at the battle. That summer he commented to friend John P. Nicholson that although he had not read all of the *Memoirs*, he had read the portions important to him. "It is very provocative of criticism," he candidly remarked, "and there is no fear that its authorship will ever be questioned." Buell had concluded that the public would certainly believe what Sherman had written, simply because of who he was and what he had achieved in the war. Nonetheless, several persons wrote to Buell appealing to him to react to Sherman's assessment of him at Shiloh. Buell had seen some articles in the *Cincin-*

nati Gazette by former officers responding to Sherman's mistreatment of the Army of the Ohio and was encouraged by these gestures of support. "I confess," he wrote to Nicholson, "that I am more moved by these appeals than I am by its [the *Memoirs*] egotistical and unfounded assumptions." Though Buell said he had no time to respond publicly, it did not lessen the anger he felt over the issue, and in due time he did reply.[22]

When Sherman's revised memoirs appeared in 1886, Buell was still dissatisfied with the treatment of Shiloh. He wrote to William F. Smith, who was compiling an article on the battle and had asked Buell for some information regarding Shiloh. Buell stated that when Sherman wrote that his advance units broke in disorder after the commencement of the battle, "it [was] one of the few cases in which he is exact." He argued that Sherman gave the impression that the battle flowed rapidly and without interruption, but Buell claimed just the opposite. "The progress of the Confederates was for the most part slow, and the effects upon the federals though inexorable, were generally gradual also," he contended, "not so much because of the *stubbornness* of the resistance, as on account of the impossibility of keeping up an effective front on such ground." He condemned Sherman for not analyzing the topography of the maps when writing the earlier version of his memoirs. "Sherman," Buell chided, "seems to have no sense, military or geographical." Buell then launched into a series of corrections dealing with Sherman's positions as he read them according to the map.[23]

Though Buell maintained self-restraint in not writing to Sherman himself, James B. Fry, Buell's former chief of staff, who in the postwar years had become a noted author and lecturer on the Army of the Cumberland, became inflamed by Sherman's bravado, which essentially eclipsed other commanders who might share any glory in the war. In 1884 Fry's *Operations of the Army under Buell* appeared, which argued that Buell's army had arrived at Shiloh just in time to save the Union from disaster. He tried to rescue Buell and the Army of the Ohio from historical obscurity. In response to Fry's volume, Sherman claimed that Buell deliberately arrived late at Shiloh to avoid fighting on the first day. "Grant's Army of the Tennessee," Sherman lashed out, "fought the first day of Shiloh without a particle of assistance from Buell." In fact, Sherman lectured to Fry, both he and Grant believed Buell had been "derelict" in coming to the battle so "slowly and deliberately," because Buell had "not [been] over anxious to share our danger. . . . *And you know it.*" The second day of the battle had been a "walkover," Sherman insisted, for which the Army of the Tennessee had not needed the Army of the Ohio.[24]

Sherman's accusations took the Shiloh debate as well as Fry's anger to new heights. Fry demanded a retraction of Sherman's charges, "which if true," he insisted, "should consign Buell, me, and others to infamy." Fry asserted that by making "deliberate, positive and specific statements" in this regard, Sherman had gone beyond a simple argument and had severely injured the reputations of many soldiers. Fry threatened to go public with Sherman's letter, which meant that Buell and others would be publicly drawn into the feud. Recognizing that he had overplayed his hand in disputing the facts of the arrival of Buell's army at Shiloh and had attacked Buell's rationale for its tardiness, Sherman penned a humble apology and withdrew his charges, asking that Fry return the offensive letter. Fry acquiesced, and the feud remained confidential.[25]

At the time Buell knew nothing of the private dispute, though Fry may have informed him later. While Buell remained silent, however, Fry continued to fuel the debate. Still, he was not the only outspoken critic of Sherman's version of Shiloh. When Grant's article on Shiloh appeared in February 1885, several of Buell's former comrades wrote him urging him to "refute in General Grant's lifetime the statements in his article" and "secure to yourself and [your] army your right place in history." Another soldier urged Buell to respond, not for his personal defense, "but simply . . . for the Truth of history and the interests of the Army of the Ohio." Thomas J. Bush, Buell's former aide-de-camp, was so incensed that he thought of making public some of the private stories he had heard from Sherman's own men about Sherman refusing to believe he had been surprised. Bush encouraged several soldiers to come forward and publicize their accounts so he would not to have to defend Buell. Sherman, Bush demanded, must be "brought up standing face to face with the truth."[26]

However much Buell was encouraged by these displays of support and encouragement, he still remained reluctant to commit anything to publication for fear that it would merely serve as a defense of his actions as opposed to an objective representation of Shiloh. Grant and Sherman were "revolutionists," Buell fumed. Still, he wrote to a friend that he could not see how "an impersonal treatment of the subject [was] altogether possible." "The history of the battle," he concluded, "has virtually been written in the official records, if no where else fairly." "The particulars were pretty fairly impressed upon the public mind," he argued, "until Grant and Sherman undertook to contradict them and make a different history of the affair." Buell thought at least a "review of their statements seems to me to be absolutely necessary."[27]

Though Buell wrote privately that he hesitated to compose an article, in truth he could no longer contain himself. He burned with resentment. The commotion caused by Grant's article was reason enough to respond. At the time the editors of the *Century Magazine* had accepted a proposal for an article on Perryville, but Grant's article caused Buell to request that a review of Shiloh was more in order. By publishing articles from Grant and Buell the editors moved the private feud into the public arena and allowed the people to decide whose version of Shiloh to accept. These kinds of war articles formed the basis of the great four-volume work titled *Battles and Leaders of the Civil War.*

Unfortunately for Buell, Grant's interpretation of the battle, whether intentional or not, corresponded with Sherman's version in his memoirs. Moreover, in 1885 Charles L. Webster and Company published the two-volume *Personal Memoirs of U. S. Grant,* which also assessed the battle of Shiloh in much the same manner as had Sherman. Grant's published memoirs appeared in 1885–86, and while they had not the luster of Sherman's, they too stirred Buell to criticism. Remarking to a friend when asked what he thought of Grant's memoirs, Buell, no doubt outraged by his article, confessed that he had not read them. However, Buell wrote, if they stated that during the war "I received, and that I resigned my commission in the army, they are so far correct."[28]

Buell's "Shiloh Reviewed" essay was an elaborately constructed justification of his actions as a commander during the battle. When the editors read his first draft, they considered calling it "The Facts about Shiloh" or "Who Fought the Battle of Shiloh?" Buell, however, feared it would appear an attack on Grant, whom in his dying condition Buell did not want to injure further. Nor did Buell want to appear "egotistical," as Sherman had. He simply wanted the article cast in a scholarly manner. He came to interpret his disagreement with Sherman and Grant as a conflict between right and wrong, or rather, justice and injustice. Playing the part of the dignified victim, of course, Buell sought to reclaim his good name. He always couched his position, however, in such a way that made it clear his words were merely on behalf of his army. His public defense simply addressed the great injustice and misrepresentation of facts as he saw it. He argued, understandably, that "scarcely less remarkable than the facts themselves are the means by which the responsible actors in the critical drama have endeavored to counteract them."[29]

Buell contended that all the attention Shiloh attracted after the war was due not to anything he had yet written but to what others had written in newspapers, journals, and memoirs, all concluding that the Army of the Ohio "was an unnecessary intruder in the battle." He registered a complaint that Sherman had revised the official map of the battle some years later to diminish the role of the Army of the Ohio. He cited proof that Sherman's map was ill conceived and wrong and, as if to settle the matter, submitted his own map as confirmation. While Buell acknowledged that Grant had decided to assume the offensive on the second day, he questioned whether Grant would have determined to do this without reinforcements from either Lew Wallace or himself. Buell made the case that Grant had not decided to attack the next day until after reinforcements had arrived. Buell also attacked Sherman's assessment that Grant's personal qualities were a guarantee for his triumph, since Grant, Buell argued, was nowhere to be found on the field of battle the first day until 10:00 A.M., by which time, according to Buell, the "determining act of the drama was completed."[30]

Buell concluded his essay by arguing that the battle of Shiloh was "full of personality" and might be called "almost properly, a personal one." He intended simply to provide a review of some of the prominent facts that "determined its character and foreshadowed its results." He emphasized that many of the facts presented by Sherman and Grant were alien to the actual battle. The tone of Buell's entire article reflected his contempt for the alleged misrepresentation of the facts. The problem for Buell, however, was that most Americans had come to believe the stories of Grant and Sherman, simply because of who they were and what they accomplished in the war.[31]

When "Shiloh Reviewed" appeared in early 1886, several friends sent Buell notes of congratulations. Although many had been convinced that before Buell's article "the whole truth of history [had] not been presented by the records," they had come to believe "that an impartial review of the campaign will prove that [Buell's] opportune arrival at Shiloh not only changed a doubtful condition into complete victory, but secured still more important results otherwise unattainable."[32] Longtime friend Thomas Gantt wrote from St. Louis that although Sherman would certainly assail Buell, "I think," he concluded, "the almost universal opinion is that your article has closed the controversy about Shiloh."[33]

Buell exhausted his thoughts and anger with the Shiloh essay, but Fry remained obsessed with getting back at Sherman. He continued to defend Buell's role and that of his army in 1862, but this only reflected poorly on Buell. At one point Fry goaded Sherman into denying he had made some disparaging remarks about the now-deceased Grant; both Fry and Sherman knew that if the remarks were ever made public, it would cost Sherman dearly. The feud continued between Sherman and Fry for several months, and Fry wrote Buell about the entire affair. For Buell, however, whatever success he could claim by arguing that he saved Grant at Shiloh was eclipsed by his failure during the war. Even in his death, Grant's brilliant career went a long way in diminishing any imperfections he might have exhibited during those few days in early April. He had even been charitable to Buell in his memoirs, characterizing Buell as brave and intelligent, with tremendous professional pride. Buell commanded respect from all who knew him, argued Grant. Still, Grant's kind words did little to secure a favorable legacy for Buell.[34]

A year after the publication of Buell's essay, in the midst of the impasse with Fry, Sherman commented to his nephew not to pay attention to Buell's anti-Grant account of Shiloh, concluding, "Let it fail still born. Thousands—millions—will read Grant's simple account who may never have the patience to compare the two accounts."[35] Almost as if to end the dispute once and for all, Buell wrote to Fry later that he personally thought the disaster at Shiloh was the responsibility of Grant and Sherman, and that Sherman's version of the battle was nothing more than self-flattery and self-glorification.[36]

Contemporary critics and later scholars characterized Buell's Shiloh debates as persistent self-aggrandizement stemming from the fact that he was relieved under a cloud of controversy and remained shelved for the duration of the war. As destitute as he was, however, Buell sought none of the personal notoriety that might have come from debating the old war stories. Had he wanted that, he might have written his memoirs or even McClellan's biography. Instead, when reminiscing about Shiloh, he remarked to Fry that the flaws in Grant's and Sherman's accounts were due partly to "ignorance" and partly "to a confusion of ideas that sometimes overtakes men in disaster."[37]

The Shiloh article was not the only essay Buell wrote. He also wrote articles on East Tennessee and the Perryville campaign and his march across northern Alabama. Though he had not intended the essay on Perryville to refute what others had said about the campaign, he nonetheless resorted to the same defense mentality. In this essay he devoted considerable attention to logistical problems and Halleck's failure to keep the Confederates occupied at other points while he marched east. As in the Shiloh essay, he hoped to present a clear and incontrovertible case for his conduct during the campaign. He felt slighted by the criticism that mounted after the battle of Perryville. Still, the focus of the essay, like that on Shiloh, was less on the events and more in pointing out the many problems he encountered, thereby demonstrating his defensive, argumentative, and confrontational attitude. Thus, while some of his friends thought him justified in his defense, his critics continued to think him petty. The articles, therefore, did little to restore his reputation as a commander or a strategist. In fact, they may have done just the opposite, since postwar critics may have viewed them as damning confirmation that he really was sympathetic to the South and feared the Confederates. If nothing more, they proved him as uncooperative and inflexible in his assessment of the events as he had been during the unfolding of them. These were exactly the traits his critics found most intolerable about him while in command. Thus, his continued insistence that he was not at fault during the Chattanooga campaign, the Kentucky campaign, or in getting to Shiloh led many to assume that he probably was.[38]

In 1885, in the midst of the war of words, President Grover Cleveland helped to relieve Buell's financial embarrassment by granting him a four-year appointment as pension agent for Kentucky, which required Buell and his daughter Nannie Mason to move to Louisville. Some viewed it as evidence of a returning sense of public justice for Buell. Louisville was a nice reprieve from the loneliness and desolation of an estate that not only had deteriorated but also was a reminder of his wife. Louisville was a bustling city with considerable distractions, and his published article in *Century Magazine* at least gave him celebrity status. Besides, the residents had always held Buell in high regard and made his stay in the city quite pleasant. Though he took few excursions outside the city, except to Airdrie, he had frequent visitors. When he returned to Airdrie in 1890 with his daughter, however, his financial burdens had worsened, although he managed to endure the hardships. The failure of his business had cost him everything, forcing him to sell almost all of his land. When Grover Cleveland returned to the presidency in 1893, Buell's close friend Thomas J. Bush unsuccessfully attempted to secure a government appointment for Buell.[39]

There were in these last years a few occasions upon which Buell came to public attention. In the same year he returned to Airdrie, the Shiloh National Park Commission was organized, and he became one of its members. Even before Congress approved the park's creation, Buell had already involved himself in the discussions to bring about the military park. He pored over Sherman's and Grant's publications of the battle and over Sherman's map, as well as other publications of soldiers who participated in the battle. In his effort to ensure that justice would be done to all who fought, Buell proved as meticulous in matters of detail as he had been during the war. He was tireless in his labors to see that the commission acquired the relevant land on which the battle was fought and interviewed residents as to geographic features at the time of the battle. He spent hours attempting to establish previous camp and burial locations and exact troop figures. He made every attempt to ensure that proper and accurate maps detailing the battle were drafted, to the point that he even prepared his own, though he died before its completion. Still, even in his waning years, Buell confided to Shiloh commissioner Col. R. F. Looney that he had "no cause to repel the false and scandalous assumptions which Grant and Sherman grew at last to put forward with unblushing affrontary." He always maintained, however, that Grant was defeated the first day and that the Army of the Ohio was responsible for the Union victory. Though his health was declining, he continued to serve on the commission until he died.[40]

Buell's last years were not happy. His ill health and financial worries restricted his mobility. In the summer of 1896, however, Buell made his last formal public appearance at an Army of the Ohio reunion, though he was physically incapable of making a speech. When he was asked to contribute an article and a photograph to the *Confederate Veteran*, he refused, not only because he lacked the physical abilities to do so, but also because he had remained so much the recluse that he had not had his picture taken for more than thirty years. Indeed, Buell was a private man.[41]

Buell spent his final years in seclusion, poverty, and obscurity. By the fall of 1898 he was completely disabled. His condition compelled Nannie Mason to carry on the correspondence with the Shiloh Battlefield commissioners. One month before his death, Buell wrote to former Union general Henry V. Boynton, president of the Society of the Army of the Cumberland, that his condition had been aggravated by the apprehension that he would not be able to complete a "suitable and faithful map of the battle of Shiloh." Without his map, he confided, the Shiloh commission would influence public opinion that the Army of the Tennessee, and Grant's and Sherman's connection with it, had eclipsed the efforts of the Army of the Ohio at that battle. A few weeks later, on the afternoon of November 19, Buell passed away. He had arranged to have his funeral services at St. Francis Xavier's Catholic Church and to be buried in Bellefontaine Cemetery in St. Louis beside his wife and her first husband, Richard Barnes Mason. Despite living in seclusion his last few years, Buell had made friends with several prominent members of the Catholic hierarchy during his lifetime, including archbishops from Philadelphia and Louisville. Though few of his wartime friends lived to see his death, those who did remembered him fondly. Letters written after his death recalled his long service as a soldier in many wars, his duty and patriotism to the Union, and his sense of justice and integrity as a gentleman and an officer. In all the years he had known Buell, "not once," wrote a friend, "did he as much as intimate to me that the Government had given him little or no reward for the services he had rendered in peace and in war." Still, the national newspapers hardly noticed his passing, and those that did failed to concede his importance as a Union commander. The *Louisville Times*, however, was among the few regional papers that devoted considerable space to his obituary. Ending what was indeed the most charitable eulogy to Buell, the editor wrote that he was "cast in the mold of Robert E. Lee, a soldier, a gentleman, a christian."[42]

Though Buell outlived Grant, Sherman, Halleck, and McClellan, he had not lasted the great race of the Civil War that Sherman had written about many years before. Obviously, the end was not all that was remembered about the Civil War. Alexander McClure, the Pennsylvania editor, legislator, attorney, assistant adjutant general, and associate of President Abraham Lincoln, wrote fondly of Buell in his 1892 volume, *Abraham Lincoln and Men of War-Times*. Buell was not only a soldier himself, wrote McClure, but "made a soldier of every man in his command as far as he could be obeyed." As if to bring closure about Shiloh, McClure argued that the battle was won only because of the timely arrival of Buell, "whose energy and skill as a soldier brought relief to Grant," who had been beaten the first day. He wrote that political clamor and not military necessity or even military expediency made the War Department relieve Buell. Buell, he argued, had been relieved as a result of the intense partisan hatred. "Thus ended," concluded McClure, "the military career of one who could and should have been one of the great military leaders of our civil war."[43] The fact remained, however, that Buell was not.

By the turn of the century, writers on the war had not forgotten Buell. Few persons wrote in simple general terms of their onetime commander. In their postwar regimentals and reminiscences, soldiers of the Army of the Ohio both reveled in and chafed at fighting under Buell. Journalists who accompanied his army reflected the same kinds of sentiments in their editorials. Politicians hardly ever favored him with a compliment. Despite whatever pleas Buell himself made or persons made on his behalf to restore his reputation for posterity, those who looked beyond the events of 1862 came to believe that Buell's removal from the race actually contributed to the victory. His refusal to return under the cloud of not wanting to fight an abolitionist war confirmed what critics wanted to believe about him. His heart was not in the war. For having repeatedly thwarted President Lincoln's attempts to end the war quickly, both by his conciliation and by his lack of aggression and battlefield success, they dubbed Buell a failure. In the celebration of the Union victory there was no celebration of Buell's role in it. Though he lasted just over a year in the war, his attitude and campaigns, like those of McClellan, were useful examples from which others drew valuable lessons. The problem for Buell, however, was that just as the Union learned from Grant's successes, so too did it learn from Buell's failures. For a commander who was positioned in perhaps the most important region to the Union and who had a major impact on the Union's handling of that region, Buell's was a negative influence and legacy. Whatever difficulties the Union had reconciling the military and political direction of the war, Buell provided perhaps the most valuable of all lessons that walking backward toward the Confederates was not going to bring success.

As a commander Buell is certainly visible in the history of the war, if only for a brief period. Few could deny that he had some remarkable qualities: his tireless energy, his personal bravery, and his unrelenting diligence in drilling, disciplining, and handling a large army. Though he made few close friends, he was nonetheless loyal to them and trusted their loyalty. As reserved and self-absorbed as he was, he was still exceedingly polite in manner and expression and sensitive to matters of the army. Still, his liabilities as a commander always eclipsed his assets. He never inspired loyalty or even devotion from his soldiers. If his appearance and tone gave evidence of aggressiveness, he never revealed the aggressive instinct. As a strategist he understood that defeating or capturing the enemy was important; he simply insisted that the occupation or defense of strategic places was more important.

Over the course of the twentieth century, scholars of the Civil War who have examined the conflict beyond the Appalachian Mountains have been unanimous in assessing Buell as a failure. Why he failed has elicited explanations that he never marched as the enemy marched, lived as the enemy lived, or fought as the enemy fought. Lincoln removed generals like Buell, wrote T. Harry Williams, because they "never fought because they never finished preparing." Allan Nevins renewed a contemporary criticism of Buell that charged he lacked initiative. "He hesitated when action was called for," wrote Nevins, "and when committed to action he still hesitated." In the end, his want of aggressive vigor ruined him, as most historians seem to agree that Buell feared combat more than he feared defeat. Most recently, James McPherson argued that Buell was too cautious and was "not the general to march and fight while living off the country." Still, Nevins conceded that "his clear-sighted activities did the Union great service."[44]

Buell lived a life of self-imposed rigid principles and fixed rules, seldom if ever recognizing that compromise might better suit some circumstances. He cared nothing for popularity or the approval of others, yet he felt compelled in his later years to defend his reputation—a reputation that had long been tarnished by the cumulative effects of failing to conform his war aims to those of his political and military superiors. In the end Buell hoped history would do him justice. Tragically, he died without recognizing that his story had been written in the collective memory of Americans who came to believe he was a failure. Consequently, Buell's life ended the way it began, in obscurity.

Notes

· ·

ABBREVIATIONS AND NOTE ON SOURCES

AGO	War Department, Adjutant General's Office
Army Returns	War Department, Adjutant General's Office, Returns from the Regular Army Infantry Regiments, Third Infantry Regiment, 1841–61
BC	Bellefontaine Cemetery, St. Louis, Mo.
Buell's Court Martial File	Records of the Office of the Judge Advocate General (Army), Court Martial Case Files, 1809–94, Don Carlos Buell File
Buell's Statement	War Department, Adjutant General's Office, Statement of Military Service, March 13, 1890, Don Carlos Buell
CCNMP	Chickamauga and Chattanooga National Military Park, Fort Oglethorpe, Ga.
CHS	Chicago Historical Society, Chicago, Ill.
CGS	Claremont Graduate School, Claremont, Calif.
CWMC	Civil War Miscellaneous Collection
CWTIC	Civil War Times Illustrated Collection
DU	Duke University, William R. Perkins Library, Durham, N.C.
FC	Filson Club, Louisville, Ky.
FDS	Florida Department of State, Division of Historical Resources Bureau of Archaeological Research, Tallahassee, Florida Master Site File
GHP	Gunston Hall Plantation, Mason Neck, Va.
GO	United States Adjutant General's Office, General Orders
HCWRTC	Harrisburg Civil War Roundtable Collection
HL	Huntington Library, San Marino, Calif.
ISHL	Illinois State Historical Library, Springfield
IHS	Indiana Historical Society, William Smith Library, Indianapolis
ISA	Indiana State Archives, Indianapolis
IU	Indiana University, Lilly Library, Archives, Bloomington
KHS	Kentucky Historical Society, Frankfort
LC	Library of Congress, Washington, D.C.
MHS	Missouri Historical Society, St. Louis
NA	National Archives and Records Administration, Washington, D.C.
OHS	Ohio Historical Society, Columbus
OR	U.S. War Department. *The War of the Rebellion: A Compilation of the Official Records of the Union and Confederate Armies.* 128 vols. Washington, D.C.: Government Printing Office, 1880–1901. All references are to series 1 unless otherwise noted.

Post Returns	War Department, Adjutant General's Office, Returns from United States Military Posts, 1800–1916, Third Infantry Regiment, 1841–61
RG	Record Group
RU	Rice University, Fondren Library, Archives, Houston, Tex.
Senate Documents	U.S. Congress. *Public Documents Printed by the Order of the Senate of the United States.* No. 71. 28th Cong., 1st sess. Serial no. 432. Vol. 2, 1843–44.
SHC	University of North Carolina, Southern Historical Collection, Wilson Library, Chapel Hill
TC	Sheila Tschumy, Private Collection, Dallas, Tex.
TSLA	Tennessee Department of State Library and Archives, Nashville
UC	University of Chicago, Joseph Regenstein Library, Archives, Chicago, Ill.
UK	University of Kentucky Library, Archives, Lexington
UMBHL	University of Michigan, Bentley Historical Library, Ann Arbor
UMWCL	University of Michigan, William L. Clements Library, Ann Arbor, Schoff Civil War Collection
UND	University of Notre Dame, Archives, South Bend, Ind.
USAMHI	United States Army Military History Institute, Carlisle Barracks, Pa.
USMA-A	United States Military Academy, Archives, West Point, N.Y.
USMA-SC	United States Military Academy, Special Collections, West Point, N.Y.
WKU	Western Kentucky University, Bowling Green, Hartford Collection
WRHS	Western Reserve Historical Society, Cleveland, Ohio

Note: Only after I had completed the manuscript did I learn that the entire Buell collection, which was in the possession of Rice University when I obtained it on microfilm in 1990, had been acquired by the Filson Club Historical Society in 1997. It is a Buell collection different from the one cited in the endnotes from the Filson Club. Thus, the citations to Rice University should now also read Filson Club, but given the untimely transfer of such an extensive collection, I simply cited the papers from where I obtained them.

CHAPTER 1

1. Welles, *Buell Family*, 1:1–25; Thomas R. Buell, *Genealogic Notes*, 5–6; Johnson and Malone, *Dictionary of American Biography*, 3:240–41.

2. Welles, *Buell Family*, 1:1–25; Schneider, *Lowell and Adams Township*, 8–9; Thomas R. Buell, *Genealogic Notes*, 5–9; Martin R. Andrews, *Marietta and Washington County*, 1:697.

3. Thomas R. Buell, *Genealogic Notes*, 5–13; Welles, *Buell Family*, 2:255–59. See also "Buell Family History," Buell Papers, RU.

4. Washington County Census, the village of Lowell had three abortive starts and several names before it was finally incorporated as Buell's Lowell in 1851. At the time of Don Carlos Buell's childhood there were two villages, Upper Lowell and Buell's Lowell, founded by the Buell brothers, Salmon and Perez Barnum. Upper Lowell eventually disappeared as a trading center, but Buell's Lowell continued to prosper.

5. Welles, *Buell Family*, 2:243–84; Thomas R. Buell, *Genealogic Notes*, 11, 31–51; Johnson and Malone, *Dictionary of American Biography*, 3:240–41; Whitelaw D. Reid, *Ohio in the War*, 2:695; "Lingering in Lowell," 1–4; Mrs. Alma Lane to Mr. Buell, June 28, 1914, Buell Papers, TC; Buell to Nellie C. Martine, December 12, 1891, Buell Papers, RU. See also *Chicago Journal of Commerce*, in Buell File, USMA-SC. This is the first appearance of the name Don Carlos in the Buell lineage, and it is most likely that Maj. Gen. Don Carlos Buell was named for him.

6. Henry Howe, *Historical Collections*, 2:777–78; Washington County Census, 1820, Washington County, Ohio, on microfilm in Washington County Public Library; Schneider, *Lowell and Adams Township*, 8–9.

7. "Buell Family History," Buell Papers, RU; "Lingering in Lowell," 2–4; Schneider, *Lowell and Adams Township*, 8–9; Mrs. Alma Lane to Mr. Buell, June 28, 1914; Buell Papers, TC.

8. Scottsman to Buell, December 29, 1881, Buell Papers, RU; Mrs. Alma Lane to Mr. Buell, June 28, 1914, Buell Papers, TC.

9. Mrs. Alma Lane to Mr. Buell, February 21, 1913, June 28, 1914, Buell Papers, TC; Schneider, *Lowell and Adams Township*, 8–9, 14; "Lingering in Lowell," 2–5; Thomas R. Buell, *Genealogic Notes*, 13–14, 31–32; Welles, *Buell Family*, 2:243–84; Scottsman to Buell, December 29, 1881, Buell Papers, RU; Martin R. Andrews, *Marietta and Washington County*, 1:697; Whitelaw D. Reid, *Ohio in the War*, 2:695. William Scottsman's correspondence to Buell several years after the Civil War was mainly a reflection of his early life with his childhood friend Don Carlos. Although it appears as though he refers to Buell's mother in a letter describing his life with Don Carlos on the Muskingum River, he was obviously referring to Buell's father.

10. Thomas R. Buell, *Genealogic Notes*, 32–34; Welles, *Buell Family*, 2:243–84; "Buell Family History," Buell Papers, RU; Whitelaw D. Reid, *Ohio in the War*, 2:695; Mrs. Alma Lane to Mr. Buell, June 28, 1914, Buell Papers, TC.

11. Welles, *Buell Family*, 2:257–84; Thomas R. Buell, *Genealogic Notes*, 11–13; *History of Dearborn and Ohio Counties*, 647–48.

12. *History of Dearborn and Ohio Counties*, 647–49; Welles, *Buell Family*, 2:257–84; Thomas R. Buell, *Genealogic Notes*, 11–13. For information relating to Lawrenceburg, Indiana, and to George Pearson Buell's business, see, for example, the local newspapers, *Indiana Spectator*, January–April 1825, and *Indiana Palladium*, August–November 1825.

13. *History of Dearborn and Ohio Counties*, 242–67, 647–49; Welles, *Buell Family*, 2:257–83; *Indiana Palladium*, November 25, 1825; *Indiana Spectator*, January 8, April 15, 1825; Whitelaw D. Reid, *Ohio in the War*, 2:695–96.

14. Whitelaw D. Reid, *Ohio in the War*, 2:695–96; Welles, *Buell Family*, 2:255–59, 280–81; *History of Dearborn and Ohio Counties*, 243–67; Mrs. Alma Lane to Mr. Buell, June 28, 1914, Buell Papers, TC.

15. Whitelaw D. Reid, *Ohio in the War*, 2:695–96.

16. Ibid.; Welles, *Buell Family*, 2:255–58; Thomas R. Buell, *Genealogic Notes*, 13–33; *History of Dearborn and Ohio Counties*, 243–67.

17. *History of Dearborn and Ohio Counties*, 243–67; Welles, *Buell Family*, 2:257–82; *Indiana Palladium*, January–November 1825.

18. Whitelaw D. Reid, *Ohio in the War*, 2:695–96.

19. *History of Dearborn and Ohio Counties*, 225–30, 250–79; Whitelaw D. Reid, *Ohio in the War*, 2:695–96; *National Tribune*, November 24, 1898; *Indiana Whig*, April 18, May 10, 1834; Mrs. Alma Lane to Mr. Buell, June 28, 1914, Buell Papers, TC.

20. Whitelaw D. Reid, *Ohio in the War*, 2:695–96.

21. Application letter for Don Carlos Buell's admission into the U.S. Military Academy at West Point from Amos Lane to Acting Secretary of War Benjamin F. Butler, December 21, 1836, USMA-A; U.S. Military Academy, Cadet Application Papers, 1806–66, Don Carlos Buell, file #24, NA.

22. Letter of recommendation by the Citizens of Lawrenceburg, Indiana, to the Acting Secretary of War Benjamin F. Butler on behalf of Don Carlos Buell's application for admission to the U.S. Military Academy, January 3, 1837, USMA-A; U.S. Military Academy, Cadet Application Papers, 1806–66, Don Carlos Buell, file #24, NA.

23. U.S. Military Academy, Cadet Application Papers, 1806–66, Don Carlos Buell, file #24, NA; Post Orders, No. 6, 1832–37, USMA-A.

24. James L. Morrison, *"Best School in the World,"* 63–65; Stephen E. Ambrose, *Duty, Honor, Country*, 83–84.

25. *Regulations of the U.S. Military Academy*, 7; Cullum, *Biographical Register*, 2:26; U.S. Military Academy, *Official Register*, June 1837, 16.

26. James L. Morrison, *"Best School in the World,"* 23–24, 37–42; Stephen E. Ambrose, *Duty, Honor, Country*, 87–105, 125–26; U.S. Military Academy, *Official Register*, June 1837, 16. For a record of the exacting disciplinary regulations and curriculum instituted by Superintendent Sylvanus Thayer, see, for example, the 1832 version of the *Regulations of the U.S. Military Academy*, 6–51. These regulations were revised in 1838, the year after Buell was admitted, which reflected the rigid disciplinary regulations instituted by superintendent Maj. Richard Delafield.

27. James L. Morrison, *"Best School in the World,"* 64–65; *Regulations of the U.S. Military Academy*, 7; Stephen E. Ambrose, *Duty, Honor, Country*, 147–66.

28. Don Carlos Buell, Academic Record While a Cadet at the U.S. Military Academy, USMA-A; U.S. Military Academy, *Official Register*, 16; *Regulations of the U.S. Military Academy*, 23–24; James L. Morrison, *"Best School in the World,"* 23–25, 61–63, 71; Stephen E. Ambrose, *Duty, Honor, Country*, 125–26.

29. Stephen E. Ambrose, *Duty, Honor, Country*, 147; U.S. Military Academy, *Official Register*, "Cadets Arranged in Order of Merit in Their Respective Classes," June 1841, 7–10; James L. Morrison, *"Best School in the World,"* 61–63. In the spring of 1840, while Buell was a cadet at West Point, the military academy came under attack by several newspapers for illegalities committed by cadets, such as trading blankets and bedding for liquor, tobacco, and cigars, and bringing "naughty" women into the barracks. See, for example, *New York Herald*, June 24, May 30, 1840; *Citizen Soldier*, May 28, 1840. Whether Buell was involved in any of these activities is uncertain, since the records on the investigation did not directly implicate him. The *Citizen Sol-*

dier continued to attack the academy not only for these illegalities but also on the academy's selection process, essentially claiming that cadets came only from wealthy families.

30. *Regulations of the U.S. Military Academy,* 22−51; Stephen E. Ambrose, *Duty, Honor, Country,* 148−64; Mrs. Alma Lane to Mr. Buell, June 28, 1914, Buell Papers, TC.

31. *Regulations of the U.S. Military Academy,* 22−51; James L. Morrison, *"Best School in the World,"* 65−78; Stephen E. Ambrose, *Duty, Honor, Country,* 148−64.

32. U.S. Military Academy, *Official Register,* 6−18; James L. Morrison, *"Best School in the World,"* 65−69. For references to those cadets who participated in the Civil War, see, for example, Warner, *Generals in Blue,* 195, 286, 374, 396; Warner, *Generals in Gray,* 22, 112, 124; Boatner, *Civil War Dictionary,* 843.

33. Post Orders, No. 6, 1832−37, June and August 1837, and No. 7, January 10, 1838, and Register of Merit, 1836−53, No. 2, January 1838, 6−23, USMA-A; *Regulations of the U.S. Military Academy,* 8−9; Buell to Irvin McDowell, September 12, 1837, Buell Papers, RU; James L. Morrison, *"Best School in the World,"* 84−94.

34. Post Orders, No. 7, Orders No. 139, 1837−39, November 27, 1837, and Register of Cadet Delinquencies, 1834−39, 1:146, USMA-A.

35. Register of Cadet Delinquencies, 1834−39, 1:146, USMA-A; James L. Morrison, *"Best School in the World,"* 65−74. Evidently Buell appealed at least once to his superiors regarding the punishment he received for an infraction of disciplinary codes; see Buell to McDowell, September 13, 1837, Buell Papers, RU. According to the explanation of the "Conduct Roll" as found in U.S. Military Academy, *Official Register,* June 1838, 20, all offenses against orders or regulations are recorded. These offenses are divided into seven grades, each of which comprises those of nearly the same degree of criminality. The degree of criminality of offenses of each grade is expressed by a number as follows: offenses of the first grade by 10; of the second grade by 8; of the third grade by 5; of the fourth grade by 4, etc. For each year (after the first year) that a cadet has been a member of the institution, his offenses are made to count more, by adding to the numbers expressing the degree of criminality of each offense: one-sixth for his second year, one-third for his third, and one-half for his fourth year. At the end of the academic year, the offenses recorded against each cadet—that is, the numbers expressive of their criminality—are added up, and the sum is recorded in the column of "Demerit." When any cadet has a demerit number greater than 200, the cadet is declared deficient in conduct and recommended by the Academic Board to the War Department for discharge.

36. Lloyd Lewis, *Fighting Prophet,* 58; Post Orders, No. 7, Orders No. 21, 1837−39, February 20, 1838, USMA-A. See also Post Orders, No. 7, Orders No. 14, January 29, 1838, and Battalion Orders, No. 15, February 16, 1838, USMA-A.

37. *Regulations of the U.S. Military Academy,* 18; U.S. Military Academy, *Official Register,* June 1837, 14−17, 20−24; Register of Merit, 1836−53, No. 2, June 1838, 6−18, and Post Orders, No. 7, 1837−39, February 19, 1838, USMA-A; Record of Books Borrowed by Cadet Buell, Library Circulation Records, 1836−41, USMA-SC; *Daily National Intelligencer,* February 23, 1838.

38. *Regulations of the U.S. Military Academy,* 25−26; James L. Morrison, *"Best School in the World,"* 75−85; Stephen E. Ambrose, *Duty, Honor, Country,* 147−66. See also Stephen E. Ambrose, "Monotonous Life."

39. Register of Cadet Delinquencies, June–August 1838, 1:146, USMA-A.

40. *National Tribune,* January 21, 1891; U.S. Military Academy, *Official Register,* June 1837, 21–24; see also June 1838, 6–18; Warner, *Generals in Gray,* 314.

41. *National Tribune,* January 21, 1891.

42. Ibid. For John Pope's tenure at West Point, see Schutz and Trenerry, *Abandoned by Lincoln,* 9–16.

43. Post Orders, No. 7, 1837–39, Orders No. 126, September 1, 1838, USMA-A; James L. Morrison, *"Best School in the World,"* 39–40; Stephen E. Ambrose, *Duty, Honor, Country,* 125–26.

44. Register of Merit, 1836–53, No. 2, January 1839, 6–23, and Post Orders, No. 7, 1837–39, January 17, 1839, USMA-A; James L. Morrison, *"Best School in the World,"* 90–94; *Regulations of the U.S. Military Academy,* 8–13.

45. Post Orders, No. 7, 1837–39, Orders No. 18, March 14, 1839, USMA-A; U.S. Military Academy, *Official Register,* June 1839, 21–24.

46. Register of Merit, 1836–53, No. 2, June 1839, 6–18, USMA-A; U.S. Military Academy, *Official Register,* June 1839, 19–24.

47. U.S. Military Academy, *Official Register,* June 1839, 6–24; Register of Merit, 1836–53, No. 2, January 1840, 6–18, USMA-A; James L. Morrison, *"Best School in the World,"* 90–98; *Regulations of the U.S. Military Academy,* 8–20. Buell ranked highest in drawing of all the courses he took at West Point. In his third year he ranked tenth in his class, while in chemistry and philosophy, for example, his scores ranked him forty-fifth and twenty-sixth, respectively.

48. Register of Merit, 1836–53, No. 2, June 1839, 6–18, and Register of Cadet Delinquencies, January–June 1840, 1:435–37 (see, for example, February 7, 9, 1840), USMA-A; U.S. Military Academy, *Official Register,* January, June 1840, 6–24; Welles, *Buell Family,* 2:255–84. Although Buell's younger sister Sallie Maria married George W. Lane (Buell's cousin) of Lawrenceburg, Indiana, in March 1840, Buell evidently did not attend the wedding, since he did not apply for a furlough that month. Given his academic and conduct record, even if he had applied for a furlough, it would have probably been denied, since he had been away without leave several times and severely reprimanded in his third year.

49. U.S. Military Academy, *Official Register,* "Explanation of the Conduct Roll, of the Roll of the Cadets Arranged According to Merit in Conduct," June 1838, 20.

50. Military Service Institute, *Letters and Addresses,* 17–18; Jordan, *Hancock,* 7–11; U.S. Military Academy, *Official Register,* "Cadets Arranged in Order of Merit in Their Respective Classes as Determined at the General Examination," June 1840, 8–9, and June 1841, 9–10.

51. U.S. Military Academy, *Official Register,* "Cadets Arranged in Order of Merit in Their Respective Classes as Determined at the General Examination," June 1840, 8–9, and June 1841, 9–10; *Regulations of the U.S. Military Academy,* 8–14; James L. Morrison, *"Best School in the World,"* 94–101; Stephen E. Ambrose, *Duty, Honor, Country,* 100–103.

52. *Regulations of the U.S. Military Academy,* 8–20; U.S. Military Academy, *Official Register,* June 1841, 9–10; Register of Merit, 1836–53, No. 2, January–June 1841, and Register of Cadet Delinquencies, September–June 1840–41, 1:436, USMA-A.

53. Register of Merit, 1836–53, No. 2, June 1841, 9–10, Roll of the Cadets

Arranged According to Merit in Conduct, 19–21; Register of Cadet Delinquencies, June–September 1840–41, 1:436; Staff Records, 1835–42, June 1841, 2:303, all in USMA-A; Phillips, *Damned Yankee*, 25.

54. Mahan to McClellan, August 3, 1861, McClellan Papers, LC; Register of Cadet Delinquencies, June–September 1840–41, 1:436, USMA-A. See Buell's Academic Record, USMA-A.

55. See, for example, Marszalek, *Sherman*, 28; Register of Cadet Delinquencies, June–September 1840–41, 1:436, USMA-A. See also Buell's Academic Record, USMA-A.

CHAPTER 2

1. Cullum, *Biographical Register*, 2:26; U.S. Military Academy, *Official Register*, June 1841, 9–22; Buell's Academic Record, USMA-A.

2. General Orders No. 47, 1–5, GO, 1837–45, RG 94, NA; Cullum, *Biographical Register*, 2:2–37; Buell File, USMA-SC; *Army and Navy Chronicle*, September 9, 1841, 286–87.

3. Army Returns, November 1841, RG 94, NA. On the unpopularity of the war, see, for example, *Daily National Intelligencer*, 1841–42; *Army and Navy Chronicle*, October 21, 1841, 385; Josephy, *Patriot Chiefs*, 177; Sidney Walter Martin, *Territorial Days*, 190–91, 236–37; Mahon, *Seminole War*, 1–17, 100–107, 294–309; Sprague, *Florida War*, 89–92, 266–348; Coffman, *Old Army*, 50–54.

4. Rodenbough and Haskin, *Army of the United States*, 434–35; Sprague, *Florida War*, 247–97, 487–88; Roberts, *Historic Forts*, 208; Army Returns, January–May, November–December 1841, RG 94, NA; Mahon, *Seminole War*, 295, 316–18; Sidney Walter Martin, *Territorial Days*, 237–38; Edward Wallace, *Worth*, 52–61; *Leon County News*, July 5, 1985; *Tallahassee Democrat*, April 12, 1964; Heitman, *Historical Register*, 1:85–87. Although the officers in command of the Third Infantry during Buell's tenure in the Seminole War included Col. James B. Many, Lieut. Ethan Allen Hitchcock, and Maj. William Lear (Capt. Philip N. Barbour was regimental adjutant June 1, 1838–October 12, 1845), the leadership of the regiment often fell on men of lesser rank.

5. General Orders No. 37, GO, 1837–45, RG 94, NA. See also Henry Wilson to Adjutant General, September 7, 9, 1841; Israel B. Richardson to Capt. L. N. Morris, November 8, 1841; Worth to Adjutant General, August 8, 27, October 9, 25, November 4, 15, 1841, Letters Received, AGO, RG 94, NA. See also Roberts, *Historic Forts*, 208; Mahon, *Seminole War*, 295, 300–309, 316–18; Sprague, *Florida War*, 247–97, 293–303, 319–20, 330–33, 354, 378–80, 396–402, 487–88; Rodenbough and Haskin, *Army of the United States*, 434–35; *Leon County News*, July 5, 1985; *Tallahassee Democrat*, April 12, 1964; Edward Wallace, *Worth*, 52–55.

6. Sprague, *Florida War*, 308, 396–99, 429–35; William Jenkins Worth to Acting Adjutant General and Commanding Officer, November 15, 1841, and Worth to Adjutant General, January 31, February 5, 18, April 21, 29, 1842, Letters Received, AGO, RG 94, NA; Roberts, *Historic Forts*, 207; Rodenbough and Haskin, *Army of the United States*, 434–35; *Leon County News*, July 5, 1985; *Tallahassee Democrat*, April 12,

1964; File Wa 103, Fort Stansbury, FDS. These records are typescripts of original reports sent to the adjutant general; on Buell's record during the Seminole War, see, for example, Post Returns, Fort Aucilla, November, December 1841, RG 94, NA. See also Army Returns, July–December 1842, RG 94, NA.

7. John H. Kendall to Buell, March 16, 1877, Buell Papers, RU. Kendall was a sergeant in the Third U.S. Infantry and was apparently in Buell's company.

8. Ibid.

9. Cullum, *Biographical Register*, 2:1–37; General Orders No. 47, August 23, 1841, 1–5, GO, 1837–45, RG 94, NA.

10. Mahon, *Seminole War*, 309–27; Sprague, *Florida War*, 440–45; Worth to Adjutant General, February 5, 1842, Letters Received, AGO, RG 94, NA; Croffut, *Fifty Years*, 166–68.

11. Mahon, *Seminole War*, 122–23, 154, 323–24; Sprague, *Florida War*, 248–60, 280–81, 469.

12. Rodenbough and Haskin, *Army of the United States*, 435; Josiah H. Vose to Adjutant General, August 20, 23, September 6, 26, 29, 1842, and Worth to Adjutant General, August 12, 1842, Letters Received, AGO, and General Orders No. 28, August 17, 1842, GO, 1837–45, RG 94, NA; Sprague, *Florida War*, 475–502; Post Returns, June–August 1842, and Army Returns, December 1842, RG 94, NA; McCall, *Letters from the Frontier*, 411–12; Powell, *Fourth Regiment*, 34–37; Edward Wallace, *Worth*, 53–61; Mahon, *Seminole War*, 309–18; Croffut, *Fifty Years*, 163–67.

13. Croffut, *Fifty Years*, 176–75; Mahon, *Seminole War*, 317–18; Sprague, *Florida War*, 498–553; Sidney Walter Martin, *Territorial Days*, 238; Reports of Ethan Allen Hitchcock, February 20, April 5, 1843, file Wa 103, FDS; Army Returns, March–April 1843, RG 94, NA.

14. Rodenbough and Haskin, *Army of the United States*, 435; Sprague, *Florida War*, 506–7, 539; Army Returns, April 1843, RG 94, NA; McCall, *Letters from the Frontier*, 411–12; Grant, *Memoirs*, 1:32–36; Croffut, *Fifty Years*, 175, 180–81; *Leon County News*, 5 July 1985; *Army and Navy Chronicle*, 20 April 1843, 476, 18 May 1843, 607–8; Webb, "Jefferson Barracks," 202–7.

15. Rodenbough and Haskin, *Army of the United States*, 435; Mahon, *Seminole War*, 317–18; Sprague, *Florida War*, 498–507; Griess and Luvas, *Centennial of the United States Military Academy*, 1:534–51; Cullum, *Biographical Register*, 2:5–37.

16. Grant, *Memoirs*, 1:32; Powell, *Fourth Regiment*, 37; Rodenbough and Haskin, *Army of the United States*, 435; Army Returns, April–June 1843, RG 94, NA; Webb, "Jefferson Barracks," 202–7; Sprague, *Florida War*, 498–507, 539. See also April 22, 1843, Letters Received, AGO, RG 94, NA; Clarke, *Kearny*, 83–91; Croffut, *Fifty Years*, 181–83.

17. Buell's Defense, June 19, 1843, Buell's Court Martial File, RG 153, NA; see also Report of Samuel Cooper, Assistant Adjutant General, July 1, 1843, and letter from Ethan Allen Hitchcock to Roger Jones, Adjutant General, February 17, 1845, ibid., regarding the death of Private Humphrey in mid-February 1845. Apparently Humphrey was killed by a citizen at Fort Jesup, Louisiana, for abrupt attitude and unmannerly conduct at a house of ill fame. Hitchcock was writing on Buell's behalf and essentially confirmed what had already been known about Private Humphrey. The actual court-martial proceedings can also be found in *Senate Documents*.

18. Buell's Defense, June 19, 1843, and Report of Samuel Cooper, July 1, 1843, Buell's Court Martial File, RG 153, NA; *Senate Documents*, 3–4, 10–14.

19. Proceedings of the Court Martial, June 14, 1843, Buell's Court Martial File, RG 153, NA; Buell conducted his own defense and the questioning of Private Humphrey. See also *Senate Documents*, 3–5.

20. Proceedings of the Court Martial, June 15, 1843, Buell's Court Martial File, RG 153, NA; General Orders No. 2, Report of Secretary of War John M. Porter, December 23, 1843, GO, 1837–45, RG 94, NA; *Army and Navy Chronicle*, March 14, 1844, 321–38.

21. Buell's Defense, June 19, 1843, and Proceedings of the Court Martial, June 10, 1843, Buell's Court Martial File, RG 153, NA; *Senate Documents*, 2–3, 10–16. Besides Major Lear, the members of the court included Capt. Henry Swartwout, Third Infantry (appointed judge advocate); Capt. Henry Bainbridge, Third Infantry; Capt. John W. Cotton, Third Infantry; Capt. Gouverneur Morris, Fourth Infantry; Capt. Charles H. Larnard (who graduated from West Point as C. H. Larned), Fourth Infantry; 1st Lt. Richard M. Cochrane, Fourth Infantry; 1st Lt. William H. Gordon, Third Infantry; 1st Lt. Douglass S. Irwin, Third Infantry; 1st Lt. Stephen D. Dobbins, Third Infantry; 2d Lt. Thomas Jordan, Third Infantry; 2d Lt. H. Ridgely, Fourth Infantry; 2d Lt. Richard H. Bacot, Third Infantry; and 2d Lt. Jenks Beaman, Fourth Infantry. See also Wilcox, *Mexican War*, 632–34; Heitman, *Historical Register*, 1:329, 616.

22. Buell's Defense, June 19, 1843, Buell's Court Martial File, RG 153, NA; *Senate Documents*, 10–11.

23. Buell's Defense, June 19, 1843, Buell's Court Martial File, RG 153, NA; *Senate Documents*, 10; Army Returns, June 1843, RG 94, NA.

24. Proceedings of the Court Martial, June 19, 1843, Buell's Court Martial File, RG 153, NA; General Orders No. 51, July 27, 1843, GO, 1837–45, RG 94, NA; *Army and Navy Chronicle*, March 14, 1844, 321–38; *Senate Documents*, 10; Army Returns, July 1843, RG 94, NA; Webb, "Jefferson Barracks," 202–7.

25. General Orders No. 4, July 10, 1843, and No. 51, July 27, 1843, Report of Adjutant General Roger Jones, GO, 1837–45, RG 94, NA; see also Report of Samuel Cooper, July 1, 10, 1843, Buell's Court Martial File, RG 153, NA; Clarke, *Kearny*, 83–91; Silver, *Gaines*, 163–64; General Orders No. 4, July 22, 1843, Report of Cooper, GO, 1837–45, RG 94, also found in Buell's Court Martial File, RG 153, NA; *Senate Documents*, 13–15; Skelton, *American Profession of Arms*, 272.

26. Proceedings of the Court Martial, July 5, 1843, Buell's Court Martial File, RG 153, NA; *Senate Documents*, 14–15; Croffut, *Fifty Years*, 183.

27. Proceedings of the Court Martial, July 5, 1843, and Report of Samuel Cooper, July 10, 1843, Buell's Court Martial File, RG 153, NA; General Orders No. 4, July 22, 1843, Report of Cooper, GO, 1837–45, RG 94, NA; Croffut, *Fifty Years*, 183.

28. Proceedings of the Court Martial, July 5, 1843, and Report of Samuel Cooper, July 10, 1843, Buell's Court Martial File, RG 153, NA; *Army and Navy Chronicle*, March 14, 1844, 321–38.

29. Report of Samuel Cooper, July 10, 1843, Buell's Court Martial File, RG 153, NA; *Senate Documents*, 16–20.

30. *Senate Documents*, 16–20; Croffut, *Fifty Years*, 183; Report of Samuel Cooper, July 10, 1843, Buell's Court Martial File, RG 153, NA.

31. Proceedings of the Court Martial, Report of General Winfield Scott, July 22, 25, 1843, Buell's Court Martial File, RG 153, NA; *Senate Documents*, 20.

32. Proceedings of the Court Martial, Report of Scott, July 22, 25, 1843, Buell's Court Martial File, RG 153, NA; *Senate Documents*, 20.

33. *Senate Documents*, 20.

34. General Orders No. 2, December 23, 1843, Report of Porter, and No. 51, Report of Jones, July 27, 1843, GO, 1837–45, RG 94, NA; *Senate Documents*, 20–21; *Army and Navy Chronicle*, March 14, 1844, 327–38; Croffut, *Fifty Years*, 183–84.

35. Ethan Allen Hitchcock to President John Tyler, June 20, 1844, Hitchcock Papers, USMA-SC; Croffut, *Fifty Years*, 183–84, 204; *Army and Navy Chronicle*, March 14, 1844, 327–32. See also Proceedings of the Court Martial, Buell's Court Martial File, RG 153, NA. Hitchcock had ordered a copy of the work on courts-martial and, after carefully examining *Simmons on Practice of Courts Martial*, claimed that "the extract furnished by the late Secretary of War to sustain the opinion he expressed is garbled and show of a material portion of the passage in Simmons and has the effect of a fraud; and if the omission of the material portion of that passage was knowingly and designedly made, I charge that the late Secretary of War was guilty of a fraud." Hitchcock made this claim by using supporting evidence from Simmons's work published in 1843, which essentially said that a prisoner "cannot legally be brought to trial a second time upon the same charge." He was concerned about the responsibility of the court and the role of the secretary of war in these matters, since he may at some point be affected by Porter's erroneous doctrine that was common to all officers. See also Edmund P. Gaines to William Wilkins, newly appointed Secretary of War, February 29, 1844, Hitchcock Papers, MHS. Gaines wrote a scathing attack on Winfield Scott's handling of the Buell case.

36. *Army and Navy Chronicle*, March 14, 1844, 333; see also Proceedings of the Court Martial, Testimony of the Witnesses, Buell's Court Martial File, RG 153, NA.

37. Proceedings of the Court Martial, Report of Samuel Cooper, July 10, 22, 1843, Buell's Court Martial File, RG 153, and General Orders No. 4, July 10, 1843, GO, 1837–45, RG 94, NA.

38. General Orders No. 2, Report of President John Tyler, January 10, 1844, GO, 1837–45, RG 94, NA; *Army and Navy Chronicle*, March 14, 1844, 329; *Senate Documents*, 14–21; Allen, *Adjutant General's Department*, 48, 66.

39. Proceedings of the Court Martial, Report of Samuel Cooper, July 10, 22, 1843, Buell's Court Martial File, RG 153, NA; *Senate Documents*, 5–20.

40. *Army and Navy Chronicle*, March 14, 1844, 321–32; Rodenbough and Haskin, *Army of the United States*, 435; Army Returns, December 1843, RG 94, NA.

41. Grant, *Memoirs*, 1:35–39; Powell, *Fourth Regiment*, 36–38; Roberts, *Historic Forts*, 341, 353–55; Croffut, *Fifty Years*, 185; Ethan Allen Hitchcock to President John Tyler, June 20, 1844, Hitchcock Papers, USMA-SC; Rodenbough and Haskin, *Army of the United States*, 435–36; Army Returns, May–June 1844, RG 94, NA; Bauer, *Mexican War*, 3–15; Bauer, *Taylor*, 11–117; *Third Infantry Day*, 9.

42. Bauer, *Mexican War*, 7–19; U.S. Congress, *Congressional Globe*, 28th Cong., 1st sess., 16–372; Mansfield, *Mexican War*, 15–21; Sellers, *Polk*, 2:215–19; Chitwood, *Tyler*, 343–66; Peterson, *Presidencies of William Henry Harrison and John Tyler*, 229–59. The joint resolution proposed by president-elect James K. Polk was essentially a

strategy to bypass the requirement of a two-thirds vote of the Senate alone, customary in ratifying a treaty.

43. Grant, *Memoirs*, 1:45; Zachary Taylor to Adjutant General, June 30, 1845, in U.S. Congress, *House Executive Documents*, 30th Cong., 1st sess., no. 60, Mexican War Correspondence, 801, 804–6; Sellers, *Polk*, 2:216–18; Croffut, *Fifty Years*, 192–95; Bauer, *Mexican War*, 18–19, 25–34; Rodenbough and Haskin, *Army of the United States*, 436; Powell, *Fourth Regiment*, 38; Justin Smith, *War With Mexico* 1:140–43; Roberts, *Historic Forts*, 355, 769; Army Returns, July–August 1845, RG 94, NA.

44. Grant, *Memoirs*, 1:56; Croffut, *Fifty Years*, 196–201.

CHAPTER 3

1. William S. Henry, *Campaign Sketches*, 11–26; Grant, *Memoirs*, 1:45; Bauer, *Mexican War*, 32; *Niles National Register*, September 20, 1845, 36; Darwin Payne, "Camp Life," 326–29; Croffut, *Fifty Years*, 195; Wilcox, *Mexican War*, 630–32; Justin Smith, *War with Mexico*, 1:140–43; Rodenbough and Haskin, *Army of the United States*, 438; Army Returns, July–August 1845, RG 94, NA.

2. Croffut, *Fifty Years*, 194, 198; *Niles National Register*, September 3, 1845, 19–20; Taylor's Army of Occupation, General Orders No. 14, September 26, 1845, AGO, RG 94, NA; Bauer, *Taylor*, 117; Darwin Payne, "Camp Life," 326–29.

3. Justin Smith, *War with Mexico*, 1:141–44; Bauer, *Taylor*, 11–19, 118–19; *Niles National Register*, May 23, October 25, November 22, 1845, 114, 178–79, 180–82; Edward Wallace, *Worth*, 66; Croffut, *Fifty Years*, 195–203; William S. Henry, *Campaign Sketches*, 27; Army Returns, December 1845, RG 94, NA; Darwin Payne, "Camp Life," 331–38; Smith and Judah, *Chronicles*, 274–76; Hill, "Army in Texas," 448–50.

4. Mrs. Alma Lane to Mr. Buell, February 21, 1913, June 28, 1914, Buell Papers, TC; Buell's Court Martial File, RG 153, NA.

5. Edward Wallace, *Worth*, 66; Justin Smith, *War with Mexico*, 1:144; Croffut, *Fifty Years*, 195–203; *Niles National Register*, January 3, 1846, 273.

6. Buell to James Grant Wilson, November 22, 1896, Buell Papers, RU; Mrs. Alma Lane to Mr. Buell, February 21, 1913, June 28, 1914, Buell Papers, TC; Edward Wallace, *Worth*, 66–67; Bauer, *Mexican War*, 34–35; William S. Henry, *Campaign Sketches*, 46; Wilcox, *Mexican War*, 632–33; Darwin Payne, "Camp Life," 338–40.

7. Bauer, *Mexican War*, 33–34, 43; Army of Occupation, General Orders No. 14 and No. 15, September 26, 28, 1845, AGO, RG 94, NA; Army Returns, October–November 1845, RG 94, NA; Edward Wallace, *Worth*, 65–71; Heidler, "Twiggs," 80–83.

8. William S. Henry, *Campaign Sketches*, 52–53; Bauer, *Taylor*, 124; Army Returns, March 1846, RG 94, NA; Frost, *Mexican War*, 11–12; *Niles National Register*, May 26, 1846, 182–88.

9. Bauer, *Mexican War*, 37–39; William S. Henry, *Campaign Sketches*, 52–53, 56–59; Frost, *Mexican War*, 11–12; Army Returns, March 1846, RG 94, NA; Croffut, *Fifty Years*, 210; Rodenbough and Haskin, *Army of the United States*, 436; Bauer, *Taylor*, 125–27; Justin Smith, *War with Mexico*, 1:164.

10. Croffut, *Fifty Years*, 213–14, 221–23; William S. Henry, *Campaign Sketches*, 56–57; *Niles National Register*, May 26, 1846, 182–83; Rodenbough and Haskin,

Army of the United States, 436; Bauer, *Mexican War*, 38–39; Rhoda Van B. Tanner Doubleday, *Barbour*, 17; Justin Smith, *War with Mexico*, 1:145–50; Bauer, *Taylor*, 147.

11. Robert Hazlitt to Sister, April 22, 1846, Hazlitt Papers, USMA-SC.

12. Croffut, *Fifty Years*, 213–14, 221–23; Army Returns, March–April 1846, RG 94, NA; Bauer, *Mexican War*, 41; Justin Smith, *War with Mexico*, 1:148–49; Rhoda Van B. Tanner Doubleday, *Barbour*, 27, 36; Wilcox, *Mexican War*, 42–46; Taylor to Adjutant General, April 26, 1846, in U.S. Congress, *House Executive Documents*, 30th Cong., 1st sess., no. 60, Mexican War Correspondence, 141, 288–89; Bauer, *Taylor*, 149–50; *Niles National Register*, May 16, 1846, 161–64.

13. Bauer, *Mexican War*, 52–71; Justin Smith, *War with Mexico*, 1:158–96; U.S. Congress, *Congressional Globe*, 29th Cong., 1st sess., 782–804; Wilcox, *Mexican War*, 53–58; Heidler, "Twiggs," 86–91; Report of Taylor, May 17, 1846, AGO, RG 94, NA; *Niles National Register*, May 23, June 6, 20, 1846, 179–83, 216–17, 249–50.

14. Croffut, *Fifty Years*, 225, 230–32; Report of Taylor, May 17, 1846, AGO, RG 94, NA; Heidler, "Twiggs," 89; *Inter-Ocean*, November 20, 1898, Chicago newspaper clipping in Buell Papers, RU; *Niles National Register*, June 20, July 4, 1846, 248–52, 276–77; Army Returns, May 1846, RG 94, NA.

15. Hazlitt to Sister, June 23, July 28, 1846, Hazlitt Papers, USMA-SC; Rhoda Van B. Tanner Doubleday, *Barbour*, 62–68, 73–75, 99–100; Bauer, *Taylor*, 171–74; Bauer, *Mexican War*, 81–87; Justin Smith, *War with Mexico*, 1:204; Wilcox, *Mexican War*, 78–86; *Niles National Register*, June 20, July 11, 1846, 246–52, 292; Rodenbough and Haskin, *Army of the United States*, 436; Army Returns, May–June 1846, RG 94, NA.

16. *Niles National Register*, July 25, 1846, 326; Justin Smith, *War with Mexico*, 1:207; Wilcox, *Mexican War*, 78; Hazlitt to Sister, June 23, 1846, Hazlitt Papers, USMA-SC.

17. William S. Henry, *Campaign Sketches*, 124–25; Justin Smith, *War with Mexico*, 1:204–11; *Niles National Register*, July 11, 1846, 292; Hazlitt to Sister, August 16, 1846, Hazlitt Papers, USMA-SC.

18. Army Returns, July–September 1846, RG 94, NA; Rhoda Van B. Tanner Doubleday, *Barbour*, 90–91; Bauer, *Mexican War*, 88–89; William S. Henry, *Campaign Sketches*, 124–25, 153–55; Wilcox, *Mexican War*, 79–90; Justin Smith, *War with Mexico*, 1:211; *Niles National Register*, October 3, 1846, 67; Bauer, *Taylor*, 175; Buell to Adjutant General, May 6, 1846, Letters Received, AGO, RG 94, NA; Heidler, "Twiggs," 91–95; Hazlitt to Sister, August 16, 24, 1846, Hazlitt Papers, USMA-SC; Edward Wallace, *Worth*, 80–83.

19. Army Returns, August–September 1846, and General Orders No. 36, August 12, 1846, AGO, RG 94, NA; Rodenbough and Haskin, *Army of the United States*, 436–37; Wilcox, *Mexican War*, 81–90.

20. Rhoda Van B. Tanner Doubleday, *Barbour*, 107; Bauer, *Mexican War*, 90–93; William S. Henry, *Campaign Sketches*, 190–91; Justin Smith, *War with Mexico*, 1:230–40; Hill Diary, 36–38, SHC.

21. Rhoda Van B. Tanner Doubleday, *Barbour*, 106–8; Justin Smith, *War with Mexico*, 1:239–40; Bauer, *Mexican War*, 92–96; Edward Wallace, *Worth*, 85–89.

22. William S. Henry, *Campaign Sketches*, 194; Justin Smith, *War with Mexico*, 1:250–54; Bauer, *Taylor*, 179–81; Heidler, "Twiggs," 96.

23. Army Returns, September, December 1846, RG 94, NA; William S. Henry,

Campaign Sketches, 194–95; Bauer, *Taylor*, 179–81; Justin Smith, *War with Mexico*, 1:250–54; Wilcox, *Mexican War*, 632–33; Heidler, "Twiggs," 96–97; Hill Diary, 35–39, SHC; *Niles National Register*, October 17, 1846, 101–2.

24. Edward Wallace, *Worth*, 96–99; William S. Henry, *Campaign Sketches*, 194–205; Justin Smith, *War with Mexico*, 1:243–50; Bauer, *Taylor*, 179–82; Wilcox, *Mexican War*, 91–110; Bauer, *Mexican War*, 98–101; *Niles National Register*, October 17, 24, 1846, 101–2, 115–16.

25. Army Returns, October, December 1846, RG 94, NA; Rodenbough and Haskin, *Army of the United States*, 437; Report of Twiggs, September 29, 1846, AGO, RG 94, NA; Hill Diary, 45, SHC; William S. Henry, *Campaign Sketches*, 195–200.

26. Wilcox, *Mexican War*, 118; Heidler, "Twiggs," 95, 105; Buell's Statement, RG 94, NA.

27. Army Returns, December 1846, February 1847, RG 94, NA; Rodenbough and Haskin, *Army of the United States*, 437; Report of Twiggs, September 29, 1846, AGO, RG 94, NA; William S. Henry, *Campaign Sketches*, 195–200; Justin Smith, *War with Mexico*, 1:259–61, 494–96; *Niles National Register*, October 17, 24, 1846, 101–2, 115–16.

28. Justin Smith, *War with Mexico*, 1:262; Bauer, *Taylor*, 188–206; William S. Henry, *Campaign Sketches*, 222–23, 245–49; Bauer, *Mexican War*, 204–5, 235–39, 240–45; Army Returns, January–February 1847, RG 94, NA; Heidler, "Twiggs," 99–100, 109; Edward Wallace, *Worth*, 116–19; Croffut, *Fifty Years*, 239–40.

29. Justin Smith, *War with Mexico*, 2:17–46; Bauer, *Mexican War*, 241–53; Croffut, *Fifty Years*, 242–48; Smith and Judah, *Chronicles*, 188–89, 194–95.

30. Bauer, *Mexican War*, 259–61; Justin Smith, *War with Mexico*, 2:37–44; Heidler, "Twiggs," 113; Croffut, *Fifty Years*, 249–51.

31. Justin Smith, *War with Mexico*, 2:44–59; Edward Wallace, *Worth*, 126–27; Croffut, *Fifty Years*, 250–53; Bauer, *Mexican War*, 259–70; *Niles National Register*, April 24, May 15, 1847, 114, 167; Stevens, *Campaigns*, 55–56; Furber, *Twelve Months Volunteer*, 579–600.

32. Report of Alexander, April 20, 1847, AGO, and Army Returns, April 1847, RG 94, NA.

33. Report of Scott, April 23, 1847, and Report of Twiggs, AGO, RG 94, NA; Justin Smith, *War with Mexico*, 2:47–59; Rodenbough and Haskin, *Army of the United States*, 438; Bauer, *Mexican War*, 267–68; *Niles National Register*, May 22, 29, 1847, 186, 199–200.

34. Bauer, *Mexican War*, 279–96; Justin Smith, *War with Mexico*, 2:60–79; Edward Wallace, *Worth*, 128–42; Croffut, *Fifty Years*, 254–71.

35. Bauer, *Mexican War*, 279–96; Justin Smith, *War with Mexico*, 2:99–107; Edward Wallace, *Worth*, 143–52; Croffut, *Fifty Years*, 271–72; Heidler, "Twiggs," 123.

36. Edward Wallace, *Worth*, 152–56; Justin Smith, *War with Mexico*, 2:99–110; Bauer, *Mexican War*, 290–98; Croffut, *Fifty Years*, 272–79; Report of Twiggs, August 23, 1847, AGO, RG 94, NA; *Niles National Register*, November 27, 1847, 202–4; Wilcox, *Mexican War*, 358–79; Gordon, "Contreras and Churubusco," 577–97.

37. Justin Smith, *War with Mexico*, 2:109.

38. Report of Twiggs, August 23, 1847, AGO, RG 94, NA; Heidler, "Twiggs," 126–29; Croffut, *Fifty Years*, 277–83; Wilcox, *Mexican War*, 387–89; Bauer, *Mexican*

War, 296–301; Furber, *Twelve Months Volunteer*, 617–18; Justin Smith, *War with Mexico*, 2:99–110; *Daily Picayune*, September 23, October 8, 14, 1847; *New York Herald*, September 16, 17, 19, 23, 1847; Gordon, "Contreras and Churubusco," 577–970.

39. Unidentified newspaper clipping, Buell Papers, RU; Charles Keeny to Buell, February 10, 1848, enclosed in Buell to Adjutant General Roger Jones, April 26, 1848, Letters Received, AGO, RG 94, NA; *New York Times*, November 12, 1861; Gordon, "Contreras and Churubusco," 577–97.

40. *St. Louis Globe-Democrat*, November 20, 1898; Jensen, "Daniel Frost's Memoirs," 221.

41. Jensen, "Daniel Frost's Memoirs," 221.

42. Report of Smith, August 23, 1847; Report of Twiggs, August 23, 1847; Report of Scott, August 28, 1847, all in AGO, RG 94, NA; unidentified newspaper clippings, Buell Papers, RU; *Niles National Register*, November 20, 27, 1847, 181–82, 200–202; Wilcox, *Mexican War*, 387–89; *New York Times*, November 12, 1861; George W. Kendall, *War between the United States and Mexico*, 31–33.

43. Army Returns, RG 94, NA; Buell's Statement, RG 94, NA; unidentified newspaper clipping, Buell File, USMA-SC; Jensen, "Daniel Frost's Memoirs," 221. Buell was not a member of the Aztec Club; see "Original List of Members Belonging to the Aztec Club," USAMHI.

44. Buell Family Genealogy Records, Buell Papers, TC; Army Returns, RG 94, NA; Buell to Adjutant General Roger Jones, April 26, 1848, Letters Received, AGO, RG 94, NA; George Lane to Buell, December 14, 1847, Buell Papers, RU; Buell's Statement, RG 94, NA.

45. Buell's Statement, RG 94, NA; Lane to Buell, December 14, 1847, Buell Papers, RU.

CHAPTER 4

1. Edmund Alexander to Roger Jones, January 28, 1848, and Buell to Jones, May 12, 1848, Letters Received, AGO, RG 94, NA.

2. Persifor Smith to Jones, January 28, 1848, Letters Received, AGO, RG 94, NA.

3. Army Returns, March–July 1847, RG 94, NA; Charles Keeny to Buell, February 10, 1848, enclosed in Buell to Adjutant General Roger Jones, April, 26, 1848, Letters Received, AGO, RG 94, NA; Mrs. Alma Lane to Mr. Buell, February 21, 1913, June 28, 1914, Buell Papers, TC; Buell to "Miss Mary Ann," September 17, 1848, Buell Papers, FC.

4. Buell's Statement, RG 94, NA; Buell to "Miss Mary Ann," September 17, October 10, 1848, Buell Papers, FC.

5. Buell's Statement, RG 94, NA; Department of Missouri, 6th Military Department, General Orders, vol. 72, Records of the U.S. Continental Commands, RG 393, NA; Heidler, "Twiggs," 150–51.

6. Buell's Statement, RG 94, NA; Buell's Letterbook, April 20, 1850–April 19, 1851, and Buell to Mrs. Hancock, May 31, 1889, Buell Papers, RU; William T. Sherman to Ellen [Ewing], September 25, 1850, Sherman Family Papers, UND. Buell and Hancock were joint owners of a tract of land below St. Louis. See also Jordan,

Hancock, 14–17, 22–23; Almira Russell Hancock, *Reminiscences,* 4–5, 252–53, 270–71; Military Service Institute, *Letters and Addresses,* 17–18, 22; Marszalek, *Sherman,* 84–86.

7. *National Tribune,* January 15, 1891; Schutz and Trenerry, *Abandoned by Lincoln,* 37–38; Department of New Mexico, General Orders, vol. 36, April 25, 1851, Records of the U.S. Continental Commands, RG 393, NA.

8. *National Tribune,* January 15, 1891; Schutz and Trenerry, *Abandoned by Lincoln,* 37–38.

9. Thomas R. Buell, *Genealogic Notes,* 32–33; Welles, *Buell Family,* 2:255; unidentified newspaper clippings, Margaret Hunter Buell Papers and Don Carlos Buell Papers, BC; *Missouri Republican,* July 27, 1850; Copeland and Macmaster, *Five George Masons,* 262; Stafford, "Mason Genealogy"; Stafford, "Graham"; Nevins, *Frémont,* 321; Jordan, *Hancock,* 23; Clarke, *Kearny,* 308–11. Buell wrote the orders notifying the soldiers at Jefferson Barracks that Mason had died.

10. Unidentified newspaper clippings, Buell Papers, RU.

11. Thomas R. Buell, *Genealogic Notes,* 32–34; Margaret Hunter Buell Papers and Don Carlos Buell Papers, BC; Buell Family Genealogy Records, Buell Papers, TC; Welles, *Buell Family,* 2:255; Federal Census, 1850, St. Louis County, Missouri, U.S. Census Records, NA; Mason Family Genealogical Records, GHP; Stafford, *Graham,* 206–13; Copeland and Macmaster, *Five George Masons,* 263. The information regarding the origin of Buell's wife is conflicting. Some records indicate she was from Mobile, Alabama, but the most conclusive evidence places her in Augusta, Georgia.

12. Federal Census, 1850, and Slave Schedules, St. Louis County, Missouri, U.S. Census Records, NA; Margaret Hunter Buell Papers and Don Carlos Buell Papers, BC; Buell Family Genealogy Records, Buell Papers, TC. See also Mrs. Alma Lane to William H. Donaldson, August 12, 1929, and Lane to Mr. Buell, June 28, 1924, Buell Papers, TC; unidentified newspaper clippings, Buell Papers, RU; Thomas R. Buell, *Genealogic Notes,* 32–34; Welles, *Buell Family,* 2:255; Buell's Statement, RG 94, NA; Stafford, "Mason Genealogy."

13. Federal Census, 1850, Slave Schedules, St. Louis County, Missouri, U.S. Census Records, NA; Buell Family Genealogy Records, and Mrs. Alma Lane to Mr. Buell, February 21, 1913, June 28, 1914, Buell Papers, TC; Buell to Nellie C. Martine, December 12, 1891, Buell Papers, RU.

14. Daniel M. Frost to Wife, January 5, 1853, Kennett Family Papers, MHS; Buell's Statement, RG 94, NA; General Orders No. 33, November 11, 1852, AGO, RG 94, NA.

15. Buell's Statement, RG 94, NA.

16. McClellan to Frederica M. English, January 1, 1853, McClellan Papers, LC; Sears, *Young Napoleon,* 35; Myers, *McClellan,* 73–77.

17. McClellan to Frederica M. English, January 1, 1853, McClellan Papers, LC; *New York Times,* November 12, 1861.

18. Sears, *Young Napoleon,* 1–35.

19. Ibid.; *OR* 1(16):30–65.

20. Department of the West, General Orders, vol. 76, no. 11, December 3, 1852; no. 25, October 31, 1853; and no. 4, November 23, 1853, Records of the U.S. Continental Commands, RG 393, NA; Buell to Thomas Lewin, March 27, 1853, Buell Papers, FC.

21. *Missouri Republican*, February 17, 1854; *Cincinnati Daily Enquirer*, November 20, 1861; Almira Russell Hancock, *Reminiscences*, 9–10; *New York Times*, November 12, 1861.

22. *Missouri Republican*, February 17, 1854; *Cincinnati Daily Enquirer*, November 20, 1861; Almira Russell Hancock, *Reminiscences*, 9–10; *New York Times*, November 12, 1861; Thomas Gantt to Emma Mason, February 16, 1854, Buell Papers, RU.

23. *Cincinnati Daily Enquirer*, November 20, 1861; *New York Times*, November 12, 1861.

24. Thomas Gantt to Emma Mason, February 16, 1854, Buell Papers, RU; *Cincinnati Daily Enquirer*, November 20, 1861; *Missouri Republican*, February 17, 1854; Almira Russell Hancock, *Reminiscences*, 9–10.

25. Almira Russell Hancock, *Reminiscences*, 9–10.

26. Ibid.

27. Buell to Wife, June 10, 1854, Buell Papers, RU; William Farrar Smith, "Don Carlos Buell," Buell File, USMA-SC.

28. William Farrar Smith, "Don Carlos Buell," Buell File, USMA-SC.

29. Crimmins, "Report of Texas," 125–35; Bender, "Military Posts in the Southwest," 130–33; Department of Texas, General Orders, vol. 1, no. 30, August 18, 1855, Records of the U.S. Continental Commands, RG 393, NA. See also Buell to R. E. Lee, May 17, 27, 1856, Letters Sent, and Post Returns, Department of Texas, May–June 1856, RG 393, NA; Roland, *Johnston*, 168–80.

30. Buell to William T. Sherman, April 24, July 26, 1857, Sherman Papers, LC; Buell's Statement, RG 94, NA; Buell to R. E. Lee, May 17, 1856, Letters Sent, Department of Texas, RG 393, NA. See also General Orders No. 3, March 23, 1857, AGO, RG 94, NA; Prucha, *Military Posts*, 59.

31. Sherman to Buell, July 13, 1857, Buell Papers, RU; Marszalek, *Sherman*, 94–115; Clarke, *Goldrush Banker*, 317–18; B. H. Liddell Hart, *Memoirs of Sherman*, 108–40; Buell to Sherman, April 24, 1857, Sherman Papers, LC; Sherman to Ellen, July 29, 1857, Sherman Family Papers, UND.

32. Margaret Buell to Joseph Lane, December 18, 1857, Buell Papers, IU; J. S. Molinard to Buell, September 14, 1857, and Samuel J. Cooper to Buell, November 11, 1857, Buell Papers, RU.

33. Margaret Buell to Joseph Lane, December 18, 1857, Buell Papers, IU.

34. Roland, *Johnston*, 185–214; Buell's Statement, RG 94, NA; Furniss, *Mormon Conflict*, 45–61; Buell's Letterbooks, June, July 1858, December 1858–January 1859, and William S. Harney to Buell, May 8, 1858, and Harney to Adjutant General, June 11, 1858, Buell Papers, RU; Department of Utah, General Orders, vol. 7, no. 12, January 1, 1858, and Department of the West, General Orders, vol. 76, no. 3, May 24, 1858, Records of the U.S. Continental Commands, RG 393, NA; Jordan, *Hancock*, 25–26; Frank Taylor to Buell, May 27, 1858, Buell Family Genealogy Records, Buell Papers, TC; Potter, *Impending Crisis*, 297–327.

35. Samuel Cooper to Buell, February 1, 1859, and Buell's Letterbooks, February 14, March 5, 1859, Buell Papers, RU; Buell's Statement, RG 94, NA.

36. Cooper to Buell, February 1, 1859, Buell Papers, RU.

37. Buell to Cooper, February 2, 1859, Letters Received by Adjutant General's Office, AGO, RG 94, NA; Cooper to Buell, February 12, 1859, Buell Papers, RU.

38. Buell's Statement, RG 94, NA; Buell's Letterbooks, February 14, March 5, 1859, and Cooper to Buell, February 12, 1859, Buell Papers, RU; Buell to Cooper, February 2, 1859, Letters Received by Adjutant General's Office, AGO, RG 94, NA.

39. Marszalek, *Sherman*, 109; Egan, *Frémont*, 421–41; Sherman to Buell, April 15, 1860, Buell Papers, RU. See also the following newspapers on the political climate in Lawrenceburg, Indiana, during Buell's early years: *Indiana Palladium, Indiana Spectator, Political Beacon.*

40. Buell Family Genealogy Records, and Letters from Margaret Hunter Mason to Richard Barnes Mason's family, July 1836 and May 1839, Buell Papers, TC; Stafford, "Mason Genealogy"; Potter, *Impending Crisis*, 154–56.

41. Auchampaugh, *Buchanan and His Cabinet*, 89; Swanberg, *First Blood*, 29; Catton, *Coming Fury*, 122; Thomas and Hyman, *Stanton*, 93–94; Cooper to Buell, February 1, 12, 1859, Buell Papers, RU.

42. As quoted in Marszalek, *Sherman*, 120–21; also found in Sherman to Buell, June 11, 1859, Sherman Papers, LC.

43. Buell to Sherman, June 17, 1859, Sherman Papers, LC.

44. Buell to Sherman, July 14, 1859, ibid.; see also Buell to Sherman, June 28, 1859, ibid. Apparently a position in the Paymaster's Department did open up, but after Sherman had applied for the position in Louisiana.

45. Buell to Sherman, July 10, 1859, ibid.

46. Stafford, "Graham," 55–56; Buell to Sherman, June 17, 1859, Sherman Papers, LC; Marszalek, *Sherman*, 120–21; Copeland and Macmaster, *Five George Masons*, 263.

47. Stafford, "Graham," 55–56; Buell to Sherman, July 31, 1859, Sherman Papers, LC.

48. Copeland and Macmaster, *Five George Masons*, 263.

49. Buell to Graham Mason, July 10, 1859, Buell Papers, RU; Stafford, "Graham," 55–56; Stafford, "Mason Genealogy."

50. Buell to Sherman, August 10, September 24, 1859, Sherman Papers, LC; Marszalek, *Sherman*, 121–23.

51. Sherman to Buell, February 21, 1860, Buell Papers, RU; Marszalek, *Sherman*, 126–36; Potter, *Impending Crisis*, 387–89; Nevins, *Ordeal of the Union*, 4:116–24; Sherman to John Sherman, November 21, 1859, Sherman Papers, LC.

52. Sherman to Buell, February 21, April 15, 1860, Buell Papers, RU; Marszalek, *Sherman*, 131–32.

53. Sherman to Buell, April 15, 1860, Buell Papers, RU.

54. Sherman to Buell, July 10, 1860, ibid.; Marszalek, *Sherman*, 132–39.

55. Marszalek, *Sherman*, 133; Nevins, *Ordeal of the Union*, 4:199–200.

56. Buell to George P. Buell, June 5, 1860, Buell Papers, RU; Thomas M. Anderson, *Political Conspiracies*, 10; Meneely, *War Department*, 38–47; Klunder, *Cass*, 297–312; Potter, *Impending Crisis*, 385–447; Nevins, *Ordeal of the Union*, 4:340–47; Catton, *Coming Fury*, 122–25.

57. Potter, *Impending Crisis*, 385–447; Nevins, *Ordeal of the Union*, 4:203–318.

58. *OR* 1(1):70–73; Swanberg, *First Blood*, 30–40; Meredith, *Storm over Sumter*, 32–35; Crawford, *Story of Sumter*, 61; Abner Doubleday, *Reminiscences*, 42; Ramsey, "Doubleday," 9–12; Meneely, *War Department*, 29–30.

59. Anderson to Cooper, November 23, 1860, *OR* 1(1):74–76; Meredith, *Storm over Sumter*, 34–36; Ramsey, "Doubleday," 9–12.

60. Anderson to Cooper, November 23, 1860, *OR* 1(1):74–76; Swanberg, *First Blood*, 39–41.

61. Anderson to Cooper, December 6, 1860, *OR* 1(1):74–77, 89; Swanberg, *First Blood*, 40–49; Meredith, *Storm over Sumter*, 38–41; Ramsey, "Doubleday," 10–13; Buell's Statement, RG 94, NA; Buell to Charles E. Bliven, December 20, 1880, December 19, 1891, Buell Papers, RU; Abner Doubleday, *Reminiscences*, 50; Crawford, *Story of Sumter*, 71–72; Thomas and Hyman, *Stanton*, 94; "Story of Sumter."

62. Abner Doubleday, *Reminiscences*, 50–51; Ramsey, "Doubleday," 56–58; Crawford, *Story of Sumter*, 72–74.

63. Catton, *Coming Fury*, 144–48; Swanberg, *First Blood*, 46–51; Crawford, *Story of Sumter*, 72–74.

64. Buell's memorandum, December 11, 1860, *OR* 1(1):89–90; Swanberg, *First Blood*, 49–51; Crawford, *Story of Sumter*, 72–74.

65. Crawford, *Story of Sumter*, 72–74; Catton, *Coming Fury*, 146–49; Ramsey, "Doubleday," 15–16; *Daily National Intelligencer*, January 4, 1861.

66. Crawford, *Story of Sumter*, 71–74.

67. Ibid., 72–75; Meredith, *Storm over Sumter*, 42–43; *Charleston Mercury*, December 13, 1860; Buell to Crawford, December 20, 1883, Buell Papers, RU.

68. Crawford, *Story of Sumter*, 72–74; Swanberg, *First Blood*, 51–59; Catton, *Coming Fury*, 148–49.

69. Catton, *Coming Fury*, 148–49; Swanberg, *First Blood*, 114; Crawford, *Story of Sumter*, 72–74; Meredith, *Storm over Sumter*, 40–41; Thomas and Hyman, *Stanton*, 94; Buchanan, *Administration*, 167–68; Philip S. Klein, *Buchanan*, 371–72; Moore, *Works of Buchanan*, 11:81–83.

70. Meredith, *Storm over Sumter*, 45–80; Swanberg, *First Blood*, 89–90; *OR* 1(1):117; Crawford, *Story of Sumter*, 74; Auchampaugh, *Buchanan and His Cabinet*, 157–60; Buchanan, *Administration*, 180–81.

71. Floyd to Anderson, December 21, 1860, *OR* 1(1):103; Swanberg, *First Blood*, 89–94; Buchanan, *Administration*, 165–67; Crawford, *Story of Sumter*, 75; Philip S. Klein, *Buchanan*, 376; Moore, *Works of Buchanan*, 11:81–83, 12:145–46.

72. Anderson to Cooper, December 26, 1860, *OR* 1(1):2, 99, 109; *Daily National Intelligencer*, January 8, 1861; Meredith, *Storm over Sumter*, 55–72; Swanberg, *First Blood*, 89–101; Auchampaugh, *Buchanan and His Cabinet*, 96–97.

73. Floyd to Anderson, December 27, 1860, *OR* 1(1):3; Crawford, *Story of Sumter*, 142–44; *Daily National Intelligencer*, December 31, 1860.

74. Crawford, *Story of Sumter*, 142–44; Nevins, *Ordeal of the Union*, 4:368–69.

75. Crawford to Buell, December 15, 1883; Bliven to Buell, December 19, 1891; and Truman Seymour to Buell, October 27, 1874, all in Buell Papers, RU; Buell to Crawford, December 1883, Buell Papers, HL; Swanberg, *First Blood*, 108–22.

76. Crawford, *Story of Sumter*, 145–46; Auchampaugh, *Buchanan and His Cabinet*, 158; Meredith, *Storm over Sumter*, 69–83; Philip S. Klein, *Buchanan*, 379–81; Moore, *Works of Buchanan*, 11:81–83; 12:145–46; *Daily National Intelligencer*, January 8, 1861.

77. Meredith, *Storm over Sumter*, 70–75; Catton, *Coming Fury*, 159–62; Swanberg,

First Blood, 64–69, 109–15; Thomas M. Anderson, *Political Conspiracies,* 20–30; Scott to Buchanan, December 30, 1860, *OR* 1(1):114, 119; James Richardson, *Messages and Papers of the Presidents,* 5:628–37; Auchampaugh, *Buchanan and His Cabinet,* 95–97; Philip S. Klein, *Buchanan,* 380.

78. Sherman to John Sherman, December 9, 1860, Sherman Papers, LC; Buell's Statement, RG 94, NA. See also General's Papers and Books, AGO, RG 94, NA.

CHAPTER 5

1. Buell to Nellie C. Martine, December 12, 1891, Buell Papers, RU; Mrs. Alma Lane to Mr. Buell, June 28, 1914, Buell Papers, TC.

2. Undated letter from Mr. Melody to Frederick A. Buell, and Mrs. Alma Lane to Mr. Buell, June 28, 1914, Buell Papers, TC; Buell to Nellie C. Martine, December 12, 1891, Buell Papers, RU.

3. Buell's Statement, RG 94, NA; General Orders No. 3, May 20, 1861, U.S. War Department, Department of the Pacific, RG 393, NA; Auchampaugh, *Buchanan and His Cabinet,* 175–80; Buchanan, *Administration,* 165–67, 180–81.

4. Davis, *Government of Our Own,* chaps. 1–5; Davis, *Davis,* 301–5.

5. George Buell to Buell, April 12, 1861, Buell Papers, RU; Sears, *Young Napoleon,* 67; Prime, *McClellan's Own Story,* 43–45.

6. Federal Census, 1860, and Slave Schedules, U.S. Census Records, NA; Buell Family Genealogy Records, Buell Papers, TC; Skelton, *American Profession of Arms,* 350–51.

7. Buell to Rockwell, July 10, 1864, Rockwell Papers, LC; Sears, *Young Napoleon,* 32; Marszalek, *Sherman,* 45–46, 59, 98–99, 123, 126. See also *Frank Leslie's Illustrated,* September 27, 1862, and *New York Daily Tribune,* October 24, 1861, for characterizations of Buell as an advocate of slavery. These articles appeared, however, when the administration was under considerable pressure to remove Buell from command.

8. Buell's Statement, RG 94, NA; Buell to Cooper, May 21, 1860, Letters Sent, AGO, RG 94, NA; Roland, *Johnston,* 238–51; *OR* 50(1):433, 456.

9. Buell's Statement, RG 94, NA; unidentified newspaper clipping, Buell File, USMA-SC.

10. General Orders No. 13, April 30, 1861, and No. 8, 23, May 20, 1861, and Letterbook, Assistant Adjutant General, June–July 1861, U.S. War Department, Department of the Pacific, RG 393, NA.

11. Sears, *Young Napoleon,* 78–94; Myers, *McClellan,* 175–95; Sears, *Papers of McClellan,* 66–67.

12. Sears, *Young Napoleon,* 113.

13. Mahan to McClellan, August 3, 1861, McClellan Papers, LC; Sears, *Young Napoleon,* 101, 113; Myers, *McClellan,* 203.

14. Mahan to McClellan, August 3, 1861, McClellan Papers, LC.

15. Gantt to Buell, August 7, 1861, Buell Papers, RU.

16. *New York Times,* November 12, 1861.

17. Anderson to Chase, September 1, 1861, and Morton to Cameron, September

12, 1861, *OR* 4(1):255–56, 257; Scott to Morton, September 3, 1861, *OR*, ser. 3, 1(1):479; Woodworth, "Indeterminate Quantities"; Marszalek, *Sherman*, 154–55; Villard, *Memoirs*, 1:204.

18. McClellan to Lincoln, September 6, 1861, as cited in Sears, *Papers of McClellan*, 94; Prime, *McClellan's Own Story*, 139–40.

19. McClellan to Cameron, September 8, 1861, *OR* 5(1):16–17, 587–89; Prime, *McClellan's Own Story*, 138–39.

20. Sears, *Young Napoleon*, 112–14; *OR* 5(1):15–17.

21. Bliven, "Reminiscences," Buell Papers, RU; *New York Times*, November 12, 1861; Rhodes, *All for the Union*, 47–48; *National Tribune*, January 15, 1891; Catton, *Terrible Swift Sword*, 61.

22. Newell, *Tenth Massachusetts*, 47–49; Roe, *Tenth Massachusetts*, 37–38; Reverdy W. Johnson, *Reminiscences*, 196–97; *OR* 5(1):15–17. Buell's division contained Batteries D and H, First Pennsylvania Artillery; Darius Couch's brigade of the Second Rhode Island; the Seventh and Tenth Massachusetts; the Thirty-sixth New York Volunteers; Lawrence Graham's brigade of the Twenty-third and Thirty-first Pennsylvania; the Sixty-seventh (First Long Island) and Sixty-fifth (First U.S. Chasseurs) New York Volunteers; John Peck's brigade of the Thirteenth and Twenty-first Pennsylvania; and the Sixty-second (Anderson Zouaves) and Fifty-fifth New York Volunteers.

23. Roe, *Tenth Massachusetts*, 39; Newell, *Tenth Massachusetts*, 49–52.

24. Roe, *Tenth Massachusetts*, 38–39.

25. Ibid.

26. Ibid., 41; Newell, *Tenth Massachusetts*, 52; Buell to James Wilson, November 22, 1896, Buell Papers, RU.

27. Rhodes, *All for the Union*, 41–47; Roe, *Tenth Massachusetts*, 42–43; Sears, *Young Napoleon*, 118–19.

28. Rhodes, *All for the Union*, 41–46; Roe, *Tenth Massachusetts*, 44; Newell, *Tenth Massachusetts*, 54.

29. Rhodes, *All for the Union*, 41–46; Roe, *Tenth Massachusetts*, 44; Newell, *Tenth Massachusetts*, 54; Genealogical Records, Margaret Hunter Buell Papers, BC; Mason Family Genealogical Records, GHP.

30. Johnson and Buel, *Battles and Leaders*, 2:123–34; Sears, *Young Napoleon*, 122–23.

31. Sears, *Young Napoleon*, 122–23.

32. Ibid., 125; Dennett, *Diaries and Letters of John Hay*, 32–33; Basler, *Works of Lincoln*, 5:9–10; Myers, *McClellan*, 219–25.

33. Buell to McClellan, November 2, 1861, McClellan Papers, LC.

34. Sears, *Young Napoleon*, 127.

35. Sears, *Papers of McClellan*, 123–24.

36. McClellan to Halleck, November 11, 1861, *OR* 3(1):568–69; Sears, *Young Napoleon*, 128; *New York Daily Tribune*, November 2, 1861; Kenneth P. Williams, *Lincoln Finds a General*, 1:131; Prime, *McClellan's Own Story*, 207–10; Stephen E. Ambrose, *Halleck*, 10–13.

37. Scribner, *How Soldiers Were Made*, 28.

38. Sherman to Garrett Davis, October 8, 1861, *OR* 4(1):297; Sherman to McClellan, November 4, 1861, and McClellan to Sherman, November 8, 1861, McClel-

lan Papers, LC; Sears, *Papers of McClellan*, 127; Marszalek, *Sherman*, 157–63; B. H. Liddell Hart, *Memoirs of Sherman*, 199–214; J. Cutler Andrews, *North Reports the War*, 116; Shanks, *Personal Recollections*, 32–33; *Cincinnati Commercial*, November 9, 1861; Lloyd Lewis, *Fighting Prophet*, 191–99; Myers, *McClellan*, 397; Buell Family Genealogy Records, Buell Papers, TC; Mason Family Genealogical Records, GHP; Dennett, *Diaries and Letters of John Hay*, 34–35; Sears, *Young Napoleon*, 132–33; *New York Daily Tribune*, November 12, 13, 1861. Buell's transfer to Kentucky triggered considerable enthusiasm in his family and hurried his daughter's marriage to Colonel Wheaton. What was surely one of the most celebrated times in Buell's life, and that of his daughter, was also one of the most remarkable episodes in the relations between McClellan and President Lincoln. On November 12, the evening of Buell's daughter's wedding, Lincoln, accompanied by Secretary of State William Seward and Lincoln's young secretary, John Hay, went to McClellan's house to pay him a visit. When the servant told them the general was attending Emma's wedding but would be back presently, they decided to wait. According to Hay, after about an hour McClellan returned, whereupon the servant greeted him and told him that the president and the secretary of state were waiting to see him. A bemused McClellan bypassed the room where they were sitting and went upstairs to bed. After another half-hour, they sent the servant to inform McClellan that they wished to see him. The servant returned with the message that the general had gone to bed. From that point on, it was clear McClellan had little time for Lincoln.

39. Sears, *Young Napoleon*, 82, 116; Mrs. Alma Lane to Mr. Buell, June 28, 1914, Buell Papers, TC; Catton, *Terrible Swift Sword*, 61.

40. *New York Times*, November 12, 1861; *Harper's Weekly*, January 11, April 12, 1862.

41. *New York Times*, November 12, 1861.

42. Rhodes, *All for the Union*, 47; Roe, *Tenth Massachusetts*, 38–47; Newell, *Tenth Massachusetts*, 49–55; *Cincinnati Daily Enquirer*, November 8, 1861.

43. Lloyd Lewis, *Fighting Prophet*, 191–99; *Cincinnati Daily Enquirer*, November 20, 1861; McClure, *Lincoln and Men of War-Times*, 212–13; Marszalek, *Sherman's Other War*, chap. 3.

44. McClellan to Buell, November 7, 1861, *OR* 4(1):342.

45. Ibid.

46. Ibid. This letter may not have reached Buell, though it was obvious from their later correspondence that Buell and McClellan had discussed these issues at length. Buell mentioned only receiving the November 12 letter of instructions, McClellan to Buell, November 12, 1861, *OR* 16(1):23. McClellan's instructions also represented Lincoln's thoughts regarding strategy in Buell's department.

47. McClellan to Buell, November 12, 1861, *OR* 16(1):23, and 4(1):355–56; see also Buell to McClellan, November 2, 1861, McClellan Papers, LC.

48. McClellan to Buell, November 12, 1861, *OR* 4(1):355–56.

49. McClellan to Buell, November 7, 1861, *OR* 4(1):342, 355–56.

50. Marszalek, *Sherman*, 160–66; *OR* 4(1):297.

51. Basler, *Works of Lincoln*, 4:263, 438–39; U.S. Congress, *Congressional Globe*, 37th Cong., 1st sess., 222–23, 258–62.

52. Reverdy W. Johnson, *Reminiscences*, 196–97.

1. Shanks, *Personal Recollections*, 245–47; Villard, *Memoirs*, 1:176–77; Catton, *Terrible Swift Sword*, 61.

2. Donald, *Why the North Won*, 42–46; T. Harry Williams, *Lincoln and His Generals*, 46–48; Sears, *Young Napoleon*, 26, 68, 201–2, 293; Stephen E. Ambrose, *Halleck*, 10–13.

3. T. Harry Williams, *Lincoln and His Generals*, 46–48; Donald, *Why the North Won*, 42–46; Stephen E. Ambrose, *Halleck*, 10–13; Glatthaar, *Partners in Command*, 236. Buell's military philosophy is best summarized in his final statement before the military commission May 5, 1863, found in *OR* 16(1):51–59.

4. Piatt, *Thomas*, 120–21; Cist, *Army of the Cumberland*, 21; Shanks, *Personal Recollections*, 247–49; Bliven, "Reminiscences," Buell Papers, RU.

5. Bliven, "Reminiscences," Buell Papers, RU; *Chicago Tribune*, November 12, 1861.

6. Bruce, "Buell's Campaign against Chattanooga," 147; *Chicago Tribune*, November 16, 1861.

7. Buell to Wife, December 10, 1861; Buell to Nellie Martine, December 12, 1891; and Bliven, "Reminiscences," all in Buell Papers, RU; Mr. Melody to Frederick A. Buell, undated, Buell Papers, TC; Piatt, *Thomas*, 120–21; *Chicago Tribune*, November 12, 1861; Hagerman, "Professionalization of George B. McClellan." According to Hagerman, the cadets at the U.S. Military Academy during the 1840s were educated at a time of public hostility, particularly on the part of Congress, toward a professional and centralized military establishment. This atmosphere rejected the definition of war as a complex problem of theory, organization, and administration in an industrial society.

8. Randall to Lincoln, May 6, 1861, *OR*, ser. 3, 1(1):167–70; Rawley, *Turning Points*, 11; Coulter, *Civil War and Readjustment in Kentucky*, 115–26.

9. Shanks, *Personal Recollections*, 225.

10. Catton, *Terrible Swift Sword*, 34; Basler, *Works of Lincoln*, 4:532.

11. *New York Times*, October 1, 1861; Basler, *Works of Lincoln*, 4:532; Rawley, *Turning Points*, 11; Coulter, *Civil War and Readjustment in Kentucky*, 115–26.

12. Coulter, *Civil War and Readjustment in Kentucky*, 126–49; Johnson and Buel, *Battles and Leaders*, 1:373–92; Van Horne, *Army of the Cumberland*, 1:4–5, 12, 16–17; Current, *Lincoln's Loyalists*, 29–30; Villard, *Memoirs*, 1:206; Speed and Pirhe, *Union Regiments of Kentucky*, 10–27; Woodworth, "Indeterminate Quantities." See also Nelson to Chase, July 16, 23, August 4, 12, 1861, Chase Papers, CGS.

13. Morton to Cameron, September 12, 1861, and Anderson to Chase, September 1, 1861, *OR* 4(1):255–57; Scott to Morton, September 3, 1861, *OR* 3(1):479; Woodworth, "Indeterminate Quantities"; Coulter, *Civil War and Readjustment in Kentucky*, 126–49; Johnson and Buel, *Battles and Leaders*, 1:373–92.

14. Shanks, *Personal Recollections*, 42–43.

15. McClellan to Halleck, November 11, 1861, *OR* 3(1):568–69; General Orders No. 1, *OR* 4(1):358–59 (officially changed the name of the Department of the Cumberland to the Department of the Ohio); Stephen E. Ambrose, *Halleck*, 11; Jefferson Davis to Howell Cobb, November 25, 1861, *OR*, ser. 4, 1(1):133; Davis, *Breckinridge*, 284–96.

16. General Orders No. 97, November 9, 1861, *OR* 4(1):348; McClellan to Halleck, November 9, 1861, *OR* 5(1):37 and 3(1):568–69; Stephen E. Ambrose, *Halleck*, 18; Kenneth P. Williams, *Lincoln Finds a General*, 3:102.

17. *Louisville Daily Journal*, November 14, 1861; Marszalek, *Sherman*, 160–61; Lloyd Lewis, *Fighting Prophet*, 198; Almon Rockwell Diary, November 12, 1861, Rockwell Papers, LC; *New York Times*, November 12, 1861.

18. *Cincinnati Commercial*, November 15, 1861.

19. Sherman to Wilbur Thomas, November 12, 1861, *OR* 4(1):353–54; Marszalek, *Sherman*, 162–63; Lloyd Lewis, *Fighting Prophet*, 197–98; Cleaves, *Rock of Chickamauga*, 89–91; McKinney, *Education in Violence*, 118–19.

20. Lloyd Lewis, *Fighting Prophet*, 197–98; *Chicago Tribune*, November 25, 1861; *OR* 4(1):340–42, 350–54.

21. Buell to McClellan, November 27, 1861, *OR* 7(1):450–51; Lloyd Lewis, *Fighting Prophet*, 198; Sherman to Thomas, November 6, 1861, *OR* 4(1):340–41; *OR*, ser. 3, 1(1):577, on the transfer of regiments. See also Assistant Secretary of War Thomas A. Scott to James Negley, October 17, 1861, and Scott to Wisconsin Governor Alexander Randall, October 17, 1861, *OR*, ser. 3, 1(1):578, 588.

22. *Cincinnati Commercial*, November 9, 1861; *Chicago Tribune*, November 9, 1861.

23. Sherman to Thomas, November 6, 1861, *OR* 4(1):340–41; Lloyd Lewis, *Fighting Prophet*, 198; Villard, *Memoirs*, 1:209–14.

24. B. H. Liddell Hart, *Memoirs of Sherman*, 203–14; *Chicago Tribune*, November 25, 1861; Boatner, *Civil War Dictionary*, 526.

25. Buell to McClellan, November 16, 1861, McClellan Papers, LC; Lloyd Lewis, *Fighting Prophet*, 198.

26. Buell to McClellan, November 16, 1861, McClellan Papers, LC.

27. Ibid. See also *OR* 16(1):51–59.

28. Buell to McClellan, November 16, 1861, McClellan Papers, LC; *OR* 16(1):51–59. See also Buell to McClellan, November 22, 1861, *OR* 7(1):443–44; Townsend to Buell, November 16, 1861, *OR* 4(1):358–59.

29. Johnson and Buel, *Battles and Leaders*, 1:385; Buell to McClellan, November 16, 1861, McClellan Papers, LC.

30. Richard W. Johnson, *Thomas*, 47–55; Cleaves, *Rock of Chickamauga*, 87–93; McKinney, *Education in Violence*, 112–21; *OR* 4(1):349–50; Samuel P. Carter to Thomas, November 12, 1861, *OR* 4(1):356; Johnson and Buel, *Battles and Leaders*, 1:376–85. See also Fry to Thomas, November 19, 1861, *OR* 7(1):439. Johnson had repeatedly urged Thomas to advance to East Tennessee, and although Thomas had justifiable reasons for not advancing, politicians and even Sherman criticized him for his reluctance. When in mid-October there was an indication that Ormsby M. Mitchel would replace Thomas, it caused a rift between Sherman, Thomas, and Mitchel. For this correspondence, see *OR* 4(1):301–6.

31. Levi Sipes, Grand Army of the Republic Application Form, Sipes Papers, CHS.

32. *OR* 16(1):23. See also Sherman's Report, November 10, 1861, *OR* 4(1):349–50; Johnson and Buel, *Battles and Leaders*, 1:376–85.

33. Schoepf's Report, December 8, 1861, *OR* 7(1):8–9.

34. Buell to McClellan, November 16, 1861, McClellan Papers, LC; *OR* 16(1):23–24.

35. Shanks, *Personal Recollections*, 42–43; *OR* 16(1):24.

36. Chumney, "Gentleman General," 30; Lloyd Lewis, *Fighting Prophet*, 194; Johnson and Buel, *Battles and Leaders*, 1:385; Stephen E. Ambrose, *Halleck*, 15.

37. *OR* 16(1):24; Buell to McClellan, November 16, 1861, McClellan Papers, LC; Fry to Thomas, November 19, 1861, *OR* 7(1):439; Cist, *Army of the Cumberland*, 21–22; Bliven, "Reminiscences," Buell Papers, RU. Bliven mentions that Buell asked permission to feed and clothe black men hanging around camps and to use them, but the administration disapproved. This is the only source, however, that makes such a claim.

38. *OR* 7(1):46–61, 460–61, 16(1):24; Buell to R. C. Wickliffe, December 25, 1861, Letters Sent, 1861–62, Department of the Ohio, AGO, RG 94, NA; Prokopowicz, "All for the Regiment," 5, 65–66.

39. Scribner, *How Soldiers Were Made*, 33; Wesley Elmore to "Dear Father and Mother," December 4, 1861, Elmore Papers, IHS.

40. Basler, *Works of Lincoln*, 5:84–85; Hunter to Cameron, "Private and Confidential," December 19, 1861, Cameron Papers, LC.

41. Prokopowicz, "All for the Regiment," 65–73, 81–82; Special Orders No. 16, November 30, 1861, Department of the Ohio, AGO, RG 94, NA; *OR* 7(1):460–61; Speed and Pirhe, *Union Regiments of Kentucky*, 58–60, 71–72.

42. General Orders No. 2, November 16, 1861, and No. 4, November 22, 1861, Department of the Ohio, AGO, RG 94, NA; Buell to Morton, December 3, 7, 1861, Telegraph Book No. 2, Morton Collection, ISA; *Louisville Daily Journal*, November 26, 1861.

43. Shanks, *Personal Recollections*, 247.

44. Ibid.; Bliven, "Reminiscences," Buell Papers, RU.

45. Cist, *Army of the Cumberland*, 21–22.

46. Ibid.

47. Bliven, "Reminiscences," Buell Papers, RU; *National Tribune*, January 15, 1891.

48. James F. Mohr to Brother, November 25, 1861, Mohr Papers, FC; Villard, *Memoirs*, 1:176–77; *National Tribune*, January 15, 1891; Prokopowicz, "All for the Regiment," 65.

49. Roderick Hooper to Brother, November 26, 1861, Hooper Papers, OHS.

50. Prokopowicz, "All for the Regiment," 84–85; Scribner, *How Soldiers Were Made*, 35, 112–14; Edwin W. Payne, *Thirty-fourth Illinois*, 8–9; Beatty, *Citizen Soldier*, 95–96; Hazen, *Narrative of Military Service*, 7–8; Athern, *Soldier in the West*, 54.

51. *Louisville Daily Journal*, December 2, 1861; Prokopowicz, "All for the Regiment," 84–85.

52. *Cincinnati Daily Enquirer*, December 5, 1861; John Love to Graham N. Fitch, December 7, 1861, Telegraph Book No. 2, Morton Collection, ISA. On one occasion Buell did allow passes to 100 ladies to advance to the outside of the camps; see *Louisville Daily Journal*, November 26, 1861.

53. Herr, *Nine Campaigns*, 29; Jesse B. Connelly Diary, December 9, 1861, Connelly Papers, IHS; John D. Inskeep Diary, December 19, 28, 1861, Inskeep Papers, OHS; Scribner, *How Soldiers Were Made*, 35; Prokopowicz, "All for the Regiment," 85–87.

54. Ulysses S. Grant to Sister, December 18, 1861, Grant Papers, UMWCL; Simon,

Papers of Grant, 3:307–8; General Orders No. 11, December 5, 1861, Department of the Ohio, AGO, RG 94, NA; Prokopowicz, "All for the Regiment," 86.

55. General Orders No. 10, December 5, 1861, and No. 13, December 9, 1861, Department of the Ohio, AGO, RG 94, NA; Buell to John Love, December 7, 1861, Telegraph Book No. 2, Morton Collection, ISA; Reverdy W. Johnson, *Reminiscences*, 196–97; Cist, *Army of the Cumberland*, 21–22; Herr, *Nine Campaigns*, 29; Bliven, "Reminiscences," Buell Papers, RU; Johnson and Buel, *Battles and Leaders*, 3:51.

56. General Orders No. 23 1//2, December 27, 1861, and No. 5, November 25, 1861, Department of the Ohio, AGO, RG 94, NA; *OR* 7(1):518; Chumney, "Gentleman General," 40.

57. *New Albany Daily Ledger*, December 13, 1861; Joseph Warren Keifer to Wife (Eliza), December 1, 1861, Keifer Papers, LC; Fry to Coburn, December 11, 1861, Selected Letters Sent, Department of the Ohio, AGO, RG 94, NA.

58. Keifer to Eliza, December 2, 12, 1861, Keifer Papers, LC.

59. Fry to Coburn, December 11, 1861, Selected Letters Sent, Department of the Ohio, AGO, RG 94, NA; Moreau to Morton, November 25, 1861, Telegraph Book No. 2, Morton Collection, ISA. See also Buell to Morton, November 25, 1861, and Morton to Buell, December 3, 1861, Telegraph Book No. 2, Morton Collection, ISA.

60. Chumney, "Gentleman General," 41–42; Fry to Negley, December 16, 1861, and Oliver Greene to Jesse Bayles, December 5, 1861, Selected Letters Sent, Department of the Ohio, AGO, RG 94, NA.

61. Villard, *Memoirs*, 1:213; Thornbrough, *Indiana in the Civil War*, 108–9; *Cincinnati Commercial*, November 16, 1861.

62. *Louisville Times*, November 16, 1861; *Cincinnati Daily Enquirer*, November 17, 1861; *OR* 16(1):51, 107.

63. Keifer to Eliza, December 31, 1861, Keifer Papers, LC; *National Tribune*, January 15, 1891.

64. Keifer to Eliza, December 1, 1861, Keifer Papers, LC; *OR* 16(1):561–69.

65. Keifer to Eliza, December 3, 1861, Keifer Papers, LC.

66. Buell to McClellan, November 22, 1861, *OR* 7(1):443–44; Lloyd Lewis, *Fighting Prophet*, 198.

67. David Davis to Cameron, October 13, 1861, "Confidential," Cameron Papers, LC; Cameron to Governor Andrew Curtin, May 22, 1861, *OR*, ser. 3, 1(1):154, 227–28, 339; Thornbrough, *Indiana in the Civil War*, 128–34, 164–67; Basler, *Works of Lincoln*, 4:402; Paludan, *"People's Contest,"* 19.

68. *OR*, ser. 3, 1(1):131, 409–10. See Cameron to previous Ohio governor William Dennison, April 29, 1861, and Yates to Cameron, August 14, 1861, ibid.; Morton to Cameron, May 10, June 22, 1861, ibid., 185, 290; Cameron to Randall, May 17, 1861, ibid., 212; Meneely, *War Department*, 167–68, 210–15; Thornbrough, *Indiana in the Civil War*, 130–34.

69. Morton to Buell, December 3, 1861, Telegraph Book No. 2, Morton Collection, ISA.

70. McClellan to Buell, November 25, 1861, *OR* 7(1):447.

71. *OR* 16(1):51; Buell to McClellan, November 22, 1861, *OR* 7(1):443–44.

72. Buell to McClellan, November 23, 1861, *OR* 7(1):445.

1. *Cincinnati Commercial,* November 15, 1861; *New York Daily Tribune,* January 18, 1862.

2. Reverdy W. Johnson, *Reminiscences,* 322; Basler, *Works of Lincoln,* 4:457–58, for Plan of Campaign; Ballard, *Military Genius of Lincoln,* 177; T. Harry Williams, *Lincoln and His Generals,* 47–48; *OR* 7(1):445, 471, 706.

3. Cooling, *Forts Henry and Donelson,* xii, 1–27; Ash, *Middle Tennessee Society,* 1–37; Noel C. Fisher, *War at Every Door,* 6–44.

4. Harris to Secretary of War, August 3, 1861, *OR,* ser. 2, 1(1):830–31; Noel C. Fisher, *War at Every Door,* 30–61; Noel C. Fisher, "Leniency Shown Them Has Been Unavailing," 276–80; Trefousse, *Johnson,* 146–47; Temple, *East Tennessee,* 366–85; McKinney, "First East Tennessee Campaign."

5. Noel C. Fisher, *War at Every Door,* 40–61; Madden, "Union Resistance to Confederate Occupation," 22–39; Lloyd Lewis, *Fighting Prophet,* 195–98; Temple, *East Tennessee,* 367–85; Trefousse, *Johnson,* 146–47; *OR* 4(1):235–49, 7(1):686–87, 690, 701; *Daily National Intelligencer,* December 24, 1861.

6. Benjamin to Wood, November 25, 1861, *OR* 7(1):701; *Cincinnati Commercial,* November 16, 1861.

7. *Cincinnati Commercial,* November 16, 1861.

8. Carter to Thomas, November 25, 1861, *OR* 7(1):448; *Cincinnati Commercial,* November 16, 1861; Noel C. Fisher, *War at Every Door,* 50–62; *New York Times,* December 11, 1861; Temple, *East Tennessee,* 375–78, 436.

9. Carter to Maynard, November 21, 25, 1861, *OR* 7(1):468–70; McKinney, *Education in Violence,* 112–22; Basler, *Works of Lincoln,* 5:31; Lloyd Lewis, *Fighting Prophet,* 206–7.

10. McClellan to Buell, November 12, 1861, McClellan Papers, LC; *OR* 4(1):355–56.

11. McClellan to Buell, November 12, 1861, McClellan Papers, LC; Sears, *Papers of McClellan,* 132; *OR* 4(1):355–56.

12. McClellan to Buell, November 12, 1861, and Buell to McClellan, November 16, 30, 1861, McClellan Papers, LC; Buell to McClellan, November 22, 1861, *OR* 7(1):443–44.

13. Lloyd Lewis, *Fighting Prophet,* 207; Kamm, "Scott," 94–95.

14. Buell to McClellan, November 22, 1861, *OR* 7(1):443–44.

15. Buell to McClellan, November 16, 30, 1861, McClellan Papers, LC; *OR* 7(1):443–44, 686–89; Trefousse, *Johnson,* 144–51; T. Harry Williams, "Johnson as a Member of the Committee on the Conduct of the War"; B. H. Liddell Hart, *Memoirs of Sherman,* 192–94; Temple, *East Tennessee,* 377–78; Lloyd Lewis, *Fighting Prophet,* 181; Ballard, *Military Genius of Lincoln,* 176–77.

16. Buell to McClellan, November 22, 1861, *OR* 7(1):443–44; Buell to McClellan, November 16, 1861, McClellan Papers, LC.

17. Buell to McClellan, November 16, 1861, McClellan Papers, LC; Buell to McClellan, November 27, 1861, *OR* 7(1):450–51; T. Harry Williams, *Lincoln and His Generals,* 49.

18. Lellyett to Buell, January 20, 25, February 4, 13, 1862, Buell Papers, RU.

19. Thomas to Schoepf, December 21, 1861, *OR* 7(1):509–10; Buell to Thomas, November 29, 1861, *OR* 7(1):458.

20. Buell to McClellan, November 22, 1861, *OR* 7(1):443–44.

21. Ibid.; Buell to McClellan, November 16, 30, 1861, McClellan Papers, LC.

22. McClellan to Buell, November 25, 1861, *OR* 7(1):447; Trefousse, *Johnson*, 147–48.

23. Sherman to Thomas, November 12, 1861, *OR* 4(1):353–54, also 420–21; Ballard, *Military Genius of Lincoln*, 176–77; Roland, *Johnston*, 261–77; Cooling, *Forts Henry and Donelson*, 12–62.

24. Cooling, *Forts Henry and Donelson*, 28–62; Roland, *Johnston*, 261–74.

25. McClellan to Buell, November 25, 1861, *OR* 7(1):447.

26. *Cincinnati Commercial*, November 16, 1861.

27. McClellan to Buell, November 25, 27, 1861, *OR* 7(1):447, 450; Prime, *McClellan's Own Story*, 215.

28. McClellan to Buell, and Buell to McClellan, November 27, 1861, *OR* 7(1):450–51.

29. Ibid. There was considerable speculation during the war and after as to who actually originated what became the Fort Henry and Fort Donelson Campaign. After the war, Buell wrote an article claiming that he, not Halleck, as Sherman had argued, had originated the idea. See D. C. Buell, "Sherman and the Spring Campaign"; Lellyett to Buell, January 20, 1862, Buell Papers, RU.

30. Buell to McClellan, November 27, 1861, *OR* 7(1):450–52; Buell to McClellan, November 16, 30, 1861, McClellan Papers, LC; Cooling, *Forts Henry and Donelson*, 65–66.

31. Buell to McClellan, November 27, 1861, *OR* 7(1):450–52; Buell to McClellan, November 16, 30, 1861, McClellan Papers, LC.

32. Halleck to McClellan, December 2, 1861, *OR* 52(1):198; Stephen E. Ambrose, *Halleck*, 15–18; on the battle of Belmont, see Hughes, *Battle of Belmont*; McClure, *Lincoln and Men of War-Times*, 212–13.

33. Halleck to McClellan, December 2, 1861, *OR* 52(1):198; Stephen E. Ambrose, *Halleck*, 15–18; Marszalek, *Sherman*, 164; Lloyd Lewis, *Fighting Prophet*, 196–207.

34. Buell to McClellan, November 30, 1861, McClellan Papers, LC.

35. Mitchel, *Mitchel*, 223, 237–41; Buell to McClellan, November 27, 1861, *OR* 7(1):450–52.

36. Buell to McClellan, November 30, 1861, McClellan Papers, LC.

37. Buell to McClellan, November 27, 1861, *OR* 7(1):451; Mitchel, *Mitchel*, 230; Hannaford, *Story of a Regiment*, 173–86.

38. Buell to McClellan, November 27, 1861, *OR* 7(1):451, 457–58.

39. McClellan to Buell, November 29, 1861, *OR* 7(1):457–58, misdated in the *OR*; see the original letter dated December 2, 1861, Buell Papers, RU. See also Kenneth P. Williams, *Lincoln Finds a General*, 3:481, for an explanation regarding this confusion.

40. McClellan to Buell, November 29, 1861, *OR* 7(1):457–58.

41. McClellan to Buell, December 3, 1861, *OR* 7(1):468–70.

42. Ibid.

43. Ibid., 468; Basler, *Works of Lincoln*, 5:54.

1. *New York Times*, December 31, 1861; Buell to McClellan, November 27, 1861, *OR* 7(1):450–52; McClellan to Buell, and Thomas to Carter, December 3, 1861, *OR* 7(1):468, 471; Johnson and Buel, *Battles and Leaders*, 1:385–86; Prokopowicz, "All for the Regiment," 126.

2. McClellan to Buell, December 5, 1861, Buell Papers, RU; also in *OR* 7(1):473–74. Also see Special Orders No. 19, December 2, 1861; Nos. 23, 24, December 5, 1861; No. 39, December 6, 1861, Department of the Ohio, AGO, RG 94, NA; *OR* 7(1):467–68.

3. Buell to McClellan, December 8, 1861, *OR* 7(1):482–83.

4. Ibid.

5. Melody to Frederick Buell, undated, Buell Papers, TC; Thornbrough, *Indiana in the Civil War*, 85–131; Stampp, *Indiana during the Civil War*, 112–15; McKinney, *Education in Violence*, 122.

6. Buell to McClellan, December 8, 1861, *OR* 7(1):482–83; see also Report of Morgan, December 7, 1861, *OR* 7(1):12–13.

7. Buell to McClellan, December 8, 1861, *OR* 7(1):482–83; Prokopowicz, "All for the Regiment," 102–3; Cist, *Army of the Cumberland*, 23–24.

8. Buell to McClellan, December 6, 1861, *OR* 7(1):477; Report of Zollicoffer, December 9, 14, 1861, *OR* 7(1):10–13; Fry to Thomas, November 19, 1861, *OR* 7(1):439; Wilbur Thomas, *Thomas*, 173–74.

9. Report of Schoepf, December 8, 1861, *OR* 7(1):8–9.

10. Buell to McClellan, December 8, 1861, *OR* 7(1):482–83.

11. *OR* 16(1):51–59; Buell to McClellan, November 16, 30, 1861, McClellan Papers, LC; Buell to Wife, December 10, 1861, Buell Papers, RU; *Louisville Daily Journal*, January 11, 1862.

12. Johnston to Benjamin, November 27, 1861, *OR* 7(1):707; Roland, *Johnston*, 274–80; *OR* 7(1):467–501; McKinney, *Education in Violence*, 123.

13. Johnson and Maynard to Buell, December 7, 1861, *OR* 7(1):480; *Chicago Tribune*, December 13, 1861.

14. Buell to Johnson and Maynard, December 8, 1861, *OR* 7(1):483.

15. Maynard to Thomas, December 8, 1861, *OR* 7(1):484–85.

16. Ibid.

17. Ibid.

18. Buell to McClellan, December 10, 1861, Buell Papers, HL; *OR* 7(1):487–89.

19. Noel C. Fisher, "Leniency Shown Them Has Been Unavailing," 280–81; Noel C. Fisher, *War at Every Door*, 50–62.

20. Buell to Wife, December 10, 1861, Buell Papers, RU.

21. Buell to McClellan, December 10, 1861, Buell Papers, HL; *OR* 7(1):487–88.

22. *OR* 7(1):487–88.

23. Ibid.

24. Trefousse, "Joint Committee"; Sears, *Young Napoleon*, 135–38; Niven, *Chase: A Biography*, 274–76; T. Harry Williams, "Committee on the Conduct of the War," 139–43.

25. Paludan, *"People's Contest,"* 89–94; Paludan, *Presidency of Lincoln*, 104; Kamm, "Scott," 94–95; *OR*, ser. 3, 1(1):710–11.

26. McClellan to Halleck, December 10, 1861, *OR* 8(1):419.

27. Frederick D. Williams, *Wild Life*, 49; Peskin, *Garfield*, 100–101; Special Orders No. 35, December 17, 1861, Department of the Ohio, AGO, RG 94, NA; *OR* 7(1):503–4; Buell to Garfield, and Lorenzo Thomas to Buell, December 17, 1861, *OR* 7(1):22, 501; Johnson and Buel, *Battles and Leaders*, 1:393–97; Cope, *Fifteenth Ohio*, 66.

28. Lorenzo Thomas to Buell, December 17, 1861, *OR* 7(1):501; Buell to McClellan, December 15, 18, 1861, *OR* 7(1):500, 504; Cope, *Fifteenth Ohio*, 59.

29. Johnson and Buel, *Battles and Leaders*, 1:386.

30. Grose, *Thirty-sixth Indiana*, 94–95.

31. Johnson and Buel, *Battles and Leaders*, 1:385–86; on Buell keeping his plans to himself, see, for example, Thomas to Schoepf, December 21, 1861, *OR* 7(1):509–10; Buell to McClellan, November 27, 1861, *OR* 7(1):450–52.

32. Buell to McClellan, December 23, 1861, *OR* 7(1):511; Report of McCook, December 17, 1861, *OR* 7(1):501; Report of Willich, December 18, 1861, *OR* 7(1):16–19; Johnson and Buel, *Battles and Leaders*, 1:385–86; Scribner, *How Soldiers Were Made*, 34–35; Cist, *Army of the Cumberland*, 23–24.

33. *New York Times*, December 19, 1861; Scribner, *How Soldiers Were Made*, 34–35; Prokopowicz, "All for the Regiment," 101–14; Kenneth P. Williams, *Lincoln Finds a General*, 3:147; *New York Times*, December 23, 1861; *Chicago Tribune*, December 18, 1861.

34. Buell to Wickliffe, December 25, 1861, *OR* 7(1):515–16; U.S. Congress, *Congressional Globe*, 37th Cong., 2nd sess., 77–110.

35. Buell to Wickliffe, December 25, 1861, *OR* 7(1):515–16.

36. Foote, *Civil War*, 1:153; Buell to McClellan, December 29, 1861, *OR* 7(1):520–21.

37. Buell to Thomas, December 23, 1861, *OR* 7(1):511–13.

38. Ibid.

39. *OR* 7(1):514; Grant to Buell, December 26, 1861, *OR* 7(1):516–17. On Grant, see McFeely, *Grant*.

40. Buell to McClellan, December 29, 1961, *OR* 7(1):520–21.

41. Ibid.; Buell to Thomas, December 28, 29, 1861, *OR* 7(1):519–21; McKinney, *Education in Violence*, 124.

42. Report of Zollicoffer, December 9, 14, 1861, *OR* 7(1):10–12.

43. Buell to McClellan, December 29, 1861, *OR* 7(1):520–21.

44. McClellan to Buell, December 29, 1861, *OR* 7(1):926.

45. Buell to McClellan, December 29, 1861, *OR* 7(1):520–21.

46. Buell to Thomas, December 29, 1861, *OR* 7(1):522; McKinney, *Education in Violence*, 124; Wilbur Thomas, *Thomas*, 174.

47. Buell to McClellan, December 29, 1861, *OR* 7(1):520–21; Roland, *Johnston*, 275–81.

48. Buell to McClellan, December 29, 1861, *OR* 7(1):520–21.

49. Ibid.

50. Buell to McClellan, December 29, 1861, *OR* 7(1):450–52.

51. Roland, *Johnston*, 275–81; Cooling, *Forts Henry and Donelson*, 41–43.

52. Catton, *Terrible Swift Sword*, 121; McClellan to Mary Ellen, November 18, 1861, McClellan Papers, LC.

1. Paludan, *"People's Contest,"* 87–88; Paludan, *Presidency of Lincoln*, 84, 104; U.S. Congress, *Congressional Globe*, 37th Cong., 1st sess., 222–23, 258–62, and 2nd sess., 6–16, 30, 32; Ash, *When the Yankees Came*, 25–26; *New York Daily Tribune,* January 3, 13, 1862.

2. *Independent,* January 23, 1862; Trefousse, *Johnson,* 148–49; U.S. Congress, *Congressional Globe*, 37th Cong., 2nd sess., 6–16, 29, 30, 32; T. Harry Williams, "Johnson as a Member of the Committee on the Conduct of the War," 70–81; Trefousse, "Joint Committee"; Trefousse, *Radical Republicans*, 184–86; T. Harry Williams, "Committee on the Conduct of the War," 139–56; Paludan, *"People's Contest,"* 64, 87–88; Paludan, *Presidency of Lincoln*, 98, 104; Sears, *Young Napoleon*, 135–39.

3. U.S. Congress, *Congressional Globe*, 37th Cong., 2nd sess., 163–65; T. Harry Williams, "Attack upon West Point during the Civil War"; Paludan, *Presidency of Lincoln*, 98; T. Harry Williams, "Johnson as a Member of the Committee on the Conduct of the War."

4. U.S. Congress, *Congressional Globe*, 37th Cong., 2nd sess., 194, 200, 206, 440–41.

5. As quoted in Paludan, *"People's Contest,"* 63; Stephen E. Ambrose, *Duty, Honor, Country,* 106–24.

6. Paludan, *"People's Contest,"* 49–52; Weigley, *American Way of War*, 38–78; Cunliffe, *Soldiers and Civilians*, 159–72; Sears, *Young Napoleon*, 84–86, 99–100, 105, 113; Hattaway and Jones, *How the North Won*, 11–25.

7. Hattaway and Jones, *How the North Won*, 11–25; Stephen E. Ambrose, *Duty, Honor, Country,* 106–24; Hagerman, *Origins of Modern Warfare*, xii-xvii, 4–39.

8. U.S. Congress, *Congressional Globe*, 37th Cong., 2nd sess., 165–202; Paludan, *"People's Contest,"* 63–65; T. Harry Williams, "Attack upon West Point during the Civil War"; T. Harry Williams, "Johnson as a Member of the Committee on the Conduct of the War"; *Independent,* January 2, 23, 1862.

9. James Richardson, *Messages and Papers of the Presidents*, 6:54; *New York Weekly Tribune,* January 18, 1862.

10. McClellan to Buell, December 29, 1861, *OR* 7(1):926; U.S. Congress, *Congressional Globe*, 37th Cong., 2nd sess., 162–202; *New York Weekly Tribune,* January 18, 1862; Paludan, *"People's Contest,"* 63–64.

11. Hattaway and Jones, *How the North Won*, 22–23; Jomini, *Summary of the Art of War,* 29–35.

12. Beale, *Diary of Bates*, 217–18.

13. *New York Times,* December 21, 1861.

14. Palmer, *Letters of Sumner*, 2:93–94; *Independent,* January 30, 1862.

15. Lincoln to Halleck, December 31, 1861, *OR* 7(1):524, 927; Sears, *Young Napoleon,* 136–37.

16. Lincoln to Buell, January 1, 1862, *OR* 7(1):525; Basler, *Works of Lincoln*, 5:86.

17. Lincoln to Halleck, January 1, 1862, *OR* 7(1):926; Paludan, *Presidency of Lincoln*, 100.

18. Buell to Lincoln, January 1, 1862, *OR* 7(1):526; Paludan, *Presidency of Lincoln*, 100.

19. Buell to Lincoln, January 1, 1862, *OR* 7(1):526.

20. Halleck to Lincoln, January 1, 1862, *OR* 7(1):527; Stephen E. Ambrose, *Halleck*, 20.

21. Halleck to Buell, January 2, 1862, *OR* 7(1):527.

22. Beale, *Diary of Bates*, 217–18.

23. McClellan to Halleck, January 3, 1862, *OR* 7(1):527–28.

24. Sears, *Young Napoleon*, 138.

25. Buell to Halleck, January 3, 1862, *OR* 7(1):528–29.

26. Ibid.

27. Ibid.

28. Halleck to Lincoln, January 6, 1862, *OR* 7(1):532–33; Stephen E. Ambrose, *Halleck*, 19; William T. Sherman, *Memoirs*, 1:219–20.

29. Halleck to Lincoln, and to Buell, January 6, 1862, *OR* 7(1):532–33.

30. Stephen E. Ambrose, *Halleck*, 21.

31. Halleck to Lincoln, and to Buell, January 6, 1862, *OR* 7(1):532–33, 583; Lincoln to Halleck, December 31, 1861, *OR* 7(1):524.

32. Lincoln to Buell, January 4, 1862, *OR* 7(1):530; Basler, *Works of Lincoln*, 5:90.

33. Buell to Lincoln, January 5, 1862, *OR* 7(1):530–31.

34. Ibid.; Buell to McClellan, January 27, 1862, *OR* 7(1):568.

35. Lincoln to Buell, January 6, 1862, *OR* 7(1):927–28.

36. Ibid.

37. McClellan to Buell, January 6, 1862, *OR* 7(1):531.

38. Ibid.

39. Sears, *Young Napoleon*, 138–39; Prime, *McClellan's Own Story*, 215.

40. Lincoln to Buell, January 6, 1862, *OR* 7(1):927–28.

41. Prime, *McClellan's Own Story*, 215.

42. Cameron to Buell, and Lincoln to Buell, January 7, 1862, *OR* 7(1):535; Basler, *Works of Lincoln*, 5:91–92.

43. Lincoln to McClellan, January 9, 1862; Basler, *Works of Lincoln*, 5:94.

44. Lincoln's Indorsement, January 10, 1862, *OR* 7(1):533.

45. As quoted in Sears, *Young Napoleon*, 139; Paludan, *Presidency of Lincoln*, 100.

46. Interestingly enough, Halleck's January 6 telegram boasted of his madness with an attempt to advance on Columbus and that if Buell were waiting on that, perhaps his own movement should be delayed. See Halleck to Buell, January 7, 10, 1862, *OR* 7(1):535, 543; Halleck to Grant, January 11, 1862, *OR* 7:544.

47. Thomas to Halleck, January 11, 1862, *OR* 7(1):545, includes the enclosure from Buell to Thomas. See also McClellan to Halleck, January 13, 1862, *OR* 7:547–48.

48. Thomas to Halleck, January 11, 1862, *OR* 7(1):545.

49. As quoted in Sears, *Young Napoleon*, 141. See also Raymond, *Life of Lincoln*, 772–77; Prime, *McClellan's Own Story*, 155–59; Montgomery Meigs, Pocket Diaries, LC; Beale, *Diary of Bates*, 218–20; Trefousse, *Radical Republicans*, 184–86; Niven, *Chase: A Biography*, 278–79; Paludan, *Presidency of Lincoln*, 102.

50. Sears, *Young Napoleon*, 141; Beale, *Diary of Bates*, 223–24; Paludan, *Presidency of Lincoln*, 102.

51. Lincoln to Buell, January 13, 1862, *OR* 7(1):928–29; Basler, *Works of Lincoln*, 5:98–99.

52. Basler, *Works of Lincoln*, 5:98–99.

53. Buell to McClellan, January 13, 1862, *OR* 7(1):548–49.

54. McClellan to Buell, January 13, 1862, *OR* 7(1):547.

55. Ibid.

56. Buell to Garfield, and Fry to Garfield, January 14, 1862, *OR* 7(1):21, 23–24; Cist, *Army of the Cumberland*, 6–8; Cope, *Fifteenth Ohio*, 66.

57. Cope, *Fifteenth Ohio*, 64.

58. Beatty, *Citizen Soldier*, 78.

59. McCook to Buell, January 10, 1862, *OR* 7(1):544.

60. Hazen, *Narrative of Military Service*, 13–14; Beatty, *Citizen Soldier*, 97; Briant, *Sixth Indiana*, 82–84; Speed and Pirhe, *Union Regiments in Kentucky*, 303–4; Ephraim S. Holloway to "Dear Father," January 21, 1862, Holloway Papers, OHS; Bishop, *Second Minnesota*, 32–33; McCook to Buell, January 10, 1862, *OR* 7(1):544; Bramlette to Thomas, December 23, 1861, *OR* 7(1):513; Prokopowicz, "All for the Regiment," 116–20; Fry to Wood, January 16, 1862, *OR* 7(1):556; Special Orders No. 4, January 8, 1862, Department of the Ohio, AGO, RG 94, NA; Crittenden to Fry, January 18, 1862, *OR* 7(1):558–59.

61. Roland, *Johnston*, 280–81; *OR* 7(1):11–12, 105–6.

62. Buell to McClellan, December 8, 17, 1861, *OR* 7(1):14–15, 482–83; Thomas to Buell, December 6, 1861, *OR* 7(1):477–78; Cist, *Army of the Cumberland*, 10–13.

63. Bircher, *Drummer Boy's Diary*, 15–16; Thomas to Buell, January 13, 1862, *OR* 7(1):550; James B. Shaw, *Tenth Indiana*, 137–38; Bishop, *Second Minnesota*, 32–36.

64. Buell to McClellan, and Thomas to Buell, January 13, 1862, *OR* 7(1):548–49, 550; James B. Shaw, *Tenth Indiana*, 137–38; McKinney, *Education in Violence*, 124–25; Bishop, *Second Minnesota*, 32–36.

65. Buell to McClellan, and to Thomas, January 13, 1862, *OR* 7(1): 548–50.

66. Bishop, *Second Minnesota*, 32–38; Cleaves, *Rock of Chickamauga*, 95; McKinney, *Education in Violence*, 124–27; Prokopowicz, "All for the Regiment," 132–43; *OR* 7(1):105–6; Cist, *Army of the Cumberland*, 15–16.

67. *OR* 7(1):79–82, 93–94; Cist, *Army of the Cumberland*, 16–18; John D. Inskeep Diary, January 19, 1862, Inskeep Papers, OHS; Cope, *Fifteenth Ohio*, 19–20; Bircher, *Drummer Boy's Diary*, 23–25; Abiah Zeller to Brother, January 22, 1862, Zeller Papers, OHS; McMurtry, "Zollicoffer and the Battle of Mill Springs."

68. Thomas M. Small Dairy, January 19, 1862, Small Papers, IHS; Grebner, *We Were the Ninth*, 84; Bishop, *Second Minnesota*, 38–47; Elmore to "Dear Father and Mother," January 23, 1862, Elmore Papers, IHS; James B. Shaw, *Tenth Indiana*, 139, 151; Bircher, *Drummer Boy's Diary*, 40; Frances Dallam Peters Diary, January 20, 21, 1862, Evans-Peters Papers, UK; Diary of James Thomson, February 5, 1862, FC; Cist, *Army of the Cumberland*, 18–19; *OR* 7(1):79–82, 93–94; Prokopowicz, "All for the Regiment," 129–59.

69. *Louisville Daily Journal*, January 21, 22, 1862.

70. Buell to Thomas, January 22, 1862, *OR* 7(1):562; Thomas to Buell, January 23, 24, 1862, *OR* 7(1):563–65.

71. Harrison Derrick to "Dear Friend Molly," January 30, 1862, Derrick Papers, IHS; Willie to Sister, January 27, 1862, "Willie" Letter, FC.

72. Cope, *Fifteenth Ohio*, 64.

73. Congratulatory Order from the President, written by Stanton, January 22, 1862, OR 7(1):102; Thomas and Hyman, *Stanton*, 150–55.

74. Fry to Thomas, January 23, 1862, OR 7(1):78; Maynard to Thomas, February 4, 1862, OR 7(1):582.

75. Buell to Lorenzo Thomas, February 9, 1862, OR 7(1):77.

76. Buell to McClellan, January 13, 1862, OR 7(1):548–49.

77. Buell to Carter, January 26, 1862, OR 7(1):567.

78. Landon C. Haynes to Jefferson Davis, January 29, 1862, OR 7(1):849.

CHAPTER 10

1. Paludan, *Presidency of Lincoln*, 105–6; Thomas and Hyman, *Stanton*, 94–96, 143–50, 169–71.

2. Thomas and Hyman, *Stanton*, 145–49; *New York Weekly Tribune*, January 18, 1862; Sears, *Young Napoleon*, 147; Sears, *Papers of McClellan*, 158; Paludan, *Presidency of Lincoln*, 104–6; Beale, *Diary of Bates*, 217, 223–24.

3. Sears, *Papers of McClellan*, 158; Sears, *Young Napoleon*, 148.

4. Sears, *Young Napoleon*, 148.

5. Buell to Lorenzo Thomas, January 27, 1862, OR 7(1):568.

6. Buell to Stanton, February 1, 1862, Stanton Papers, LC; Trefousse, "Joint Committee."

7. Trefousse, "Joint Committee"; Cope, *Fifteenth Ohio*, 68; Paludan, *Presidency of Lincoln*, 104–8; Thomas and Hyman, *Stanton*, 169–76.

8. Basler, *Works of Lincoln*, 5:111–12.

9. Ibid.; Sears, *Young Napoleon*, 149–53; Sears, *Papers of McClellan*, 162–70; OR 5(1):42–45.

10. Stephen E. Ambrose, *Halleck*, 17–25.

11. Buell to McClellan, December 10, 1861, Buell Papers, HL; OR 7(1):487–88.

12. Roland, *Johnston*, 264–86; Stephen E. Ambrose, *Halleck*, 17–25.

13. Buell to McClellan, December 10, 1861, Buell Papers, HL; Buell to McClellan, December 29, 1861, OR 7(1):520–21; Buell to Halleck, January 3, 1862, OR 7(1):528–29; Buell to Lorenzo Thomas, January 27, 1862, OR 7(1):568.

14. Halleck to Lincoln, January 1, 6, 1862, OR 7(1):526, 532–33; Halleck to Buell, January 2, 6, 10, 1862, OR 7(1):527, 533, 543; Stephen E. Ambrose, *Halleck*, 19–25.

15. Stephen E. Ambrose, *Halleck*, 21; Halleck to Grant, January 22, 1862, OR 7(1):561–62.

16. Long, *Memoirs of Grant*, 1:147; Stephen E. Ambrose, *Halleck*, 23–25.

17. McClellan to Halleck, January 29, 1862, OR 7(1):571.

18. Halleck to McClellan, January 20, 1862, OR 8(1):508–11; Stephen E. Ambrose, *Halleck*, 22–24.

19. Halleck to McClellan, January 20, 1862, OR 8(1):508–11.

20. Ibid.; Stephen E. Ambrose, *Halleck*, 23–25.

21. Buell to Halleck, January 3, 1862, OR 7(1):528–29.

22. Halleck to McClellan, January 20, 1862, OR 8(1):509–11; Halleck to Grant,

and to McClellan, January 30, 1862, *OR* 7(1):571–72; see also the telegrams of the next few days, *OR* 7(1):572–79.

23. Buell to McClellan, and to Halleck, January 30, 1862, *OR* 7(1):572–74; Lellyett to Buell, January 30, February 4, 1862, Buell Papers, RU.

24. Buell to Halleck, January 30, 1862, *OR* 7(1):574.

25. Halleck to Buell, January 31, 1862, *OR* 7(1):574; McClellan to Halleck, January 29, 1862, *OR* 7(1):930–31; Halleck to Buell, February 1, 1862, *OR* 7(1):576.

26. Buell to Halleck, January 31, 1862, *OR* 7(1):574.

27. Buell to Thomas, January 31, 1862, *OR* 7(1):576; Buell to Halleck, February 5, 1862, *OR* 7(1):936–37.

28. Halleck to Buell, February 2, 1862, *OR* 7(1):578–79; Buell to Halleck, February 3, 5, 1862, *OR* 7(1):580–83.

29. Halleck to Buell, February 1, 1862, *OR* 7(1):576.

30. Buell to McClellan, February 1, 1862, *OR* 7(1):931–32.

31. Ibid.

32. Ibid.

33. Stanton to Buell, February 9, 1862, *OR* 7(1):937–38.

34. Halleck to Buell, February 2, 1862, *OR* 7(1):578–79; Grant to Halleck, January 31, 1862, *OR* 7(1):575.

35. Buell to Thomas, February 2, 1862, *OR* 7(1):580.

36. Halleck to Buell, February 5, 1862, *OR* 7(1):583; Stephen E. Ambrose, *Halleck*, 26.

37. Buell to Halleck, February 5, 1862, *OR* 7(1):583.

38. Ibid., 584; Halleck to McClellan, February 5, 1862, *OR* 7(1):583–84; McClellan to Buell, and Buell to McClellan, February 5, 1862, *OR* 7(1):584; Stephen E. Ambrose, *Halleck*, 27.

39. Buell to Halleck, February 5, 1862, *OR* 7(1):936–37.

40. Buell to McClellan, February 5, 1862, *OR* 7(1):585.

41. McClellan to Buell, February 6, 1862, *OR* 7(1):586.

42. Buell to McClellan, February 5, 1862, *OR* 7(1):585.

43. McClellan to Morton, February 6, 7, 1862, Telegraph Book No. 3, Morton Collection, ISA; McClellan to Buell, and Halleck to McClellan, February 6, 1862, *OR* 7(1):586–87; Stephen E. Ambrose, *Halleck*, 27.

44. McClellan to Halleck, and Halleck to McClellan, February 6, 1862, *OR* 7(1):587.

45. Scott to Stanton, February 1, 2, 4, 6, 1862, Stanton Papers, LC; Thomas and Hyman, *Stanton*, 172–73; Nicolay and Hay, *Complete Works*, 5:188; Kamm, "Scott," 93.

46. *Memphis Daily Avalanche* and *Nashville Republican Banner*, February 8, 1862; Scott to Stanton, February 6, 7, 1862, and "Private and Confidential," February 7, 1862, Stanton Papers, LC; Kamm, "Scott," 93.

47. Scott to Stanton, Reports from February 5–21, 1862, esp. "Private and Confidential," February 7, 1862, Stanton Papers, LC; Kamm, "Scott," 93–95; Thomas and Hyman, *Stanton*, 172–73; Buell to Halleck, February 6, 1862, *OR* 7(1):589.

48. Scott to Stanton, and "Private and Confidential," February 7, 1862, Stanton Papers, LC; Kamm, "Scott," 95–96; *Louisville Daily Journal*, January 22, 1862.

49. Scott to Stanton, February 7, 1862; "Private and Confidential," February 7,

1862; and Stanton's Letterbook No. 4, 95–96, all in Stanton Papers, LC; Kamm, "Scott," 95–96, 108.

50. Buell to McClellan, February 6, 1862, *OR* 7(1):587–88; Buell to Halleck, February 5, 6, 1862, *OR* 7(1):584, 588.

51. Bruce, "Donelson Campaign," 19–20.

CHAPTER 11

1. Cooling, *Forts Henry and Donelson*, 101–11; Roland, *Johnston*, 284–91; Lellyett to Buell, February 4, 1862, Buell Papers, RU.

2. Halleck to Buell, February 7, 1862, *OR* 7(1):590; Cooling, *Forts Henry and Donelson*, 103–13.

3. Halleck to McClellan, February 7, 1862, *OR* 7(1):590.

4. Cooling, *Forts Henry and Donelson*, 103–11; Peter Franklin Walker, "Command Failure."

5. Halleck to Buell, February 7, 1862, *OR* 7(1):592.

6. Ibid.

7. Halleck to McClellan, February 7, 1862, *OR* 7(1):590–91.

8. Ibid.

9. Buell to Halleck, February 7, 1862, *OR* 7(1):593; Stephen E. Ambrose, *Halleck*, 27.

10. Buell to McClellan, February 7, 8, 1862, *OR* 7(1):593–94.

11. Halleck to McClellan, February 8, 1862, *OR* 7(1):595.

12. Halleck to Stanton, February 9, and to Scott, February 12, 1862, Stanton Papers, LC; Halleck to McClellan, February 10, 1862, *OR* 7(1):599; Stephen E. Ambrose, *Halleck*, 30; Sears, *Young Napoleon*, 180; McClellan to Halleck, February 14, 1862, *OR* 7(1):614.

13. Scott to Stanton, February 13, 14, 1862, "Private and Confidential," Stanton Papers, LC; Kamm, "Scott," 108–9.

14. Buell to Thomas, February 8, 1862, *OR* 7(1):597.

15. Cope, *Fifteenth Ohio*, 73; *OR* 7(1):597–627; Scribner, *How Soldiers Were Made*, 34–36.

16. McClellan to Buell, February 13, 1862, *OR* 7(1):608–9; Buell to Halleck, February 12, 1862, 7(1):607–8.

17. Halleck to Buell, February 13, 1862, *OR* 7(1):609; Halleck to McClellan, February 14, 1862, *OR* 7(1):612.

18. Grant to Halleck, Buell to McClellan, and McClellan to Halleck, February 14, 1862, *OR* 7(1):612–14.

19. Halleck to McClellan, and Buell to Halleck, February 15, 1862, *OR* 7(1):616, 621.

20. Buell to McClellan, and to Nelson, February 15, 1862, *OR* 7(1):619–20, 623; Lellyett to Buell, February 13, 1862, Buell Papers, RU.

21. McClellan to Buell, February 15, 1862, *OR* 7(1):620.

22. Halleck to McClellan, February 15, 1862, *OR* 7(1):617.

23. Halleck to Buell, February 15, 1862, *OR* 7(1):621–22.

24. Scott to Stanton, February 14, 1862, Stanton Papers, LC; Sears, *Young Napoleon*, 153.

25. McClellan to Halleck, February 15, 1862, *OR* 7(1):617–18.

26. Halleck to McClellan, February 16, 1862, *OR* 7(1):624.

27. Roland, *Johnston*, 282–301; Cooling, *Forts Henry and Donelson*, 129.

28. Sears, *Papers of McClellan*, 182.

29. Lincoln to Halleck, February 16, 1862, *OR* 7(1):624.

30. Buell to McClellan, February 16, 1862, *OR* 7(1):627.

31. Grant to Halleck, February 16, 1862, *OR* 7(1):625; Cooling, *Forts Henry and Donelson*, 122–224; Roland, *Johnston*, 291–99.

32. George W. Johnson to Wife, February 15, 1862, Johnson Papers, KHS; Durham, *Nashville*, 6–39; McKee, *Great Panic*, 20–28.

33. Roland, *Johnston*, 295–99; Cooling, *Forts Henry and Donelson*, 224–37; McKee, *Great Panic*, 20–28; Durham, *Nashville*, 6–39.

34. Halleck to McClellan, February 17, 1862, *OR* 7(1):628; Stephen E. Ambrose, *Halleck*, 33; *Chicago Tribune*, February 18, 1862.

35. Halleck to McClellan, February 17, 1862, *OR* 7(1):627–28.

36. D. P. Dougherty to "My Dear Wife," February 16, 1862, Dougherty Papers, OHS; Mitchel to Buell, February 14, 1862, *OR* 7(1):615; McClellan to Halleck, and Buell to Halleck, February 17, 1862, *OR* 7(1):628, 630; Mitchel, *Mitchel*, 248; Cist, *Army of the Cumberland*, 24; Prime, *McClellan's Own Story*, 243.

37. Buell to McClellan, February 15, 1862, *OR* 7(1):620; Buell to Halleck, February 17, 18, 1862, *OR* 7(1):630, 632.

38. Halleck to Buell, February 18, 1862, *OR* 7(1):632–33.

39. Buell to Halleck, February 18, 1862, *OR* 7(1):634; Lellyett to Buell, February 13, 1862, Buell Papers, RU.

40. Buell to Halleck, February 19, 1862, *OR* 7(1):639; Kamm, "Scott," 112; Stanton to Scott, February 21, 1862, Stanton Papers, LC; Halleck to Cullum, February 19, 1862, and to Scott, February 20, 1862, *OR* 7(1):636, 642; Thomas and Hyman, *Stanton*, 175.

41. Halleck to McClellan, February 19, 20, 1862, *OR* 7(1):636, 641.

42. James B. McPherson to Grant, February 21, 1862, as quoted in Simon, *Papers of Grant*, 4:222–23.

43. Halleck to Scott, February 20, 1862, *OR* 7(1):643; McClellan to Halleck, and Halleck to McClellan, February 21, 1862, *OR* 7(1):645–47; Nicolay and Hay, *Complete Works*, 5:307–8.

44. McClellan to Buell, February 20, 1862, General's Papers, AGO, RG 94, NA.

45. Halleck to McClellan, February 21, 1862, *OR* 7(1):647.

46. Stanton to Scott, February 21, 1862, Stanton Papers, LC; Kamm, "Scott," 112; Thomas and Hyman, *Stanton*, 172–75.

47. Stanton to Scott, February 21, 1862, Stanton Papers, LC.

48. Ibid.; Niven, *Chase: A Biography*, 285; Kamm, "Scott," 112; Thomas and Hyman, *Stanton*, 172–75.

49. Scribner, *How Soldiers Were Made*, 34–36; Villard, *Memoirs*, 1:219–23.

50. Thomas to Buell, February 21, 1862, *OR* 7(1):653; Mitchel, *Mitchel*, 242; Fry to McClellan, February 20, 1862, *OR* 7(1):642; Cope, *Fifteenth Ohio*, 78–83.

51. Mitchel, *Mitchel*, 242; R. Delavan Mussey to Joseph Barrett, February 21, 1862, Mussey Papers, Lincoln Collection, UC.

52. Henry Seys to "My Dear Wife," January 25, 1862, Seys Papers, UMWCL.

53. Briant, *Sixth Indiana*, 96–97.

54. Prokopowicz, "All for the Regiment," 167–70; W. R. Holloway to Buell, and Buell to Morton, February 8, 1862, Telegraph Book No. 2, Morton Collection, ISA; Buell to McClellan, February 17, 1862, *OR* 7(1):629; Colburn to Buell, February 15, 1862, *OR* 7(1):622; Cope, *Fifteenth Ohio*, 78–83.

55. *Memphis Daily Avalanche*, February 8, 1862.

56. Mussey to Barrett, February 21, 1862, Mussey Papers, Lincoln Collection, UC.

57. Scribner, *How Soldiers Were Made*, 36–38; Villard, *Memoirs*, 1:222–23; Cope, *Fifteenth Ohio*, 78–83.

58. Samuel Thomas Davis Diary, February 17, 1862, Davis Papers, WKU; George Botkin to "Friend Sid [Baker]," February 24, 1862, Baker Papers, OHS; Cope, *Fifteenth Ohio*, 78–83; Prokopowicz, "All for the Regiment," 174–76.

59. Buell to McClellan, February 14, 1862, *OR* 7(1):611; Cope, *Fifteenth Ohio*, 80–82; *National Tribune*, July 14, 1862.

60. *OR* 7(1):642, 651–57; Hannaford, *Story of a Regiment*, 199–201.

61. Halleck to Fry, February 23, 1862, *OR* 7(1):658.

62. Halleck to Stanton, February 24, 1862, *OR* 7(1):660.

63. McClellan to Buell, February 24, 1862, *OR* 7(1):660; Fry to McClellan, February 22, 1862, *OR* 7(1):652.

64. McClellan to Buell, February 20, 1862, *OR* 7(1):640.

65. McClellan to Buell, February 25, 1862, *OR* 7(1):664.

66. Garfield to Fry, February 24, 1862, *OR* 7(1):663–64.

67. McClellan to Halleck, February 24, 1862, *OR* 7(1):661; Buell to Halleck, March 1, 1862, *OR* 7(1):675.

68. McKee, *Great Panic*, 29–30; Keifer to Eliza, February 24, 1862, Keifer Papers, LC; Frances Dallam Peters Diary, February 26, 1862, Evans-Peters Papers, UK; *Memphis Daily Avalanche*, February 25, 1862; *Indianapolis Daily Journal*, March 4, 1862; *OR* 7(1):425–28, 431–32; Hannaford, *Story of a Regiment*, 197–203; Clift, "From the Archives"; Durham, *Nashville*, 1–45; Villard, *Memoirs*, 1:230–31; Stanley F. Horn, "Nashville during the War"; Lucy Virginia French Diary, February 22, 1862, 45, French Papers, TSLA; *New York Daily Tribune*, March 6, 1862; Hardison, "In the Toils of War," 64–67; Maslowski, *Treason Must Be Made Odious*, 15; Cooling, *Fort Donelson's Legacy*, 15–25.

69. Hannaford, *Story of a Regiment*, 201–6; Villard, *Memoirs*, 1:225–27; Beatty, *Citizen Soldier*, 86–89.

70. Hannaford, *Story of a Regiment*, 202–5; *New York Daily Tribune*, March 6, 1862.

71. *OR* 7(1):424, 425, 659–60, 668–69; Mitchel, *Mitchel*, 251–52; *Indianapolis Daily Journal*, March 4, 1862; McKee, *Great Panic*, 32–33; Hannaford, *Story of a Regiment*, 203–6; Durham, *Nashville*, 1–3; Hardison, "In the Toils of War," 64–67.

72. Report of Buell, February 26, 1862, *OR* 7(1):425; Villard, *Memoirs*, 1:228.

73. *New York Daily Tribune*, February 22, 26, 1862; *Frank Leslie's Illustrated*, March 8, 1862.

74. Report of Buell, February 26, 1862, *OR* 7(1):425, 670–71; Villard, *Memoirs*, 1:230–31; Durham, *Nashville*, 51–52; Cooling, *Fort Donelson's Legacy*, 19–25.

75. Grant, *Memoirs*, 1:217; Simon, *Papers of Grant*, 4:344.

76. *OR* 7(1):425, 668–69, 670–71, 674; Simon, *Papers of Grant*, 4:299, 5:293; Hardison, "In the Toils of War," 64–67; Roland, *Johnston*, 299–302.

77. Halleck to Buell, February 28, 1862, *OR* 7(1):671; Report of Buell, February 26, 1862, *OR* 7(1):425.

78. Keifer to Eliza, February 28, 1862, Keifer Papers, LC.

79. Villard, *Memoirs*, 1:225–26.

80. Ibid.; Hardison, "In the Toils of War," 64–67.

81. Durham, *Nashville*, 3–10; Hardison, "In the Toils of War," 64–67; Stanley F. Horn, "Nashville during the War"; Villard, *Memoirs*, 1:225–26.

82. Grant to Julia, February 24, 1862, Grant Papers, Federal Collection, TSLA; *OR* 7(1):661; Cooling, *Forts Henry and Donelson*, 225–26; Roland, *Johnston*, 298–302; Cooling, *Fort Donelson's Legacy*, 20–25.

83. *New York Herald*, March 6, 1862; *Frank Leslie's Illustrated*, March 8, 22, 1862; Cooling, *Forts Henry and Donelson*, 224.

CHAPTER 12

1. Maslowski, "From Reconciliation to Reconstruction," 281–84; Paludan, *"People's Contest,"* 62–88.

2. Ash, *When the Yankees Came*, 25–27; Grimsley, *Hard Hand of War*, 23–38, 47–63; Cooling, *Fort Donelson's Legacy*, 22–25.

3. Foner, *Reconstruction*, 43–45; Maslowski, "From Reconciliation to Reconstruction"; Ash, *Middle Tennessee Society*, 97–98; Ash, *When the Yankees Came*, 25–27; *New York Times*, March 21, 1862; *New York Daily Tribune*, March 8, 1862; *Chicago Tribune*, March 8, 15, 1862.

4. Maslowski, "From Reconciliation to Reconstruction," 281–95; Gerteis, *From Contraband to Freedom*, 14–19.

5. James B. Shaw, *Tenth Indiana*, 163; Villard, *Memoirs*, 1:223–34; *OR* 7(1):654–55; Scott to Stanton, March 1, 1862, Stanton Papers, LC; *New York Times*, March 21, 23, 1862; *New York Daily Tribune*, March 6, 1862; *Chicago Tribune*, March 8, 15, 1862; Ash, *Middle Tennessee Society*, 84–85.

6. As quoted in Durham, *Nashville*, 18–20, 47; *Chicago Tribune*, March 3, 1862, as reprinted in the *Missouri Republican*.

7. Botkin to "Friend Sid," March 7, 1862, Baker Papers, OHS; Villard, *Memoirs*, 1:223–24.

8. Thomas J. Wright, *Eighth Kentucky*, 41–43.

9. *National Tribune*, July 14, 1921.

10. Scott to Stanton, March 1, 1862, Stanton Papers, LC.

11. Thomas J. Wright, *Eighth Kentucky*, 44; *Indianapolis Daily Journal*, March 4, 1862; *New York Daily Tribune*, March 17, 18, 1862; *Chicago Tribune*, March 4, 8, 15, 1862.

12. *OR* 7(1):669–70.

13. Ibid.

14. Scribner, *How Soldiers Were Made*, 40.

15. *New York Daily Tribune*, March 6, 18, 1862.

16. Smart, *Radical View*, 1:115; Durham, *Nashville*, 53; Ash, "Sharks in an Angry Sea," 224–25; Botkin to "Friend Sid," March 7, 1862, Baker Papers, OHS; Villard, *Memoirs*, 1:228–29. See also William Nelson to Salmon P. Chase, February 28, 1862, Chase Papers, CGS.

17. *Memphis Daily Avalanche*, March 18, 1862.

18. Buell to McClellan, February 28, 1862, *OR* 7(1):671.

19. Ibid.

20. Scott to Stanton, March 1, 2, 4, 1862, Stanton Papers, LC.

21. Scott to Stanton, March 1, 2, 4, 1862, Stanton Papers, LC; *OR* 7(1):675; *New York Daily Tribune*, March, 1862; *New York Times*, March 24, 1862; Mitchel, *Mitchel*, 254; *Chicago Tribune*, March 8, 1862; James B. Shaw, *Tenth Indiana*, 163; Durham, *Nashville*, 54–56.

22. DeWitt Clinton Loudon to Hannah, March 13, 1862, Loudon Papers, OHS; *Chicago Tribune*, March 15, 1862.

23. MacKenzie, *"Maggie!,"* 8.

24. Ibid., 8–9.

25. Ellen McClung to "Dear Mother," March 6, 1862, Campbell Family Papers, DU.

26. *New York Times*, March 16, 1862.

27. Ibid.

28. Ibid., March 23, 1862.

29. Buell to McClellan, March 2, 1862, *OR*, 7(1):679; Scott to Stanton, March 1, 1862, Stanton Papers, LC; *New York Times*, March 16, 1862; Villard, *Memoirs*, 1:228–29; *New York Daily Tribune*, March 6, 1862.

30. McClellan to Buell and Halleck, March 2, 1862, *OR* 7(1):678; Sears, *Young Napoleon*, 154–57; U.S. Congress, *Congressional Globe*, 37th Cong., 2nd sess., 162–202.

31. Buell to McClellan, March 3, 1862, *OR* 7(1):679.

32. Scott to Stanton, March 1, 1862, Stanton Papers, LC.

33. Buell to Halleck, March 6, 1862, *OR* 10(2):10 and 7(1):676, 679–80, 682; Stephen E. Ambrose, *Halleck*, 36–39.

34. Buell to McClellan, March 3, 1862, *OR* 7(1):679.

35. MacKenzie, *"Maggie!,"* 9; *OR* 16(1):633; Maslowski, *Treason Must Be Made Odious*, 26; Hall, *Johnson*, 40–41.

36. *OR* 16(1):59–60.

37. Scott to Stanton, March 1, 4, 6, 1862, Stanton Papers, LC; *New York Daily Tribune*, March 8, 17, 1862; Durham, *Nashville*, 62–63; Hardison, "In the Toils of War," 180–81. According to Hardison, this editor may have been George Baber of the *Nashville Republican Banner*, who cooperated with the Johnson administration.

38. *New York Times*, March 16, 1862; Keifer to Eliza, March 10, 11, 1862, Keifer Papers, LC.

39. *New York Daily Tribune*, March 17, 31, 1862; *Memphis Daily Appeal*, March 8, 27, 1862; Cooling, *Fort Donelson's Legacy*, 49–50.

40. Cooling, *Fort Donelson's Legacy*, 49–50; *New York Daily Tribune*, March 17, 31, 1862; *Memphis Daily Appeal*, March 8, 27, 1862.

41. Nelson to Chase, February 28, 1862, Chase Papers, CGS; Trefousse, *Johnson*, 152–53. Several newspapers carried the rumor that Johnson would be appointed to military governor even before the appointment. See *Chicago Tribune*, February 21, 1862; *Cincinnati Daily Enquirer*, February 20, 1862; *New York Daily Tribune*, March 8, 1862; Maslowski, *Treason Must Be Made Odious*, 78.

42. Scott to Stanton, March 4, 1862, Stanton Papers, LC.

43. Garrett Davis to Buell, February 14, 1862, with enclosure W. W. Trimble to Dr. W. O. Smith, February 11, 1862, Davis Papers, FC; *New York Daily Tribune*, March 6, May 31, October 13, 1862.

44. *Memphis Daily Avalanche*, January 30, March 11, 18, 1862; Scott to Stanton, March 4, 1862, Stanton Papers, LC.

45. Scott to Stanton, March 4, 1862, Stanton Papers, LC; Trefousse, *Johnson*, 152–53; Hall, *Johnson*, 36–38.

46. Keifer to Wife, March 11, 1862, Keifer Papers, LC; Trefousse, *Johnson*, 152–53.

47. *New York Times*, March 4, 1862; Trefousse, *Johnson*, 152–53; Hardison, "In the Toils of War," 178.

48. Graf, Haskins, and Bergeron, *Papers of Johnson*, 5:177; Trefousse, *Johnson*, 152–53.

49. Trefousse, *Johnson*, 152–57.

50. Buell to McClellan, March 6, 1862, *OR* 10(2):611.

51. McClellan to Buell, March 7, 1862, *OR* 10(2):611.

52. *OR* 7(1):669.

53. Beatty, *Citizen Soldier*, 77–78.

54. Ibid.; Mitchel to Chase, March 2, 1862, Chase Papers, CGS; Mitchel, *Mitchel*, 241–59.

55. Mitchel, *Mitchel*, 243; Mitchel to Chase, March 2, 1862, Chase Papers, CGS; Grimsley, *Hard Hand of War*, 64–65.

56. Mitchel to Chase, March 2, 1862, Chase Papers, CGS; *Indianapolis Daily Journal*, March 4, 1862; Grimsley, *Hard Hand of War*, 64–65.

57. Mitchel to Chase, March 2, 1862, Chase Papers, CGS; Grimsley, *Hard Hand of War*, 64–65.

58. Fry to Mitchel, March 1, 1862, *OR* 7(1):675–76.

59. Mitchel to Chase, March 10, 1862, Chase Papers, CGS.

60. Keifer to Eliza, March 10, 11, 1862, Keifer Papers, LC.

61. Halleck to Scott, March 6, 1862, *OR* 10(2):10; Buell to Halleck, March 3, 1862, *OR* 7(1):680; Halleck to Buell, March 4, 1862, *OR* 7(1):682.

62. Halleck to Wife, March 5, 1862, Halleck Papers, Federal Collection, TSLA.

63. Scott to Stanton, March 4, 1862, Stanton Papers, LC.

64. Scott to Halleck, March 6, 1862, *OR* 10(2):10; Halleck to McClellan, March 3, 4, 1862, *OR* 7(1):679–80; Buell to McClellan, March 2, 1862, *OR* 7(1):679.

65. Buell to Halleck, March 6, 1862, *OR* 10(2):10–11.

66. Halleck to Scott, March 7, 1862, *OR* 10(2):16.

67. Scott to Stanton, March 4, 6, 1862, Stanton Papers, LC.

68. Carter to Fry, March 9, 1862, *OR* 10(2):23.

69. Garfield to Fry, March 7, 1862, *OR* 10(2):17–18.

70. Buell to Underwood, March 6, 1862, *OR* 10(2):15; *New York Times*, March 25, 1862; Cimprich, "Slave Behavior"; U.S. Congress, *Congressional Globe*, 37th Cong., 2nd sess., 492–96, 1049–54, 1137–41; Hubbard and Lewis, "Shiloh Letters," 28–29; Berlin, *Destruction of Slavery*, 50–52, 493–96.

71. *New York Weekly Tribune*, April 5, 1862, letter from a special correspondent dated March 17, 1862; *Louisville Daily Journal*, March 20, 1862; *New York Daily Tribune*, March 27, 31, 1862; Hubbard and Lewis, "Shiloh Letters," 28–29; *Chicago Tribune*, March 15, 1862; Ash, "Sharks in an Angry Sea," 217–26; Ash, *When the Yankees Came*, 25–36; Grimsley, *Hard Hand of War*, 49, 123–29; Berlin, *Destruction of Slavery*, 17–19, 26–27; Cooling, *Fort Donelson's Legacy*, 40.

72. Harvey S. Ford, *Beatty*, 91–92. Although Beatty's original work is cited earlier in this text, this edited version of his memoirs contains some useful endnotes.

73. Ibid.

74. Buell to Mitchel, March 11, 1862, *OR* 10(2):31.

75. Harvey S. Ford, *Beatty*, 91–92.

76. *OR* 16(1):138–45; *New York Daily Tribune*, January 20, March 17, 27, 1862; *New York Weekly Tribune*, April 5, 1862; *Louisville Daily Journal*, March 20, 1862.

77. Edwin W. Payne, *Thirty-fourth Illinois*, 14–15.

78. Ibid.; Mitchel, *Mitchel*, 251–52; Berlin, *Destruction of Slavery*, 280–81.

79. General Orders, March 19, 1862, Department of the Ohio, AGO, RG 94, NA; *OR*, ser. 3, 1(1):937–38; Keifer to Wife, March 20, 22, 1862, Keifer Papers, LC; U.S. Congress, *Congressional Globe*, 37th Cong., 2nd sess., 101–7; Donald, *Sumner*, 48–49.

80. Halleck to McClellan, March 10, 1862, *OR* 10(2):24–25.

81. Stanton to Scott, March 8, 1862, *OR* 10(2):20.

82. Graf, Haskins, and Bergeron, *Papers of Johnson*, 5:195–96; Johnson to Buell, March 10, 1862, *OR* 10(2):26, 612.

83. Trefousse, *Johnson*, 154; Buell to Johnson, March 11, 1862, *OR* 10(2):612; Curry, *Four Years*, 30. The group traveling with Johnson included his son Robert, Horace Maynard, Emerson Etheridge, and William A. Browning.

84. Graf, Haskins, and Bergeron, *Papers of Johnson*, 5:195–96; *New York Times*, March 21, 1862; Maslowski, "From Reconciliation to Reconstruction," 289–95; Cooling, *Fort Donelson's Legacy*, 45–46.

85. Villard, *Memoirs*, 1:232–34; Trefousse, *Johnson*, 155; Durham, *Nashville*, 59–61; Maslowski, "From Reconciliation to Reconstruction," 289–95.

86. Buell to Scott, March 7, 1862, *OR* 10(2):611.

87. Buell to Halleck, March 9, 1862, *OR* 10(2):22–23; Halleck to Buell, March 13, 1862, *OR* 10(2):613; Basler, *Works of Lincoln*, 5:155.

88. Buell to Halleck, March 10, 1862, *OR* 10(2):27.

89. Halleck to Buell, March 13, 1862, *OR* 10(2):33.

90. Keifer to Eliza, March 14, 1862, Keifer Papers, LC; Sears, *Young Napoleon*, 164–67.

91. *OR* 10(2):613; Halleck to Buell, March 13, 1862, *OR* 10(2):33; Thomas and Hyman, *Stanton*, 185–87; Croffut, *Fifty Years*, 437–40.

92. T. Harry Williams, *Lincoln and the Radicals*, 192–93; *Chicago Tribune* as quoted in *Frank Leslie's Illustrated*, September 27, 1862; *New York Daily Tribune*, May 31, October 24, 1862; T. Harry Williams, "Johnson as a Member of the Committee on the Conduct of the War."

93. Keifer to Wife, March 7, 1862, Keifer Papers, LC.

CHAPTER 13

1. *New York Weekly Tribune*, April 5, 1862; Maslowski, "From Reconciliation to Reconstruction," 281–95; Cooling, *Fort Donelson's Legacy*, 45–46.

2. Trefousse, *Johnson*, 154–57; Durham, *Nashville*, 62–65; *New York Weekly Tribune*, April 5, 1862; Cooling, *Fort Donelson's Legacy*, 45–46.

3. Johnson and Maynard to Stanton, March 14, 1862, *OR* 10(2):38; *OR* 10(2):28–29 for President's War Order No. 3, March 11, 1862.

4. Halleck to Buell, March 16, 1862, *OR* 10(2):42, 44; Buell to Halleck, March 9, 14, 17, 1862, *OR* 10(2):22–23, 37–38, 44.

5. Buell to Donn Piatt, October 12, 1890, Buell Papers, RU; Buell to Johnson, March 19, 1862, *OR* 10(2):47.

6. Buell to Halleck, March 15, 1862, *OR* 10(2):39; Buell to Dumont, March 20, 1862, *OR* 10(2):54–55, also 47–48.

7. Durham, *Nashville*, 67–69; Maury Klein, *Louisville and Nashville Railroad*, 39–40; *OR* 52(1):228.

8. Buell to Mitchel, March 27, 1862, *OR* 10(2):71–72; Mitchel, *Mitchel*, 261–69.

9. *OR* 10(2):68–76; Van Horne, *Army of the Cumberland*, 1:99–100; Dodge, *Old Second Division*, 163; Keifer to Wife, March 20, 1862, Keifer Papers, LC; Mitchel, *Mitchel*, 261–69.

10. Buell to McCook, March 18, 1862, *OR* 10(2):46; Johnson and Buel, *Battles and Leaders*, 1:489–91.

11. Lincoln to Buell, March 10, 1862, *OR* 10(2):612.

12. Buell to Stanton, March 23, 1862, *OR* 10(2):59; Johnson and Buel, *Battles and Leaders*, 1:491.

13. Halleck to Grant, March 21, 1862, *OR* 10(2):55–56.

14. Ibid., 50–51.

15. Buell to Halleck, March 19, 20, 1862, *OR* 10(2):48, 52; Villard, *Memoirs*, 1:236–37.

16. Johnson to Stanton, March 21, 1862, *OR* 10(2):56.

17. Stanton to Halleck, March 22, 1862, *OR* 10(2):57–58; Stanton to Buell, March 23, 1862, *OR* 10(2):59.

18. Buell to Halleck, and to Stanton, March 23, 1862, *OR* 10(2):59–61.

19. Lizzie Rogers to Capt. George W. Gordon, May 18, 1862, Gordon and Avery Family Papers, TSLA.

20. Buell to Halleck, March 24, 27, 1862, *OR* 10(2):64–65, 70–71, also (1):329–31; Johnson and Buel, *Battles and Leaders*, 1:490–92; Van Horne, *Army of the Cumberland*, 1:102; Dodge, *Old Second Division*, 31; Briant, *Sixth Indiana*, 98–99;

Chase, *Fourteenth Ohio*, 24–25; Villard, *Memoirs*, 1:236–37; Prokopowicz, "All for the Regiment," 187–88.

21. Halleck to Buell, March 26, 1862, *OR* 10(2):66.

22. Ibid.

23. Buell to Halleck, March 28, 1862, *OR* 10(2):75.

24. T. J. Bush to Buell, January 16, 1886, Buell Papers, RU; Halleck to Buell, March 16, 17, 26, 1862, and Buell to Halleck, March 18, 1862, General's Papers, AGO, RG 94, NA; *OR* 10(2):44.

25. Halleck to Buell, March 29, April 2, 1862, *OR* 10(2):77, 617; Thomas J. Bush to Buell, January 16, 1866, Buell Papers, RU.

26. Buell to Halleck, March 29, 1862, *OR* 10(2):77.

27. Hannaford, *Story of a Regiment*, 231; *OR* 10(1):329–31 and (2):64–65, 70–71; Johnson and Buel, *Battles and Leaders*, 1:490–92; Van Horne, *Army of the Cumberland*, 1:102; Dodge, *Old Second Division*, 31; Briant, *Sixth Indiana*, 98–99; Villard, *Memoirs*, 1:238–40; Jacob H. Smith, *Personal Reminiscences*, 7; Curry, *Four Years*, 35–36; Edgar Kellog, April 6, 1862, "Recollections of Civil War Service," CWMC, USAMHI; Bush to Buell, January 16, 1866, Buell Papers, RU.

28. Johnson to Stanton, March 29, 1862, *OR* 10(2):76.

29. Stanton to Halleck, March 30, 1862, *OR* 10(2):79; Durham, *Nashville*, 67–68.

30. Stanton to Buell, March 30, 31, 1862, *OR* 10(2):81; Buell to Stanton, March 25, 31, 1862, *OR* 10(2):81–82, 616.

31. Grant to Sherman, April 4, 1862, *OR* 10(2):91; Hazen, *Narrative of Military Service*, 24; Van Horne, *Army of the Cumberland*, 1:102–3; Curry, *Four Years*, 32–34; Kerwood, *Fifty-seventh Indiana*, 47–48.

32. *OR* 10(1):329–31; Johnson and Buel, *Battles and Leaders*, 1:491; Hazen, *Narrative of Military Service*, 24; Curry, *Four Years*, 32–34; Villard, *Memoirs*, 1:237–40; Van Horne, *Army of the Cumberland*, 1:101–3; Dodge, *Old Second Division*, 166–68, 173; Briant, *Sixth Indiana*, 98–100; Hannaford, *Story of a Regiment*, 237–38; Horace Cecil Fisher, *Staff Officer*, 349; Daniel, *Shiloh*, 140; Bush to Buell, January 16, 1866, Buell Papers, RU. In a postwar editorial, Buell agreed that he could have marched to Savannah faster than he did, but under the circumstances he thought it best to set the rate of march "to suit the object in view." "When there is no pressing emergency, the health and discipline of the troops are the controlling consideration." "Under the circumstances, when no serious obstacles have to be overcome," he argued, "twelve miles a day for many days in succession is a very good average for large bodies of troops" (*New York World*, April 6, 1886, in Buell Papers, RU; Chumney, "Gentleman General," 90).

33. Grant to Buell, and Sherman to Grant, April 5, 1862, *OR* 10(2):91–95; Johnson and Buel, *Battles and Leaders*, 1:490–92; *OR* 10(1):330–31.

34. Johnson and Buel, *Battles and Leaders*, 1:466–67, 491–92, 519; *OR* 10(2):94–95; Buell to Halleck, March 22, 1862, General's Papers, AGO, RG 94, NA; *OR* 10(1):330–32; Hannaford, *Story of a Regiment*, 236–40; Villard, *Memoirs*, 1:240–41.

35. Halleck to Stanton, April 5, 1862, *OR* 10(2):93; Daniel, *Shiloh*, 117–30; McDonough, *Shiloh*, 56–69; T. Harry Williams, *Beauregard*, 125–32; Roland, *Johnston*, 304–17.

36. Niven, *Chase Papers*, 1:406–7; Donald, *Inside Lincoln's Cabinet*, 163–64; Roland, *Johnston*, 317–19; McDonough, *Shiloh*, 56–69.

37. *OR* 10(1):385–88, 396–97; Roland, *Johnston*, 317–25; Daniel, *Shiloh*, 118–45; T. Harry Williams, *Beauregard*, 124–34; McDonough, *Shiloh*, 64–85.

38. *OR* 10(1):89, 183–85, 291–92; Simon, *Papers of Grant*, 5:17; Johnson and Buel, *Battles and Leaders*, 1:467–68, 492; Kenneth P. Williams, *Lincoln Finds a General*, 3:360; Daniel, *Shiloh*, 173–75.

39. John K. Duke, *Fifty-third Ohio*, 41–42; *OR* 10(2):93–94, 248–54; Johnson and Buel, *Battles and Leaders*, 1:468; Lloyd Lewis, *Fighting Prophet*, 219–20; Daniel, *Shiloh*, 130–60; McDonough, *Shiloh*, 86–91.

40. Lloyd Lewis, *Fighting Prophet*, 219–20; Marszalek, *Sherman*, 176–79; William T. Sherman, *Memoirs*, 1:230; Daniel, *Shiloh*, 143–219.

41. *OR* 10(2):95–96; Throne, *Diary of Cyrus Boyd*, 32–36; Daniel, *Shiloh*, 143–219; McDonough, *Shiloh*, 120–24.

42. Johnson and Buel, *Battles and Leaders*, 1:492; *OR* 10(1):291–92, 302, 330–32; Rerick, *Forty-fourth Indiana*, 45; Sword, *Shiloh*, 214–15; Daniel, *Shiloh*, 242–43.

43. As quoted in Frank and Reaves, *"Seeing the Elephant,"* 73.

44. *OR* 10(1):331.

45. Todd M. Oliphant Diary, April 7, 1862, Oliphant Papers, OHS; Andrew F. Davis to Brother, April 21, 1862, Davis Papers, and Levi Wagner Diary, April 7, 1862, Wagner Papers, CWTIC, USAMHI.

46. Briant, *Sixth Indiana*, 82–84; Johnson and Buel, *Battles and Leaders*, 1:492; Horace Cecil Fisher, *Staff Officer*, 10; Villard, *Memoirs*, 1:241; Tapp and Klotter, *Kentucky Captain's Account*, 81; Bircher, *Drummer Boy's Diary*, 32; Dodge, *Old Second Division*, 174; Curry, *Four Years*, 35; *OR* 10(1):291–92.

47. Samuel B. Franklin, April 16, 1862, "Memoirs of a Civil War Veteran," Franklin Papers, HCWRTC, USAMHI.

48. Presley Judson Edwards, "Autobiography," 73–74, Edwards Papers, CHS.

49. McDonough, *Shiloh*, 161. See also Jacob Ammen to A. B. Martin, April 8, 9, 1862, Ammen Papers, USMA-SC; Villard, *Memoirs*, 1:242; Daniel, *Shiloh*, 242–43.

50. Johnson and Buel, *Battles and Leaders*, 1:492; *OR* 10(1):323.

51. Hannaford, *Story of a Regiment*, 241–48.

52. Johnson and Buel, *Battles and Leaders*, 1:491–92; *OR* 10(1):291–92, 331–32; Jacob H. Smith, *Personal Reminiscences*, 8; Ammen to Martin, April 8, 9, 1862, Ammen Papers, USMA-SC.

53. *OR* 10(2):95; Johnson and Buel, *Battles and Leaders*, 1:492; Hannaford, *Story of a Regiment*, 248–49; Sword, *Shiloh*, 221; Daniel, *Shiloh*, 243.

54. *OR* 10(1):292; Johnson and Buel, *Battles and Leaders*, 1:492–93; Daniel, *Shiloh*, 243.

55. Daniel, *Shiloh*, 243; Johnson and Buel, *Battles and Leaders*, 1:492–94.

56. Grant, *Memoirs*, 1:345; *OR* 10(1):291–92; Johnson and Buel, *Battles and Leaders*, 1:474; *Cincinnati Gazette*, April 9, 1862; *Indianapolis Daily Journal*, April 15, 16, 1862; John Eicker, Memoir, Eicker Papers, HCWRTC, USAMHI.

57. Johnson and Buel, *Battles and Leaders*, 1:493–94; *OR* 10(1):186.

58. *OR* 10(1):291–92; Johnson and Buel, *Battles and Leaders*, 1:474; Z. Payson

Shumway Diary, May 1, 1862, Shumway Papers, ISHL; *Indianapolis Daily Journal,* April 15, 16, 1862; unidentified newspaper clippings, Buell Papers, RU.

59. Johnson and Buel, *Battles and Leaders,* 1:494–95; Rerick, *Forty-fourth Indiana,* 241; Throne, "Letters from Shiloh," 266.

60. *OR* 10(1):292–93, 323–24, 331–32; Johnson and Buel, *Battles and Leaders,* 1:492–507; Daniel, *Shiloh,* 244; McDonough, *Shiloh,* 112–34.

61. Roland, *Johnston,* 334–39; *OR* 10(1):277–80; T. Harry Williams, *Beauregard,* 133–40; McDonough, *Shiloh,* 154–67; Kenneth P. Williams, *Lincoln Finds a General,* 3:367–71.

62. Johnson and Buel, *Battles and Leaders,* 1:569–603; Obreiter, *Seventy-seventh Pennsylvania,* 78–79; Daniel, *Shiloh,* 243–49; McDonough, *Shiloh,* 243–49.

63. McCann, *Bierce's Civil War,* 17.

64. Villard, *Memoirs,* 1:246; *OR* 10(1):333; Jacob H. Smith, *Personal Reminiscences,* 8–11.

65. Shanks, *Personal Recollections,* 43.

66. As cited in Throne, *Diary of Cyrus Boyd,* 33; Smart, *Radical View,* 1:149–50.

67. *OR* 10(1):324; Villard, *Memoirs,* 1:244–45; Edgar Kellog, April 6, 1862, "Recollections of Civil War Service," CWMC, USAMHI; Throne, *Diary of Cyrus Boyd,* 33; Jacob H. Smith, *Personal Reminiscences,* 10–11; Frank and Reaves, "Seeing the Elephant," 109.

68. Horace Cecil Fisher, *Staff Officer,* 13; Partridge, *Alms,* 41–42; Albert D. Richardson, *Grant,* 247.

69. Dodge, *Old Second Division,* 183; *OR* 10(1):332–33; Hannaford, *Story of a Regiment,* 256–57.

70. Hannaford, *Story of a Regiment,* 256–57.

71. Grose, *Thirty-sixth Indiana,* 104–6; *OR* 10(1):337–39; William T. Sherman to John W. Draper, September 24, 1867, Draper Papers, LC; Kenneth P. Williams, *Lincoln Finds a General,* 3:378–79; Daniel, *Shiloh,* 248–49.

72. *OR* 10(1):384; T. Harry Williams, *Beauregard,* 139–43; McDonough, *Shiloh,* 180–82.

73. Grant, *Memoirs,* 1:354; George Carrington Diary, April 6, 7, 1862, Carrington Papers, CHS; Z. Payson Shumway Diary, April 13, 1862, Shumway Papers, ISHL; *OR* 10(1):324; Daniel, *Shiloh,* 248–52; McDonough, *Shiloh,* 183.

74. William T. Sherman, *Memoirs,* 1:246; Johnson and Buel, *Battles and Leaders,* 1:519–20; Van Horne, *Army of the Cumberland,* 1:109; William T. Sherman to Prof. Henry Coppee, in John Sherman, "Battle of Pittsburg Landing"; Lloyd Lewis, *Fighting Prophet,* 228; Briant, *Sixth Indiana,* 107; Daniel, *Shiloh,* 265–66.

75. Grant, *Memoirs,* 1:354.

76. *OR* 10(1):324–55; Samuel B. Franklin, April 16, 1862, "Memoirs of a Civil War Veteran," HCWRTC, USAMHI; McCann, *Bierce's Civil War,* 17; Johnson and Buel, *Battles and Leaders,* 1:474; J. Amos Glover Diary, April 6, 7, 1862, Glover Papers, OHS; *Indianapolis Daily Journal,* April 15, 16, 1862; *Cincinnati Commercial,* April 16, 1862.

77. *OR* 10(1):355; Smart, *Radical View,* 1:158.

78. Hazen, *Narrative of Military Service,* 25; Villard, *Memoirs,* 1:246–47; *OR*

10(1):302–6; James F. Mohr to Brother, April 10, 1862, Mohr Papers, FC; Samuel Thomas Davis Diary, April 6, 7, 1862, Davis Papers, WKU.

79. Van Horne, *Army of the Cumberland*, 1:109; Briant, *Sixth Indiana*, 107; Johnson and Buel, *Battles and Leaders*, 1:519; Monroe Cockrell to Kenneth P. Williams, May 16, 1952, Fulkerson Cockrell Papers, DU.

80. Johnson and Buel, *Battles and Leaders*, 1:602–3.

81. *OR* 10(1):293; William H. Fitzhugh, "On Shiloh," Payne Papers, USMA-SC.

82. *OR* 10(1):292–94, 335, 355–56; Todd M. Oliphant Diary, April 7, 1862, Oliphant Papers, OHS; Mohr to Brother, April 10, 1862, Mohr Papers, FC; William H. Fitzhugh, "On Shiloh," Payne Papers, USMA-SC.

83. Johnson and Buel, *Battles and Leaders*, 1:495–97; Frank and Reaves, *"Seeing the Elephant,"* 87–91, 105; Prokopowicz, "All for the Regiment," 198–99.

84. Throne, "Letters from Shiloh," 275; *OR* 10(1):293–94, 324–25, 341, 346, 351, 354–55, 372–73; Johnson and Buel, *Battles and Leaders*, 1:526–32; Jacob H. Smith, *Personal Reminiscences*, 10–13; Partridge, *Alms*, 42–43; Daniel, *Shiloh*, 267–69.

85. Almon Rockwell Diary, April 7, 1862, Rockwell Papers, LC; Frederick D. Williams, *Wild Life*, 50; *Daily Nashville Union*, April 23, 1862.

86. Hannaford, *Story of a Regiment*, 572–73.

87. Reynolds to William Orland Bourne, January 23, 1866, Bourne Papers, LC.

88. Levi Sipes, Application Records, Grand Army of the Republic, CHS.

89. Mohr to Brother, April 10, 1862, Mohr Papers, FC; Throne, *Diary of Cyrus Boyd*, 35–36.

90. Edwin W. Payne, *Thirty-fourth Illinois*, 29.

91. *OR* 10(1):251–52, 307–10, 317–18; Daniel, *Shiloh*, 283–84.

92. *OR* 10(1):251–52, 307–10.

93. *OR* 10(1):252; Edwin W. Payne, *Thirty-fourth Illinois*, 20–21; Briant, *Sixth Indiana*, 108; Jacob Van Zwaluwenberg Memoir, UMWCL; Johnson and Buel, *Battles and Leaders*, 1:527–30; *OR* 10(1):251–52, 303–6, 307–10, 388–89; Dodge, *Old Second Division*, 200; Horace Cecil Fisher, *Staff Officer*, 15–16; McDonough, *Shiloh*, 200–208.

94. William H. Harder Diary, April 7, 1862, Leeds Collection; Johnson and Buel, *Battles and Leaders*, 1:603; T. Harry Williams, *Beauregard*, 145; McDonough, *Shiloh*, 207–8; *OR* 10(1):388; McWhiney, "General Beauregard's 'Complete Victory' at Shiloh."

95. *OR* 10(1):263, 268, (2):96–97; McDonough, *Shiloh*, 208–10.

96. H. H. Giesy to Brother, Sister, and Mother, April 9, 1862, Giesy Papers, WKU.

97. *New York Daily Tribune*, April 16, 1862; *Indianapolis Daily Journal*, April 14, 15, 16, 1862; Ammen to Martin, April 8, 9, 1862, Ammen Papers, USMA-SC.

98. Alexander Varian to Father, April 10, 1862, and to Mary, April 18, 1862, Varian Papers, WRHS; David H. Thomas to Brother and Sister, April 8, 14, 1862, Thomas Papers, OHS.

99. Thomas Prickett to Matilda, April 18, 1862, Prickett Papers, IHS.

100. *New York Daily Tribune*, April 16, 1862.

101. Frederick D. Williams, *Wild Life*, 83–86.

102. Nelson to Chase, April 10, 1862, Chase Papers, CGS.

103. Torah W. Sampson to Mother, April 12, 1862, Sampson Papers, FC; Charles B. Tompkins to Wife, April 8, 14, 1862, Tompkins Papers, DU.

104. Davis to Brother, April 21, 1862, Davis Papers, CWTIC, USAMHI.

105. Samuel Thomas Davis Diary, April 15, 1862, Davis Papers, WKU; Henry M. Osborn Diary, April 9, 1862, Osborn Papers, OHS; Bircher, *Drummer Boy's Diary*, 32–35; *OR* 10(1):336; Henry Franklin Huffer Diary, April 10, 1862, Huffer Papers, HCWRTC, USAMHI.

106. Tapp and Klotter, *Kentucky Captain's Account*, 88; Reynolds to Bourne, January 23, 1866, Bourne Papers, LC; *Frank Leslie's Illustrated*, May 24, 1862; Bircher, *Drummer Boy's Diary*, 32–35; Samuel B. Franklin, April 16, 1862, "Memoirs of a Civil War Veteran," HCWRTC, USAMHI; Cyrus F. Leasher to Uncle, April 11, 1862, Leasher Papers, Mann Collection, USAMHI.

107. Todd M. Oliphant Diary, April 9, 1862, Oliphant Papers, OHS; Davis to Brother, April 21, 1862, Davis Papers, CWTIC, USAMHI; Sam to Cousin Aquors, April 9, 1862, Aquors Papers, DU; Curry, *Four Years*, 36–39.

108. As quoted in Throne, "Letters from Shiloh," 238, 275.

109. *OR* 16(1):135; Levi Wagner, "Recollections of an Enlistee," Wagner Papers, CWTIC, USAMHI.

110. Nelson to Chase, April 10, 1862, Chase Papers, CGS.

111. Rousseau to Chase, April 15, 1862, ibid.

112. Throne, *Diary of Cyrus Boyd*, 257; *Indianapolis Daily Journal*, April 16, 1862; *Nashville Republican Banner*, April 10, 1862; *Cincinnati Daily Enquirer*, April 15, 1862; *Daily National Intelligencer*, April 10, 1862; *Memphis Daily Avalanche*, April 7, 1862; *Chicago Tribune*, April 10, 1862; Frank and Reaves, *"Seeing the Elephant,"* 143–44; William H. Fitzhugh, "On Shiloh," Payne Papers, USMA-SC.

113. Buell to Wife, April 8, 1862, Buell Papers, RU; also reprinted in *North American Review* (December 1885–February 1886) in Buell Papers, RU.

114. Louis M. Buford to Charles Buford Jr., April 21, 1862, Buford Papers, LC; *OR* 10(1):356; *New York Daily Tribune*, May 9, 1862; Varian to Wife, April 9, 1862, Varian Papers, WRHS; Davis to Brother, April 21, 1862, Davis Papers, CWTIC, USAMHI.

115. Rousseau to Chase, April 15, 1862, Chase Papers, CGS; *New York Daily Tribune*, May 9, 1862; *Indianapolis Daily Journal*, April 14, 15, 16, 1862; *Cincinnati Commercial*, April 16, 1862.

116. Blaisdell to Sister and Brother, April 12, 1862, Blaisdell Papers, CWMC, USAMHI; Keil, *Thirty-fifth Ohio*, 64–66; Davis to Brother, April 21, 1862, Davis Papers, CWTIC, USAMHI; Marion Morrison, *Ninth Illinois*, 34; William H. Fitzhugh, "On Shiloh," Payne Papers, USMA-SC.

117. Tompkins to Wife, April 8, 1862, Tompkins Papers, DU; Throne, *Diary of Cyrus Boyd*, 42; Z. Payson Shumway Diary, April 13, 1862, Shumway Papers, ISHL.

118. Nelson to Chase, April 10, 1862, Chase Papers, CGS.

119. Frederick D. Williams, *Wild Life*, 82.

120. *Frank Leslie's Illustrated*, May 10, 1862; Keil, *Thirty-fifth Ohio*, 64–66; Rousseau to Chase, April 15, 1862, Chase Papers, CGS.

121. *Cincinnati Commercial*, April 16, 1862; *Indianapolis Daily Journal*, April 16, 1862.

122. Nelson to Chase, April 10, 1862, Chase Papers, CGS; *OR* 10(1):115–21, 169–73; Shanks, *Personal Recollections*, 43; *Indianapolis Daily Journal*, April 15, 1862;

Cincinnati Commercial, April 14, 16, 1862; *Cincinnati Gazette,* April 14, 1862; Eugene Marshall Diary, April 8, 1862, Marshall Papers, DU; William Farrar Smith, "Don Carlos Buell," Buell Papers, USMA-SC.

123. *OR* 10(1):297.

124. Shanks, *Personal Recollections,* 247; Prokopowicz, "All for the Regiment," 240–42.

125. *OR* 10(1):336; Ammen to Martin, April 8, 9, 1862, Ammen Papers, and William H. Fitzhugh, "On Shiloh," Payne Papers, USMA-SC; Fry, *Military Miscellanies,* 305.

126. Rousseau to Chase, April 15, 1862, Chase Papers, CGS.

127. Marszalek, *Sherman,* 172–83; McFeely, *Grant,* 11–13; Lloyd Lewis, *Fighting Prophet,* 211–13, 232–33; William H. Fitzhugh, "On Shiloh," Payne Papers, USMA-SC.

128. Thorndike, *Sherman Letters,* 143–45; *New York Herald,* May 3, 1862; Shanks, *Personal Recollections,* 102.

129. Sherman to Draper, September 27, 1862, Draper Papers, LC.

130. John Sherman, "Battle of Pittsburg Landing."

131. T. J. Bush to Buell, February 4, 1885, January 16, 1886; Thomas Gantt to Buell, May 26, 1886; Robert Hunter to Buell, January 22, 1885; Buell to Hunter, January 29, 1885; Buell to Editor of *Century Magazine,* January 29, 1885; James M. Rogers to Buell, March 19, 1886; Robert M. Wilson to Buell, February 16, 1886, all in Buell Papers, RU; Fellman, *Citizen Sherman,* 329–31; Marszalek, *Sherman,* 460–66.

132. Stanton to Halleck, April 23, 1862, *OR* 10(1):98–99.

133. Halleck to Stanton, April 13, 23, 24, 1862, *OR* 10(1):98–99; Stephen E. Ambrose, *Halleck,* 45–46; *New York Daily Tribune,* May 9, 1862.

134. Daniel, *Shiloh,* 322.

CHAPTER 14

1. *New York Daily Tribune,* May 9, 1862; Stephen E. Ambrose, *Halleck,* 45.

2. Halleck to Stanton, May 2, 1862, *OR* 10(1):99.

3. Tompkins Diary, May 5, 1862, Tompkins Papers, DU.

4. Grant to Pope, April 15, 1862, *OR* 10(2):107–8; Stephen E. Ambrose, *Halleck,* 46–49.

5. *OR* 10(2):106, 117.

6. Johnson to Stanton, April 11, 1862, *OR* 10(2):101; Stanton to Johnson, April 17, 1862, *OR* 10(2):110–11; Trefousse, *Johnson,* 157–59; Durham, *Nashville,* 73–80.

7. Johnson to Maynard, April 24, 1862, *OR* 10(2):126; Trefousse, *Johnson,* 156–59; Durham, *Nashville,* 73–80.

8. Johnson to Buell, April 24, 1862, General's Papers, AGO, RG 94, NA.

9. Graf, Haskins, and Bergeron, *Papers of Johnson,* 5:330.

10. Halleck to Buell, April 26, 1862, *OR* 10(2):128.

11. Graf, Haskins, and Bergeron, *Papers of Johnson,* 5:334.

12. Buell to Halleck, April 26, 1862, *OR* 10(2):129.

13. Johnson to Lincoln, April 26, 1862, *OR* 10(2):129; Trefousse, *Johnson,* 157–59; Durham, *Nashville,* 73–80.

14. Lincoln to Johnson, April 27, 1862, *OR* 10(2):131.

15. Buell to Mitchel, March 27, 1862, *OR* 10(2):71–72; Mitchel to Buell, April 13, 1862, *OR* 10(2):617; Beatty, *Citizen Soldier*, 95–103; Van Horne, *Army of the Cumberland*, 1:136–38; Johnson and Buel, *Battles and Leaders*, 2:701–8, 709–16.

16. Mitchel, *Mitchel*, 270–75.

17. *OR* 10(2):104, 111, 117, 118–19, 124–35, 618–19; Johnson and Buel, *Battles and Leaders*, 2:702–4; Beatty, *Citizen Soldier*, 102–7; Cist, *Army of the Cumberland*, 31–33; Mitchel, *Mitchel*, 269–77, 335–38.

18. Buell to Halleck, April 30, 1862, *OR* 10(2):144–45.

19. *OR* 10(2):117; Cope, *Fifteenth Ohio*, 144–51; Hannaford, *Story of a Regiment*, 284–310; Joseph Phillips Diary, May 12, 1862, Phillips Papers, OHS; William Mitchell Diary, May 18, 1862, Mitchell Papers, OHS; Stephen E. Ambrose, *Halleck*, 48–49.

20. Halleck to Buell, May 17, 1862, *OR* 10(2):197–99; Buell to Halleck, May 18, 1862, *OR* 10(2):201, also 196–99.

21. Stanton to Mitchel, May 1, 1862, *OR* 10(2):156; Mitchel to Stanton, May 4, 1862, *OR* 10(2):162–63; Mitchel to Chase, April 20, 1862, Chase Papers, CGS; *New York Daily Tribune*, May 9, 1862.

22. Beatty, *Citizen Soldier*, 111.

23. Mitchel, *Mitchel*, 271.

24. Beatty, *Citizen Soldier*, 111–14.

25. Keil, *Thirty-fifth Ohio*, 11; Frederick D. Williams, *Wild Life*, 89; Harvey S. Ford, *Beatty*, 102–8; Cope, *Fifteenth Ohio*, 170; Canfield, *Twenty-first Ohio Volunteer*, 45–47; Grebner, *We Were the Ninth*, 106; Mitchel, *Mitchel*, 269–85, 319–23, 325–29; Grimsley, *Hard Hand of War*, 79–81; Berlin, *Destruction of Slavery*, 256–57.

26. *OR* 10(2):212–13; Beatty, *Citizen Soldier*, 107; Thomas McBeath to Nannie, July 2, 1862, McBeath Papers, UK; Prokopowicz, "All for the Regiment," 233–34; Grimsley, *Hard Hand of War*, 79–83.

27. Keifer to Wife, March 20, 1862, Keifer Papers, LC; Harvey S. Ford, *Beatty*, 102–4, 108–10; Mitchel, *Mitchel*, 318–19; Mitchel to Stanton, May 4, 1862, *OR* 10(2):163; Mitchel to Chase, March 2, 10, April 20, 1862, Chase Papers, CGS; Johnson and Buel, *Battles and Leaders*, 2:707; General Orders No. 27, March 27, 1862, *OR*, ser. 3, 1(1):937–38; Prokopowicz, "All for the Regiment," 224–27; Berlin, *Destruction of Slavery*, 26, 256.

28. Keifer to Wife, March 22, 1862, Keifer Papers, LC.

29. Mitchel to Chase, June 19, 1862, Chase Papers, CGS.

30. John Fox to Wife, May 1, 1862, Fox Papers, OHS.

31. Frederick D. Williams, *Wild Life*, 87–91.

32. Ibid.

33. Harvey S. Ford, *Beatty*, 103; Frederick D. Williams, *Wild Life*, 87–91.

34. Keifer to Wife, March 22, 1862, Keifer Papers, LC.

35. Mitchel to Buell, May 20, 1862, *OR* 10(2):206; Stanton to Mitchel, May 22, 1862, *OR* 10(2):209.

36. Mitchel to Stanton, May 28, 1862, *OR* 10(2):222; Mitchel to Chase, March 10, 1862, Chase Papers, CGS.

37. Ephraim Holloway to Wife, May 25, 1862, Holloway Papers, OHS.

38. Halleck to Buell, May 27, 1862, *OR* 10(2):219, 223; Luther P. Bradley Diary,

May 20, 1862, Bradley Papers, USAMHI; Cope, *Fifteenth Ohio*, 150−52; Hannaford, *Story of a Regiment*, 284−310; David H. Thomas to Father and Mother, May 26, 28, 1862, Thomas Papers, OHS; C. S. Bolton Diary, May 1862, Bolton Papers, OHS; Mohr to Brother, May 12, 1862, Mohr Papers, FC; Stephen E. Ambrose, *Halleck*, 51−53.

39. Hannaford, *Story of a Regiment*, 303−8; Cope, *Fifteenth Ohio*, 152−53; James B. Shaw, *Tenth Indiana*, 167−69; Villard, *Memoirs*, 1:274−78; Henry M. Osborn Diary, May 29, 1862, Osborn Papers, OHS.

40. James Easton to Family, May 30, 1862, Easton Papers, OHS.

41. Stanton to Halleck, June 2, 1862, *OR* 10(2):242.

42. Stephen E. Ambrose, *Halleck*, 54.

43. *OR* 10(2):233−34.

44. Halleck to Buell, May 31, June 2, 1862, *OR* 10(2):232−33, 244, 288; Stephen E. Ambrose, *Halleck*, 55; Kenneth P. Williams, *Lincoln Finds a General*, 3:418−20.

45. Mitchel to Chase, April 20, June 5, 1862, Chase Papers, CGS; Mitchel to Buell, June 4, 8, 1862, *OR* 10(2):257, 275; Cist, *Army of the Cumberland*, 32−35; Kenneth P. Williams, *Lincoln Finds a General*, 3:424−27.

46. *OR* 10(2):278, 280−81, 16(2):8; Villard, *Memoirs*, 1:282−83; McDonough, *War in Kentucky*, 42; Kenneth P. Williams, *Lincoln Finds a General*, 4:27.

47. Johnson to Halleck, June 5, 1862, *OR* 10(2):261; Trefousse, *Johnson*, 156−59.

48. Halleck to Johnson, June 5, 1862, in Graf, Haskins, and Bergeron, *Papers of Johnson*, 5:442.

49. Stephen E. Ambrose, *Halleck*, 56−57; Trefousse, *Johnson*, 157−58.

50. Morton to Buell, June 5, 1862, *OR* 10(2):630; Buell to Morton, June 6, 1862, *OR* 10(2):631; Morton to Buell, June 4, 1862, Telegraph Book No. 3, Morton Collection, ISA.

51. Stanton to Buell, June 9, 1862, *OR* 10(2):285.

52. Buell to Stanton, ibid.

53. Mitchel to Chase, April 20, 1862, Chase Papers, CGS; *OR* 10(2):244, 254, 281, 16(2):30−31; Don Carlos Buell, *Statement of Buell*, 10−11; Fry, *Operations under Buell*, 81; Cope, *Fifteenth Ohio*, 160−62; Villard, *Memoirs*, 1:288; Prokopowicz, "All for the Regiment," 226−28.

54. *OR* 16(2):5−8; Hannaford, *Story of a Regiment*, 313; Cope, *Fifteenth Ohio*, 160−61; Cist, *Army of the Cumberland*, 35−40; Villard, *Memoirs*, 1:282−83; McDonough, *War in Kentucky*, 40; Stephen E. Ambrose, *Halleck*, 56−57; Kenneth P. Williams, *Lincoln Finds a General*, 4:27.

55. Halleck to Buell, June 11, 1862, *OR* 16(2):9; Don Carlos Buell, *Statement of Buell*, 10−11; *OR* 16(2):30−31; Cist, *Army of the Cumberland*, 41−42; Fry, *Operations under Buell*, 81; Stephen E. Ambrose, *Halleck*, 56−57; Prokopowicz, "All for the Regiment," 223−27.

56. Kenneth P. Williams, *Lincoln Finds a General*, 4:27; Bruce, "Buell's Campaign against Chattanooga," 104; Cope, *Fifteenth Ohio*, 160−61; *OR* 16(2):9; Villard, *Memoirs*, 1:288; Lew Wallace, *Autobiography*, 2:653.

57. William M. Ferry Diary, May 14, 1862, Ferry Papers, UMBHL.

58. As quoted in *New York Daily Tribune*, May 31, 1862; Hannaford, *Story of a Regiment*, 312−13.

1. Basler, *Works of Lincoln*, 5:295; Black, *Railroads of the Confederacy*, 180–82; Bruce, "Buell's Campaign against Chattanooga," 106, 110–15; Stephen E. Ambrose, *Halleck*, 57–58; Robert S. Henry, "Chattanooga and the War," 222–26.

2. Halleck to Buell, June 12, 1862, *OR* 16(2):15; Bruce, "Buell's Campaign against Chattanooga," 110–15; Stephen E. Ambrose, *Halleck*, 57–59; Prokopowicz, "All for the Regiment," 226–27; *OR* 10(2):232–33, 244, 254, 267–68, 280–81, 16(1):30–31; Hattaway and Jones, *How the North Won*, 214–17; Cope, *Fifteenth Ohio*, 160–62; Villard, *Memoirs*, 1:288–89; Hannaford, *Story of a Regiment*, 313. Buell knew the railroads could not be defended, but the degree to which this knowledge affected his march to Chattanooga is debatable. According to Kenneth P. Williams, "One of the great myths of the war was that Buell's Chattanooga campaign failed because Halleck required him to rebuild the Memphis and Charleston Railroad as he advanced." The myth originated from the commission in which Buell made this statement regarding his advance. In June 1862 Halleck magnified the role that the Memphis and Charleston Railroad played in supplying Buell, but he stated in his endorsement of the commission's report that Buell had not been "delayed an hour beyond what he himself deemed necessary to secure his supplies." "Moreover," wrote Halleck, "his lines of supply were those which he himself selected." The truth was that Buell was slowed not primarily by the need to move along the railroad but by the need to draw supplies from it, which partly implicated Halleck in Buell's dilemmas (see Kenneth P. Williams, *Lincoln Finds a General*, 4:27–28). In his autobiography, Lew Wallace claimed that Halleck's Indorsement to the Commission was "wholly without proof." He further implied that Halleck was partially to blame for the failed Chattanooga campaign and that he was responsible for losing the commission's opinion after the war, perhaps to exonerate himself from any blame about the failed offensive (see Lew Wallace, *Autobiography*, 2:653; *OR* 16(1):12, 31). In "Buell's Campaign against Chattanooga," 104, Bruce argues that the controversy over whether or not repairing the Memphis and Charleston Railroad delayed Buell's march to Chattanooga was irrelevant, since the railroad was completed and put in use by June 29. He argued that it was the use, not the repair, of the railroad that slowed Buell, since Halleck had diverted his engineer forces to the track extending from Memphis to Columbus instead of east as he had promised Buell. He further blamed Halleck for not making sufficient preparations for the movement east. The commission also revealed that in June the divisions of McCook and Crittenden crossed the Tennessee River at Florence and marched through Athens without repairing the railroad. Furthermore, Nelson's division, after making some repairs on the line near Iuka, followed those of McCook and Crittenden without any interval of time. Wood's division alone advanced along the railroad, and it arrived at Decatur only two days after the head of the other column had passed through Athens.

3. Buell to Mitchel, June 11, 12, 1862, and Buell to Anderson, June 12, 1862, *OR* 16(2):10, 16–17; McDonough, *War in Kentucky*, 42; Bruce, "Buell's Campaign against Chattanooga," 110–15; Cist, *Army of the Cumberland*, 40–44.

4. Briant, *Sixth Indiana*, 138; John D. Inskeep Diary, June 11, 1862, Inskeep Papers, OHS; Hannaford, *Story of a Regiment*, 313.

5. Buell to Halleck, June 14, 1862, and Halleck to Buell, June 16, 1862, *OR* 16(2):22–23, 27.

6. Mitchel to Buell, June 15, 1862, *OR* 16(2):19, 24; Cist, *Army of the Cumberland*, 40–41.

7. Rerick, *Forty-fourth Indiana*, 267–68; *OR* 16(2):25–26, 28, 40; Hannaford, *Story of a Regiment*, 314.

8. *OR* 16(2):28–31.

9. Buell to Halleck, June 17, 1862, *OR* 16(2):53; Mitchel to Buell, June 16, 24, 1862, *OR* 16(2):30, 58; Kenneth P. Williams, *Lincoln Finds a General*, 4:36–37.

10. Halleck to Buell, June 17, 1862, *OR* 16(2):33–34.

11. Ibid.; *OR* 16(2):34–35.

12. Johnson to Halleck, June 17, 1862, *OR* 16(2):36–37; Trefousse, *Johnson*, 157–59.

13. Lincoln to Halleck, June 18, 1862, *OR* 16(2):37; Stanton to Johnson, June 21, 1862, *OR* 16(2):47.

14. Halleck to Lincoln, and to Buell, June 21, 1862, *OR* 16(2):43–44.

15. Ibid.

16. Buell to Halleck, June 21, 1862, *OR* 16(2):44.

17. Ibid., June 22, 1862, *OR* 16(2):48.

18. Morgan to Buell and Stanton, June 18, 1862, *OR* 16(2):38, 49–52.

19. Mitchel to Stanton, and Stanton to Mitchel, June 21, 1862, *OR* 16(2):46; Mitchel, *Mitchel*, 269–300.

20. *OR* 10(2):628, 16(1):32–34, 247–50, 516–602, 603–11, 709, 16(2):22–23, 41–44, 68–69, 77, 85; Kenneth P. Williams, *Lincoln Finds a General*, 4:27; Chumney, "Gentleman General," 102–3; McDonough, *War in Kentucky*, 45.

21. Bingham to Fry, June 16, 1862, *OR* 16(2):15, 31, 127; Hagerman, *Origins of Modern Warfare*, 176–85.

22. Frederick D. Williams, *Wild Life*, 114.

23. Hagerman, *Origins of Modern Warfare*, 178; *OR* 16(2):2–5, 10(2):235.

24. Hagerman, *Origins of Modern Warfare*, 175–76; Prokopowicz, "All for the Regiment," 245–47; Bruce, "Buell's Campaign against Chattanooga," 117; General Orders No. 26, June 24, 1862, Department of the Ohio, AGO, RG 94, NA; *OR* 16(2):23, 32–35, 39, 54, 60–65, 73; *New York Daily Tribune*, June 30, 1862; Dee Alexander Brown, *Bold Cavaliers*, 103.

25. Beatty, *Citizen Soldier*, 103.

26. *OR* 16(2):41–42, 53, 57–58, 63, 73, 77–79; Fry, *Operations under Buell*, 15; Hannaford, *Story of a Regiment*, 318–19; Cleaves, *Rock of Chickamauga*, 107–8; Kenneth P. Williams, *Lincoln Finds a General*, 4:29.

27. Mitchel, *Mitchel*, 339–43; Benson J. Lossing to Mrs. Susan Wallace, September 1, 1862, Buell Papers, HL; Berlin, *Destruction of Slavery*, 256–58.

28. Stanton to Halleck, June 28, 1862, and Halleck to Stanton, June 30, 1862, *OR* 16(2):69–70, 74–75.

29. Stanton to Halleck, June 28, 1862, *OR* 16(2):69–70; Stephen E. Ambrose, *Halleck*, 57.

30. Stanton to Halleck, and Lincoln to Halleck, June 30, 1862, *OR* 16(2):75; Stephen E. Ambrose, *Halleck*, 58; Fry, *Operations under Buell*, 17–18.

31. Halleck to Buell, and Buell to Halleck, June 30, 1862, *OR* 16(2):75–77, 78; Fry, *Operations under Buell*, 14.

32. Halleck to Buell, June 30, 1862, *OR* 16(2):77.

33. *OR* 16(1):30–34, 472–81, 16(2):124; Bruce, "Buell's Campaign against Chattanooga," 106; Chumney, "Gentleman General," 107; Don Carlos Buell, *Statement of Buell*, 14–15; Fry, *Operations under Buell*, 29; Cope, *Fifteenth Ohio*, 169–71; *Cincinnati Commercial*, July 15, 1862; Kimberly and Holloway, *Forty-first Ohio*, 30–31.

34. *OR* 4(1):342, 355–56, 16(1):23; Kenneth P. Williams, "Buell's March to Chattanooga," 9–10, Williams Papers, IU; Kenneth P. Williams, *Lincoln Finds a General*, 4:33; Prokopowicz, "All for the Regiment," 232.

35. *OR* 16(1):474, 485–96, 324–63; Cope, *Fifteenth Ohio*, 169–72; Hannaford, *Story of a Regiment*, 318–20.

36. Halleck to Buell, July 3, 1862, and to Lincoln, July 5, 1862, *OR* 16(2):92–93, 95; Fry, *Operations under Buell*, 19; Halleck to Stanton, July 3, 1862, *OR* 17(2):67.

37. Buell to Boyle, July 14, 1862, *OR* 16(1):739.

38. *OR* 16(1):635–39, 16(2):97, 99, 104; Cope, *Fifteenth Ohio*, 169–72; Robert McBeath to Nannie, July 2, 1862, McBeath Papers, UK; Prokopowicz, "All for the Regiment," 233–35; Grimsley, *Hard Hand of War*, 82; Cooling, *Fort Donelson's Legacy*, 75–76.

39. Beatty, *Citizen Soldier*, 117–18.

40. Prokopowicz, "All for the Regiment," 236.

41. Frederick D. Williams, *Wild Life*, 119, 121; *Daily National Intelligencer*, July 16, 1862; Mary Ione Chadick Diary, July 1, 1862, Chadick Papers, DU; *OR* 16(2):99; Beatty, *Citizen Soldier*, 116–23; Grimsley, *Hard Hand of War*, 83–85.

42. Beatty, *Citizen Soldier*, 119–20; *OR* 16(2):277; Mary Ione Chadick Diary, July 27, 1862, Chadick Papers, DU; Keifer to Wife, July 10, 18, 19, 1862, Keifer Papers, LC; Otis, "Kentucky Campaign," 122–47; *Cincinnati Gazette*, July 7, 22, 24, 25, 1862; Grimsley, *Hard Hand of War*, 83–85.

43. Prokopowicz, "All for the Regiment," 237–40.

44. Frederick D. Williams, *Wild Life*, 114–17; Bishop, *Second Minnesota*, 60–61; *Daily Nashville Union*, July 23, 1862; William Oglevie Diary, July 24, 1862, Oglevie Papers, OHS; Piatt, *Memories of Men*, 200–208; Mary Ione Chadick Diary, June 1, 1862, Chadick Papers, DU; Prokopowicz, "All for the Regiment," 237–40.

45. Prokopowicz, "All for the Regiment," 241–53; Johnson and Buel, *Battles and Leaders*, 1:482; *New York Daily Tribune*, June 30, November 12, 1862; Cope, *Fifteenth Ohio*, 176–77; Frances Dallam Peters Diary, August 28, 1862, Evans-Peters Papers, UK; *Cincinnati Commercial*, July 14, 29, 1862; *New Albany Daily Ledger*, July 30, 1862.

46. Halleck to Buell, July 8, 1862, *OR* 16(2):75, 104.

47. Bruce, "Buell's Campaign against Chattanooga," 118; *OR* 16(2):104; Stephen E. Ambrose, *Halleck*, 59.

48. Buell to Halleck, July 11, 1862, *OR* 16(2):122–23, 16(1):33; Black, *Railroads of the Confederacy*, 180.

49. Buell to Halleck, July 11, 1862, *OR* 16(2):122–23.

50. Johnson to Lincoln, July 10, 1862, *OR* 16(2):118–19; Trefousse, *Johnson*, 144–48; Graf, Haskins, and Bergeron, *Papers of Johnson*, 5:549–50.

51. Basler, *Works of Lincoln*, 5:313–14.

52. Halleck to Buell, July 12, 1862, *OR* 16(2):128.

53. Ibid.; Stephen E. Ambrose, *Halleck*, 61.

54. Keifer to Wife, July 5, 6, 8, 1862, Keifer Papers, LC.

55. Frederick D. Williams, *Wild Life*, 117–18.

56. John W. Switzer Diary, July 20, 1862, Switzer Papers, IHS.

57. Ibid., July 9, 1862; Reuben D. Mussey to William H. Smith, July 6, 1862, William H. Smith Papers, OHS.

58. Keifer to Eliza, July 12, 1862, Keifer Papers, LC; Frederick D. Williams, *Wild Life*, 123.

59. Keifer to Eliza, July 14, 1862, Keifer Papers, LC; Henry Seys to Wife, July 12, 1862, Seys Papers, UMWCL.

60. James B. Shaw, *Tenth Indiana*, 185–86; *OR* 16(1):635–39; *New Albany Daily Ledger*, July 14, 1862; Mungo P. Murray to Parents, August 20, 1862, Murray Papers, CWTIC, USAMHI.

61. *Indianapolis Daily Journal*, July 16, 1862; J. Cutler Andrews, *North Reports the War*, 286–87.

62. *Daily Nashville Union*, July 23, 1862.

63. *Cincinnati Gazette*, July 7, 1862; *Indianapolis Daily Journal*, July 18, 1862; *Chicago Tribune*, July 11, 1862; *Cincinnati Commercial*, July 12, 16, 24, 1862; *New York Herald*, August 24, September 6, October 3, 4, 10, 1862; J. Cutler Andrews, *North Reports the War*, 286–87.

64. As quoted in J. Cutler Andrews, *North Reports the War*, 286–87.

65. Graf, Haskins, and Bergeron, *Papers of Johnson*, 5:575–76; *Daily Nashville Union*, July 23, 1862; *Daily National Intelligencer*, July 29, 1862.

66. *OR* 17(1):150.

67. Beatty, *Citizen Soldier*, 121–22; Basler, *Works of Lincoln*, 5:433–36; Niven, *Chase Papers*, 3:231–32; Keifer to Wife, July 22, 1862, Keifer Papers, LC; T. Harry Williams, *Lincoln and the Radicals*, 141–47, 164–68; U.S. Congress, *Congressional Globe*, 37th Cong., 2nd sess., 1720, 1896, 1917–20, 3006.

68. *OR* 11(1):73–74; Prime, *McClellan's Own Story*, 487–89; T. Harry Williams, *Lincoln and the Radicals*, 146–47.

69. *OR* 16(2):128–35; Kenneth P. Williams, *Lincoln Finds a General*, 4:437–39.

70. Fry to Greene, July 14, 1862, and Fry to Swords, July 15, 1862, *OR* 16(2):144–52; William Blair to Margaret, August 31, 1862, Blair Papers, IHS; Hannaford, *Story of a Regiment*, 322–23; Cist, *Army of the Cumberland*, 43–44; Prokopowicz, "All for the Regiment," 249–53.

71. Cope, *Fifteenth Ohio*, 177.

72. Fry to Swords, July 13, 1862, Buell Papers, RU.

73. Buell to Halleck, July 15, 1862, *OR* 16(2):151.

74. Buell to Halleck, and Halleck to Buell, July 16, 1862, *OR* 16(2):159–60.

75. Beatty, *Citizen Soldier*, 124; *OR* 20(2):350–53.

76. *OR* 16(1):815–17, 16(2):143, 169, 176; Kenneth P. Williams, *Lincoln Finds a General*, 4:41.

77. Buell to Negley, July 22, 1862, *OR* 16(2):199.

78. *OR* 16(2):197–211, 221–25, 236, 240–41; Kenneth P. Williams, *Lincoln Finds a General*, 4:40–41.

79. Buell to Halleck, July 31, 1862, *OR* 16(2):236–49; McWhiney, *Bragg*, 268–71.

80. Niven, *Chase Papers*, 1:35–60; Donald, *Inside Lincoln's Cabinet*, 20, 103, 107–8; Niven, *Chase: A Biography*, 294; Stephen E. Ambrose, *Halleck*, 88.

81. Niven, *Chase Papers*, 1:355–60.

82. Nelson to Chase, July 30, 1862, Chase Papers, CGS.

83. Halleck to Buell, August 6, 1862, *OR* 16(2):265.

84. Buell to Halleck, August 6, 1862, *OR* 16(2):265–66.

85. Cleaves, *Rock of Chickamauga*, 108.

86. Ibid.; Buell to Halleck, August 7, 1862, *OR* 16(2):278; Maslowski, *Treason Must Be Made Odious*, 44–47.

87. Bruce, "Buell's Campaign against Chattanooga," 125–30; *OR* 16(2):292; Buell to Morton, August 8, 1862, Telegraph Book No. 2, Morton Collection, ISA.

88. *OR* 17(2):160, 16(2):302–3; Simon, *Papers of Grant*, 5:277–78; McWhiney, *Bragg*, 268–71.

89. Halleck to Buell, August 12, 1862, *OR* 16(2):314–15.

90. Ibid.

91. Boyle to Morton, August 17, 1862, Telegraph Book No. 2, Morton Collection, ISA.

92. Graf, Haskins, and Bergeron, *Papers of Johnson*, 5:617–18, 604–5; Yates to Morton, July 16, 1862, Telegraph Book No. 2, and Morton to Stanton, August 13, 1862, General Dispatch Book, Morton Collection, ISA; Johnson to Buell, August 11, 1862, General's Papers, AGO, RG 94, NA; Maslowski, *Treason Must Be Made Odious*, 44–47; Cleaves, *Rock of Chickamauga*, 108–9.

93. Graf, Haskins, and Bergeron, *Papers of Johnson*, 5:617–18; Cleaves, *Rock of Chickamauga*, 108–9.

94. *OR* 16(2):287, 290–91; Cist, *Army of the Cumberland*, 46–47; Keifer to Eliza, August 14, 1862, Keifer Papers, LC; Terah W. Sampson to Mother, August 19, 1862, Sampson Papers, FC; Dee Alexander Brown, *Bold Cavaliers*, 111–12; Kenneth P. Williams, *Lincoln Finds a General*, 4:43.

95. *OR* 16(2):290.

96. Ramage, *Rebel Raider*, 111; McDonough, *War in Kentucky*, 56–58; Hagerman, *Origins of Modern Warfare*, 117; Bruce, "Buell's Campaign against Chattanooga," 119; *OR* 16(2):322, 328–30; *New York Daily Tribune*, August 7, 1862; McWhiney, *Bragg*, 266–75.

97. Beatty, *Citizen Soldier*, 129–30; Villard, *Memoirs*, 1:300; Bircher, *Drummer Boy's Diary*, 40–41; Cist, *Army of the Cumberland*, 48–53; *Cincinnati Commercial*, August 23, 1862.

98. *OR* 16(2):348; Johnson and Buel, *Battles and Leaders*, 3:39; McDonough, *War in Kentucky*, 117–22.

99. Keifer to Eliza, July 3, 1862, Keifer Papers, LC.

100. *Cincinnati Commercial*, August 5, 1862.

101. Ibid., July 12, 1862; Keifer to Eliza, August 16, 1862, Keifer Papers, LC; *Indianapolis Daily Journal*, August 20, 1862; *Daily Nashville Union*, August 3, 1862; Mary Ione Chadick Diary, August 15–19, 1862, Chadick Papers, DU.

102. *Cincinnati Gazette*, August 18, 1862.

103. Halleck to Buell, August 18, 1862, *OR* 16(2):360; Niven, *Chase: A Biography*, 292–94.

104. Buell to Halleck, August 18, 1862, *OR* 16(2):360–61; Fry, *Operations under Buell*, 30.

105. Buell to Halleck, August 24, 1862, *OR* 16(2):406–7; Chumney, "Gentleman General," 119–21; McWhiney, *Bragg*, 270–75; Cleaves, *Rock of Chickamauga*, 109.

106. Bragg to Smith, August 15, 1862, *OR* 16(2):758–59, 344–48, 353–57, 405–7, 16(1):371–72; Johnson and Buel, *Battles and Leaders*, 3:39–43; Don Carlos Buell, *Statement of Buell*, 20; Fry, *Operations under Buell*, 40–43; Prokopowicz, "All for the Regiment," 257, 266–69; Kenneth P. Williams, *Lincoln Finds a General*, 4:45, 472.

107. Halleck to Wright, August 25, 1862, *OR* 16(2):421.

108. Buell to Halleck, August 25, 1862, *OR* 16(2):434, 449; Hannaford, *Story of a Regiment*, 327–36.

109. *OR* 16(1):134, 16(2):387–88; Fry, *Operations under Buell*, 41–44; Cist, *Army of the Cumberland*, 49–53; *Daily National Intelligencer*, July 29, 1862; Graf, Haskins, and Bergeron, *Papers of Johnson*, 5:637; Cleaves, *Rock of Chickamauga*, 109–10; McWhiney, "Controversy in Kentucky," 5–14.

110. T. Harry Williams, *Lincoln and His Generals*, 151.

111. *OR* 16(1):354–55.

112. *Cincinnati Commercial*, July 26, 1862.

113. Cope, *Fifteenth Ohio*, 178.

114. Keifer to Eliza, August 27, 1862, Keifer Papers, LC; unidentified newspaper clippings, Buell Papers, RU; Berlin, *Destruction of Slavery*, 258–59, 288–89.

CHAPTER 16

1. Day, *One Hundred and First Ohio*, 35.

2. Bircher, *Drummer Boy's Diary*, 41.

3. McWhiney, *Bragg*, 281–85; McDonough, *War in Kentucky*, 121–48.

4. Graf, Haskins, and Bergeron, *Papers of Johnson*, 6:4–6; *New York Daily Tribune*, September 1, 1862; Shanks, *Personal Recollections*, 254–56; Stanley F. Horn, "Nashville during the War," 12–14; Trefousse, *Johnson*, 158–60.

5. Lucy Virginia French Diary, September 14, 1862, French Papers, TSLA.

6. J. W. King to Jenny, September 10, 1862, King Papers, Federal Collection, TSLA; Henry M. Osborn Diary, September 7, 1862, Osborn Papers, OHS; Lines L. Parker Diary, September 8, 1862, Parker Papers, ISHL; James E. Love to Molly, September 9, 11, 28, 1862, Love Papers, MHS.

7. Buell to Halleck, and Halleck to Buell, September 2, 1862, *OR* 16(2):470–71, 505.

8. William E. Patterson Diary, September 26, 1862, Patterson Papers, ISHL; John Tilford Diary, September 15, 1862, Tilford Papers, FC; William R. Stuckey Diary, September 13, 1862, Stuckey Papers, IHS; John Fox to Wife, September 14, 28, 1862, Fox Papers, OHS; Charles Coburn Diary, September 15, 1862, Coburn Papers, OHS; Cope, *Fifteenth Ohio*, 196–99; Horrall, *Forty-second Indiana*, 138, 145; Briant, *Sixth Indiana*, 147–48; *OR* 16(1):641; Herr, *Nine Campaigns*, 105; Prokopowicz, "All for the Regiment," 279–81.

9. Buell to Lincoln, September 10, 1862, *OR* 16(2):497, 500; McWhiney, *Bragg,* 282–83; Parks, *Smith,* 225–26.

10. *OR* 16(2):476, 502–10, 514, 516, 521–22; Stanton to Governor Tod, September 7, 1862, Tod Papers, OHS; Johnson and Buel, *Battles and Leaders,* 3:46; *Cincinnati Gazette,* September 5, 1862; *New Albany Daily Ledger,* September 22, 1862; *New York Daily Tribune,* September 12, 1862; Orville T. Chamberlain to Father, September 28, 1862, Chamberlain Papers, IHS; Griese, "Louisville Tragedy," 134–35; J. Cutler Andrews, *North Reports the War,* 291; Bennett and Haigh, *Thirty-sixth Illinois,* 236–37; Stampp, *Indiana during the Civil War,* 153.

11. Buell to Halleck, September 14, 1862, *OR* 16(2):515–16; McWhiney, *Bragg,* 283–84; Tourgée, *Story of a Thousand,* 83–94; Cope, *Fifteenth Ohio,* 197–99.

12. *OR* 16(1):134, 173–74, 182–83, 221–22; Tourgée, *Story of a Thousand,* 83–94; Bircher, *Drummer Boy's Diary,* 42–44; Cope, *Fifteenth Ohio,* 197–99; Otis, "Kentucky Campaign," 140–41; James B. Shaw, *Tenth Indiana,* 184; Prokopowicz, "All for the Regiment," 277–78; Hafendorfer, *Perryville,* 44–49.

13. Johnson and Buel, *Battles and Leaders,* 3:41–42; *OR* 16(1):205, 209–10, 212, 214, 692–93; McWhiney, *Bragg,* 285–86; Harrison, "Battle of Munfordville"; John Fox Diary, September 10–19, 1862, Fox Papers, OHS; Hannaford, *Story of a Regiment,* 350–53; Griese, "Louisville Tragedy," 135–37.

14. *OR* 16(1):968; *New Albany Daily Ledger,* September 30, 1862; *Indianapolis Daily Journal,* September 15, 23, 1862; Day, *One Hundred and First Ohio,* 35–36; Parks, *Smith,* 225–26; McWhiney, *Bragg,* 286; McDonough, *War in Kentucky,* 182–84.

15. Johnson and Buel, *Battles and Leaders,* 3:41–42; William Herbert to Parents, September 25, 1862, Herbert Papers, FC; McWhiney, *Bragg,* 286; McDonough, *War in Kentucky,* 182–84.

16. McWhiney, *Bragg,* 286–87; John D. Inskeep Diary, September 10–20, 1862, Inskeep Papers, OHS; Graf, Haskins, and Bergeron, *Papers of Johnson,* 6:13; *OR* 16(2):511–12, 522–23, 527; Johnson and Buel, *Battles and Leaders,* 3:42; Hafendorfer, *Perryville,* 49–55.

17. Villard, *Memoirs,* 1:304.

18. John A. Duncan Diary, September 13, 18, 1862, Duncan Papers, CWTIC, USAMHI; *New Albany Daily Ledger,* September 23, 24, 1862; *OR* 16(2):132–34. Other rumors included that Buell had a son-in-law in Bragg's army; see, for example, Becker and Thomas, *Hearth and Knapsack,* 53.

19. Halleck to Buell, September 20, 1862, *OR* 16(2):530; Don Carlos Buell, *Statement of Buell,* 32–34.

20. Buell to Nelson, September 22, 1862, *OR* 16(2):533–34; Otis, "Kentucky Campaign," 137.

21. Buell to Halleck, September 25, 1862, *OR* 16(2):542–43.

22. Bishop, *Second Minnesota,* 68–69.

23. Barnes, Carnaham, and McCain, *Eighty-sixth Indiana,* 49–50; Tourgée, *Story of a Thousand,* 94–95; Harden, *Ninetieth Ohio,* 16; Kerwood, *Fifty-seventh Indiana,* 120–21; Villard, *Memoirs,* 1:301; Bircher, *Drummer Boy's Diary,* 43–44; Day, *One Hundred and First Ohio,* 36–37.

24. *Cincinnati Commercial,* July 25, 30, September 30, 1862; Bennett and Haigh,

Thirty-sixth Illinois, 237; Cope, Fifteenth Ohio, 199–200; Hannaford, Story of a Regiment, 346; Villard, Memoirs, 1:257–58; Weisberger, Reporters for the Union, 234–35.

25. Day, One Hundred and First Ohio, 36–37; New Albany Daily Ledger, September 5, 29, 1862; Cope, Fifteenth Ohio, 200–203; Johnson and Buel, Battles and Leaders, 3:46.

26. James B. Shaw, Tenth Indiana, 186; Rerick, Forty-fourth Indiana, 69–70, 270–71; Hannaford, Story of a Regiment, 354.

27. Rerick, Forty-fourth Indiana, 270–71; Cincinnati Commercial, October 1, 1862.

28. Frank Leslie's Illustrated, September 27, 1862; Chicago Tribune, September 25, 1862; Cincinnati Commercial, July 25, 30, September 30, 1862; New York Daily Tribune, October 1, 4, 8, 1862; Boston Journal, August 1, October 24, 1862; Weisberger, Reporters for the Union, 198–99, 234–35.

29. Independent, September 25, 1862.

30. Louisville Daily Journal, October 11, 1862; Chicago Times, October 12, 1862; New York Herald, October 3, 4, 10, 20, 1862.

31. James Love to Molly, September 9, 11, 28, 1862, Love Papers, MHS.

32. Tourgée, Story of a Thousand, 110–11.

33. Tapp and Klotter, Kentucky Captain's Account, 125; Thomas Small Diary, September 22, 1862, Small Papers, IHS.

34. Thomas J. Wright, Eighth Kentucky, 61.

35. James B. Shaw, Tenth Indiana, 185.

36. Thomas J. Wright, Eighth Kentucky, 61.

37. Thomas Small Diary, September 22, 1862, Small Papers, IHS.

38. Mussey to Joseph R. Barrett, September 30, 1862, Mussey Papers, Lincoln Collection, UC. See also Alva C. Griest Diary, September 26, 1862, Griest Papers, HCWRTC, USAMHI; Lathrop, Fifty-ninth Illinois, 154; Dodge, Old Second Division, 327–28; Mungo P. Murray Diary, September 29, 1862, Murray Papers, CWTIC, USAMHI; Prokopowicz, "All for the Regiment," 283–84.

39. Love to Molly, October 2, 1862, Love Papers, MHS; Day, One Hundred and First Ohio, 36–37; Cincinnati Commercial, October 1, 1862; Cope, Fifteenth Ohio, 200–205; Hazen, Narrative of Military Service, 54–55.

40. OR 16(1):105, 107, 16(2):546, 549; Mungo P. Murray Diary, September 29, 1862, Murray Papers, CWTIC, USAMHI; Levi A. Ross to Father, September 16, 1862, Ross Papers, ISHL.

41. OR 16(1):124, 544–45, 591–96, 16(2):558–59; Johnson and Buel, Battles and Leaders, 3:45; Frederick Marion to Sister, September 12, 1862, Marion Papers, ISHL; Shanks, Personal Recollections, 252; Prokopowicz, "All for the Regiment," 289–95.

42. Kerwood, Fifty-seventh Indiana, 120.

43. OR 16(1):372–73; Stone, "Operations of Buell," 278; Herr, Nine Campaigns, 110; James B. Shaw, Tenth Indiana, 170; Johnson and Buel, Battles and Leaders, 3:45; Prokopowicz, "All for the Regiment," 284–89.

44. Herr, Nine Campaigns, 107; Foulke, Morton, 1:193–94; Chicago Tribune, October 10, 1862; W. R. Holloway to George K. Steele, October 9, 27, 1862, Morton Papers, ISA; Stampp, Indiana during the Civil War, 154–55.

45. Villard, Memoirs, 1:308–9; Johnson and Buel, Battles and Leaders, 3:60–61; Tapp, "Assassination of Nelson," 195–201; Jenkins, "Shooting at the Galt House"; OR 16(2):566–67; James P. Jones, "'Bull' and the Damned Puppy."

46. Johnson and Buel, *Battles and Leaders*, 3:60–61; John Fox Diary, September 29, 1862, Fox Papers, OHS; J. Cutler Andrews, *North Reports the War*, 296; *Louisville Daily Journal*, September 30, 1862; Hannaford, *Story of a Regiment*, 368–69; *Indianapolis Daily Journal*, September 30, 1862.

47. Coburn to Father, September 30, 1862, Coburn Papers, OHS; John Tilford Diary, September 27, 1862, Tilford Papers, FC.

48. Johnson and Buel, *Battles and Leaders*, 3:42–43, 60–61; Tourgée, *Story of a Thousand*, 70–71, 104–5; Hannaford, *Story of a Regiment*, 358–69; Otis, "Kentucky Campaign," 139–41; Foulke, *Morton*, 1:194–96.

49. Fry, *Military Miscellanies*, 489; Fry, *Killed by a Brother Soldier*, 7.

50. *OR* 16(1):638–40, 16(2):537–55; *New York Daily Tribune*, October 28, 1862; Thomas and Hyman, *Stanton*, 227; Stephen E. Ambrose, *Halleck*, 90–91.

51. McKibbin to Halleck, September 29, 1862, *OR* 16(2):549–56; Halleck to McKibbin, September 24, 1862, *OR* 16(2):538–39, 549; McKinney, *Education in Violence*, 152–54; Stephen E. Ambrose, *Halleck*, 90–91.

52. Frederick D. Williams, *Wild Life*, 154; Niven, *Chase Papers*, 1:412–14; Stampp, *Indiana during the Civil War*, 153–54; *Indianapolis Daily Journal*, September 26, 1862; *OR*, ser. 2, 4(1):562, and ser. 3, 2(1):590. Morton was so infuriated that he tried to get Indiana troops furloughed so they could vote to put pressure on Lincoln.

53. Chandler to P. C. Watson, September 10, 1862, Stanton Papers, LC; Yates to Morton, September 23, 1862, Telegraph Book No. 2, Morton Collection, ISA; *New York Daily Tribune*, September 25, 1862; T. Harry Williams, *Lincoln and the Radicals*, 192–94.

54. *OR* 16(2):549, 554–55, 557, 59; T. Harry Williams, *Lincoln and the Radicals*, 192–94.

55. Otis, "Kentucky Campaign," 142–43; Mussey to Barrett, September 30, 1862, Mussey Papers, Lincoln Collection, UC; *OR* 16(2):555, 544–45; Johnson and Buel, *Battles and Leaders*, 3:44; *Indianapolis Daily Journal*, October 6, 1862; Eben P. Sturgis Diary, October 4, 1862, Sturgis Papers, and Murray to Parents, Sister, Brothers, September 29, 1862, Murray Papers, CWTIC, USAMHI; *Cincinnati Commercial*, October 10, 1862; James A. Price Diary, September 21, 1862, Price Papers, CWMC, USAMHI. See also Cleaves, *Rock of Chickamauga*, 112–13.

56. Frederick D. Williams, *Wild Life*, 154.

57. Cist, *Army of the Cumberland*, 75–77; Shanks, *Personal Recollections*, 247–57; Thomas and Hyman, *Stanton*, 227–28; *OR* 16(2):555–59.

58. *OR* 16(2):560; Otis, "Kentucky Campaign," 139–43; James B. Shaw, *Tenth Indiana*, 174; Cist, *Army of the Cumberland*, 75–77; Aten, *Eighty-fifth Illinois*, 43–45; Shanks, *Personal Recollections*, 257–58; Villard, *Memoirs*, 1:307–10; *Cincinnati Commercial*, October 1, 1862; *New York Daily Tribune*, November 12, 1862; Prokopowicz, "All for the Regiment," 296–98.

59. Stone, "Operations of Buell," 272–79; Otis, "Kentucky Campaign," 138–43; Tapp, "Assassination of Nelson"; Johnson and Buel, *Battles and Leaders*, 3:60–61.

60. Tourgée, *Story of a Thousand*, 113–14; Thatcher, *Hundred Battles*, 73; Day, *One Hundred and First Ohio*, 42.

61. George W. Morris, *Eighty-first Indiana*, 13.

62. Thatcher, *Hundred Battles*, 73; Herr, *Nine Campaigns*, 110; Tourgée, *Story of a Thousand*, 113–14.

63. *OR* 16(2):564; Briant, *Sixth Indiana*, 152–53; Keil, *Thirty-fifth Ohio*, 96–98; Hartpence, *Fifty-first Indiana*, 87; Johnson and Buel, *Battles and Leaders*, 3:33; Prokopowicz, "All for the Regiment," 299–302.

64. Bennett and Haigh, *Thirty-sixth Illinois*, 243; Keil, *Thirty-fifth Ohio*, 96–98; Dodge, *Old Second Division*, 345–53; George W. Morris, *Eighty-first Indiana*, 13–15; Barnes, Carnaham, and McCain, *Eighty-sixth Indiana*, 60–61; Johnson and Buel, *Battles and Leaders*, 3:45–47; *OR* 16(2):566, 575–76, 578–79.

65. James B. Fry to Buell, January 13, 1889, Buell Papers, RU; *New York Daily Tribune*, November 12, 1862; *National Tribune*, February 16, 1888; Levi A. Ross Diary, October 3, 1862, Ross Papers, ISHL; Everett F. Abbott Diary, October 7, 1862, Chamberlain Papers, IHS; Perry Hall Diary, October 7, 1862, Hall Papers, IHS; Stone, "Operations of Buell," 281; Prokopowicz, "All for the Regiment," 310; Overmyer, *Stupendous Effort*, 35–37.

66. Fry to Buell, January 13, 1889, Buell Papers, RU; Hafendorfer, *Perryville*, 117–20.

67. *OR* 16(2):580–81, 585–88; Cist, *Army of the Cumberland*, 63–65; Johnson and Buel, *Battles and Leaders*, 3:47–49, 52–53; McKinney, *Education in Violence*, 158–61; Hafendorfer, *Perryville*, 120–22.

68. *OR* 16(1):1072–74, 16(2):580–81; Johnson and Buel, *Battles and Leaders*, 3:47–49, 52–54; McDonough, *War in Kentucky*, 219–25.

69. *OR* 16(1):641.

70. *OR* 16(1):125, 135–36, 138, 221; McDonough, *War in Kentucky*, 223–24.

71. Johnson and Buel, *Battles and Leaders*, 3:47–49; McWhiney, *Bragg*, 300–301; McDonough, *War in Kentucky*, 226–56; McKinney, *Education in Violence*, 160–62.

72. Johnson and Buel, *Battles and Leaders*, 3:47–49, 53; *OR* 16(1):1072–74, 16(2):597–99; Hafendorfer, *Perryville*, 146–53; Roy Morris Jr., *Sheridan*, 89–93.

73. *OR* 16(1):1038–40, 1072–74; Cist, *Army of the Cumberland*, 63–66; Shanks, *Personal Recollections*, 250–51; Hafendorfer, *Perryville*, 136–73; McDonough, *War in Kentucky*, 266–69.

74. *OR* 16(1):88–91, 1038–40, 1072–74; Lewis C. Dougherty Diary, October 8, 1862, Dougherty Papers, ISHL; Levi A. Ross Diary, October 8, 9, 1862, Ross Papers, ISHL.

75. Day, *One Hundred and First Ohio*, 51–54; Tourgée, *Story of a Thousand*, 117–20; Bennett and Haigh, *Thirty-sixth Illinois*, 250–58; Hafendorfer, *Perryville*, 187–215.

76. *OR* 16(1):1038–41; Bennett and Haigh, *Thirty-sixth Illinois*, 251–58; Tourgée, *Story of a Thousand*, 117–23; Day, *One Hundred and First Ohio*, 51–54; Hafendorfer, *Perryville*, 197–217.

77. Bennett and Haigh, *Thirty-sixth Illinois*, 254–58; Villard, *Memoirs*, 1:318; *OR* 16(1):1072–74; Cist, *Army of the Cumberland*, 65–67.

78. Johnson and Buel, *Battles and Leaders*, 3:57; *OR* 16(1):284; Otis, "Kentucky Campaign," 104; James B. Shaw, *Tenth Indiana*, 172–73; *New York Daily Tribune*, November 12, 1862.

79. *OR* 16(1):1072–74, 1079–83; Johnson and Buel, *Battles and Leaders*, 3:47–50; Cist, *Army of the Cumberland*, 66–68; Henry M. Hempstead Diary, October 8, 1862, Hempstead Papers, UMBHL.

80. *OR* 16(1):1072–74, 1079–83; Johnson and Buel, *Battles and Leaders*, 3:47–50; Henry M. Hempstead Diary, October 8, 1862, Hempstead Papers, UMBHL; Bennett

and Haigh, *Thirty-sixth Illinois*, 257–71; Herr, *Nine Campaigns*, 112–15; O'Connor, *Sheridan*, 80–82; McDonough, *War in Kentucky*, 266–69; Hafendorfer, *Perryville*, 271–84.

81. Cleaves, *Rock of Chickamauga*, 114–16; Hafendorfer, *Perryville*, 271–84.

82. Sheridan, *Memoirs*, 1:198–99; Roy Morris Jr., *Sheridan*, 95–97; *Cincinnati Daily Enquirer*, October 30, 1862.

83. *OR* 16(1):102–3, 345.

84. Johnson and Buel, *Battles and Leaders*, 3:61; *OR* 16(1):187–88; Otis, "Kentucky Campaign," 145–46, 150–51; *Cincinnati Daily Enquirer*, October 30, 1862; Van Horne, *Army of the Cumberland*, 1:186.

85. McDonough, *War in Kentucky*, 289; Roy Morris Jr., *Sheridan*, 96.

86. Henry F. Perry, *Thirty-eighth Indiana*, 37; Charles Carr to Sarah, October 25, 1862, Carr Papers, CHS; Amos Flegel Diary, October 19, 1862, Flegel Papers, UK; John A. Duncan Diary, October 8, 1862, Duncan Papers, CWTIC, USAMHI.

87. James B. Shaw, *Tenth Indiana*, 186.

88. Thomas J. Frazee to Parents, October 16, 1862, Frazee Papers, ISHL.

89. Henry M. Kendall, "Battle of Perryville," 12; Lathrop, *Fifty-ninth Illinois*, 162–63, 170–72; Kerwood, *Fifty-seventh Indiana*, 140; *Cincinnati Commercial*, October 22, 1862; Love to Molly, October 17, 1862, Love Papers, MHS; Thomas J. Wright, *Eighth Kentucky*, 102.

90. Lathrop, *Fifty-ninth Illinois*, 172.

91. David Smith to Father, n.d., ca. October 1862, Smith Papers, FC. On losses, see *OR* 16(1):1112, 1033–36; Hafendorfer, *Perryville*, 452–59.

92. *OR* 16(1):63; McKinney, *Education in Violence*, 164–65; Chumney, "Gentleman General," 175–76.

93. Shanks, *Personal Recollections*, 250–51; Prokopowicz, "All for the Regiment," 347–57.

94. McWhiney, *Bragg*, 319–21; *OR* 16(1):63; Cist, *Army of the Cumberland*, 67–71.

95. Mussey to Barrett, October 16, 1862, Mussey Papers, Lincoln Collection, UC; Thaddeus A. Minshall to Friend, October 24, 1862, Minshall Papers, FC; Keil, *Thirty-fifth Ohio*, 101; John D. Inskeep Diary, October 15, 1862, Inskeep Papers, OHS; Frances Dallam Peters Diary, October 21, 24, 1862, Evans-Peters Papers, UK; Kaiser, "Civil War Letters of Charles W. Carr," 267–69; Bearss, "Bragg Abandons Kentucky"; McWhiney, *Bragg*, 321–26.

96. Buell to Halleck, October 16, 1862, *OR* 16(2):619; Lincoln to Boyle, October 11, 1862, *OR* 16(2):606, 608, 613, 16(1):1022–23; Niven, *Chase Papers*, 1:419.

97. Buell to Robinson, October 16, 1862, *OR* 16(2):622–23; Buell to Halleck, October 16, 17, 1862, *OR* 16(2):619–22; Bearss, "Bragg Abandons Kentucky."

98. Buell to Halleck, October 18, 1862, *OR* 16(2):621–22.

99. Niven, *Chase Papers*, 3:294–95.

100. Halleck to Buell, October 18, 1862, *OR* 16(2):623.

101. Ibid., October 19, 1862, *OR* 16(2):626–27.

102. Buell to Halleck, October 22, 1862, *OR* 16(2):637.

103. Aten, *Eighty-fifth Illinois*, 43.

104. Halleck to Buell, October 23, 1862, *OR* 16(2):638; Stephen E. Ambrose, *Halleck*, 91.

105. Morton to Lincoln, October 21, 1862, *OR* 16(2):634; Johnson and Buel, *Battles and Leaders*, 3:31; Foulke, *Morton*, 1:196–97.

106. Tod to Stanton, and Stanton to Tod, October 30, 1862, *OR* 16(2):652.

107. White to Lincoln, October 22, 1862, Lincoln Collection, LC.

108. Bainbridge to Holt, October 22, 1862, Holt Papers, LC.

109. Buell to Rockwell, July 10, 1864, Rockwell Papers, LC; Samuel Shellabarger to Lincoln, October 22, 1862, Lincoln Collection, LC; Trefousse, *Radical Republicans*, 251–52; Frederick D. Williams, *Wild Life*, 161, 169; *New York Daily Tribune*, October 23, 1862; T. Harry Williams, *Lincoln and the Radicals*, 179–95.

110. Halleck to Buell, October 23, 1862, *OR* 16(2):638.

111. Buell to Halleck, October 29, 1862, *OR* 16(2):651; Stephen E. Ambrose, *Halleck*, 92; *New York Daily Tribune*, October 23, 1862.

112. *OR* 16(1):654, 16(2):654.

113. *New York Daily Tribune*, November 12, 1862.

114. Buell to Thomas, October 30, 1862, *OR* 16(2):654.

115. Guthrie to Halleck, October 27, 1862, *OR* 16(2):646–47.

116. Bell to Holt, November 1, 1862, and Thomas E. Nelson to Holt, October 17, 1862, Holt Papers, LC.

117. *New Albany Daily Ledger*, October 28, 1862.

118. Rosecrans to Buell, October 30, 1862, *OR* 16(2):653.

119. Yates and Morton to Lincoln, October 25, 1862, *OR* 16(2):642; Mark S. Skinner to Stanton, October 20, 1862, Stanton Papers, LC; *New York Daily Tribune*, October 25, 1862.

120. Palmer to Trumbull, November 15, 1862, Trumbull Papers, LC.

121. Niven, *Chase Papers*, 3:304–5.

122. Halleck to Rosecrans, October 24, 1862, *OR* 16(2):641–42.

CHAPTER 17

1. *New Albany Daily Ledger*, October 2, 24, 1862.

2. As reprinted in *Frank Leslie's Illustrated*, November 24, 1862; *New Albany Daily Ledger*, November 24, 1862.

3. Keifer to Wife, November 12, 1862, Keifer Papers, LC.

4. Basler, *Works of Lincoln*, 5:509–10.

5. Donald, *Why the North Won*, 33–55.

6. *Cincinnati Daily Enquirer*, December 2, 1862; *New Albany Daily Ledger*, November 5, December 3, 1862; *New York Times*, December 5, 1862; Thomas L. Crittenden to John Watson, December 11, 1862, Watson Papers, LC; Thomas Bush to Almon Rockwell, November 14, 1862, Rockwell Papers, LC; Stanton to Halleck, November 4, 1862, *OR* 16(1):6–7; Thomas and Hyman, *Stanton*, 260.

7. *Cincinnati Daily Enquirer*, December 2, 1862; *New Albany Daily Ledger*, December 3, 1862; *New York Times*, December 5, 1862; Crittenden to Watson, December 11, 1862, Watson Papers, LC; Bush to Rockwell, November 14, 1862, Rockwell Papers, LC; unidentified newspaper clippings, Buell Papers, RU.

8. *OR* 16(1):6; Peine, "Buell Commission," 84–87.

9. Peine, "Buell Commission," 84–87.

10. Fry, *Operations under Buell*, 116; *Chicago Times*, November 19, 1862; Piatt, *Thomas*, 178; Thomas and Hyman, *Stanton*, 260; F. Case to Buell, November 28, 1862, Buell Papers, RU.

11. Stanton to Halleck, November 4, 1862, *OR* 16(1):6–7; Lew Wallace, *Autobiography*, 2:643; Morton to Piatt, November 4, 29, 1862, Telegraph Book No. 2, Morton Collection, ISA. See also Theisen, "Public Career of Wallace."

12. Wallace to Wife, December 14, 1862, Wallace Papers, IHS.

13. Taken from *New York World*, November 18, 1862, and *Washington Capital*, n.d., in Buell Papers, RU; unsigned letter to Buell, November 21, 1862, and Case to Buell, November 28, 1862, Buell Papers, RU; Lew Wallace, *Autobiography*, 2:643; McKinney, "Trial of Buell," 165; Niven, *Chase Papers*, 1:198, 204, 396; Chumney, "Gentleman General," 11–13.

14. Fry to Buell, November 23, 1862, Buell Papers, RU; McKinney, "Trial of Buell," 166–67; Wallace to Wife, December 14, 1862, Wallace Papers, IHS; Chumney, "Gentleman General," 12–13.

15. Everett to Buell, December 17, 1862, Buell Papers, RU.

16. Wallace to Wife, December 14, 1862, Wallace Papers, IHS.

17. Lew Wallace, *Autobiography*, 2:641–45; Peine, "Buell Commission," 77–78.

18. Lew Wallace, *Autobiography*, 2:641–45; Chumney, "Gentleman General," 11–13.

19. Peine, "Buell Commission," 78–80.

20. Ibid., 79–83; U.S. War Department, *Military Laws of the United States*, 23, 27, 36–38, 120–21; U.S. War Department, *Revised Regulations for the Army of the United States*, 499–516.

21. *OR* 16(1):21–22; *New Albany Daily Ledger*, December 15, 1862; Thomas and Hyman, *Stanton*, 260.

22. Wallace to Wife, December 8, 1862, Wallace Papers, IHS; *OR* 16(1):413–14.

23. Peine, "Buell Commission," 87–88; Donald, *Why the North Won*, 39–50; Grimsley, *Hard Hand of War*, 67–105.

24. *OR* 16(1):390–415, 472–85; Peine, "Buell Commission," 90–93.

25. Peine, "Buell Commission," 90–93; *OR* 16(1):515–28, 602–4.

26. *OR* 16(1):571–75; Peine, "Buell Commission," 92–93.

27. *OR* 16(1):13.

28. Ibid., 671–73; Peine, "Buell Commission," 93.

29. *OR* 16(1):709–10.

30. Ibid., 381.

31. Ibid., 134; Peine, "Buell Commission," 97–100.

32. *OR* 16(1):132–43.

33. Ibid., 450–52; Peine, "Buell Commission," 97–103.

34. *OR* 16(1):182–83; Piatt, *Thomas*, 180–81.

35. *OR* 16(1):102–3, 141–45, 535–41; Peine, "Buell Commission," 103–6.

36. *OR* 16(1):347.

37. Ibid., 55–60; Grimsley, *Hard Hand of War*, 317–35.

38. *OR* 16(1):269–71, 500, 636; Peine, "Buell Commission," 108–14.

39. *OR* 16(1):139–40.

40. Ibid., 674–75.

41. Ibid., 59.

42. Lucy Virginia French Diary, January 13, 1863, French Papers, TSLA; *OR* 16(1):481, 501–5.

43. Wallace to Wife, December 22, 1862, February 6, 1863, Wallace Papers, IHS; Lew Wallace, *Autobiography,* 2:643–46; McClure, *Lincoln and Men of War-Times,* 383–89.

44. Graf, Haskins, and Bergeron, *Papers of Johnson,* 6:113, 127–29, 215–17; *OR* 16(1):419–20, 542, 591–600, 638–42; Lew Wallace, *Autobiography,* 2:643; Stampp, *Indiana during the Civil War,* 160; Chumney, "Gentleman General," 16–17; McKinney, "Trial of Buell," 167–68.

45. Lew Wallace, *Autobiography,* 2:642–44.

46. *Washington Capital,* n.p., Buell Papers, RU; McKinney, "Trial of Buell," 165.

47. Piatt, *Thomas,* 179.

48. Lew Wallace, *Autobiography,* 2:643–44.

49. Ibid.

50. Ibid., 2:643.

51. Shanks, *Personal Recollections,* 257.

52. Lew Wallace, *Autobiography,* 2:643–44; Piatt, *Thomas,* 179.

53. Unidentified newspaper clipping, Buell Papers, RU.

54. *New York Daily Tribune,* May 16, 29, 1863; Basler, *Works of Lincoln,* 5:509–11.

55. *New York Daily Tribune,* May 29, 1863.

56. As quoted in Chumney, "Gentleman General," 17; *OR* 16(1):9–13; McClure, *Lincoln and Men of War-Times,* 383–89.

57. Lellyett to Buell, March 24, 1863, Buell Papers, RU.

58. Ibid., April 14, 1863.

59. Thorndike, *Sherman Letters,* 181–82.

60. Shanks to Buell, April 1863, Buell Papers, RU.

61. Reverdy W. Johnson to Buell, May 20, 1863, ibid.

62. Resolution of thanks to Buell from the Commonwealth of Kentucky, March 2, 1863, ibid.

63. Buell to Stanton, May 20, 1863, Stanton Papers, LC.

64. Lellyett to Buell, June 3, 1863, Buell Papers, RU; see also unidentified newspaper clippings, ibid.

65. Bush to Buell, July 23, 1863, ibid.

66. Unidentified newspaper clippings, ibid.

67. Ibid.

68. Sherman to Wright, September 2, October 14, 1863, ibid.; Lloyd Lewis, *Fighting Prophet,* 301–2; *OR* 30(3):294–95, 30(4):357–58.

69. *OR* 30(3):294–95, 30(4):357–58; Lloyd Lewis, *Fighting Prophet,* 301–2; Sherman to Wright, September 2, October 14, 1863, Buell Papers, RU.

70. Graf, Haskins, and Bergeron, *Papers of Johnson,* 6:660–61.

71. Ibid., 664.

72. Halleck to Grant, April 11, 1864, *OR* 35(2):48; Grant to Halleck, April 9, 1864, *OR* 35(1):46, 35(3):289, 292, 304; Stephen E. Ambrose, *Halleck,* 168; McClure, *Lincoln and Men of War-Times,* 386–89.

73. *OR* 39(2):38–39.

74. Crittenden to Watson, December 11, 1863, Watson Papers, LC; Buell to Rockwell, July 10, 1864, Rockwell Papers, LC; McClure, *Lincoln and Men of War-Times*, 386–89; Fry, *Operations under Buell*, 200–201; *OR* 36(2):694–95, 746, 34(3):532.

75. Grant, *Memoirs*, 2:121.

76. Buell to Rockwell, July 10, 1864, Rockwell Papers, LC; *New York Times*, August 7, 1864; Ephraim Otis to [?], May 28, 1864, General's Papers, RG 94, NA; Chumney, "Gentleman General," 191.

77. *New York Times*, August 7, 19, 20, 1864.

78. McClellan to Buell, November 11, 1864, Buell Papers, RU.

79. Johnson and Buel, *Battles and Leaders*, 3:51.

80. *National Tribune*, January 15, 1891.

EPILOGUE

1. Business Logs and Mining Company Books, and Miscellaneous Newspapers, Buell Papers, RU; Miscellaneous Genealogical Papers, Buell Papers, TC; Buell to William Lindsay, December 4, 1895, Lindsay Papers, UK; Rothert, *Muhlenberg County*, 242–45.

2. Buell to Lindsay, December 4, 1895, Lindsay Papers, UK; Rothert, *Muhlenberg County*, 241–45.

3. *New York World*, February 18, 1865; John Sherman, "Battle of Pittsburg Landing."

4. John Sherman, "Battle of Pittsburg Landing"; *New York World*, February 18, 1865.

5. John Sherman, "Battle of Pittsburg Landing"; *New York World*, February 18, 1865.

6. *New York World*, February 18, 1865.

7. Ibid.

8. Ibid.; see also *Chicago Tribune*, July 11, 1891, for an article in defense of Buell.

9. Wright to Buell, September 14, 1865, Buell Papers, RU, and *New York World*, February 18, 1865.

10. George H. Thomas to Buell, December 13, 1865; Stephen Jones to Buell, January 8, 1866, Buell Papers, RU.

11. *New York Herald*, August 3, 1865, April 3, 1866; Simon, *Papers of Grant*, 5:447–49; McFeely, *Grant*, 233; Grant, *Memoirs*, 1:359.

12. James Russell Young, *Around the World with General Grant*, 2:289.

13. William Farrar Smith, "Don Carlos Buell," Buell Papers, USMA-SC; B. B. Lewis to Buell, May 31, 1879, Buell Papers, RU.

14. Richard R. Bolling to Buell, March 12, 1867, and William Smith to Buell, April 21, 1877, Buell Papers, RU; O'Curry, *Radicalism, Racism, and Party Realignment*, 121–41.

15. Smith to Buell, April 21, 1877, Buell Papers, RU.

16. Buell to D. S. Richardson, September 1871, and Report of Regulations, Kentucky A and M College, Buell Papers, RU.

17. Buell to Roscoe Conkling, January 15, 1870; N. G. Ordway to Buell, May 18,

1872; Buell to Charles Eaves, March 29, 1874, all in Buell Papers, RU; Miscellaneous Genealogical Records, Buell Papers, TC; Trefousse, *Johnson*, 361–62; *New York Times*, May 25, June 4, 1872.

18. Eaves to Buell, November 16, 1874, and William B. Franklin to Buell, April 29, 1877, Buell Papers, RU; Rothert, *Muhlenberg County*, 238–41.

19. S. A. Buell to Buell, August 22, 1881, Buell Papers, RU; Rothert, *Muhlenberg County*, 238–41; Burial Certificate, Margaret Hunter Buell Papers, BC.

20. Eaves to Buell, November 16, 1874; Bush to Buell, April 29, 1877; Franklin to Buell, April 14, 1884, Scientific American Patent Department, November 25, 1876, all in Buell Papers, RU; Rothert, *Muhlenberg County*, 238–41.

21. Samuel W. Crawford to Buell, December 15, 1883; Buell to Crawford, December 20, 1883; Robert Hunter to Buell, June 9, 1879; Buell to T. Seymour, October 27, 1874; Edward Richardson to Buell, November 10, 1893; Buell to Nannie Mason, April 20, 1897; Buell to Walter Belas, February 8, 1894; R. N. Scott to Buell, February 18, 1880; A. H. Markland to Buell, August 17, 1881; Buell to J. Grant Wilson, January 27, 1895; Buell to Robert Johnson, April 21, 1888; S. A. Buell to Buell, August 22, 1881, all in Buell Papers, RU.

22. Buell to John P. Nicholson, June 4, 1875, Buell Papers, FC; Hunter to Buell, June 9, 1876, Buell Papers, RU.

23. Buell to William F. Smith, April 1, 23, 1886, Buell Papers, FC.

24. Lloyd Lewis, *Fighting Prophet*, 228; Fellman, *Citizen Sherman*, 329–30; Marszalek, *Sherman*, 475–76; Fry to Buell, January 8, 1886, Buell Papers, RU; Fry, *Operations under Buell*.

25. Fellman, *Citizen Sherman*, 329–31; Marszalek, *Sherman*, 475–76; Fry to Buell, January 8, 1886, Buell Papers, RU.

26. Bush to Buell, February 4, 1885; Hunter to Buell, January 22, 1885; T. C. Cory to Buell, July 17, 1885; Fry to Buell, August 25, 1885; B. B. Stone to Buell, March 6, 1885, all in Buell Papers, RU; Grant, "Battle of Shiloh," 593–613; Johnson and Buel, *Battles and Leaders*, 1:465–86; D. C. Buell, "Sherman and the Spring Campaign," 74–82.

27. Buell to Hunter, January 29, 1885, Buell Papers, RU.

28. Buell to Fry, March 28, 1889, and Buell to Editor, *Century Magazine*, January 29, 1885, Buell Papers, RU; D. C. Buell, "Shiloh Reviewed." See also Johnson and Buel, *Battles and Leaders*, 1:487–536.

29. Buell to Editor, *Century Magazine*, December 18, 1885, Buell Papers, RU.

30. Johnson and Buel, *Battles and Leaders*, 1:487–536.

31. Ibid.

32. W. G. Eliot to Buell, November 20, 1885, Buell Papers, RU.

33. Thomas Gantt, to Buell, May 11, June 2, 1886, Buell Papers, RU. See also *Chicago Tribune*, July 11, 1891, for an article in defense of Buell.

34. Grant, *Memoirs*, 1:358; Fry to Buell, January 8, 1886, Buell Papers, RU; Fellman, *Citizen Sherman*, 331–33; Marszalek, *Sherman*, 475–77.

35. As quoted in McFeely, *Grant*, 504.

36. Buell to Fry, March 28, 1889, Buell Papers, RU.

37. Ibid.; see, for example, Fellman, *Citizen Sherman*, 329–31.

38. Johnson and Buel, *Battles and Leaders*, 2:701–8, 3:31–51.

39. Bush to President Cleveland, March 28, 1893, Buell Papers, RU.

40. Buell to Looney, August 21, 1895, October 20, 1896, and Buell to General H. V. Boynton, October 29, 1898, Buell-Shiloh Battlefield Commission Papers, CCNMP; Buell to S. A. Cunningham, March 19, 1895, Buell Papers, UK; unidentified letter from the War Department to Buell, March 12, 1895, and certificate of Buell's appointment, January 25, 1894, Buell Papers, RU; Rothert, *Muhlenberg County*, 238–43; Hopkins, *University of Kentucky*, 121; Howard, *History of Shiloh*, 169.

41. Charles Lafland to Buell, July 13, 1896; *Louisville Times*, November 21, 1898; miscellaneous newspaper clippings, all in Buell Papers, RU.

42. Atwell Thompson to Buell, October 20, 1898, and *Louisville Times*, November 21, 1898, Buell Papers, RU; *Louisville Daily Journal*, November 30, 1898; Buell to Boynton, October 29, 1989, Buell-Shiloh Commission Battlefield Commission Papers, CCNMP; Buell File, USMA-SC; Rothert, *Muhlenberg County*, 245; Don Carlos Buell Papers and Margaret Hunter Buell Papers, BC.

43. McClure, *Lincoln and Men of War-Times*, 381–89.

44. T. Harry Williams, *Lincoln and His Generals*, 184; Nevins, *War for the Union*, 2:13; McPherson, *Battle of Freedom*, 522, 579.

Bibliography

· ·

MANUSCRIPTS

Note: Manuscript sources below have been listed by name only however they may have been designated (i.e., as collections, diaries, or papers) by the various repositories.

Bellefontaine Cemetery, St. Louis, Mo.
   Don Carlos Buell
   Margaret Hunter Buell
Chicago Historical Society, Chicago, Ill.
   Don Carlos Buell
   Charles W. Carr
   George D. Carrington
   Presley Judson Edwards
   Henry Halleck
   Roger W. Hanson
   Douglass Hapemann
   William J. Hardee
   Jacob G. Lauman
   James W. Lawrence
   John Alexander McClernand
   Duncan Chambers Milner
   William Weston Patton
   Andrew C. Rankin
   William H. Ross
   Tomas Benton Roy
   George Sawin
   Levi H. Sipes
   U.S. History, Civil War
   Lewis Wallace
   James R. Zearing
Chickamauga and Chattanooga National Military Park, Fort Oglethorpe, Ga.
   Buell-Shiloh Battlefield Commission
Claremont Graduate School, Claremont, Calif.
   Salmon P. Chase microfilm edition
Duke University, William R. Perkins Library, Durham, N.C.
   Eglantine Aquors
   Marvin B. Butler

Campbell Family
Mary Ione Chadick
Frederick W. Clark
Monroe Fulkerson Cockrell
James Andrew Mann
John Euclid Magee
Eugene Marshall
William Massee
H. H. Price
John Wesley Timmons
Charles Brown Tompkins
James H. Wiswell
Filson Club, Louisville, Ky.
Ben Albert
Braxton Bragg
Don Carlos Buell
Lincoln Conkey
Johnson W. Culp
Garrett Davis
Conrad Lewis Diehl
Dudley Family
Foote Family
George Herbert
J. Stoddard Johnston
Humphrey Marshall
Thaddeus A. Minshall
James F. Mohr
William Nelson
Alfred Pirtle
Pope-Humphrey
Torah W. Sampson
David Smith
James Thomson
John Tilford
Todd Family
"Willie" Letter
Florida Department of State, Division of Historical Resources, Bureau of
    Archaeological Research, Tallahassee
Florida Master Site File
Gunston Hall Plantation, Mason Neck, Va.
Mason Family
Huntington Library, San Marino, Calif.
Don Carlos Buell
Illinois State Historical Library, Springfield
Bruce Family
David Bunn

Charles E. Calkins
J. G. Cavis
Salmon P. Chase
George A. Cummins
Lewis C. Dougherty
James F. Drish
Edward E. Fielding
Thomas J. Frazee
James C. Howlett
Edson W. Lyman
Frederick Marion
Geza Mihalotzy
Olin H. Miner
Thaddeus B. Packard
Lines L. Parker
William E. Patterson
Edwin and Ira Payne
Levi A. Ross
John H. Sackett
Z. Payson Shumway
Dietrich C. Smith
Augustine Vieira
Philip Welschimer
Indiana Historical Society, William Smith Library, Indianapolis
Henry H. Aye
Judson W. Bishop
William W. Blair
Bower Collection
    Williamson D. Ward
Stanton J. Brumfield
Joseph and Orville Chamberlain
    Everett F. Abbott
Jesse B. Connelly
Wylie J. Daniels
Harrison Derrick
Wesley Elmore
William D. Evritt
Lancelot Chapman Ewbank
Nathan T. Fuller
Alva Griest
Joseph Gullian
Perry Hall
Ballard Hardin
John J. Hardin
James H. Jones
Journal by unidentified member of the 79th Indiana

George W. Lambert
Garrett Larew
Andrew J. McGarrah
Benjamin B. Mabrey
William B. Miller
Elizah R. Mitchell
Louis Nettelhaust
William Orr
Thomas Prickett
Benjamin Franklin Scribner
Oliver Shelly
Thomas M. Small
Thomas J. Stephenson
William R. Stuckey
John W. Switzer
Lew Wallace
Indiana State Archives, Indianapolis
Oliver P. Morton
Indiana State Library, Indianapolis
Samuel Shepherdson Family
Jean Simmonds
William Innis
Indiana University, Lilly Library, Archives, Bloomington
Don Carlos Buell
Kenneth P. Williams
Kansas State Historical Society, Topeka
John A. Martin
Kentucky Historical Society, Frankfort
Orlando Brown
Don Carlos Buell
Robert H. Earnest
Emilie Todd Helm
George W. Johnson
Metcalfe Collection
Howard Smith
Kentucky Military History Museum, Frankfort
Adjutant General's Office, letter books
Kentucky Quartermaster Records, 1860–65
Morgan Proclamation
Records Related to Kentucky Volunteer Infantry Regiments
Kentucky State Archives, Frankfort
Beriah Magoffin
Emily Stockard Leeds, Private Collection, Fort Lauderdale, Fla.
William H. Harder
Library of Congress, Washington, D.C.
William Orland Bourne

Charles M. Buford
Simon Cameron
Zachariah Chandler
Salmon P. Chase
John J. Crittenden
John W. Draper
Henry Halleck
Ethan Allen Hitchcock
Joseph Holt
Joseph Warren Keifer
Robert Todd Lincoln
George B. McClellan
McCook Family
Montgomery Meigs
Reed Family
Almon F. Rockwell
John Sherman
William T. Sherman
Edwin M. Stanton
Lyman Trumbull
Elihu B. Washburne
John C. Watson
Missouri Historical Society, St. Louis
Richard Graham
Ethan Allen Hitchcock
Kennett Family
James E. Love
National Archives and Records Administration, Washington, D.C.
Record Group 94
Records of the Adjutant General's Office, General's Papers, Don Carlos Buell, Letters and Telegrams Sent and Received, December 1861–December 1862
United States Adjutant General's Office
General Orders, 1837–45
General Orders, 1846–49
General Orders, 1849–51
General Orders, 1852–56
General Orders, 1857–61
United States Military Academy, Cadet Application Papers, 1806–66, Don Carlos Buell, file #24
War Department, Adjutant General's Office
General Correspondence and Related Records, Miscellaneous File, Papers concerning the Department of the Ohio
General's Papers and Books, Don Carlos Buell, 1861–63, 1865, Special Civil War Collection
Letters Received by Adjutant General's Office, 1841–64
Orders of the War Department and of Military Commands, General

Orders, Department of the Ohio, by Command of General Don
Carlos Buell
Returns from the Regular Army Infantry Regiments, Third Infantry
Regiment, 1841–61
Returns from United States Military Posts, 1800–1916, Third Infantry
Regiment, 1841–61
Staff Papers
Statement of Military Service, March 13, 1890, Don Carlos Buell
War Department, Engineer Department, United States Military
Academy Papers, Don Carlos Buell
War Department, Letters Received by the Secretary of War, Main Series
A–W, January 1843–44
Record Group 153
Records of the Office of the Judge Advocate General (Army), Court Martial
Case Files, 1809–94
Record Group 393
Records of the United States Continental Commands, pt. 1
Department of Missouri, 6th Military Department, General Orders, vol. 72
Department of New Mexico, General Orders, vol. 36
Department of Texas, General Orders, vol. 1
Department of the West, General Orders, vol. 76
Department of Utah, General and Special Orders and Circulars, vol. 7
United States War Department, Headquarters, Department of the Pacific,
San Francisco, General Orders, May 20–August 9, 1861
War Department, Adjutant General's Office, Records of the United States
Army Commands, Department of the Ohio, Letters and Telegrams Sent
and Received, 1861–62
United States Census Records
Slave Schedules
Oberlin College, Archives, Oberlin, Ohio
Jacob Colson Cox
Ohio Historical Society, Columbus
Jacob Ammen
Robert Baird
Sidney Baker
John W. Baldwin
William Ballentine
C. S. Bolton
Don Carlos Buell
Charles Coburn
D. P. Dougherty
Joseph Easton
Nancy Ann Emerson
Samuel T. Evans
Nathan Finegan
John G. Fox

A. L. Gierhart
J. Amos Glover
Frank A. Hardy
Samuel J. Harrison
Ephraim Holloway
Roderick Hooper
John D. Inskeep
Patrick Keran
Lewis Family
DeWitt Clinton Loudon
Edwin L. Lybarger
Lewis Mathewson
James B. Mitchell
William Mitchell
William Oglevie
Todd Oliphant
James O'Halligan
Henry M. Osborn
William Parkinson
Joseph Phillips
Asa B. Smith
William H. Smith
James Stillwell
E. P. Sturges
David H. Thomas
David Tod
Julius B. Work
Abia Zeller
Pennsylvania Historical and Museum Commission and State Archives, Harrisburg
Harris-Fisher
Ross A. Hickok
Rice University, Fondren Library, Archives, Houston, Tex.
Don Carlos Buell
Charles B. Bliven, "Reminiscences: A Paper Read at a Meeting of the Resident
Members of the Loyal Legion held at the Residence of Major General
Rutherford B. Hayes," February 28, 1885
Shiloh National Park and Historical Commission, Shiloh, Tenn.
Records Relating to Buell as Park Commissioner
State Historical Society of Wisconsin, Madison
George B. Bingham
Hans Christian Hegg
Oscar F. Pinney
Tennessee Department of State Library and Archives, Nashville
Gordon and Avery Family
Don Carlos Buell
George P. Buell/James Smith Brien

Benjamin Franklin Cheatham
Federal Collection
George M. Beck
Colburn
U. S. Grant
Henry W. Halleck
James W. King
Joseph Dimmit Thompson
Virginia L. French
George Washington Gordon and William Tecumseh
Harding-Jackson
James Winchester
Sheila Tschumy, Private Collection, Dallas, Tex.
Don Carlos Buell
Buell Family Genealogy Records
United States Army Military History Institute, Carlisle Barracks, Pa.
"Original List of Members Belonging to the Aztec Club, Founded in the City of
Mexico, A.A., 1847, by the Officers of the Army of the United States, 1879"
Luther Bradley
Henry S. Briggs
Andrew S. Burt
George Cheney
Civil War Miscellaneous
Timothy M. Blaisdell
Hugh T. Carlisle
Jason W. Culp
Thomas Finley
George W. Garratt
Edward Hill
Edgar Kellogg
James A. Price
Ephraim G. Wagley
R. Hoyt Winslow
Civil War Times Illustrated
Jacob Behm
Emerson Calkins
Andrew F. Davis
John A. Duncan
Mungo P. Murray
Edward H. Reynolds
Eben P. Sturgis
Levi Wagner
Harrisburg Civil War Roundtable
John Eicker
W. R. Eddington
Henry M. Erisman

Samuel B. Franklin
Alva C. Griest
Henry F. Huffer
John S. Walker
William B. Hazen
Richard F. Mann
Cyrus F. Leasher
William Stahl
MOLLUS Collection
Pennsylvania Save the Flag
Larew Phisterer
Murray J. Smith
United States Military Academy, West Point, N.Y.
Archives
Application for Admission and Recommendation
Cadets Admitted to the USMA, 1800–1845
Descriptive List of Candidates for Admission into the USMA
General Orders and Special Orders, Headquarters, 1836–43
Miscellaneous Book, 1838–68
Post Orders, 1832–42
Register of Cadet Delinquencies
Register of Merit, 1836–43
Staff Records, 1837–87
Special Collections
Jacob Ammen
Don Carlos Buell
William Farrar Smith, "Don Carlos Buell," twelve-page manuscript on Buell's
life, presented for the annual reunion, June 7, 1899
William Payne
General Orders, Adjutant General's Office, 1837–87
Robert Hazlitt
Ethan Allen Hitchcock
Library Circulation Records, Cadets, Officers, 1824–67
Jeremiah Mason Scarritt
Thirteenth Annual Reunion of the Association and Graduates of the USMA
University of Chicago, Joseph Regenstein Library, Archives, Chicago, Ill.
Abraham Lincoln
R. Delavan Mussey
University of Kentucky Library, Archives, Lexington
James Blanton
Don Carlos Buell
Mary E. Dan Meter
Evans-Peters
Amos Flegel
Gunn Family
Hunt-Morgan

William Lindsay
Thomas Robert McBeath
Means Family
University of Michigan, Bentley Historical Library, Ann Arbor
William Montague Ferry
Henry Mortimer Hempstead
Asa Slayton
University of Michigan, William L. Clements Library, Ann Arbor
Schoff Civil War Collection
Aaron Cooke
Ulysses S. Grant
Henry Seys
Jacob Van Zwaluwenberg
University of North Carolina, Southern Historical Collection, Wilson Library,
Chapel Hill
William Birnie
Elias Brady
Alexander D. Coffee
Chesley D. Evans
Daniel Harvey Hill
Cornelius J. Madden
C. Irvin Walker
Chauncey B. Welton
University of Notre Dame, Archives, South Bend, Ind.
Don Carlos Buell
Sherman Family
Washington County Public Library, Marietta, Ohio
"Lingering in Lowell"
Washington County Census Records, Probate Records
Western Kentucky University, Bowling Green
Hartford Collection
H. H. Giesy
Samuel Thomas Davis
Western Reserve Historical Society, Cleveland, Ohio
Alexander Varian Jr.

PRINTED PRIMARY MATERIAL

Ambrose, D. Leib. *History of the Seventh Regiment Illinois Volunteer Infantry.* Springfield: Illinois Journal Co., 1868.
Ammen, Daniel B. *The Old Navy and the New.* Philadelphia: Lippincott, 1891.
Anderson, Thomas M. *The Political Conspiracies Preceding the Rebellion; or, The True Stories of Pickens and Sumter.* New York: Putnam's, 1882.
Andrews, Martin R. *History of Marietta and Washington County, Ohio, and Representative Citizens.* 2 vols. Chicago: Biographical Pub. Co., 1902.

Angle, Paul, ed. *Three Years in the Army of the Cumberland: The Letters and Diary of Major James A. Connolly.* Bloomington: Indiana University Press, 1959.

Annals of the Fifty-seventh Regiment Indiana Volunteers. Dayton, Ohio: W. J. Shuey, 1868.

Armstrong, Zella. *The History of Hamilton County and Chattanooga, Tennessee.* Chattanooga: Lookout Publishing, 1931.

Aten, Henry J. *History of the Eighty-fifth Regiment Illinois Volunteer Infantry.* Hiawatha, Kans.: n.p., 1901.

Athern, Robert G., ed. *Soldier in the West: The Civil War Letters of Alfred Lacey Hough.* Philadelphia: University of Pennsylvania Press, 1957.

Barnes, James A., James R. Carnaham, and Thomas H. B. McCain. *The Eighty-sixth Regiment, Indiana Volunteer Infantry.* Crawfordville, Ind.: Journal Co., 1895.

Basler, Roy P., ed. *Collected Works of Abraham Lincoln.* 8 vols. New Brunswick, N.J.: Rutgers University Press, 1953–55.

Beale, Howard K., ed. *The Diary of Edward Bates, 1859–1866.* Washington, D.C.: Government Printing Office, 1933.

Beatty, John. *The Citizen Soldier; or, Memoirs of a Volunteer.* Cincinnati: Wilstach, Baldwin, 1879.

Becker, Carl M., and Ritchie Thomas, ed. *Hearth and Knapsack: The Ladley Letters, 1857–1880.* Athens: Ohio University Press, 1988.

Bennett, L. G., and William M. Haigh. *History of the Thirty-six Regiment Illinois Volunteers.* Aurora, Ill.: Knickerbocker and Hodder, 1876.

Bevens, W. E. *Reminiscences of a Private, Company "G," First Arkansas Regiment.* Newport, Ark.: W. E. Bevens, 1913.

Bircher, William. *A Drummer Boy's Diary.* St. Paul, Minn.: St. Paul Book Co., 1889.

Bishop, Judson W. *The Story of a Regiment: Being a Narrative of the Service of the Second Regiment Minnesota Veteran Volunteer Infantry.* St. Paul, Minn.: Published by the Regiment, 1890.

Blegen, Theodore C., ed. *The Civil War Letters of Colonel Hans Christian Heg.* Northfield, Minn.: Norwegian-American Historical Association, 1936.

Bowman, Thornton Hardie. *Reminiscences of an ex-Confederate Soldier.* Austin, Tex.: Gammel-Stateman, 1904.

Brewer, A. T. *History of the Sixty-first Regiment Pennsylvania Volunteers.* Pittsburgh: Art Engraving and Printing, 1911.

Briant, Charles C. *History of the Sixth Regiment Indiana Volunteer Infantry.* Indianapolis: W. B. Burford, 1891.

Brooks, Nathan C. *A Complete History of the Mexican War.* Baltimore: Hutchinson and Seebold, 1849.

Brown, Alonzo L. *History of the Fourth Regiment Minnesota Infantry Volunteers.* St. Paul, Minn.: Pioneer Press, 1892.

Bryan, Edwin Eustace. *History of the Third Regiment of Wisconsin Veteran Volunteer Infantry.* Madison, Wis.: Veteran Association, 1891.

Bryner, Byron C. *Bugle Echoes: The Story of the Illinois Forty-seventh.* Springfield, Ill.: Phillips Brothers, 1905.

Buchanan, James. *Buchanan's Administration.* New York: Appleton, 1866.

Buell, Don Carlos. *Statement of Major General Buell in Review of the Evidence Before the*

Military Commission Appointed by the War Department in November, 1862. Campaign in Kentucky, Tennessee, Northern Mississippi, and North Alabama in 1861 and 1862. Cincinnati: n.p., 1863.

Burdette, Robert J. *The Drums of the Forty-seventh.* Indianapolis: Bobbs-Merrill, 1914.

Butler, Watson H., ed. *Letters Home: B. Jay Caldwell Butler.* Birmingham, N.Y.: n.p., 1930.

Canfield, Silas S. *History of the Twenty-first Regiment Ohio Volunteer Infantry in the War of the Rebellion.* Toledo, Ohio: Vrooman, Anderson and Bateman, 1903.

Chamberlin, W. H. *History of the Eighty-first Regiment Ohio Infantry Volunteers during the War of the Rebellion.* Cincinnati: Gazette Steam Printing House, 1865.

Chase, John A. *History of the Fourteenth Ohio Regiment.* Toledo, Ohio: St. John Print House, 1881.

Chronister, Elza. *Reminiscences of Army Life.* Eagle Grove, Iowa: n.p., 1909.

Cist, Henry M. *The Army of the Cumberland: The Campaigns of the Civil War.* New York: Scribner's, 1882.

Clark, Charles M. *The History of the Thirty-ninth Regiment Illinois Volunteer Veteran Infantry.* Reprint, Bowie, Md.: Heritage Books, 1994.

Clark, Olynthus B., ed. *Downing's Civil War Diary.* Des Moines: Historical Department of Iowa, 1916.

Clowes, Walter F. *The Detroit Light Guard: A Complete Record of the Organization.* Detroit: John F. Eby, 1900.

Cluett, William W. *History of the Fifth-seventh Regiment Illinois Volunteer Infantry.* Princeton, N.J.: Lessee Republican Job Department, 1886.

Connelly, Thomas H. *History of the Seventieth Ohio Regiment.* Cincinnati: Peak Brothers, 1902.

Coons, John W. *Indiana at Shiloh.* Indianapolis: Shiloh National Park Commission, 1904.

Cope, Alexis. *The Fifteenth Ohio Volunteers.* Columbus, Ohio: Edward T. Miller, 1916.

Crawford, Samuel W. *Genesis of the Civil War: The Story of Sumter, 1860–1861.* New York: Charles L. Webster, 1887.

Croffut, W. A. *Fifty Years in Camp and Field: Diary of Major-General Ethan Allen Hitchcock.* New York: Putnam's, 1909.

Cullum, George W. *Biographical Register of the Officers and Cadets of the United States Military Academy at West Point.* 3 vols. New York: D. Van Nostrand, 1868.

Curry, William. *Four Years in the Saddle.* Columbus, Ohio: Champlin, 1898.

Curtis, George T. *Life of James Buchanan.* 2 vols. New York: Harper and Brothers, 1883.

Damon, Herbert C. *History of the Milwaukee Light Guard.* Milwaukee: Sentinel, 1875.

Dannett, Sylvia G. *She Rode with the Generals.* New York: Thomas Nelson and Sons, 1960.

Day, Lewis W. *Story of the One Hundred and First Ohio Infantry.* Cleveland: W. M. Bayne, 1894.

Dennett, Tyler, ed. *Lincoln and the Civil War in the Diaries and Letters of John Hay.* New York: Dodd, Mead, 1939.

Dodge, William Summer. *History of the Old Second Division, Army of the Cumberland. Commanders: M'Cook, Sill, and Johnson.* Chicago: Church and Goodman, 1864.

————. *A Waif of the War: The History of the Seventy-fifth Illinois Infantry.* Chicago: Church and Goodman, 1866.

Donald, David, ed. *Inside Lincoln's Cabinet: The Civil War Diaries of Salmon P. Chase.* New York: Longmans, Green, 1954.

Doubleday, Abner. *Reminiscences of Forts Sumter and Moultrie in 1860–1861.* New York: Harper and Brothers, 1876.

Doubleday, Rhoda Van B. Tanner. *Journals of the Late Brevet Major Phillip Norbourne Barbour.* New York: Putnam's, 1936.

Driggs, George W. *Opening of the Mississippi; or, Two Years Campaigning in the Southwest.* Madison, Wis.: William J. Park, 1864.

Duke, Basil W. *Reminiscences of General Basil Duke, C.S.A.* Garden City, N.Y.: Doubleday, Page, 1911.

Duke, John K. *History of the Fifty-third Ohio Volunteer Infantry.* Portsmouth, Ohio: Blade Printing, 1900.

The Eagle Regiment: Eighth Wisconsin Infantry Volunteers. Belleville, Wis.: Recorder Print, 1890.

Eastham, Tarrant. *The Wild Riders of the First Kentucky Cavalry.* Louisville, Ky.: R. H. Carothers, 1894.

Esarey, Logan. *History of Indiana from Its Exploration to 1922.* 4 vols. Dayton, Ohio: Dayton Historical Pub. Co., 1924.

Evelyn, Sarah E. *The Female Spy of the Union Army.* Boston: DeWolfe Fiske, 1864.

Federico, Bianca, ed. *Civil War: The Letters of John Holbrook Morse, 1861–1865.* Washington, D.C.: n.p., 1975.

Farley, Edwin. *Experience of a Soldier, 1861–1865.* Paducah, Ky.: Billings Printing, 1918.

Fertig, James Walter. *Secession and Reconstruction of Tennessee.* Chicago: University of Chicago Press, 1898.

Fisher, Horace Cecil, ed. *A Staff Officer's Story: The Personal Experiences of Colonel Horace Newton Fisher in the Civil War.* Boston: Todd, 1960.

Fitch, John. *Annals of the Army of the Cumberland.* Philadelphia: Lippincott, 1864.

Floyd, David B. *History of the Seventy-fifth Regiment of Indiana Infantry Volunteer.* Philadelphia: Lutheran Publication Society, 1893.

Ford, Harvey S., ed. *John Beatty: Memoirs of a Volunteer.* New York: Norton, 1946.

Ford, Thomas J. *With the Rank and File: Incidents and Anecdotes during the War of the Rebellion.* Milwaukee: Press of the Evening Wisconsin, 1898.

Foulke, William D. *Life of Oliver P. Morton.* 2 vols. Indianapolis: Bowen-Merrill, 1898–99.

Frost, John. *The Mexican War and Its Warriors.* New Haven: H. Mansfield, 1850.

Fry, James B. *Killed by a Brother Soldier.* New York: Putnam's, 1885.

————. *Military Miscellanies.* New York: Brentano's, 1889.

————. *Operations of the Army under Buell.* New York: D. Van Nostrand, 1884.

Furber, George C. *The Twelve Months Volunteer; or, Journal of a Private in the Tennessee Regiment of Cavalry in the Campaign in Mexico, 1846–47.* Cincinnati: J. A. and U. P. James, 1848.

Goodrich, Dewitt, and Charles Tuttle. *An Illustrated History of the State of Indiana.* Indianapolis: Richard S. Peale, 1875.

Gorham, George C. *Life and Public Service of Edwin M. Stanton.* 2 vols. New York: Houghton Mifflin, 1899.

Graf, LeRoy P., Ralph W. Haskins, and Paul H. Bergeron, eds. *The Papers of Andrew Johnson.* 13 vols. Knoxville: University of Tennessee Press, 1967–89.

Graham, Bernice, and Elizabeth Cottle. *Abstract of Probate Records, Washington County, Ohio.* Marietta, Ohio: Washington County Historical Society, 1982.

Grant, Ulysses Simpson. *Personal Memoirs of U. S. Grant.* 2 vols. New York: Charles L. Webster, 1885.

Grebner, Constantin. *We Were the Ninth: A History of the Ninth Regiment, Ohio Volunteer Infantry, April 17, 1861, to June 7, 1864.* Translated and edited by Frederic Trautmann. Kent, Ohio: Kent State University Press, 1897.

Grose, William. *The Story of the Marches, Battles and Incidents of the Thirty-sixth Regiment Indiana Volunteer Infantry.* New Castle, Ind.: Courier Company Press, 1891.

Halleck, Henry W. *Elements of Military Art and Science.* 2nd ed. New York: Appleton, 1862.

Hancock, Almira Russell. *Reminiscences of Winfield Scott Hancock.* New York: Charles L. Webster, 1887.

Hancock, John. *The Fourteenth Wisconsin.* Indianapolis: Engle, 1895.

Hannaford, Edwin. *The Story of a Regiment: A History of the Campaigns and Association in the Field of the Sixth Regiment Ohio Volunteer Infantry.* Cincinnati: Published by the Author, 1868.

Harden, Henry O. *History of the Ninetieth Ohio Volunteer Infantry in the War of the Great Rebellion.* Stoutsville, Ohio: Fanfield-Pickaway News, 1902.

Hardie, James A. *Memoir: James Allen Hardie, Inspector General, United States Army.* Washington, D.C.: n.p., 1877.

Hart, B. H. Liddell, ed. *The Memoirs of General William T. Sherman: By Himself.* Bloomington: Indiana University Press, 1957.

Hart, Ephraim. *History of the Fortieth Illinois Infantry.* Cincinnati: H. S. Bosworth, 1864.

Hartpence, William R. *History of the Fifty-first Indiana Veteran Volunteer Infantry.* Cincinnati: Robert Clarke, 1894.

Hazen, William B. *A Narrative of Military Service.* Boston: Ticknor and Fields, 1885.

Henry, William S. *Campaign Sketches of the War with Mexico.* New York: Harper and Brothers, 1847.

Herr, George W. *Nine Campaigns in Nine States: The History of the Fifty-ninth Regiment Illinois Veteran Volunteer Infantry.* San Francisco: Bancroft, 1890.

Hinman, Wilbur F. *The Story of the Sherman Brigade.* Alliance, Ohio: Daily Review, 1897.

Historical Memoranda Fifty-second Regiment Illinois Infantry Volunteer. Elgin, Ill.: Gilbert and Post, 1868.

History of Dearborn and Ohio Counties, Indiana. Chicago: F. E. Weakley, 1885.

History of the Seventy-ninth Regiment Indiana Volunteer Infantry. Indianapolis: Hellenkeck Press, 1899.

History of Trumbull and Mahoning Counties. Cleveland: H. Z. Williams and Brothers, 1882.

Hittle, J. D., ed. *Jomini and His Summary of the Art of War*. Harrisburg, Pa.: Stackpole Books, 1964.

Hobart, Edwin L. *The Truth about Shiloh*. Denver: Hicks-Fairall, 1909.

Holmes, James T. *Fifty-second O.V.I. Then and Now*. Columbus, Ohio: Berlin Printing, 1898.

Holmes, Meade. *A Soldier of the Cumberland: Memoir of Meade Holmes*. Boston: American Tract Society, 1864.

Horrall, Spillard. *History of the Forty-second Indiana Volunteer Infantry*. Chicago: Horrall, 1892.

Howe, Daniel W. *Civil War Times by Daniel Wait Howe*. Indianapolis: Bowen-Merrill, 1892.

Howe, Henry. *Historical Collections of Ohio*. 2 vols. Cincinnati: C. J. Krehbiel, 1900.

Hubert, Charles F. *History of the Fiftieth Regiment Illinois Volunteer Infantry*. Kansas City, Mo.: Western Veteran Pub. Co., 1894.

Humes, Thomas W. *The Loyal Mountaineers of Tennessee*. Knoxville: Ogden Brothers, 1888.

Hunter, Alfred G. *History of the Eighty-second Indiana Volunteer Infantry*. Indianapolis: W. B. Burford, 1893.

Hutchinson, Nelson. *History of the Seventh Massachusetts Volunteer Infantry*. Taunton, Mass.: n.p., 1890.

Indiana Historical Society Publication. 2 vols. Indianapolis: Bowen-Merrill, 1897.

Johnson, Reverdy W. *A Soldier's Reminiscences in Peace and War*. Philadelphia: Lippincott, 1886.

Johnson, Richard W. *Memoir of Major General George H. Thomas*. Philadelphia: Lippincott, 1881.

Johnson, Robert U., and Clarence C. Buel, eds. *Battles and Leaders of the Civil War*. 4 vols. New York: Century, 1887.

Johnston, Margaret. *The Young Chaplain: William Curtis Johnston*. New York: N. Tibbals and Sons, 1876.

Jomini, Henri Antoine. *Summary of the Art of War*. Translated by G. H. Mendell and W. P. Craighill. Philadelphia: Lippincott, 1863.

Keil, Frederick. *Thirty-fifth Ohio: A Narrative of Service from August 1861–1864*. Fort Wayne, Ind.: Archer, Housh, 1894.

Kelley, R. M., and Alfred Pirtle. *The Union Regiments of Kentucky*. Louisville, Ky.: Courier-Journal Job Printing, 1897.

Kendall, Amos. *Letters Exposing the Mismanagement of Public Affairs by Abraham Lincoln*. Washington, D.C.: Constitutional Union Office, 1864.

Kendall, George W. *The War between the United States and Mexico*. New York: Appleton, 1851.

Kern, Albert. *History of the First Regiment Ohio Volunteer Infantry*. Dayton, Ohio: Curt Dalton, 1918.

Kerwood, Asbury L. *Annals of the Fifty-seventh Regiment Indiana Volunteers*. Dayton, Ohio: W. J. Shuey, 1868.

Kimberly, Robert L., and Ephraim S. Holloway. *The Forty-first Ohio Veteran Volunteer Infantry in the War of the Rebellion*. Cleveland: W. R. Smellie, 1897.

Lathrop, David. *The History of the Fifty-ninth Regiment Illinois Volunteers.* Indianapolis: Hall and Hutchinson, 1865.

Lawton, Eba A. *Major Robert Anderson and Fort Sumter, 1861.* New York: Knicker-bocker Press, 1911.

Lindsey, T. J. *Ohio at Shiloh.* Cincinnati: C. J. Krehbiel, 1903.

Long, E. B., ed. *Personal Memoirs of Ulysses S. Grant.* 2 vols. Cleveland: World Pub. Co., 1952.

Longstreet, James. *From Manassas to Appomattox: Memoirs of the Civil War in America.* New York: Lippincott, 1908.

Lyon, William Penn. *Reminiscences of the Civil War.* San Jose, Calif.: William P. Lyon, 1907.

McCall, George A. *Letters from the Frontier.* Philadelphia: Lippincott, 1868.

McCann, William. *Ambrose Bierce's Civil War.* Chicago: Gateway Editions, 1956.

McClure, Alexander K. *Abraham Lincoln and Men of War-Times.* Philadelphia: Times Pub. Co., 1892.

McKee, John Miller. *The Great Panic, Being Connected with Two Weeks of the War in Tennessee.* Nashville: Johnson and Whiting, 1862.

MacKenzie, Muriel Davis, ed. *"Maggie!" Maggie Lindsley's Journal, Nashville, 1864, Washington, D.C., 1865.* Southberry, Conn.: M. D. MacKenzie, 1977.

Magdeburg, F. H. *Wisconsin at Shiloh: Report of the Commission.* Milwaukee: Riverside, 1909.

Mahan, Dennis Hart. *An Elementary Treatise on Advanced Guard, Out Post, and Detach-ment Service of Troops.* New York: Wiley and Putnam, 1847.

Mansfield, Edward D. *The Mexican War: A History of Its Origin.* Cincinnati: Derby, Bradley, 1848.

Marshall, John Wesley. *Civil War Journal of John Wesley Marshall.* New York: n.p., 1958.

Martin, John A. *Military History of the Eighth Kansas Veteran Volunteer Infantry.* Leav-enworth: Daily Bulletin, 1869.

Meade, George G. *The Life and Letters of George Gordon Meade.* 2 vols. New York: Scribner's, 1913.

Meek, Howard Samuel. *The Illustrated Comprehensive History of the Great Battle of Shiloh.* Kansas City, Mo.: Press of Franklin Hudson Publishing, 1921.

Merrill, Samuel. *The Seventieth Indiana Volunteer Infantry.* Indianapolis: Bowen-Merrill.

Military Service Institute. *Letters and Addresses in Memory of Winfield Scott Hancock.* New York: Putnam's, 1886.

Miller, Charles G. *Donn Piatt: His Works and His Ways.* Cincinnati: Robert Clarke, 1893.

Mitchel, F. A. *Ormsby MacKnight Mitchel: Astronomer and General.* New York: Houghton Mifflin, 1887.

Moore, John Bassett, ed. *The Works of James Buchanan.* 12 vols. New York: Antiquar-ian Press, 1960.

Morris, George W. *History of the Eighty-first Regiment of Indiana Volunteer Infantry.* Louisville, Ky.: Franklin Printing Co., 1901.

Morrison, Marion. *A History of the Ninth Regiment Illinois Volunteer Infantry.* Mon-mouth, Ill.: John S. Clark, 1864.

Morse, Loren, ed. *Civil War Diaries of Bliss Morse*. Pittsburg, Kans.: Pittcraft, 1964.

Newell, Keith. *"Ours" Annals of the Tenth Regiment Massachusetts Volunteers in the Rebellion*. Springfield, Mass.: C. A. Nichols, 1875.

Newlin, William Henry, ed. *A History of the Seventy-third Regiment of Illinois Infantry Volunteers*. Springfield, Ill.: Regimental Reunion Association, 1890.

Newton, H. William. *The Indiana Banker Has Posted His Books*. Detroit: Free Press, 1866.

Nicolay, John G., and John Hay, eds. *Complete Works of Abraham Lincoln*. 12 vols. New York: Francis D. Tandy, 1905.

Niven, John, ed. *Salmon P. Chase Papers*. 4 vols. Kent, Ohio: Kent State University Press, 1993– .

Obreiter, John. *The Seventy-seventh Pennsylvania at Shiloh*. Harrisburg, Pa.: Harrisburg Publications, 1905.

Ovrey, S. Barrett. *Reminiscences of Incidents, Battles, Marches, and Camplife of the Old Fourth Michigan Infantry in the War of the Rebellion*. Detroit: W. S. Ostler, 1888.

Palmer, Beverly Wilson, ed. *The Selected Letters of Charles Sumner*. 2 vols. Boston: Northeastern University Press, 1990.

Partridge, Warren G. *Life of Frederick H. Alms*. Cincinnati: Jennings and Graham, 1904.

Payne, Edwin W. *History of the Thirty-fourth Illinois Infantry*. Clinton, Iowa: Allen Printing, 1902.

Perrin, W. H., and J. H. Battle. *History of Logan County and Ohio*. Chicago: O. L. Baskin, 1880.

Perry, Henry F. *History of the Thirty-eighth Regiment Indiana Volunteer Infantry*. Palo Alto, Calif.: F. A. Stuart, 1906.

Perry, Oran. *Indiana in the Mexican War*. Indianapolis: W. B. Burford, 1908.

Piatt, Donn. *General George H. Thomas: A Critical Biography*. Cincinnati: Robert Clarke, 1893.

———. *Memories of Men Who Saved the Union*. New York: Belford, Clarke, 1887.

Polk, J. J. *Autobiography of Dr. J. J. Polk*. Louisville, Ky.: John P. Morton, 1867.

Polk, William M. *Leonidas Polk, Bishop and General*. New York: Longmans, Green, 1915.

Powell, William H. *A History of the Organization and Movements of the Fourth Regiment of Infantry*. Washington, D.C.: M'Gill and Witherow, 1871.

Prime, William C., ed. *McClellan's Own Story*. New York: Charles L. Webster, 1887.

Rabb, Kate M., and William Herschell. *An Account of Indianapolis and Marion County*. 4 vols. Dayton, Ohio: Dayton Historical Pub. Co., 1924.

Raymond, Henry J. *The Life and Public Service of Abraham Lincoln*. New York: Stevens, 1865.

Record of the Ninety-fourth Regiment Ohio Volunteer Infantry in the War of the Rebellion. Cincinnati: Ohio Valley Press, [1894].

Reed, David. *Campaigns and Battles of the Twelfth Regiment Iowa Veteran Volunteer Infantry*. N.p.: n.d.

Regimental Association Committee. *History of the Fifteenth Regiment Iowa Veteran Volunteer Infantry*. Keokuk, Iowa: R. B. Ogden and Son, 1887.

Regulations of the U.S. Military Academy at West Point. West Point, N.Y.: J. and J. Harper, 1833.

Reid, H. T. *History of the Fifteenth Regiment Iowa Veteran Volunteer Infantry.* Keokuk, Iowa: R. B. Ogden and Son, 1887.

Reid, Whitelaw D. *Battle of Shiloh and the Organization Engaged.* Washington, D.C.: Government Printing Office, 1903.

———. *Ohio in the War: Her Statesmen, Generals, and Soldiers.* 2 vols. Columbus, Ohio: Eclectic Publishing, 1893.

Rerick, John H. *The Forty-fourth Indiana Volunteer Infantry.* LeGrange, Ind.: Published by the Author, 1880.

Rhodes, Robert Hunt. *All for the Union: A History of the Second Rhode Island Volunteer Infantry in the War of the Rebellion.* Lincoln, R.I.: Andrew Mowbray, 1985.

Rich, Joseph. *The Battle of Shiloh.* Iowa City: State Historical Society of Iowa, 1911.

Richardson, James. *A Compilation of the Messages and Papers of the Presidents, 1789–1897.* 10 vols. Washington, D.C.: Government Printing Office, 1896–99.

Ripley, Roswell. *The War with Mexico.* 2 vols. New York: Harper and Brothers, 1849. Reprint, New York: Burt Franklin, 1970.

Robertson, Charles. *History of Morgan County, Ohio.* Chicago: L. H. Watkins, 1886.

Roe, Alfred S. *The Tenth Regiment Massachusetts Volunteer Infantry.* Springfield, Mass.: Tenth Regiment Veteran Association, 1909.

Rogers, Robert. *The 125th Regiment Illinois Volunteer Infantry.* Champaign, Ill.: Gazette Steam Print, 1882.

Rothert, Otto A. *A History of Muhlenberg County, Kentucky.* Louisville, Ky.: J. P. Morton, 1913.

Scribner, Benjamin F. *How Soldiers Were Made; or, The War as I Saw It under Buell, Rosecrans, Thomas, Grant, and Sherman.* New Albany, Ind.: Donahue and Henneberry, 1887.

Sears, Stephen. *The Civil War Papers of George B. McClellan.* New York: Da Capo Press, 1992.

Shanks, William F. B. *Personal Recollections of Distinguished Generals.* New York: Harper and Brothers, 1866.

Shannon, Fred A. *The Organization and Administration of the Union Army, 1861–1865.* Cleveland: Arthur H. Clarke, 1928.

Shaw, Archibald, ed. *History of Dearborn County, Indiana.* Indianapolis: B. F. Bowen, 1915. Reprint, Evansville, Ind.: Unigraphic, 1980.

Shaw, James B. *History of the Tenth Regiment Indiana Volunteer Infantry.* Lafayette, Ind.: n.p., 1912.

Sheridan, Philip H. *Personal Memoirs of P. H. Sheridan, General, United States Army.* 2 vols. New York: Charles L. Webster, 1888.

Sherman, William T. *Memoirs.* 2 vols. New York: Appleton, 1875.

Simmons, Louis. *The History of the Eighty-fourth Regiment Illinois Vols.* Macomb, Ill.: Hampton Brothers, 1866.

Simon, John Y., ed. *The Papers of Ulysses S. Grant.* 18 vols. Carbondale: Southern Illinois University Press, 1967–91.

Smart, James G., ed. *A Radical View: The "Agate" Dispatches of Whitelaw Reid, 1861–1865.* 2 vols. Memphis: Memphis State University Press, 1976.

Smith, Harry V., ed. *The Life and Letters of Pvt. Samuel Thomas Smith, Fifteenth Indiana Regiment Volunteer, Civil War*. Bloomington, Ind.: Monroe County Historical Society, 1976.

Smith, Jacob H. *Personal Reminiscences Three Weeks Prior, during 10 Days after the Battle of Shiloh*. Detroit: Winn and Hammond, 1894.

Smith, John Thomas. *A History of the Thirty-first Regiment of Indiana Volunteer Infantry in the War for the Rebellion*. Cincinnati: Western Methodist Book Concern, 1900.

Smith, Theodore C. *Life and Letters of James A. Garfield*. 2 vols. New Haven: Yale University Press, 1935.

Speed, Thomas. *The Union Cause in Kentucky, 1860–1865*. New York: Putnam's, 1907.

Speed, Thomas, R. H. Kelly, and Alfred Pirhe. *The Union Regiments of Kentucky*. Louisville, Ky.: Courier-Journal Job Printing, 1897.

Sprague, John T. *The Origin, Progress, and Conclusion of the Florida War*. 1848. Reprint, Gainesville: University Presses of Florida, 1964.

Stevens, Isaac I. *Campaigns of the Rio Grande and of Mexico*. New York: Appleton, 1851.

Stewart, Nixon B. *Dan McCook's Regiment, Fifty-second O.V.I.* [Alliance, Ohio]: Published by the author, 1900.

Stuart, A. A. *Iowa Colonels and Regiments: Being a History of Iowa Regiments in the War of the Rebellion*. Des Moines: Mills and Co., 1865.

Sulgrove, Berry R. *History of Indianapolis and Marion Counties, Indiana*. Philadelphia: L. H. Everts, 1854.

Sunderland, Glenn W. *Five Days to Glory*. New York: A. S. Barnes, 1970.

Tapp, Hambleton, and James C. Klotter, eds. *The Union, the Civil War, and John W. Tuttle: A Kentucky Captain's Account*. Frankfort: Kentucky Historical Society, 1980.

Tarrant, Sergeant E. *The Wild Riders of the First Kentucky Cavalry*. N.p.: published by the Regiment, 1894.

Temple, Oliver P. *East Tennessee and the Civil War*. Cincinnati: Robert Clarke, 1888.

Thatcher, Marshall P. *A Hundred Battles in the West*. Detroit: Published by the Author, 1884.

Third Infantry Day. Fort Snelling, Minn.: n.p., 1929.

Thoburn, Thomas Crawford. *My Experiences during the Civil War*. Cleveland: Lyle Thoburn, 1963.

Thorndike, Rachel Sherman, ed. *The Sherman Letters: Correspondence between General and Senator Sherman from 1837 to 1891*. New York: Scribner's, 1894.

Throne, Mildred, ed. *The Civil War Diary of Cyrus F. Boyd: Fifteenth Iowa Infantry, 1861–1863*. Iowa City: State Historical Society of Iowa, 1953.

Tourgée, Albion Winegar. *The Story of a Thousand, Being a History of the 105th Ohio Volunteer Infantry*. Buffalo, N.Y.: McGerald and Son, 1896.

Turner, George E. *Victory Rode the Rails: The Strategic Plan of Railroads in the Civil War*. New York: Bobbs-Merrill, 1953.

Tutorow, Norman E. *The Mexican American War in Annotated Bibliography*. Westport, Conn.: Greenwood Press, 1981.

Vandiver, Frank E., ed. *The Civil War Diary of General Josiah Gorges*. University: University of Alabama Press, 1947.

Van Horne, Thomas V. *History of the Army of the Cumberland: Its Organization, Campaigns, and Battles.* 3 vols. Cincinnati: Robert Clarke, 1875.

Villard, Henry. *Memoirs of Henry Villard, Journalist and Financier, 1835–1900.* 2 vols. Boston: Houghton Mifflin, 1904.

Walker, Charles M. *Sketch of the Life, Character, and Public Services of Oliver P. Norton.* Indianapolis: Indianapolis Journal, 1878.

Wallace, Edward. *General William Jenkins Worth: Monterrey's Forgotten Hero.* Dallas, Tex.: Southern Methodist University Press, 1953.

Wallace, Isabel. *Life and Letters of General W. H. L. Wallace.* Chicago: R. R. Donnelley and Sons, 1909.

Wallace, Lew. *Lew Wallace: An Autobiography.* 2 vols. New York: Harper and Brothers, 1906.

Waterloo, Stanley. *Illinois at Shiloh.* Chicago: M. A. Donohue, 1905.

Wilcox, Cadmus. *History of the Mexican War.* Washington, D.C.: Church News Pub. Co., 1892.

Williams, Frederick D., ed. *The Wild Life of the Army: Civil War Letters of James A. Garfield.* East Lansing: Michigan State University Press, 1964.

Williams, H. Z. *History of Washington County, Ohio.* Cleveland: W. W. Williams, 1881.

Winters, Erastus. *In the Fiftieth Ohio Serving Uncle Sam.* East Walnut Hills: n.p., 1905.

Wittke, Carl. *The Ninth Ohio Volunteer.* Columbus, Ohio: F. S. Heer, 1926.

Worley, Ted R., ed. *The War Memoirs of Captain John W. Lavender, C.S.A.* Pine Bluff, Ark.: Southern Press, 1956.

Worthington, C. J. *The Woman in Battle.* Hartford, Conn.: T. Belnag, 1876.

Wright, Charles. *A Corporal's Story: Experiences in the Ranks of Company C, Eighty-first Ohio Volunteer Infantry.* Philadelphia: n.p., 1887.

Wright, Marcus J. *Tennessee in the War, 1861–1865.* New York: A. Lee Pub. Co., 1908.

Wright, Thomas J. *History of the Eighth Regiment Kentucky, Vol. Infantry.* St. Joseph, Mo.: St. Joseph Steam Printing, 1880.

Young, James Russell. *Around the World with General Grant.* 2 vols. New York: Subscription Book Department, American News Co., 1879.

Young, Jesse B. *What a Boy Saw in the Army.* New York: Hunt and Eaton, 1894.

PRINTED GOVERNMENT DOCUMENTS

Allen, Jeremiah. *Adjutant General's Department: Subject Index of the General Orders of the War Department from January 1, 1809, to December 31, 1860.* Washington, D.C.: Government Printing Office, 1886.

Dyer, Frederick H. *Compendium of the War of the Rebellion.* 3 vols. New York: Thomas Yoseloff, 1959.

U.S. Congress. *Congressional Globe.*

———. House. *House Executive Documents.* 29th Cong., 1st sess.

———. House. *House Executive Documents.* 30th Cong., 1st sess.

———. *Public Documents Printed by the Order of the Senate of the United States.* No. 71. 28th Cong., 1st sess. Serial no. 432. Vol. 2, 1843–44.

————. Senate. *Senate Executive Documents.* 29th Cong., 1st sess.

————. Senate. *Senate Executive Documents.* 30th Cong., 1st sess.

U.S. Military Academy. *Official Register of the Officers and Cadets of the United States Military Academy, 1818–1850.* West Point, N.Y.: United States Military Academy, 1852.

————. *Regulations Established for the Organization and Government of the Military Academy at West Point.* New York: Wiley and Putnam, 1839.

U.S. War Department. *The Military Laws of the United States.* Washington, D.C.: George Templeman, 1846.

————. *Report of the Secretary of War Showing Names of the Officers and Men Killed, Wounded, or Missing in the Battles of Palo Alto and Resaca de La Palma.* Washington, D.C.: Government Printing Office, 1846.

————. *Revised Regulations for the Army of the United States, 1861.* Philadelphia: Lippincott, 1862.

————. *The War of the Rebellion: A Compilation of the Official Records of the Union and Confederate Armies.* 128 vols. Washington, D.C.: Government Printing Office, 1880–1901.

NEWSPAPERS

Army and Navy Chronicle (Washington, D.C.)

Aurora (Ind.) Commercial

Baltimore American and Commercial Advertiser

Boston Journal

Charleston Courier

Charleston Mercury

Chicago Times

Chicago Tribune

Cincinnati Commercial

Cincinnati Daily Enquirer

Cincinnati Gazette

Cincinnati Times

Citizen Soldier (Norwich, Vt.)

Corpus Christi Gazette

Daily Nashville Union

Daily National Intelligencer

Frankfort (Ky.) Yeoman

Frank Leslie's Illustrated (New York, N.Y.)

Freedom's Champion (Atchison, Kans.)

Fremont (Ohio) Daily Journal

Harper's Weekly (New York, N.Y.)

Independent (New York, N.Y.)

Indiana Palladium (Lawrenceburg, Ind.)

Indiana Spectator (Lawrenceburg, Ind.)

Indiana Whig (Lawrenceburg, Ind.)

Indianapolis Daily Journal
Ironton (Ohio) Register
Knoxville Weekly Register
Lawrenceburg (Ind.) Register
Leon County News (Tallahassee, Fla.)
Lexington Daily News
Louisville Daily Journal
Louisville Post
Louisville Times
Missouri Republican (St. Louis)
Memphis Daily Appeal
Memphis Daily Avalanche
Memphis Press-Scimitar
Nashville Republican Banner
Nashville Times
Nashville Union and American
National Tribune (Washington, D.C.)
New Albany (Ind.) Daily Ledger
New Orleans Crescent
New Orleans Daily Picayune
New York Daily News
New York Daily Tribune
New York Herald
New York Mirror
New York Times
New York Weekly Tribune
New York World
Niles National Register (Baltimore, Md.)
Owensboro (Ky.) Messenger
Philadelphia Public Ledger
Political Beacon (Lawrenceburg, Ind.)
St. Louis Globe-Democrat
Tallahassee (Fla.) Democrat
Times Argus (Central City, Ky.)
Tuscaloosa (Ala.) Gazette
Western Statesmen (Lawrenceburg, Ind.)

SECONDARY MATERIAL: BOOKS

Adams, Michael C. *Fighting for Defeat: Union Military Failure in the East, 1861–1865.* Lincoln: University of Nebraska Press, 1992.

———. *Our Masters the Rebels: A Speculation on Union Military Failure in the East, 1861–1865.* Cambridge: Harvard University Press, 1978.

Ambrose, Stephen E. *Duty, Honor, Country: A History of West Point.* Baltimore: Johns Hopkins University Press, 1966.

———. *Halleck: Lincoln's Chief of Staff.* Baton Rouge: Louisiana State University Press, 1962.

Anderson, Charles C. *Fighting by Southern Federals.* New York: Neale Pub. Co., 1912.

Andrews, J. Cutler. *The North Reports the Civil War.* Pittsburgh: University of Pittsburgh Press, 1955.

Armstrong, Zella. *The History of Hamilton County and Chattanooga, Tennessee.* 2 vols. Johnson City, Tenn.: Overmountain Press, 1931.

Ash, Stephen V. *Middle Tennessee Society Transformed, 1860–1870.* Baton Rouge: Louisiana State University Press, 1988.

———. *When the Yankees Came: Conflict and Chaos in the Occupied South, 1861–1865.* Chapel Hill: University of North Carolina Press, 1995.

Auchampaugh, Philip G. *James Buchanan and His Cabinet on the Eve of Secession.* Boston: J. S. Canner, 1965.

Ballard, Colin R. *The Military Genius of Abraham Lincoln.* London: Oxford University Press, 1926.

Bauer, K. Jack. *The Mexican War, 1846–1848.* New York: Macmillan, 1974.

———. *Zachary Taylor: Soldier, Planter, Statesman of the Old Southwest.* Baton Rouge: Louisiana State University Press, 1985.

Berlin, Ira, Barbara J. Fields, Thavolia Glymph, Joseph P. Reidy, and Leslie Rowland, eds. *The Destruction of Slavery.* Vol. 1 of *Freedom: A Documentary History of Emancipation, 1861–1867.* New York: Cambridge University Press, 1985.

Black, Robert C., III. *The Railroads of the Confederacy.* Chapel Hill: University of North Carolina Press, 1952.

Blue, Frederick J. *Salmon P. Chase: A Life in Politics.* Kent, Ohio: Kent State University Press, 1987.

Boatner, Mark M., III. *The Civil War Dictionary.* New York: David McKay, 1959.

Brown, Dee Alexander. *The Bold Cavaliers: Morgan's Second Kentucky Cavalry Raiders.* Philadelphia: Lippincott, 1959.

Buell, Thomas R. *Genealogic Notes on Buell Family.* Effingham, Ill.: E. W. Petty, 1971.

Burt, Jesse C. *Nashville: Its Life and Times.* Nashville: Tennessee Book Co., 1959.

Catton, Bruce. *The Coming Fury.* Garden City, N.Y.: Doubleday, 1961.

———. *Terrible Swift Sword.* Garden City, N.Y.: Doubleday, 1963.

Chitwood, Oliver Perry. *John Tyler: Champion of the Old South.* New York: Russell and Russell, 1964.

Clark, Thomas D. *A History of Kentucky.* Lexington, Ky.: John Bradford Press, 1950.

Clarke, Dwight L. *Stephen Watts Kearny: Soldier of the West.* Norman: University of Oklahoma Press, 1961.

———. *William Tecumseh Sherman: Gold Rush Banker.* San Francisco: California Historical Society, 1969.

Cleaves, Freeman. *Rock of Chickamauga: The Life of General George H. Thomas.* Norman: University of Oklahoma Press, 1948.

Coffman, Edward M. *The Old Army: A Portrait of the American Army in Peacetime, 1784–1898.* New York: Oxford University Press, 1986.

Collins, Richard H. *History of Kentucky.* 2 vols. Frankfort: Kentucky Historical Society, 1966.

Cooling, Benjamin Franklin. *Fort Donelson's Legacy: War and Society in Kentucky and Tennessee, 1862–1863*. Knoxville: University of Tennessee Press, 1997.

———. *Forts Henry and Donelson: The Key to the Confederate Heartland*. Knoxville: University of Tennessee Press, 1987.

Copeland, Pamela C., and Richard K. Macmaster. *The Five George Masons: Patriots and Planters of Virginia and Maryland*. Charlottesville: University Press of Virginia, 1975.

Cortissoz, Royal. *The Life of Whitelaw Reid*. 2 vols. New York: Scribner's, 1921.

Coulter, E. Merton. *Civil War and Readjustment in Kentucky*. Chapel Hill: University of North Carolina Press, 1926.

Cunliffe, Marcus. *Soldiers and Civilians: The Martial Spirit in America, 1775–1865*. Boston: Little, Brown, 1968.

Current, Richard N. *Lincoln's Loyalists: Union Soldiers From the Confederacy*. Boston: Northeastern University Press, 1992.

Daniel, Larry. *Shiloh: The Battle That Changed the Civil War*. New York: Simon and Schuster, 1997.

Davis, William C. *Battle at Bull Run: A History of the First Major Campaign of the Civil War*. Baton Rouge: Louisiana State University Press, 1977.

———. *Breckinridge: Soldier, Statesman, Symbol*. Baton Rouge: Louisiana State University Press, 1974.

———. *A Government of Our Own: The Making of the Confederacy*. New York: Free Press, 1994.

———. *Jefferson Davis, the Man and His Hour: A Biography*. New York: Harper Collins, 1991.

Dillahunty, Albert. *Shiloh, National Military Park, Tennessee*. National Park Service Historical Handbook Series, No. 10. Washington, D.C.: U.S. National Park Service, 1961.

Donald, David. *Charles Sumner and the Rights of Man*. New York: Knopf, 1970.

———. *Lincoln Reconsidered: Essays on the Civil War Era*. New York: Knopf, 1956.

———. *Why the North Won*. Baton Rouge: Louisiana State University Press, 1960.

Dupuy, R. Ernest. *Where They Have Trod: The West Point Tradition in American Life*. New York: Frederick A. Stokes, 1940.

Durham, Walter T. *Nashville: The Occupied City*. Nashville: Tennessee Historical Society, 1985.

Dyer, John. *"Fightin' Joe Wheeler."* Baton Rouge: Louisiana State University Press, 1941.

Egan, Ferol. *Frémont: Explorer for a Restless Nation*. Garden City, N.Y.: Doubleday, 1977.

Fellman, Michael. *Citizen Sherman: A Life of William Tecumseh Sherman*. New York: Random House, 1995.

Fisher, Noel C. *War at Every Door: Partisan Politics and Guerrilla Violence in East Tennessee, 1860–1869*. Chapel Hill: University of North Carolina Press, 1997.

Folmar, John Kent. *From That Terrible Field: Civil War Letters of J. M. Williams*. Tuscaloosa: University of Alabama Press, 1981.

Foner, Eric. *Reconstruction: America's Unfinished Revolution, 1863–1877*. New York: Harper and Row, 1988.

Foote, Shelby. *The Civil War: A Narrative.* 3 vols. New York: Random House, 1958.

Frank, Joseph A., and George K. Reaves. *"Seeing the Elephant": Raw Recruits at the Battle of Shiloh.* New York: Greenwood Press, 1989.

Furniss, Norman F. *The Mormon Conflict, 1850–1859.* New Haven: Yale University Press, 1960.

Gerteis, Louis S. *From Contraband to Freedom: Federal Policy towards Southern Blacks, 1861–1865.* Westport, Conn.: Greenwood Press, 1973.

Glatthaar, Joseph T. *Partners in Command: The Relationship between Leaders in the Civil War.* New York: Free Press, 1994.

Griess, Thomas E., and Jay Luvas. *The Centennial of the United States Military Academy at West Point, New York.* New York: Greenwood Press, 1969.

Grimsley, Mark. *The Hard Hand of War: Union Military Policy toward Southern Civilians, 1861–1865.* Cambridge: Cambridge University Press, 1995.

Hafendorfer, Kenneth A. *Perryville: Battle for Kentucky.* Louisville, Ky.: Kenneth Hafendorfer Press, 1991.

Hagerman, Edward. *The American Civil War and the Origins of Modern Warfare: Ideas, Organization, and Field Command.* Bloomington: Indiana University Press, 1992.

Hall, Clifton R. *Andrew Johnson, Military Governor of Tennessee.* Princeton, N.J.: Princeton University Press, 1916.

Hassler, Warren W. *General George B. McClellan: Shield of the Union.* Baton Rouge: Louisiana State University Press, 1957.

Hattaway, Herman, and Archer Jones. *How the North Won: A Military History of the Civil War.* Champaign: University of Illinois Press, 1983.

Heitman, Francis B. *Historical Register and Dictionary of the United States Army.* 2 vols. Washington, D.C.: Government Printing Office, 1903.

Hesseltine, William B. *Lincoln and the War Governors.* New York: Knopf, 1948.

Holland, Cecil Fletcher. *Morgan and His Raiders: Biography of the Confederate General.* New York: Macmillan, 1943.

Hopkins, James F. *The University of Kentucky: Origins and Early Years.* Lexington: University of Kentucky Press, 1951.

Horn, Stanley F. *The Army of Tennessee.* Norman: University of Oklahoma Press, 1955.

Howard, Samuel Meek. *The Illustrated Comprehensive History of the Great Battle of Shiloh.* Kansas City, Mo.: Franklin Hudson, 1921.

Hughes, Nathaniel Cheairs, Jr. *The Battle of Belmont: Grant Strikes South.* Chapel Hill: University of North Carolina Press, 1991.

Johnson, Allen, and Dumas Malone. *Dictionary of American Biography.* 20 vols. New York: Scribner's, 1937–43.

Jones, Archer. *Civil War Command and Strategy: The Process of Victory and Defeat.* New York: Free Press, 1992.

Jordan, David M. *Winfield Scott Hancock: A Soldier's Life.* Bloomington: Indiana University Press, 1988.

Josephy, Alvin M., Jr. *The Patriot Chiefs: A Chronicle of American Indian Leadership.* New York: Viking Compass, 1961.

Klein, Maury. *History of the Louisville and Nashville Railroad.* New York: Macmillan, 1972.

Klein, Philip S. *President James Buchanan: A Biography*. University Park: Pennsylvania State University Press, 1962.

Klunder, Willard C. *Lewis Cass and the Politics of Moderation*. Kent, Ohio: Kent State University Press, 1996.

Lewis, Alvin F. *History of Higher Education in Kentucky*. Washington, D.C.: Government Printing Office, 1899.

Lewis, Lloyd. *Sherman, Fighting Prophet*. New York: Harcourt, Brace, 1932.

Lingering in Lowell. Marietta, Ohio: n.p., 1977.

McDonough, James Lee. *Shiloh: In Hell before Night*. Knoxville: University of Tennessee Press, 1977.

————. *War in Kentucky: From Shiloh to Perryville*. Knoxville: University of Tennessee Press, 1994.

McFeely, William S. *Grant: A Biography*. New York: Norton, 1981.

McKinney, Francis F. *Education in Violence: The Life of George H. Thomas and the History of the Army of the Cumberland*. Chicago: American House, 1991.

McPherson, James M. *Battle Cry of Freedom: The Civil War Era*. New York: Oxford University Press, 1988.

————. *Ordeal by Fire: The Civil War and Reconstruction*. New York: McGraw-Hill, 1992.

McVey, Frank L. *The Gates Open Slowly: A History of Education in Kentucky*. Lexington: University of Kentucky Press, 1949.

McWhiney, Grady. *Braxton Bragg and Confederate Defeat*. New York: Columbia University Press, 1969.

Mahon, John K. *History of the Second Seminole War, 1835–42*. Gainesville: University of Florida Press, 1967.

Marszalek, John F. *Sherman: A Soldier's Passion for Order*. New York: Free Press, 1993.

————. *Sherman's Other War: The General and the Civil War Press*. Memphis: Memphis State University Press, 1981.

Martin, Sidney Walter. *Florida during the Territorial Days*. Athens: University of Georgia Press, 1944.

Maslowski, Peter. *Treason Must Be Made Odious: Military Occupation and Wartime Reconstruction in Nashville, Tennessee, 1862–1865*. Millwood, N.J.: KTO Press, 1978.

Maurice, Sir Frederick. *Statesmen and Soldiers of the Civil War: A Study in the Conduct of the War*. Boston: Little, Brown, 1926.

Meneely, A. Howard. *The War Department, 1861: A Study in Mobilization and Administration*. New York: Columbia University Press, 1928.

Meredith, Roy. *Storm over Sumter: The Opening Engagement of the Civil War*. New York: Simon and Schuster, 1957.

Morris, Roy, Jr. *The Life and Wars of General Phil Sheridan*. New York: Crown, 1992.

Morrison, James L. *"The Best School in the World": West Point, the Pre–Civil War Years, 1833–1866*. Kent, Ohio: Kent State University Press, 1986.

Morrison, Olin D. *Indiana's Care for Her Soldiers in the Field, 1861–1865*. Bloomington: Indiana University, 1926.

Myers, William S. *General George B. McClellan: A Study in Personality*. New York: Appleton Century, 1934.

Nevins, Allan. *Frémont: Pathmaker of the West*. New York: Appleton Century, 1939.

————. *The Ordeal of the Union.* 4 vols. New York: Scribner's, 1947–50.

————. *The War for the Union.* 4 vols. New York: Scribner's, 1959–71.

Nicolay, Helen. *Lincoln's Secretary: A Biography of John G. Nicolay.* Westport, Conn.: Greenwood Press, 1949.

Niven, John. *Salmon P. Chase: A Biography.* New York: Oxford University Press, 1995.

O'Connor, Richard. *Sheridan: The Inevitable.* New York: Bobbs-Merrill, 1953.

O'Curry, Richard O., ed. *Radicalism, Racism, and Party Realignment: The Border States during Reconstruction.* Baltimore: Johns Hopkins University Press, 1969.

Overmyer, Jack K. *A Stupendous Effort: The Eighty-seventh Indiana in the War of the Rebellion.* Bloomington: Indiana University Press, 1997.

Paludan, Phillip Shaw. *"A People's Contest": The Union and the Civil War, 1861–1865.* Lawrence: University Press of Kansas, 1988.

————. *The Presidency of Abraham Lincoln.* Lawrence: University Press of Kansas, 1994.

Parks, Joseph H. *General Edmund Kirby Smith, C.S.A.* Baton Rouge: Louisiana State University Press, 1954.

————. *General Leonidas Polk, C.S.A.: The Fighting Bishop.* Baton Rouge: Louisiana State University Press, 1962.

Patton, James W. *Unionism and Reconstruction in Tennessee, 1860–1869.* Chapel Hill: University of North Carolina Press, 1934.

Peskin, Allan. *Garfield.* Kent, Ohio: Kent State University Press, 1978.

Peterson, Norma. *The Presidencies of William Henry Harrison and John Tyler.* Louisville, Ky.: American Printing House for the Blind, 1994.

Phillips, Christopher. *Damned Yankee: The Life of General Nathaniel Lyon.* Columbia: University of Missouri Press, 1990.

Potter, David. *The Impending Crisis, 1848–1861.* New York: Harper and Row, 1976.

Prucha, Francis P. *Guide to the Military Posts of the United States, 1789–1895.* Madison: State Historical Society of Wisconsin, 1964.

Ramage, James A. *Rebel Raider: The Life of John Hunt Morgan.* Lexington: University Press of Kentucky, 1986.

Rawley, James A. *Turning Points of the Civil War.* Lincoln: University of Nebraska Press, 1966.

Reed, David W. *The Battle of Shiloh and the Organizations Engaged.* Washington, D.C.: Government Printing Office, 1903.

Richardson, Albert D. *A Personal History of Ulysses S. Grant.* Hartford, Conn.: Winter and Hatch, 1885.

Roberts, Robert B. *Encyclopedia of Historic Forts: The Military, Pioneer, and Trading Posts of the United States.* New York: Macmillan, 1988.

Rodenbough, Theophilus, and William Haskin. *The Army of the United States.* New York: Maynard, Merrill, 1896.

Roland, Charles. *Albert Sidney Johnston: Soldier of Three Republics.* Austin: University of Texas Press, 1964.

Ropes, John C., and W. R. Livermore. *The Story of the Civil War.* 8 vols. New York: Putnam's, 1894–1913.

Royster, Charles. *The Destructive War: William Tecumseh Sherman, Stonewall Jackson, and the Americans.* New York: Knopf, 1991.

Schneider, Norris F. *History of Lowell and Adams Township.* Lowell, Ohio: Midwest Book Co., 1946.

Schutz, Wallace J., and Walter N. Trenerry. *Abandoned by Lincoln: A Military Biography of General John Pope.* Urbana: University of Illinois Press, 1990.

Sears, Stephen. *George B. McClellan: The Young Napoleon.* New York: Ticknor and Fields, 1988.

Sellers, Charles. *James K. Polk: Continentalist, 1843–1846.* 2 vols. Princeton, N.J.: Princeton University Press, 1966.

Shannon, Fred A. *The Organization and Administration of the Union Army, 1861–1865.* 2 vols. Cleveland: Arthur H. Clarke, 1928.

Silver, James W. *Edmund Pendelton Gaines: Frontier General.* Baton Rouge: Louisiana State University Press, 1949.

Simpson, Brooks D. *Let Us Have Peace: Ulysses S. Grant and the Politics of War and Reconstruction, 1861–1868.* Chapel Hill: University of North Carolina Press, 1991.

Skelton, William B. *An American Profession of Arms: The Army Officers Corps, 1784–1861.* Lawrence: University Press of Kansas, 1992.

Smith, Elbert B. *The Presidency of James Buchanan.* Lawrence: University Press of Kansas, 1975.

Smith, George W., and Charles Judah. *Chronicles of the Gringos: The U.S. Army in the Mexican War, 1846–1848.* Albuquerque: University of New Mexico Press, 1968.

Smith, Justin. *The War with Mexico.* 2 vols. New York: Macmillan, 1919.

Stafford, George Mason Graham. *General George Mason Graham of Tyrone Plantation and His People.* New Orleans: Pelican, 1947.

Stampp, Kenneth M. *Indiana Politics during the Civil War.* Bloomington: Indiana University Press, 1949. Reprint, 1978.

Stickles, Arndt M. *Simon Bolivar Buckner: Borderland Knight.* Chapel Hill: University of North Carolina Press, 1940.

Swanberg, W. A. *First Blood: The Story of Fort Sumter.* New York: Dorset Press, 1957.

Sword, Wiley. *Shiloh: Bloody April.* New York: William Morrow, 1974.

Thomas, Benjamin P. *Abraham Lincoln: A Biography.* New York: Modern Library, 1968.

Thomas, Benjamin P., and Harold M. Hyman. *Stanton: The Life and Times of Lincoln's Secretary of War.* New York: Knopf, 1962.

Thomas, Wilbur. *George H. Thomas: The Indomitable Warrior.* New York: Exposition Press, 1964.

Thornbrough, Emma Lou. *Indiana in the Civil War Era, 1850–1880.* Indianapolis: Indiana Historical Bureau and Indiana Historical Society, 1965.

Trefousse, Hans L. *Andrew Johnson: A Biography.* New York: Norton, 1989.

———. *The Radical Republicans: Lincoln's Vanguard for Racial Justice.* New York: Knopf, 1969.

Tucker, Glenn. *Hancock the Superb.* Indianapolis: Bobbs-Merrill, 1960.

Vandiver, Frank E. *Ploughshares into Swords: Josiah Gorges and Confederate Ordnance.* Austin: University of Texas Press, 1952.

Warner, Ezra J. *Generals in Blue: Lives of the Union Commanders.* Baton Rouge: Louisiana State University Press, 1964.

———. *Generals in Gray: The Lives of Confederate Commanders.* Baton Rouge: Louisiana State University Press, 1959.

Weber, Thomas. *The Northern Railroads in the Civil War, 1861–1865.* New York: King's Crown Press, 1952.

Weigley, Russell F. *The American Way of War: A History of United States Military Strategy and Policy.* Bloomington: Indiana University Press, 1973.

———. *Quartermaster General of the Union Army: A Biography of M. C. Meigs.* New York: Columbia University Press, 1959.

———. *Towards an American Army: Military Thought from Washington to Marshall.* New York: Columbia University Press, 1962.

Weisberger, Bernard A. *Reporters for the Union.* Boston: Little, Brown, 1953.

Welles, Albert, ed. *History of the Buell Family.* 2 vols. New York: New-York Historical Society Library, 1881.

Wilbur, Thomas. *General George A. Thomas.* New York: Exposition Press, 1964.

Williams, Kenneth P. *Lincoln Finds a General: A Military Study of the Civil War.* 4 vols. New York: Macmillan, 1949–59.

Williams, T. Harry. *Lincoln and His Generals.* New York: Knopf, 1952.

———. *Lincoln and the Radicals.* Madison: University of Wisconsin Press, 1960.

———. *P. G. T. Beauregard: Napoleon in Gray.* Baton Rouge: Louisiana State University Press, 1954.

Wills, Brian Steel. *A Battle from the Start: The Life of Nathan Bedford Forrest.* New York: Harper Collins, 1992.

Wilson, Mindwell C., ed. *Indiana Battle Flags and a Record of Indiana Organizations in the Mexican Civil and Spanish-American Wars.* Indianapolis, n.p., 1929.

The Works of Hubert Howe Bancroft: A History of California, 1848–1859. San Francisco: History Company Publishers, 1888.

Wright, J. Marcus. *Tennessee in the War, 1861–1865.* New York: Ambrose Lee, 1908.

SECONDARY MATERIAL: ARTICLES, DISSERTATIONS, AND THESES

Ambrose, Stephen E. "The Monotonous Life." *American History Illustrated* 8 (August 1971): 22–32.

Ash, Stephen V. "Sharks in an Angry Sea: Civilian Resistance and Guerrilla Warfare in Occupied Middle Tennessee, 1862–1865." *Tennessee Historical Quarterly* 45 (Fall 1986): 217–29.

Bearss, Edwin C. "General Bragg Abandons Kentucky." *Register of the Kentucky Historical Society* 59 (July 1961): 217–44.

Bender, Averam B. "Frontier Defense in the Territory of New Mexico, 1846–1853." *New Mexico Historical Review* 9 (July 1934): 249–72.

———. "Military Posts in the Southwest, 1848–1860." *New Mexico Historical Review* 16 (April 1941): 125–47.

Bruce, George A. "The Donelson Campaign." In *Campaigns in Kentucky and Tennessee, Including the Battle of Chickamauga, 1862–1864. Papers of the Military Historical Society of Massachusetts.* Vol. 7. Boston: Military Historical Society of Massachusetts, 1910, 3–29.

————. "General Buell's Campaign against Chattanooga." In *Campaigns in Kentucky and Tennessee, Including the Battle of Chickamauga, 1862–1864. Papers of the Military Historical Society of Massachusetts.* Vol. 7. Boston: Military Historical Society of Massachusetts, 1910, 99–148.

Buell, D. C. "Major-General William T. Sherman and the Spring Campaign of 1862 in the West." *Historical Magazine* 8 (July 1870): 74–83.

————. "Shiloh Reviewed." *Century Magazine* 9 (1886): 749–81.

Burt, Jesse C. "Sherman's Logistics and Andrew Johnson." *Tennessee Historical Quarterly* 15 (September 1956): 195–215.

Campbell, Bernard T. "Shiloh National Military Park." *Tennessee Historical Quarterly* 21 (March 1962): 3–18.

Carr, Charles. "Civil War Letter of the Twenty-first Wisconsin." *Wisconsin Magazine of History* 43 (1959–60): 264–72.

Chumney, James, Jr. "Don Carlos Buell: Gentleman General." Ph.D. diss., Rice University, 1964.

Cimprich, John. "Slave Behavior during the Federal Occupation of Tennessee, 1862–1865." *Historian* 44 (March 1982): 335–47.

Clift, Glenn G. "From the Archives." *Register of the Kentucky Historical Society* 60 (July 1962): 209–23.

Crimmins, M. L. "Colonel J. F. K. Mansfield's Report of the Inspection of the Department of Texas, 1856." *Southwestern Historical Quarterly* 42 (October 1938–April 1939): 122–48, 215–57, 351–87.

Cunningham, Edward O. "Shiloh and the Western Campaign of 1862." Ph.D. diss., Louisiana State University, 1966. Ann Arbor, Mich., University Microfilms.

Dawson, Henry B. "The Conflicts of the War of Secession: The Story of Fort Sumter." *Historical Magazine* 1 (January 1872): 34–53.

Dillon, Rodney E., Jr. "Don Carlos Buell and the Union Leadership." *Lincoln Herald* 82 (1980): 363–73.

East, Ernest E. "Lincoln's Russian General." *Journal of Illinois State Historical Society* 52 (Spring 1959): 106–22.

Engle, Stephen D. "Don Carlos Buell: Military Philosophy and Command Problems in the West." *Civil War History* 41 (June 1995): 89–115.

Ferguson, Edward. "The Army of the Cumberland under Buell." In *War Papers: Being Papers Read before the Commandery of the State of Wisconsin.* Milwaukee: A. Ross Houston, Recorder, for the Military Order of the Loyal Legion of the United States, 1891, 425–43.

Fisher, Noel C. "The Leniency Shown Them Has Been Unavailing." *Civil War History* 40 (December 1994): 275–91.

"General M. C. Meigs on the Conduct of the War." *American Historical Review* 26 (January 1921): 285–303.

Gildrie, Richard P. "Guerrilla Warfare in the Lower Cumberland River Valley, 1862–1865." *Tennessee Historical Quarterly* 49 (1990): 161–76.

Gordon, George H. "The Battles of Contreras and Churubusco." In *Papers of the Military Historical Society of Massachusetts.* Vol. 13. Boston: Military Historical Society of Massachusetts, 1913, 561–98.

Grant, Ulysses S. "The Battle of Shiloh." *Century Magazine* 39 (1885): 593–613.

Griese, Arthur A. "A Louisville Tragedy, 1862." *Filson Club Quarterly* 26 (April 1952): 133–54.

Grimsley, Mark. "Conciliation and Its Failure, 1861–1862." *Civil War History* 39 (December 1993): 317–35.

Hagerman, Edward. "Field Transportation and Strategic Mobility in the Union Armies." *Civil War History* 34 (June 1988): 143–71.

———. "The Professionalization of George B. McClellan and Early Civil War Field Command." *Civil War History* 21 (June 1975): 113–35.

Hardison, Edwin T. "In the Toils of War: Andrew Johnson and the Federal Occupation of Tennessee, 1862–1865." Ph.D. diss., University of Tennessee, 1981.

Harrison, Lowell H. "The Battle of Munfordville." *Civil War Times Illustrated* 13 (June 1974): 4–9, 45–47.

———. "Mill Springs: The Brilliant Victory." *Civil War Times Illustrated* 10 (January 1972): 4–9, 44–47.

Hays, John B. "An Incident at Shiloh." *Tennessee Historical Quarterly* 9 (1925–26): 264–65.

Heidler, Jeannie. "The Military Career of David Emmanuel Twiggs." Ph.D. diss., Auburn University, 1989.

Henry, Robert S. "Chattanooga and the War." *Tennessee Historical Quarterly* 19 (September 1960): 222–30.

Hill, Daniel H. "The Army in Texas." *Southern Quarterly Review* 9 (April 1946): 434–57.

Horn, Stanley F. "Nashville during the Civil War." *Tennessee Historical Quarterly* 4 (March 1945): 3–22.

Horn, Stanley T. "Perryville." *Civil War Times Illustrated* 4 (February 1966): 4–11, 42–47.

Hubbard, Paul, and Christine Lewis, eds. "The Shiloh Letters of George W. Lennard." *Indiana Magazine of History* 76 (March 1980): 21–53.

Jenkins, Kirk C. "A Shooting at the Galt House: The Death of General William Nelson." *Civil War History* 43 (June 1997): 101–18.

Jensen, Dana O. "Daniel Frost's Memoirs." *Missouri Historical Society Bulletin* 26, pt. 3 (April 1970): 200–226.

Jones, D. Lloyd. "The Battle of Shiloh: Reminiscences of D. Lloyd Jones." In *War Papers: Being Papers Read before the Commandery of the State of Wisconsin*, 51–60. Milwaukee: A. Ross Houston, Recorder, for the Military Order of the Loyal Legion of the United States, 1914.

Jones, James P. "'Bull' and the Damned Puppy: A Civil War Tragedy." *American History Illustrated* 7 (July 1972): 12–21.

———. "Jefferson Davis in Blue." Master's thesis, University of Florida, 1954.

Kaiser, Leo M. "Civil War Letters of Charles W. Carr of the Twenty-first Wisconsin Volunteers." *Wisconsin Magazine of History* 43 (1959–60): 264–72.

Kamm, Samuel R. "The Civil War Career of Thomas A. Scott." Ph.D. diss., University of Pennsylvania, 1940.

Kendall, Henry M. "The Battle of Perryville." In *War Papers: Being Papers Read before the Commandery of the District of Columbia*, 27–48. N.p.: Military Order of the Loyal Legion of the United States, 1902.

McKinney, Francis F. "The First East Tennessee Campaign." *Michigan Alumnus Quarterly Review* 59 (May 23, 1953): 213–21.

———. "The Trial of General Buell." *Michigan Alumnus Quarterly Review* 64 (March 7, 1956): 163–68.

McMurtry, Gerald R. "Zollicoffer and the Battle of Mill Springs." *Filson Club Quarterly* 29 (October 1955): 303–19.

McWhiney, Grady. "Controversy in Kentucky: Braxton Bragg's Campaign of 1862." *Civil War History* 6 (March 1960): 5–41.

———. "General Beauregard's 'Complete Victory' at Shiloh: An Interpretation." *Journal of Southern History* 3 (August 1983): 421–34.

Madden, David. "Union Resistance to Confederate Occupation: The Bridge-Burners of East Tennessee." *East Tennessee Historical Society Publications* 52 (1980): 42–53; 53 (1981): 22–39.

Maslowski, Peter. "From Reconciliation to Reconstruction: Lincoln, Johnson, and Tennessee." *Tennessee Historical Quarterly* 42 (Fall 1983): 281–98.

Otis, Ephraim. "Recollections of the Kentucky Campaign of 1862." In *Military Essays and Recollections: Papers Read before the Commandery of the State of Illinois*, 122–47. Military Order of the Loyal Legion of the United States. Chicago: Cozzens and Beaton, 1907.

Payne, Darwin. "Camp Life in the Army of Occupation: July 1845–March 1846." *Southwestern Historical Quarterly* 72 (1970): 326–42.

Peine, Mark A. "The Buell Military Commission." Master's thesis, University of North Dakota, 1977.

Prokopowicz, Gerald. "All for the Regiment: Unit Cohesion and Tactical Stalemate in the Army of the Ohio, 1861–1862." Ph.D. diss., Harvard University, 1994.

Ramsey, David M. "The 'Old Sumpter Hero': A Biography of Major-General Abner Doubleday." Ph.D. diss., Florida State University, 1980.

———. "Robert Anderson in the Civil War." Master's thesis, Florida State University, 1974.

Raney, Matthew A. "The Early Political and Military Career of Governor John Alexander Martin of Kansas." Master's thesis, Kansas State University, 1984.

Reid, Brian Holden. "The Crisis at Fort Sumter in 1861 Reconsidered." *History* 77 (1992): 2–32.

Robertson, James I. "An Indiana Soldier in Love and War: The Civil War Letters of John V. Hadley." *Indiana Magazine of History* 59 (September 1963): 189–288.

Sanders, Robert Lee. "Military Career of Don Carlos Buell during the Civil War." Master's thesis, University of Kentucky, 1937.

Sherman, John. "An Address Commemorative of General William T. Sherman." *War Papers: Being Papers Read before the New York Commandery*, 1–23. N.p.: Military Order of the Loyal Legion of the United States, 1892.

———. "The Battle of Pittsburg Landing: A Letter from General Sherman." *United States Service Magazine* 3 (January 1865): 1–4.

Stafford, George Mason Graham. "The Autobiography of George Mason Graham." *Louisiana Historical Quarterly* 20 (1937): 43–57.

———. "Mason Genealogy." *Tyler's Quarterly Historical and Genealogical Magazine* 23 (1942): 193–203.

Stampp, Kenneth M. "The Impact of the Civil War upon Hoosier Society." *Indiana Magazine of History* 38 (March 1942): 1–16.

———. "Kentucky's Influence upon Indiana in the Crisis of 1861." *Indiana Magazine of History* 39 (September 1943): 263–76.

Stone, Henry. "The Operations of General Buell in Kentucky and Tennessee in 1862." In *Campaigns in Kentucky and Tennessee, Including the Battle of Chickamauga, 1862–1864. Papers of the Military Historical Society of Massachusetts*, 7:255–91. Boston: Military Historical Society of Massachusetts, 1908.

"The Story of Sumter." *Historical Magazine* 1 (January 1872): 34–53.

Tapp, Hambleton. "The Assassination of General William Nelson, September 29, 1862, and Its Ramifications." *Filson Club Quarterly* 19 (October 1945): 195–207.

———. "The Battle of Perryville, 1862." *Filson Club Quarterly* 9 (July 1935): 158–81.

———, ed. "The Battle of Perryville, October 8, 1862, as described in the Diary of Captain Robert B. Taylor." *Register of the Kentucky Historical Society* 60 (October 1962): 255–92.

Theisen, Lee Scott. "The Public Career of General Lew Wallace, 1845–1905." Ph.D. diss., University of Arizona, 1973.

Throne, Mildred, ed. "Letters from Shiloh." *Iowa Journal of History and Politics* 52 (July 1954): 235–80.

Trefousse, Hans L. "The Joint Committee on the Conduct of the War." *Civil War History* 10 (March 1964): 5–19.

Walker, Peter Franklin. "Command Failure: The Fall of Forts Henry and Donelson." *Tennessee Historical Quarterly* 16 (December 1957): 335–60.

Webb, Henry W. "The Story of Jefferson Barracks." *New Mexico Historical Review* 21 (July 1946): 185–208.

Williams, T. Harry. "Andrew Johnson as a Member of the Committee on the Conduct of the War." *East Tennessee Historical Society Publications* 12 (1940): 70–83.

———. "The Attack upon West Point during the Civil War." *Mississippi Valley Historical Review* 25 (March 1939): 491–504.

———. "The Committee on the Conduct of the War." *Journal of the American Military Institute* 3 (1939): 139–59.

Woodworth, Steven E. "The Indeterminate Quantities: Jefferson Davis, Leonidas Polk, and the End of Kentucky Neutrality, September, 1861." *Civil War History* 38 (December 1992): 289–97.

Index

· ·

Bruce, Sanders, 174
Bryantsville, Ky., 312
Buchanan, James, 54, 61, 62
Buckner, Simon Bolivar, 68, 83, 107, 305
Buell, Ann Lane (aunt), 5
Buell, Auriela Ann (sister), 3, 5
Buell, Don Carlos: historical evaluation of, xi–xiv; early life, 3–8; at West Point, 11–19; joins Third U.S. Infantry, 20; in Second Seminole War, 20–23; stands trial, 23–28; in Mexican War, 34–46; wounded at Churubusco, 40, 43, 44; assigned to adjutant general's office, 44; assigned to Department of New Mexico, 45; promoted to major, 45; meets Sherman and Hancock, 45–46; marries Margaret Hunter Mason, 47–48; assigned to Eighth Military Department, 48; attitude toward slaves, 48, 66; meets McClellan, 48–49; injured aboard *Kate Kearney*, 50; and financial affairs, 50–51; assigned to Department of the West, 52; ordered to War Department, 54; friendship with Sherman, 55–56; memorandum to Anderson, 61; assigned to the Department of the Pacific, 65; ordered to Washington, D.C., 69; promoted to brigadier general, 69–70; as divisional commander, 73; assigned to Department of the Ohio, 74; comparison with Halleck, 79–80; professional attitude of, 80–81; attitude toward East Tennessee, 87–89, 112, 118, 119; arrives in Louisville, 87–88; as disciplinarian, 92; and state governors, 94–97, 115–16; philosophy of war of, 116–17, 128–30; meets Thomas, 123–24; lack of collaboration with Halleck, 131–41 passim; and Nashville, 135, 138–39, 141; and political pressure regarding East Tennessee, 140, 141–43, 145; and battle of Mill Springs,
142–45; attitude toward Halleck's river campaign, 152–57, 169–71; and Guthrie, 160; and Fort Henry, 164; captures Bowling Green, 171; captures Nashville, 178; and Lincoln's reconstruction efforts, 183–87, 190–92, 195; and General Orders 13a, 184–86; confronts slavery, 201–3; promoted to major general, 204; under Halleck's command, 205, 220; and battle of Shiloh, 220–34; hailed a hero of Shiloh, 234–37; advances to Corinth, 242–48; and Chattanooga campaign, 253–58; meets Mitchel in Huntsville, 264, 269; and politics, 273–75; and Bragg, 284–85; and Kentucky campaign, 287, 289–91, 312; and Munfordville, 289–92; temporarily relieved of command, 298–300; and battle of Perryville, 304–12; fails to pursue Bragg, 312–18; permanently relieved of command, 318; comparison with McClellan, 321–23; requests court of inquiry, 323, 328; resigns, 343–45; after the war, 347–61
Buell, Elizabeth (mother), 2
Buell, Elizabeth Mary Ann Mason (stepdaughter), 48
Buell, Emma Twiggs Mason (stepdaughter), 48
Buell, George Pearson (uncle), 5
Buell, Margaret (wife), 45, 51, 52
Buell, Perez Barnum (uncle), 2
Buell, Sallie Maria (sister), 3, 5
Buell, Salmon (grandfather), 2, 3
Buell, Salmon A., Jr. (father), 2
Buell, Thomas (cousin), 3
Buell, Timothy (uncle), 2
Buena Vista, Mexico, 38
Buford, Louis M., 236
Bull Run, First, battle of, 68
Bush, Asahel, K., 308
Bush, Thomas J., 355, 359
Butler, Benjamin F., 8